MONETARY
THEORY AND
POLICY

MONETARY THEORY AND POLICY

Major Contributions to Contemporary Thought

edited by **Richard S. Thorn**
University of Pittsburgh

Praeger Publishers · New York

Monetary Theory and Policy is based on the editor's earlier publication of the same title published by Random House in 1966.

Published in the United States of America in 1976 by Praeger Publishers, Inc., 111 Fourth Avenue, New York, N.Y. 10003

© 1976 by Praeger Publishers, Inc.

Library of Congress Cataloging in Publication Data

Thorn, Richard S.   ed.
  Monetary theory and policy.
  Includes bibliographies.
    1. Money—Addresses, essays, lectures.
2. Monetary policy—Addresses, essays, lectures.
I. Title.
HG221. T44   1976   332.4   75–41865
ISBN 0–275–22800–2
ISBN 0–275–64470–7 pbk.

Printed in the United States of America

To My Parents

PREFACE

The earlier edition of this work attempted to present a representative sampling of the leading developments in monetary theory and policy. This is no longer possible. The literature in monetary economics has been growing in numerous directions at an exponential rate so that it is now impossible to collect in a single volume a satisfactory survey.

The objective of this work is more pedagogic than that of its predecessor. It is an attempt to present the advanced student with a cross section of some key developments in the field of monetary theory and policy against the background of some seminal articles written in the postwar period. Several decades ago Schumpeter was able to survey the entire field of economics from his lofty perch. Harry Johnson, a decade and a half ago, in his article reprinted in this volume was able to present an elegant and brilliant survey of most of monetary economics. Today, the best that can be offered is a few peepholes through which one may see some of the larger trees which we hope suggest something of the shape of the forest.

The articles in this volume have been chosen with the advanced student in mind, with a view to giving him an entrance into the vast and growing literature of monetary economics. Needless to say, even a minimum basic reading list in monetary economics would be much longer. The choices of articles presented must, of necessity, be somewhat personal and are based on the editor's perception of the direction in which monetary economics is moving.

The format of the book is similar to that of the earlier edition. The selections have been placed under six conventional divisions of monetary economics, but several of the articles cut across the subject matter of several or all of the sections. The introductions that appear at the beginning of each division are designed to give the reader some background to the central issues and to maintain some continuity in the exposition.

The article by Paul Smith on control theory is not strictly a piece on monetary economics. However, the use of control theory in dealing with problems of monetary policy has become so widespread that it was thought useful to present the student with some minimum tools in order to make this literature accessible rather than attempt to survey this voluminous literature.

Due to the limited space available, personal acknowledgements by the authors have been omitted. In many instances authors have used this opportunity to make minor revisions in their articles, eliminating misprints or minor errors.

In view of the vastness of the literature in this edition more weight has been given to survey articles in contrast to leading theoretical articles. The replacement of many articles which appeared in the previous edition of this work does not mean they are less important today but rather reflects an attempt to focus on the literature of the past decade.

I am grateful to the authors and publishers for their kind permission to reprint the articles appearing herein and wish to thank Professor Thomas Mayer of the University of California, Davis, and Jonas Prager of Hunter College of the City of New York for their helpful suggestions. My research assistant Kevin Zaney assisted in checking the bibliographical references and in preparing the manuscript for publication. Mrs. Esther Zavos, my secretary, as usual, made a substantial editorial contribution.

Finally, I would like to express my appreciation to my colleagues and graduate students at the University of Pittsburgh for their constant stimulation.

RICHARD S. THORN

CONTENTS

Part **I**

Introduction

The intellectual impact of Keynes' *General Theory of Employment, Interest and Money* (1936) with its persuasive arguments for the wider use of fiscal policy in the circumstances of the great depression was overwhelming, and the subsequent absorption of economists with the problems of wartime finance and postwar reconstruction was so intense as to result in a virtual neglect of monetary theory and policy in the immediate prewar and postwar periods. It was not until the 1950's that monetary problems once again attracted the attention of a large number of economists. This renewed interest was largely the result of the rebirth of monetary policy in Europe under the impact of postwar inflation. The renaissance of monetary policy in the United States occurred somewhat later when the Federal Reserve, under the terms of the Federal-Reserve Treasury Accord of 1951, was relieved of the responsibility for maintaining the prices of government securities.

As has frequently occurred in the history of economic doctrine, academic interest in monetary theory arose out of the challenge of specific policy problems. This attention was greatly stimulated by the Patman Hearings held in 1951[1] and subsequently by two large-scale reports, one by the Radcliffe Committee in the United Kingdom in 1959,[2] the other by the Commission on Money and Credit in the United States in 1961.[3] During the course of these inquiries large numbers of economists and other interested persons were called upon to express their views and interpretations of contemporary monetary problems and many special memoranda and studies were commissioned.

The central theoretical theme of this renaissance has been the integration of monetary theory with value and capital theory. Economists picked up the reins where Keynes and his critics dropped them at the

[1] U.S. Congress, Joint Economic Committee, *Monetary Policy and the Management of the Public Debt,* 2 vols., 82nd Congress, 2nd Session (Washington, 1952).

[2] Committee on the Working of the Monetary System (Chairman: The Rt. Hon. Lord Radcliffe), *Report* (London, 1959).

[3] Commission on Money and Credit, *Money and Credit: Their Influence on Jobs, Prices, and Growth* (Englewood Cliffs, N.J., 1961).

outset of the war and tried to bridge the dichotomy between "real" economics and "monetary" economics. Money, as Wicksell long ago discovered, is not a veil but a raiment which clothes the economy and forever alters its appearance. Much of the development in monetary theory in recent years is a result of the generalization of the Wicksell-Pigou Effect[4] which in essence stated that volume of monetary assets, measured in terms of the general price level, can affect "real" phenomena, such as consumption, investment, and income, not only through the rate of interest but also through its effect on the amount and composition of desired wealth portfolios.

The recognition that consumers' behavior may be influenced by their income and stock of wealth, just as entrepreneurs' investment decisions are influenced by their income and stock of capital, opened the door to the possibility that both consumption theory and investment theory may be assimilated into a general theory of expenditure. Another important development is the tendency to depart from the broad macroeconomic level to a detailed analysis of how monetary policy affects the spending and saving decisions of various groups and sectors in the economy, thus providing monetary theory with a firmer behavioral basis. This attempt at disaggregation has brought about renewed interest in the flow-of-funds analysis as a general framework within which to reconcile sectoral financial behavioral analysis.

The past decade has seen monetary theory grow in several different directions. The marriage of monetary theory with growth theory begun by Metzler has raised a new set of general problems centering around the optimum rate of growth of the money supply. General equilibrium theory has expanded its purview to monetary economics and raised several new questions, the most interesting of which is the relevance of Walrasian general equilibrium in models in which expectations play an important role. This has led to the formulation of so-called disequilibrium theories. The new disequilibrium theory takes as its point of departure the notion that individual decisions based on present market prices cannot be realized unless these prices are, in fact, an equilibrium set of prices. The new theory rejects as unrealistic the Walrasian process of tâtonnement to arrive at a new equilibrium set of prices from a point of disequilibrium.

Jevons and again Tinbergen pointed out that the introduction of lagged variables into economics models can generate cyclical behavior depending on the values of the parameters of the model. Until recently

[4] Although Pigou is generally credited with injecting what Patinkin called the "real balance effect" into contemporary monetary discussions, Wicksell gave a classical description of the effect in his *Interest and Prices* (Jena, 1898, reprinted by Augustus M. Kelley, New York, 1965, trans.), pp. 39–40. Since the term "Pigou Effect" is most commonly used by the authors in this volume, I shall employ the same terminology. Although other writers at various times have also described real balance effects.

this possibility had been largely confined to a consideration of lags in the policymaking and transmission process. Expectations (both rational and adaptive) and stock-adjustment processes have been introduced into a wide variety of monetary behavioral models. This type of behavior results in the appearance of lagged variables in formal econometric models resulting in a considerable amount of ambiguity in the theoretical results. A recurrent phrase in descriptions of these models is that the outcome depends on the values of the parameters. It would seem that under these conditions econometricians would become the true arbiters of economics. Unfortunately, many nagging problems relating to uncertainty and autoregressivity result in econometricians speaking with more than one voice, leaving policy-makers to fall back on subjective and political evaluations to guide their decisions.

Economic theory has always been influenced by current issues, and without question the most important influence on monetary economics in the past decade has been inflation and particularly a new variant, stagflation—inflation without aggregate excess demand. What in 1956 was looked upon as a minor aberration in the U.S. economy has become the dominant worldwide monetary problem. Much of this discussion has renewed interest in the relation of the labor market to monetary variables—a market Keynes' *General Theory* omitted by the convenient device of expressing all real quantities in terms of wage units. Much of the recent theoretical discussion of inflation has not concerned monetary theory so much as labor theory centering on the existence or nonexistence of a trade-off between employment and rising prices, the now famous Phillips Curve.

The renewed interest in inflation has also stimulated interest in how expectations (particularly price expectations) are formed. Economists have resorted to many of the tools employed in the much earlier controversy over the theory of the term structure of interest rates in dealing with this problem. All this has led to the rediscovery of Irving Fisher by a new generation of economists. Fisher's early exploration of the trade-off between employment and inflation, and his early recognition of the relationship between inflation and the rate of interest, have given rise to a wide variety of models which attempt to explain the current stagflation.

The theory of economic public policy had shown little development until the middle fifties when there appeared two important works, Tinbergen's *Theory of Economics Policy* (1956) and A. W. Phillips trailblazing article applying control theory to economic policymaking.[5] An important result of this period was the demonstration that equivalent policies in deterministic models are not necessarily so in an uncertain world with imperfect information. Control theory, in the manner

---

[5] A. W. Phillips, "Stabilisation Policy in a Closed Economy," *Economic Journal* 64:290–323 (June 1954).

in which it formulates the policy problem, seems to be the answer to a policy-maker's prayer. Unfortunately, the mathematical assumptions under which it labors are highly restrictive and the results are sensitive to the imperfectly known lags in the economic models employed. The possible extension of control theory to uncertain situations, however, seems promising.

The two most important questions of policy yet to be resolved are: what is it reasonable to expect monetary policy to do in the economy given the available instruments and are monetary rules superior to discretionary monetary policy?

If one were to base one's opinion of the future of monetary policy theory solely on the quantity and variety of work being undertaken, one would be optimistic about future progress. However, there remain methodological problems which raise doubts about how efficiently the wheat is being separated from the chaff.

The familiar line tagged onto many papers that further empirical testing is needed to validate or discredit the theory in question today sounds more like yearning than expectation. The early optimism that econometrics aided by the computer would resolve all issues has faded. Further substantial improvement in economics methodology is required before we may discriminate effectively between useful and useless theories. Further recourse to the type of empirical testing we now know is likely to be inadequate for the job.

1 Recent Developments in Monetary Theory

Harry G. Johnson *University of Chicago*

I. *Introduction*

The Radcliffe Committee initiated its investigations into the working of the British monetary system at a time when the intellectual environment could be characterized as the high tide of Keynesian scepticism about the importance of monetary policy and the relevance of monetary theory. By the time its Report was published, however, that tide had begun markedly to ebb, a fact which accounts for the unexpectedly harsh reception the Report received even from what might have been expected to be intellectually sympathetic quarters. In the ensuing ten years, the tide has set markedly in the opposite direction, towards emphasis on the importance of monetary policy and concern with the theory of money (as distinct from the theory of income and employment), to the point where contemporary controversy centres on the so-called "rise of monetarism."

The purpose of this chapter is to survey developments in monetary theory since the Radcliffe Report, with particular emphasis on developments subsequent to two previous surveys of mine, written in 1961–62 and 1963 (Johnson [29, 30]). The first of those surveys, designed to provide a comprehensive overview of the field for graduate

Reprinted from David R. Croome and Harry G. Johnson (eds.), *Money in Britain, 1959–1969* (Oxford University Press, 1970), Ch. III, pp. 83–114. © Oxford University Press 1970. Reprinted by permission of the publisher.

students and nonspecialist professional economists, organized the material presented within the broad analytical framework of demand for and supply of money. The second, an essay in personal interpretation unrestricted by the obligation of representation by population, took as its organizational focus six problems originating in Keynes's *General Theory,* and emphasized the two themes of the application of capital theory to monetary theory and the trend towards dynamic analysis.

For the purposes of this chapter, the type of approach of the second survey referred to seems the more suitable. Accordingly, I will discuss recent developments under a series of topical headings chosen to represent themes considered to be of general interest to monetary economists. However, in comparison with the 1963 survey, emphasis is placed rather less on unifying strands of thought and rather more on current controversy. Also, certain themes are treated in exceptional detail, in view of their presumed interest to British readers—particularly the first two, the revival of monetarism and the rehabilitation of Keynes. The remaining topics are the fundamentals of monetary theory, the problems associated with financial intermediation, money in growth models, and the theory of inflation and economic policy.

II. *The Revival of the Quantity Theory and the Rise of "Monetarism"*

As already remarked, the dominant feature of the post-Radcliffe era, in the American if not quite yet the British literature, has been the revival of the quantity theory of money and the rise of the associated "monetarist" approach to economic policy—an approach which stresses the explanatory and controlling power of changes in the quantity of money, in contrast to the Keynesian emphasis on fiscal policy, and as regards monetary policy on credit and interest-rate policies. It may be useful, though it risks the accusation of putting an unwarranted motivational construction on a process of scientific development, to trace the stages in the intellectual revival of the quantity theory, which has been almost exclusively the work of Milton Friedman.

The Keynesian revolution left the quantity theory thoroughly discredited, on the grounds either that it was a mere tautology (the quantity equation), or that it "assumed full employment" and that the velocity factor it emphasized was in fact highly unstable. The revival of a quantity theory that could claim to rival the Keynesian theory required a restatement of it that would free it from these objections and give it an empirical content. Such a restatement was provided by Milton Friedman's classic article [13], which redefined the quantity theory as a theory of the demand for money (or velocity) and not a theory of prices or output, and made the essence of the theory the existence of a stable functional relation between the quantity of real balances demanded and a limited number of independent variables, a relation deduced from capital theory. This version of the quantity theory, Friedman asserted, had been handed down through the "oral tradition" of the University of Chicago. In fact, as Don Patinkin [47] has recently shown conclusively, it is to be found neither in the written tradition of Chicago—which on the contrary stressed the quantity equation and the cumulative instability of velocity—nor in the oral tradition of Chicago as Patinkin himself experienced it: "What Friedman has actually presented is an elegant exposition of the modern portfolio approach to the demand for money which . . . can only be seen as a continuation of the Keynesian theory of liquidity preference" (p. 47). In recent writings, Friedman has ceased to refer to the Chicago oral tradition, and has admitted that his reformulation of the quantity theory was "much influenced by the Keynesian liquidity analysis."[1]

Redefinition of the quantity theory as hypothesizing a stable demand function for money not only gave it an empirical content subject to testing,[2] but facilitated the interpretation by researchers of good statistical results as evidence in favour of the quantity theory and against the rival "income-expenditure" theory (the Chicago term for the prevalent version of Keynesian economics). The next stage was to devise a set of tests of the rival theories against one another; this was the subject of the Friedman-Meiselman study for the Commission on Money and Credit [8] of "The Relative Stability of Monetary Velocity and the Investment Multiplier in the United States, 1898–1958."

The tests in question rested on some fundamental—and debatable— methodological principles; and the failure of the critics to understand these principles, as well as to appreciate the depth of the intellectual effort put into the tests, made their criticisms and attempted refutations less powerful and persuasive than they might have been. The crucial principle is that the test of good theory is its ability to predict something large from something small, by means of a simple and stable theoretical relationship; hence the essence of the quantity theory was specified to be the velocity function relating income to money, and the essence of the income-expenditure theory was specified to be the multiplier relationship relating income to autonomous expenditure (for the purposes of the tests, these relationships were redefined in terms of consumption rather than income, to avoid pseudo-correlation). This principle is in sharp contrast to the more common view that the purpose of theory in this context is to lay out the full structure of a general-equilibrium model in the detail necessary to produce an adequately good statistical "fit." A second principle is that behavioural relationships should be invariant to institutional and historical change; hence the Friedman-Meiselman emphasis on a long run of data. A third principle, whose practical application has given rise to legitimate criticism, is that since Keynesian theory does not specify exactly what is to be treated as "autonomous" and what as "induced" in an economy with governmental and foreign trade sectors, the classification must be effected by statistical tests of independence and interdependence.

According to the Friedman-Meiselman tests, the quantity theory consistently out-performed the Keynesian theory, with the exception of the 1930s sub-period. A conscientious, or nonchalant, Keynesian might well have interpreted these results as confirming the master's insight, insofar as the tests could be considered relevant at all. Instead a number were provoked into attempting to disprove the findings; and, as mentioned, their efforts were generally vitiated in their impact by violation of one or another of the rules of the game as laid down by Friedman and Meiselman [18].[3]

As restated by Friedman, the quantity theory still laboured under the handicap of two potentially powerful criticisms. The first was the long-standing traditional criticism of the quantity theory, that the theory is irrelevant because the quantity of money supplied responds passively to the demand for it—the "Banking School" position which remains strong in popular thinking on monetary policy. This criticism was quelled by the publication of the long-awaited, monumental volume by Friedman and Schwartz [14] on the monetary history of the United States, and the companion volume by Cagan [5] on the supply of money in the United States. These works demonstrated both the independent determination of the supply of money, and the significant influence of monetary changes on U.S. economic history. The second criticism stemmed from the strongly-held belief that the great depression of 1929 and after was the consequence of the collapse of the willingness to invest and proved conclusively the inability of monetary policy to remedy mass unemployment. The Friedman-Schwartz volume demonstrated as conclusively as possible the causal role played by rapid and substantial monetary contraction in the depression of the 1930s, and thus paved the way for a dismissal of the Keynesian analysis as based on a misinterpretation of the facts of experience.[4] There remains, however, acute controversy over the interpretation of the emergence of large holdings of excess reserves by the American banking system in the latter part of the 1930s.

While, as already mentioned, Friedman's restatement of the quantity theory of money should probably be interpreted as an appropriation of portfolio-balance analysis on Keynesian lines for use against those Keynesians who have neglected the monetary side of Keynes's theory in favor of the income-expenditure side, there is one important difference between the Friedman (quantity-theory) approach and the Keynesian approach to that analysis which is of considerable importance both theoretically and practically. This difference is that the restated quantity theory introduces explicitly, and emphasizes, expected changes in the price level as an element in the cost of holding money and other assets fixed as to both capital value and yield in money terms, whereas Keynesian portfolio-balance theory almost invariably starts from the assumption of an actual or expected stable price level (though this assumption may subsequently be modified).[5] The assumption in question has the great theoretical advantage of endowing money with an absolutely certain yield of zero per cent, and hence making it a fixed point of reference for portfolio choices; but this advantage is bought at the cost of giving money in the portfolio attributes of safety which in general it does not possess. Moreover, from the standpoint of application of monetary theory to the interpretation of actual events and policies, the assumption is likely to be consistently misleading, because it encourages practitioners of the approach to interpret changes in market interest rates on monetary assets as indicators of changes in monetary ease or tightness, without proper allowance for the effects on the relation between money and real rates of interest of changes in expected rates of inflation or deflation.

This difference is in an important sense the essence of the differentiation between the "monetarist" and the alternative "Keynesian" approach to problems of economic policy. The monetarist approach stresses the unreliability of money interest rate changes as economic indicators, owing to the influence on them of price expectations, and concentrates instead on changes in the money supply as a variable over which the monetary authority has control and whose meaning is theoretically clear. In addition, and more fundamentally, the monetarist approach rests on the assumption that velocity rather than the multiplier is the key relationship in the understanding of macro-economic developments in the economy. This was the point of the Friedman-Meiselman test already discussed. Subsequently, the focus of the controversy has shifted from autonomous expenditure versus money supply to fiscal policy versus monetary policy as the subject of empirical testing. In this connection, tests performed at the Federal Reserve Bank of St. Louis at the initiative of the Bank's staff have been advanced in support of the monetarist as against the Keynesian approach; but these tests too have been the subject of considerable criticism.[6]

As mentioned above, Friedman's restatement of the quantity theory obtained the immediate tactical advantage of freeing it from the Keynesian criticism of assuming an automatic tendency towards full employment in the economy, by making it a theory of the demand for money without commitment to the analysis of prices and employment. This advantage, however, has proved something of an embarrassment subsequently, given the success of the quantity-theory counter-attack on Keynesianism and the rise of the monetarist approach to economic policy, since it apparently leaves the quantity theorist with nothing to say about the relative impact of short-run variations in the money supply, and hence in aggregate demand, on money prices on the one hand and physical output on the other. (It may be noted that a similar problem arises for the Keynesian theory, under conditions of near full employment, which the Phillips curve analysis seeks to resolve but which it resolves rather unsatisfactorily—see below.) The obvious answer to this problem, in neo-quantity terms, lies in an application of expectations theory to the determination of the division of an increase in monetary demand between changes in money wages and prices and changes in employment and output; but thus far no satisfactory theory along these lines has been produced.[7]

In concluding this section, a brief reference should be made to recent extensions of the monetarist approach to problems of balance-of-payments analysis and policy. As regards individual countries, prevailing theory emphasizes the balance of aggregate demand and aggregate supply capacity on the one hand, and the relation between domestic and foreign price levels on the other, as the key determinants of the balance of payments. A monetarist approach, on the other hand, as reflected in the new IMF-inspired emphasis of British economic policy on "Domestic Credit Expansion," emphasizes the relation between the growth of domestic demand for money and the growth of supply intended by the monetary authority as the key determinant of international reserve gains or losses. As regards the international monetary system as a whole, the monetarist approach emphasizes the relation between the growth of total desired reserves and the growth of overall reserve supplies as determining the need for some countries to have deficits, and the relation between national growth of desired money balances and national expansion of domestic credit as determining which countries will have the necessary deficits.[8]

III. *The Rehabilitation of Keynes*

The quantity-theory counter-revolution discussed in section II has been directed against the so-called "income–expenditure" school, by which is meant those economists in the Keynesian tradition who have concentrated their analysis and policy prescriptions on the income–expenditure side of the Keynesian general-equilibrium apparatus. (This focus has been the dominant impact of the Keynesian revolution on governmental and other practical thinking on economic forecasting and policy-making.) There is, it should be remarked, nothing to prevent the absorption of the empirical evidence of a stable demand function for money into the corpus of the Keynesian general-equilibrium model—a stable demand function for money is in fact implicit in the liquidity-preference component of the standard Hicksian *IS–LM* diagram—other than the conditioned Keynesian reflex against the "quantity-theory" label and the conditioned Keynesian belief that 'money does not matter' (or, at least, "does not matter much").

"Keynesian economics" came very rapidly to be epitomized by the *IS–LM* diagram of the textbooks, in terms of which Keynesian under-employment equilibrium depends either on the rigidity of money wages or on the special case of the "liquidity trap" (a perfectly interest-elastic liquidity-preference function) keeping the rate of interest above that consistent with full-employment equilibrium between saving and investment; and this special case was disposed of by the critics through the introduction of the "Pigou effect" of a falling price level on the real value of money balances and hence on real wealth and consumption. As a result, Keynes has become "the greatest economist of modern times" (an obituary remark indicating that his contribution was so indisputable as to require no explanation) and the *General Theory* has been shelved as a "classic" (meaning an acknowledged great book that no one reads, for fear of discovering that the author was himself not clear about the message his disciples derived from his work). Put differently, Keynes has been assigned to the shadow regions, as one who had a tremendous influence on popular (i.e. undergraduate-level) economic theory and on the thinking of the makers of public policy, but whose theoretical contribution considered at the highest scientific level was shamefully amateurish, if not downright clownish, and is best passed over with a curt but fulsome general acknowledgement.

The position thus assigned to Keynes in contemporary economic folklore has been challenged in a recently-published, monumentally scholarly work of exegesis and interpretation of the *General Theory* by Axel Leijonhufvud [35]. Leijonhufvud distinguishes sharply between "Keynesian economics"—essentially the *IS–LM* analysis summarized above—and "the economics of Keynes," as represented by the *General Theory* and the *Treatise on Money,* on which the *General Theory* built to a greater extent than Keynes's followers have appreciated; and he seeks to show that the latter economics is both quite different from, and far more subtle and profound than, the former. In this endeavour he draws heavily on some very recent work unfamiliar to most monetary economists, notably R. W. Clower's attack on the extension of the Walrasian general-equilibrium apparatus to a monetary economy by Patinkin and others (to be discussed subsequently), and the work of Alchian and others on the economic theory of market information and search; and the structure of his argument rests importantly on one proposition that readers who think they have understood Keynes may have difficulty in accepting as essential to Keynes's thought, namely the assertion of a "second psychological law of consumption," according to which a fall in the rate of interest increases consumption by increasing the "perceived wealth" of the community (described as Keynes's "windfall effect").

Leijonhufvud's re-interpretation of Keynes's economics, and differentiation of it from "Keynesian economics," can be briefly but crudely summarized in the following propositions. First, what Keynes was challenging, and what he found most difficult to escape from, was the concentration of received economic theory on a dynamic adjustment process in which prices moved instantaneously to equilibrate markets. His dynamic adjustment process focused on quantity adjustments; and quantity adjustments by producers give rise to destabilizing feedback processes, epitomized in the multiplier analysis. If Walras's Law held in reality, any excess supply of one commodity (or labour or money) would imply an excess demand for others, and produce an adjustment process consistent with full employment. But in a monetary economy, Walras's Law refers to potential and not to "effective" demands, because goods and labour are exchanged proximately for money and only ultimately for labour and goods; there is an "income-constrained process" by which an excess supply of labour ("involuntary unemployment") appears not as an excess demand for goods signalling to producers the need to increase output and demand for labour, but as an equilibrium position in which the excess demands of the unemployed either proximately for money or ultimately for goods are not "effective" and hence do not work to restore full-employment equilibrium.

Second, the core of Keynes's analysis is "liquidity preference," the unwillingness of asset holders to allow an equilibrating fall in the rate of interest, motivated by inelastic expectations about future rates of interest based on past experience. The cause of underemployment equilibrium is neither interest inelasticity of investment demand—because Keynes aggregated bonds and real assets, and a fall in the rate of interest means a rise in the demand price for real capital—nor interest inelasticity of saving—because while Keynes discounted the pure intertemporal substitution effect of interest-rate changes, he attached (or so Leijonhufvud asserts) considerable importance to the "windfall effect" described above—but the prevention by liquidity preference of the equilibrating fall in interest rates necessary to counteract a decline in the inducement to invest. For economic policy it follows that, for an economy in the neighbourhood of full-employment equilibrium, stabilization policy should rely primarily on monetary policy, to keep market rates of interest in line with the "natural rate." But for an economy in deep depression, interest rates may well be low enough for consistency with full-employment equilibrium, and the problem may instead by depression of entrepreneurial expectations requiring fiscal policy of a pump-priming nature to restore a full-employment level of activity. For a near-full-employment economy, however, Leijonhufvud [36] reasons that the logic of the "income-constrained process" implies that fiscal policy will not be a powerful tool, because, short of a general liquidity crisis, the public will be able to maintain its normal consumption levels by drawing on its financial assets. Leijonhufvud, incidentally, argues that Keynes in fact recognized the real balance effect of a reduction in wages and prices, but attached predominant importance to the interest-rate effect precisely because he believed that both investment and saving were highly sensitive to the influence of lower interest rates in raising the values of real assets.

Leijonhufvud's rehabilitation of Keynes is virtually certain to be widely acclaimed by economists of most persuasions, not merely on the scientific account of its scholarly grasp and range, but also for the broadly political reason that it writes "Keynesian economics" as it has been developed by mathematical economists, primarily in America, out of the "true" Keynesian tradition, and that it does so by the application of concepts and approaches either developed by or congenial to contemporary quantity theorists—especially, the application of the "human capital" approach to labour and wage determination and of expectations theory to the determination of wages and interest rates. Hence it provides common ground of an intellectually appealing kind on which both "old-line" Keynesian revolutionaries (such as Joan Robinson) and neoquantity-theory counter-revolutionaries (such as Milton Friedman) can unite in condemnation of their common enemy, the dominant school of orthodox macro-economic theory based on the *IS–LM* model. From the point of view of scientific progress in the understanding of macro-economics and monetary theory, Leijonhufvud's work provides an extremely useful assemblage and conspectus of emerging concepts and approaches on which further theoretical work is required, and also clears the air of a number of prevailing myths about the true nature of the Keynesian revolution. In a very broad sense, his work carries forwards the process of transformation of monetary theory by the application of capital-theory concepts and the analysis of dynamic processes discussed in my 1963 survey.

IV. *Fundamental Issues in Monetary Theory*

As recorded in my 1962 survey (Johnson [30]) one of the major contributions to the development of monetary theory consequent on the Keynesian revolution was Patinkin's integration of monetary and value theory within the framework of Hicksian general-equilibrium analysis. That integration rested on the conception of money as "outside money"—an asset of the community matched by

no corresponding debt of the community to a monetary institution—
and the mechanics of the analysis depended heavily on the real-
balance (real-wealth) effect of a change in the money price level.
Subsequently, Gurley and Shaw developed an alternative "inside-
money" model, in which the mechanics of the analysis rested instead
on the substitution effect of a change in the ratio of privately-held
money to privately-held assets of other kinds. The "neutrality of
money" issue on which the Patinkin-Gurley and Shaw controversy
focused need not detain us here, since the essential rules of the game
are clear enough in retrospect. What is more relevant from the contemporary perspective is the distinction introduced by the debate
between "inside" and "outside" money, and the ensuing proclivity of
monetary theorists to distinguish between models built on the two
alternative assumptions about the institutional nature of money, one
involving both a wealth and a substitution effect and the other involving only a substitution effect.

The validity of the distinction between "inside" and "outside"
money has been successfully challenged in a recent book by Boris
Pesek and Thomas Saving [48], distinguished on the one hand by its
insight into relevant questions and on the other by analytical confusions into which it stumbles. Put very briefly, Pesek and Saving have
shown that, for purposes of model-building, the relevant distinction is
not between "inside" and "outside" money, but between money bearing a zero rate of interest (or more generally money bearing a rate of
interest fixed in nominal terms, of which zero interest is a special
case), and money bearing an interest rate competitive with rates of
return on other available assets. In the former case the services of
money, being "monopolized" in a sense, have a scarcity value for the
community and hence a wealth value for the community as a whole;
in the latter case the services of money become a free good and hence
have no wealth value, though the fact that they are a free good maximizes community welfare. Unfortunately Pesek and Saving fail to
understand the distinction between a zero alternative opportunity
cost of money services to money holders, and a zero purchasing power
of money itself in terms of goods and services: the former involves the
payment of competitive interest on real balances, the latter will result
from the absence of any restriction in the freedom of the banking
system to expand its issue of (assumedly costless) paper credit.[9] Hence
the initial insight, which has important implications for the efficiency
of monetary arrangements and for various monetary-theoretic problems such as optimal monetary growth (see below), is vitiated by il-
logical analysis and absurd conclusions.

The main purpose of the Pesek and Saving analysis, however, was
to establish an *a priori* theoretical definition of what should and
what should not be counted in practice as part of the money stock

for purposes of monetary analysis, and in particular to establish the medium-of-exchange function as decisive (i.e. to validate the conventional definition of money as currency in circulation plus deposits subject to cheque). A parallel attempt has been made by Newlyn [45], and subsequently by Yeager [59], to arrive at an *a priori* definition of money in terms of "neutrality," by which is meant that the use of the monetary item can affect aggregate expenditure on goods and services without affecting the market for loans, rather than in terms of non-interest-bearingness. Friedman and Schwartz [19] have recently shown that both efforts rest on special sets of assumptions—about the banking system in the former case and about the nature of relevant monetary transactions in the latter—and that properly interpreted both lead back to the identification of money with the cash base provided by the central bank. The definition of money for purposes of empirical application of monetary theory therefore remains an empirical question.

Patinkin's integration of monetary and value theory rested on a particular way of incorporating money into the general-equilibrium framework, namely through the attribution of "utility" to the services provided by real money balances. As has long been recognized, money can be incorporated into a general-equilibrium system in an alternative way, as part of the budget restraint that conditions the maximization of utility from the consumption of real goods and services. This alternative approach is represented by the inventory-theoretic analysis of transactions demand for cash developed by Baumol and Tobin. It has significant implications for the national income accounting aspects of monetary theory,[10] important in some theoretical contexts (see below on money in growth models). Though the concept of money as a producers' good (as well as a consumer's good), which incorporates the essence of the inventory approach, has long been a part of the neo-quantity-theory conceptual approach to monetary theory (Friedman [19]), the lines of battle between contemporary quantity theorists and Keynesians have gradually been drawing up on the issue of the "utility approach" versus the "transactions-cost approach" to monetary theory.[11] This line of division is unlikely to prove fruitful in the advancement of knowledge in the field. On the one hand, the utility approach is to be interpreted as an "as if" or "revealed preference" means of introducing the notion that the demand for money is subject to the ordinary analytics of choice among rival assets; it is thus unspecific enough to absorb any more specific theory based on the precise circumstances of choice. On the other hand, insofar as there is an empirically resolvable conflict between the two approaches, it must imply either a prediction as to which of alternative empirical variables will produce the better econometric results (e.g. measured current income as a proxy for transactions versus "permanent" income as a proxy for wealth), or a prediction of the empirical magnitude of a statistical elasticity coefficient (e.g. the transactions approach predicts interest and scale elasticities of the demand for real balances significantly below unity); and the empirical studies of demand for money available so far provide little clear support for the transactions-cost approach.[12] In addition, the inventory approach is open to the general theoretical objection that it takes the patterns of payments and receipts as given, whereas these patterns can be construed instead as an optimizing response to the social usefulness of money as a medium of exchange and store of value.

The integration of monetary and value theory that has ensued on the Keynesian revolution, the work of Lange, Patinkin, and many others, has built on the Hicksian formulation of general-equilibrium theory. As applied by these writers, the approach treats money as parallel to any other good that is the object of utility-maximizing choice. In my 1962 survey, I called attention to certain difficulties that arise in treating money—as a capital good with a service flow—on a par with current flows of perishable consumption goods in a utility-maximization process subject to a budget constraint involving both current income and inherited money capital. More recently, Robert Clower [7] has attacked this type of formulation of the economic theory of a monetary economy, as making money just like any other good and therefore omitting from the analysis the essence of the difference between a monetary and a barter economy, which is precisely that in a barter economy goods exchange for other goods without differentiation of the goods, whereas in a monetary economy money plays a unique role distinct from that of goods, because goods have to be exchanged for money and money for goods. In consequence of this difference, economic actors have to be considered as constrained in their choices, not by the potential worth of their initial endowments of goods and money, but as purchasers by their initial cash balances (the "expenditure constraint") and as sellers by the value of desired intra-period receipts of money income (the "income constraint"). The outcome is a drastic reformulation of the general-equilibrium theory of a monetary economy, some of the implications of which have been discussed above in connection with Leijonhufvud's rehabilitation of Keynes. It may be remarked that in its own way Hicks's [27] recent re-examination of the transactions demand for money, intended indirectly to support the Radcliffe Report position, has attempted to cope with the same problem, though Hicks has been justly criticized for failing to realize that the transactions demand for money is conditional on and inseparable from its characteristics as a store of value, and that the pattern of use of money for transactions is, in anything longer than the very short run, the resultant of acts of choice and therefore not "involuntary."[13] Similar questions can be raised about Clower's sharp distinction between purchasers and sellers and between the budget constraints to which they are subject.

V. *Financial Intermediaries and the "New View" of Monetary Theory and Policy*[14]

As mentioned in section I, the Radcliffe Committee's emphasis on "the liquidity of the economy" as the key variable for monetary analysis and policy represented the high tide of Keynesian disbelief in the practical relevance and theoretical importance of money as formulated in traditional monetary theory, and as such met a harsh critical reception from the spokesmen of resurgent monetarism. In my 1962 survey I remarked that one important group working in the Keynesian liquidity-preference tradition had yet to be heard from: those pursuing the Markowitz "portfolio-balance" approach to monetary analysis under the leadership of James Tobin at Yale University. The collective works of this group have recently been published in three Cowles Commission monographs (Hester [24, 25, 26]), which constitute something of a delayed Yale counter-blast against the Chicago School's famous *Studies in the Quantity Theory of Money* (Friedman [12]). These monographs, and especially Monograph 21, *Financial Markets and Economic Activity*,[15] may be interpreted as providing belatedly the intellectual foundations of the Radcliffe Committee's position on monetary theory and policy—what has come to be described in the American literature, following a phrase in Tobin's important essay on "Commercial Banks as Creators of 'Money,'" (Carson [6]) as the "new view" of money.

In the general approach of the Yale School, "monetary theory broadly conceived is simply the theory of portfolio management by economic units: households, businesses, financial institutions, and governments. It takes as its subject matter stocks of assets and debts (including money proper) and their values and yields; its accounting framework is the balance sheet. It can be distinguished from branches of economic theory which take the income statement as their accounting framework and flows of income, saving, expenditure, and production as their subject matter." This distinction is admitted to be artificial, but useful because "the processes which determine why one balance sheet or portfolio is chosen in preference to another are just beginning to be studied and understood."[16] One of the major implications of this approach is the necessity "to regard the structure of interest rates, asset yields, and credit availabilities rather than the quantity of money as the linkage between monetary and financial institutions on the one hand and the real economy on the other"— hence the relevance to Radcliffe.

The crucial distinction for the Yale School, then (as for the Radcliffe Committee), is between the financial sector and the real sector (or between stock and flow analysis) rather than between the banking system and the rest of the economy (as various versions of the contemporary quantity theory would have it) or between liquid and illiquid assets (which Leijonhufvud interprets to be the essential distinction drawn in Keynes's own theory). Their central contribution is an elaborate analysis of the competition between banks and non-bank financial intermediaries—acknowledged to stem from the earlier work of Gurley and Shaw[17]—from which emerges the conclusions that "the quantity of money as conventionally defined is not an autonomous variable controlled by governmental authority but an endogenous or 'inside' quantity reflecting the economic behaviour of banks and other private economic units"; that "commercial banks differ . . . from other financial units less basically in the nature of their liabilities than in the controls over reserves and interest rates to which they are legally subject";[18] and that controls over non-bank financial intermediaries may increase the effectiveness of monetary policy in influencing the real sector.[19]

As its authors acknowledge, this last proposition is not particularly impressive or useful, since there is no obvious economic gain discernible in enabling the monetary authority to operate on the economy by smaller rather than larger monetary-policy operations. The main argument for controls on financial intermediaries is in fact the rather disreputable one of shielding the interest cost of the public debt from the impact of general economic policy, and so forcing the burden of adjustment to changes in general economic policy on to the private sector; and the practice of such controls raises the question of the effects on the efficiency of the economic system as a whole. It is the first two propositions that raise fundamental issues in monetary theory.

Both of these propositions are rendered difficult to deal with by the strict separation of the monetary and the real sectors assumed by the basic approach, and particularly by the assumption of prices of real goods and services fixed autonomously in terms of money, on which the analysis rests, and which precludes consideration of many of the aspects of the problem that would naturally occur to a quantity theorist. The second proposition on its positive side is essentially that controls on banks place the latter in the position of making a "monopoly" profit on marginal business, so that an increase in reserves will automatically induce them to expand the scale of their operations, whereas other institutions are marginally in equilibrium so that their response to changes effected by monetary policy or otherwise will involve a general-equilibrium adjustment in asset values and yields. This is certainly a possibility. But it fits easily into the general framework of analysis of the efficiency effects of controls mentioned in the previous paragraph (and also into the Pesek–Saving analysis of the wealth effect of an expansion of "inside" money discussed in section IV); and it does not suffice to equate banks in the really relevant respects with non-bank financial intermediaries, the negative side of the proposition. Further, what it implies is only that on impact an increase in bank reserves will have a wealth effect on the economy; when all the repercussions of an increase in the cash base are taken into account (including the repercussions on prices) there should be no change in the relative size of the banking sector, in spite of the marginal excess profitability of banking.

The crux of the matter is the first proposition, that the quantity of money as conventionally defined is an endogenous variable. This proposition derives its force by contrast with a straw man, the "text-book" old view that the quantity of bank deposits is determined by a mechanical multiplier process operating on bank reserves, in which the preferences of the public play no part. Even in theoretical analyses of the determination of the money supply long pre-dating the Keynesian revolution, the preferences of the public, in the form of the desired ratio of currency to deposits, played an essential part in the determination of the volume of bank deposits erectable on a given cash base provided by the monetary authority.[20] The contemporary theory of money supply, which has developed very rapidly since my 1962 survey, has incorporated all the relevant influences of the choices of the public among competing monetary and near-monetary liabilities and of the financial institutions (both bank and non-bank) among reserves and other assets in the theory of the relation of the conventionally-measured money supply to the cash base provided by the central bank.[21] The crucial issue is whether the interrelationships (deduced from rational maximizing behaviour on the part of all economic actors) in the financial sector are stable enough to permit changes in the monetary base (or, more proximately, changes in the conventionally-measured quantity of money) to be used to analyse and predict changes in the real sector (including both output and price level changes), or whether detailed understanding of the financial sector and the effects of monetary changes on the "structure of interest rates, asset yields, and credit availabilities" is a necessary prerequisite of this endeavour. In this connection, the "new view" is long on elegant analysis of theoretical possibilities, but remarkably short on testable or tested theoretical propositions about the way the economy works, and specifically how it responds to monetary impulses, when the interaction of the monetary and the real sectors is taken into account.

VI. *Money in Growth Models and Monetary Efficiency*

In concluding my (Johnson [30]) 1962 survey, I remarked that "almost nothing has yet been done to break monetary theory loose from the mould of short-run equilibrium analysis . . . and to integrate it with the rapidly developing literature on economic growth." The period since has seen a rapid development of theorizing in this direction, to the point where a whole issue of the new *Journal of Money, Credit and Banking* has been devoted to publication of the proceedings of a conference held on this precise subject.[22] This literature has raised in a fresh form many of the fundamental problems of monetary theory, notably those of the role and functions of money in the economy; as yet, however, it has barely approached the question of quantification of the influence of money and monetary policy on economic growth. It does, however, overlap with an emerging body of analysis dealing with the requirements of efficiency in the organization of the monetary and financial sector, of considerably more relevance to practical economic policy.

The starting point of the latter body of analysis is the proposition that money, as an instrument of exchange and an item of wealth, is socially virtually costless to create (though not necessarily socially costless to use) and hence that the stock of it should be maintained at the satiety level for society. In the context of the problem of monetary efficiency, this proposition implies that taxes on the use of money, such as are involved in the imposition of required reserves in the form of non-interest-bearing currency and deposits at the central bank and other restrictions on commercial banking, as well as restrictions on the freedom of competition among financial intermediaries, restrict the use of money and money substitutes to sub-optimal levels and hence reduce the efficiency of the economy. (If restrictions are applied to commercial banks only, there may be an extra-optimal resort to non-bank intermediary services.[23]) This proposition refers to optimization of the holding of real balances; if banks are left free to compete without restriction in providing nominal money, the gains from using costless paper as a medium of exchange and store of value will be dissipated through inflation. The proposition also abstracts from the practical point that the payment of interest on currency holdings is infeasible.[24] If this last point is taken as being of predominating importance, monetary efficiency requires the establishment of a zero money rate of interest on other financial claims to parallel the assumedly inherently institutionally necessary zero money rate of return on currency. To analyse the condition for accomplishing this, the analysis must move from a static to a dynamic framework, and appeal to the Fisherian distinction between the real and the money rate of interest, as separated by the expected rate of inflation or deflation. The conclusion then emerges that monetary efficiency and the optimization of social welfare require management of the growth of the money supply so as to cause the price level to fall at a rate equal to the real rate of return on capital.[25]

Recent work on the problem of introducing money and monetary policy into models of economic growth, however, has started from a quite different analytical framework, namely the artificial conventions of "real" growth models. These models postulate a constant ratio of savings to income (real output), and proceed to determine (i) the conditions under which the model will converge on a steady-state growth path, the rate of growth being determined by the exogenously-given rates of growth of the population and of technological efficiency, and (ii) that savings ratio which will maximize consumption per head along the steady-state growth path. The problem of introducing money into such a model presents itself as the problem of incorporating money and monetary growth into the concept of "income" to which the assumed fixed savings ratio is to be applied, and deducing the influence of variation in the rate of monetary expansion (or proximately the trend rate of change of prices) on the proportion of physical output available for investment in additions to the physical capital stock. It has been recognized that this problem has a close affinity to Metzler's [42] classic article on the neutrality of money in a short-run Keynesian system. A subsidiary problem has been the interpretation of the welfare implications of the consumption-maximizing savings ratio, epitomized in "the golden rule of accumulation" Phelps [49]. So long as the actual savings ratio is above the consumption-maximizing ratio, no problem results, because by reducing the savings ratio society can increase its consumption level at all points of time, present, and future, which must be accounted an indisputable welfare gain; but if the actual ratio falls short of the consumption-maximizing ratio, the welfare implications of a movement towards the latter are ambiguous, because the move involves a sacrifice of present consumption for the sake of future consumption, and the model contains no specification of the terms on which such an intertemporal substitution between present and future consumption can be analysed.

Subtleties of welfare analysis apart, the problem is how to introduce money and monetary growth into the "real" model of accumulation described above. For this purpose, "money" has been generally defined as an asset bearing interest at a rate fixed in monetary terms—usually taken as zero by convention—so that its real rate of return is determined by the (assumed to be fully expected) rate of inflation or deflation determined by monetary policy. The original analysis of the problem by Tobin [57] treated money as an asset pure and simple, contributing nothing to real income and welfare; hence monetary growth entered the model purely as a capital gain additional to current production, which added to perceived income but subtracted from the saving available for real investment, and hence reduced real output per head. Thus inflation appeared to be "a good thing," if the savings ratio fell short of the consumption-maximizing ratio and the intertemporal choice problem was ignored.

My own analysis of the problem (Johnson [33]) stressed the necessity of allowing money a function in a monetary economy, and therefore of attributing to the presence of money an increase in economic welfare and so in the base to which the assumed constant savings ratio was applied, thus introducing two conflicting terms in the effect of the presence of money and the exercise of monetary policy—the Tobin capital-gains effect of real monetary growth reducing the real savings ratio and the Johnson consumption-of-cash-balance-services effect raising it—with an ambiguous result for the specification of optimal monetary policy. My contribution violated some of the canons of sound national income accounting in attempting to capture intra-marginal consumers' surplus in the representation of the income-augmenting effect of cash-balance services. Levhari and Patinkin [37] have subsequently explored the implications of a more conventional valuation of the services of cash balances (at their marginal value) for income and consumption accounting, with the predictable consequence of making their conclusions depend on the elasticity or inelasticity of demand for cash-balance services.

Other writers, especially the late Miguel Sidrauski [54], have departed from the confining influence of the Metzler assumption that saving is inversely related to wealth, and placed their analytical emphasis on time preference, i.e. on some minimum acceptable rate of interest as the ultimate determinant of the accumulation of material capital per head. In such a theoretical framework, or in one in which the savings ratio is regarded as amenable to influence by fiscal policy, the analysis must return to regarding the optimization of the quantity of money at any point of time as a separable problem from that of maximizing consumption of real goods and services per head, in which case its solution (again assuming the infeasibility of paying explicit interest on currency) must be management of the money supply so as to produce a rate of price decline equal to the real rate of interest—as pointed out above in connection with the static problem of monetary efficiency. In this connection, it should be noted, the same conclusions follow whether money is regarded as "productive," and/or yielding utility, or whether it is treated on transactions-demand theory lines as the cheapest means of reconciling different temporal patterns of receipts and payments—in which latter case money balance holdings affect economic welfare via the observable flow of goods and services rather than via the "utility" yielded by money services.

VII. *The Theory of Inflation and of Economic Policy*

The objectives of macro-economic policy for the government of a contemporary "mixed-capitalist" country have come to be formulated as the maintenance of high employment without inflation, consistently with the achievement of an adequate rate of economic growth and the preservation of balance-of-payments equilibrium. In this context a major contribution to the theory of economic policy—in my judgement the only significant contribution to emerge from post-Keynesian theorizing—has been the "Phillips curve" [51]. The Phillips curve is an empirical relationship between the rate of unemployment (taken as an index of demand conditions in the labour market) and other variables on the one hand, and the rate of increase of money wages on the other. From it can be deduced, through the assumption that the trend of prices is determined by the trend of wages via the deduction of the rate of increase of productivity, a "trade-off function" between the rate of inflation and the rate of unemployment; and the policy-makers can either be assumed to choose a point on this function according to their or the community's preferences, or advised to choose a point on it that maximizes social welfare (minimizes social loss).[26]

Much work has been done on the econometric refinement and testing of the Phillips curve. Recently there has been a recurrence of the initial doubts about the concept, namely about whether the assumed rounded-L shape of the curve does not represent an arbitrary and illegitimate linkage of the behaviour of the labour market under conditions of approximately full employment and of mass unemployment.[27] More fundamentally, the concept of the curve has been attacked as being logically inconsistent in ignoring the influence on the wage-fixing process of expectations about the rate of wage and price inflation, which expectations themselves are derived by a learning process from past experience of the rate of inflation chosen by the policy-makers. On the assumption that inflation eventually becomes fully expected and translated into wage- and price-fixing behaviour, the trade-off for the policy-makers is not between a "permanent" rate of unemployment and a "permanent" rate of inflation, but between the gains from less unemployment now and the losses from more inflation later (Phelps [50]). The most elegant statement of this position is to be found in Milton Friedman's [15] Presidential Address to the 1967 Meetings of the American Economic Association, which argues forcefully that in the long run monetary policy cannot control real variables—notably the real rate of interest and the level of unemployment—but can only control nominal money variables—the behaviour of the price level and of the money rate of interest.

The Friedman argument from the quantity theory of money raises the empirical question of the effects of introducing the expected rate of inflation into the estimation of the Phillips curve. If the coefficient of the expected rate of inflation is unity, the Phillips curve vanishes, and only one rate of unemployment—"the natural rate of unemployment," in Friedman's terminology—is consistent with a constant rate of inflation (which may—and may as well—be zero) in the long run. While various recent writers have attempted to investigate this empirical question, the most thorough examination of it is to be found in a rather obscure source, a symposium held at New York University on January 31, 1968 (Rousseas [53]). Empirical evidence produced by Robert M. Solow strongly supports, and evidence produced by Phillip Cagan (on a somewhat different methodological approach) does not effectively refute, a coefficient for expected inflation significantly below unity (in the neighbourhood of one-half). The outcome is a "sophisticated" Phillips curve, based on a dynamic version of "money illusion," which still offers a trade-off to the policy-makers, though its slope is steeper than that implied by the "naive" Phillips curve.

Recognition of the Phillips curve relationship has prompted governments, particularly in the United Kingdom, to resort to "incomes policy" as a way to alter the Phillips curve and permit the achievement of fuller employment consistently with the maintenance of price stability. The Phillips curve approach has suggested an obvious test of the effectiveness of incomes policy as practised on past occasions, namely its effectiveness in shifting the Phillips curve to the left in the standard diagram. Such tests have almost invariably shown incomes policy to have been of negligible effectiveness in terms of the relevant policy objective. Very recently, R. G. Lipsey [38] has argued that this formulation of the problem is wrong, and that the purpose of incomes policy is to change the slope of the Phillips curve (specifically, to flatten it) rather than to change the constant term that determines its location. The empirical work on the British data by Lipsey and Parkin[28] shows that incomes policy, interpreted this way, has in fact been successful; but that because the policy-makers have reduced the level of employment simultaneously with the introduction of incomes policy, they have in fact achieved the pessimum result of increasing both the level of unemployment and the rate of inflation.

VIII. *Concluding Comments*

Since the Radcliffe Committee was appointed, and even more since it reported, there has been a tremendous surge of interest in and research into the general field of monetary economics. This chapter has attempted to survey the major topics of probable interest to British readers. One topic important for the development of British monetary economics has been deliberately omitted as not yet lending itself to generalization: the long and frequently confused debate over the theory of the money-supply process in the United Kingdom and the role and objectives of the Bank of England, a debate sparked by the Radcliffe Report itself and strongly influenced by the development of theory and research in the United States. Of the topics surveyed, the one probably of greatest current interest is the rise of monetarism and particularly the implications of monetarism for the theory of the balance of payments. Perhaps the greatest disservice that Keynes rendered to the development of economics in Britain was to develop the theory of macro-economics and money on the assumption of a closed economy. The extension of Keynesian theory to an open economy—which has been largely the work of economists in other countries, though the classic contribution of James Meade [39] must be recognized—has been built on the manifestly unsatisfactory assumption of money illusion on the part of the wage-earners, which assumption is necessary to permit exchange rate changes to be treated as producing changes in real-price relationships. Much work remains to be done in developing a monetary economics appropriate to the analytical and policy problems of the British economy.

NOTES

1. M. Friedman [16], p. 73. (My personal hypothesis is that, as a result of his studies of the Marshallian demand curve and his year as a visitor in Cambridge, Friedman became enamoured of the "Cambridge oral tradition" as a concept permitting the attribution to an institution of a wisdom exceeding that displayed in its published work, and unconsciously stole a leaf from Cambridge's book for the benefit of his own institution.)

2. For a review of the relevant empirical studies, see David Laidler [34] and Laurence Harris [21].

3. See Hester [23], Ando [2], de Prano [10], also Friedman [18] and Rejoinders in same issue. For a commentary on the issues, see Stephanie K. Edge [11].

4. See Milton Friedman [15].

5. See, for example, James Tobin [57].

6. See Leonall C. Andersen and Jerry L. Jordan [1]; further discussion may be found in the April 1969 and August 1969 issues of the *Review.*

7. The issue is discussed in Milton Friedman [17].

8. For an example of the monetary approach to balance-of-payments theory, see R. A. Mundell [44].

9. On these issues see also "Comment."

10. See Don Patinkin [46], Ch. VII.

11. See, for example, James Tobin [58].

12. See, for example, David W. Laidler [34].

13. See Gibson, "Foundations of Monetary Theory: A Review Article," *The Manchester School of Economic and Social Studies,* Vol. XXXVII, No. 1 (March 1969), pp. 59–75; and Laurence Harris, "Professor Hicks and the Foundations of Monetary Economics," *Economica,* Vol. 36, No. 142 (May 1969), pp. 196–208.

14. For an extended treatment of the subject matter of this and the following section, see Allan H. Meltzer [41].

15. Monographs 19 and 20 (Hester [24, 25]) are concerned with applications of the portfolio-balance approach to the micro-economics of investor and of institutional behaviour, and hence fall outside the field of interest of this chapter.

16. Quotations from "Foreword" (to the series), Monograph 21, pp. v–vi.

17. In connection with the discussion of the work (Johnson [30]) of Gurley and Shaw in my 1962 survey, it may be remarked that the empirical volume that was to have validated their theoretical work on financial intermediation has not yet appeared.

18. Quotations from "Foreword," Monograph 21, p. viii; these two propositions are developed in Hester [26].

19. See Tobin [56] and Brainard [3].

20. See, for example, J. E. Meade [40].

21. For discussion see Brunner [4].

22. *Journal of Money, Credit and Banking,* Vol. I, No. 2 (May 1969).

23. Recognition of these points motivated, at least in part, the *Report on Bank Charges* of the National Board for Prices and Incomes, which argued against traditional methods of monetary control in the United Kingdom and in favour of more competition in banking.

24. On these issues see Johnson [31].

25. For a recent analysis leading to this conclusion, couched in quantity theory terms and rich in the application of relevant capital theory, see M. Friedman [16]. Besides being misleadingly titled, since the analysis refers to a growing and not a static economy, this essay is rather distracting in its pursuit of theoretical side issues suggested by past controversies and its intrusive concern for a quantification of potential welfare gains which is provided only fragmentarily and inconclusively; the need for the rather embarrassing "final schizophrenic note" could have been avoided by presenting the argument more frankly as a logical exercise. It may be recalled that the pre-Keynesian quantity theorists recognized the problem of the

optimal trend of the price level, but tended to interpret it as a problem of social justice in the division of the gains from technical progress between the active and the retired population, because they failed to understand the link between the money and the real rate of interest provided by the expected rate of inflation.

26. See, for example, G. L. Reuber [52].

27. See, for example, Bernard Corry and David Laidler [9]; also A. G. Hines [28].

28. See, for example, David C. Smith [55].

REFERENCES

1. Andersen, Leonall C., and Jerry Jordan, "Monetary and Fiscal Actions: A Test of Their Relative Importance in Economic Stabilization," *Federal Reserve Bank of St. Louis Review,* 50: 11–23 (November 1968).

2. Ando, Albert, and Franco Maligliani, "Velocity and the Investment Multiplier," *American Economic Review,* 55: 693–728 (September 1965).

3. Brainard, William C., "Financial Intermediaries and a Theory of Monetary Control," *Yale Economic Essays,* 4: 431–82 (Fall 1964).

4. Brunner, Karl, "Yale and Money," *Journal of Finance,* 26: 165–75 (March 1971).

5. Cagan, Phillip, *Determinants and Effects of Changes in the Stock of Money, 1867–1960* (New York: Columbia University Press, 1965).

6. Carson, Deane (ed.), *Banking and Monetary Studies* (Homewood, Ill.: Richard D. Irwin, 1963).

7. Clower, R. W., "Reconsideration of the Microfoundations of Monetary Theory," *Western Economic Journal,* 6: 1–8 (December 1967).

8. Commission of Money and Credit, *Stabilization Policies* (Englewood Cliffs, N.J.: Prentice-Hall, 1963).

9. Corry, Bernard, and David Laidler, "The Phillips Relation: A Theoretical Explanation," *Economica,* 34: 189–97 (May 1967).

10. de Prano, Michael, and Thomas Mayer, "Autonomous Expenditure and Money," *American Economic Review,* 55: 729–52 (September 1965).

11. Edge, Stephanie K. "The Relative Stability of Monetary Velocity and the Investment Multiplier," *Australian Economic Papers,* 6: 192–207 (December 1967).

12. Friedman, Milton, *Studies in the Quantity Theory of Money* (University of Chicago Press, 1956).

13. Friedman, Milton, "The Quantity Theory of Money: A Restatement," in Milton Friedman (ed.), *Studies in the Quantity Theory of Money* (University of Chicago Press, 1956) [reprinted in this volume—Ed.].

14. Friedman, Milton, and Anna J. Schwartz, *A Monetary History of The United States, 1867–1960* (Princeton, N.J.: Princeton University Press, 1963).

15. Friedman, Milton, "The Role of Monetary Policy," *American Economic Review,* 58: 1–17 (March 1968). Reprinted in M. Friedman,

The Optimum Quantity of Money (London: Aldine, 1969), Ch. 5, pp. 95–110.

16. Friedman, Milton, *The Optimum Quantity of Money* (London: Aldine, 1969).

17. Friedman, Milton, "A Theoretic Framework for Monetary Analysis," *Journal of the Political Economy,* 78: 193–238 (March/April 1970).

18. Friedman, Milton, and David Meiselman, "Reply to Ando et al.," *American Economic Review* 55: 693–728 (September 1965).

19. Friedman, Milton, and Anna J. Schwartz, "The Definition of Money: Net Wealth and Neutrality as Criteria," *Journal of Money, Credit and Banking,* 1: 1–14 (February 1969).

20. Gibson, N. J., "Foundations of Monetary Theory: A Review Article," *Manchester School,* 37: 59–75 (March 1969).

21. Harris, Laurence, "Regularities and Irregularities in Monetary Economics," in C. R. Whittlesey and J. S. G. Wilson (eds.), *Essays in Money and Banking in Honour of R. S. Sayers* (New York: Clarendon Press, 1968).

22. Harris, Laurence, "Professor Hicks and the Foundations of Monetary Economics," *Economica,* 36: 196–208 (May 1969).

23. Hester, Donald, "Keynes and the Quantity Theory: A Comment on the Friedman-Meiselman CMC Paper," and M. Friedman and D. Meiselman, "Reply to Donald Hester," *Review of Economics and Statistics,* 46: 364–76 (November 1964).

24. Hester, Donald D., and James Tobin (eds.), *Risk Aversions and Portfolio Choice,* Cowles Foundation Monograph 19 (New York: Wiley and Sons, 1967).

25. Hester, Donald D., and James Tobin, *Studies in Portfolio Behavior,* Cowles Foundation Monograph 20 (New York: Wiley and Sons, 1967).

26. Hester, Donald D., and James Tobin, *Financial Markets and Economic Activity,* Cowles Foundation Monograph 21 (New York: Wiley and Sons, 1967).

27. Hicks, John R., *Critical Essays in Monetary Theory* (New York: Clarendon Press, 1967).

28. Hines, A. G., "Unemployment and the Rate of Change of Money Wages in the United Kingdom 1862–1963: A Reappraisal," *Review of Economics and Statistics,* 50: 60–67 (February 1968).

29. Johnson, Harry G., "Monetary Theory and Policy," *American Economic Review,* 52: 335–84 (June 1962) [reprinted in this volume—Ed.].

30. Johnson, Harry G., "Recent Developments in Monetary Theory," *Indian Economic Review,* 6: 1–28 (August 1963). Reprinted in H. G. Johnson, *Essays in Monetary Economics* (London: Allen & Unwin, 1969).

31. Johnson, Harry G., "Problems of Efficiency in Monetary Management," *Journal of Political Economy,* 76: 971–90 (September/October 1968).

32. Johnson, Harry G., "Inside Money, Outside Money, Income, Wealth, and Welfare in Monetary Theory," *Journal of Money, Credit and Banking,* 1: 30–45 (February 1969); also "Comment."

33. Johnson, Harry G. "Money in a Neo-Classical One-Sector Growth Model," in Johnson, *Essays in Monetary Economics* (London: Allen & Unwin (1969).

34. Laidler, David, *The Demand for Money* (Scranton, Pa.: International Textbook, 1969).

35. Leijonhufvud, Axel, *On Keynesian Economics and the Economics of Keynes* (London: Oxford University Press, 1968).

36. Leijonhufvud, Axel, *Keynes and the Classics,* Occasional Paper 30 (Institute of Economic Affairs, 1969).

37. Levhari, D., and D. Patinkin, "The Role of Money in a Simple Growth Model," *American Economic Review,* 58: 713–53 (September 1968).

38. Lipsey, R. G., and J. M. Pankin, "Incomes Policy: A Reappraisal," *Economica,* 37: 115–38 (May 1970).

39. Meade, J. E., *The Theory of International Economic Policy,* Vol. I: *The Balance of Payments;* Vol. II: *Trade and Welfare* (London: Oxford University Press, 1951 and 1955).

40. Meade, J. E., "The Amount of Money and the Banking System," *Economic Journal,* 44: 77–83 (1934). Reprinted in American Economic Association, *Readings in Monetary Theory* (Homewood, Ill.: Richard D. Irwin, 1951).

41. Meltzer, Allan, "Money, Intermediation, and Growth," *Journal of Economic Literature,* 7: 27–56 (March 1969).

42. Metzler, Lloyd A., "Wealth, Saving and the Rate of Interest," *Journal of Political Economy,* 59: 93–116 (April 1951) [reprinted in this volume—Ed.].

43. Moore, Basil J., *An Introduction to the Theory of Finance: Asset-holder Behaviour under Uncertainty* (London: Macmillan, 1968).

44. Mundell, R. A., "Real Gold, Dollars and Paper Gold," *American Economic Review, Papers and Proceedings,* 59: 324–31 (May 1968).

45. Newlyn, W. T., "Definitions and Classifications," *Theory of Money* (New York: Clarendon Press, 1962).

46. Patinkin, Don, *Money, Interest, and Prices: An Integration of Monetary and Value Theory* (New York: Harper & Row, 1965).

47. Patinkin, Don, "The Chicago Tradition, The Quantity Theory and Friedman," *Journal of Money, Credit and Banking,* 1: 46–70 (February 1969).

48. Pesek, Boris P., and Thomas Saving. *Money, Wealth and Economic Theory* (New York: Macmillan, 1967).

49. Phelps, E. S., "The Golden Rule of Accumulation: A Fable for Growthman," *American Economic Review,* 51: 638–48 (September 1961).

50. Phelps, E. S., "Philips Curves, Expectations of Inflation and Optimal Unemployment Over Time," *Economica,* 34: 254–81 (August 1967).

51. Phillips, A. W., "The Relation between Unemployment and the Rate of Change of Money Wages in the United Kingdom, 1862–1957," *Economica,* 25: 283–99 (December 1958).

52. Reuber, G. L., "The Objectives of Canadian Monetary Policy,

1949–61: Empirical 'Tradeoffs' and the Reaction Function of the Authorities," *Journal of Political Economy,* 72: 109–32 (April 1964).

53. Rousseas, Stephen W. (ed.), *Proceedings of Symposium on Inflation: Its Causes, Consequences and Control* (Calvin K. Kazanjian Economics Foundation, 1969).

54. Sidrauski, Miguel, "Inflation and Economic Growth," *Journal of Political Economy,* 75: 796–810 (December 1967).

55. Smith, David C., "Incomes Policy," in R. E. Cases and associates, *Britain's Economic Prospects* (Washington, D.C.: Brookings Institution and London: Allen & Unwin, 1968).

56. Tobin, James, and William C. Brainard, "Financial Intermediaries and the Effectiveness of Monetary Controls," *American Economic Review,* 52: 383–400 (May 1963).

57. Tobin, James, "Money and Economic Growth," *Econometrica,* 33: 671–84 (October 1965).

58. Tobin, James, "Notes on Optimal Monetary Growth," *Journal of Political Economy,* 76: 833–59 (July/August 1968).

59. Yeager, Leland B., "Essential Properties of the Medium of Exchange," *Kyklos,* 21: 45–69 (1968).

2 *Monetary Theory and Policy*

Harry G. Johnson *University of Chicago*

In order to isolate a field of study clearly enough demarcated to
be usefully surveyed, it is necessary to define monetary theory as
comprising theories concerning the influence of the quantity of
money in the economic system, and monetary policy as policy employing the central bank's control of the supply of money as an
instrument for achieving the objectives of general economic policy.
In surveying the field thus narrowly defined fourteen years ago,
Henry Villard [124] began by remarking on the relative decline in
the significance attached to it as compared with the offshoot fields
of business cycle and fiscal (income and employment) theory, a
decline related to the experience of the 1930's, the intellectual impact of Keynes' *General Theory* [66], and the inhibiting effects of the
wartime expansion of public debt on monetary policy. While this
division of labor has continued, and has indeed been accentuated
by the emergence of the cross-cutting field of economic growth and
development as an area of specialization, the field of money has
been increasingly active and has received increasing attention in
the past fourteen years.

This recent activity in the money field can be explained in part
by the general logic of scientific progress, according to which disputed issues are investigated with the aid of more powerful theoretical tools, and the implications of new approaches are explored
in rigorous detail. Thus, in monetary theory, the issues raised by
Keynes' attack on "classical" monetary theory have been worked

Reprinted from *American Economic Review*, Vol. 52 (June 1962), 335–84, by
permission of the author and the American Economic Association.

33

over with the apparatus of general equilibrium analysis developed by J. R. Hicks [60] (to the gradual eclipse of the Robertsonian and Swedish period analysis once considered most promising), and Keynes' emphasis on treating money as an asset has been followed by subsequent theorists as a means of bringing money within the general framework of the theory of choice. In larger part, the revival of interest in money is a reflection of external developments —the postwar inflation, the consequent revival of monetary policy, and the persistence of inflation in the face of unemployment— together with recognition of the problems posed for both policy and theory by certain institutional characteristics of the modern economy (notably the widespread holding of liquid assets) and by potential conflicts between the diverse policy objectives now accepted as responsibilities of governmental policy.

The interest of professional economists in these matters has also been directly enlisted in the preparation of testimony and studies for a succession of large-scale enquiries into monetary policy and institutions, most recently the Radcliffe Report in Britain [128] and the Report [129] of the Commission on Money and Credit established by the Committee for Economic Development in the United States.[1] Finally, recent work on both theory and policy has been strongly influenced by the increased postwar emphasis on (and capacity for) econometric model-building and testing, and stimulated by the availability of new data—especially Raymond Goldsmith's data on saving [47] and financial intermediaries [48] in the United States, the Federal Reserve System's flow-of-funds accounts ([127] and subsequent publications), and Milton Friedman and Anna Schwartz' historical series of the United States money supply, forthcoming in [42].

While the impact of Keynes' *General Theory* has been so great that most of recent theory and research on money can be classified either as application and extension of Keynesian ideas or as counter-revolutionary attack on them, it seems preferable in a survey of the field to organize the material according to the main areas of research rather than according to the issues Keynes raised. Readers interested in the present status of Keynes' contributions to economics are referred to anniversary assessments by William Fellner and Dudley Dillard [32], James Schlesinger [103], H. G. Johnson [61], and R. E. Kuenne [71]. This survey deals with four broad topics: the neutrality of money; the theory of demand for money, which becomes the theory of velocity of circulation when the demand for money is related to income; the theory of money supply, monetary control, and monetary dynamics; and monetary policy. In companion articles G. L. S. Shackle has surveyed the theory of interest [106; see also page 419, in this volume], and

Martin Bronfenbrenner and Franklyn Holzman have surveyed the theory of inflation [*American Economic Review*, 53: 593–661 (September 1963)].

The Classical Dichotomy and the Neutrality of Money

From the standpoint of pure theory, the most fundamental issue raised by Keynes in the *General Theory* lay in his attack on the traditional separation of monetary and value theory, the "classical dichotomy" as (following Don Patinkin [95]) it has come to be called, according to which relative prices are determined by the "real" forces of demand and supply and the absolute price level is determined by the quantity of money and its velocity of circulation. Keynes' attack has been followed by a protracted, often confused, and usually intensely mathematical investigation of the "consistency" or "validity" of the classical dichotomy, the requirements of a consistent theory of value in a monetary economy, and the conditions under which money will or will not be "neutral" (in the sense that a change in the quantity of money will not alter the real equilibrium of the system—relative prices and the interest rate). In the course of the controversy at least as much has been learned about the difficulty of extracting theoretical conclusions from systems of equations as has been contributed to usable monetary theory. The argument, it should be noted, has been concerned throughout with a monetary economy characterized by minimal uncertainty, whereas Keynes was concerned with a highly uncertain world in which money provides a major link between present and future (on this point see Shackle [106, p. 211]).

THE INTEGRATION OF MONETARY AND VALUE THEORY

The early history of what is often described as "the Patinkin controversy" is not worth recounting in detail; an annotated bibliography of it may be found in Valavanis [123], and Patinkin's own summary in [91; see also page 268 in this volume]. It began with Oskar Lange's argument [72] that Say's Law (which in this context is the principle that people sell goods only for the purpose of buying goods) logically precludes any monetary theory, since in combination with Walras' Law (that the total supply of goods and money to the market must be equal to the total demand for goods and money from the market) it implies that the excess demand for money on the market is identically zero regardless of the absolute price level, which therefore is indeterminate. Patinkin took up this charge, shifting the object of criticism to the classical assumption that the demand and supply functions for commodities are homogeneous of degree zero in commodity prices (that is, a doubling of all commodity prices will leave quantities demanded and supplied unchanged—in other words, quantities demanded depend only on relative prices). This criticism was refined and its mathematical formulation clarified in response to subsequent critical contributions, of which the most important was Karl Brunner's demonstration [17] that a consistent monetary theory could be constructed without assigning utility to money.

In its final form at this stage [91], Patinkin's criticism of the classical dichotomy was that there was a logical contradiction between classical value theory, in which demands and supplies of commodities depended only on relative prices and not on the real value of people's cash balances, and the quantity theory of money, in which the dependence of spending on the real value of money balances provides the mechanism by which the quantity of money determines a stable equilibrium absolute price level, a contradiction which could be removed neither by resort to Say's Law nor by abandonment of the quantity theory in favor of some other monetary theory. But, Patinkin argued, the contradiction could be removed, and classical theory reconstituted, by making the demand and supply functions depend on real cash balances as well as relative prices; while this would eliminate the dichotomy, it would preserve the basic features of classical monetary theory, and particularly the invariance of the real equilibrium of the economy (relative prices and the rate of interest) with respect to changes in the quantity of money.

The integration of monetary and value theory through the explicit introduction of real balances as a determinant of behavior, and the reconstitution of classical monetary theory, is the main theme and contribution of Patinkin's monumentally scholarly work, *Money, Interest, and Prices* [94]. The first part of the book ("Microeconomics") develops the theory of the real balance effect (the effect of a change in the price level on the real value of money balances and hence on expenditure) in terms of a Hicksian exchange economy in which the individual starts each week with an endowment of commodities that must be consumed within the week and a stock of fiat money, and plans to exchange these for commodities to be consumed during the week and cash balances with which to start the next week. The demand for cash balances is a demand for real balances, derived rather artificially from the assumption that though equilibrium prices are fixed at the beginning of the week, cash payments and receipts are randomly distributed over the week and the individual attaches disutility to the prospect of being unable to pay cash on demand. A rise in prices lowers the real value of an individual's initial cash holding and, provided that neither goods nor real balances are "inferior," reduces his demand for both (implying a less than unit-elastic demand curve for money with respect to its purchasing power); but a proportional rise in prices accompanied by an equiproportional increase in the individual's initial money stock does not alter his behavior. Extended to the market as a whole, the first property ensures the stability of the money price level, the second yields the quantity theory result that a doubling of everyone's money stock will double prices but leave the real equilibrium unchanged. When lending and borrowing by means of bonds are introduced, this latter result requires a doubling of everyone's initial bond assets or liabilities as well as his money holdings. Patinkin's chief criticism of the classical economists has now been reduced to their failure to analyze the role of the real balance effect in ensuring price level stability; the charge of definite inconsistency can only be fairly pinned to a few specific writers of later vintage.

Carefully worked out as it is, Patinkin's analysis of the real balance effect is conceptually inadequate and crucially incomplete; both defects are attributable to an unsatisfactory analysis of stock-flow relationships. The conceptual inadequacy is inherent in the lumping together of the stock of cash and the week's income of goods into a total of disposable resources and the application of the conventional concept of inferiority to the possible effects of changes in this hybrid total on the quantities of real balances and goods demanded.[2] The incompleteness is inherent in Patinkin's restriction of his analysis of the effects of a disturbance to the single week in which it occurs. Archibald and Lipsey [2; see also page 297 in this volume] have shown that over succeeding weeks an individual whose real balances differed from their desired level would accumulate or decumulate balances by spending less or more than his income until real balances attained the desired level, at which point expenditure would once again equal income. Thus, they argue, the real balance effect is a transient phenomenon, relevant only to short-run disequilibrium situations. If positions of long-run equilibrium are compared, the effect of a change in the quantity of money does not depend on its initial distribution (since individuals will redistribute it among themselves in adjusting their real balances to the desired level) and the demand for money with respect to its purchasing power has the classical unitary elasticity; finally, real balances can be dropped from the equations determining equilibrium, which can be written as functions of relative prices only.

On the basis of this last result, Archibald and Lipsey attacked the Lange-Patinkin charge of inconsistency in classical theory, and showed that a consistent system could be constructed using demand and supply functions homogeneous of degree zero in prices, supplemented by the quantity equation, though this system would not conform to Walras' Law when out of equilibrium. Earlier, Valavanis [123] had disputed Patinkin's apparent victory in the dichotomy debate, and shown that if the (in my opinion, misnamed) Cambridge equation is interpreted as an independent restraint on behavior rather than as a behavior relationship conflicting with Walras' Law, there is no inconsistency. J. Encarnación has since shown [31] that Lange's mathematical proof of inconsistency is invalid, and Patinkin's rests on a misuse of the term "consistency."

As a subsequent symposium [7] on the Archibald-Lipsey article has helped to show, these demonstrations, while justified perhaps by Patinkin's continued emphasis on the "inconsistency" theme, are really beside the main point. While a formally consistent theory can be constructed by interpreting velocity as an externally imposed restraint on monetary behavior (an interpretation for which there is ample precedent in the literature) this treatment not only leaves velocity itself unexplained on economic grounds, but precludes any analysis of monetary dynamics and the stability of monetary equilibrium by its inability to specify behavior in disequilibrium conditions. As the better classical monetary theorists saw, these problems are most easily handled by assuming that money balances yield services of utility to their holders; and Patinkin's major contribution has been to elaborate a rigorous formal theory of this approach.

THE NEUTRALITY AND NONNEUTRALITY OF MONEY

The second part of Patinkin's book reformulates the argument in terms of a short-run macroeconomic system, Keynesian in structure[3] but based on "classical" behavior assumptions, and arrives at the classical result that relative prices and the rate of interest are independent of the quantity of money. The significance of this demonstration lies mainly in the assumptions required to establish the neutrality of money [94, Ch. 12]: wage and price flexibility, inelastic expectations, absence of "money illusion," absence of "distribution effects," homogeneity of "bonds," and absence of government debt or open-market operations.[4] This rarefied set of assumptions is the main object of attack in J. G. Gurley and E. S. Shaw's *Money in a Theory of Finance* [52], a central purpose of which is to elucidate the conditions under which money will not be neutral.

Mention must first be made of an earlier, and influential, article by L. A. Metzler [84; see also page 324 in this volume], whose analysis underlies the final assumption listed above. Metzler argued that the wealth-saving relationship assumed in the use of the Pigou effect by Keynes' critics to demonstrate that price flexibility would maintain full employment in the Keynesian model[5] implied a theory in which changes in the quantity of money could affect the rate of interest (and consequently the rate of growth). Assuming for simplicity that government obligations are fixed in real terms, and that interest on government holdings of its own debt is returned as income to the community, Metzler showed that the price increase consequent on monetary expansion effected by open-market purchase of government debt would leave the community with a smaller stock of real assets and a greater willingness to save, thus lowering the equilibrium interest rate, though monetary expansion effected through the printing press would not alter the equilibrium interest rate. As Haberler shortly pointed out [54], Metzler's analysis of open-market operations implicitly rests on a distribution effect (the private sector but not the government being assumed to be influenced by a change in the latter's real debt); but subsequent writers, including Patinkin, have accepted this as a legitimate assumption, and Gurley and Shaw's analysis builds on it.

Gurley and Shaw's book is related to their earlier work on financial intermediaries in relation to economic growth and monetary policy; these aspects of their analysis will be taken up in the appropriate context. Their contribution to the neutrality discussion, apart from their insistence that rigidities, money illusion, expectations, and distribution effects may be quite important in actuality, consists in bringing back into the analysis the monetary and financial structure and the differing liquidity characteristics of different assets excluded by assumption in Patinkin's models. They begin by constructing a simple model alternative to Patinkin's, in which money is not itself government debt but is issued by the monetary authority against private debt ("inside" money, as contrasted with "outside" money), and showing that in this model the price level is determinate[6] and money is neutral. They then show that money will not be neutral in a system containing inside and outside money, outside bonds, or a variety of securities against which money can be created. The key to these results is that in these cases an increase in the quantity of money of either variety, accompanied by a proportional increase in the prices of goods and private debts, alters the relative quantities of the various assets to be held by the public; and their significance to the neutrality debate can be reduced to any arbitrarily low level by arguing that they depend on a distribution effect, and that the appropriate test of neutrality is an equiproportional change in inside money, the assets backing it, and outside assets (see Patinkin [92, p. 108]). It may also be remarked that the results depend in no way on the presence of financial intermediaries.

Gurley and Shaw's analysis follows the tradition of Metzler and Patinkin in relating nonneutrality to the existence of government debt; their inside-money analysis merely makes noninterest-bearing as well as interest-bearing government debt a disturber of neutrality. This tradition leaves modern formal monetary theory rather awkwardly dependent on adventitious institutional or historical details; and the question naturally arises whether this is the best that can be done. The source of the difficulty lies in the implicit distribution effect introduced by the recognition that, unlike other debtors, the government does not have to worry about the size of its debts. For this difference there are two reasons: (1) the government can always pay its debts by issuing fresh debts, since it controls the money supply, (2) the government can always command the resources required to pay the interest on its debts, since it possesses the taxing power. The latter is the reason relevant to the level of theoretical generality of the neutrality discussion; and at that level it provides grounds for denying that interest-bearing government debt should be treated as net assets of the public. The existence of government debt implies the levying of taxes to pay the interest on it, and in a world of reasonable certainty these taxes would be capitalized into liabilities equal in magnitude to the government debt; hence, if distribution effects between individuals are ignored, a change in the real amount of government debt will have no wealth-effect.[7] Finally, if this logic applies to interest-bearing government debt, why should it not apply to the limiting case of noninterest-bearing government debt, which is equally a debt of the public to itself, and to commodity moneys, which are the same thing though based on custom rather than law?

This line of reasoning suggests that the more elegant approach to monetary theory lies along inside-money rather than outside-money lines, and that the foundation of the theory of monetary equilibrium and stability should be the substitution effect rather than the (in this case nonexistent) wealth effect of a change in real balances. It also has implications for the dichotomy debate: in the inside-money case the economy can be validly dichotomized into a real and a money sector, since the real-balance effect reduces to a change in the relative quantities of real balances and real debt (see Franco Modigliani [58, pp. 183–84] and Patinkin [92, p. 107]). Finally, it suggests an opportunity for a reassessment of Keynes' theory of employment, which is guiltless of the charges brought against it by

Pigou and elaborated by Patinkin and others if interpreted as applying to an inside-money world.

The Demand for Money and the Velocity of Circulation

As Villard remarked in his earlier survey [124, pp. 316–24], the equation-of-exchange approach to monetary theory was eclipsed by the income-expenditure approach[8] after 1930 largely because of the prevailing tendency to treat velocity as determined in principle by institutional factors governing the rapidity of circulation of the medium of exchange and as in practice a constant—a treatment clearly contradicted by experience in the 1930's. The alternative theory expounded by Keynes emphasized the determinants of expenditure; but it also contained a monetary theory founded on the function of money as a store of value and on the special characteristics of money as a form of holding wealth. This theory has been refined and elaborated by subsequent writers in the Keynesian tradition. In the process, Keynes' most extreme departure from previous analysis of the demand for money—his emphasis on the speculative demand for money at the expense of the precautionary—has been gradually abandoned (as has his awkward separation of the transactions and speculative demand for money), and the speculative motive has been relegated to the short run and reabsorbed into the general theory of asset holding. On the other side, the treatment of velocity as determined by payments institutions, while prominent in some expositions of the quantity theory, was by no means the core of classical monetary theory, which clearly recognized the opportunity cost of holding wealth in monetary form; and modern followers of the classical tradition, building on this foundation, treat velocity explicitly as reflecting a demand for money derived from preferences concerning the disposition of wealth.

In consequence, contemporary monetary theorists, whether avowedly "Keynesian" or "quantity," approach the demand for money in essentially the same way, as an application of the general theory of choice, though the former tend to formulate their analysis in terms of the demand for money as an asset alternative to other assets, and the latter, in terms of the demand for the services of money as a good. Aside from some conceptual perplexities concerning the relation between capital and income in this context, the chief substantive issues outstanding are three: first, what specific collection of assets corresponds most closely to the theoretical concept of money—an issue that arises as soon as the distinguishing characteristic of money ceases to be its function as a medium of exchange; second, what the variables are on which the demand for money so defined depends; and third, whether the demand for money is sufficiently stable to provide, in conjunction with the quantity of money, a better explanation of observed movements of money income and other aggregates than is provided by models built around income-expenditure relationships. These are essentially empirical issues, to which empirical research has as yet produced no conclusive answers; and they clearly have an important practical bearing on monetary policy.

DEVELOPMENTS IN LIQUIDITY PREFERENCE THEORY

To begin with the recent development of Keynesian analysis of the demand for money, subsequent contributions have been concerned with four aspects of Keynes' treatment of this subject: the separation of the demand into a transactions demand dependent on income and a liquidity-preference demand dependent on the rate of interest; the emphasis on the speculative element in liquidity preference; the neglect of wealth as a determinant of liquidity preference; and the aggregation of all assets other than money into bonds implicit in the use of a single (long-term) rate of interest.

The separation of the demand for money into two parts, besides being mathematically inelegant, incorporated the mechanical treatment of transactions demand that Keynes had criticized in the quantity theory. Keynesian writers (for example, Alvin Hansen [56, pp. 66–67]) began to treat transactions demand as reflecting economic behavior and particularly as being interest-elastic, from which it was a short step to making the demand for money as a whole depend on income and the rate of interest. The logic of treating transactions demand as reflecting rational choice was subsequently provided by W. J. Baumol [9; see also page 165 in this volume] and James Tobin [118], the former's analysis being more interesting in that it links the problem to inventory theory. Both authors show that an economic unit starting a period with a transactions balance to be spent evenly over the period, and having the opportunity of investing idle funds at interest and withdrawing them as needed at a cost partly fixed per withdrawal, will disinvest at more frequent intervals (carry a lower average cash balance) the higher the rate of interest. They also show that the average cash balance held by the unit will be higher the higher the amount of the initial transactions balance, but less than proportionately higher.[9]

Keynes' emphasis on the extremely short-run speculative motive as the source of interest-elasticity in the liquidity demand for money was one of the main targets of Keynes' critics. Subsequent Keynesian writing has stressed Keynes' alternative explanation of liquidity preference, which rests this interest-elasticity on uncertainty about the future interest rate rather than on a definite expectation about its level; this explanation is really the precautionary motive in disguise (see Johnson [61, p. 8]). An elegant exposition of both explanations, using the theory of portfolio management, has been provided by Tobin [116; see also page 178 in this volume].

The introduction of the value of wealth, which itself depends on the rate of interest, as an explicit determinant of the demand for money was part of a more general process of freeing Keynes' theory from its short-period equilibrium assumptions. It implied for the theory of liquidity preference, as noticed by Lloyd Metzler [84; see also page 128 in this volume], Ralph Turvey [121] and Frank Brechling [10], that the liquidity-preference curve would be different for a change in the quantity of money brought about by fiscal policy than for a change effected by open-market operations (these two curves, and a third corresponding to constant wealth, are discussed in Turvey [122, Ch. 2]). It also introduces the difficulty, noted earlier by Borje Kragh [69], that the speculative demand curve for money traced out by open-market operations will differ according to the size of the units in which these are conducted, since the effects on wealth will differ. The wealth effects of discontinuity in open-market operations are exploited in Sidney Weintraub's recent contention [125, pp. 156–60] that the speculative demand curve is irreversible, as Richard Davis [30] has subsequently pointed out. At a far more fundamental level, the analysis of the demand for money that emerges from these developments, in which the demand for money depends on the interrelated variables income, the rate of interest, and wealth, raises important conceptual (and econometric) difficulties not always fully appreciated by monetary theorists; these difficulties will be referred to later in connection with Milton Friedman's restatement of the quantity theory.

The fourth development stemming from Keynes' theory of the demand for money has been the disaggregation of assets other than money and the elaboration of liquidity preference theory into a general theory of the relative prices of (rates of return on) assets of different types. The chief contributions in the direct line of Keynes' own thought, by Joan Robinson [99] and Richard Kahn [63], are primarily concerned with reasserting Keynes' view that the long-term rate of interest is determined by expectations about the future long-term rate, against Hicks' dismissal of it as a bootstrap theory and his attempt to explain the long-term rate as an average of expected short-term rates [60, pp. 163–64]. Robinson and Kahn both employ a division of assets into cash, bills, bonds, and equities, and a classification of asset-holders into contrasting types according to whether their asset preferences are dominated by capital-uncertainty or income-uncertainty; but Robinson is concerned to set the argument against the background of a growing economy, while Kahn concentrates on a rather subtle analysis of the interaction of the precautionary and speculative motives.

In contrast, U.S. contributions have been prompted by concern with the problems posed for monetary, fiscal, and debt-management policy by the wartime legacy of a large public debt of short average maturity; two early articles influential in subsequent thinking were those of Roland McKean [81] and Richard Musgrave [88]. The common feature of subsequent work is the treatment of assets as possessing varying degrees of liquidity, and the application of general equilibrium theory to the determination of their relative prices (yields), which are treated as the outcome of the interaction of asset preferences and the relative quantities of the different assets available. This approach (which is also central in the analysis of Robinson and Kahn just mentioned) is exemplified in W. L. Smith's study of debt management for the Joint Economic Committee [111] and Ralph Turvey's book on interest rates and asset prices [122]. The latter is notable for its explicit general equilibrium approach and its careful attention to the requirements of consistent aggregation. The formulation of monetary theory as part of a more general theory of asset holding has been carried farthest by the group working at Yale University under the inspiration of James Tobin; their "portfolio-balance" approach has been strongly influenced by Harry Markowitz's work on rational investor behavior (notably [78]). Unfortunately little of this group's work is yet available in print (see, however, Tobin [114; 116; 117; see also page 205 in this volume]).

The formulation of the general equilibrium approach to the theory of asset prices and yields in the literature just described has some implicit biases which are apt to mislead the unwary, especially in its application to the analysis of the term structure of interest rates.[10] In the first place, there is a tendency to follow too closely Hicks' original sketch of the approach [59] in identifying the typical asset-holder with a bank, borrowing for a shorter term than it lends and therefore preferring the shorter-term assets. In the second place, emphasis on the slippery and ill-defined quality of liquidity as the characteristic differentiating alternative assets tends to divert attention from the linkage of asset markets by speculation, and so to exaggerate the sensitivity of the interest-rate pattern to changes in the relative quantities of assets.[11] In this connection it is

appropriate to refer briefly[12] to some recent work on the term structure of interest rates by John Culbertson [29] and Joseph Conard
[24, Part III], which on its empirical side contributes to filling the
gap noted by Villard [124, pp. 336–37] between the theory and the
historical facts of interest-rate behavior. Both authors arrive at
essentially the same major result, that short and long rates tend to
move together in a rational way, though Culbertson regards his
analysis as contradicting the classical "expectations" theory whereas Conard regards his as confirming a modified version of it. The
explanation of this difference is ьat Culbertson identifies accepted
theory with the incorrect Hicks-Lutz formulation of it, according
to which the investor is depicted as choosing between holding a
bond to maturity and investing in successive short-term loans over
the same period, whereas Conard identifies it with the correct
formulation, in which the investor compares the expected yields
(including interest and changes in capital value) of alternative
assets over the period for which he expects or is obliged to remain
invested. A more recent study by David Meiselman [82] advances
both the theory and explanation of the rate structure (and incidentally refutes one of Culbertson's main arguments against the
expectations theory) by interpreting the yield curve as expressing
expected future short-term rates and explaining changes in it as
the market's reaction to errors of expectation.

RESTATEMENT OF THE QUANTITY THEORY

While Keynes' formulation of the theory of demand for money
has been evolving in the directions just described, a fundamentally
very similar formulation has been developed by a group of scholars
associated with the University of Chicago, inspired by Milton
Friedman and claiming allegiance to the quantity theory as handed
down in the oral tradition of that institution. The most complete
statement of this group's basic theory—which tends usually to be
mentioned only briefly in the course of presenting the results of
empirical research—is contained in the condensed and rather
cryptic restatement of the quantity theory by Friedman that
introduces four of their empirical studies [41; see also page 67 in
this volume], a restatement that takes the reader at a hard pace
from the fundamental theory to the simplifications required for its
empirical application. The central points in the restatement are
that the quantity theory is a theory of the demand for money, not
of output, money income, or prices; and that money is an asset or
capital good, so that the demand for it is a problem in capital
theory. In formulating the demand for money as a form of capital,
however, Friedman differs from the Keynesian theorists in starting

from the fundamentals of capital theory. He begins with the broad concept of wealth as comprising all sources of income, including human beings, and relates the demand for money to total wealth and the expected future streams of money income obtainable by holding wealth in alternative forms. Then, by a series of mathematical simplifications, approximations of nonobservable variables (of which the most important is the representation of the influence of human wealth by the ratio of nonhuman to human wealth), simplifying economic assumptions, and rearrangements of variables, he arrives at a demand function for money which depends on the price level, bond and equity yields, the rate of change of the price level, income, the ratio of nonhuman to human wealth, and a taste variable; finally, he makes neat use of the homogeneity assumption to show that the demand for real balances depends only on real variables and that it can be reformulated as a velocity function depending on the same variables.

In its final form, Friedman's demand function for money is hard to distinguish from a modern Keynesian formulation, especially in view of his remark that the nonhuman to human wealth ratio "is closely allied to what is usually defined as the ratio of wealth to income" [41, p. 8]. The apparent similarity is misleading, however, because what comes out as income originally entered as wealth, i.e. capitalized income, the process of capitalizing it being absorbed by Friedman's simplifications into the yield and wealth-ratio arguments of the function; and, as Friedman indicated by various remarks and has since demonstrated by the application of his permanent income concept to the explanation of the behavior of velocity [38; see also page 86 in this volume], the "income" relevant to this equation is not income as measured in the national accounts but income conceived of as the net return on a stock of wealth, or wealth measured by the income it yields. The use of "income" to represent what is really a wealth variable has incidentally contributed to some minor confusions of stock and flow concepts in the writings of Chicago monetary theorists, especially in the alternative formulation of the theory of demand for money as an application of demand theory developed by Richard Selden [105], where money rather than its services is described as the good demanded, the elasticity relating changes in the stock of money demanded to changes in the flow of income is described as an income-elasticity, and money is classed on the basis of the empirical magnitude of this elasticity as a luxury good.

Friedman's application to monetary theory of the basic principle of capital theory—that income is the yield on capital, and capital the present value of income—is probably the most important development in monetary theory since Keynes' *General Theory*.

Its theoretical significance lies in the conceptual integration of wealth and income as influences on behavior: Keynes ignored almost completely the influence of wealth, as was legitimate in short-period analysis; and while subsequent writers in the Keynesian tradition have reintroduced wealth they have generally followed the Cambridge practice of restricting wealth to nonhuman property, a practice which encourages uncritical treatment of wealth and income as entirely independent influences on behavior. In consequence, as mentioned earlier, much of the recent monetary literature contains formulations of the demand for money relating it to income, wealth, and the rate of interest, variables which are in fact interdependent and the use of which in this way involves inelegant redundancy and promotes errors in both theoretical reasoning and empirical applications.

The most important implication of Friedman's analysis, however, concerns not the formulation of monetary theory but the nature of the concept of "income" relevant to monetary analysis, which, as explained above, should correspond to the notion of expected yield on wealth rather than the conventions of national income accounting. This concept Friedman has elaborated under the name of "permanent income," and employed in his theory of the consumption function [35] and subsequent empirical work on the demand for money [38]. The statistical application of it has involved estimating expected income from past income, which means that empirically the theory is very similar to theories employing lagged income as a determinant of behavior.[13] This similarity exemplifies a serious problem in the empirical application and testing of economic theories—the theoretical interpretation of empirical results—which is especially acute in the interpretation of empirical findings on the demand for money because of the interrelationship of income, wealth, and interest.

THE DISTINGUISHING CHARACTERISTICS OF MONEY

While the treatment of money as an asset distinguished from other assets by its superior liquidity is common ground among contemporary theorists, the transition from the conception of money as a medium of exchange to money as a store of value has raised new problems for debate among monetary theorists. These problems result from recognition of the substitutability between money (conventionally defined as medium of exchange) and the wide range of alternative financial assets provided by government debt and the obligations of financial institutions, and between money and the access to credit provided by an elaborate credit system, in a financially advanced economy. They concern the related empirical questions of the definition of an appropriate monetary magnitude, and the specification of the variables on which the demand for the selected magnitude depends, questions that pose little difficulty when money is defined as the medium of exchange and its velocity is assumed to be determined by institutional factors. These questions lead into the fundamental question of the importance of the quantity of money in monetary theory and monetary policy, since unless the demand for money—defined to correspond to some quantity the central bank can influence—can be shown to be a stable function of a few key variables, the quantity of money must be a subordinate and not a strategic element in both the explanation and the control of economic activity. Argument and opinion about these issues have frequently been clouded by confusion between constant velocity and a stable velocity function, and between elasticity and instability of the function. In discussing them, it is convenient to describe first the main schools of thought on these issues,[14] and then the empirical research bearing on them.

At the cost of some arbitrary oversimplification, one can distinguish broadly four main schools of thought. At one extreme are those who continue to find the distinguishing characteristic of money in its function as medium of exchange, and define it as currency plus demand deposits adjusted [73; see also page 118 in this volume]. Next to them are the Chicago quantity theorists, who define the function of money more broadly as a temporary abode of purchasing power,[15] and in their empirical work define money as currency plus total commercial bank deposits adjusted, largely to obtain a consistent long statistical series [105; 38]. Both schools believe that there is a stable demand for money (velocity function), though they define money differently. A third school, at the opposite extreme, consists of those, usually specially interested in monetary policy rather than theory as such, who carry recognition of the similarity between money and other realizable assets or means of financing purchases to the point of rejecting money in favor of some much broader concept, measurable or unmeasurable. A measurable concept is exemplified by the long-established Federal Reserve Board theory that what matters is the total amount of credit outstanding, the quantity of money exercising an influence only because bank credit is a component of total credit (see for example [57, pp. 261–63 and 272–76]). An unmeasurable concept is exemplified by the Radcliffe Committee's concept of the liquidity of the economy [128, Ch. 6], the theory of which was left unexplained in its Report but has since been expounded by Richard Sayers [102]; according to this more extreme theory velocity is a meaningless number, the economy being able to economize on money by substituting credit for it without limit [128, p. 133]. This school, in both its variants, does not so much advance a theory as assert a position that implies a highly elastic, complex, or unstable velocity function. The serious controversy of recent years has been aroused by a fourth school, in between those already mentioned, which has been concerned with the implications for velocity of the presence of a substantial volume of liquid assets closely substitutable for money. In the early years after the war, this school was mainly concerned with the influence of short-term public debt; since the mid-fifties, the centre of attention has shifted to the liabilities of nonbank financial intermediaries.

The leading figures in this last development are J. G. Gurley and E. S. Shaw, who in a series of contributions [50; 51; 53; see also page 363 in this volume] culminating in a major theoretical work [52] have developed an analysis of the role of finance and particularly of nonbank financial intermediaries in economic development which has important implications for monetary theory. Gurley and Shaw start from the fact that real economic development is accompanied by a process of financial development in which primary securities (those issued to finance expenditure) become differentiated and there emerge financial intermediaries—of which commercial banks are only one variety—whose function is to enable asset holders to hold primary securities indirectly in the more attractive forms of liabilities issued by the intermediaries. Contrary to the main stream of both classical and Keynesian monetary theory, which treats the financial structure as of secondary importance and relates the demand for money to the long-term rate of interest or to the rate of return on real capital, Gurley and Shaw maintain that monetary theory must take account of these details of financial organization and development, since they affect the demand for money. In particular, they argue that because nonbank financial intermediaries generally offer liabilities which are closer substitutes for money than for primary securities, and hold small reserves of money themselves, their growth tends to reduce the demand for money. One implication of this analysis, which comes out more strongly in their remarks on monetary policy than in their theory,[16] but to which they do not in fact commit themselves, is that the "quantity of money" relevant for monetary theory and policy should include the liabilities of nonbank financial intermediaries.

Gurley and Shaw's work has provoked a number of critical journal articles, but those most specifically concerned with their theoretical analysis of the influence of nonbank intermediaries on the demand for money (by Culbertson [27] and Aschheim [3]) misunderstand both Gurley and Shaw's argument and the theory of credit creation.[17] The important question Gurley and Shaw raise is the empirical one of whether explanation of the demand for money requires introduction of the amounts of or yields on non-bank intermediary liabilities. This requires an elaborate statistical analysis of the demand for money and other assets which they have not yet produced. In [53] they show only that the facts of financial development in the United States can be rationalized by their theory; and Gurley's independent demonstration [49] that interest rates in the postwar period can be explained on the assumption that an increase in liquid assets reduces the demand for money by half as much—that is, that a correspondingly weighted sum of money and liquid assets can be used to represent the "quantity of money" in applying monetary theory—does not prove that money alone would do less well; indeed Gurley explains in an Appendix why money alone could have been used. The results of recent empirical research on the demand for money and velocity by other economists described below tend to contradict Gurley and Shaw's contention, since the writers concerned find it possible to explain the demand for money without reference to the variety of alternative assets and do not discover the downward trend in demand for money implied by Gurley and Shaw's thesis. This is, however, only an indirect test; and the empirical research in question is itself controversial.

EMPIRICAL RESEARCH ON THE DEMAND FOR MONEY

Prior to the *General Theory*, empirical research on velocity was primarily concerned with the measurement of the institutional determinants of transactions velocity; since then, attention has shifted to econometric explanation of income velocity and its alternative formulation, the demand for money,[18] one of the prime objects being to determine the existence or otherwise of the Keynesian liquidity trap. An influential early contribution by James Tobin [115] followed Keynes' theory in estimating idle balances by subtracting from total deposits an estimate of active balances derived from the maximum recorded velocity of circulation, and found a rough hyperbolic relationship between idle balances and interest rates, implying a liquidity trap. This relationship broke down for the postwar years, one reason being its failure to include the influence of total wealth; and subsequent researchers have generally preferred to avoid its assumption of a separable and proportional transactions demand in favor of analyzing the total demand for money. Tobin's method has, however, been employed in a more sophisticated form in a recent major study by Martin Bronfenbrenner and Thomas Mayer [13], which relates the demand for idle money (total money being defined as currency plus demand deposits adjusted) to the short-term interest rate, wealth, and idle balances of the previous year. They find that the last two variables explain most of the fluctuations in idle balances, and that the demand for idle balances is interest-inelastic with no tendency for the elasticity to increase as the rate falls. They interpret this last result as evidence against the liquidity trap; the validity of this inference depends on whether the liquidity trap is identified with infinite elasticity at some positive interest rate or an unlimited increase in the quantity of money demanded as the interest rate falls.

Estimates of the total demand function for money, besides avoiding arbitrary assumptions about transactions velocity, are easier to relate to income velocity than estimates of the Tobin type, since they usually use income as one of the explanatory variables.[19] Among a number of such estimates the two most important, in terms of length of period covered, simplicity of the demand function fitted, and intrinsic theoretical interest, are those by Henry Latané [73] and Milton Friedman [38]. Latané, adopting what he called a pragmatic approach to the constant-velocity and Keynesian formulations of demand for money, found that a simple linear relationship between the ratio of money (currency plus demand deposits) to income and the reciprocal of high-grade long-term interest rates fitted the historical data closely. Friedman's contribution builds on Selden's earlier finding [105] that the secular decline in velocity could be explained by the hypothesis that the demand for money (currency plus total commercial bank deposits) increases more rapidly than income (money is a "luxury good"), a finding apparently inconsistent with the fact that income and velocity vary together over the cycle. Friedman resolves the paradox by hypothesizing that the demand for real balances is an elastic function of permanent income, and showing that the apparent inconsistency of the cyclical behavior of velocity with this hypothesis disappears when the expected income and expected prices indicated by the theory are used instead of their observed counterparts; moreover, since this empirical analysis explains velocity without introducing interest rates into the demand function for money, it seems to dispose of the liquidity trap.

These two empirical demand functions for money apparently conflict, in that Latané's depends on both income (with a unitary income-elasticity) and the long-term interest rate, whereas Friedman's depends only on income, with an income-elasticity substantially above unity. But there is no necessary conflict, since Friedman's definition of money includes time deposits, and may therefore absorb most of the substitution between demand deposits and currency and interest-bearing assets induced by interest-rate changes. The real issue is which definition of money gives the better empirical results. Latané has since shown [74] that his formulation fits the subsequent data well. He explains the difference between the income-elasticities of the two functions by the facts that over the period covered by Friedman's calculations time deposits (whose inclusion he questions on theoretical grounds) grew more rapidly than demand deposits, and the long-term interest rate declined from 6.4 to 2.9 per cent. (Latané also adduces evidence for the existence of a liquidity trap, though he prefers to explain it by the cost of bond transactions rather than by Keynes' speculative motive.) Friedman's demand function, by contrast, does not fit the subsequent data, since the secular decline in velocity has reversed itself (Latané's analysis would attribute this to the subsequent upward movement of interest rates). Friedman has since been experimenting with an extended permanent income hypothesis that allows for changes in the confidence with which expectations are held [37]. Latané's demand function, incidentally, can be used to illustrate the difficulty of interpretation mentioned earlier: if wealth is assumed to be measured by income capitalized at the long-term interest rate, the quantity of money demanded in Latané's function can be expressed alternatively as a function of interest and wealth or of wealth and income,[20] thus being consistent with a variety of theoretical formulations.

The empirical studies of demand for money just discussed have a bearing on the fundamental issue, the subject of continued controversy in the history of monetary theory: whether monetary theory is more usefully formulated in terms of the demand for and supply of money or of the influence of money on expenditure and income—the equation-of-exchange approach or the income-expenditure approach. This issue, which Keynes' promulgation of the propensity to consume as a behavior relationship more stable than the discredited velocity of circulation seemed to have settled finally in favor of the income-expenditure approach, has become less settled with the postwar failure of the simple consumption function and the increasing complexity of Keynesian models on the one hand, and the increasing sophistication of modern adherents of the velocity approach on the other.

The counterattack on Keynesian income theory first launched by Friedman [36; 41] has been carried further in an article by Friedman and Gary Becker [43], which argues that the proper test of Keynesian theory is not the stability of the consumption function but its ability to predict consumption from investment, and produces some evidence that the investment multiplier is a poorer predictor of consumption than is the trend of consumption. In reply, Lawrence Klein [67] and John Johnston [62] have argued that a proper test should be concerned with the sophisticated and not the naive version of a theory, and should test the predictive power of the complete model and not just one part of it. This preliminary skirmish probably indicates the main lines of the battle that is likely to follow publication of a major study by Friedman and David Meiselman [44], which shows by exhaustive statistical tests on U.S. data since 1897, that except for the 1930's, the quantity of money has been a better predictor of consumption than has autonomous spending.

These results pose an important theoretical problem, since they imply that a change in the quantity of money that has no wealth-effect nevertheless will have an effect on consumption even though it has no effect on interest rates. The difficulty of understanding how this can be prompted the dissatisfaction of Keynes, Wicksell, and other income-expenditure theorists with the quantity theory, and provides the hard core of contemporary resistance to it. Friedman and Meiselman's explanation of their results may therefore initiate a new and possibly fruitful debate on how money influences activity.

The Supply of Money, Monetary Control, and Monetary Dynamics

THE SUPPLY OF MONEY

The theory of money supply is virtually a newly discovered area of monetary research. The general practice in monetary theory has been to treat the quantity of money as determined directly by the monetary authority, without reference to the links intervening between reserves provided by the central bank on the one hand, and the total of currency and bank deposits on the other. This treatment has rested on a mechanical analysis of the determination of money supply, very similar to the outmoded treatment of velocity, in which the money supply is related to the reserve base by a multiplier determined by the reserve ratio observed by the banking system, and the ratio between currency and deposits held by the public. In conformity with developments on the side of demand, the trend of recent research on money supply has been towards treating these ratios as behavior relationships reflecting asset choices rather than as exogenous variables, and elaborating the analysis to include the part played by other financial intermediaries than commercial banks, in the process evolving a less mechanical theory of central bank control. In part, recent developments in this area reflect a more general tendency to formulate the dynamics of monetary change in terms of the adjustment of actual to desired stocks rather than in terms of changes in flows.

Though Keynes followed convention in treating the quantity of money as a direct policy variable, other monetary theorists (an early example is Kragh [70]) applied the notion of liquidity preference to the reserve behavior of banks, and the same idea has been incorporated in various Keynesian models (not always consistently) by making the money supply vary with the rate of interest. Theorists concerned with the money supply have, however, tended until recently to stick to the mechanical "money multiplier" approach, extending it to allow for the different reserve requirements against time and demand deposits and the demand for money by financial intermediaries; and empirical research has followed the same line, partitioning changes in the quantity of money among changes in the currency-deposit and reserve-deposit ratios and the reserve base, and changes in the reserve base among changes in reserve bank liabilities and assets. These techniques can be extremely fruitful—notable examples are Donald Shelby's investigation of the monetary implications of the growth of financial intermediaries [108], and Brunner's empirical study of U.S. monetary policy in the middle 1930's [15]—but asset ratios are a crude technique for representing behavior relationships.

Philip Cagan's study of the demand for currency relative to the total money supply [19] has broken new ground in attempting an economic explanation of the ratio of currency to currency plus total deposits. Cagan examines a number of possible determining factors, and finds that expected real income per capita explains most of the decline in the ratio from 1875 to 1919, while changes in the net cost of holding currency instead of deposits explain most of the variation in the ratio from 1919 to 1955, though the rate of personal income tax (taken to represent the possible gain from tax evasion permitted by using currency for transactions) is required to explain the rise in the currency ratio in the Second World War.

Other researchers have concerned themselves with the response of the banking system to changes in reserves, though so far the published results have been theoretical rather than empirical. Recent work on this problem has departed from the "money-multiplier" approach in three respects: first, in basing the analysis on the behavior of the individual bank instead of the banking system; second, in applying economic theory to the explanation of the level of reserves desired by the bank and relating its behavior in expanding or contracting its assets to the difference between its actual and its desired reserves; and third, in treating the loss of reserves consequent on expansion as a stochastic process. These innovations are exemplified in two recent articles, both intended as a basis for empirical research: Brunner's schema for the supply theory of money [16], the central feature of which is a relationship between a bank's surplus reserves and its desired rate of change in its asset portfolio, formulated in terms of a "loss coefficient" measuring the (probable) loss of surplus reserves per dollar of asset expansion; and Daniel Orr and W. J. Mellon's analysis of bank credit expansion [90], which applies inventory theory to the bank's holding of reserves against cash losses (which are assumed to be random and normally distributed). Orr and Mellon show, in contrast to the results of money-multiplier analysis, that the marginal expansion ratio will be lower than the average for a monopoly bank, and lower for a banking system than for a monopoly bank; and that for a banking system the marginal expansion ratio depends on the distribution of the additional reserves among banks.

MONETARY CONTROL: A THEORETICAL ISSUE

The research just mentioned is concerned with introducing into the theory of money supply recognition of the fact that commercial banks are profit-maximizing institutions with economic behavior patterns on which the central bank must operate to control the money supply. The fact that monetary control operates in this way is the source of one group of issues in recent discussions of monetary policy, to be described in the next section; it also poses the interesting theoretical question of what powers the central bank needs to control the price level. This question has been raised and discussed by Gurley and Shaw [52, Ch. 6], who conclude their book by contrasting monetary control in a private commercial banking system with their standard case, in which the government determines the nominal quantity of money and the deposit rate on it. Unfortunately their argument is nonrigorous and inconsistent: having shown [52, pp. 261–62] that control of the nominal quantity of bank reserves and the rate of interest paid on these reserves is sufficient for control of the price level (though they argue that this control is weaker than in their standard case because bank liquidity preferences or deposit rates may change independently of central bank action), they conclude their discussion of the technical apparatus of monetary control with the statement that "of three indirect techniques—fixing nominal reserves, setting the reserve-balance rate, and setting members' own deposit rate—the Central Bank can get along with any two in regulating all nominal variables in the economic system" [52, pp. 274–75].[21] Patinkin [92, pp. 112–16] has shown that this statement is incorrect, and that the central bank needs to control nominal reserves and one of the interest rates.[22]

MONETARY DYNAMICS

As mentioned above, one of the recent innovations in the theory of money supply is the analysis of bank response to changes in reserves in terms of the adjustment of actual to desired reserves. This way of stating the problem reflects a more general tendency towards the formulation of monetary dynamics in terms of adjustment of actual to desired stocks, associated in turn with the formulation of monetary theory in terms of asset choices as described in the previous section. This tendency has developed somewhat apart from, and has been concerned with more fundamental issues than, the controversy over the interrelated issues of stock versus flow analysis and liquidity-preference versus loanable-funds theories that has broken out anew since the war. Much of the relevant literature on the latter subject has been surveyed by Shackle [106]; unfortunately, Shackle's discussion of the issues is vitiated by the erroneous belief that the presence of both a stock of old securities and a flow of new securities implies a conflict of forces—stock demand and supply, and flow demand and supply—operating on the interest rate, and that this conflict poses a dilemma for monetary theory that can only be resolved by the postulation of two rates of interest. It is therefore necessary to describe the controversy briefly, before turning to the more important development in monetary dynamics.

Modern controversy over liquidity-preference versus loanable-funds theories starts from Hicks' demonstration of the formal equivalence of the two [60, pp. 160–62]; Hicks used the fact that Walras' Law permits the elimination of one of the equations in a general equilibrium system to argue that one can omit either the excess-demand-for-money equation, leaving a loanable-funds theory of interest, or the excess-demand-for-securities equation, leaving a liquidity-preference theory of interest. The omitted equations are flow equations; William Fellner and Harold Somers [33] subsequently showed that they could be identified with the desired change in the stock of money or securities over the market period, so that flow analysis and stock analysis of monetary equilibrium were equivalent. Fellner and Somers also argued in favor of the loanable-funds theory and against the liquidity-preference theory that, as the rate of interest is the price of securities, it is more sensible to regard it as determined by the demand for and supply of securities than by the demand for and supply of money. This led to a controversy with L. R. Klein [68], who objected to Fellner and Somers' assumption that the period of analysis starts with equilibrium between actual and desired stocks as begging the question of stock versus flow theory, and declared that the real difference between the liquidity-preference and loanable-funds theories was a dynamic one, liquidity-preference theory maintaining that the rate of interest would change in response to an excess demand for or supply of money, not an excess supply of or demand for securities [68, pp. 236–41].[23]

In commenting on the controversy, Brunner [68, pp. 247–51] pointed out that Fellner and Somers' analysis, while correct, evaded the real issue that Klein was raising—that there is a difference between the dynamic adjustment processes of markets in which the object of demand is primarily a stock to be held, and of those in which the object of demand is primarily a flow to be consumed; but he sided with Fellner and Somers against Klein on the dynamic determinants of interest-rate changes. Earlier, Lerner had produced a much-quoted but untraceable objection to Hicks' original argument: that if the excess demand equation for some commodity (Lerner chose peanuts) is eliminated by Walras' Law, the resulting system includes both a loanable-funds and a money equation, one of which must be used to determine the price of the excluded commodity.

Subsequent contributors to the debate can be classed as those who maintain the identity of the two theories, and those who maintain that the liquidity-preference theory is different from (and superior to) the loanable-funds theory. To clarify the issues, it is convenient to discuss these groups in order. Among the former group, S. C. Tsiang [120], W. L. Smith [112], and Don Patinkin [93] deserve mention—Smith for his compact exposition and explicit recognition of the difference between stock and flow theories of behavior.

Tsiang objects to the Hicks-Fellner and Somers use of Walras' Law to establish the equivalence of the two theories on the Lerner grounds that this law only permits the elimination of one of the general equilibrium equations, and maintains that to establish the equivalence it is necessary to show that the individual can only demand or supply securities by supplying or demanding money. He also objects that the flow demand and supply of money in the Fellner-Somers analysis bears no relation to the stock demand and supply of Keynesian theory. To get around these difficulties (which, as Patinkin [93] shows, are of Tsiang's own creating) Tsiang chooses a period so short that the economic unit cannot plan on using its proceeds from planned sales of commodities to finance planned purchases of them; by this arbitrary device the flow and stock demands for money are equated and the only choice left to the unit is between holding cash (as an idle balance or for spending) and holding securities, so that identity of the two theories (in Tsiang's sense) necessarily follows.

Patinkin's article is an elegant restatement of the Hicksian position. Patinkin argues that the Lerner objection merely means that
it is wrong to classify interest theories by the equation omitted, and
that the two theories are simply alternative formulations of one
general equilibrium theory of interest. He disposes of Tsiang's
objection to the Fellner-Somers analysis by showing that the excess
flow-demand for money is identical with the excess stock-demand
for money for the period (Patinkin slips in not making explicit
that to translate a desired change in a stock over a period into a
flow during the period it is necessary to divide the change by the
length of the period). Finally, he disposes of Klein's statement of
the difference between the two theories by showing that this difference refers to the dynamic behavior of the same market—the
securities market—so that the choice of which market to eliminate
is not relevant.

Patinkin goes on to argue, with the help of the apparatus of
dynamic theory developed in his book, that the Klein hypothesis
concerning the dynamics of the interest rate is inherently implausible, since it implies that the interest rate will fall (rise) in the
face of excess supply (demand) in the securities market. This argument, appealing as it is, is restricted by its dependence on Patinkin's
dynamic apparatus, which permits simultaneous disequilibrium in
all markets and relates the direction of movement of individual
prices to the excess demand or supply in the corresponding markets.
It can be objected both that there is no reason why the movement
of price in a market should be dominated by the excess demand or
supply in that market (Brunner's argument against Klein recognized this point [68, p. 251]) and that a dynamic analysis of price
movements in one market requires specification of how disequilibria
in the remaining markets are resolved.[24] Further, in setting up a
dynamic analysis—particularly a period analysis—explicitly allowing for the (temporary) resolution of disequilibrium, it is possible
and sometimes convenient to define the relationships in such a way
that Walras' Law does not hold. This is the procedure that has been
adopted (implicitly or explicitly) by recent defenders of the
liquidity-preference theory: Joan Robinson's exposition of it [99]
employs a period analysis in which retailers confronted with un-
intended increases in inventories finance themselves by releasing
cash or securities, and Hugh Rose's dynamic version of Keynes'
theory [101] (which behaves according to Klein's hypothesis) uses
the same model with inventories being financed by security issues.
In both cases the demand and supply of goods are equated *ex post*
by the accommodating behavior of retailers, but this behavior is
not included in the *ex ante* description of disturbances to equilib-

rium. F. H. Hahn's reformulation of the liquidity-preference theory as a theory of the ratios in which cash and securities are held [55] employs a similar but more subtle device—a distinction between the investment-planning period, and a shorter "investment-financing" period during which the loanable-funds but not the liquidity-preference theory applies—to reconcile the two theories dynamically.

Elegant as it is, Patinkin's analysis is confined to the determination of equilibrium in a single period, and ignores the effects of the changes in stocks determined in that period on the equilibrium determined in the next period. Other participants in the controversy have followed him (or rather Keynes) in abstracting from the process of accumulation of real and financial wealth. The discussion has therefore stopped short of the issue raised by Klein, and elaborated on by Brunner, of the dynamics of price in a market characterized by a large stock and small demand-and-supply flows per period. Brunner [68, pp. 247–49] sketched a theory of such a market; in this theory price is determined at every moment by the demand for the existing stock, but at this price there may be a net flow demand or supply which gradually changes the existing stock and therefore the price; and full equilibrium requires a price which both equates the stock demand and supply and induces a zero net flow.[25] A very similar theory has since been elaborated by Robert Clower [22], who uses it to argue that productivity and thrift have only an indirect effect on interest (through the net flow of new securities) unless they affect the stock demand for securities directly by changing expectations. Clower and D. W. Bushaw [23] have produced a general theory of price for an economy that includes commodities appearing only as stocks, commodities appearing only as flows, and commodities appearing as both stocks and flows; in this theory the equilibrium price in the market for a stock-flow commodity must equate both the desired and actual stock and the flow demand and supply, and in the dynamic analysis the rate of change of price depends on both the excess-stock and excess-flow demands.[26]

Neither the Brunner-Clower nor the Clower-Bushaw theory really solves the stock-flow problem: the former subordinates the flow analysis entirely to the stock, the latter simply adds stock and flow analyses together. The defect common to both is the absence of a connection between the price at which a stock will be held and the current rate of change of the stock held, and correspondingly between the price at which a stock will be supplied and the current rate of change of the stock supplied; such connections would yield a simultaneous equilibrium of stock and flow evolving towards full stock equilibrium (zero net flow).[27] The addition of such connections would require treating savings and investment as processes of adding to stock, rather than as flows as they have customarily been treated in the post-Keynesian literature.[28]

This is the approach to monetary dynamics that has been emerging in the past few years, from both "Keynesian" and "quantity" theorists, as an outgrowth of the formulation of monetary theory as part of a general theory of asset holding. The essence of the new approach, elements of which are to be found in recent works of such diverse writers as Cagan [20], Tobin [117], Friedman [40, pp. 461–63] and Brunner [18; see also page 540 in this volume], is to view a monetary disturbance as altering the terms on which assets will be held (by altering either preferences among assets or the relative quantities of them available), and so inducing behavior designed to adjust the available stocks of assets to the changed amounts desired.[29] The new approach has been aptly summarized, from the point of view of monetary policy, by Brunner [18, p. 612]:

> Variations in policy variables induce a reallocation of assets (or liabilities) in the balance sheets of economic units which spills over to current output and thus affect the price level. Injections of base-money (or "high-powered" money) modify the composition of financial assets and total wealth available to banks and other economic units. Absorption of the new base money requires suitable alterations in asset yields or asset prices. The banks and the public are thus induced to reshuffle their balance sheets to adjust desired and actual balance-sheet position.
>
> The interaction between banks and public, which forms the essential core of money-supply theory, generates the peculiar leverage or multiplier effect of injections of base money on bank assets and deposits and, correspondingly, on specific asset and liability items of the public's balance sheet. The readjustment process induces a change in the relative yield (or price) structure of assets crucial for the transmission of monetary policy-action to the rate of economic activity. The relative price of base money and its close substitutes falls, and the relative price of other assets rises.
>
> The stock of real capital dominates these other assets. The increase in the price of capital relative to the price of financial assets simultaneously raises real capital's market value relative to the capital stock's replacement costs and increases the desired stock relative to the actual stock. The relative increase in the desired stock of capital induces an adjustment in the actual stock through new production. In this manner current output and prices of durable goods are affected by the readjustments in the balance sheets and the related price movements set in motion by the injection of base money. The wealth, income, and relative price effects involved in the whole transmission process also tend to raise demand for non-durable goods.

Monetary Policy

There is probably no field of economics in which the writings of economists are so strongly influenced by both current fashions in opinion and current problems of economic policy as the field of monetary policy. In the period immediately after the war, economists writing on monetary policy were generally agreed that monetary expansion was of little use in combating depression. Skepticism about the effectiveness of monetary restraint in combating inflation was less marked, though some took the extreme view that monetary restraint would either prove ineffective or precipitate a collapse. But it was generally thought that the wartime legacy of a large and widely-held public debt was a major obstacle to the application of monetary restraint, both because it was feared that abandonment of the bond-support program adopted to assist war financing would destroy public confidence in government debt, and because the transfer from the government to the private banking system that would result from an increase in the interest payable on the latter's large holdings of public debt was regarded as undesirable. Economists therefore divided into those who advocated schemes for insulating bank-held government debt from general interest-rate movements, as a means of clearing the way for monetary restraint, and those who argued for an extension of selective credit controls.

The inflation that accompanied the Korean War forced the termination of the bond-support program, and thereafter monetary policy became the chief instrument for controlling short-run fluctuations. The nonmaterialization of the disastrous consequences that some had predicted would follow the termination of the bond-support program, together with the development of the availability doctrine (which enlisted liquidity preference on the side of monetary policy and made a widely-held public debt a help rather than a hindrance) strengthened confidence in the power of monetary restraint to control inflation, though the availability doctrine also provided ammunition to advocates of selective controls by depicting monetary policy as achieving its results through irrational and discriminatory mechanisms. Subsequent experience, together with empirical and theoretical research, has fairly conclusively disposed of the availability doctrine's most appealing feature—the proposition that the central bank can produce large reductions in private spending by means of small increases in interest rates—and research has tended to refute the contention that monetary policy operates discriminatorily. Nevertheless, the availability doctrine has left its mark on the field, inasmuch as the majority of monetary economists would probably explain how monetary policy influences the economy by reference to its effects on the availability and cost of credit, with the stress on availability. Trust in the power of monetary restraint to control inflation has been further reduced by the coexistence of rising prices and higher average unemployment in the late 1950's, and the associated revival and elaboration of cost-push theories of inflation. On the other hand, experience of monetary policy in three mild business cycles has revived confidence in the efficacy of monetary expansion in combating recessions and dispelled the belief that monetary restraint in a boom will do either nothing or far too much. In fact, the wheel has come full circle, and prevailing opinion has returned to the characteristic 1920's view that monetary policy is probably more effective in checking deflation than in checking inflation.[30]

Changing fashions in prevailing opinion apart, the revival of monetary policy as a major branch of economic policy has stimulated much controversy, thought, and research on all aspects of monetary policy. In addition, the legacy of war debt and the increased size and frequency of government debt operations that it has entailed, together with the difficulties created for the Treasury by "bills only" and other Federal Reserve and governmental policies, has brought the whole subject of debt management within the purview of monetary economists as a special form of open-market operations. It is neither possible nor worthwhile to attempt to survey all the issues discussed in this voluminous literature: the Report of the Commission on Money and Credit [129] contains a consensus of informed professional opinion on most of them, the usefulness of which is much reduced by the absence of documentation of empirical statements and precise references to conflicting points of view; Friedman's *A Program for Monetary Stability* [34] discusses many of the issues within a consistent theoretical framework; and a 1960 *Review of Economics and Statistics* symposium [57] assembles the views of a variety of monetary specialists. The remainder of this part will instead concentrate on what seem to be the significant developments in three areas: the objectives of economic policy and the instrumental role of monetary policy; the means by which monetary policy influences the economy and their effectiveness; and the adequacy of the tools of monetary policy.

THE OBJECTIVES AND INSTRUMENTAL ROLE OF
MONETARY POLICY

In pre-Keynesian days, monetary policy was the single established instrument of aggregative economic policy, and price stability was its established objective. The Keynesian revolution introduced an alternative instrument, fiscal policy, and a second objective, maintenance of full employment (now more commonly described as economic stability), which might conflict with the objective of price stability. Since the war, debt management has been added almost universally to the list of instruments; and since the middle 1950's many economists have added a third item—adequately rapid economic growth—to the list of objectives. In recent years the balance-of-payments problem has been forcing the admission of a fourth objective—international balance—and may eventually establish a fourth instrument—foreign economic policy.

Recognition of several objectives of economic policy introduces the possibility of a conflict of objectives requiring resolution by a compromise. This possibility and its implications have been more clearly recognized elsewhere (for example by the Radcliffe Committee [128, pp. 17–18]), than in the United States, where there has been a tendency to evade the issue by denying the possibility of conflict[31] or by insisting that conflicts be eliminated by some other means than sacrifice of the achievement of any of the objectives.[32] Where a conflict of objectives has been clearly recognized —notably in the criticisms directed at the anti-inflationary emphasis of Federal Reserve policy in 1957–60—the arguments about alternative compromises have been qualitative and nonrigorous; rigorous theoretical exploration and quantitative assessment of the costs and benefits of alternative compromises between conflicting policy objectives remain to be undertaken.

The availability of alternative policy instruments introduces the question of their absolute and comparative effectiveness; research on this range of problems has been undertaken by a number of economists, but has not progressed far towards an accepted body of knowledge. As already mentioned, monetary policy since 1951 has resumed a large part of the responsibility for short-run economic stabilization—a consequence of both the inadaptability of the budgetary process to the requirements of a flexible fiscal policy and the domination of the budget by other objectives of national policy than stabilization. Reliance on monetary policy for this purpose has raised the question of how effectively the task is likely to be performed. The argument for using monetary policy is usually expressed in terms of the "flexibility" of monetary policy, by which is often meant no more than that monetary policy can be changed quickly. But the real issues are whether the monetary authorities are likely to take appropriate action at the right time, and whether the effects of monetary action on the economy occur soon enough and reliably enough to have a significant stabilizing effect.

As to the first question, there is general agreement that the Federal Reserve has committed errors in the timing, extent, and duration of policy changes. Most economists seem inclined to trust the System to improve its performance with experience and the benefit of their criticism. Some, however, are so distrustful of discretionary authority in principle, or so skeptical of the feasibility of effective stabilization by monetary means, as to advocate that the Federal Reserve should not attempt short-run stabilization, but should confine itself (or be confined) to expanding the money supply at a steady rate appropriate to the growth of the economy (for variants of this proposal, see Friedman [34, pp. 84–99], Angell [57, pp. 247–52], and Shaw [107]). The proposal to substitute a monetary rule for the discretion of the monetary authority is not of course new—Henry Simons' classic statement of the case for it [109] appeared in the 1930's—but the definition of the rule in terms of the rate of monetary expansion rather than stability of a price index reflects both the modern concern with growth and a more sophisticated understanding of the stabilization problem.

Whether such a rule would have produced better results than the policy actually followed in the past is a difficult matter to test. Friedman [34, pp. 95–98] discusses the difficulties and describes some abortive tests that tend to favor his (4 per cent annual increase) rule. Martin Bronfenbrenner has devised a more elaborate series of tests of alternative rules, including discretionary policy; his results for annual data 1901–1958 (excluding the Second World War) [11] show that a 3 per cent annual increase rule comes closest to the "ideal pattern" defined by price stability, though his subsequent tests on quarterly data from 1947 on [12] suggest the superiority of a "lag rule" relating changes in the money supply to prior changes in the labor force, productivity, and velocity. These tests are subject to statistical and theoretical objections, but they open up an interesting new line of research. In the absence of a definitely specified standard of comparison, discussions of the appropriateness of the central bank's monetary policy tend to fall back on textual criticism of its explanation of its actions or the exercise of personal judgment about what policy should have been (see, for example, the contributions of Weintraub, Samuelson, and Fellner to [57]).

The question of the extent of the stabilizing effect that monetary action may be expected to achieve was first raised, at the formal theoretical level, by Friedman [39], who argued that policies intended to stabilize the economy might well have destabilizing effects because of the lags involved in their operation. Subsequent work and discussion of this aspect of monetary policy has concentrated on the length and variability of the lag in the effect of monetary policy, and has become enmeshed in intricate arguments about the proper way of measuring the lag. Two alternative approaches to the measurement of the lag have been employed, direct estimate and statistical inference. The outstanding example of the first is Thomas Mayer's study of the inflexibility of monetary policy [80; see also page 594 in this volume]. Mayer estimates the lag in the reaction of investment expenditure and consumer credit outstanding to monetary policy changes, sector by sector, and, taking into account lags in monetary-policy changes and the multiplier process, concludes that monetary policy operates on the economy much too slowly for its effects to be quickly reversed; from a computation of the effect that an optimally-timed monetary policy would have had on the stability of industrial production over six business cycles, he concludes that monetary policy is too inflexible to reduce the fluctuation of industrial production by more than about 5 to 10 per cent on the average [80, p. 374]. W. H. White [126; see also page 628 in this volume] has since argued that Mayer seriously overestimates the average lag, and that the correct estimate would provide almost ideal conditions for effective anti-cyclical policy; White also remarks that Mayer's results do not show the destabilizing effects indicated as possible by Friedman's analysis.

Statistical inference is the basis of Friedman's contention that monetary policy operates with a long and variable lag, a contention which figures largely in his opposition to discretionary monetary policy. Friedman's preliminary references to his results [42; see also page 86 in this volume], made it appear that this contention rested mostly on a comparison of turning points in the rate of change of the money stock with turning points in National Bureau reference cycles (that is, in the level of activity); this comparison automatically yields a lag a quarter of a cycle longer than does a comparison of turning points in the level of the money stock with reference-cycle turning points, the comparison that Friedman's critics regard as the proper one to make. In reply to criticisms by J. M. Culbertson [26], Friedman has produced a lengthy defense of his measure of the lag, together with other supporting evidence [40]. This defense indicates that the measurement of the lag raises much more subtle and fundamental theoretical and methodological issues than appear at first sight; but the majority of monetary economists competent to judge is likely to agree with Culbertson [28] in finding Friedman's arguments unpersuasive.

Statistical inference is also employed in the study of lags in fiscal and monetary policy conducted for the Commission on Money and Credit by Brown, Solow, Ando and Kareken [14]. These authors claim that Friedman's comparison of turning points in the rate of change of the money stock with turning points in the level of activity involves a methodological *non sequitur*, and find from a comparison of turning points in the rates of change of money with the rate of change of aggregate output that the money stock and aggregate output move roughly simultaneously over the cycle. Their own work attempts to estimate the lag between the indication of a need for a change in monetary policy and the effect of the resulting change in policy on output, and finds that a substantial stabilizing effect is achieved within six to nine months. They also find that fiscal policy operating on disposable income is a more powerful stabilizer, achieving as much as half of its effect within six months.

This research on the lag in effect of monetary policy has been orientated towards determining the efficacy of monetary policy as a stabilizer, on the assumption that monetary policy is decided with reference to contemporaneous economic conditions. Little if any research has been devoted to the more ambitious task of designing optimal systems of changing monetary policy in response to movements of relevant economic indicators. A. W. Phillips [96] and more recently W. J. Baumol [8] have shown that what seem like sensible procedures for changing a policy variable in response to changing conditions may well aggravate instability; Phillips has applied the theory and concepts of control systems to the analysis of the effects of alternative operating rules of stabilization policy.

THE EFFECTIVENESS OF MONETARY POLICY

To turn from the instrumental role of monetary policy to the related but broader questions of how monetary action influences the economy, and how effectively, the prevailing tendency has been to approach these questions by analyzing how monetary policy, and particularly open-market operations, affect the spending decisions of particular sectors of the economy. This formulation of the problem is a natural corollary of Keynesian theory, and the evolution of the analysis since the war has closely reflected the evolution of monetary theory, though with a perceptible lag; but the analysis has also been strongly influenced by the availability doctrine. That doctrine, the formulation of which was largely the work of Robert Roosa [100; see also page 559 in this volume], emerged in the later years of the bond-support program as a solution to the conflict between the belief that a large widely-held public debt obliged the central bank to confine interest-rate movements to narrow limits and the belief that large interest-rate changes were necessary to obtain significant effects on spending.

The doctrine comprised two central propositions. The first was that widespread holding of public debt, particularly by financial institutions and corporations, facilitates monetary control by transmitting the influence of interest-rate changes effected by open-market operations throughout the economy. The second was that small interest-rate changes could, by generating or dispelling uncertainty about future rates and by inflicting or eliminating capital losses that institutions were unwilling to realize by actual sales ("the pinning-in effect"), achieve significant effects on spending even if the demands of spenders for credit were interest-inelastic—these effects being achieved by influencing the willingness of lenders to lend or, put another way, by influencing the availability of credit to borrowers by altering the terms of credit and the degree of credit rationing. The second proposition has turned out on subsequent investigation to depend on incorrect empirical assumptions about institutional behavior, particularly with respect to "the pinning-in effect" (see Warren Smith [113]) and on a doubtful asymmetry between the reactions of lender and borrower expectations to interest-rate changes (see Dennis Robertson [98]), as well as to involve some logical inconsistencies (see John Kareken [64], and for a theoretical defense of the availability doctrine, Ira Scott [104; see page 585 in this volume]). Nevertheless, the doctrine and discussion of it have helped to popularize the concept of "availability of credit" as one of the main variables on which monetary policy operates.

"Availability" actually comprises a number of disparate elements—the liquidity of potential lenders' and spenders' assets, the terms on which lenders will extend or borrowers can obtain credit, and the degree to which credit is rationed among eligible borrowers (see Kareken [64]). Emphasis on these factors as influences on spending has provided new arguments for those who favor selective credit controls—specific arguments for controls where the terms of credit rather than the cost of credit seem the effective determinant of spending decisions, as in the case of installment credit, and a general defensive argument based on the discriminatory character of credit rationing. The most powerful attack on the discriminatory character of allegedly general methods of economic control has come from J. K. Galbraith [45], who has maintained that the use of monetary and fiscal policy has favored the monopolistic at the expense of the competitive sectors of the economy to an extent comparable to repeal of the antitrust laws. Others have maintained that monetary restraint discriminates against small business. Empirical studies by Bach and Huizenga [6] and Allen Meltzer [83] show that this is not true of bank credit; Meltzer's study finds that while small firms have greater difficulty in obtaining nonbank credit in tight periods than large firms, this discrimination tends to be offset by extension of trade credit from large firms to small.

The emphasis on the availability of credit as a determinant of expenditure has led to a critical re-examination of the business-attitude survey findings that formerly were used as evidence that business investment is insensitive to monetary policy. In addition, monetary theorists have tended to raise their estimates of the sensitivity of business investment to changes in the cost of credit. These reassessments have been based on the opinion that investors' expected profits are more finely and rationally calculated than used to be thought, rather than on any impressive new empirical evidence of such sensitivity. The most definite new empirical evidence there is confirms the long-time theoretically established sensitivity of residential construction to interest-rate changes, and even this sensitivity has been attributed in part to the influence of ceiling rates on federally-guaranteed mortgages on the willingness of institutional lenders to lend on such mortgages [129, p. 51]. The failure of empirical research to disclose such sensitivity may, as Brunner has suggested [18, p. 613], be the consequence of too simple a theoretical approach, the attempt to relate a flow of expenditure on assets to the cost of credit without adequate recognition of the range of alternative assets or the complexities of stock-adjustment processes. The new approach to monetary dynamics described in the previous part suggests that a more sophisticated theory of real investment is necessary for successful empirical work; on the other hand, some of the empirical work described in the first part suggests that better results might be achieved by working with changes in the quantity of money than by attempting to determine the influence of changes in interest rates on particular categories of spending.

The discussion of the effectiveness of monetary policy just described has been concerned with monetary policy operating in a given institutional environment. Since the middle 1950's a new debate has been opened up, concerned with the fact that traditional methods of monetary control are primarily directed at commercial bank credit, and the possibility that institutional change stimulated by monetary restriction may reduce the effectiveness of traditional techniques of monetary control. The main debate has been concerned with Gurley and Shaw's contention [50, pp. 537–38] that the growth of financial intermediaries, prompted in part by the competitive handicaps imposed on commercial banks for purposes of monetary control, progressively provides close substitutes for money the presence of which weakens the grip of monetary policy on the economy; and with their suggestion that the controlling powers of the central bank should be extended beyond the commercial banks to other financial institutions.[33] The debate has ranged over a wide territory, including such matters as whether existing controls over commercial banks are really discriminatory, given that banks enjoy the privilege of creating money (Aschheim [3] and Shelby [108]) and whether imposition of credit controls on financial intermediaries would in fact improve the effectiveness of monetary policy or the competitive position of the banks (David Alhadeff [1]). From the point of view of monetary policy, the central issue is not whether financial development leads to a secular decline in the demand for money—by itself, this would increase the leverage of monetary policy (Shelby [108]) and could readily be assimilated by the monetary authorities ([129, pp. 80–81] and Axilrod [5])—but whether the liabilities of financial intermediaries are such close substitutes for money that monetary restriction is substantially offset through substitution for bank deposits of other financial claims backed by only a small fractional reserve of money —in short, whether financial intermediaries substantially increase the interest-elasticity of demand for money. This is an empirical question; and the empirical evidence so far is that shifts by the public from money into thrift assets in periods of monetary restraint have not had a significant influence on velocity ([129, pp. 78–80]; see also Smith [111]).

THE ADEQUACY OF THE TOOLS OF MONETARY POLICY

The revival of monetary policy as an instrument of short-run stabilization has provoked a great deal of discussion not only of the use and effectiveness of monetary policy, but also of the use and efficiency of the Federal Reserve's traditional instruments of monetary control—open-market operations, rediscount rates, and reserve requirements. Controversy about open-market operations has centered on the "bills only" policy—the policy of conducting open-market operations in Treasury bills only, adopted by the Federal Reserve in 1953, modified later to "bills usually," and abandoned in 1961. Both the availability doctrine and the assets approach to the theory of interest rates imply that the central bank can obtain differential effects on credit conditions according to the maturity of government debt in which it chooses to conduct open-market operations, and can alter the structure of interest rates by switching between short and long maturities. The bills-only policy therefore appeared to most academic economists as an undesirable renunciation by the central bank of an important technique of monetary control, and the reason given for it—the desire to improve the "depth, breadth and resiliency" of the government bond market by eliminating arbitrary central bank intervention in it— as a shallow excuse masking the unwillingness of the Federal Reserve to risk unpopularity with the financial community by overtly subjecting it to capital losses. The surrender of power entailed in bills-only was probably greatly exaggerated by many of its opponents: Winfield Riefler [97] has pointed out that the central bank's choice of securities only contributes about one-eighth of the total effect of its open-market operations, the remaining seven-eighths being determined by the asset choices of the banks whose reserves are altered by the operations; and has produced some evidence that substantial changes in the maturity composition of the public debt have had little effect on the rate structure. On the other side of the argument, Dudley Luckett [76] has shown that the empirical evidence fails to indicate any improvement in "depth, breadth and resiliency" since bills-only was adopted.

While much of the discussion of bills-only has been concerned exclusively with Federal Reserve policy, the fundamental issue involved was the division of responsibility for the maturity composition of government debt held by the public between the Federal Reserve and the Treasury. Bills-only assigned this responsibility, and the associated responsibility for smoothing the impact of debt-management operations on the market, to the Treasury. One school of thought, represented for example by A. G. Hart [57, pp. 257–58], has maintained strongly that this is an inappropriate division of responsibility, since the Federal Reserve has both the powers and the continual contact with the market required for the purpose and the Treasury has not. (The limited ability of the Treasury to conduct open-market operations has been demonstrated by Deane Carson's study [21] of debt management after the adoption of bills-only.) Others have seen the source of the trouble in the Treasury's debt-management practices, particularly the practice of issuing debt in large blocks at irregular intervals, at fixed prices and with maturities "tailored" to market requirements. Carson [21] and Friedman [34, Ch. 3] have proposed similar schemes for replacing present practice by a system of auctioning long-term government debt issues; Culbertson [25] and Friedman [34, Ch. 3] have propounded plans for regularizing the timing and composition of debt issues to reduce the market disturbance of government financing. The difficulties the Treasury has experienced with debt management in the postwar period, in consequence not only of bills-only but of other developments adverse to easy Treasury financing,[34] have led many economists to become skeptical of the practicability of a countercyclical debt-management program. Such a program, which would involve issuing long-term debt in booms and short-term debt in depressions, would in any case have a countercyclical influence only insofar as the interest-rate structure is sensitive to change in the composition of the debt, and this sensitivity seems to be too small to yield important stabilizing effects (see Riefler [97] and Meiselman [82]).

Though the growth of the public debt has definitely established open-market operations as the chief instrument of day-to-day monetary control, the revival of monetary policy has been accompanied by a revival of rediscounting and the use of rediscount rates as a control instrument. Controversey over rediscount policy has mainly been concerned with whether rediscount policy is a useful auxiliary instrument of control, or whether the possibility of rediscounting creates an unnecessary and troublesome loophole in the control over member banks afforded by reserve requirements and open-market operations. It can be argued (see Friedman [34, pp. 35–35]) that rediscount rates are a treacherous control instrument, since their restrictiveness depends on their relationship with shifting market rates of interest, and that the growth of bank holdings of public debt and the postwar development of the federal funds market make it unnecessary for the Federal Reserve to continue to perform the function of lender of last resort for its members.[35] There has also been some argument about whether control of the rediscounting privilege gives the Federal Reserve undesirable arbitrary authority over member banks.

Apart from the debate concerning the desirability of rediscounting, a number of writers have criticized the asymmetry of the present reserve-requirement and rediscount-rate system, under which member banks receive no interest on reserves or excess reserves but pay a penalty rate on reserves borrowed to meet deficiencies, and have proposed payment of interest on reserves or excess reserves. Tobin, for example [57, pp. 276–79], has recommended payment of interest at the discount rate on excess reserves, and coupled this with the recommendation to terminate the prohibition of demand-deposit interest and the ceilings on time- and savings-deposit interest, arguing that the justification for intervention in the fixing of deposit rates—to protect depositors by preventing excess competition among banks—has been removed by federal deposit insurance.[36]

The power to change reserve requirements gives the central bank a method of changing the quantity of bank deposits alternative to open-market operations. The chief differences between the two methods[37] are, first, that reserve-requirement changes, being discontinuous, are apt to have disturbing effects on securities markets requiring auxiliary open-market operations; and second, that credit expansion by open-market purchases is less costly for the government and less profitable for the banks than credit expansion by reduction of reserve requirements (and vice versa). The discontinuity and disturbing effects of reserve-requirement changes, dramatically exemplified by their misuse in 1936–37 (see Brunner [15]), have led most economists to believe that they should be used sparingly if at all, especially in restraining credit expansion. The differential effects of the two methods of control on governmental interest costs and bank profits have been the focus of controversy over the policy of lowering reserve requirements followed by the Federal Reserve since 1951. In the course of time the balance of the argument has tilted in favor of reduction of reserve requirements, as the postwar sentiment against high bank profits derived from interest on the public debt has given way to the more recent fear that banks are unduly handicapped by reserve requirements and interest ceilings on deposits in competing with other financial intermediaries.

The controversy has raised the more general issue of how the secular growth of the money supply should be provided for. George Tolley, who first raised this issue [119; see also page 382 in this volume], has shown that the choice between open-market operations and reserve-requirement variation involves some intricate theoretical issues, since in addition to its implications for debt management and the ease of government financing this choice influences the efficiency of allocation of resources to the provision of the supply of deposit money.

Some attention has also been given to the efficiency of the present system of reserve requirements as an instrument of monetary control. Frank Norton and Neil Jacoby [89] have revived the 1930's Federal Reserve proposal to relate required reserve ratios to deposit turnover rates as a means of introducing an automatic offset to changes in the velocity of circulation. The preponderance of professional opinion, however, seems opposed to any system of reserve requirements that discriminates between banks or affects their profits differentially, and in favor of the removal of inequities among banks by the standardization of reserve requirements.

Concluding Remarks

The main impression that emerges from this survey of monetary theory and policy is not only that the field has been extremely active, especially in the past few years, but that it has been on the move towards interesting and important new developments. To summarize what is already a summary is a difficult task, and prediction of the direction of future scientific progress is a risky business; but in the literature surveyed in the preceding sections, two broad trends are evident. One is the trend towards the formulation of monetary theory as a part of capital theory, described on pages 13–25 (and implicitly on pages 7–13). As mentioned on pages 25–44, this trend has only just begun to manifest itself in the formulation of monetary dynamics. More important, almost nothing has yet been done to break monetary theory loose from the mould of short-run

equilibrium analysis, conducted in abstraction from the process of
growth and accumulation; and to integrate it with the rapidly developing theoretical literature on economic growth (important exceptions are the models of Tobin [114] and Enthoven [52, App.]). The
other trend is that towards econometric testing and measurement of
monetary relationships. As is evident on pages 33–44, econometric
methods have barely begun to be applied to the study of relationships relevant to the management of monetary policy.

NOTES

1. For a list of Congressional documents bearing on monetary policy,
see Friedman [34, pp. 103–40]; to Friedman's list should be added the
Staff Report on Employment, Growth and Price Levels [130] and the accompanying *Staff Studies*.
2. For example, inferiority of real balances implies that if an individual's initial stock of real balances is reduced, his initial commodity
endowment being unchanged, he will reduce his planned consumption
in the current week sufficiently to increase his planned real balances.
By shortening the week and reducing the individual's weekly endowment of commodities proportionately, a procedure which leaves the rate
of flow of the individual's income unchanged, it can be made impossible
for the individual to cut his commodity consumption sufficiently to increase his planned balances. "Inferiority" of real balances is therefore
not invariant with respect to the time unit of the analysis. Further,
inferiority of real balances would imply that any disturbance to an individual's initial equilibrium would be followed by a "cobweb" adjustment of his real balances and consumption in succeeding weeks, a pattern
difficult to rationalize. I am indebted to the oral tradition of the University of Chicago Money and Banking Workshop for these points.
3. Goods are produced as well as exchanged; net saving and investment occur but their effects on wealth and productive capacity are ab-
stracted from; for analysis the economy is aggregated into four markets,
those for labor services, commodities, bonds, and money. Patinkin uses
the dynamic development of this model to investigate Keynes' theory of
involuntary unemployment, a subject not considered here; his analytical
methods have been adopted by several subsequent writers.
4. Absence of money illusion means that behavior depends on the real
and not the money values of income, balances, and bonds; absence of
distribution effects, that behavior is unaffected by redistributions of total
real income, balances, and bonds among individuals, such as result from
price-level changes; homogeneity of bonds, that behavior is affected only
by the net creditor position of the private sector, not by the totals and
composition of its assets and liabilities; absence of government debt or
open-market operations, that the net creditor position of the private
sector consists in its holding of fiat money, or that, if government debt

fixed in real terms is introduced (the Metzler case discussed below), its quantity does not alter when the quantity of money changes. The assumption of absence of distribution effects might seem unnecessary, on the Archibald-Lipsey argument, but that argument does not apply to this model, which by construction cannot be in full stationary equilibrium: see Ball and Bodkin's criticism of Archibald and Lipsey, which the latter accept [7, pp. 44–49].

5. The Pigou effect in modern usage is the effect on the demand for goods of a change in private real wealth resulting from the effect of a change in the price level on the real value of net private financial assets, the latter consisting of net government debt outstanding (including fiat money) and the part of the money supply backed by gold; it is the real balance effect corrected for the presence of government debt and money issued against private debt.

6. Their insistence on the determinacy of the price level, in contrast to what they take to be the implication of Patinkin's approach (which they term "net money doctrine") [52, p. 76], rests on an understandable misunderstanding. Patinkin's analysis of price-level stability throws the emphasis on the wealth effect of a change in real balances resulting from a price-level change, an effect which only exists when money is a net asset; but it also provides for a substitution effect. Gurley and Shaw's demonstration that the substitution effect is sufficient to determine the price level therefore does not conflict with Patinkin's analysis (for Patinkin's views, see [92, pp. 100–9]), though it does show that Patinkin's emphasis on the wealth effect is misplaced and misleading. The broader implications of this point are discussed below.

7. In an elegant recent article [87] R. A. Mundell has extended Metzler's analysis by considering explicitly the tax remissions resulting from open-market purchases of government debt. He assumes that corporate taxes are capitalized in the price of equities but that personal income taxes are not capitalized (there being no market for human capital); he allows for the effect of corporate taxation on the incentive to invest; and he demonstrates that Metzler's conclusion is valid if income taxes are remitted, but reversed if corporate taxes are remitted. The non-marketability of human capital seems an inadequate reason for assuming that people do not feel richer when income taxes are reduced; consideration of the incentive effects of tax changes introduces an interesting new aspect of the neutrality problem but one that lies at a somewhat lower level of abstraction.

8. These terms are intended to distinguish the two main (and historically long-established) schools of thought in monetary theory, one of which formulates its analysis in terms of the quantity of money and its velocity of circulation and the other in terms of the determinants of money expenditure, without ensnaring the exposition in the rights and wrongs of Keynes' protracted quarrel with what he understood by "the quantity theory." As this section explains, neither the quantity theory nor the Keynesian theory is now what it was in the 1930's; in particular, the modern quantity theorist is committed to neither full employment nor the constancy of velocity, and his theory is a theory of the relation

between the stock of money and the level of money income, that is, a theory of velocity and not of prices and employment.

9. Ralph Turvey [122, p. 33], following Richard Selden [105, pp. 209–10], argues that the interest-elasticity conclusion does not extend to aggregate behavior because a change in the interest rate will have the opposite effect on the demand for cash of a unit facing a maturing debt and having the alternatives of holding cash in the interim or spending it and borrowing later. This argument involves an elementary confusion between saving behavior and asset management: savings effects of interest-rate changes aside, the unit in question would have the same alternative of investing its idle cash at interest, and react the same way. Turvey also argues [122, pp. 28–30] that an increase in the level of a unit's transactions will raise transactions demand only in a probability sense, since there may be an offsetting change in the timing-structures of the unit's payments and receipts.

10. This phrase has reference to the pattern of rates on loans of successively longer maturity; statistically it is represented by the "yield curve," which charts the yields on government debts against their maturities. In the English literature the problem appears as that of the relation between the long and the short rate of interest (the bill rate and the bond rate), a reflection of the institutional fact that the British government obtains its short-term financing predominantly by three-months bills of exchange, and has a substantial volume of perpetual debt ("consols") outstanding.

11. The sensitivity of the rate pattern to changes in the relative quantities of short-term and long-term debt is the crucial empirical issue in some recent controversies about monetary policy, especially the "bills only" policy.

12. Shackle's survey of interest theory [106], to which the reader has been referred in the introduction, unfortunately makes very little reference to rate-structure theory, presumably because it has not been discussed recently in English journals. The interested reader is referred to Conard's useful book [24].

13. These brief remarks do justice neither to Friedman nor to other consumption theorists, a number of whom have been working towards similar theories (see Johnson [61]).

14. To keep the bibliography within reasonable bounds, the references below are confined as far as possible to authors who have supported their theories with empirical research, or to recent writings.

15. The phrase is Milton Friedman's.

16. Gurley and Shaw believe that present methods of credit control discriminate against banks in their competition with nonbank intermediaries, weakening the effectiveness of monetary policy over the long run, and unlike most of their critics are prepared to contemplate extension of the central bank's regulatory powers.

17. Patinkin's review [92] of the book translates Gurley and Shaw's argument into his own language and interprets the effect of financial intermediation as an increase in the liquidity of bonds which decreases the demand for money and increases its interest-elasticity. Alvin Marty's

review [79] makes the interesting theoretical point that the introduction of a substitute does not necessarily increase the elasticity of demand. Neither reviewer notices that Gurley and Shaw infer increased elasticity only in the special case of an unfunding of government debt, and present a satisfactory reason for it [52, pp. 162–66].

18. For discussion of the earlier literature, see Villard [124] and Selden [105]; a useful survey of the econometric studies preceding their own work is given by Bronfenbrenner and Mayer [13]. The more traditional type of research on transactions velocity has been continued by a number of contemporary economists, notably George Garvey [46].

19. An interesting exception is Harold Lydall's derivation of the demand for money from the hypothesis of a constant ratio of liquidity to wealth [77].

20. In [74] Latané uses a linear relationship between income velocity and the rate of interest, $V = .77r + .38$, where $V = Y/M$, the quantity of money divided into income. This yields the demand function for money, $M = Y/(.77r + .38)$. Using the definition $W = Y/r$, this can be written equivalently as

$$M = \frac{W}{.77 + .38/r} \quad \text{or} \quad M = \frac{W}{.77 + .38W/Y}.$$

21. Gurley and Shaw also state as a prerequisite of monetary control that the authorities take steps to ensure the moneyness of bank deposits; the necessity for this is debatable.

22. Patinkin goes on to argue that price-level determinacy requires fixity of one nominal quantity and one yield, and would be secured by fixity of the nominal quantity of (noninterest-bearing) outside money; and that therefore Gurley and Shaw should have considered the means by which the central bank changes the price level, instead of the powers required to determine it. This argument raises the question discussed earlier, of the usefulness of founding monetary theory on the real-balance effect.

23. An excess demand for money does not necessarily imply an excess supply of securities, since it may be accompanied by an excess supply of goods.

24. Patinkin recognized these difficulties in the discussion of dynamic stability in his book [94, pp. 157–58], and admitted that they made stability a matter of assumption rather than of proof; but he overlooked them in applying his dynamic apparatus to the liquidity-preference loanable-funds controversy.

25. In describing a mathematical model of this theory, Brunner admits two possible situations of partial equilibrium—stock equilibrium and flow disequilibrium and the converse—but nevertheless asserts that the stock relation determines momentary price in both. This inconsistency, which was presumably prompted by his intention to contrast the adjustment processes of markets dominated respectively by stocks and flows, is the source of the dilemma Shackle finds between stock and flow equilibrium as the determinant of price [106, p. 222].

26. Cliff Lloyd [75] has argued that the presence of two equilibrium equations for a stock-flow commodity may invalidate the Hicksian proof of the equivalence of the loanable-funds and liquidity-preference theories. It may be noted that the Clower-Bushaw theory provides a formal solution to the apparent dilemma created by Brunner's alternative partial equilibria.

27. In one passage [106, p. 223] Shackle outlines a solution to his dilemma along these lines, but does not pursue it further. The Brunner-Clower theory can (with some difficulty) be interpreted as a special case of the general theory, one in which the price at which a stock is held is independent of the current rate of change in the stock.

28. This observation refers to the literature on the Keynesian general equilibrium system, and not to the specialist work on consumption and investment, where the treatment of saving and investment as processes of adding to stock has become well established since the war.

29. While this approach can be described as new in relation to the time period included in this survey, it can from another point of view be regarded as a development of certain strands in Keynes' thought [65, Vol. 1, pp. 200–9] [66, Ch. 11].

30. This account refers, of course, to developments in the United States (compare Paul Samuelson [57, pp. 263–69]). A parallel evolution of opinion has occurred in other countries, though in Britain prevailing opinion, as reflected notably in the Radcliffe Report [128, Ch. 6], has remained skeptical of the efficacy and usefulness of monetary policy; this difference in prevailing opinion is partly responsible for the generally critical reception of the Report by U.S. commentators. Limitations of space make it necessary to confine this section to developments in the United States.

31. This can always be done by giving priority to one objective and defining the others in terms that implicitly impose consistency with the favored objective; an example is the concept of "sustainable economic growth" promulgated by the Federal Reserve System.

32. One example of this type of evasion is the affirmation that balance-of-payments difficulties should not be allowed to hinder the achievement of domestic policy, an affirmation rarely accompanied by specification of any obviously efficacious solution to these difficulties. Another is the expression of trust that policies designed to increase the competitiveness and efficiency of the economy will eliminate the possibility of conflict between high employment, price stability, and adequate growth. Both are contained in the Report of the Commission on Money and Credit [129, pp. 45, 227].

33. A related but different argument has been advanced by Hyman Minsky [86], to the effect that monetary restriction stimulates financial innovations that progressively reduce the demand for money, increase the velocity of circulation, and threaten to make the money market unstable; Minsky recommends extension of the lender-of-last-resort function to the whole market and not merely the commercial banks. Arguments similar to those of Gurley and Shaw and Minsky may be found in Smith [113].

34. For a comprehensive survey of these developments see Erwin Miller [85].
35. The controversy has aroused some interest in the Canadian innovation of setting the discount rate at a fixed margin above the weekly average tender rate on Treasury bills. In England, where the rediscount rate is the chief instrument of monetary policy, recognition of the loophole in monetary control afforded by rediscounting has led to the promulgation of the theory that the liquidity ratio of the commercial banks and the supply of bills, rather than the cash ratio and the quantity of central bank deposits, determine the amount of commercial bank deposits.
36. The fact that this justification was fallacious to begin with has not prevented the Commission on Money and Credit from endorsing the continuation of control of these rates [129, pp. 167–68].
37. For a fuller analysis, see Aschheim [4, Ch. 2].

REFERENCES

1. Alhadeff, D. A., "Credit Controls and Financial Intermediaries," *American Economic Review*, 50: 655–71 (September 1960).
2. Archibald, G. C., and R. G. Lipsey, "Monetary and Value Theory: A Critique of Lange and Patinkin," *Review of Economic Studies*, 26: 1–22 (October 1958) [reprinted in this volume—Ed.].
3. Aschheim, J., "Commercial Banks and Financial Intermediaries: Fallacies and Policy Implications," *Journal of Political Economy*, 67: 59–71 (February 1959).
4. ———, *Techniques of Monetary Control* (Baltimore, 1961).
5. Axilrod, S. H., "Liquidity and Public Policy," *Federal Reserve Bulletin*, 47: 1161–77 (October 1961).
6. Bach, G. L., and C. J. Huizenga, "The Differential Effects of Tight Money," *American Economic Review*, 51: 52–80 (March 1961).
7. Baumol, W. J., R. W. Clower and M. L. Burstein, F. H. Hahn, R. J. Ball and R. Bodkin, G. C. Archibald and R. G. Lipsey, "A Symposium on Monetary Policy," *Review of Economic Studies*, 28: 29–56 (October 1960).
8. Baumol, W. J., "Pitfalls in Contracyclical Policies: Some Tools and Results," *Review of Economics and Statistics*, 43: 21–26 (February 1961).
9. ———, "The Transactions Demand for Cash: An Inventory Theoretic Approach," *Quarterly Journal of Economics*, 66: 545–56 (November 1952) [reprinted in this volume—Ed.].
10. Brechling, F. P. R., "A Note on Bond-Holding and the Liquidity Preference Theory of Interest," *Review of Economic Studies*, 24: 190–97 (June 1957).
11. Bronfenbrenner, M., "Statistical Tests of Rival Monetary Rules," *Journal of Political Economy*, 69: 1–14 (February 1961).
12. ———, "Statistical Tests of Rival Monetary Rules: Quarterly Data Supplement," *Journal of Political Economy*, 69: 621–25 (December 1961).
13. ———, and T. Mayer, "Liquidity Functions in the American Economy," *Econometrica*, 28: 810–34 (October 1960).

14. Brown, E. C., R. M. Solow, A. Ando and J. H. Kareken, *Lags in Fiscal and Monetary Policy*, Commission on Money and Credit (Englewood Cliffs, N.J., 1963).

15. Brunner, K., "A Case Study of U.S. Monetary Policy: Reserve Requirements and Inflationary Gold Flows in the Middle 30's," *Schweizerische Zeitschrift für Volkswirtschaft und Statistik*, 94: 160–201 (1958).

16. ———, "A Schema for the Supply Theory of Money," *International Economic Review Papers*, 2: 79–109 (January 1961).

17. ———, "Inconsistency and Indeterminacy in Classical Economics," *Econometrica*, 19: 152–73 (April 1951).

18. ———, "The Report of the Commission on Money and Credit," *Journal of Political Economy*, 69: 605–20 (December 1961) [reprinted in this volume—Ed.].

19. Cagan, P., "The Demand for Currency Relative to the Total Money Supply," *Journal of Political Economy*, 66: 303–28 (August 1958).

20. ———, "Why Do We Use Money in Open Market Operations?" *Journal of Political Economy*, 66: 34–46 (February 1958).

21. Carson, D., "Treasury Open Market Operations," *Review of Economics and Statistics*, 41: 438–42 (November 1959).

22. Clower, R. W., "Productivity, Thrift and the Rate of Interest," *Economic Journal*, 64: 107–15 (March 1954).

23. ———, and D. W. Bushaw, "Price Determination in a Stock-Flow Economy," *Econometrica*, 22: 328–43 (July 1954).

24. Conard, J. W., *Introduction to the Theory of Interest* (Berkeley, 1959).

25. Culbertson, J. M., "A Positive Debt Management Program," *Review of Economics and Statistics*, 41: 89–98 (May 1959).

26. ———, "Friedman on the Lag in Effect of Monetary Policy," *Journal of Political Economy*, 68: 617–21 (December 1960).

27. ———, "Intermediaries and Monetary Theory: A Criticism of the Gurley-Shaw Theory," *American Economic Review*, 48: 119–31 (March 1958).

28. ———, "The Lag in Effect of Monetary Policy: Reply," *Journal of Political Economy*, 69: 467–77 (October 1961).

29. ———, "The Term Structure of Interest Rates," *Quarterly Journal of Economics*, 71: 485–517 (November 1957).

30. Davis, R. M., "A Re-examination of the Speculative Demand for Money," *Quarterly Journal of Economics*, 73: 326–32 (May 1959).

31. Encarnación, J., "Consistency between Say's Identity and the Cambridge Equation," *Economic Journal*, 68: 827–30 (December 1958).

32. Fellner, W., and D. Dillard, "Keynesian Economics after Twenty Years," *American Economic Review Proceedings*, 47: 67–87 (May 1957).

33. ———, and H. M. Somers, "Note on 'Stocks' and 'Flows' in Monetary Interest Theory," *Review of Economics and Statistics*, 31: 145–46 (May 1949) [reprinted in this volume—Ed.].

34. Friedman, M., *A Program for Monetary Stability* (New York, 1960).

35. ———, *A Theory of the Consumption Function* (Princeton, 1957).

36. ———, "Price, Income and Monetary Changes in Three Wartime Periods," *American Economic Review Proceedings*, 42: 612–25 (May 1952).

37. ———, "The Demand for Money," *American Philosophical Society Proceedings*, 105: 259–64 (June 1961).

38. ———, "The Demand for Money: Some Theoretical and Empirical Results," *Journal of Political Economy*, 67: 327–51 (August 1959) [reprinted in this volume—Ed.].

39. ———, "The Effects of a Full-Employment Policy on Economic Stability: A Formal Analysis," in *Essays in Positive Economics* (Chicago, 1953), pp. 117–32.

40. ———, "The Lag in Effect of Monetary Policy," *Journal of Political Economy*, 69: 447–66 (October 1961).

41. ———, "The Quantity Theory of Money—A Restatement," in M. Friedman (ed.), *Studies in the Quantity Theory of Money* (Chicago, 1956), pp. 3–21 [reprinted in this volume—Ed.].

42. ———, and A. J. Schwartz, *The Stock of Money in the United States 1867–1960, The Secular and Cyclical Behavior of the Stock of Money in the United States, 1867–1960*. National Bureau of Economic Research and *A Monetary History of the United States, 1870–1960* (Princeton, 1963).

43. ———, and G. S. Becker, "A Statistical Illusion in Judging Keynesian Models," *Journal of Political Economy*, 65: 64–75 (February 1957).

44. ———, and D. Meiselman, *The Relative Stability of Monetary Velocity and the Investment Multiplier in the United States, 1897–1958*. Commission on Money and Credit. *Stabilization Policies* (Englewood Cliffs, N.J., 1963), pp. 165–268.

45. Galbraith, J. K., "Market Structure and Stabilization Policy," *Review of Economics and Statistics*, 39: 124–33 (May 1957).

46. Garvey, G., *Deposit Velocity and its Significance* (New York, 1959).

47. Goldsmith, R. W., *A Study of Saving in the United States* (Princeton, 1955).

48. ———, *Financial Intermediaries in the American Economy Since 1900* (Princeton, 1958).

49. Gurley, J. G., *Liquidity and Financial Institutions in the Postwar Economy*, Study Paper 14, Joint Economic Committee, 86th Congress, 2nd Session (Washington, 1960).

50. ———, and E. S. Shaw, "Financial Aspects of Economic Development," *American Economic Review*, 45: 515–38 (September 1955).

51. ——— and ———, "Financial Intermediaries and the Saving-Investment Process," *Journal of Finance*, 11: 257–76 (May 1956) [reprinted in this volume—Ed.].

52. ——— and ———, *Money in a Theory of Finance*. With a mathematical appendix by A. C. Enthoven (Washington, 1960).

53. ——— and ———, "The Growth of Debt and Money in the United States, 1800–1950: A Suggested Interpretation," *Review of Economics and Statistics*, 39: 250–62 (August 1957).

54. Haberler, G., "The Pigou Effect Once Again," *Journal of Political Economy*, 60: 240–46 (June 1952).

55. Hahn, F. H., "The Rate of Interest and General Equilibrium Analysis," *Economic Journal*, 65: 52–66 (March 1955).

56. Hansen, A. H., *Monetary Theory and Fiscal Policy* (New York, 1949).

57. Harris, S. E., J. W. Angell, W. Fellner, A. H. Hansen, A. G. Hart, H. Neisser, R. V. Roosa, P. A. Samuelson, W. L. Smith, W. Thomas,

J. Tobin, and S. Weintraub, "Controversial Issues in Recent Monetary Policy: A Symposium," *Review of Economics and Statistics*, 42: 245–82 (August 1960).

58. Hazlitt, H. (ed.), *The Critics of Keynesian Economics* (Princeton, 1960).

59. Hicks, J. R., "A Suggestion for Simplifying the Theory of Money," *Economica*, 2: 1–19 (February 1935). Reprinted in F. A. Lutz and L. W. Mints (eds.), *Readings in Monetary Theory* (Homewood, Ill., 1951), pp. 13–32.

60. ———, *Value and Capital* (Oxford, 1939).

61. Johnson, H. G., "The General Theory after Twenty-five Years," *American Economic Review Proceedings*, 51: 1–17 (May 1961). Reprinted in H. G. Johnson, *Money, Trade and Economic Growth* (London, 1962).

62. Johnston, J., "A Statistical Illusion in Judging Keynesian Models: Comment," *Review of Economics and Statistics*, 40: 296–98 (August 1958).

63. Kahn, R. F., "Some Notes on Liquidity Preference," *Manchester School of Economics and Social Studies*, 22: 229–57 (September 1954).

64. Kareken, J. H., "Lenders' Preferences, Credit Rationing, and the Effectiveness of Monetary Policy," *Review of Economics and Statistics*, 39: 292–302 (August 1957).

65. Keynes, J. M., *A Treatise on Money* (London and New York, 1930).

66. ———, *The General Theory of Employment, Interest and Money* (London and New York, 1936).

67. Klein, L. R., "The Friedman-Becker Illusion," *Journal of Political Economy*, 66: 539–45 (December 1958).

68. ———, W. Fellner, H. M. Somers, and K. Brunner, "Stock and Flow Analysis in Economics," *Econometrica*, 18: 236–52 (July 1950).

69. Kragh, B., "The Meaning and Use of Liquidity Curves in Keynesian Interest Theory," *International Economic Papers*, 5: 155–69 (1955).

70. ———, "Two Liquidity Functions and the Rate of Interest: A Simple Dynamic Model," *Review of Economic Studies*, 17: 98–106 (February 1950).

71. Kuenne, R. E., "Keynes's Identity, Ricardian Virtue, and the Partial Dichotomy," *Canadian Journal of Economics and Political Science*, 27: 323–36 (August 1961).

72. Lange, O., "Say's Law: A Restatement and Criticism," in O. Lange, F. McIntyre, and T. O. Yntema (eds.), *Studies in Mathematical Economics and Econometrics* (Chicago, 1942), pp. 49–68.

73. Latané, H. A., "Cash Balances and the Interest Rate—A Pragmatic Approach," *Review of Economics and Statistics*, 36: 456–60 (November 1954) [reprinted in this volume—Ed.].

74. ———, "Income Velocity and Interest Rates: A Pragmatic Approach," *Review of Economics and Statistics*, 42: 445–49 (November 1960).

75. Lloyd, C. L., "The Equivalence of the Liquidity Preference and Loanable Funds Theories and the *New* Stock-Flow Analysis," *Review of Economic Studies*, 27: 206–9 (June 1960).

76. Luckett, D. G., " 'Bills Only': A Critical Appraisal," *Review of Economics and Statistics*, 42: 301–6 (August 1960).

77. Lydall, H. F., "Income, Assets and the Demand for Money," *Review of Economics and Statistics*, 40: 1–14 (February 1958).

78. Markowitz, H. M., *Portfolio Selection: Efficient Diversification of Investments* (New York, 1959).

79. Marty, A. L., "Gurley and Shaw on Money in a Theory of Finance," *Journal of Political Economy*, 69: 56–62 (February 1961).

80. Mayer, T., "The Inflexibility of Monetary Policy," *Review of Economics and Statistics*, 40: 358–74 (November 1958) [reprinted in this volume—Ed.].

81. McKean, R. N., "Liquidity and a National Balance Sheet," *Journal of Political Economy*, 57: 506–22 (December 1949). Reprinted in F. A. Lutz and L. W. Mints (eds.), *Readings in Monetary Theory* (Homewood, Ill., 1951), pp. 63–88.

82. Meiselman, D., *The Term Structure of Interest Rates* (Englewood Cliffs, N.J., 1962).

83. Meltzer, A. H., "Mercantile Credit, Monetary Policy and Size of Firm," *Review of Economics and Statistics*, 42: 429–37 (November 1960).

84. Metzler, L. A., "Wealth, Saving and the Rate of Interest," *Journal of Political Economy*, 59: 93–116 (April 1951) [reprinted in this volume—Ed.].

85. Miller, E., "Monetary Policies in the United States Since 1950: Some Implications of the Retreat to Orthodoxy," *Canadian Journal of Economics and Political Science*, 27: 205–22 (May 1961).

86. Minsky, H. P., "Central Banking and Money Market Changes," *Quarterly Journal of Economics*, 71: 171–87 (May 1957).

87. Mundell, R. A., "The Public Debt, Corporate Income Taxes, and the Rate of Interest," *Journal of Political Economy*, 68: 622–26 (December 1960).

88. Musgrave, R. A., "Money, Liquidity and the Valuation of Assets," in *Money, Trade and Economic Growth*, in honor of John Henry Williams (New York, 1951), pp. 216–42.

89. Norton, F. E., and N. H. Jacoby, *Bank Deposits and Legal Reserve Requirements* (Los Angeles, 1959).

90. Orr, D., and W. J. Mellon, "Stochastic Reserve Losses and Expansion of Bank Credit," *American Economic Review*, 51: 614–23 (September 1961).

91. Patinkin, D., "Dichotomies of the Pricing Process in Economic Theory," *Economica*, 21: 113–28 (May 1954).

92. ———, "Financial Intermediaries and the Logical Structure of Monetary Theory," *American Economic Review*, 51: 95–116 (March 1961).

93. ———, "Liquidity Preference and Loanable Funds: Stock and Flow Analysis," *Economica*, 25: 300–18 (November 1958).

94. ———, *Money, Interest and Prices* (Evanston, Ill., 1956).

95. ———, "The Indeterminacy of Absolute Prices in Classical Economic Theory," *Econometrica*, 17: 1–27 (January 1949).

96. Phillips, A. W., "Stabilization Policy in a Closed Economy," *Economic Journal*, 64: 290–323 (June 1954).

97. Riefler, W., "Open Market Operations in Long-Term Securities," *Federal Reserve Bulletin*, 44: 1260–74 (November 1958).

98. Robertson, D. H., "More Notes on the Rate of Interest," *Review of Economic Studies*, 21: 136–41 (February 1954).

99. Robinson, J., "The Rate of Interest," *Econometrica*, 19: 92–111 (April 1951). Reprinted in J. Robinson, *The Rate of Interest and Other Essays* (London, 1952).

100. Rosa [Roosa], R. V., "Interest Rates and the Central Bank," in *Money, Trade and Economic Growth*, in honor of John Henry Williams (New York, 1951), pp. 270–95 [reprinted in this volume—Ed.].

101. Rose, H., "Liquidity Preference and Loanable Funds," *Review of Economic Studies*, 24: 111–19 (February 1957).

102. Sayers, R. S., "Monetary Thought and Monetary Policy in England," *Economic Journal*, 70: 710–24 (December 1960).

103. Schlesinger, J. R., "After Twenty Years: The General Theory," *Quarterly Journal of Economics*, 70: 581–602 (November 1956).

104. Scott, I. O., "The Availability Doctrine: Theoretical Under-pinnings," *Review of Economic Studies*, 25: 41–48 (October 1957) [reprinted in this volume—Ed.].

105. Selden, R. T., "Monetary Velocity in the United States," in M. Friedman (ed.), *Studies in the Quantity Theory of Money* (Chicago, 1956), pp. 179–257.

106. Shackle, G. L. S., "Recent Theories Concerning the Nature and Role of Interest," *Economic Journal*, 71: 209–54 (June 1961) [reprinted in this volume—Ed.].

107. Shaw, E. S., "Money Supply and Stable Economic Growth," in *United States Monetary Policy* (New York, 1958), pp. 49–71.

108. Shelby, D., "Some Implications of the Growth of Financial Intermediaries," *Journal of Finance*, 13: 527–41 (December 1958).

109. Simons, H. C., "Rules versus Authorities in Monetary Policy," *Journal of Political Economy*, 44: 1–30 (February 1936). Reprinted in H. C. Simons, *Economic Policy for a Free Society* (Chicago, 1948), pp. 160–83.

110. Smith, W. L., *Debt Management in the United States*, Study Paper No. 19, Joint Economic Committee, 86th Congress, 2nd Session (Washington, 1960).

111. ———, "Financial Intermediaries and Monetary Controls," *Quarterly Journal of Economics*, 73: 533–53 (November 1959).

112. ———, "Monetary Theories of the Rate of Interest: A Dynamic Analysis," *Review of Economics and Statistics*, 40: 15–21 (February 1958).

113. ———, "On the Effectiveness of Monetary Policy," *American Economic Review*, 46: 588–606 (September 1956).

114. Tobin, J., "A Dynamic Aggregative Model," *Journal of Political Economy*, 63: 103–15 (April 1955) [reprinted in this volume—Ed.].

115. ———, "Liquidity Preference and Monetary Policy," *Review of Economics and Statistics*, 29: 124–31 (May 1947).

116. ———, "Liquidity Preference as Behavior Towards Risk," *Review of Economic Studies*, 25: 65–86 (February 1958) [reprinted in this volume—Ed.].

117. ———, "Money, Capital and Other Stores of Value," *American Economic Review Proceedings*, 51: 26–37 (May 1961).

118. ———, "The Interest-Elasticity of Transactions Demand for Cash," *Review of Economics and Statistics*, 38: 241–47 (August 1956).

119. Tolley, G. S., "Providing for Growth of the Money Supply," *Journal of Political Economy*, 65: 465–85 (December 1957) [reprinted in this volume—Ed.].

120. Tsiang, S. C., "Liquidity Preference and Loanable Funds Theories, Multiplier and Velocity Analysis: A Synthesis," *American Economic Review*, 46: 539–64 (September 1956).

121. Turvey, R., "Consistency and Consolidation in the Theory of Interest," *Economica*, 21: 300–7 (November 1954).

122. ———, *Interest Rates and Asset Prices* (London, 1960).

123. Valavanis, S., "A Denial of Patinkin's Contradiction," *Kyklos*, 4: 351–68 (1955).

124. Villard, H. H., "Monetary Theory," in H. S. Ellis (ed.), *A Survey of Contemporary Economics* (Philadelphia, 1948), pp. 314–51.

125. Weintraub, S., *An Approach to the Theory of Income Distribution* (Philadelphia, 1958).

126. White, W. H., "The Flexibility of Anticyclical Monetary Policy," *Review of Economics and Statistics*, 43: 142–47 (May 1961) [reprinted in this volume—Ed.].

127. "A Flow-of-Funds System of National Accounts: Annual Estimates, 1939–54," *Federal Reserve Bulletin*, 41: 1085–1124 (October 1955).

128. Committee on the Working of the Monetary System (Chairman: The Rt. Hon. The Lord Radcliffe, G.B.E.), *Report* (London, 1959).

129. *Money and Credit: Their Influence on Jobs, Prices and Growth* (Englewood Cliffs, N.J., 1961).

130. U.S. Congress Joint Economic Committee, *Staff Report on Employment, Growth and Price Levels* (Washington, 1959).

Part **II**

The Demand
For Money

The analysis of the demand for money prior to the General Theory centered about the quantity theory of money, which has had a venerable reputation, receiving its classical presentation in David Hume's essay *On Money*. The modern discussion of the quantity theory has taken as its point of departure Irving Fisher's equation-of-exchange which stated that the quantity of money, M, times the transaction velocity of money, V', equals the value of transactions, $p'T$, where p' is an index of prices and T is the volume of real transactions measured in base period prices:

$$MV' = p'T$$

An alternative formulation of Fisher's equation, which proved theoretically and empirically more manageable, employed the real value of income measured in base period prices, Y, in place of the volume of real transactions, and employed the income velocity of money, V, in place of transaction velocity, with a suitable redefinition of the price index, p:

$$MV = pY$$

The equation-of-exchange was a truism and was always satisfied by the manner in which the variables were defined. The quantity theory of money was transformed into a theory of demand for money by assuming that velocity was determined largely by institutional factors and that in the short-run it could be treated as a constant. This view was expressed by rewriting the equation-of-exchange in a form that has come to be known as the cash balance or "Cambridge equation":

$$M = kpY$$

where k, the reciprocal of the income velocity of money, can be interpreted as the average length of time money is held between transactions. This interpretation emphasized the role of money as a medium of exchange and implied that money would not be held except to finance transactions.

Keynes' analysis of the demand for money in the *General Theory of Employment, Interest and Money* emphasized the role of money as a store of value and distinguished a "speculative" demand for money. The speculative demand for money, as introduced by Keynes and subsequently elaborated upon by Tobin, was explained by the logic that in an uncertain world in which interest rates fluctuated, a wealthholder investing in interest-bearing financial assets undertook the risk of a capital loss if the rate of interest rose and if he should at the same time require money to make unforeseen payments (a precautionary motive) or if he wished to take advantage of future investment opportunities (a speculative motive). Thus the risk and the rate of return an individual receives on his stock of wealth is dependent on the rate of interest and on the proportion of his wealth held in the form of interest-yielding assets (securities). If the rate of interest declines, the rate of return on an individual's stock of wealth would no longer offset the risk he undertakes, both because the return is low, and because an "abnormally" low rate of interest may be thought more likely to rise. A wealthholder will reduce his risk by increasing the proportion of wealth he holds in the form of money. It is possible that the rate of interest may be so low that any increases in the stock of money will simply be held by wealthholders as "idle balances."

For analytical convenience Keynes combined the precautionary and transactions motives for holding money since he believed both to be determined largely by the level of income (although as may be seen above, the precautionary motive can just as easily be combined with the speculative demand for money). Keynes' formulation of the demand for money may be written as:

$$M/p = k'Y + L'(i)$$

where $k'Y$ is the transactions demand and $L'(i)$ the speculative demand for money which varies inversely with the rate of interest, i. This manner of expressing the Keynesian demand for money follows Patinkin in that it assumes that both the speculative and transactions demand for money are, for any given income, proportional to the price level. Keynes rejected the idea that for practical purposes velocity in the short-run could be treated as a constant. The main thrust of his speculative demand for money was to suggest that there are conditions under which the price mechanism and, specifically, the interest rate mechanism, will not work to restore full employment.

TRANSACTIONS APPROACH

Baumol and Tobin demonstrated that the transactions demand for money was also interest-elastic, so that the demand for money could be written as:

$$M/p = L_1(i, Y) + L_2(i)$$

or more generally as

$$M/p = L(i, Y)$$

Miller and Orr analyzed the transaction demand for when income and expenditure were subject to uncertainty and arrived at similar results to Baumol and Tobin. Transaction costs were still the necessary condition for holding money, only now income was replaced in the argument for the transaction demand for money by the variance in cash balances so the demand function for money becomes

$$M/p = L_1(i, \sigma_M) + L_2(i)$$

Thorn attempts to synthesize the transaction demand and asset demand for money into a general transaction demand for money under uncertainty which does not depend on transaction costs for its existence by attaching a cost to running out of money balances. This expected cost will vary inversely with the size of cash balances. As long as cash balances cannot be restored instantly, then some cash will generally be held even if there are no transaction costs. Furthermore, if the opportunity cost of holding cash balances is defined as the marginal rate of return on wealth portfolios, then the demand for money may be integrated with the theory of portfolio selection. Changes in risk aversion or interest rates result in changes in the composition of wealth portfolios which change the marginal rate of return on wealth portfolios which constitutes the opportunity cost of holding money and therefore affects the holding of cash balances.

If the variance in cash balances is functionally related to income, then the general form of the demand for money may be written in the familiar form:

$$M/p = L(W, Y, i)$$

Wide agreement has been arrived at by both "quantity" and "Keynesian" monetary theorists in recent years that: (1) money has utility as a store of value in an uncertain world; (2) the demand for money is part of a theory of asset preference; and (3) that the major determinants of the demand for money are wealth, W, income, and the rate of interest (although considerable difference of opinion exists about the relative importance of the variables).

The theoretical differences that have arisen between the "Keynesian," or what has more recently been called the "portfolio," approach and the "quantity" approach are mainly differences of emphasis. The "portfolio" approach emphasized the substitution effects of money as an alternative to other financial assets and "dethrones" money from the central position it has occupied, by treating it symmetrically with other assets which yield services. Thus it attempts to treat the theory of money with the tools of the theory of consumer choice. The "quantity" approach as exemplified by Friedman emphasized income effects as the principal explanation for the variation in the demand for money, assigning substitution effects a secondary role. This approach attempts to treat the theory of money as a subject within capital theory.

RESTATEMENT OF THE QUANTITY THEORY

The modern restatement of the quantity theory as an asset preference theory, as expounded by Professor Friedman, attempts to integrate monetary theory into value theory via the theory of capital. Friedman following Irving Fisher treats all factor income as emanating from capital. The source of human income is human capital. Friedman makes the demand for money depend on the real rate of interest on financial assets, the rate of return on nominal money which is taken to be the rate of change of price level, $\Delta p/p$, real income, the ratio of non-human capital to human capital, w, and a taste variable, u, so that the demand for money may be written:

$$M/p = L(i, \Delta p/p, Y, w, u)$$

In the empirical application of his theory, Friedman has made clear that he believes that substitution effects are secondary to the role of income effects. He takes the observed decline in velocity to the Second World War as evidence that money is a luxury good and that at higher levels of income proportionally more cash balances are demanded. However, in his study with Anna Schwartz of *The History of Money in the United States* (Princeton 1964), Friedman found a contradiction between the secular and the cyclical behavior of money. Over long periods of time, Friedman and Schwartz found real income and velocity tended to move in opposite directions (i.e., money-holding grew faster than income) while over the business cycle they tended to move in the same direction. The trend and the cycle also differed in the relative importance of the factors, money-holding and velocity with respect to money income. The nominal stock of money statistically tended to dominate the long swings in money income while in the business cycle changes in velocity were of comparable statistical importance in determining changes in money income. To reconcile this contradiction, Friedman introduced the explanation that per capita demand for money, M', was determined by permanent per capita income Y', and the permanent price level, p'', so that the demand for money may be written:

$$M'/p'' = a(Y'/p'')^b$$

where a and b are constants.

The cyclical behavior of velocity was reconciled with the secular behavior by the fact that in the expansionary phase nominal income increases more than permanent income (the level of income which people expect will be sustained), so that *measured* velocity exceeds permanent velocity. Permanent velocity may even be declining while measured velocity is rising. Friedman through a series of statistical manipulations and approximations tested his theory against the data for the United States and found that his computed measured velocity closely approximated observed velocity for most of the period. This explanation was intended to supplant cyclical variations in the interest rate (substitution effect) as the chief determinant of the observed cyclical change in velocity. However, since 1950, observed measured velocity has risen while Friedman's computed measured velocity has fallen.

THE PORTFOLIO APPROACH

The portfolio approach, largely developed by Professor Tobin, retains the Keynesian two-stage approach to wealth accumulation; saving is largely determined by income, but the types of assets in which savings are held are determined by the expected relative yields and the expected yield variability of the different types of wealth assets. If the theory were extended to the stock of human capital, the portfolio approach would not differ much from Friedman's quantity theory. This theory extended still further could embrace consumption theory as well by treating the demand for assets as being determined by their relative yields and existing stocks. Consumption goods would be treated simply as assets of which there were always zero stocks. Most portfolio theorists have fallen short of this sweeping generalization, however, preferring to retain the dichotomy of consumption and saving. The portfolio approach in its rigorous form has no special place for money except possibly as a policy variable. The denial of any unique qualities to money as an asset does not necessarily deny to money a unique role as a policy instrument. As long as one believes that the composition of wealth assets can affect spending decisions and if one were limited to the possibility of altering the stock of only one type of asset, money would have some special properties to commend it, such as the ease with which its stock may be significantly changed and the pervasiveness of money in wealth portfolios of all sectors of the economy.

Goldfeld has found, as Duesenberry[1] discovered earlier, that the empirical behavior of the demand for money by the various sectors of the economy differs significantly.

THE RECONCILIATION OF THE QUANTITY AND PORTFOLIO APPROACHES

We may conclude from this discussion above and the selections that follow that there is a wide agreement on the variables that affect the demand for money. The reformulated quantity theory, and the extension of the liquidity preference theory into one of maintaining an optimum portfolio of wealth assets, can in large measure be reconciled. Whether substitution or income effects dominate the demand for money is an empirical question.

From the point of view of policy the important question is, does there exist some collection of liquid assets, the stock of which may be influenced by monetary authorities, which has a stable functional relationship with income; and, whether the quantitative significance of this relationship is sufficiently great to be useful as a major instrument of economic policy, or, on the other hand, whether policies should be sought that will influence more directly investment and consumption.

After two decades of discussion and empirical research most economists would answer in the affirmative to these questions. However, they do not agree on what monetary aggregate is the most valuable, nor on the specification of the functional relationship, nor on the quantitative significance of the relationship between money and income. Furthermore, there is some doubt whether these questions can in fact be settled empirically.[2]

---

[1] See J. S. Duesenberry, "The Portfolio Approach to the Demand for Money and Other Assets," *Review of Economics and Statistics,* 45:9–24 (February 1963) [reprinted in the first edition of this work].

[2] Cf. David A. Pierce, "Relationships—and the Lack Therefore—between Economic Time Series, with Special Reference to Money, Reserves, and Interest Rates," *Special Studies Paper,* No. 55, Division of Research and Statistics, Federal Reserve Board, Washington, D.C., February 3, 1975.

A. Transactions Theory

3 The Transactions Demand for Cash: An Inventory Theoretic Approach

William J. Baumol *New York University*

A stock of cash is its holder's inventory of the medium of exchange, and like an inventory of a commodity, cash is held because it can be given up at the appropriate moment, serving then as its possessor's part of the bargain in an exchange. We might consequently expect that inventory theory and monetary theory can learn from one another. This note attempts to apply one well-known result in inventory control analysis to the theory of money.[1]

A Simple Model

We are now interested in analyzing the transactions demand for cash dictated by rational behavior, which for our purposes means the holding of those cash balances that can do the job at minimum cost. To abstract from precautionary and speculative demands let us consider a state in which transactions are perfectly foreseen and occur *in a steady stream*.

Suppose that in the course of a given period an individual will pay out T dollars in a steady stream. He obtains cash either by

Reprinted from *Quarterly Journal of Economics*, Vol. 66 (Cambridge, Mass.: Harvard University Press, November 1952), 545–56, by permission of the author and publisher. Copyright, 1952, by the President and Fellows of Harvard College.

borrowing it, or by withdrawing it from an investment, and in either case his interest cost (or interest opportunity cost) is i dollars per dollar per period. Suppose finally that he withdraws cash in lots of C dollars spaced evenly throughout the year, and that each time he makes such a withdrawal he must pay a fixed "broker's fee" of b dollars.[2] Here T, the value of transactions, is predetermined, and i and b are assumed to be constant.

In this situation any value of C less than or equal to T will enable him to meet his payments equally well provided he withdraws the money often enough. For example, if T is \$100, he can meet his payments by withdrawing \$50 every six months or \$25 quarterly, etc.[3] Thus he will make $\dfrac{T}{C}$ withdrawals over the course of the year, at a total cost in "brokers' fees" given by $\dfrac{bT}{C}$.

In this case, since each time he withdraws C dollars he spends it in a steady stream and draws out a similar amount the moment it is gone, his average cash holding will be $\dfrac{C}{2}$ dollars. His annual interest cost of holding cash will then be $\dfrac{iC}{2}$.

The total amount the individual in question must pay for the use of the cash needed to meet his transaction when he borrows C dollars at intervals evenly spaced throughout the year will then be the sum of interest cost and "brokers' fees" and so will be given by

$$\frac{bT}{C} + \frac{iC}{2}. \tag{1}$$

Since the manner in which he meets his payments is indifferent to him, his purpose only being to pay for his transactions, rationality requires that he do so at minimum cost, i.e., that he choose the most economical value of C. Setting the derivative of (1) with respect to C equal to zero we obtain[4]

$$-\frac{bT}{C^2} + \frac{i}{2} = 0,$$

i.e.,

$$C = \sqrt{\frac{2bT}{i}}. \tag{2}$$

Thus, in the simple situation here considered, the rational individual will, given the price level,[5] demand cash in proportion to the square root of the value of his transactions.

Before examining the implications of this crude model we may note that, as it stands, it applies to two sorts of cases: that of the individual (or firm) obtaining cash from his invested capital and that of the individual (or firm) spending out of borrowing in anticipation of future receipts. Since our problem depends on non-coincidence of cash receipts and disbursements, and we have assumed that cash disbursements occur in a steady stream, one other case seems possible, that where receipts precede expenditures. This differs from the first case just mentioned (living off one's capital) in that the individual now has the option of withholding some or all of his receipts from investment and simply keeping the cash until it is needed. Once this withheld cash is used up the third case merges into the first: the individual must obtain cash from his invested capital until his next cash receipt occurs.

We can deal with this third case as follows. First, note that any receipts exceeding anticipated disbursements will be invested, since, eventually, interest earnings must exceed ("brokerage") cost of investment. Hence we need only deal with that part of the cash influx which is to be used in making payments during the period between receipts. Let this amount, as before, be T dollars. Of this let I dollars be invested, and the remainder, R dollars, be withheld, where either of these sums may be zero. Again let i be the interest rate, and let the "broker's fee" for withdrawing cash be given by the linear expression $b_w + k_w C$, where C is the amount withdrawn. Finally, let there be a "broker's fee" for investing (depositing) cash given by $b_d + k_d I$ where the b's and the k's are constants.

Since the disbursements are continuous, the $R = T - I$ dollars withheld from investment will serve to meet payments for a fraction of the period between consecutive receipts given by $\dfrac{T-I}{T}$. Moreover, since the average cash holding for that time will be $\dfrac{T-I}{2}$, the interest cost of withholding that money will be $\dfrac{T-I}{T} i \dfrac{T-I}{2}$. Thus the total cost of withholding the R dollars and investing the I dollars will be

$$\frac{T-I}{2} i \frac{T-I}{T} + b_d + k_d I.$$

Analogously, the total cost of obtaining cash for the remainder of the period will be

$$\frac{C}{2} i \frac{I}{T} + (b_w + k_w C) \frac{I}{C}.$$

Thus the total cost of cash operations for the period will be given by the sum of the last two expressions, which when differentiated partially with respect to C and set equal to zero once again yields our square root formula, (2), with $b = b_w$.

Thus, in this case, the optimum cash balance after the initial cash holding is used up will again vary with the square root of the volume of transactions, as is to be expected by analogy with the "living off one's capital" case.

There remains the task of investigating $R/2$, the (optimum) average cash balance before drawing on invested receipts begins. We again differentiate our total cost of holding cash, this time partially with respect to I, and set it equal to zero, obtaining

$$-\frac{T - I}{T} i + k_d + \frac{Ci}{2T} + \frac{b_w}{C} + k_w = 0,$$

i.e.,

$$R = T - I = \frac{C}{2} + \frac{b_w T}{Ci} + \frac{T(k_d + k_w)}{i},$$

or since from the preceding result, $C^2 = 2Tb_w/i$, so that the second term on the right-hand side equals $C^2/2C$,

$$R = C + T\left(\frac{k_w + k_d}{i}\right).$$

The first term in this result is to be expected, since if *everything* were deposited at once, C dollars would have to be withdrawn at that same moment to meet current expenses. On this amount two sets of "brokers' fees" would have to be paid and no interest would be earned—a most unprofitable operation.[6]

Since C varies as the square root of T and the other term varies in proportion with T, R will increase less than in proportion with T, though more nearly in proportion than does C. The general nature of our results is thus unaffected.[7]

Note finally that the entire analysis applies at once to the case of continuous receipts and discontinuous payments, taking the period to be that between two payments, where the relevant decision is the frequency of investment rather than the frequency of withdrawal. Similarly, it applies to continuous receipts and payments where the two are not equal.

Some Consequences of the Analysis

I shall not labor the obvious implications for financial budgeting by the firm. Rather I shall discuss several arguments which have been presented by monetary theorists, to which our result is relevant.

The first is the view put forth by several economists,[8] that in a stationary state there will be no demand for cash balances since it will then be profitable to invest all earnings in assets with a positive yield in such a way that the required amount will be realized at the moment any payment is to be made. According to this view no one will want any cash in such a stationary world, and the value of money must fall to zero so that there can really be no such thing as a truly static monetary economy. Clearly this argument neglects the transactions costs involved in making and collecting such loans (the "broker's fee").[9] Our model is clearly compatible with a static world and (2) shows that it will generally pay to keep some cash. The analysis of a stationary monetary economy in which there is a meaningful (finite) price level does make sense.

Another view which can be reëxamined in light of our analysis is that the transactions demand for cash will vary approximately in proportion with the money value of transactions.[10] This may perhaps even be considered the tenor of quantity theory though there is no necessary connection, as Fisher's position indicates. If such a demand for cash balances is considered to result from rational behavior, then (2) suggests that the conclusion cannot have general validity. On the contrary, the square root formula implies that demand for cash rises less than in proportion with the volume of transactions, so that there are, in effect, economies of large scale in the use of cash.

The magnitude of this difference should not be exaggerated, however. The phrase "varying as the square" may suggest larger effects than are actually involved. Equation (2) requires that the average transactions velocity of circulation vary exactly in proportion with the quantity of cash, so that, for example, a doubling of the stock of cash will *ceteris paribus*, just double velocity.[11]

A third consequence of the square root formula is closely connected with the second. The effect on real income of an injection of cash into the system may have been underestimated. For suppose that (2) is a valid expression for the general demand for cash, that there is widespread unemployment, and that for this or other reasons prices do not rise with an injection of cash. Suppose, moreover, that the rate of interest is unaffected, i.e., that none of the new cash is used to buy securities. Then so long as transactions do not rise so as to maintain the same proportion with the square of the quantity of money, people will want to get rid of cash. They will use it to demand more goods and services, thereby forcing the volume of transactions to rise still further. For let ΔC be the quantity of cash injected. If a proportionality (constant velocity) assumption involves transactions rising by $k\Delta C$, it is easily shown that (2) involves transactions rising by more than twice as much, the magnitude of the excess increasing with the ratio of the injection to the initial stock of cash. More precisely, the rise in transactions would then be given by[12]

$$2k\Delta C + \frac{k}{C}\Delta C^2.$$

Of course, the rate of interest would really tend to fall in such circumstances, and this would to some extent offset the effect of the influx of cash, as is readily seen when we rewrite (2) as

$$T = C^2 i/2b. \tag{3}$$

Moreover, prices will rise to some extent,[13] and, of course, (3) at best is only an approximation. Nevertheless, it remains true that the effect of an injection of cash on, say, the level of employment, may often have been underestimated.[14] For whatever may be working to counteract it, the force making for increased employment is greater than if transactions tend, *ceteris paribus*, toward their original proportion to the quantity of cash.

Finally the square root formula lends support to the argument that wage cuts can help increase employment, since it follows that the Pigou effect and the related effects are stronger than they would be with a constant transactions velocity. Briefly the phenomenon which has come to be called the Pigou effect[15] may be summarized thus: General unemployment will result in reduction in the price level which must increase the purchasing power of the stock of cash provided the latter does not itself fall more than in proportion with prices.[16] This increased purchasing power will augment demand for commodities[17] or investment goods (either directly, or because it is used to buy securities and so forces down the rate of interest). In any case, this works for a reduction in unemployment.

Now the increase in the purchasing power of the stock of cash which results from fallen prices is equivalent to an injection of cash with constant prices. There is therefore exactly the same reason for suspecting the magnitude of the effect of the former on the volume of transactions has been underestimated, as in the case of the latter. Perhaps this can be of some little help in explaining why there has not been more chronic unemployment or runaway inflation in our economy.

The Simple Model and Reality

It is appropriate to comment on the validity of the jump from equation (2) to conclusions about the operation of the economy. At best, (2) is only a suggestive oversimplification, if for no other reason, because of the rationality assumption employed in its derivation. In addition the model is static. It takes the distribution of the firm's disbursements over time to be fixed, though it is to a large extent in the hands of the entrepreneur how he will time his expenditures. It assumes that there is one constant relevant rate of interest and that the "broker's fee" is constant or varies linearly with the magnitude of the sum involved. It posits a steady stream of payments and the absence of cash receipts during the relevant period. It deals only with the cash demand of a single economic unit and neglects interactions of the various demands for cash in the economy.[18] It neglects the precautionary and speculative demands for cash.

These are serious lacunae, and without a thorough investigation we have no assurance that our results amount to much more than an analytical curiosum. Nevertheless I offer only a few comments in lieu of analysis, and hope that others will find the subject worth further examination.

1. It is no doubt true that a majority of the public will find it impractical and perhaps pointless to effect every possible economy in the use of cash. Indeed the possibility may never occur to most people. Nevertheless, we may employ the standard argument that the largest cash users may more plausibly be expected to learn when it is profitable to reduce cash balances relative to transactions. The demand for cash by the community as a whole may then be affected similarly and by a significant amount. Moreover, it is possible that even small cash holders will sometimes institute some cash economies instinctively or by a process of trial and error not explicitly planned or analyzed.

2. With variable b and i the validity of our two basic results— the non-zero rational transactions demand for cash, and the less than proportionate rise in the rational demand for cash with the real volume of transactions, clearly depends on the nature of the responsiveness of the "brokerage fee" and the interest rate to the quantity of cash involved. The first conclusion will hold generally provided the "broker's fee" never falls below some preassigned level, e.g., it never falls below one mill per transaction, and provided the interest rate, its rate of change with C and the rate of change of the "broker's fee" all (similarly) have some upper bound, however large, at least when C is small.

The second conclusion will not be violated persistently unless the "brokerage fee" tends to vary almost exactly in proportion with C (and it pays to hold zero cash balances) except for what may roughly be described as a limited range of values of C. Of course, it is always possible that this "exceptional range" will be the one relevant in practice. Variations in the interest rate will tend to strengthen our conclusion provided the interest rate never decreases with the quantity of cash borrowed or invested.[19]

It would perhaps not be surprising if these sufficient conditions for the more general validity of our results were usually satisfied in practice.

3. If payments are lumpy but foreseen, cash may perhaps be employed even more economically. For then it may well pay to obtain cash just before large payments fall due with little or no added cost in "brokers' fees" and considerable savings in interest payments. The extreme case would be that of a single payment during the year which would call for a zero cash balance provided the cash could be loaned out profitably at all. Cash receipts during the relevant period may have similar effects, since they can be used to make payments which happen to be due at the moment the receipts arrive. Here the extreme case involves receipts and payments always coinciding in time and amounts in which case, again, zero cash balances would be called for. Thus lumpy payments and receipts of cash, with sufficient foresight, can make for economies in the use of cash, i.e., higher velocity. This may not affect the rate of increase in transactions velocity with the level of transactions, but may nevertheless serve further to increase the effect of an injection of cash and of a cut in wages and prices. With imperfect foresight, however, the expectation that payments may be lumpy may increase the precautionary demand for cash. Moreover, the existence of a "broker's fee" which must be paid on lending or investing cash received during the period is an added inducement to keep receipts until payments fall due rather than investing, and so may further increase the demand for cash.

4. The economy in a single person's use of cash resulting from an increase in the volume of his transactions may or may not have its analogue for the economy as a whole. "External economies" may well be present if one businessman learns cash-economizing techniques from the experiences of another when both increase their transactions. On the diseconomies side it is barely conceivable that an infectious liquidity fetishism will permit a few individuals reluctant to take advantage of cash saving opportunities to block these savings for the bulk of the community. Nevertheless, at least two such possible offsets come to mind: (a) The rise in the demand for brokerage services resulting from a general increase in transactions may bring about a rise in the "brokerage fee" and thus work for an increase in average cash balances (a decreased number of visits to brokers). If cash supplies are sticky this will tend to be offset by rises in the rate of interest resulting from a rising total demand for cash, which serve to make cash more expensive to hold. (b) Widespread cash economizing might require an increase in

precautionary cash holdings because in an emergency one could rely less on the ability of friends to help or creditors to be patient. This could weaken but not offset the relative reduction in cash holdings entirely, since the increase in precautionary demand is contingent on there being some relative decrease in cash holdings.

5. A priori analysis of the precautionary and the speculative demands for cash is more difficult. In particular, there seems to be little we can say about the latter, important though it may be, except that it seems unlikely that it will work consistently in any special direction. In dealing with the precautionary demand, assumptions about probability distributions and expectations must be made.[20] It seems plausible offhand, that an increase in the volume of transactions will make for economies in the use of cash for precautionary as well as transactions purposes by permitting increased recourse to insurance principles.

Indeed, here we have a rather old argument in banking theory which does not seem to be widely known. Edgeworth,[21] and Wicksell[22] following him, suggested that a bank's precautionary cash requirements might also grow as the square root of the volume of its transactions (!). They maintained that cash demands on a bank tend to be normally distributed.[23] In this event, if it is desired to maintain a fixed probability of not running out of funds, precautionary cash requirements will be met by keeping on hand a constant multiple of the standard deviation (above the mean). But then the precautionary cash requirement of ten identical banks (with independent demands) together will be the same as that for any one of them multiplied by the square root of ten. For it is a well-known result that the standard deviation of a random sample from an infinite population increases as the square root of the size of the sample.

NOTES

1. T. M. Whitin informs me that the result in question goes back to the middle of the 1920's when it seems to have been arrived at independently by some half dozen writers. See, e.g., George F. Mellen, "Practical Lot Quantity Formula," *Management and Administration*, Vol. 10 (September 1925). Its significant implications for the economic theory of inventory, particularly for business cycle theory, seems to have gone unrecognized until recently when Dr. Whitin analyzed them in *The Theory of Inventory Management* (Princeton, N.J.: Princeton University Press, 1963) which, incidentally, first suggested the subject of this note to me. See also, Dr. Whitin's "Inventory Control in Theory and Practice" (*Quarterly Journal of Economics* [November 1952], p. 502), and Kenneth J. Arrow, Theodore Harris, and Jacob Marschak, "Optimal Inventory Policy," *Econometrica*, Vol. 19 (July 1951), especially pp. 252–55.

2. The term "broker's fee" is not meant to be taken literally. It covers all non-interest costs of borrowing or making a cash withdrawal. These include opportunity losses which result from having to dispose of assets just at the moment the cash is needed, losses involved in the poor resale price which results from an asset becoming "second-hand" when purchased by a non-professional dealer, administrative costs, and psychic costs (the trouble involved in making a withdrawal) as well as payment to a middleman. So conceived it seems likely that the "broker's fee" will, in fact, vary considerably with the magnitude of the funds involved, contrary to assumption. However, *some* parts of this cost will not vary with the amount involved—e.g., postage cost, bookkeeping expense, and, possibly, the withdrawer's effort. It seems plausible that the "broker's fee" will be better approximated by a function like $b + kC$ (where b and k are constants), which indicates that there is a part of the "broker's fee" increasing in proportion with the amount withdrawn. As shown in a subsequent footnote, however, our formal result is completely unaffected by this amendment.

We must also extend the meaning of the interest rate to include the value of protection against loss by fire, theft, etc., which we obtain when someone borrows our cash. On the other hand, a premium for the risk of default on repayment must be deducted. This protection obtained by lending seems to be mentioned less frequently by theorists than the risk, yet how can we explain the existence of interest-free demand deposits without the former?

3. In particular, if cash were perfectly divisible and no elapse of time were required from withdrawal through payment he could make his withdrawals in a steady stream. In this case he would never require any cash balances to meet his payments and C could be zero. However, as may be surmised, this would be prohibitive with any b greater than zero.

4. This result is unchanged if there is a part of the "broker's fee" which varies in proportion with the quantity of cash handled. For in this case the "broker's fee" for each loan is given by $b + kC$. Total cost in "brokers' fees" will then be

$$\frac{T}{C}(b + kC) = \frac{T}{C}b + kT.$$

Thus (1) will have the constant term, kT, added to it, which drops out in differentiation.

5. A doubling of *all* prices (including the "broker's fee") is like a change in the monetary unit, and may be expected to double the demand for cash balances.

6. Here the assumption of constant "brokerage fees" with $k_d = k_w = 0$ gets us into trouble. The amount withheld from investment then is never greater than C dollars only because a strictly constant "broker's fee" with no provision for a discontinuity at zero implies the payment of the fee even if nothing is withdrawn or deposited. In this case it becomes an overhead and it pays to invest for any interest earning greater than zero.

For a firm, *part* of the "broker's fee" may, in fact, be an overhead in this way. For example, failure to make an anticipated deposit will sometimes involve little or no reduction in the bookkeeping costs incurred in keeping track of such operations.

7. If we replace the linear functions representing the "brokers' fees" with more general functions $f_w(C)$ and $f_d(I)$ which are only required to be differentiable, the expression obtained for R is changed merely by replacement of k_w, and k_d by the corresponding derivatives $f_{w'}(C)$ and $f_{d'}(I)$.

8. See, e.g., Frank H. Knight, *Risk, Uncertainty and Profit* (Preface to the Re-issue), No. 16 in the series of Reprints of Scarce Tracts in Economic and Political Science (London: The London School of Economics and Political Science, 1933), p. xxii; F. Divisia, *Économique Rationelle* (Paris: G. Doin, 1927), Chapter 19 and the Appendix; and Don Patinkin, "Relative Prices, Say's Law and the Demand for Money," *Econometrica*, Vol. 16 (April 1948), 140–45. See also, P. N. Rosenstein-Rodan, "The Coordination of the General Theories of Money and Price," *Economica*, N. S., Vol. 3 (August 1936), Part 2.

9. It also neglects the fact that the transfer of cash takes time so that in reality we would have to hold cash at least for the short period between receiving it and passing it on again.

It is conceivable, it is true, that with perfect foresight the difference between money and securities might disappear since a perfectly safe loan could become universally acceptable. There would, however, remain the distinction between "real assets" and the "money-securities." Moreover, there would be a finite price for, and non-zero yield on the former, the yield arising because they (as opposed to certificates of their ownership) are not generally acceptable, and hence not perfectly liquid, since there is trouble and expense involved in carrying them.

10. Marshall's rather vague statements may perhaps be interpreted to support this view. See, e.g., Book 1, Chapter 4 in *Money, Credit and Commerce* (London 1923). Keynes clearly accepts this position. See *The General Theory of Employment, Interest and Money* (New York 1936), p. 201. It is also accepted by Pigou: "As real income becomes larger, there is, prima facie, reason for thinking that, just as, up to a point, people like to invest a larger proportion of their real income, so also they like to hold real balances in the form of money equivalent to a larger proportion of it. On the other hand, as Professor Robertson has pointed out to me, the richer people are, the cleverer they are likely to become in finding a way to *economize* in real balances. On the whole then we may, I think, safely disregard this consideration . . . for a close approximation . . . " (*Employment and Equilibrium*, 1st ed. [London 1941], pp. 59–60). Fisher, however, argues: "It seems to be a fact that, at a given price level, the greater a man's expenditures the more rapid his turnover; that is, the rich have a higher rate of turnover than the poor. They spend money faster, not only absolutely but relatively to the money they keep on hand. . . . We may therefore infer that, if a nation grows richer per capita, the velocity of circulation of money will increase. This proposition of course, has no reference to *nominal* increase of expenditure" (*The Purchasing Power of Money* [New York 1922], p. 167).

11. Since velocity equals $\dfrac{T}{C} = \dfrac{i}{2b} C$ by (2).

12. This is obtained by setting $k = Ci/2b$ in (3), below, and computing ΔT by substituting $C + \Delta C$ for C.

13. Even if (2) holds, the demand for cash may rise only in proportion with the money value of transactions when all prices rise exactly in proportion, the rate of interest and transactions remaining unchanged. For then a doubling of all prices and cash balances leaves the situation unchanged, and the received argument holds. The point is that b is then one of the prices which has risen.

14. But see the discussions of Potter and Law as summarized by Jacob Viner, *Studies in the Theory of International Trade* (New York 1937), pp. 37–39.

15. See A. C. Pigou, "The Classical Stationary State," *Economic Journal*, Vol. 53 (December 1943).

16. Presumably the "broker's fee" will be one of the prices which falls, driven down by the existence of unemployed brokers. There is no analogous reason for the rate of interest to fall, though it will tend to respond thus to the increase in the "real stock of cash."

17. The term "Pigou effect" is usually confined to the effects on consumption demand while the effect on investment demand, and (in particular) on the rate of interest is ordinarily ascribed to Keynes. However, the entire argument appears to antedate Pigou's discussion (which, after all, was meant to be a reformulation of the classical position) and is closely related to what Mr. Becker and I have called the Say's Equation form of the Say's Law argument. See our article "The Classical Monetary Theory: The Outcome of the Discussion," *Economica* (November 1952).

18. I refer here particularly to considerations analogous to those emphasized by Duesenberry in his discussion of the relation between the consumption functions of the individual and the economy as a whole in his *Income, Saving and the Theory of Consumer Behavior* (Cambridge, Mass. 1950).

19. For people to want to hold a positive amount of cash, the cost of cash holding must be decreasing after $C = 0$. Let b in (1) be a differentiable function of C for $C > 0$ (it will generally be discontinuous and equal to zero at $C = 0$). Then we require that the limit of the derivative of (1) be negative as C approaches zero from above, where this derivative is given by

$$-b\frac{T}{C^2} + \frac{T}{C}b' + \frac{i + i'C}{2}. \tag{i}$$

Clearly this will become negative as C approaches zero provided b is bounded from below and b', i, and i' are all bounded from above.

The second conclusion, the less than proportionate rise in minimum cost cash holdings with the volume of transactions, can be shown, with only b not constant, to hold if and only if $b - b'C + b''C^2$ is positive. This result is obtained by solving the first order minimum condition (obtained by setting (i), with the i' term omitted, equal to zero) for $\dfrac{T}{C}$

and noting that our conclusion is equivalent to the derivative of this ratio with respect to C being positive.

Now successive differentiation of (i) with the i' term omitted yields as our second order minimum condition $2(b - b'C) + b''C^2 > 0$ (note the resemblance to the preceding condition). Thus if our result is to be violated we must have

$$b - Cb' \lessgtr - b''C^2 < 2(b - Cb'), \tag{ii}$$

which at once yields $b'' \leq 0$. Thus if b' is not to become negative (a decreasing *total* payment as the size of the withdrawal increases!) b'' must usually lie within a small neighborhood of zero, i.e., b must be approximately linear. However we know that in this case the square root formula will be (approximately) valid except in the case $b = kC$ when it will always [by (i)] pay to hold zero cash balances. Note incidentally that (ii) also yields $b - Cb' \geq 0$ which means that our result must hold if ever the "brokerage fee" increases more than in proportion with C.

Note, finally, that if i varies with C the first order condition becomes a cubic and, provided $\infty > i' > 0$, our conclusion is strengthened, since T now tends to increase as C^2.

20. See Arrow, Harris, and Marschak, *op. cit.* for a good example of what has been done along these lines in inventory control analysis.

21. F. Y. Edgeworth, "The Mathematical Theory of Banking," *Journal of the Royal Statistical Society*, Vol. 51 (1888), especially pp. 123–27. Fisher (*op. cit.*) points out the relevance of this result for the analysis of the cash needs of the public as a whole. The result was independently rediscovered by Dr. Whitin (*op. cit.*) who seems to have been the first to combine it and (2) in inventory analysis.

22. K. Wicksell, *Interest and Prices* (London 1936), p. 67.

23. The distribution would generally be approximately normal if its depositors were large in number, their cash demands independent and not very dissimilarly distributed. The independence assumption, of course, rules out runs on banks.

4 A Model of the Demand for Money by Firms

Merton H. Miller *University of Chicago*
and Daniel Orr *University of California, San Diego*

I. *Introduction*

Economists have long recognized the similarity between the problem of managing a cash balance and that of managing an inventory of some physical commodity. An early attempt to exploit this analogy was provided by Baumol [2] who applied to cash holdings the classical "lot size" model of inventory management that Whitin [16] had earlier brought to the attention of economists. Since that time, the analysis of the firm's control of physical stocks has been vastly extended by economists and others; but no parallel advance has occurred on the cash balance front. The Baumol model in its original or some more refined version (such as that of Tobin [14]) has remained the dominant tool for analyzing the "transactions" demand for money at the micro level.

Since the Baumol model will serve as the point of departure and of contrast for the results to be presented in this paper, it will be helpful first to summarize briefly the main assumptions and properties of that model. In essence, the decision-maker is pictured as holding two distinct types of asset: (1) an earning asset such as a savings deposit or

Reprinted from the *Quarterly Journal of Economics,* Vol. 79 (Cambridge, Mass.: Harvard University Press, November 1966), 413–35, by permission of the authors and publisher, Copyright, 1966, by the President and Fellows of Harvard College.

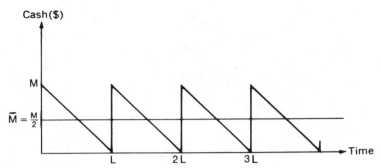

Figure 1a.

"bond" which bears interest at given rate of, say, v per dollar per day; and (2) a noninterest bearing cash balance into which periodic receipts of income are deposited and from which a steady flow of expenditures is made at the constant rate of, say, m dollars per day.[1] Transfers of funds between the two accounts are permissible at any time, but only at a cost which, in the simplest version of the model, is taken as a constant, γ, independent of the amount transferred.[2] The precise nature of this transfer cost will vary depending on the context to which the model is being applied, but in all cases it is to be interpreted as including both the direct expenses of effecting the transfer (such as postage or bank service charges) and any opportunity costs (such as time spent waiting at the teller's window or in making and communicating decisions about purchases and sales of portfolio assets).

Given these conditions, an optimal cash management policy will call for the investment of the periodic receipts in the earning asset followed by a regularly timed sequence of security sales that transfers M dollars every $L = M/m$ days from the earning to the cash account. The operating cash balance will thus have the "sawtooth" form shown in Figure 1a. If the decision-maker assigns a relatively large value to M, transfers will be infrequent; but the average cash balance $\dfrac{M}{2}$ will also be high with a consequent substantial loss of interest earnings. If he assigns a low value to M, then the interest loss on idle funds is reduced, but the gains thereby realized may be eaten up by the in-and-out costs. The minimum cost solution, balancing these opposing forces, is given by the familiar "square root rule," viz., transfer $M^* = \left(\dfrac{2\gamma m}{v}\right)^{\frac{1}{2}}$ dollars every $L^* = \left(\dfrac{2\gamma}{mv}\right)^{\frac{1}{2}}$ days, implying an average cash balance (or long-run demand for money) of $\bar{M}^* = \dfrac{M^*}{2} = \left(\dfrac{\gamma m}{2v}\right)^{\frac{1}{2}}.$[3]

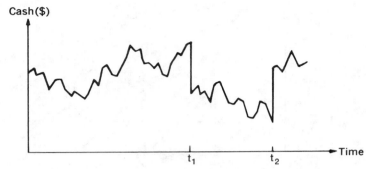

Figure 1b.

Simple as it is, this inventory model of cash management, with its emphasis on the cost of putting idle cash to work, does capture the essence of one fundamental element underlying the demand for money—perhaps the single most important element in an economy such as ours with a wide variety of interest-bearing securities of very low risk and very quickly convertible to cash. Moreover, the assumptions with respect to cash flows underlying the Baumol model apply reasonably well to much of the household sector, particularly to salary-earning households. The model, however, is much less satisfactory, both from the positive and normative points of view when applied to business firms (and to entrepreneurial and professional households) who hold about half of the total money stock.

For many business firms, the typical pattern of cash management is not the simple, regular one of Figure 1a, but a more complex one which might appear as in Figure 1b. The cash balance fluctuates ir-regularly (and to some extent unpredictably) over time in *both* directions—building up when operating receipts exceed expenditures and falling off when the reverse is true. If the build-up is at all pro-longed, a point is eventually reached (such as that indicated at t_1) at which the financial officer decides that cash holdings are excessive, and transfers a sizable quantity of funds either to the control of the portfolio staff for temporary investment or to loan retirement. In the other direction, in the face of a prolonged net drain, a level will be reached (as at t_2) at which the portfolio managers will be instructed to liquidate securities, or the firm will borrow to restore the cash balance to an "adequate working level."

The main purpose of this paper is to develop a simple, analytic model that incorporates both this "up and down" cash balance move-ment characteristic of business operations *and* the critical, lumpy transfer cost feature of the Baumol model. Note that we say *a* model, since for cash management as well as inventory management a wide variety of models will ultimately have to be developed by finance specialists and monetary theorists to cover all of the many important and interesting variations.[4]

II. *A Model of Cash Flows and the Costs of Cash Management for Business Firms*

We shall begin by listing the main assumptions underlying the model. Some of these will be recognized as mere technical simplifications. Others, however, are of a more substantive nature and will inevitably raise questions about the range of applicability of the model. Although we shall comment on certain of the substantive assumptions briefly here in passing, fuller consideration of the matter of applicability is best postponed until Section III, after the model and its major empirical implications have been set forth.

1. THE ASSUMPTIONS UNDERLYING THE MODEL

A first group of assumptions represents the analogues and necessary extensions of those in the Baumol model. Specifically, we suppose: (1) that we continue to have a "two-asset" setting, one asset being the firm's cash balance and the other a separately managed portfolio of liquid assets (such as Treasury bills, certificates of deposit, commercial paper or other money market instruments) whose marginal and average yield is v per dollar per day; (2) that transfers between the two asset accounts may take place at any time at a given marginal cost of γ per transfer, independent of the size of the transfer, the direction of the transfer or of the time since the previous transfer;[5] and (3) that such transfers may be regarded as taking place instantaneously, i.e., that the "lead-time" involved in portfolio transfers is short enough to be ignored.

The third assumption serves, among other things, to eliminate the need for a precautionary "buffer stock" whose function in stochastic inventory problems is to protect against runouts during the lead-time. While an assumption of zero lead-time may seem quite strong at first glance, it is actually not unrealistic, at least for the larger firms with specialized staffs that monitor the cash balance and the portfolio closely. Transactions in most of the major money market instruments can be initiated by such firms merely by placing a telephone call, with delivery for the start of the next business day (and in some special cases even during the same day).[6]

Consistent with present-day banking arrangements we shall further assume that there is a definite minimum level below which a firm's cash balance is not permitted to fall. Zero, of course, would be an absolute minimum since overdrafts are rarely allowed for business firms: even firms with open lines of credit must go through the formality (and expense) of a transfer to the cash balance before an overdrawn check will be cleared. In practice, required minimum balances are normally substantially greater than zero. The precise amount of the required minimum in any particular instance is negotiated between the parties and depends basically on the amount of banking services—mainly check processing and loan accommodation—that the firm actually uses. Since this required minimum is primarily a form of compensation to the bank in lieu of service charges we shall here regard it as completely exogenous to the problem of cash balance management and focus attention entirely on the discretionary holdings over and above the required minimum.[7] For further simplicity in notation we shall designate the required minimum level as zero.

A third group of assumptions specifies the nature of the fluctuations in the cash balance. In contrast to the completely deterministic Baumol model we shall here make the opposite extreme assumption that the net cash flows are completely stochastic; and, specifically, that they behave as if they were generated by a stationary random walk. Given this framework, it is convenient and yet sufficiently general for our purposes to suppose that the random behavior of the cash flows can be characterized as a sequence of independent Bernoulli trials. In particular, let $1/t$ = some small fraction of a working day such as $\frac{1}{8}$, i.e., an "hour." We suppose that during any such hour the cash balance will either increase by m dollars with probability p, or decrease by m dollars with probability $q = 1 - p$.[8] Over a longer interval of, say, n days, the observable distribution of changes in the cash balance will thus have mean $\mu_n = ntm(p - q)$ and variance $\sigma_n^2 = 4ntpqm^2$; and this distribution in turn will approach normality as n increases. Most of the subsequent discussion in the text will focus on the special symmetric or zero-drift case in which $p = q = \frac{1}{2}$ (with the derivations for more complicated nonsymmetric cases relegated to the Appendix). For this special case, $\mu_n = 0$, $\sigma_n^2 = nm^2t$ and $\sigma^2 = \dfrac{\sigma_n^2}{n} = m^2t =$ the variance of daily changes in the cash balance.

The Bernoulli process is by no means as restrictive in this context as it may appear at first glance. The properties of the Bernoulli process that are crucial for present purposes are not the implied regular timing or constant size of transaction; the critical features are rather serial independence, stationarity and the absence of discernible, regular swings in the cash balance. Any of a number of other familiar generating processes with these features might equally well have been used, all leading to the same solution as the one we present.[9]

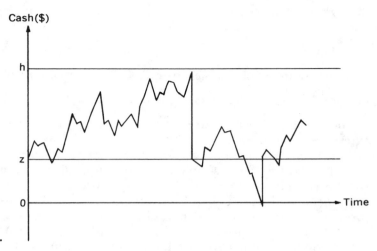

Figure 2.

The final set of assumptions concerns the firm's objective function. Here, following a standard practice in inventory theory we shall assume that the firm seeks to minimize the long-run average cost of managing the cash balance under some "policy of simple form."[10] In the present context, the simplest and most natural such policy is the two-parameter control-limit policy illustrated in Figure 2. That is, the cash balance will be allowed to wander freely until it reaches either the lower bound, zero, or an upper bound, h, at which times a portfolio transfer will be undertaken to restore the balance to a level of z.[11] Hence, the policy implies that when the upper bound is hit there will be a lump sum transfer *from* cash of $(h - z)$ dollars; and when the lower limit is triggered, a transfer *to* cash of z dollars.

Given this (h, z) policy structure, and our other assumptions, the expected cost per day of managing the firm's cash balance over any finite planning horizon of T days can be expressed formally as:

$$\epsilon(c) = \gamma \frac{\epsilon(N)}{T} + \nu\epsilon(M) \qquad (1)$$

where $\epsilon(N)$ = the expected number of portfolio transfers (in either direction) during the planning period; γ = the cost per transfer; $\epsilon(M)$ = the average daily cash balance; and ν = the daily rate of interest earned on the portfolio.[12] The firm's objective is that of minimizing $\epsilon(\bar{c})$ with respect to the control variables afforded by the chosen policy; the upper bound on cash holdings, h, and the intermediate return point, z.

2. THE OPTIMAL VALUES OF THE POLICY PARAMETERS

Turning now to the solution, consider first the term $\frac{\epsilon(N)}{T}$, the expected number of transfers per day. The derivation of an expression for $\frac{\epsilon(N)}{T}$ in terms of the decision variables z and h will be performed in two parts. First the mean number of transfers will be expressed in terms of the average time interval between transfers; and then this average interval will be related to z and h.

As for the first part, suppose that the successive time intervals (measured in days) $x_1, x_2, \ldots$, between portfolio transfers are independent random drawings from a population with a well-defined probability distribution. In particular, let this distribution have mean D and finite variance. If T is a fixed planning horizon and N is a random variable denoting the number of transfers that occur during the horizon period, then (by the definition of N)

$$x_1 + x_2 + \cdots + x_N \leq T < x_1 + x_2 + \cdots + x_{N+1}. \quad (1)$$

Or, taking expectations

$$\epsilon(x_1 + x_2 + \cdots + x_N) \leq T < \epsilon(x_1 + x_2 + \cdots + x_{N+1}).$$

Wald [15] has proved that under the assumed conditions on $\{x_i\}$

$$\epsilon(x_1 + x_2 + \cdots + x_N) = \epsilon(x)\epsilon(N) = D\epsilon(N)$$

from which the inequalities

$$D\epsilon(N) \leq T < D\epsilon(N) + D$$

are seen to hold. These in turn imply

$$\frac{1}{D} - \frac{1}{T} < \frac{\epsilon(N)}{T} \leq \frac{1}{D}. \quad (2)$$

Hence as T is allowed to grow unboundedly large, the ratio $\frac{\epsilon(N)}{T}$, the expected number of transfers per day, approaches $\frac{1}{D}$.[13]

We next seek an expression for D in terms of z and h, and here we can make direct use of classical results reviewed by Feller [3]. In particular, for a symmetric $(p = q = 1/2)$ Bernoullian random walk with unit transaction "steps" originating at z and terminating at either 0 or h, Feller proves (a) that the duration of the walk is a random variable whose distribution has the properties we assumed to hold for the $\{x_i\}$; and (b) that the expected value of the duration,

$D(z, h)$, is given by

$$D(z, h) = (z)(h - z). \tag{3}$$

The above expression states the expected duration in terms of number of trials. To convert the time unit to days, we need merely divide by t, the number of operating cash transactions per day. To convert z and h from unit steps to dollars we define new variables z' and h' in dollars with $z' = z \cdot m$ and $h' = h \cdot m$. Hence, the expected duration stated in days and with the bounds in dollar units is:

$$D(z', h') = \frac{(z')(h' - z')}{m^2 t}. \tag{4}$$

Having shown that $\frac{\epsilon(N)}{T}$ approaches $1/D(z, h)$ for sufficiently large T, the transfer cost term of the long-run average cost function (1.1) can thus be written as the product of γ and the reciprocal of the right-hand side of (4). [To simplify the notation we shall hereafter omit the primes on z and h in expressions based on (4) since the presence of m and t will indicate that dollar rather than transaction step units are the appropriate dimension.]

The second term of the cost function requires an expression for the long-run average cash balance in terms of z and h. This balance is simply the mean of the steady-state distribution of cash holdings. Following the usual procedure for deriving this distribution (Feller [3]) the probability that the cash balance will contain precisely x units is obtained from the difference equations:

$$f(x) = pf(x - 1) + qf(x + 1) \qquad x \neq z \tag{5}$$

with boundary conditions

$$f(z) = p[f(z - 1) + f(h - 1)] + q[f(z + 1) + f(1)] \tag{6}$$

and

$$f(0) = 0, \qquad f(h) = 0 \tag{7}$$

and the density condition

$$\sum_{x=0}^{n} f(x) = 1. \tag{8}$$

For the special case $p = q = \frac{1}{2}$, the system (5) has a solution of the form

$$f(x) = A_1 + B_1 x \qquad 0 \leq x \leq z$$
$$f(x) = A_2 + B_2(h - x) \tag{9}$$

The linearity of (9) and the conditions (6) and (7) imply that the steady-state distribution of cash holdings is of discrete triangular form with base h and mode z. The mean of such a distribution is $\dfrac{h + z}{3}$. [14]

Combining both segments of the expected cost function, and letting $Z = h - z$, the problem can now be stated as:

$$\min_{Z,z} \epsilon(c) = \frac{\gamma m^2 t}{zZ} + \frac{\nu(Z + 2z)}{3} . \tag{10}$$

The necessary conditions for a minimum are

$$\frac{\partial \epsilon(c)}{\partial z} = -\frac{\gamma m^2 t}{z^2 Z} + \frac{2\nu}{3} = 0$$

$$\frac{\partial \epsilon(c)}{\partial Z} = -\frac{\gamma m^2 t}{Z^2 z} + \frac{\nu}{3} = 0$$

which together yield the optimal values[15]

$$z^* = \left(\frac{3\gamma m^2 t}{4\nu}\right)^{\frac{1}{3}} \tag{11}$$

and

$$Z^* = 2z^* \tag{12}$$

or in terms of the original parameters

$$h^* = 3z^*. \tag{13}$$

3. SOME PROPERTIES OF THE SOLUTION

This solution has a number of interesting and in some respects quite surprising properties. Notice first that despite the symmetry of the generating process and of the cost of returning the system to z, the control rules turn out to be asymmetrical. The optimal return point lies substantially *below* the midpoint of the range over which the cash balance is permitted to wander. To put it another way, sales of portfolio assets will take place with greater average frequency and in smaller "lots" than purchases.[16] Some insight into the economic rationale of this result can be gained from Figure 3 in which the transfer cost and the holding cost are plotted separately as functions of z for some given $h = h_0$. The transfer cost is a symmetric U-shaped function with its minimum at the midpoint, $z = \frac{1}{2} h_0$. The idle balance cost, by contrast, is a linear increasing function of z through-

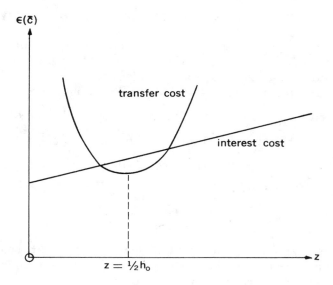

Figure 3.

out. Hence, it would obviously be uneconomical to set z greater than $h_0/2$ since both costs would be increasing in that range. But in the other direction some cost reduction can be achieved by reducing z since the transfer cost function, though rising as z moves below $\frac{1}{2} h_0$, is relatively flat in the region of its minimum.

An even more surprising aspect of the optimal solution is that z^* always lies at $\frac{1}{3} h^*$, regardless of the relative magnitudes of the cost coefficients γ and ν. Changes in these costs serve only to shrink or dilate the system as a whole with no change in the internal balance between z and h. The explanation of this result lies in the structure of the cost function (2.10). Note that z and Z enter symmetrically into the transfer cost component, but that z enters with twice as much weight as Z in the holding cost component. This means that if $Z > 2z$, we can add a small amount, $\triangle$, to z and subtract $2\triangle$ from Z with no resulting change in the holding cost term $\nu(Z + 2z)/3$. These changes, however, will transform the denominator of the transfer cost term to

$$(Z - 2\triangle)(z + \triangle) = Zz + \triangle(Z - 2z) - 2\triangle^2 > Zz$$

the last inequality necessarily holding for some small value of $\triangle$ so long as $Z > 2z$. Thus, it would pay to increase z by $\triangle$ and to reduce Z by $2\triangle$ since the higher value of the denominator implies a lower value for the transfer cost term. Similar reasoning applies to the case of $Z < 2z$ so that only if $Z = 2z$ is no such cost-reducing substitution possible.

4. IMPLICATIONS FOR THE DEMAND FOR MONEY BY FIRMS

For economists, the major interest in the solution lies in its implications for the demand for money by firms. In the present context, that demand can be identified with the average cash balance realized when operating under a policy (h,z) and hence will be given by $\dfrac{h+z}{3}$. Substituting the optimal values of h^* and z^* from (2.11) and (2.13) and recalling (from page 110 above) that $\sigma^2 = \dfrac{\sigma_n^2}{n} = m^2 t =$ the variance of the daily change in the cash balance, we obtain

$$\bar{M}^* = \frac{4}{3}\left(\frac{3\gamma m^2 t}{4\nu}\right)^{\frac{1}{3}} = \frac{4}{3}\left(\frac{3\gamma}{4\nu}\sigma^2\right)^{\frac{1}{3}} \tag{1}$$

as an expression for the firm's optimal average cash balance (or long-run average demand for money) in terms of the cost parameters γ and ν and the (observable) variance of daily cash flows, σ^2. As in the case of the Baumol model the demand for money is an increasing function of the cost of transferring funds to and from the earning portfolio, and a decreasing function of the interest rate or opportunity cost of the funds held in the cash balance. The novel aspect of the money demand equation (1) is the presence of σ^2, a term directly representing the variability of the cash balance, or the degree of the "lack of synchronization" between cash receipts and payments.

The fact that the variance of daily net cash flows serves as the "transactions" variable in the money demand function raises the question of how equation (1) is related to the kind of demand function typically used in empirical studies of money holdings by firms in which total sales or some closely related concept is taken as the measure of transactions. That there is a relation between total sales and the variance of changes in the cash balance is clear enough since total sales are approximately the positive changes in the cash balance summed over a time interval. But the relation is a loose one, and no precise value can be established for the elasticity of the demand for cash with respect to sales that is implied by our model. The difficulty in specifying the sales elasticity stems from the fact that even with unchanging prices sales may change in any of several ways, each with a different impact on the firm's need for cash. At one extreme, a doubling of sales may be due to a doubling of each separate receipt and expenditure invoice. In terms of the model, this is equivalent to raising the transaction step size from m to $2m$ and implies that the optimal average balance will rise by a factor of $2^{2/3}$. At the other extreme, a doubling of sales may take the form of a doubling in the frequency of transactions (i.e., a doubling of t), with the average invoice size unchanged. In this case, because of the increased opportunity for offsetting changes, the desired balance increases only by a factor of $2^{1/3}$. The range of elasticities, of course, becomes even larger when we allow for the possibility of increases in transaction magnitude accompanied by decreases in transaction frequency, or vice versa.

The existence of such a wide range for the sales elasticity in our (h, z) model is in sharp contrast to the prediction of the Baumol model where the elasticity of average cash holdings with respect to sales (assuming constant prices) is always and precisely $\frac{1}{2}$. This uniformity of prediction is one of the most obvious weaknesses of Baumol-type models as applied to corporate cash balances. Studies of intersectoral velocities (Selden [12]) show substantial differences between industries; and there is simply no convincing way of accounting for such differences in the Baumol framework. Whether our variability term provides the answer we cannot say; but it does at least offer a plausible (and testable) explanation for the observed systematic inter-industry differences.

Further questions arise about the relation of our demand function (1) to the "classical" quantity theory of money and to the so-called "modern" quantity theory (running in terms of such variables as "permanent income" or wealth). As to the former, if we regard as the essence of the classical position that the demand for money in real terms be independent of the absolute price level, then equation (1) is consistent with that position. Like the Baumol model, it is homogeneous of degree one in prices, that is, it implies that a doubling of all prices (including those impounded in γ) will lead to a doubling of the quantity of money demanded. With respect to the modern quantity theory, however, the relation is much less clear. Certainly it is hard to see any direct relevance for concepts such as permanent income or wealth in the decision process at the level of the firm. But this, of course, does not rule out the possibility that *aggregate* permanent income or wealth might nevertheless be effective proxies for the level of transactions in macro models of the demand for money.

5. EXTENSION TO ALLOW FOR NON-ZERO DRIFT

Although the no-drift case is likely to be one of the greatest interest to monetary theorists, the model can be extended to incorporate systematic drift in the cash balance (in either direction).[17] The analytical expressions leading to the optimal solution values for h, z and $\bar{M}$ in the presence of drift turn out to be extremely cumbersome and hard to interpret,[18] but the main qualitative properties of the solutions as a function of drift can easily be seen from constructed numerical examples. Two sets of such numerical results are presented

TABLE 1   Optimal Solution Values as a Function of Drift

A. For $\gamma/\nu = 50$

p	z^*	h^*	$\bar{M}^*$	$|\mu|$	σ^2
1.0	1.0	11.0	5.5	1.0	0.00
0.9	1.2	10.6	5.3	0.9	0.36
0.8	1.5	10.0	5.1	0.8	0.64
0.7	1.9	9.5	4.8	0.7	0.84
0.6	2.5	9.4	4.6	0.6	0.96
0.5	3.3	10.0	4.5	0.5	1.00
0.4	4.7	11.7	4.4	0.6	0.96
0.3	6.3	13.9	4.4	0.7	0.84
0.2	7.7	16.1	4.7	0.8	0.64
0.0	11.0	—	5.5	1.0	0.00

B. For $\gamma/\nu = 500$

p	z^*	h^*	$\bar{M}^*$	$|\mu|$	σ^2
1.0	1.0	32.6	16.3	1.0	0.00
0.9	1.6	30.4	15.4	0.9	0.36
0.8	2.2	27.4	14.0	0.8	0.64
0.7	2.9	24.1	12.4	0.7	0.84
0.6	4.1	20.9	10.6	0.6	0.96
0.5	7.2	21.6	9.6	0.5	1.00
0.4	14.2	31.0	9.6	0.6	0.96
0.3	20.0	44.7	11.2	0.7	0.84
0.2	24.5	—	13.1	0.8	0.64
0.0	32.6	—	16.3	1.0	0.00

Francis Nourie set up and carried out the computations for this table.

in Table 1, the first for a case in which the critical cost ratio γ/ν has the extremely low value of 50; and the second for one in which it has the higher and more reasonable value of 500 (the values of m and t being taken as unity in both cases).

For extreme positive drift (the case $p = 1$) the stochastic element in the cash flow vanishes and we are, in effect, dealing with a Baumol model of the pure uniform-flow-of-receipts variety. The cash balance builds up steadily to h and then is returned to its lowest possible value (which is zero, in principle, but which we have had to set at one unit for purposes of computer calculation). As p falls, and hence as the upward drift becomes less pronounced and then changes to downward drift, the optimal "return point" z^* increases steadily in value. The behavior of the optimal upper bound, h^*, however, is somewhat surprising. As p falls, h^* first falls slowly; reaches a minimum while still in the zone of net upward drift (in the neighborhood of $p = .6$); then rises again at an increasing rate once the zone of downward drift ($p < q$) is entered. As the downward drift increases and p approaches zero, the probability of ever hitting h^* becomes microscopic, and when

p reaches zero, h^* becomes entirely irrelevant to the solution. We have returned to the one-parameter Baumol model, this time of the pure uniform-flow-of-expenditures variety.

The column headed $\bar{M}^*$ in the table relates the average cash balance to drift. Starting from $p = 1$ (extreme upward drift) the optimal cash balance declines steadily with p, and is still falling in the neighborhood of the no-drift case. The minimum of $\bar{M}^*$ actually occurs somewhat beyond the no-drift point and within the zone of net downward drift (at about $p = .4$ in both panels).[19] Thereafter the optimal average balance rises again reaching the same level at $p = 0$ as obtained at $p = 1$ (which is as expected since the extreme cases are Baumol models differing only in the direction of the cash flow).

Some insight into why cash holdings are a U-shaped function of drift can be gained by relating drift to the mean and variance of the distribution of cash balance changes (shown in the last two columns of the table). In these terms, our no-drift case can be thought of as an "all variance—no mean" model; while the pure Baumol models for extreme drift are essentially "all mean—no variance" models. Starting near a zero value for the drift, increases in drift (in either direction) imply smaller values for the variance of daily changes in cash and this, by itself, would tend to reduce cash needs. But higher values of drift also imply larger mean daily changes in cash and this, by itself, would tend to raise average holdings. Since the mean rises faster than the variance falls; and since the responsiveness of cash holdings to the mean is greater (a square-root as opposed to a cube-root effect), the net effect of substantial amounts of drift in either direction is to increase optimal average cash balances.

III. *The Applicability of the Model*

Now that the model of cash management by business firms has been developed and the main properties and implications of that model have been sketched, we may turn to consider the previously postponed questions regarding the realism and empirical relevance of the model. As noted earlier, the various assumptions underlying the model fall into two categories. On the one hand are those that define the basic framework; the assumptions of a "two-asset" structure, of a lumpy component in the cost of transfers between the assets; of a negligible lead time in transfers; and, especially, of a stationary random walk for the cash flows. On the other are the special assumptions introduced primarily to simplify either the proofs or the economic interpretation of the results, such as the assumption of a constant marginal transfer cost independent of the size or direction of the transfer, or the assumption that the cash balance changes by a constant positive or negative amount at regular intervals. Insofar as the latter assumptions are concerned, many interesting variations with respect to the cost structure or the distribution of cash changes can and should be explored. Such variations will certainly lead to more complicated control rules and change other matters of detail, but the general qualitative picture is unlikely to be much altered as long as the basic framework is maintained.[20] Attention here will therefore be focused primarily on the more fundamental question of whether the framework itself constitutes a useful and meaningful way of describing the demand for money by business firms.[21]

In this connection some reservations must certainly be entered with respect to the realism of the simple two-asset dichotomy. Business firms typically hold many different liquid securities in their portfolios, frequently even at the same time that they are issuing short-term claims such as commercial paper or bank loans. If this were the only problem, however, we doubt that it would constitute any very serious limitation for present purposes. In principle, it is possible to extend the model to allow for more than one portfolio asset each with its own γ and ν (and, presumably, with γ higher for those with higher yields). Analytical results for such extensions are hard to obtain, but from such limited experimentation as we have conducted with models of this type we would conjecture that the system will turn out to be very loosely coupled.

Much more serious than lumping all earning assets into a single portfolio asset is the lumping of all cash holdings into a single cash balance. Most firms do maintain an identifiable central bank balance, but they also hold many separate smaller accounts. This is particularly true of large, divisionalized firms.[22] Transfers take place not only between the field accounts and the central balance but also among the local balances and between these balances and the portfolio. For such a setting, a more appropriate inventory model might be one of the multi-stage factory-warehouse system variety—though models of the general type developed here might still be expected to govern the behavior of some of the separate components of the system. How much a multi-stage approach would affect our main conclusions is hard to say—because results to date in inventory theory with such models have been meager, and because we still have very little precise information about the relative importance of field and central balances or the cost savings that field balances permit. At the very least, however, we would expect to find smaller economies of scale than those implied under our single-balance framework.

Many will regard the assumption that the cash generating mechanism is entirely stochastic as an even more serious limitation on the approach taken here. And certainly this can hardly be defended as being literally descriptive. The size and timing of many of the important individual transactions comprising the cash flow are under the direct control of the management (e.g., dividend payments). Other transactions are the foreseeable fulfillments of past commitments (such as payments on trade accounts or tax payments). Even where genuinely random changes do occur they are usually superimposed on some systematic and at least partially forecastable movements (e.g., payroll disbursements).[23] This is, however, not a very useful way of evaluating the random walk assumption or the model based on it. The decisive question is how well the assumption serves on an "as if" basis; and here the case against it is by no means an obvious one.

For normative applications, models can certainly be developed to utilize available information about local "patterns" in the cash flow. The lumpy component of transfer cost, however, may present a serious obstacle to the derivation of optimal decision rules under some kinds of programming approaches and the derivation of rules under any such approach would definitely be greatly complicated by the presence of both stochastic and deterministic elements in the cash flow. Because of these difficulties it is by no means certain here, as elsewhere in inventory theory, that the gains from exploiting more of the local information about the flows are large enough to offset the added costs of model development and implementation.

For positive applications, the usefulness of a simple stochastic model of cash management depends mainly on how closely its conditional predictions of the average frequency and size of transfer and of average cash balances correspond to those actually observed. Tolerably accurate predictions of these items are entirely possible even though firms use more complicated, *ad hoc* decision procedures based on detailed forecasts or cash budgets. In terms of operating characteristics, the main effect of such procedures and forecasts is likely to be to transform the bounds on cash holdings into zones rather than the simple limits as in our model. For example, there will be occasions when the firm will not transfer funds to the portfolio even though current cash holdings are larger than h, because it knows or predicts that a "turnaround" will occur in the very near future. In the other direction, it may pay the firm to make a transfer even when holdings are below h if a reasonably long "quiet" period is anticipated. Because these tendencies are partially offsetting, no decisive case against a stochastic model with single-valued bounds can be established on a priori grounds.[24] Final judgment must await the results of empirical testing.

Meltzer [8] argues that the empirical decision has already been rendered by recent cross-sectional studies of the corporate demand for money. The failure of these studies to find any significant economies of scale in cash holdings with respect to total sales or total assets is seen as running directly counter to predictions based on inventory models either of the Baumol variety or of the (h, z) type developed here. Such a conclusion, however, would be unwarranted. Quite apart from the difficulties noted previously in the use of sales or assets as measures of transactions,[25] recall that our (h, z) model is intended to explain only the "discretionary" part of the firm's cash balance over and above its required minimum balance. Despite the fact that such minimum balance requirements in lieu of service charges have long been a conspicuous feature of banking arrangements for business firms in this country, little precise information is available about the absolute size of such balances or how they vary between firms and over time. As we noted earlier, however, it is at least clear that the cost-trade-offs and other strategic elements involved in determining minimum balances differ in important respects from those relating to the active transactions balances. Consequently, the empirical cross-sectional elasticities of money holdings with respect to sales represent only an average (with unknown weights) over the two very different processes.[26] In the absence of evidence, therefore, either that the negotiated minimum balances are a considerably smaller part of the total than the finance literature would lead one to believe; or that minimum balances increase substantially less than proportionally with size of firm, the issue of the validity of inventory models in representing the transactions demand for money by firms must be regarded as still very much an open one.[27]

Appendix

In general, the occupancy probabilities of a Bernoullian cash balance which drifts between 0 and h, and is returned instantly to z upon encountering either barrier, are given by the difference equation

$$f(x, t + 1) = pf(x - 1, t) + qf(x + 1, t)$$

and the boundary conditions

$$f(z, t + 1) = p[f(z - 1, t) + f(h - 1, t)]$$
$$+ q[f(z + 1, t) + f(1, t)]$$
$$f(0, t + 1) = 0$$
$$f(h, t + 1) = 0$$
$$\sum_{x=0}^{h} f(x, t + 1) = 1.$$

To ascertain the steady-state occupancy probabilities, we pass to the limit in time, to obtain the system

$$f(x) = pf(x-1) + qf(x+1) \tag{1}$$
$$f(z) = p[f(z-1) + f(h-1)] + q[f(z+1) + f(1)] \tag{2}$$
$$f(0) = f(h) = 0, \qquad \sum_{x=0}^{h} f(x) = 1.$$

The general solution for the case $p \neq q$

$$\begin{aligned} f(x) &= A + B(p/q)^x & 0 \leq x \leq z \\ f(x) &= C + D(p/q)^x & z \leq x \leq h \end{aligned} \tag{3}$$

contains four arbitrary constants, which are evaluated via the four boundary conditions.

Since $f(0) = 0$, it follows that

$$0 = A + B, \qquad B = -A. \tag{4}$$

Similarly,

$$D = -C(p/q)^{-h}. \tag{5}$$

Substitution of (3), (4) and (5) in (2) yields the relation

$$C = A \left[\frac{1 - (p/q)^z}{1 - (p/q)^{z-h}} \right]. \tag{6}$$

Finally, the density condition on the summed occupancy probabilities

$$1 = \sum_{x=0}^{h} f(x) = \sum_{x=0}^{z} A[1 - (p/q)^x]$$
$$+ \sum_{x=z+1}^{h} [1 - (p/q)^{x-h}] A \left[\frac{1 - (p/q)^z}{1 - (p/q)^{z-h}} \right]$$

yields the result

$$A = \frac{1 - (p/q)^{z-h}}{z[1 - (p/q)^{z-h}] + (h-z)[1 - (p/q)^z]}. \tag{7}$$

The values (6) and (7) may be combined to obtain a specific expression for the stationary occupancy probabilities of x, in terms of p and q.

Expression of the density permits explicit evaluation of the expected steady-state cash balance:

$$E(x) = \sum_{x=0}^{h} xf(x) = \sum_{x=0}^{z} xA[1 - (p/q)^x] + \sum_{x=z+1}^{h} xC[1 - (p/q)^{x-h}].$$

Use of the values (6) and (7), and resort to the identity

$$\sum_{x=1}^{h-1} x(p/q)^{x-1} \equiv d/d(p/q) \sum_{x=0}^{h} (p/q)^x$$

$$\equiv \frac{1 - h(p/q)^h - (p/q)^h - h(p/q)^{h+1}}{[1 - (p/q)]^2}$$

for $q > p$, yields the value

$$E(x) = \frac{1}{2} \left\{ \frac{1}{q-p} + h + z \right.$$

$$\left. - \frac{hz[1 - (p/q)^{z-h}]}{z[1 - (p/q)^{z-h} + (h-z)[1 - (p/q)^z]]} \right\}.$$

For the other segment of the cost function, the expression for the expected duration between passages of either 0 or h is derived in Feller [3]: it is

$$D(z) = \frac{z}{q-p} - \frac{h}{q-p} \cdot \frac{1 - (p/q)^z}{1 - (p/q)^h} \qquad q > p.$$

NOTES

1. The Baumol model [2] may also be applied to the opposite situation in which receipts from operations flow steadily into the cash balance at a constant rate per day subject to periodic large withdrawals for operating expenditures.

2. Although γ represents what would ordinarily be called a "transaction cost" we shall refer to it throughout as a "transfer" cost, reserving the term "transactions" for the receipts and payments exogenous to the model.

3. The expressions given are optimal only under the further assumption that the transfer costs under the policy are less than the interest earnings on the amounts transferred. If not, receipts should be kept entirely in cash and the average cash balance will be one-half the periodic receipt. Some additional difficulties arise with respect to the solution as developed by Baumol if the size of the periodic cash receipt is not an integer multiple of the optimal amount transferred. Tobin [14] presents a modified solution in which M is optimized subject to this "adding up" constraint. For further discussion and characterization of the minimum cost conditions see Teigen [13] and Johnson [6].

4. In fact, there are already in the literature models that advance matters beyond the original Baumol model (such as Johnson [6]), including some which allow for both positive and negative net changes in the cash balance. One such is the model developed by Patinkin [10], Chap. VII, and further elaborated by Dvoretzky in the appendix to that book. It is essentially a "buffer stock" model focusing on the size of the initial cash

balance needed to reduce the probability of cash run-outs during a "period" to some given, small level (transfers from other assets to cash being permitted only at the start of a period). The analysis is also restricted by the assumptions that total cash flows net out to zero in every period and that the total volume of transactions over the period is known in advance. More recently, Orr and Mellon [9] have developed a model in the context of reserve holdings by banks, but otherwise similar in a number of respects to the model to be developed here. The main difference comes from the assumption in the Orr-Mellon model of a fixed settlement period for reserves—the Federal Reserve bi-weekly Wednesday call— which permits their problem to be treated as a series of independent, one-period decisions rather than as a single problem, continuous in time. Mention should also be made of a model for cash holdings by firms, very similar in spirit to ours, developed independently by Melvin Greenball, currently a student at the Graduate School of Business, University of Chicago.

5. Another cost component proportional to the amount transferred might be added to allow for the brokerage charges typically incurred when securities are sold before maturity. Such an extension is fairly easily handled in the context of the Baumol model. See Tobin [14]. Analytical results for the present problem, however, are much harder to obtain under that form of cost structure and would require methods different and considerably more complex than those to be used here.

6. To say that the model contains no buffer stock does not mean that we are ignoring the so-called "precautionary" motive for holding cash. While cash can be obtained instantaneously in the event of an unexpectedly large cash drain, it can only be obtained by incurring a transfer cost. Hence the possibility of such drains and consequent costs will affect the size of the optimal cash balance even though no specific part of the optimal holding can be separately identified as the precautionary balance. As for the so-called "speculative" motive, we would expect under present day conditions (where securities of very short maturity are always readily available) that most of any speculation on a fall in interest rates would take the form of shortening the maturity structure of the portfolio rather than of building up cash holdings. But the optimal cash holding might be affected indirectly by speculation, however, to the extent that the prospect of speculative gains were reflected in the value of v.

7. Little of importance is lost, we feel, by treating the minimum as exogenous and "suboptimizing" in terms of the "discretionary" balance only. Although a firm can certainly affect its required minimum to some extent by altering its use of bank services, the interaction of policies is likely to be extremely weak since the cost trade-offs involved and the speed with which adjustments can be made are of a very different kind in the two cases.

To the extent that a firm's required minimum balance changes over time—and it will do so periodically in response to changes in the level of activity in the account as well as to changes in the agreed interest rate used for computing the stock-equivalent of the service charge flows—we assume in effect that the whole discretionary balance is instantly and costlessly moved up or down by an appropriate transfer to or from the portfolio.

8. These increments or decrements represent only "operating" cash transactions and are to be regarded as exclusive of cash flows stemming from the portfolio, either transfers or run-offs of securities held. The proceeds of matured individual securities are assumed to be immediately reinvested.

9. That the results are not dependent on the assumed Bernoulli process can be verified by reference to a forthcoming paper by Antelman and Savage [1] on the "surveillance problem," a special case of which is very similar to and has the same solution as our cash balance problem. The Antelman-Savage paper uses a Wiener process as the generating mechanism; in an earlier paper, Savage [11] derives the same solution for a Poisson process. Our reason for relying on the Bernoulli process here is its great simplicity, which permits the solution to be developed with only the most elementary methods.

10. For the rationalization of this approach see Karlin [7], esp. p. 223.

11. Such a policy is simpler and more "natural" than, say, one involving different return points after a purchase and a sale—a policy form that might be appropriate if the transfer cost were assumed to differ depending on the direction of the transfer, or if the cost of transfer were in part proportional to the size of the transfer.

12. The expression (1), like the loss functions in similar inventory models, is only an approximation, though normally a very close (see Hadley [5] to the flow equivalent of the discounted present value of costs. The discrepancy comes from neglecting the interest on the transfer costs and on the interest itself as well as from averaging rather than integrating over the cash holdings.

13. This result can be derived exactly rather than asymptotically if the cash balance changes are assumed to be generated by a continuous rather than a discrete probability mechanism. However, by maintaining discrete framework, the stationary cash balance density, which underlies the calculation of holding cost, is far easier to derive; and since we are dealing with a steady state model, derivation of (2) as an asymptotic result is not in any sense a shortcoming.

14. Derivations for the case $p \neq q$ are sketched in the Appendix.

15. Sufficient conditions also hold for these values.

16. Despite this asymmetry in the size and frequency of transfers, it is reassuring to note that no drift is thereby communicated to the volume of earning assets held in the firm's portfolio. This property follows directly from the probabilities of passage in a symmetric Bernoullian process; viz.,

Prob (first passage at 0 when process originates at z) $= \dfrac{h - z}{h}$ and Prob

(first passage at h when process originates at z) $= 1 - \dfrac{h - z}{h} = \dfrac{z}{h}$. See

Feller [3].

Although the portfolio has no drift, nothing in the model prevents the portfolio from becoming negative if the sales called for by the policy happen to precede or exceed the purchases over some period of time. In such cases, the firm is presumed to utilize a line of credit or some other short-term borrowing arrangement (i.e., the portfolio securities it sells are its own).

17. Drift models might be appropriate even where there was no overall net drift in the operating cash balance, but simply a heavy concentration of receipts or expenditures at regularly recurring intervals. If a firm, for example, gets 75 per cent of its monthly receipts on the tenth of the month, then the process over the remaining days might be characterized as one with $p = .25$ and $q = .75$. And similarly, in the other direction, for cases involving large, regularly recurring payments such as tax or dividend payments.

18. Cf. the Appendix.

19. The fact that the minimum occurs in both cases very near the value $p = .4$ is entirely an artifact of the particular numbers used. As successively higher values of the ratio γ/v are used, the minimum tends to move steadily closer to the no-drift point, $p = .5$.

20. This has certainly proved to be the case with the Baumol model and, in fact, with classes of inventory models generally.

21. In one sense, the single most crucial assumption in shaping the whole analysis is that substantial lump sum portfolio transfer costs exist. Here, however, we feel that no extended defense is really necessary even though we would concede that those costs may be hard to estimate in practical applications. Their existence seems amply demonstrated by the very large minimum trading units in all the standard money market instruments (e.g., currently $100,000 for commercial bank negotiable Certificates of Deposit).

22. The results of a recent survey of cash balances practices of large corporations by Gibson [4] indicate that the average number of separate bank balances maintained is currently about 200 per firm with some firms actually holding more than 2,300 individual accounts. Gibson's data, however, give no indication of the size distribution of the balances and many accounts undoubtedly are of only nominal size. Even so, the extent of significant multiple holding is clearly quite substantial.

23. To the extent that the systematic component is in the form of a simple trend then a non-zero drift model might meet the need. Even seasonal components might be incorporated by an alternating sequence of drift models, provided the seasonal movements persisted long enough relative to the mean time between transfers to avoid excessive violence to the steady-state assumptions that underlie the objective function.

24. Another possibility that might more seriously affect the predictive power of the model would be systematic efforts to obtain closer synchronization between receipts and payments by influencing the timing of receipts and payments (e.g., by increasing discounts for early payment when interest rates rise). Such direct adjustments in timing are admittedly quite common among small firms where there is often no alternative to such brute force methods of synchronization as delaying payments to some creditors until sufficient cash receipts have been accumulated. For larger

firms, however, it is unlikely to be economic to tinker with the details of the receipt and payment structure in the short run though from time to time the whole system will be re-examined (and of course, such re-examinations are likely to be made more frequently in periods of high interest rates).

25. See Section II above. On a priori grounds, one would suspect that within any given industry the variance of daily cash changes would probably tend to increase less than proportionally with sales, thus strengthening the presumption of scale economies with respect to sales under the inventory approach. The "industries" studied tend to be quite heterogeneous, however, so that it may be well to withhold judgment until some direct empirical evidence on variability in relation to size is available.

Although our concern in this paper is primarily with the demand for money by business firms it may perhaps be worth pointing out that somewhat similar problems with respect to interpreting cross-sectional elasticities arise in the case of households. In particular, it does not follow that a finding of an elasticity of money holdings with respect to *income* of unity or even greater is inconsistent with the "inventory" approach. For one thing, many (perhaps, most) households have incomes too small or too frequently received to justify moving off the "corner solution" and over this range the implied income elasticity is unity. For those with incomes large enough to warrant temporary investment of idle cash, income will be the relevant "transactions" variable provided that the only portfolio purchases and sales made by the household are those transfers required by the inventory model. Where, however, the household engages in autonomous portfolio activity (such as switching in and out of investments) an additional "transactions" demand for cash balances is generated over and above that involved in spending income on current account. If the amount and frequency of such autonomous financial transactions tend to rise more than proportionally with income (which is certainly not improbable), then an income elasticity of cash holdings greater than unity might well be observed over this range even though substantial economies of scale were present with respect to total transactions.

26. Although the functions governing the two kinds of balances are different, they are likely to have some arguments in common. In particular, our transaction-frequency variable t is closely related to the "activity" variable used in negotiating minimum balances. Both functions also contain an interest rate variable, though not necessarily the same one for the two cases.

27. For the sake of argument, we accept here the proposition that existing cross-section studies do not show significant economies of scale in cash holdings though, in fact, we have some reservations about these findings. The main one is that these studies typically fit a single money demand relation over the whole range of available size classes of firms including the very smallest sizes; whereas inventory models of the type developed here are at best applicable only for reasonably large firms. With respect to the larger size classes, the case for the existence of economies of

scale does seem to be somewhat stronger (Selden [12]), though there are too few cells in the usual *Statistics of Income* or F.T.C.-S.E.C. tabulations to permit any reliable estimates of the elasticity in this range of size classes.

REFERENCES

1. Antelman, G., and I. R. Savage, "Surveillance Problems: Weiner Process," Technical Report No. 32 (University of Minnesota, Department of Statistics, January 1962).

2. Baumol, William, "The Transaction Demand for Cash: An Inventory Theoretic Approach," *Quarterly Journal of Economics,* 66: 545–56 (November 1952).

3. Feller, W., *An Introduction to Probability Theory and Its Applications,* 2nd ed., Vol. I (New York: Wiley, 1957).

4. Gibson, W. E., "Compensating Balance Requirements," *National Banking Review,* 2: 387–96 (March 1965).

5. Hadley, G., "A Comparison of Order Quantities Computed Using the Average Annual Cost and the Discounted Cost," *Management Science,* 10: 472–76 (April 1964).

6. Johnson, Harry G., "Notes in the Theory of Transaction Demand for Cash," *Indian Journal of Economics,* 44: 1–11 (July 1963).

7. Karlin, S., "Steady State Solutions," in Arrow, Karlin, and Scarf (eds.), *Studies in the Mathematical Theory of Inventory and Production* (Stanford, Ca.: Stanford University Press, 1958).

8. Meltzer, Allan H., "The Demand for Money: A Cross-Section Study of Business Firms," *Quarterly Journal of Economics,* 77: 405–22 (August 1963).

9. Orr, Daniel, and W. G. Mellon, "Stochastic Reserve Losses and Expansion of Bank Credit," *American Economic Review,* 51: 614–23 (September 1961).

10. Patinkin, Don, *Money, Interest and Prices* (New York: Harper & Row, 1956).

11. Savage, I. R., "Surveillance Problem," *Naval Research Logistics Quarterly,* 9: 187–209 (September/December 1962).

12. Selden, R., "The Postwar Rise in the Velocity of Money," Occasional Paper #78 (National Bureau of Economic Research, 1962).

13. Teigen, R. L., "Demand and Supply Functions for Money in the United States: Some Structural Estimates," *Econometrica,* 32: 476–509 (October 1964).

14. Tobin, James, "The Interest Elasticity of Transaction Demand for Cash," *Review of Economics and Statistics,* 38: 241–47 (August 1956).

15. Wald, A., *Sequential Analysis* (New York: Wiley, 1947).

16. Whitin, T. M., *The Theory of Inventory Management* (Princeton, N.J.: Princeton University Press, 1953).

5 A Transaction Theory of the Demand for Money

Richard S. Thorn *University of Pittsburgh*

The object of this paper is to show that the demand for active and idle cash balances can be derived from the transaction demand for money eliminating the dichotomization of the demand for money without resort to the introduction of risk aversion or volatility of capital values resulting from interest rate fluctuations. Risk aversion and interest rate fluctuations do influence the demand for money, but there will be a demand for active money balances and idle money balances even when interest rates are unchanged and risk aversion is absent. A second objective is to clarify the interrelationship between portfolio theory and the theory of the demand for money.

Active cash balances following Tobin are defined as those cash balances held for the purpose of making expected (planned) expenditures, and idle cash balances are all those held in excess of all expected seasonal excesses of cumulative expenditures over cumulative receipts during the year ahead. Keynes identified the demand for idle balances with the speculative and precautionary motives for holding money and the demand for active balances with the transaction demand for money. Keynes analyzed the demand for speculative balances separately and he linked this demand to the unknown behavior of future interest rates. Tobin [14] attempted to show that even when the expected capital gain or loss was zero, individual economic units

Reprinted from the *Weltwirtschaftliches Archiv,* Band 110, Heft 3 (Institut fur Weltwirtschaft Kiel, 1974), 430–44, Hubertus Muller-Groeling, editor, by permission of the publisher.

(households and firms) would still desire to hold positive idle money balances as long as the variance of the market value of bonds was not zero and the units possessed risk aversion. In the absence of risk aversion there would be no speculative demand for money.

Following Keynes, Baumol [1] and Tobin [13] analyzed the transactions demand for money separately from the demand for idle balances. Their analyses were based on the assumption that expenditures are perfectly foreseen and occur in a steady stream. This analysis was extended by Matthews [10] and Miller and Orr [11] to the case where there is uncertainty concerning future income receipts and expenditure plans. Borch [2], Feldstein [4], and Tsiang [16] criticized Tobin's specific use of Markowitz's [9] mean-variance analysis to establish a demand for idle cash.

Keynes chose to relate the precautionary demand for money to the level of income. Many monetary theorists simply ignored it. Notable exceptions were Dvoretzky [3], Hicks [6], and Tsiang [15]. These latter analyses indicated that the existence of unforeseen expenditures leads to a demand for idle cash balances.

In the two asset money-consol world of Baumol and Tobin the dichotomy between the transaction demand for money and the asset demand for money can only be maintained if the composition of the portfolio in no way affects the net flow of funds in the future (Matthews [10] and Ochs [12]). In general, portfolio decisions do affect the future stream of cash receipts and therefore individuals' choice of optimal cash balances for transactions purposes. The independence of the transactions demand and asset demand for money is not possible except under very restrictive assumptions. Stochastic variation in interest rates implies stochastic variation in income and, therefore, stochastic variation in cash balances. Increased variance of cash balances results in increased demand for cash balances so that asset portfolio decisions are not independent, in general, of the demand for transaction balances.

Tsiang [16] demonstrated that Tobin's mean-variance analysis is not capable of explaining the demand for idle cash in an investment portfolio except under highly restrictive and implausible assumptions.

Another criticism of treating the demand for idle money balances as being independent of the transactions demand is that the loss assumed in the portfolio approach can only occur if bonds are converted into cash. Bonds will never be converted into cash in a three asset model in order to reduce risk when there is a relatively riskless asset such as treasury bills.

The only circumstance under which an economic unit will incur a capital loss through the sale of a bond before maturity that is not more than offset by an increase in total wealth through investment of the proceeds is when a bond is sold in order to make a current transaction. This latter circumstance will occur as a result of unplanned income or expenditure. The relevance of risk in Tobin's portfolio analysis of the demand for money exists only in the context of an uncertain transactions demand for money.

Interest rate uncertainty and risk aversion are shaky foundations upon which to build a theory of the demand for idle cash balances. A surer foundation is to be found in a transaction theory based on receipts and expenditures subject to uncertainty which does not dichotomize money balances into transactions, and asset balances. Money is part of an individual's stock of wealth, and his entire stock of wealth can be converted into money for transaction purposes if it is desired.

A Transaction Theory

It will be assumed that money is held only for the purpose of making payments. Money is the sole medium of exchange and its value as a wealth asset is derived from this function. Money has no commodity value. If money no longer served as a medium of exchange, it would not be held in wealth portfolios. As a form of wealth, it is assumed that money is dominated by at least one very short term asset which has the characteristics that it has a positive yield and the variance of its market value is so negligible that it may be assumed to be zero. Only money and this very short term asset are assumed to be held in wealth portfolios.

Individuals' receipts and expenditures consist of two components: a certain or planned component and a stochastic component with a given distribution. In each decision period, it is assumed that, for each economic unit, planned receipts equal planned expenditures and the mean of the distribution of stochastic components of receipts and expenditures is zero so that expected receipts equal expected expenditures. Included in planned expenditures and receipts are any borrowing costs involved in covering a temporary cumulative net planned expenditure deficit and any net income obtained from the temporary investment of a planned excess of cumulative receipts over cumulative expenditures.

We assume that advanced notice is required for borrowing and the sale of securities. If during any decision period the cumulative sum of actual expenditures exceeds the cumulative sum of receipts and sufficient cash balances are not held to cover the deficit, expenditures cannot be made. They must either be foregone or postponed, incurring, in either case, an economic cost. The stochastic component in receipts and expenditures therefore gives rise to a demand for money resulting from the possibility of being unable to make planned current expenditures as a result of unforeseen reduction in receipts or as a result of having to make unplanned current expenditures (Keynes's precautionary motive). The asset (speculative) motive for holding idle money balances arises from two possibilities: one, of not being able to make planned capital expenditures as a result of an unforeseen reduction of receipts; and, two, loss of opportunities to increase net wealth by liquidating assets currently held in order to purchase new assets, because the sale of current assets without adequate notice results in a loss which offsets the increase in wealth that would otherwise occur if adequate notice were given and a better price obtained from the sale of the currently held asset.[1]

The Costs of Holding Money

There are three costs identified with the holding of money balances:

(1) *opportunity costs* are the costs of holding money, which yields no monetary return instead of an income yielding asset

(2) *the stockout costs*[2] which are the costs of running out of money and not being able to carry out planned or unplanned expenditures

(3) *conversion costs* which are the costs of converting unwanted money balances into income yielding assets or the costs of converting assets into money

Conversion costs correspond to what has generally been called transaction costs in the literature. The term transaction costs has been avoided here since, in fact, all three of the costs described may be regarded as transaction costs.

It is further assumed that the conversion of nonmonetary assets into money is not instantaneous. This last assumption is necessary in order for stockout costs to exist. If nonmonetary assets could always be instantaneously converted into money there would be no risk of having insufficient cash balances to make planned or unplanned expenditures. These costs of holding money shall now be considered in more detail.

THE OPPORTUNITY COST

In order to hold money an economic unit must forego the income it could obtain if that portion of its wealth held as money were invested in income yielding assets. This total opportunity cost (C_1) is a function of the rate of return on alternative income yielding assets (i)

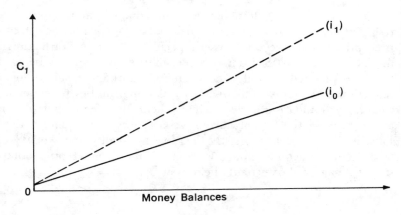

Figure 1. *Opportunity Cost of Holding Money*

and the average size of money balances (M) held per period of time.

$$C_1 = f_1(M, i) \tag{1}$$

The total opportunity cost is assumed to increase with the size of money balances held. The only restriction placed on this cost function is that it rise monotonically as a function of cash balances. This general relationship is shown in Figure 1 where the total opportunity cost is shown as a linear function of the size of cash balances per unit time period for geometric simplicity.

THE STOCKOUT COST

Cash balances may become unexpectedly exhausted because of the occurrence of an unplanned reduction income or an unplanned increase in expenditures. When this occurs an economic unit must postpone expenditures until it receives additional cash receipts, arranges for a loan, or converts some of its income yielding assets into cash, possibly incurring a capital loss. The exhaustion of cash balances is costly in that the inability to carry out planned expenditures prevents the most efficient allocation of one's expenditures. It either results in a less efficient allocation of current resources, or, it results in a loss of an investment opportunity which would have increased total wealth had it been taken advantage of.

Perhaps the greatest costs of a reduced cash position are not the direct costs of the exhaustion of cash balances, but the indirect costs resulting from outsiders' subjective reappraisal of the probable solvency of the economic unit if knowledge of its weak cash position is known. If a firm's cash position falls significantly below what conventional wisdom regards as normal, it may find itself confronted with a whole host of adverse events. Lenders may be unwilling to lend to it. If willing to lend, they may charge a higher interest rate and make the lending conditional upon the acceptance of certain restrictions in the firm's freedom of action. Creditors of the firm concerned about the deterioration in its cash position may accelerate their demands for payment, aggravating the original situation. The costs resulting from the weakening of an economic unit's cash position mount steadily as its cash balances decline and are never known with complete certainty beforehand. For analytical convenience, however, it is assumed that these costs are discrete (given the firm's asset portfolio) in that they are only incurred when the firm can no longer make payments, i.e., when its cash balances are zero. While this assumption appears somewhat awkward, it preserves the essential elements of the problem. The replacement of this assumption by a more realistic set of assumptions would complicate the analysis at this point. Therefore as simplification it is assumed that the actual cost of running out of cash (C_2), i.e., being unable to make planned expenditures, is fixed for each decision period.

For a person who holds cash balances of size M at the outset of each period, the expected stockout cost $\{\epsilon(C_2)\}$ equals $C_2 \cdot P_m$ where P_m represents the probability that cash balances will go below some small finite amount during the relevant time period. In general, P_m is a decreasing function of M but an increasing function of σ, where σ represents the standard deviation of cash balances resulting from the combined variance of receipts and expenditures. Thus, $\epsilon(C_2)$ is a monotonic decreasing function of M.

$$\epsilon(C_2) = f_2(M, \sigma), \frac{\partial f_2}{\partial M} < 0 \qquad (2)$$

If cash balances are very large $\epsilon(C_2)$ approaches zero and if they are very small $\epsilon(C_2)$ approaches some finite sum. The general relationship is shown in Figure 2.

The curve in Figure 2 has a kink which results from the assumption that the stockout costs in any decision period are fixed. At some finite stock of money (m) the probability of a stockout will be unity.

The remainder of the analysis will be confined to the portion of the total cost curve to the right of the kink.

THE TOTAL COST OF HOLDING MONEY

By adding the opportunity cost of holding any size money balances to the expected stockout cost for holding the same size money balances one may derive the total expected cost of holding any size

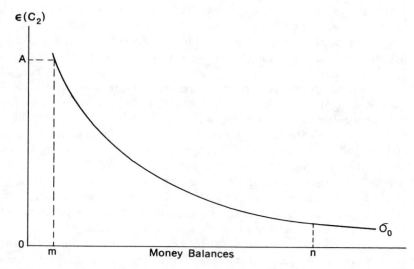

Figure 2. *Expected Stockout Cost of Holding Money*

money balance (ϵC), given the variance of receipts and expenditures.

$$\epsilon(C) = C_1 + \epsilon(C_2)$$

$$\epsilon(C) = f_1(M, i) + f_2(M, \sigma), \qquad (3)$$

subject to the condition $\dfrac{\partial f_1}{\partial M} + \dfrac{\partial f_2}{\partial M} < 0$, for $M = m$

The addition of the two cost functions will produce the nonsymmetrical U-shaped cost curve shown in Figure 3 which possesses a well-defined minimum cost of holding cash balances associated with the level of cash balances z.

CONVERSION COSTS

The last cost element in our model is conversion cost. These costs are the costs incurred in converting cash into other assets or noncash assets into money. These costs may be symmetrical, or asymmetrical with the direction of the transaction, independent of the amount of assets converted, proportional to the amount of assets converted, or exhibit economies or diseconomies of scale. The essential characteristic of conversion costs is that they are discrete and only incurred when a conversion is made.

For the sake of simplicity, we shall assume that conversion costs (a) are independent of the amount of assets converted, symmetrical, and are constant per act of conversion.

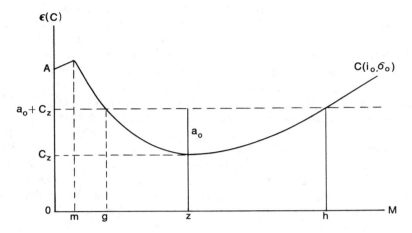

Figure 3. *Total Expected Cost of Holding Money Balances*

The Complete Model

A general transaction theory of the demand for money can now be formulated on the basis of the three costs concepts introduced and the stochastic behavior of cash balances. It shall be assumed that at the end of each investment decision period of length T that each economic unit decides if it wishes to make any rearrangement of its portfolio; if not, it leaves its wealth portfolio unchanged until the end of the next decision period when it is again reexamined. In practice the period T is chosen on the basis of an optimization calculation so that over some long period of time (a multiple of T) the expected returns from reviewing the portfolio over the expected costs of review will be maximized. The theoretical solution to the determination of T is difficult. For our purposes, it shall simply be assumed that the period T can be determined. At the outset, it is assumed that money balances are at their minimum cost level z. During each decision period the level of money balances varies as a consequence of planned income and receipts and unplanned income and receipts. At the end of the decision period the economic unit is left with some level of cash balances, M. Based on this level of cash balances it calculates its average expected total cost of holding cash over the next period. If the expected cost $\{\epsilon(C)\}$ minus the minimum cost (C_z) is less than the average cost of conversion (a) no change in the portfolio is made, if it is greater than the average cost of conversion then we will convert sufficient assets to restore the level of cash balances to their optimum level (z).

If we make the assumption that our economic unit makes its esti-

mate of the opportunity cost of holding money based on the level of
cash balances it actually holds at the end of each decision period,
then we can employ Figure 3 to illustrate the operation of the model.
The horizontal line represents the average transaction costs (a_0) plus
the minimum cost of holding cash balances (C_z) under the assumption they are fixed. Money balances at the end of each period are
measured on the abscissa and the average expected cost of holding
money is measured on the ordinate. If at the end of a decision period
(t), $M > g$ and $M < h$, no adjustment of cash balances is made. If
$M < g$ or $M > h$ cash balances are set equal to z. Idle money balances in Tobin's sense may be identified with the quantity Og. Adequate money balances may be defined as any level of money balances
lying between g and h. Optimum money balances may be defined as
equal to z.

Average observed idle money balances may be greater or less than
Og in Figure 3 since adjustment is not instantaneous and is made
only at the end of the decision period. There is even a small, but
finite, probability that cash balances may become zero for an individual economic unit. The optimum level of money balances (z) and
observed average cash balances ($\bar{M}$) will seldom coincide. Furthermore, since the total cost function of holding money, in general, is
asymmetrical, it is unlikely except under very special assumptions
concerning the stochastic behavior of cash balances that the observed
cumulative average of cash balances will converge on z. A realistic
characteristic of the model is that over some range of cash balances
economic units will undertake no action to adjust to their cash
balances.

RISE IN THE OPPORTUNITY COST

A rise in the opportunity cost of holding money from (i_0) to (i_1)
will result in a rotation upward of the ray Oi_0 as shown in Figure 1.
This will have the effect of shifting the total cost curve of holding
money upward as shown in Figure 4. If the average transaction and
stockout costs remain unchanged, g and h will decline but h will decline relatively more than g, and z will also decline. The result of this
is that lower average cash balances will be held. The observed frequency of conversion of money into securities will rise relative to the
conversion of securities into money. The demand for money is
interest-elastic.

RISE IN CONVERSION COSTS

A rise in conversion costs results in a widening of the range of
the adjustment points g and h but does not effect the optimum level

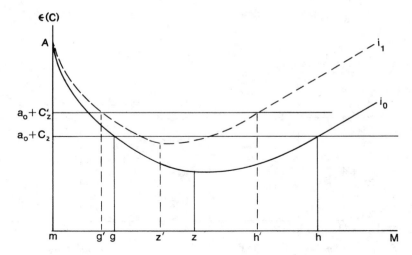

Figure 4. *Effect of a Rise in Opportunity Cost*

of cash balances. In our particular model, it will tend to raise the average amount of cash balances held $(\tilde{M})$ by raising the limit h relatively more than the decline in the limit g as a consequence of the asymmetry of the total cost curve. These results can readily be inferred from Figure 3.

A RISE IN THE VARIABILITY OF CASH BALANCES

A rise in the standard deviation (σ) of cash balances given i results in a higher expected probability of a stockout at every level of money balances with a consequent increase in the total expected cost attached to holding each level of cash balances. This situation is shown in Figure 5 as an upward shift and flattening out of the cost curve since it is anchored at point A. The new total cost curve lies completely above the original cost curve. Given the conversion costs, for $\sigma < k$, k to be defined in the next section, the lower and upper adjustment points, g and h, will shift to the right. But in this particular case g will shift more than h. The optimum level of cash balances, z, will also shift to the right. This implies a rise in average cash balances and a smaller frequency of adjustment transactions since the new expected cost curve is shallower. However since g shifts to the right relatively more than h there will be a rise in the number of conversions of securities into money relative to the conversion of money into securities.

For $\sigma > k$ the elasticity of optimum cash balances with respect to σ will become *negative* or zero, i.e., completely inelastic. The proof of

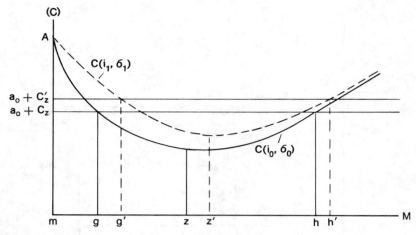

Figure 5. *Effect of an Increase in the Variance of Cash Balances*

this somewhat novel result cannot be shown easily by means of a graph and requires more analytical apparatus which we shall now develop.

The Demand Function for Money

At this point we shall examine more formally the demand function for money that is implied in the above model. One may write right away

$$M^d = D(i, \sigma), \; D_i < 0, \; D_\sigma > 0, \; \sigma \geq 0, \; i > 0, \; i < 1 \quad (4)$$

We wish to obtain the relevant elasticities D_i and D_0 if every economic unit holds the optimum money balance, $M^d = z$. To determine z from (3) assuming $f_1 = iM$ we write,

$$\frac{dC}{dM} = i + \frac{df_2}{dM} = 0$$

$$-i = \frac{df_2}{dM}, \text{ at } z \quad (5)$$

and thus

$$\frac{d^2 f_2}{dM^2} \, dz = -di$$

whence,

$$D_i = \frac{i}{z} \frac{dz}{di} = \frac{i}{z} \frac{1}{\dfrac{d^2 f_2}{dM^2}} = 1 \left/ \frac{M}{\dfrac{df_2}{dM}} \frac{d}{dM}\left(\frac{df_2}{dM}\right) \right. \quad (6)$$

The interest rate elasticity of the demand for money evaluated at the point of optimum cash balances (z) is equal to the reciprocal of the elasticity of $\dfrac{df_2}{dM}$ with respect to M.

To obtain a more precise idea of the demand for money we shall assume somewhat arbitrarily that the chance of a stockout occurring has an exponential probability distribution of the following form: $P_m = e^{\frac{-M}{\sigma}}$. There is a probability of one that a stockout will occur when no money balances are held. This probability approaches zero asymptotically as money balances are increased. At some finite level of cash balances this probability becomes so small as to be negligible. The expected cost of incurring the stockout cost (A) is then

$$f_2 = Ae^{\frac{-M}{\sigma}}, \quad A \geq 1, \ M \geq 0 \tag{7}$$

$$\frac{df_2}{dM} = -\frac{1}{\sigma} Ae^{\frac{-M}{\sigma}} \tag{8}$$

The elasticity of (7) is $\dfrac{-M}{\sigma} < 0$, as $M \to \infty$, (8) approaches 0, hence from (5) $i \to 0$ and the elasticity approaches $-\infty$. This is analogous to the Keynesian demand function for money (except that Keynes postulated an asymptote as some positive value of i). If the expected stockout cost should become zero for M above a sufficient large amount $(C_2 = 0, \ M > n)$, the demand for money would become inelastic at this point. This is a monetary analogy to the Pigou Effect; it implies that above some level of money balances, all additions to cash will be employed either to increase consumption or acquire income yielding wealth assets, i.e., there would be a floor to the velocity of money.

The elasticity D_σ at z has an interesting behavior. Substituting (8) in (5) we have,

$$i = \frac{Ae^{\frac{-M}{\sigma}}}{\sigma}$$

taking logs of both sides and rearranging terms,

$$M = -\sigma \left[\ln \sigma + \ln i - \ln A \right], \quad M = z \tag{9}$$

evaluating the elasticity D_σ at z,

$$\frac{\sigma}{z}\frac{dz}{d\sigma} = \frac{1}{\ln \sigma + \ln i - \ln A} + 1 \tag{10}$$

When $\sigma = 0$, $M = 0$. When there is no uncertainty concerning either payments or receipts no planned cash balances are held. When

$\sigma > 0$ and $\sigma < A/i$, $M > 0$. For $\sigma > A/i$ *no* money balances are held. Furthermore for $\sigma < A/ie$ the elasticity (10) is positive and for $\sigma > A/ie$, the elasticity is *negative*. As the variance of cash balances increases, at first more money balances are held, but beyond a certain point further increases in the variance result in *less* money balances being held until at the point $\sigma^2 = A/i$, no cash balances are held.

This somewhat novel result that increasing uncertainty can result in a reduction as well as an increase in money balances is not as surprising as it might first appear and may be given a plausible intuitive explanation. Money balances may be looked upon as a form of insurance that one does not run out of cash in any given period. The income foregone on these balances is like an insurance premium. As the stochastic variation of cash balances becomes very large, requiring a very large balance to avoid a high risk of running out of money, the insurance premium also becomes very high, and approaches the expected cost of running out of cash. The cost of running out of cash in any one period is fixed by assumption so that at some sufficiently large value of σ, the marginal insurance premium exceeds any marginal reduction in expected stockout cost and no cash balances are held. The optimum strategy in this case is to plan to hold zero cash balances and earn as much income as possible before a stockout occurs and the stockout cost A is incurred.

Conclusion

It has been shown that a demand for both active and idle cash balances can be derived from the transaction demand for money and that this demand is elastic with respect to the opportunity cost of holding money. The important result has been derived that as long as the cost of running out of cash is finite, increased variance of cash balances resulting from stochastic variation of either receipts or expenditures will at first increase the demand for money balances, but beyond a certain point greater stochastic variation of cash balances will actually decrease the demand for cash balances.

Risk aversion is not necessary or sufficient for the existence of a demand for idle money balances. The relevance of risk aversion for the demand for money is the effect that it has on the composition of the portfolios of income yielding assets of individual economic units and thereby on the marginal opportunity cost of holding money and the cost of conversion of income yielding assets into cash. Economic units do not have to reduce risk in their wealth portfolios by holding more money but may reduce risk by increasing the proportion of less risky to more risky income yielding assets changing the marginal and average rate of return on their wealth. It is this marginal rate of return on wealth that represents the opportunity cost of holding cash balances that is relevant for the demand for money and *not the market rates of interest,* although there is an obvious connection between the two. At any point in time the opportunity cost of holding money may differ from one economic unit to another depending on the marginal rate of return to their wealth portfolios. An answer is provided to Leontieff's [8] contention that the demand for idle cash balances must necessarily be zero in equilibrium. As long as receipts and expenditures are subject to stochastic disturbances there will be a demand for idle cash balances even if there is no expectation that rates of interest will change.

The demand for money affects portfolio selection primarily through its effect on the determination of the probability that wealth assets will be required to be converted into cash without adequate notice. If cash balances are sufficiently large so that the probability of being caught short of cash is negligible, then the risk of capital loss resulting from the unplanned sale of wealth assets may be disregarded in portfolio selection. A complete theory of portfolio selection must weigh the risk of variations of the capital value of each income yielding asset by the probability that it will be necessary to convert the asset into cash without adequate notice.

The fact that there may be a considerable range of cash balances over which economic units do not adjust their cash balances and that observed cash balances are likely to be a biased estimate of optimum cash balances should caution one in the evaluation of the results of deductive investigations of the demand for money.

The theory presented here eliminates the dichotomy between a transactions demand and a speculative demand for money in a model which is consistent with many of the empirical regularities observed with respect to the aggregate demand for money while providing a simpler and more complete microeconomic foundation.

NOTES

1. This view follows Hicks's [6] discussion of liquidity.
2. This term is borrowed from inventory theory which is closely related to the analysis that follows.

REFERENCES

1. Baumol, W. J., "The Transaction Demand for Cash: An Inventory Theoretical Approach," *Quarterly Journal of Economics,* 66: 545–56 (November 1952) [reprinted in this volume—Ed.].

2. Borch, K., "A Note on Uncertainty and Indifference Curves," *Review of Economic Studies,* 36: 1–4 (January 1969).

3. Dvoretsky, A., in Patinkin, D., *Money, Interest and Prices: An Integration of Monetary and Value Theory,* 2nd ed. (New York, 1965).

4. Feldstein, M. S., "Mean-Variance Analysis in the Theory of Liquidity Preference and Portfolio Selection," *Review of Economic Statistics,* 36: 5–12 (January 1969).

5. Hicks, J. R., "Liquidity," *Economic Journal,* 72: 787–808 (December 1962).

6. Hicks, J. R., *Critical Essays in Monetary Theory,* Lecture III (London, 1967).

7. Johnson, H., *Essays in Monetary Economics,* 2nd ed. (London, 1969).

8. Leontieff, W., "Postulates: Keynes' *General Theory* and the Classicists," in S. E. Harris (ed.), *The New Economics* (New York, 1947).

9. Markowitz, H., *Portfolio Selection* (New York, 1959).

10. Matthews, R. C. O., "Expenditure Plans and the Uncertainty Motive for Holding Money," *Journal of Political Economy,* 71: 201–18 (June 1963).

11. Miller, M. H., and Orr, D., "A Model of the Demand for Money by Firms," *Quarterly Journal of Economics,* 79: 413–35 (November 1966) [reprinted in this volume—Ed.].

12. Ochs, J., "The Transaction Demand for Money and Choices Involving Risk," *Journal of Political Economy,* 76: 289–91 (March 1968).

13. Tobin, J., "The Interest Elasticity of Transactions Demand for Cash," *Review of Economics and Statistics,* 38: 241–47 (August 1956).

14. Tobin, J., "Liquidity Preference as Behavior Toward Risk," *Review of Economics Studies,* 25: 65–86 (February 1958).

15. Tsiang, S. C., "The Precautionary Demand for Money: An Inventory Theoretical Analysis," *Journal of Political Economy,* 77: 99–117 (January 1969).

16. Tsiang, S. C., "The Rationale of the Mean-Standard Deviation Analysis, Skewness Preference, and the Demand for Money," *American Economic Review,* 62: 354–71 (June 1972).

B. Asset Preference Theory

6 Liquidity Preference as Behavior Towards Risk

James Tobin *Yale University*

One of the basic functional relationships in the Keynesian model of the economy is the liquidity preference schedule, an inverse relationship between the demand for cash balances and the rate of interest. This aggregative function must be derived from some assumptions regarding the behavior of the decision-making units of the economy, and those assumptions are the concern of this paper. Nearly two decades of drawing downward-sloping liquidity preference curves in textbooks and on classroom blackboards should not blind us to the basic implausibility of the behavior they describe. Why should anyone hold the non-interest bearing obligations of the government instead of its interest bearing obligations? The apparent irrationality of holding cash is the same, moreover, whether the interest rate is 6%, 3% or $\frac{1}{2}$ of 1%. What needs to be explained is not only the existence of a demand for cash when its yield is less than the yield on alternative assets but an inverse relationship between the aggregate demand for cash and the size of this differential in yields.[1]

1. *Transactions balances and investment balances.*

Two kinds of reasons for holding cash are usually distinguished: transactions reasons and investment reasons.

1.1 *Transactions balances: size and composition.* No economic unit— firm or household or government—enjoys perfect synchronization

Reprinted from *Review of Economic Studies*, Vol. 25 (February 1958), 65–86, by permission of the author and publisher.

between the seasonal patterns of its flow of receipts and its flow of expenditures. The discrepancies give rise to balances which accumulate temporarily, and are used up later in the year when expenditures catch up. Or, to put the same phenomenon the other way, the discrepancies give rise to the need for balances to meet seasonal excesses of expenditures over receipts. These balances are *transactions balances*. The aggregate requirement of the economy for such balances depends on the institutional arrangements that determine the degree of synchronization between individual receipts and expenditures. Given these institutions, the need for transactions balances is roughly proportionate to the aggregate volume of transactions.

The obvious importance of these institutional determinants of the demand for transactions balances has led to the general opinion that other possible determinants, including interest rates, are negligible.[2] This may be true of the size of transactions balances, but the composition of transactions balances is another matter. Cash is by no means the only asset in which transactions balances may be held. Many transactors have large enough balances so that holding part of them in earning assets, rather than in cash, is a relevant possibility. Even though these holdings are always for short periods, the interest earnings may be worth the cost and inconvenience of the financial transactions involved. Elsewhere[3] I have shown that, for such transactors, the proportion of cash in transactions balances varies inversely with the rate of interest; consequently this source of interest-elasticity in the demand for cash will not be further discussed here.

1.2 *Investment balances and portfolio decisions.* In contrast to transactions balances, the investment balances of an economic unit are those that will survive all the expected seasonal excesses of cumulative expenditures over cumulative receipts during the year ahead. They are balances which will not have to be turned into cash within the year. Consequently the cost of financial transactions— converting other assets into cash and vice versa—does not operate to encourage the holding of investment balances in cash.[4] If cash is to have any part in the composition of investment balances, it must be because of expectations or fears of loss on other assets. It is here, in what Keynes called the speculative motives of investors, that the explanation of liquidity preference and of the interest-elasticity of the demand for cash has been sought.

The alternatives to cash considered, both in this paper and in prior discussions of the subject, in examining the speculative motive for holding cash are assets that differ from cash only in having a variable market yield. They are obligations to pay stated cash amounts at future dates, with no risk of default. They are, like cash, subject to changes in real value due to fluctuations in the price level. In a broader perspective, all these assets, including cash, are merely minor variants of the same species, a species we may call monetary assets—marketable, fixed in money value, free of default risk. The differences of members of this species from each other are negligible compared to their differences from the vast variety of other assets in which wealth may be invested: corporate stocks, real estate, unincorporated business and professional practice, etc. The theory of liquidity preference does not concern the choices investors make between the whole species of monetary assets, on the one hand, and other broad classes of assets, on the other.[5] Those choices are the concern of other branches of economic theory, in particular theories of investment and of consumption. Liquidity preference theory takes as given the choices determining how much wealth is to be invested in monetary assets and concerns itself with the allocation of these amounts among cash and alternative monetary assets.

Why should any investment balances be held in cash, in preference to other monetary assets? We shall distinguish two possible sources of liquidity preference, while recognizing that they are not mutually exclusive. The first is inelasticity of expectations of future interest rates. The second is uncertainty about the future of interest rates. These two sources of liquidity preference will be examined in turn.

2. Inelasticity of interest rate expectations.

2.1 *Some simplifying assumptions.* To simplify the problem, assume that there is only one monetary asset other than cash, namely consols. The current yield of consols is r per "year." $1 invested in consols today will purchase an income of $\$r$ per "year" in perpetuity. The yield of cash is assumed to be zero; however, this is not essential, as it is the current and expected differentials of consols over cash that matter. An investor with a given total balance must decide what proportion of this balance to hold in cash, A_1, and what proportions in consols, A_2. This decision is assumed to fix the portfolio for a full "year."[6]

2.2 *Fixed expectations of future rate.* At the end of the year, the investor expects the rate on consols to be r_e. This expectation is assumed, for the present, to be held with certainty and to be independent of the current rate r. The investor may therefore expect with certainty that every dollar invested in consols today will earn over the year ahead not only the interest $\$r$, but also a capital gain or loss g:

$$g = \frac{r}{r_e} - 1 \tag{2.1}$$

For this investor, the division of his balance into proportions A_1 of cash and A_2 of consols is a simple all-or-nothing choice. If the current rate is such that $r + g$ is greater than zero, then he will put everything in consols. But if $r + g$ is less than zero, he will put everything in cash. These conditions can be expressed in terms of a critical level of the current rate r_c, where:

$$r_c = \frac{r_e}{1 + r_e} \tag{2.2}$$

At current rates above r_c, everything goes into consols; but for r less than r_c, everything goes into cash.

2.3 *Sticky and certain interest rate expectations.* So far the investor's expected interest-rate r_e has been assumed to be completely independent of the current rate r. This assumption can be modified so long as some independence of the expected rate from the current

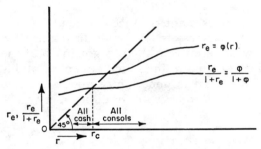

Figure 1. *Stickiness in the Relation between Expected and Current Interest Rate*

rate is maintained. In Figure 1, for example, r_e is shown as a function of r, namely $\varphi(r)$. Correspondingly $\dfrac{r_e}{1 + r_e}$ is a function of r.

As shown in the figure, this function $\dfrac{\varphi}{1 + \varphi}$ has only one intersection with the 45° line, and at this intersection its slope $\dfrac{\varphi'}{(1 + \varphi)^2}$ is less than one. If these conditions are met, the intersection determines a critical rate r_c such that if r exceeds r_c the investor holds no cash, while if r is less than r_c he holds no consols.

2.4 *Differences of opinion and the aggregate demand for cash.* According to this model, the relationship of the individual's investment demand for cash to the current rate of interest would be the discontinuous step function shown by the heavy vertical lines *LMNW* in Figure 2. How then do we get the familiar Keynesian liquidity preference function, a smooth, continuous inverse relationship

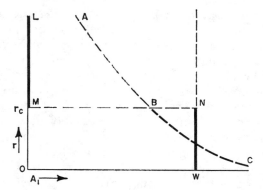

Figure 2. *Individual Demand for Cash Assuming
Certain but Inelastic Interest Rate
Expectations*

between the demand for cash and the rate of interest? For the
economy as a whole, such a relationship can be derived from
individual behaviour of the sort depicted in Figure 2 by assuming
that individual investors differ in their critical rates r_c. Such an
aggregate relationship is shown in Figure 3.

At actual rates above the maximum of individual critical rates
the aggregate demand for cash is zero, while at rates below the
minimum critical rate it is equal to the total investment balances
for the whole economy. Between these two extremes the demand
for cash varies inversely with the rate of interest r. Such a relationship is shown as $LMN\Sigma W$ in Figure 3. The demand for cash
at r is the total of investment balances controlled by investors
whose critical rates r_c exceed r. Strictly speaking, the curve is a
step function; but, if the number of investors is large, it can be
approximated by a smooth curve. Its shape depends on the distribution of dollars of investment balances by the critical rate of
the investor controlling them; the shape of the curve in Figure 3
follows from a unimodal distribution.

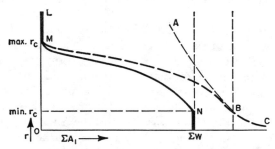

Figure 3. *Aggregate Demand for Cash Assuming Differences
Among Individuals in Interest Rate Expectations*

2.5 *Capital gains or losses and open market operations.* In the foregoing analysis the size of investment balances has been taken as independent of the current rate on consols r. This is not the case if there are already consols outstanding. Their value will depend inversely on the current rate of interest. Depending on the relation of the current rate to the previously fixed coupon on consols, owners of consols will receive capital gains or losses. Thus the investment balances of an individual owner of consols would not be constant at W but would depend on r in a manner illustrated by the curve ABC in Figure 2.[7] Similarly, the investment balances for the whole economy would follow a curve like ABC in Figure 3, instead of being constant at ΣW. The demand for cash would then be described by $LMBC$ in both figures. Correspondingly the demand for consols at any interest rate would be described by the horizontal distance between $LMBC$ and ABC. The value of consols goes to infinity as the rate of interest approaches zero; for this reason, the curve BC may never reach the horizontal axis. The size of investment balances would be bounded if the monetary assets other than cash consisted of bonds with definite maturities rather than consols.

According to this theory, a curve like $LMBC$ depicts the terms on which a central bank can engage in open-market operations, given the claims for future payments outstanding in the form of bonds or consols. The curve tells what the quantity of cash must be in order for the central bank to establish a particular interest rate. However, the curve will be shifted by open-market operations themselves, since they will change the volume of outstanding bonds or consols. For example, to establish the rate at or below $min\ r_c$, the central bank would have to buy all outstanding bonds or consols. The size of the community's investment balances would then be independent of the rate of interest; it would be represented by a vertical line through, or to the right of, B, rather than the curve ABC. Thus the new relation between cash and interest would be a curve lying above LMB, of the same general contour as $LMN\Sigma W$.

2.6 *Keynesian theory and its critics.* I believe the theory of liquidity preference I have just presented is essentially the original Keynesian explanation. The *General Theory* suggests a number of possible theoretical explanations, supported and enriched by the experience and insight of the author. But the explanation to which Keynes gave the greatest emphasis is the notion of a "normal" long-term rate, to which investors expect the rate of interest to return. When he refers to uncertainty in the market, he appears to mean disagreement among investors concerning the future of the rate rather than subjective doubt in the mind of an individual investor.[8] Thus Kaldor's correction of Keynes is more verbal than substantive when he says, "It is . . . not so much the *uncertainty* concerning future interest rates as the *inelasticity* of interest expectations which is responsible for Mr. Keynes' 'liquidity preference function,' . . . "[9]

Keynes' use of this explanation of liquidity preference as a part of his theory of underemployment equilibrium was the target of important criticism by Leontief and Fellner. Leontief argued that liquidity preference must necessarily be zero *in equilibrium*, regardless of the rate of interest. Divergence between the current and expected interest rate is bound to vanish as investors learn from experience; no matter how low an interest rate may be, it can be accepted as "normal" if it persists long enough. This criticism was a part of Leontief's general methodological criticism of Keynes, that unemployment was not a feature of equilibrium, subject to analysis by tools of static theory, but a phenomenon of disequilibrium requiring analysis by dynamic theory.[10] Fellner makes a similar criticism of the logical appropriateness of Keynes' explanation of liquidity preference for the purposes of his theory of underemployment equilibrium. Why, he asks, are interest rates the only variables to which inelastic expectations attach? Why don't wealth owners and others regard pre-depression price levels as "normal" levels to which prices will return? If they did, consumption and investment demand would respond to reductions in money wages and prices, no matter how strong and how elastic the liquidity preference of investors.[11]

These criticisms raise the question whether it is possible to dispense with the assumption of stickiness in interest rate expectations without losing the implication that Keynesian theory drew from it. Can the inverse relationship of demand for cash to the rate of interest be based on a different set of assumptions about the behaviour of individual investors? This question is the subject of the next part of the paper.

3. *Uncertainty, risk aversion, and liquidity preference.*

3.1 *The locus of opportunity for risk and expected return.* Suppose that an investor is not certain of the future rate of interest on consols; investment in consols then involves a risk of capital gain or loss. The higher the proportion of his investment balance that he holds in consols, the more risk the investor assumes. At the same time, increasing the proportion in consols also increases his expected return. In the upper half of Figure 4, the vertical axis represents expected return and the horizontal axis risk. A line such as OC_1 pictures the fact that the investor can expect more return if he assumes more risk. In the lower half of Figure 4, the left-hand

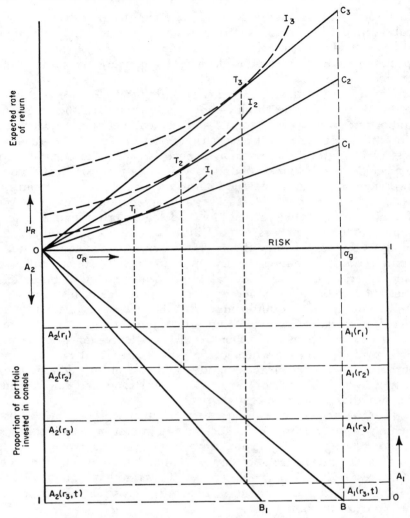

Figure 4. *Portfolio Selection at Various Interest Rates and Before and After Taxation*

vertical axis measures the proportion invested in consols. A line like OB shows risk as proportional to the share of the total balance held in consols.

The concepts of expected return and risk must be given more precision.

The individual investor of the previous section was assumed to have, for any current rate of interest, a definite expectation of the capital gain or loss g [defined in expression (2.1) above] he would obtain by investing one dollar in consols. Now he will be assumed instead to be uncertain about g but to base his actions on his estimate of its probability distribution. This probability distribution, it will be assumed, has an expected value of zero and is independent of the level of r, the current rate on consols. Thus the investor considers a doubling of the rate just as likely when rate is 5% as when it is 2%, and a halving of the rate just as likely when it is 1% as when it is 6%.

A portfolio consists of a proportion A_1 of cash and A_2 of consols, where A_1 and A_2 add up to 1. We shall assume that A_1 and A_2 do not depend on the absolute size of the initial investment balance in dollars. Negative values of A_1 and A_2 are excluded by definition; only the government and the banking system can issue cash and government consols. The return on a portfolio R is:

$$R = A_2(r + g) \qquad 0 \le A_2 \le 1 \qquad (3.1)$$

Since g is a random variable with expected value zero, the expected return on the portfolio is:

$$E(R) = \mu_R = A_2 r \qquad (3.2)$$

The risk attached to a portfolio is to be measured by the standard deviation of R, σ_R. The standard deviation is a measure of the dispersion of possible returns around the mean value μ_R. A high standard deviation means, speaking roughly, high probability of large deviations from μ_R, both positive and negative. A low standard deviation means low probability of large deviations from μ_R; in the extreme case, a zero standard deviation would indicate certainty of receiving the return μ_R. Thus a high-σ_R portfolio offers the investor the chance of large capital gains at the price of equivalent chances of large capital losses. A low-σ_R portfolio protects the investor from capital loss, and likewise gives him little prospect of unusual gains. Although it is intuitively clear that the risk of a portfolio is to be identified with the dispersion of possible returns, the standard deviation is neither the sole measure of dispersion nor the obviously most relevant measure. The case for the standard deviation will be further discussed in section 3.3 below.

The standard deviation of R depends on the standard deviation of g, σ_g, and on the amount invested in consols:

$$\sigma_R = A_2 \sigma_g \qquad 0 \le A_2 \le 1 \qquad (3.3)$$

Thus the proportion the investor holds in consols A_2 determines both his expected return μ_R and his risk σ_R. The terms on which the investor can obtain greater expected return at the expense of assuming more risk can be derived from (3.2) and (3.3):

$$\mu_R = \frac{r}{\sigma_g} \sigma_R \qquad 0 \le \sigma_R \le \sigma_g \qquad (3.4)$$

Such an *opportunity locus* is shown as line OC_1 (for $r = r_1$) in Figure 3.1. The slope of the line is $\dfrac{r_1}{\sigma_g}$. For a higher interest rate r_2, the opportunity locus would be OC_2; and for r_3, a still higher rate, it would be OC_3. The relationship (3.3) between risk and investment in consols is shown as line OB in the lower half of the figure. Cash holding $A_1(= 1 - A_2)$ can also be read off the diagram on the right-hand vertical axis.

3.2 *Loci indifference between combinations of risk and expected return.* The investor is assumed to have preferences between expected return μ_R and risk σ_R that can be represented by a field of in-difference curves. The investor is indifferent between all pairs (μ_R, σ_R) that lie on a curve such as I_1 in Figure 4. Points on I_2 are preferred to those on I_1; for given risk, an investor always prefers a greater to a smaller expectation of return. Conceivably, for some investors, *risk-lovers*, these indifference curves have nega-tive slopes. Such individuals are willing to accept lower expected return in order to have the chance of unusually high capital gains afforded by high values of σ_R. *Risk-averters*, on the other hand, will not be satisfied to accept more risk unless they can also expect greater expected return. Their indifference curves will be posi-tively sloped. Two kinds of risk-averters need to be distinguished. The first type, who may be called *diversifiers* for reasons that will become clear below, have indifference curves that are concave up-ward, like those in Figure 4. The second type, who may be called *plungers*, have indifference curves that are upward sloping, but either linear or convex upward.

3.3 *Indifference curves as loci of constant expected utility of wealth.* The reader who is willing to accept the indifference fields that have just been introduced into the analysis may skip to section 3.4 without losing the main thread of the argument. But these in-difference curves need some explanation and defence. Indifference curves between μ_R and σ_R do not necessarily exist. It is a simpli-fication to assume that the investor chooses among the alternative probability distributions of R available to him on the basis of only two parameters of those distributions. Even if this simplification is accepted, the mean and standard deviation may not be the pair of parameters that concern the investor.

3.3.1 One justification for the use of indifference curves be-tween μ_R and σ_R would be that the investor evaluates the future of consols only in terms of some two-parameter family of prob-ability distributions of g. For example, the investor might think in terms of a range of equally likely gains or losses, centered on zero. Or he might think in terms that can be approximated by a normal distribution. Whatever two-parameter family is assumed—uniform, normal, or some other—the whole probability distribution is determined as soon as the mean and standard deviation are specified. Hence the investor's choice among probability distributions can be analyzed by μ_R-σ_R indifference curves; any other pair of independent parameters could serve equally well.

If the investor's probability distributions are assumed to belong to some two-parameter family, the shape of his indifference curves can be inferred from the general characteristics of his utility-of-return function. This function will be assumed to relate utility to R, the percentage growth in the investment balance by the end of the period. This way of formulating the utility function makes the investor's indifference map, and therefore his choices of proportions of cash and consols, independent of the absolute amount of his initial balance.

On certain postulates, it can be shown that an individual's choice among probability distributions can be described as the maximization of the expected value of a utility function.[12] The ranking of probability distributions with respect to the expected value of utility will not be changed if the scale on which utility is measured is altered either by the addition of a constant or by multiplication by a positive constant. Consequently we are free to choose arbitrarily the zero and unit of measurement of the utility function $U(R)$ as follows: $U(0) = 0$; $U(-1) = -1$.

Suppose that the probability distribution of R can be described by a two-parameter density function $f(R; \mu_R, \sigma_R)$. Then the expected value of utility is:

$$E[U(R)] = \int_{-\infty}^{\infty} U(R)f(R; \mu_R, \sigma_R)\, dR \qquad (3.5)$$

Let

$$z = \frac{R - \mu_R}{\sigma_R}$$

$$E[U(R)] = E(\mu_R, \sigma_R) = \int_{-\infty}^{\infty} U(\mu_R + \sigma_R z)f(z; 0, 1)\, dz. \qquad (3.6)$$

An indifference curve is a locus of points (μ_R, σ_R) along which expected utility is constant. We may find the slope of such a locus by differentiating (3.6) with respect to σ_R:

$$0 = \int_{-\infty}^{\infty} U'(\mu_R + \sigma_R z)\left[\frac{d\mu_R}{d\sigma_R} + z\right] f(z; 0, 1)\, dz$$

$$\frac{d\mu_R}{d\sigma_R} = -\frac{\int_{-\infty}^{\infty} zU'(R)f(z; 0, 1)\, dz}{\int_{-\infty}^{\infty} U'(R)f(z; 0, 1)\, dz} \qquad (3.7)$$

$U'(R)$, the marginal utility of return, is assumed to be everywhere non-negative. If it is also a decreasing function of R, then the slope of the indifference locus must be positive; an investor with such a utility function is a risk-averter. If it is an increasing function of R, the slope will be negative; this kind of utility function characterizes a risk-lover.

Similarly, the curvature of the indifference loci is related to the shape of the utility function. Suppose that (μ_R, σ_R) and (μ'_R, σ'_R) are on the same indifference locus, so that $E(\mu_R, \sigma_R) = E(\mu_R, \sigma_R)$. Is $\left(\dfrac{\mu_R + \mu'_R}{2}, \dfrac{\sigma_R + \sigma'_R}{2} \right)$ on the same locus, or on a higher or a lower one? In the case of declining marginal utility we know that for every z:

$$\tfrac{1}{2}U(\mu_R + \sigma_R z) + \tfrac{1}{2}U(\mu'_R + \sigma'_R z)$$

$$< U\left(\frac{\mu_R + \mu'_R}{2} + \frac{\sigma_R + \sigma'_R}{2} z \right)$$

Consequently $E\left(\dfrac{\mu_R + \mu'_R}{2}, \dfrac{\sigma_R + \sigma'_R}{2} \right)$ is greater than $E(\mu_R, \sigma_R)$ or $E(\mu'_R; \sigma'_R)$, and $\left(\dfrac{\mu_R + \mu'_R}{2}, \dfrac{\sigma_R + \sigma'_R}{2} \right)$, which lies on a line between (μ_R, σ_R) and (μ'_R, σ'_R), is on a higher locus than those points. Thus it is shown that a risk-averter's indifference curve is necessarily concave upwards, provided it is derived in this manner from a two-parameter family of probability distributions and declining marginal utility of return. All risk-averters are diversifiers; plungers do not exist. The same kind of argument shows that a risk-lover's indifference curve is concave downwards.

3.3.2 In the absence of restrictions on the subjective probability distributions of the investor, the parameters of the distribution relevant to his choice can be sought in parametric restrictions on his utility-of-return function. Two parameters of the utility function are determined by the choice of the utility scale. If specification of the utility function requires no additional parameters, one parameter of the probability distribution summarizes all the information relevant for the investor's choice. For example, if the utility function is linear $[U(R) = R]$, then the expected value of utility is simply the expected value of R, and maximizing expected utility leads to the same behaviour as maximizing return in a world of certainty. If, however, one additional parameter is needed to specify the utility function, then two parameters of the probability distribution will be relevant to the choice; and so on. Which parameters of the distribution are relevant depends on the form of the utility function.

Focus on the mean and standard deviation of return can be justified on the assumption that the utility function is quadratic. Following our conventions as to utility scale, the quadratic function would be:

$$U(R) = (1 + b)R + bR^2 \qquad (3.8)$$

Here $0 < b < 1$ for a risk-lover, and $-1 < b < 0$ for a risk-averter. However (3.8) cannot describe the utility function for the whole range of R, because marginal utility cannot be negative. The function given in (3.8) can apply only for:

$$(1 + b) + 2bR \geq 0;$$

that is, for:

$$R \geq - \left(\frac{1 + b}{2b}\right)(b > 0) \qquad \text{(Risk-lover)}$$

$$R \leq - \left(\frac{1 + b}{2b}\right)(b < 0) \qquad \text{(Risk-averter)} \qquad (3.9)$$

In order to use (3.8), therefore, we must exclude from the range of possibility values of R outside the limits (3.9). At the maximum investment in consols ($A_2 = 1$), $R = r + g$. A risk-averter must be assumed therefore, to restrict the range of capital gains g to which he attaches non-zero probability so that, for the highest rate of interest r to be considered:

$$r + g \leq - \left(\frac{1 + b}{2b}\right) \qquad (3.10)$$

The corresponding limitation for a risk-lover is that, for the lowest interest rate r to be considered:

$$r + g \geq - \left(\frac{1 + b}{2b}\right) \qquad (3.11)$$

Given the utility function (3.8), we can investigate the slope and curvature of the indifference curves it implies. The probability density function for $R, f(R)$, is restricted by the limit (3.10) or (3.11); but otherwise no restriction on its shape is assumed.

$$E[U(R)] = \int_{-\infty}^{\infty} U(R)f(R)\, dR = (1 + b)\mu_R + b(\sigma_R^2 + \mu^2{}_R) \qquad (3.12)$$

Holding $E[U(R)]$ constant and differentiating with respect to σ_R to obtain the slope of an indifference curve, we have:

$$\frac{d\mu_R}{d\sigma_R} = \frac{\sigma_R}{-\dfrac{1 + b}{2b} - \mu_R} \qquad (3.13)$$

For a risk-averter, $-\dfrac{1+b}{2b}$ is positive and is the upper limit for

R, according to (3.9); $-\dfrac{1+b}{2b}$ is necessarily larger than μ_R.

Therefore the slope of an indifference locus is positive. For a risk-lover, on the other hand, the corresponding argument shows that the slope is negative.

Differentiating (3.13) leads to the same conclusions regarding curvature as the alternative approach of section 3.3.1, namely that a risk-averter is necessarily a diversifier.

$$\frac{d^2\mu_R}{d\sigma^2{}_R} = \frac{1 + \left(\dfrac{d\mu_R}{d\sigma_R}\right)^2}{-\dfrac{1+b}{2b} - \mu_R} \tag{3.14}$$

For a risk-averter, the second derivative is positive and the indifference locus is concave upwards; for a risk-lover, it is concave downwards.

3.4 *Effects of changes in the rate of interest.* In section 3.3 two alternative rationalizations of the indifference curves introduced in section 3.2 have been presented. Both rationalizations assume that the investor (1) estimates subjective probability distributions of capital gain or loss in holding consols, (2) evaluates his prospective increase in wealth in terms of a cardinal utility function, (3) ranks alternative prospects according to the expected value of utility. The rationalization of section 3.3.1 derives the indifference curves by restricting the subjective probability distributions to a two-parameter family. The rationalization of section 3.3.2 derives the indifference curves by assuming the utility function to be quadratic within the relevant range. On either rationalization, a risk-averter's indifference curves must be concave upwards, characteristic of the diversifiers of section 3.2, and those of a risk-lover concave downwards. If the category defined as *plungers* in 3.2 exists at all, their indifference curves must be determined by some process other than those described in 3.3.

The opportunity locus for the investor is described in Figure 4 and summarized in equation (3.4). The investor decides the amount to invest in consols so as to reach the highest indifference curve permitted by his opportunity locus. This maximization may be one of three kinds:

I. Tangency between an indifference curve and the opportunity locus, as illustrated by points T_1, T_2, and T_3 in Figure 4. A regular maximum of this kind can occur only for a risk-averter, and will lead to diversification. Both A_1, cash holding, and A_2, consol holding, will be positive. They too are shown in Figure 4, in the bottom half of the diagram, where, for example, $A_1(r_1)$ and $A_2(r_1)$ depict the cash and consol holdings corresponding to point T_1.

II. A corner maximum at the point $\mu_R = r$, $\sigma_R = \sigma_g$, as illustrated in Figure 5. In Figure 5 the opportunity locus is the ray OC, and point C represents the highest expected return and risk obtainable by the investor, i.e. the expected return and risk from holding his entire balance in consols. A utility maximum at C can occur either for a risk-averter or for a risk-lover. I_1 and I_2 represent indifference curves of a diversifier; I_2 passes through C and has a lower slope, both at C and everywhere to the left of C, than the opportunity locus. I_1' and I_2' represent the indifference curves of a risk-lover, for whom it is clear that C is always the optimum position. Similarly, a plunger may, if his indifference curves stand with respect to his opportunity locus as in Figure 6 (OC_2) plunge his entire balance in consols.

III. A corner maximum at the origin, where the entire balance is held in cash. For a plunger, this case is illustrated in Figure 6 (OC_1). Conceivably it could also occur for a diversifier, if the slope of his indifference curve at the origin exceeded the slope of the opportunity locus. However, case III is entirely excluded for investors whose indifference curves represent the constant-expected-utility loci of section 3.3. Such investors, we have already noted, cannot be plungers. Furthermore, the slope of all constant-expected-utility loci at $\sigma_R = 0$ must be zero, as can be seen from (3.7) and (3.13).

We can now examine the consequences of a change in the interest rate r, holding constant the investor's estimate of the risk of capital gain or loss. An increase in the interest rate will rotate

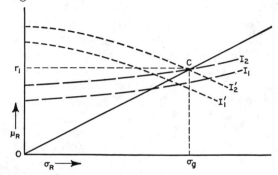

Figure 5. *"Risk-lovers" and "Diversifiers": Optimum Portfolio at Maximum Risk and Expected Return*

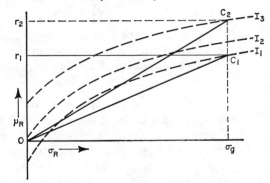

Figure 6. *"Plungers"—Optimum Portfolio at Minimum or Maximum Risk and Expected Return*

the opportunity locus OC to the left. How will this affect the investor's holdings of cash and consols? We must consider separately the three cases.

I. In Figure 4, OC_1, OC_2, and OC_3 represent opportunity loci for successively higher rates of interest. The indifference curves I_1, I_2, and I_3 are drawn so that the points of tangency T_1, T_2, and T_3, correspond to successively higher holdings of consols A_2. In this diagram, the investor's demand for cash depends inversely on the interest rate.

This relationship is, of course, in the direction liquidity preference theory has taught us to expect, but it is not the only possible direction of relationship. It is quite possible to draw indifference curves so that the point of tangency moves left as the opportunity locus is rotated counter-clockwise. The ambiguity is a familiar one in the theory of choice, and reflects the ubiquitous conflict between income and substitution effects. An increase in the rate of interest is an incentive to take more risk; so far as the substitution effect is concerned, it means a shift from security to yield. But an increase in the rate of interest also has an income effect, for it gives the opportunity to enjoy more security along with more yield. The ambiguity is analogous to the doubt concerning the effect of a change in the interest rate on saving; the substitution effect argues for a positive relationship, the income effect for an inverse relationship.

However, if the indifference curves are regarded as loci of constant expected utility, as derived in section 3.3, part of this ambiguity can be resolved. We have already observed that these loci all have zero slopes at $\sigma_R = 0$. As the interest rate r rises from zero, so also will consol holding A_2. At higher interest rates, however, the inverse relationship may occur.

This reversal of direction can, however, virtually be excluded in the case of the quadratic utility function (section 3.3.2). The condition for a maximum is that the slope of an indifference locus as given by (3.13) equal the slope of the opportunity locus (3.4).

$$\frac{r}{\sigma_g} = \frac{A_2 \sigma_g}{-\dfrac{1+b}{2b} - A_2 r} \; ; \; A_2 = \frac{r}{r^2 + \sigma_g^2}\left(-\frac{1+b}{2b}\right) \qquad (3.15)$$

Equation (3.15) expresses A_2 as a function of r, and differentiating gives:

$$\frac{dA_2}{dr} = \frac{\sigma_g^2 - r^2}{(\sigma_g^2 + r^2)^2}\left(-\frac{1+b}{2b}\right); \; \frac{r}{A_2}\frac{dA_2}{dr} = \frac{\sigma_g^2 - r^2}{\sigma_g^2 + r^2} \qquad (3.16)$$

Thus the share of consols in the portfolio increases with the interest rate for r less than σ_g. Moreover, if r exceeds σ_g, a tangency maximum cannot occur unless r also exceeds g_{max}, the largest capital gain the investor conceives possible (see 3.10).[13] The demand for consols is less elastic at high interest rates than at low, but the elasticity is not likely to become negative.

II and III. A change in the interest rate cannot cause a risk-lover to alter his position, which is already the point of maximum risk and expected yield. Conceivably a "diversifier" might move from a corner maximum to a regular interior maximum in response either to a rise in the interest rate or to a fall. A "plunger" might find his position altered by an increase in the interest rate, as from r_1 to r_2 in Figure 6; this would lead him to shift his entire balance from cash to consols.

3.5 *Effects of changes in risk.* Investor's estimates σ_g of the risk of holding monetary assets other than cash, "consols," are subjective. But they are undoubtedly affected by market experience, and they are also subject to influence by measures of monetary and fiscal policy. By actions and words, the central bank can influence investors' estimates of the variability of interest rates; its influence on these estimates of risk may be as important in accomplishing or preventing changes in the rate as open-market operations and other direct interventions in the market. Tax rates, and differences in tax treatment of capital gains, losses, and interest earnings, affect in calculable ways the investor's risks and expected returns. For these reasons it is worth while to examine the effects of a change in an investor's estimate of risk on his allocation between cash and consols.

In Figure 7, T_1 and $A_2(r_1, \sigma_g)$ represent the initial position of an investor, at interest rate r_1 and risk σ_g. OC_1 is the opportunity locus (3.4), and OB_1 is the risk-consols relationship (3.3). If the

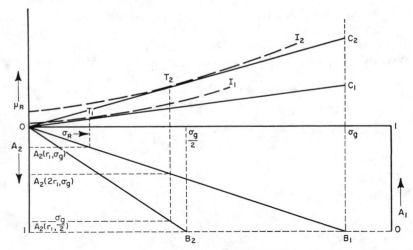

Figure 7. *Comparison of Effects of Changes in Interest Rate (r) and in "Risk"*
(σ_g) on Holding of Consols

investor now cuts his estimate of risk in half, to $\dfrac{\sigma_g}{2}$, the opportunity

locus will double in slope, from OC_1 to OC_2, and the investor will
shift to point T_2. The risk-consols relationship will have also
doubled in slope, from OB_1 to OB_2. Consequently point T_2 cor-

responds to an investment in consols of $A_2\left(r_1, \dfrac{\sigma_g}{2}\right)$. This same

point T_2 would have been reached if the interest rate had doubled
while the investor's risk estimate σ_g remained unchanged. But in
that case, since the risk-consols relationship would remain at OB_1,
the corresponding investment in consols would have been only
half as large, i.e., $A_2(2r_1, \sigma_g)$. In general, the following relationship
exists between the elasticity of the demand for consols with respect
to risk and its elasticity with respect to the interest rate:

$$\frac{\sigma_g}{A_2}\frac{dA_2}{d\sigma_g} = -\frac{r}{A_2}\frac{dA_2}{dr} - 1 \qquad (3.17)$$

The implications of this relationship for analysis of effects of
taxation may be noted in passing, with the help of Figure 7. Suppose that the initial position of the investor is T_2 and $A_2(2r_1, \sigma_g)$.
A tax of 50% is now levied on interest income and capital gains
alike, with complete loss offset provisions. The result of the tax is
to reduce the expected net return per dollar of consols from $2r_1$ to
r_1 and to reduce the risk to the investor per dollar of consols from
σ_g to $\sigma_g/2$. The opportunity locus will remain at OC_2, and the investor will still wish to obtain the combination of risk and ex-

pected return depicted by T_2. To obtain this combination, however, he must now double his holding of consols, to $A_2(r_1, \sigma_g/2)$;
the tax shifts the risk-consols line from OB_1 to OB_2. A tax of this
kind, therefore, would reduce the demand for cash at any market
rate of interest, shifting the investor's liquidity preference schedule
in the manner shown in Figure 8. A tax on interest income only,
with no tax on capital gains and no offset privileges for capital
losses, would have quite different effects. If the Treasury began to
split the interest income of the investor in Figure 7 but not to share
the risk, the investor would move from his initial position, T_2 and
$A_2(2r_1, \sigma_g)$; to T_1 and $A_2(r_1, \sigma_g)$. His demand for cash at a given
market rate of interest would be increased and his liquidity preference curve shifted to the right.

3.6 *Multiple alternatives to cash.* So far it has been assumed that
there is only one alternative to cash, and A_2 has represented the
share of the investor's balance held in that asset, "consols." The
argument is not essentially changed, however, if A_2 is taken to be
the aggregate share invested in a variety of non-cash assets, e.g.,
bonds and other debt instruments differing in maturity, debtor,
and other features. The return R and the risk σ_g on "consols" will
then represent the average return and risk on a composite of these
assets.

Suppose that there are m assets other than cash, and let $x_i(i =
1, 2, \ldots, m)$ be the amount invested in the ith of these assets. All
x_i are non-negative, and $\sum_{i=1}^{m} x_i = A_2 \leqq 1$. Let r_i be the ex-

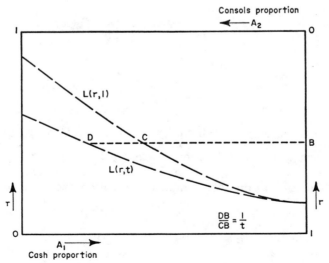

Figure 8. *Effect of Tax (at Rate* 1-t *) on Liquidity Preference*
Function

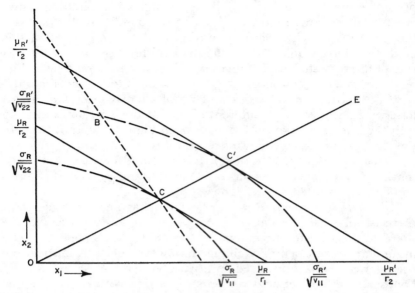

Figure 9. *Dominant Combinations of Two Assets*

pected yield, and let g_i be the capital gain or loss, per dollar invested in the ith asset. We assume $E(g_i) = 0$ for all i. Let v_{ij} be the variance or covariance of g_i and g_j as estimated by the investor.

$$v_{ij} = E(g_i g_j) \quad (i, j, = 1, 2, \ldots, m) \tag{3.18}$$

The over-all expected return is:

$$\mu_R = A_2 r = \sum_{i=1}^{m} x_i r_i \tag{3.19}$$

The over-all variance of return is:

$$\sigma_R^2 = A_2^2 \sigma_g^2 = \sum_{i=1}^{m} \sum_{j=1}^{m} x_i x_j v_{ij}. \tag{3.20}$$

A set of points x_i for which $\sum\limits_{i=1}^{m} x_i r_i$ is constant may be defined as a *constant-return locus*. A constant-return locus is linear in the x_i. For two assets x_1 and x_2, two loci are illustrated in Figure 9. One locus of combinations of x_1 and x_2 that give the same expected return μ_R is the line from $\dfrac{\mu_R}{r_2}$ to $\dfrac{\mu_R}{r_1}$, through C; another locus, for a higher constant, μ_R', is the parallel line from $\dfrac{\mu_R'}{r_2}$ to $\dfrac{\mu_R'}{r_1}$, through C'.

A set of points x_i for which σ_R^2 is constant may be defined as a *constant-risk locus*. These loci are ellipsoidal. For two assets x_1 and

x_2, such a locus is illustrated by the quarter-ellipse from $\dfrac{\sigma_R}{\sqrt{v_{22}}}$ to $\dfrac{\sigma_R}{\sqrt{v_{11}}}$, through point C. The equation of such an ellipse is:

$$x_1^2 v_{11} + 2x_1 x_2 v_{12} + x_2^2 v_{22} = \sigma_R^2 = \text{constant}$$

Another such locus, for a higher risk level, σ_R', is the quarter-ellipse from $\dfrac{\sigma_R'}{\sqrt{v_{22}}}$ to $\dfrac{\sigma_R'}{\sqrt{v_{11}}}$ through point C'.

From Figure 9, it is clear that C and C' exemplify *dominant* combinations of x_1 and x_2. If the investor is incurring a risk of σ_R, somewhere on the ellipse through C, he will have the highest possible expectation of return available to him at that level of risk. The highest available expected return is represented by the constant-expected-return line tangent to the ellipse at C. Similarly C' is a dominant point: it would not be possible to obtain a higher expected return than at C' without incurring additional risk, or to diminish risk without sacrificing expected return.

In general, a dominant combination of assets is defined as a set x_i which minimizes σ_R^2 for μ_R constant:

$$\sum_i \left(\sum_j v_{ij} x_j \right) x_i - \lambda \left(\sum_i r_i x_i - \mu_R \right) = \min \qquad (3.21)$$

where λ is a Lagrange multiplier. The conditions for the minimum are that the x_i satisfy the constraint (3.19) and the following set of m simultaneous linear equations, written in matrix notation:

$$[v_{ij}][x_i] = [\lambda r_i] \qquad (3.22)$$

All dominant sets lie on a ray from the origin. That is, if $[x_i^{(0)}]$ and $[x_i^{(1)}]$ are dominant sets, then there is some non-negative scalar κ such that $[x_i^{(1)}] = [\kappa x_i^{(0)}]$. By definition of a dominant set, there is some $\lambda^{(0)}$ such that:

$$[v_{ij}][x_i^{(0)}] = [\lambda^{(0)} r_i]$$

and some $\lambda^{(1)}$ such that:

$$[v_{ij}][x_i^{(1)}] = [\lambda^{(1)} r_i]$$

Take $\kappa = \dfrac{\lambda^{(1)}}{\lambda^{(0)}}$. Then:

$$[v_{ij}][\kappa x_i^{(0)}] = [\kappa \lambda^{(0)} r_i] = [\lambda^{(1)} r_i] = [v_{ij}][x_i^{(1)}]$$

At the same time, $\sum_i r_i x_i^{(0)} = \mu_R^{(0)}$ and $\sum_i r_i x_i^{(1)} = \mu_R^{(1)}$.

Hence, $\mu_R^{(1)} = \kappa \mu_R^{(0)}$. Conversely, every set on this ray is a dominant set. If $[x_i^{(0)}]$ is a dominant set, then so is $[\kappa x_i^{(0)}]$ for any non-negative constant κ. This is easily proved. If $[x_i^{(0)}]$ satisfies (3.19) and (3.22) for $\mu_R^{(0)}$ and $\lambda^{(0)}$, then $[\kappa x_i^{(0)}]$ satisfies (3.19) and (3.22) for $\lambda^{(\kappa)} = \kappa \lambda^{(0)}$ and $\mu_R^{(\kappa)} = \kappa \mu_R^{(0)}$. In the two-dimensional case pictured in Figure 9, the dominant pairs lie along the ray $OCC'E$.

There will be some point on the ray (say E in Figure 9) at which the investor's holdings of non-cash assets will exhaust his investment balance ($\sum_i x_i = 1$) and leave nothing for cash hold-ing. Short of that point the balance will be divided among cash and non-cash assets in proportion to the distances along the ray; in Figure 9 at point C for example, $\dfrac{OC}{OE}$ of the balance would be non-cash, and $\dfrac{CE}{OE}$ cash. But the convenient fact that has just been proved is that the proportionate composition of the non-cash assets is independent of their aggregate share of the investment balance. This fact makes it possible to describe the investor's decisions as if there were a single non-cash asset, a composite formed by combining the multitude of actual non-cash assets in fixed proportions.

Corresponding to every point on the ray of dominant sets is an expected return μ_R and risk σ_R; these pairs (μ_R, σ_R) are the op-portunity locus of sections 3.1 and 3.4. By means of (3.22), the opportunity locus can be expressed in terms of the expected return and variances and covariances of the non-cash assets: Let:

$$[V_{ij}] = [V_{ij}]^{-1}$$

Then:

$$\mu_R = \lambda \sum_i \sum_j r_i r_j V_{ij} \tag{3.23}$$

$$\sigma_R^2 = \lambda^2 \sum_i \sum_j r_i r_j V_{ij}. \tag{3.24}$$

Thus the opportunity locus is the line:

$$\mu_R = \sigma_R \sqrt{\sum_i \sum_j r_i r_j V_{ij}} = \sigma_R \frac{r}{\sigma_g}. \tag{3.25}$$

This analysis is applicable only so long as cash is assumed to be a riskless asset. In the absence of a residual riskless asset, the in-vestor has no reason to confine his choices to the ray of dominant sets. This may be easily verified in the two-asset case. Using Figure 9 for a different purpose now, suppose that the entire investment balance must be divided between x_1 and x_2. The point (x_1, x_2) must fall on the line $x_1 + x_2 = 1$, represented by the line through BC in the diagram. The investor will not necessarily choose point

C. At point *B*, for example, he would obtain a higher expected yield as well as a higher risk; he may prefer *B* to *C*. His opportunity locus represents the pairs (μ_R, σ_R) along the line through $BC(x_1 + x_2 = 1)$ rather than along the ray *OC*, and is a hyperbola rather than a line. It is still possible to analyze portfolio choices by the apparatus of (μ_R, σ_R) indifference and opportunity loci, but such analysis is beyond the scope of the present paper.[14]

It is for this reason that the present analysis has been deliberately limited, as stated in section 1.2, to choices among monetary assets. Among these assets cash is relatively riskless, even though in the wider context of portfolio selection, the risk of changes in purchasing power, which all monetary assets share, may be relevant to many investors. Breaking down the portfolio selection problem into stages at different levels of aggregation—allocation first among, and then within, asset categories—seems to be a permissible and perhaps even indispensable simplification both for the theorist and for the investor himself.

4. Implications of the analysis for liquidity preference theory.

The theory of risk-avoiding behaviour has been shown to provide a basis for liquidity preference and for an inverse relationship between the demand for cash and the rate of interest. This theory does not depend on inelasticity of expectations of future interest rates, but can proceed from the assumption that the expected value of capital gain or loss from holding interest-bearing assets is always zero. In this respect, it is a logically more satisfactory foundation for liquidity preference than the Keynesian theory described in section 2. Moreover, it has the empirical advantage of explaining diversification—the same individual holds both cash and "consols"—while the Keynesian theory implies that each investor will hold only one asset.

The risk aversion theory of liquidity preference mitigates the major logical objection to which, according to the argument of section 2.6, the Keynesian theory is vulnerable. But it cannot completely meet Leontief's position that in a strict stationary equilibrium liquidity preference must be zero unless cash and consols bear equal rates. By their very nature consols and, to a lesser degree, all time obligations contain a potential for capital gain or loss that cash and other demand obligations lack. Presumably, however, there is some length of experience of constancy in the interest rate that would teach the most stubbornly timid investor to ignore that potential. In a pure stationary state, it could be argued, the interest rate on consols would have been the same for so long that investors would unanimously estimate σ_g to be zero. So stationary a state is of very little interest. Fortunately the usefulness of comparative statics does not appear to be confined to comparisons of states each of which would take a generation or more to achieve. As compared to the Keynesian theory of liquidity preference, the risk aversion theory widens the applicability of comparative statics in aggregative analysis; this is all that need be claimed for it.

The theory, however, is somewhat ambiguous concerning the direction of relationship between the rate of interest and the demand for cash. For low interest rates, the theory implies a negative elasticity of demand for cash with respect to the interest rate, an elasticity that becomes larger and larger in absolute value as the rate approaches zero. This implication, of course, is in accord with the usual assumptions about liquidity preference. But for high interest rates, and especially for individuals whose estimates σ_g of the risk of capital gain or loss on "consols" are low, the demand for cash may be an increasing, rather than a decreasing, function of the interest rate. However, the force of this reversal of direction is diluted by recognition, as in section 2.5, that the size of investment balances is not independent of the current rate of interest r. In section 3.4 we have considered the proportionate allocation between cash and "consols" on the assumption that it is independent of the size of the balance. An increase in the rate of interest may lead an investor to desire to shift towards cash. But to the extent that the increase in interest also reduces the value of the investor's consol holdings, it automatically gratifies this desire, at least in part.

The assumption that investors expect on balance no change in the rate of interest has been adopted for the theoretical reasons explained in section 2.6 rather than for reasons of realism. Clearly investors do form expectations of changes in interest rates and differ from each other in their expectations. For the purposes of dynamic theory and of analysis of specific market situations, the theories of sections 2 and 3 are complementary rather than competitive. The formal apparatus of section 3 will serve just as well for a non-zero expected capital gain or loss as for a zero expected value of g. Stickiness of interest rate expectations would mean that the expected value of g is a function of the rate of interest r, going down when r goes down and rising when r goes up. In addition to the rotation of the opportunity locus due to a change in r itself, there would be a further rotation in the same direction due to the accompanying change in the expected capital gain or loss. At low interest rates expectation of capital loss may push the opportunity locus into the negative quadrant, so that the optimal position is clearly no consols, all cash. At the other extreme, expectation of capital gain at high interest rates would increase sharply the slope of the opportunity locus and the frequency of no cash, all consols positions, like that of Figure 6. The stickier the investor's expectations, the more sensitive his demand for cash will be to changes in the rate of interest.

NOTES

1. ". . . in a world involving no transaction friction and no uncertainty, there would be no reason for a spread between the yield on any two assets, and hence there would be no difference in the yield on money and on securities . . . in such a world securities themselves would circulate as money and be acceptable in transactions; demand bank deposits would bear interest, just as they often did in this country in the period of the twenties." (Paul A. Samuelson, *Foundations of Economic Analysis* [Cambridge: Harvard University Press, 1947], p. 123). The section, pp. 122–24, from which the passage is quoted makes it clear that liquidity preference must be regarded as an explanation of the existence and level not of the interest rate but of the differential between the yield on money and the yields on other assets.

2. The traditional theory of the velocity of money has, however, probably exaggerated the invariance of the institutions determining the extent of lack of synchronization between individual receipts and expenditures. It is no doubt true that such institutions as the degree of vertical integration of production and the periodicity of wage, salary, dividend, and tax payments are slow to change. But other relevant arrangements can be adjusted in response to money rates. For example, there is a good deal of flexibility in the promptness and regularity with which bills are rendered and settled.

3. "The Interest Elasticity of the Transactions Demand for Cash," *Review of Economics and Statistics*, Vol. 38 (August 1956), 241–47.

4. Costs of financial transactions have the effect of deterring changes from the existing portfolio, whatever its composition; they may thus operate against the holding of cash as easily as for it. Because of these costs, the *status quo* may be optimal even when a different composition of assets would be preferred if the investor were starting over again.

5. For an attempt by the author to apply to this wider choice some of the same theoretical tools that are here used to analyze choices among the narrow class of monetary assets, see "A Dynamic Aggregative Model," *Journal of Political Economy*, Vol. 63 (April 1955), 103–15.

6. As noted above, it is the costs of financial transactions that impart inertia to portfolio composition. Every reconsideration of the portfolio involves the investor in expenditure of time and effort as well as of money. The frequency with which it is worth while to review the portfolio will obviously vary with the investor and will depend on the size of his portfolio and on his situation with respect to costs of obtaining information and engaging in financial transactions. Thus the relevant "year" ahead for which portfolio decisions are made is not the same for all

investors. Moreover, even if a decision is made with a view to fixing a portfolio for a given period of time, a portfolio is never so irrevocably frozen that there are no conceivable events during the period which would induce the investor to reconsider. The fact that this possibility is always open must influence the investor's decision. The fiction of a fixed investment period used in this paper is, therefore, not a wholly satisfactory way of taking account of the inertia in portfolio composition due to the costs of transactions and of decision making.

7. The size of their investment balances, held in cash and consols, may not vary by the full amount of these changes in wealth; some part of the changes may be reflected in holdings of assets other than monetary assets. But presumably the size of investment balances will reflect at least in part these capital gains and losses.

8. J. M. Keynes, *The General Theory of Employment, Interest and Money* (New York: Harcourt Brace & Co., 1936), Chapters 13 and 15, especially pp. 168–72 and 201–3. One quotation from page 172 will illustrate the point: "It is interesting that the stability of the system and its sensitiveness to changes in the quantity of money should be so dependent on the existence of a *variety* of opinion about what is uncertain. Best of all that we should know the future. But if not, then, if we are to control the activity of the economic system by changing the quantity of money, it is important that opinions should differ."

9. N. Kaldor, "Speculation and Economic Stability," *Review of Economic Studies*, Vol. 7 (October 1939), 15.

10. W. Leontief, "Postulates: Keynes' *General Theory* and the Classicists," Chapter 19 in S. E. Harris (ed.), *The New Economics* (New York: Knopf, 1947), pp. 232–42. Section 6, pp. 238–39, contains the specific criticism of Keynes' liquidity preference theory.

11. W. Fellner, *Monetary Policies and Full Employment* (Berkeley: University of California Press, 1946), p. 149.

12. See J. Von Neumann and O. Morgenstern, *Theory of Games and Economic Behavior*, 3rd ed. (Princeton: Princeton University Press, 1953), pp. 15–30, 617–32; I. N. Herstein and J. Milnor, "An Axiomatic Approach to Measurable Utility," *Econometrica*, Vol. 23 (April 1953), 291–97; J. Marschak, "Rational Behavior, Uncertain Prospects, and Measurable Utility," *Econometrica*, Vol. 18 (April 1950), 111–41; M. Friedman and L. J. Savage, "The Utility Analysis of Choices Involving Risk," *Journal of Political Economy*, Vol. 56 (August 1948), 279–304; and "The Expected Utility Hypothesis and the Measurability of Utility," *Journal of Political Economy*, Vol. 60 (December 1952), 463–74. For a treatment which also provides an axiomatic basis for the subjective probability estimates here assumed, see L. J. Savage, *The Foundations of Statistics* (New York: Wiley, 1954).

13. For this statement and its proof, I am greatly indebted to my colleague Arthur Okun. The proof is as follows:

If $r^2 \geq \sigma_g^2$, then by (3.15) and (3.10):

$$1 \geq A_2 \geq \frac{r}{2r^2}\left(-\frac{1+b}{2b}\right) \geq \frac{1}{2r}(r + g_{max})$$

From the two extremes of this series of inequalities it follows that $2r \geqq r + g_{max}$ or $r \geqq g_{max}$. Professor Okun also points out that this condition is incompatible with a tangency maximum if the distribution of g is symmetrical. For then $r \geqq g_{max}$ would imply $r + g_{min} \geqq 0$. There would be no possibility of net loss on consols and thus no reason to hold any cash.

14. Harry Markowitz's *Techniques of Portfolio Selection* (New York 1959), treats the general problem of finding dominant sets and computing the corresponding opportunity locus, for sets of securities all of which involve risk. Markowitz's main interest is prescription of rules of rational behaviour for investors; the main concern of this paper is the implications for economic theory, mainly comparative statics, that can be derived from assuming that investors do in fact follow such rules. For the general nature of Markowitz's approach, see his article, "Portfolio Selection," *Journal of Finance*, Vol. 7 (March 1952), 77–91.

7 A Dynamic Aggregative Model

James Tobin *Yale University*

Contemporary theoretical models of the business cycle and of economic growth typically possess two related characteristics: (1) they assume production functions that allow for no substitution between factors, and (2) the variables are all real magnitudes; monetary and price phenomena have no significance. Because of these characteristics, these models present a rigid and angular picture of the economic process: straight and narrow paths from which the slightest deviation spells disaster, abrupt and sharp reversals, intractable ceilings and floors. The models are highly suggestive, but their representation of the economy arouses the suspicion that they have left out some essential mechanisms of adjustment.

The purpose of this paper is to present a simple aggregative model that allows both for substitution possibilities and for monetary effects. The growth mechanism in the model is not radically different from the accelerator mechanism that plays the key role in other growth models. But it is unlike the accelerator mechanism in that there is not just one tenable rate of growth. As in accelerator models, growth is limited by the availability of factors other than capital. But here these limitations do not operate so abruptly, and they can be tempered by monetary and price adjustments that the accelerator models ignore.

The cyclical behavior of the model is similar to the nonlinear cyclical processes of Kaldor, Goodwin, and Hicks.[1] But the cycle

Reprinted from *Journal of Political Economy*, Vol. 63 (April 1955), 103–15, by permission of the author and The University of Chicago Press. Copyright 1955 by The University of Chicago Press.

172

in the present model depends in an essential way on the inflexibility of prices, money wages, or the supply of monetary assets.

Furthermore, the model to be described here does not restrict the economic process to two possibilities, steady growth or cycles. An alternative line of development is continuing underemployment—"stagnation" during which positive investment increases the capital stock and possibly the level of real income. This outcome, like the cycle, depends on some kind of price or monetary inflexibility.

In Part I the structure of the model will be described, and in Part II some of its implications will be examined.

I

The building blocks from which this model is constructed are four in number: (1) the saving function; (2) the production function; (3) asset preferences; and (4) labor-supply conditions.

THE SAVING FUNCTION

At any moment of time output is being produced at a rate Y, consumption is occurring at a rate C, and the capital stock, K, is growing at the rate $\dot{K}$, equal to $Y - C$. The saving function tells how output is divided between consumption and net investment:

$$\dot{K} = S(Y). \tag{1}$$

This relationship is assumed to hold instantaneously. That is, consumption is adjusted without lag to the simultaneous level of output; any output not consumed is an addition to the capital stock. Whether or not it is a welcome addition is another matter, which depends on the asset preferences of the community, discussed below.

Of the saving function, it is assumed that $S'(Y)$ is positive and that $S(Y)$ is zero for some positive Y. Otherwise the shape of the saving function is not crucial to the argument. Variables other than Y—for example, W, total real wealth—could be assumed to affect the propensity to save without involving more than inessential complications.

THE PRODUCTION FUNCTION

The rate of output, Y, depends jointly on the stock of capital in existence, K, and the rate of input of labor services, N:

$$Y = P(K, N). \tag{2}$$

The production function is assumed to be linear homogeneous. It follows that the marginal products are homogeneous functions of degree zero of the two factors; in other words, the marginal products depend only on the proportions in which the two inputs are being used. The real wage of labor, w, is equated by competition to the marginal product of labor; and the rent, r, per unit of time earned by ownership of any unit of capital is equated to the marginal product of capital:

$$w = P_N(K, N), \tag{3}$$

$$r = P_K(K, N). \tag{4}$$

If labor and capital expand over time in proportion, then output will expand in the same proportion, and both the real wage and the rent of capital will remain constant. If capital expands at a faster rate than labor, its rent must fall, and the real wage must rise.

A production function with constant returns to scale, both at any moment of time and over time, is a convenient beginning assumption. In judging the appropriateness of this kind of production function to the model, it should be remembered that, if it ignores technical improvement, on the one hand, it ignores limitations of other factors of production, "land," on the other. In the course of the argument the consequences of technological progress will be briefly discussed.

ASSET PREFERENCES

Only two stores of value, physical capital and currency, are available to owners of wealth in this economy. The own rate of return on capital is its rent, r, equal to its marginal product. Currency is wholly the issue of the state and bears an own rate of interest legally and permanently established. This rate will be assumed to be zero. The stock of currency, M, is exogenously determined and can be varied only by budget deficits or surpluses. The counterpart of this "currency" in the more complex asset structure of an actual economy is not money by the usual definition, which includes bank deposits corresponding to private debts. It is, for the United States, currency in circulation plus government debt plus the gold stock.[2]

If p is the price of goods in terms of currency, the community's total real wealth at any moment of time is

$$W = K + \frac{M}{p}. \tag{5}$$

Given K, M, and p, the community may be satisfied to split its wealth so that it holds as capital an amount equal to the available stock, K, and as currency an amount equal to the existing real supply, M/p. Such a situation will be referred to as "portfolio balance."

Portfolio balance is assumed to be the necessary and sufficient condition for price stability ($\dot{p} = 0$). If, instead, owners of wealth desire to hold more goods and less currency, they attempt to buy goods with currency. Prices are bid up ($\dot{p} > 0$). If they desire to shift in the other direction, they attempt to sell goods for currency ($\dot{p} < 0$). These price changes may, in turn, be associated with changes in output and employment; but that depends on other parts of the model, in particular on the conditions of labor supply.

What, then, determines whether an existing combination of K and M/p represents a situation of portfolio balance or imbalance? Portfolio balance is assumed in this model to be defined by the following functional relationship:

$$\frac{M}{p} = L(K, r, Y), \qquad L_K \gtreqless 0, \qquad L_r < 0, \qquad L_Y > 0. \qquad (6)$$

Requirements for transactions balances of currency are assumed, as is customary, to depend on income; this is the reason for the appearance of Y in the function. Given their real wealth, W, owners of wealth will wish to hold a larger amount of capital, and a smaller amount of currency, the higher the rent on capital, r. Given the rent on capital, owners of wealth will desire to put some part of any increment of their wealth into capital and some part into currency. It is possible that there are levels of r (e.g., negative rates) so low that portfolio balance requires all wealth to be in the form of currency and that there is some level of r above which wealth owners would wish to hold no currency. But the main argument to follow in part II concerns ranges of r between those extremes.

The assumption about portfolio balance has now been stated, and the reader who is more interested in learning its consequences than its derivation can proceed to the next section. But since this is the one of the four building blocks of the model that introduces possibly unconventional and unfamiliar material into the structure, it requires some discussion and defense.

The theory of portfolio balance implicit in most conventional aggregative economic theories of investment implies that rates of return on all assets must be equal. Applied to the two assets of the mythical economy of this paper, this theory would go as follows: Owners of wealth have a firm, certain, and unanimous expectation of the rate of price change, $\dot{p}_e$. This may or may not be the same as the actual rate of price change $\dot{p}$ at the same moment of time.[3] The rate at which a unit of wealth is expected to grow if it is held in the form of currency is, therefore, $-\dot{p}_e/p$.

Similarly, owners of wealth have a firm and unanimous view of the rate at which wealth will grow if it is held as physical capital. This rate is r_e, the expected market rent, which may or may not be the same as r. Owners of wealth will choose that portfolio which makes their wealth grow at the fastest rate. If $-\dot{p}_e/p$ were to exceed r_e, they would desire to hold all currency and no capital; if r_e were greater than $-\dot{p}_e/p$, they would desire to hold all capital and no currency. Only if the two rates are equal will they be satisfied to hold positive amounts of both assets; and, indeed, in that case, they will not care what the mix of assets is in their portfolios. On this theory of asset preferences the relative supplies of the assets do not matter. Whatever the supplies, portfolio balance requires that the real expected rates of return on the assets be equal. In particular, if $r_e = r$ and $\dot{p}_e = 0$, equilibrium requires that $r = 0$.

Keynes departed from this theory in his liquidity-preference explanation of the choice between cash balances and interest-bearing monetary assets. He was able to show that, given uncertainty or lack of unanimity in the expectations of wealth owners, the rate of interest that preserves portfolio balance between cash and "bonds" is not independent of the supplies of the two kinds of assets. But he did not apply the same reasoning to the much more important choice between physical goods or capital, on the one hand, and monetary assets, on the other. His theory of investment was orthodox in requiring equality between the marginal efficiency of capital and the rate of interest.

The assumptions behind the portfolio-balance equation in the present model, equation (6), may be briefly stated. Each owner of wealth entertains as possibilities numerous values of both r_e and $-\dot{p}_e/p$, and to each possible pair of values he attaches a probability. The expected value of r_e, that is, the mean of its marginal probability distribution, is assumed to be r. The expected value of $-\dot{p}_e/p$ is assumed to be zero. In other and less precise words, the owner of wealth expects *on balance* neither the rent of capital nor the price level to change. But he is not sure. The dispersions of possible rents and price changes above and below their expected values constitute the risks of the two assets.

Owners of wealth, it is further assumed, dislike risk. Of two portfolios with the same expected value of rate of return, an investor will prefer the one with the lower dispersion of rate of return.[4] The principle of "not putting all your eggs in one basket" explains why a risk-avoiding investor may well hold a diversified portfolio even when the expected returns of all the assets in it are not identical. For the present purpose it explains why an owner of wealth will hold currency in excess of transactions requirements, even when its expected return is zero and the expected return on capital is positive. It also explains why, given the risks associated with the two assets, an investor may desire to have more of his wealth in capital the larger is r. The higher the prospective yield of a portfolio, the greater is the inducement to accept the additional risks of heavier concentration on the more remunerative asset.[5]

LABOR SUPPLY

The behavior of the model depends in a crucial way on assumptions regarding the relations of the supply of labor to the real wage, to the money wage, and to time. It will be convenient, therefore, to introduce alternative assumptions in the course of the argument of part II.

II

STATIONARY EQUILIBRIUM

The model would be of little interest if its position of stationary equilibrium were inevitably and rapidly attained, but, for the sake of completeness, this position will be described first. There are any number of combinations of labor and capital that can produce the zero-saving level of output. To each combination corresponds a marginal productivity of labor, to which the real wage must be equal; this marginal productivity is higher the more capital-intensive the combination. Suppose there is a unique relation between the supply of labor and the real wage. An equilibrium labor-capital combination is one that demands labor in an amount equal to the supply forthcoming at the real wage corresponding to that combination. The equilibrium absolute price level is then determined by the portfolio-balance equation. Given the rent and amount of capital in the equilibrium combination and the supply of currency, portfolio balance must be obtained by a price level that provides the appropriate amount of real wealth in liquid form.

BALANCED GROWTH

Proportional growth of capital, income, and employment implies, according to the assumed production function, constancy of capital rent, r, and the real wage, w. Maintenance of portfolio balance requires, therefore, an increase in M/p. Given the supply of currency, the price level must fall continuously over time. Balanced growth requires an expanding labor supply, available at the same real wage and at an ever decreasing money wage.

GROWTH WITH CAPITAL DEEPENING

In this model, unlike those of Harrod, Hicks, and others, failure of the labor supply to grow at the rate necessary for balanced growth does not mean that growth at a slower rate is impossible. If the real wage must rise in order to induce additional labor supply, the rent of capital must, it is true, fall as capital grows. Portfolio balance requires, therefore, that a given increment of capital be accompanied by a greater price decline than in the case of balanced growth. But there is some rate of price decline that will preserve portfolio balance, even in the extreme case of completely inelastic labor supply. Although the rate of price decline per increment of capital is greater the less elastic the supply of labor with respect to the real wage and with respect to time, the time rate of price decline is not necessarily faster. The growth of income, saving, and capital is slower when labor is less elastic, and it takes longer to achieve the same increment of capital.

TECHNOLOGICAL PROGRESS AND PRICE DEFLATION

The preceding argument has assumed an unchanging production function with constant returns to scale. In comparison with that case, technological progress is deflationary to the extent that a more rapid growth of income augments transactions requirements for currency. But technological progress has offsetting inflationary effects to the extent that it raises the marginal productivity of capital corresponding to given inputs of capital and labor. Conceivably technical improvement can keep the rent on capital rising even though its amount relative to the supply of labor is increasing. This rise might even be sufficient to keep the demand for real currency balances from rising, in spite of the growth of the capital stock and of transactions requirements. At the other extreme, it is possible to imagine technological progress that fails to raise or even lowers the marginal productivity of capital corresponding to given inputs of the two factors. Progress of this kind contains nothing to counteract the deflationary pressures of a growing capital stock, declining capital rent, and increasing transactions needs.

MONETARY EXPANSION AS AN ALTERNATIVE TO PRICE DEFLATION

Growth with continuous price deflation strains the assumption that wealth owners expect, on balance, the price level to remain constant. The process itself would teach them that the expected value of the real return on currency is positive, and it would perhaps also reduce their estimates of the dispersion of possible returns on currency. This lesson would increase the relative attractiveness of currency as a store of value and thus force an ever faster rate of price decline.

An alternative to price deflation is expansion of the supply of currency. As noted above, monetary expansion cannot, in this model, be accomplished by monetary policy in the conventional sense but must be the result of deficit financing.[6] Assume that the government deficit $\dot{M}$ takes the form of transfer payments. Then equation (1) must be changed to read:

$$\dot{K} + \frac{\dot{M}}{p} = S\left(Y + \frac{\dot{M}}{p}\right). \tag{7}$$

The normal result is that consumption will be a larger and investment a smaller share of a given level of real income. Thus, the greater is $\dot{M}$, the slower will be the rate of capital expansion. At the same time the growth of the currency supply meets growing transactions requirements and satisfies the desire of wealth owners to balance increased holdings of capital, possibly yielding lower rents, with enlarged holdings of liquid wealth.

That there is a time path of M compatible with price stability may be seen by considering the inflationary consequences of large values of $\dot{M}$. There is presumably a value of $\dot{M}$ large enough so that the desire of the community to save at the disposable income level $Y + \dot{M}/p$ would be satisfied by saving at the rate $\dot{M}/p$. Then the capital stock would remain constant, its marginal product would stay constant, and transactions requirements would remain unchanged. Portfolio balance could then be maintained only by inflation at the same rate as $\dot{M}/M$. Somewhere between this value of $\dot{M}$ and zero there is a rate of growth of the currency supply compatible with price stability.

WAGE INFLEXIBILITY AS AN OBSTACLE TO GROWTH

If the currency supply grows too slowly, the necessity that price deflation—probably an ever faster price deflation—accompany growth casts considerable doubt on the viability of the growth processes described above. This doubt arises from the institutional limits on downward flexibility of prices, in particular money wage rates, characteristic of actual economies. The purpose of this and the two following sections is to analyze the behavior of the system when money wage rates are inflexible.

For this analysis it is convenient to work with two relationships between the price level, p, and employment of labor, N. Both relationships assume a constant capital stock, K. The first, called the "labor market balance" (LMB) relation, gives for any level of employment, N, the price level, p, that equates the marginal productivity of labor to the real wage. Given the money wage, this p is higher for larger values of N, because the marginal product of labor declines with employment with a given capital stock. This relation is shown in Figures 1a and 1b as curve LMB. The level of employment N_f is the maximum labor supply that can be induced at the given money wage. At that level of employment the money wage becomes flexible upward. If the money wage is raised or lowered, the LMB curve will shift up or down proportionately. If the capital stock is expanded, the LMB curve will shift downward, because an addition to capital will raise the marginal product of labor at any level of employment.

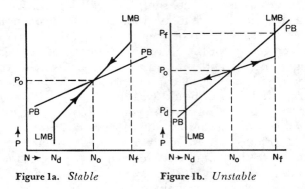

Figure 1a. *Stable*   **Figure 1b.** *Unstable*

The second relation between the same two variables, p and N, is the "portfolio balance" relation PB, also shown in Figures 1a and 1b. As the name indicates, it shows for any level of employment the price level required for portfolio balance between the given stock of capital K and the given supply of currency M. Its slope may be either positive or negative. The marginal productivity of the given stock of capital, and hence the rent of capital, is greater the higher the volume of employment. Currency is thus a relatively less attractive asset at higher levels of employment; so far as this effect is concerned, the price level must be higher at higher levels of employment in order to reduce the real supply of currency. The transactions relation of demand for currency to the level of real income works, however, in the opposite direction. Whatever its slope, the PB curve will, for obvious reasons, shift upward if currency supply M is expanded, and downward if capital expands.

It is not possible to establish a priori which curve, LMB or PB, has the greater slope. The two possibilities are shown in Figures 1a and 1b. In Figure 1a the LMB curve has the greater slope; both curves are drawn with positive slopes, but the *PB* curve could equally well have a negative slope. In Figure 1b the *PB* curve has the greater slope. As indicated by the arrows, the intersection (p_0, N_0) is a stable short-run equilibrium in Figure 1a but an unstable one in Figure 1b. This follows from the assumption that $\dot{p}$ will be positive, zero, or negative, depending on whether wealth owners regard their currency holdings as too large, just right, or too small.[7] In Figure 1b (p_f, N_f) is a stable short-run equilibrium. And there may be another stable intersection (p_d, N_d). Here N_d would be a level of employment so low and, correspondingly, a real wage so high that the rigidity of the money wage breaks down.

Capital expansion shifts both the *LMB* and the *PB* curve downward. How does capital expansion affect the point (p_0, N_0)? The following results are proved in the Appendix: When the intersection (p_0, N_0) is an unstable point (Figure 1b), capital expansion increases both N_0 and p_0. The *PB* curve shifts more than the *LMB* curve, and their intersection moves northeast. The qualitative effect of capital expansion may be depicted graphically by imagining the *PB* curve to shift downward while the *LMB* curve stays put. The same argument shows that capital accumulation moves a point like (p_f, N_f) or (p_d, N_d) in Figure 1b downward, while capital decumulation moves it upward. When the intersection (p_0, N_0) is a stable point (Figure 1a), the argument of the Appendix indicates that capital expansion necessarily lowers p_0 but may either increase or decrease N_0; the intersection may move either southeast or southwest. It is, in other words, not possible to say which curve shifts more as a consequence of a given change in the capital stock.

These results permit consideration of the question whether growth with full employment of labor is compatible with a floor on the money-wage rate. Except in the case where labor supply grows as rapidly as capital or more rapidly, the growth process brings about an increase of the real wage. A certain amount of price deflation is therefore compatible with rigidity of the money wage. But, according to the results reported in the previous paragraph, certainly in the unstable case and possibly in the stable case, too, the amount of price deflation needed to maintain portfolio balance is too much to enable employment to be maintained at a rigid money wage. Capital growth shifts the *PB* curve down more than the *LMB* curve. However, it is also possible in the stable case that the *LMB* curve shifts more than the *PB* curve, so that employment could be maintained and even increased while the money wage remains rigid and prices fall. But even this possibility depends on the assumption that wealth owners balance their portfolios on the expectation that the price level will remain the same.

As noted above, it is only realistic to expect that a process of deflation would itself teach owners of wealth to expect price deflation rather than price stability. Such expectations would inevitably so enhance the relative attractiveness of currency as an asset that the process could not continue without a reduction of the money-wage rate.

WAGE INFLEXIBILITY AND CYCLICAL FLUCTUATIONS

It is the situation depicted in Figure 1b that gives rise to the possibility of a cycle formally similar to those of Kaldor, Goodwin, and Hicks. Suppose the economy is at point (p_f, N_f). Capital expansion will sooner or later cause this point to coincide with (p_0, N_0) at a point like R in Figure 2. This day will be hastened by any inflation in the money-wage floor fostered by full employment; it may be that, once having enjoyed the money wage corresponding to (p_f, N_f) in Figure 1b, labor will not accept any lower money wage. Once R is reached, any further capital expansion will require a price decline that will push the real wage of labor, given that the money wage cannot fall, above its marginal productivity. Employers will therefore contract employment. But this does not obviate the necessity of price deflation. Indeed, it aggravates it, because the reduction of employment lowers the marginal productivity of capital. Balance cannot be restored both in the labor market and in wealth holdings until a level of employment is reached at which the wage rate becomes flexible downward (N_d in Figure 2).

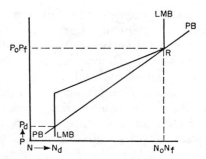

Figure 2.

The permanence of this "floor" equilibrium depends upon the saving function. If positive saving occurs at the levels of income produced by labor supply N_d, capital expansion will continue; and so also will price and wage deflation. Increase of employment then depends on the willingness of labor to accept additional employment at the low level to which severe unemployment has driven the money wage. Willingness to accept additional employment at this money wage may be encouraged by the increase in the real wage due to continued capital accumulation. A sufficient lowering of the money-wage rate demanded for increased employment would result in a situation like that represented by point S in Figure 3, and full employment could be restored.

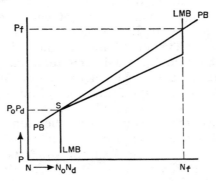

Figure 3.

Alternatively, the "floor" may correspond to a level of income at which there is negative saving. The gradual attrition of the capital stock will then move the PB curve up relative to the LMB curve. As capital becomes scarcer, its marginal product rises; and for both reasons its attractiveness relative to that of currency increases. Whatever happens to the money-wage terms on which labor will accept additional employment, the decumulation of capital will eventually lead to a position like S in Figure 3.

Once S is reached, any further reduction in the money wage, or any further decumulation of capital, will lead to an expansion of employment. But increasing employment only enhances the relative attractiveness of the existing stock of capital, causing the price level to rise and employment to be still further increased. As Figure 3 shows, the only stopping point is (p_f, N_f). Once N_f is reached, the money wage becomes flexible upward and follows the price level upward until portfolio balance is restored at the price level p_f. The cycle then repeats itself.

The floor in this model is provided by a level of employment so low, and a real wage correspondingly so high, that money-wage rates become flexible downward. The breakdown of money-wage rigidity may also be interpreted as a function of time; as Leontief has suggested, money-wage rigidity may not reflect any persistent "money illusion" on the part of workers and their organizations but only a lag in their perception of the price level to use in reckoning their real wage.[8] Trouble occurs at full employment, even when real wages are increasing, because the time rate of price deflation becomes too fast in relation to this lag. Likewise, contraction of employment can be stopped and even reversed when money-wage demands have had time to catch up with what has been happening to the price level.

In this discussion of the floor it has been assumed that the rate of capital decumulation is controlled by the saving function. An interesting question arises when the saving function indicates dissaving at a rate higher than that at which the capital stock can physically decumulate. In the models of Goodwin and Hicks, in fact, the floor is the level of income at which dissaving equals the maximum possible rate of capital decumulation.

A physical limit on the rate of capital decumulation cannot really be handled within the framework of an aggregative model that takes account of only one industry, one commodity, and one price level. Such a model assumes that the output of the economy is essentially homogeneous and can equally well be consumed or accumulated in productive stocks, from which it can be withdrawn at will. If capital goods and consumers' goods are regarded as less than perfect substitutes, it is necessary to imagine that they have different price levels. Encountering a Goodwin-Hicks floor would then mean that the two price levels diverge. At any lower level of income the community would be unable to consume capital at the rate at which it wished to dissave. Consequently, the community would dissave from its holdings of currency. This would stop the fall in the price level of consumption goods and make the Goodwin-Hicks floor an equilibrium level of employment and income. The price of capital goods would continue to fall as owners of wealth attempted to convert capital into either currency or consumption. This fall in the value of capital goods would restore portfolio balance—even though consumers' goods prices ceased to fall and money-wage rates remained rigid—by making capital a smaller proportion of the community's wealth.

With the model thus amended, the physical limit on capital decumulation provides a floor that will stop and eventually reverse a contraction even if the money-wage rate is intractable. But the contraction need not proceed to this extreme, if the wage-flexibility floor described above occurs at a higher level of employment and output.

WAGE INFLEXIBILITY AND STAGNATION

The cycle just described arises from the situation depicted in Figure 1b. But the situation of Figure 1a, where the LMB curve has an algebraically greater slope than the PB curve and the intersection (p_0, N_0) is a stable equilibrium, also is a possibility. In this case the intersection may move to the left as the capital stock increases. Growth of capital is accompanied by reduction of employment, so long as the money-wage rate is maintained. This process may end in a stationary equilibrium position if it entails such a reduction in output (or, if wealth is relevant to the saving function, such an increase in wealth) as to reduce saving to zero. But it is also possible that a process with positive saving, growth of capital, and increasing unemployment will continue indefinitely.

SUMMARY

The simple aggregative model that has been presented here differs from others used in discussions of growth and cycles in two main respects. The production function allows for substitution between capital and labor. The willingness of the community to hold physical capital depends on its rate of return and on the value of the liquid wealth held by the community. These two assumptions provide a link, generally absent in other models, between the world of real magnitudes and the world of money and prices. This link provides the model with some adjustment mechanisms ignored in other growth and cycle models. The following conclusions result:

1. Growth is possible at a great variety of rates and is not necessarily precluded when the labor supply grows slowly or remains constant.

2. The course of the price level as capital grows depends on (*a*) the accompanying rate of expansion of the labor force, (*b*) the rate at which the supply of currency is augmented by government deficits, and (*c*) the rate of technological progress. The first two factors are both inflationary. Technological progress has mixed effects. In the absence of monetary expansion and technological progress, price deflation is a necessary concomitant of growth even when the labor supply is increasing just as rapidly as capital. In these circumstances, therefore, growth with stable or increasing employment cannot continue if the money-range rate is inflexible downward.

3. Given wage inflexibility, the system may alternate between high and low levels of employment and, concurrently, between periods of price inflation and deflation. The ceiling to this cyclical process is provided by inelasticity of the labor supply. The floor may be provided either by the breakdown of the rigid money wage or by physical limits on the rate of consumption of capital. Alternatively, the system may "stagnate" at less than full employment, quite conceivably with capital growth and reduction of employment occurring at the same time. Whether the system behaves in this manner or with cyclical fluctuations depends on the relation between the conditions of portfolio balance and the rate of return

on capital. The greater the shift in portfolios that owners of wealth wish to make when the rate of return on capital changes, the more likely it is that the system will have a cyclical solution.

Appendix

The equation of the labor-market-balance curve, for given K, is

$$pP_N(K, N) = w_0, \tag{1}$$

where w_0 is the rigid money-wage rate. The slope of this curve is

$$\left(\frac{dp}{dN}\right)_{LMB} = \frac{-p^2 P_{NN}}{w_0}. \tag{2}$$

Since $P_{NN} < 0$, this slope is positive.

The equation of the portfolio-balance curve, for given K and M, is

$$M = pL(K, r, Y)$$
$$= pL(K, P_K[K, N], P[K, N]). \tag{3}$$

The slope of this curve is

$$\left(\frac{dp}{dN}\right)_{PB} = \frac{-p^2}{M}(L_r P_{KN} + L_Y P_N). \tag{4}$$

Since $L_r < 0$, $P_{KN} > 0$, and $L_Y > 0$, this slope may be either positive or negative.

The point (p_0, N_0) is determined by the intersection of (1) and (3). The problem is to find the changes in p_0 and N_0 associated with an increase in K.

Differentiating (1) and (3) with respect to K gives

$$\frac{\partial p_0}{\partial K}\left(\frac{w_0}{p_0}\right) + \frac{\partial N_0}{\partial K}(p_0 P_{NN}) = -p_0 P_{NK}, \tag{5}$$

$$\frac{\partial p_0}{\partial K}\left(\frac{M}{p_0}\right) + \frac{\partial N_0}{\partial K}(p_0 L_r P_{KN} + p_0 L_Y P_N)$$
$$= -p_0 L_K - p_0 L_r P_{KK} - p_0 L_Y P_K. \tag{6}$$

Equations (5) and (6) give the following solutions:

$$\frac{\partial p_0}{\partial K} = -\frac{p^2}{D}(P_{NK}^2 L_r - P_{NN} P_{KK} L_r$$
$$- L_K P_{NN} + P_{NK} P_N L_Y - P_{NN} P_K L_Y), \tag{7}$$

$$\frac{\partial N_0}{\partial K} = -\frac{1}{D}(w_0 L_K + w_0 L_r P_{KK} - M P_{NK} + w_0 L_Y P_K), \tag{8}$$

where

$$D = w_0 L_r P_{KN} - M P_{NN} + w_0 L_Y P_N. \tag{9}$$

From (2), (4), and (9), it can be concluded that D will be positive, zero, or negative according as the slope of the LMB curve is greater than, equal to, or less than the slope of the PB curve. In the stable case (Figure 1a), D is positive. In the unstable case (Figure 1b), D is negative.

The production function is assumed to be homogeneous of degree one. Consequently,

$$P_N N + P_K K = P.$$

Differentiating this with respect to N and K gives

$$P_{NN} N + P_{KN} K = 0, \tag{10}$$

$$P_{NK} N + P_{KK} K = 0. \tag{11}$$

Using (10) and (11) in (7) gives

$$\frac{\partial p_0}{\partial K} = \frac{-p_0^2}{D} (P_{NN} L_K + P_{NK} P_N L_Y - P_{NN} L_K L_Y). \tag{12}$$

Since P_{NN} is negative, this derivative has the opposite sign of D. Consequently, in the stable case it is negative, and in the unstable case it is positive.

Using (9), (10), and (11) in (8) gives

$$\frac{\partial N_0}{\partial K} = \frac{1}{D} \left(\frac{N}{K} D - w_0 L_K - w_0 L_Y \frac{Y}{K} \right), \tag{13}$$

where L_K and L_Y are positive. Consequently, if D is negative—the unstable case—$\partial N_0 / \partial K$ must be positive. But if D is positive—the stable case—the derivative may have either sign.

A point like (p_f, N_f) represents the intersection of the portfolio-balance curve (3) with a vertical labor-market-balance curve. To find out whether employment can be maintained at N_f when K is increased, it is necessary only to find $\partial w_0 / \partial K$ for fixed N_f from (1) and (3). If this $\partial w_0 / \partial K$ is negative, then maintenance of employment is not consistent with maintenance of portfolio balance unless the money-wage floor w_0 is lowered. If the derivative is zero or positive, then employment can be maintained or indeed increased even though the money-wage rate remains fixed or rises. Differentiating (1) and (3) with respect to K, for fixed N, gives:

$$\frac{\partial w_0}{\partial K} - \frac{\partial p_f}{\partial K} \left(\frac{w_0}{p_f} \right) = p_f P_{NK}, \tag{14}$$

$$\frac{\partial p_f}{\partial K} \left(\frac{M}{p_f} \right) = -p_f L_K - p_f L_r P_{KK} - p_f L_Y P_K. \tag{15}$$

Therefore:

$$\frac{\partial w_0}{\partial K} = \frac{-w_0 L_K - w_0 L_r P_{KK} - w_0 L_Y P_K + M P_{NK}}{M / p_f}. \tag{16}$$

Comparing (8) and (16),

$$\left(\frac{\partial w_0}{\partial K}\right)_{N\text{const.}} = \frac{D}{M/p_f}\left(\frac{\partial N_0}{\partial K}\right)_{w_0\text{const.}} \tag{17}$$

From the conclusions previously reached with the aid of (13), it follows that, when D is negative (unstable case), $\partial w_0/\partial_K$ is negative. But when D is positive (stable case), $\partial w_0/\partial K$ may have either sign.

NOTES

1. N. Kaldor, "A Model of the Trade Cycle," *Economic Journal,* Vol. 50 (March 1940), 78–92; R. Goodwin, "The Nonlinear Accelerator and the Persistence of Business Cycles," *Econometrica,* Vol. 19 (January 1951), 1–17, and "Econometrics in Business Cycle Analysis," in A. H. Hansen, *Business Cycles and National Income* (New York: W. W. Norton & Co., 1951), Chapter 22; J. R. Hicks, *A Contribution to the Theory of the Trade Cycle* (Oxford: Oxford University Press, 1950).

2. This is the same concept developed in connection with discussions of the "Pigou effect"; see Herbert Stein, "Price Flexibility and Full Employment: Comment," *American Economic Review,* Vol. 39 (June 1949), 725–26; and Don Patinkin, "Price Flexibility and Full Employment: Reply," *American Economic Review,* Vol. 39 (June 1949), 726–28.

3. An individual may be assumed to know the historical course of prices $p(t)$ up to the present (for $t \lesseqgtr t_0$) and to expect a future course of prices $p_e(t)$ (for $\gtreqless t_0$). Presumably the expected course starts at the same price at which the historical course ends ($p[t_0] = p_e[t_0]$). But there is no reason that one should start with the same slope with which the other ends: $p'(t_0)$, referred to in the text as $\dot{p}$, is not necessarily the same as $p'_e(t_0)$, referred to in the test as $\dot{p}_e$.

4. Risk aversion in this sense may be deduced from the assumption of generally declining marginal utility of income. Here, however, it is not necessary to go into the question of the usefulness of the concept of cardinal utility in explaining behavior under uncertainty.

5. There is an "income effect" working in the opposite direction. The portfolio-balance function, equation (6), assumes the substitution effect to be dominant.

6. The implications of the approach of this paper concerning the effects of conventional monetary policy are left for discussion elsewhere. Clearly such a discussion requires the introduction of additional types of assets, including bank deposits and private debts.

7. Employment has been assumed always to be at the point where the marginal product of labor equals the real wage. But the conclusions on the stability of (p_0, N_0) in Figures 1a and 1b would not be altered if it were assumed instead that $\dot{N}$ is positive, zero, or negative depending on whether the marginal product of labor exceeds, equals, or is less than the real wage.

8. W. Leontief, "Postulates: Keynes' *General Theory* and the Classicists," in S. E. Harris (ed.), *The New Economics* (New York: Knopf, 1947), Chapter 19.

8 The Demand for Money Revisited

Stephen M. Goldfeld *Princeton University*

The money market is a critical component of virtually all theories that explain the evolution of aggregate economic activity. More particularly, an accurate understanding and portrayal of this market is essential both to the analysis of past monetary policies and to the formulation of appropriate contemporary policy. This paper focuses on one aspect of the money market, the demand side, and provides an extensive review of the current state of the art concerning the demand for money. The emphasis will be unabashedly empirical, with concentration on the short term, taken here to be quarterly, since this horizon appears to be the most relevant to policy purposes.[1]

There has been a substantial amount of past research on the demand for money and several survey pieces as well.[2] Nevertheless, a number of good reasons argue for embarking on another broad empirical effort. In the first instance, until recently research with quarterly data had not been that extensive. Consequently, most of the received wisdom on the subject stems from empirical work with long-term annual data[3] whose relevance for short-term purposes is questionable.[4]

A second reason for undertaking a broad empirical effort is that much of the existing evidence stems from the work of researchers who have each used a different sample period, measurement method, and

Reprinted from *Brookings Papers on Economic Activity,* Arthur M. Okun and George L. Perry, editors (1973, no. 3), 576–638, by permission of the author and publisher. © 1973 by the Brookings Institution, Washington, D.C.

estimating technique. There is much to be said for attacking the substantial range of issues that I wish to examine in a homogeneous and consistent manner. This procedure seems all the more desirable since it will permit me to use the latest data uniformly, which seems important in view of the varied behavior of money and interest rates in recent years.[5]

A final motivation for this paper is that recent events have raised the question, in both the popular and the professional press, as to whether the conventional money demand formulation is adequate to explain the monetary experience of the seventies. For example, from early to mid-1971 the money stock rose rapidly but so did short-term interest rates. Over roughly the next half-year money grew at a meager 1 percent rate but interest rates fell below their early 1971 lows. Both during this period and subsequently, observers questioned whether the economy had experienced short-run shifts in the demand for money. More recently, the first half of 1973 saw sharply rising interest rates. But while the money stock rose only marginally in the first quarter, it spurted ahead at the annual rate of 11 percent in the second quarter. Once again the press has referred to the puzzling behavior of the demand for money. The basic issue is whether the demand function for money can be assumed by the policy maker to be essentially stable in the short run. This issue, which has not been examined previously in any great detail, will receive particular emphasis in this paper.

Outline

The plan of the paper is as follows. The next section briefly spells out the conventional story on the origins and general nature of the demand for money and then reports estimates of one simple and common version of the money demand function. The estimates are then analyzed with primary focus on the following two questions:

1. Is there any evidence of economies of scale in aggregate money holdings? Is there any indication, as previously has been suggested, that the income elasticity is difficult to pin down from quarterly data?

2. Has the demand function for money remained stable over the postwar period? Put another way, is there any evidence of either systematic long-run shifts or marked short-run instabilities that makes historically estimated relationships unsuitable for forecasting purposes?

The results of that section will serve as a rough standard for considering other important issues on the proper specification of the money demand function that are taken up in the third section:

3. What degree of aggregation is appropriate with respect to currency, demand deposits, and time deposits?

4. What sorts of lags appear to be present in the adjustment of money holdings and what rationale can be offered to explain these lags?

5. Is there any evidence that expected rates of inflation measured either directly or indirectly influence the demand for money?

6. Should income, or wealth, or perhaps both, be used in the demand function?

In the fourth section a number of more technical issues are explored:

7. Which interest rates work best in explaining the demand for money?

8. Are estimated demand-for-money functions sensitive to the time unit used to construct the aggregate data?

9. How important are the problems of serial correlation and simultaneous equations bias in the demand for money?

10. Is the demand for money homogeneous with respect to prices or population?

The fifth section examines the problems of disaggregation in somewhat more detail, using the flow of funds data on holdings by type of holder (business and consumers and the rest). The basic question is whether separate analysis of more homogeneous groups of money holders can improve understanding of the money demand process and the ability to forecast the demand for money. The paper concludes with a summary of the main results and an attempt to draw some lessons from them.

As the outline suggests, I shall cover a fairly broad range of issues on the specification and properties of the demand-for-money function. While these questions are clearly interrelated, simultaneous consideration of all of them would be a strategic and expositional monstrosity. Consequently, except where it seems particularly warranted, I shall try to avoid a flood of permutations and alternative specifications. Even so, some may regard the output as a "junior encyclopedia" if not the full-fledged thing.

Some Underpinnings

The conventional textbook formulation of the demand for money typically relates the demand for real money balances, $m = M/P$, assumed to be noninterest bearing[6]—to "the" interest rate, r, and some measure of economic activity such as real GNP, $y = Y/P$, where M = money holdings, P = the price level, and Y = gross national product. Thus

$$m = f(r, y). \tag{1}$$

A variety of stories can explain the origins of equation (1). Perhaps the most satisfying is the transactions view, in which the demand for money evolves from a lack of synchronization between receipts and payments and the existence of a transactions cost in exchanging money for interest-bearing assets (usually taken to be short term).

One example of this approach is the well-known Baumol-Tobin formulation which readily leads to an equation of the form of (1). Its simplest version is the so-called square root law of money holdings,[7]

$$m = ky^{\frac{1}{2}}r^{-\frac{1}{2}}, \tag{1'}$$

where k is related to the transactions cost. This implies that the income elasticity of the demand for money is $\frac{1}{2}$ while the interest elasticity is $-\frac{1}{2}$.

Other analyses of the demand for money emphasize speculative, precautionary, or utility considerations in addition to the transactions motive.[8] These tend to blur the specific predictions of income and interest rate elasticities that emerge from the simple transactions approach, but they are broadly consistent with the general form of equation (1).[9]

At an empirical level such an equation has underpinned estimation in a number of studies of the demand for money. This has typically been the case where annual data are involved. With quarterly data, empirical workers have generally resorted to a more complicated version of (1) involving lagged as well as current variables. At least two motivations—not necessarily conflicting—have been offered for modifying (1) in this way, the partial adjustment mechanism and expectations formation. For the present only the former justification is explored, but the expectational lag will be considered more extensively below.

The ubiquitous partial adjustment assumption usually proceeds by interpreting (1) as setting a "desired" value for money holdings, say m^*, as in

$$m^* = f(r, y) \tag{2}$$

Portfolio adjustment costs, both pecuniary and nonpecuniary, are then assumed to prevent a full, immediate, adjustment of actual money holdings to desired levels. Depending upon the functional form of (2), actual money holdings are assumed to adjust linearly or logarithmically to the gap between desired holdings and last period's holdings; that is,

$$m_t - m_{t-1} = \gamma(m_t^* - m_{t-1}), \tag{3}$$

or

$$\ln m_t - \ln m_{t-1} = \gamma(\ln m_t^* - \ln m_{t-1}), \tag{3'}$$

where γ is the coefficient of adjustment. While, as demonstrated below, the partial adjustment model is not without its shortcomings, it seems, in view of its widespread use, a convenient starting point for empirical work.

A CONVENTIONAL EQUATION

The first step is estimating an equation following the format of (3') and (1') above. Detailed definitions of the variables are found in the appendix but a few words on the matter are in order here. The narrow money stock (currency plus demand deposits, M_1) is used as the dependent variable; it is measured as a quarterly average of monthly data and deflated by the implicit GNP deflator. Income was defined as real GNP and the interest rate was measured in two ways—by the rate on commercial paper (RCP) and by the rate on time deposits (RTD). The results obtained with ordinary least squares, using the Cochrane-Orcutt technique to adjust for serial correlation, are given below (the numbers in parentheses here and in following equations are t-statistics):

$$\ln m = 0.271 + 0.193 \ln y + 0.717 \ln m_{-1}$$
$$\quad\;\; (2.2) \quad\; (5.3) \qquad\quad (11.5)$$

$$- \ 0.019 \ln RCP - 0.045 \ln RTD. \quad (4)$$
$$(6.0) \qquad\qquad\;\; (4.0)$$

$R^2 = 0.995$; $\rho = 0.414$; standard error $= 0.0043$; Durbin-Watson statistic $= 1.73$.
Sample period $= 1952:2–1972:4$.[10]

At first glance this equation seems quite reasonable. Both the commercial paper rate and the time deposit rate are significant, with long-run elasticities of 0.07 and 0.16, respectively. The coefficient of adjustment—that is, γ in (3')—is 0.283 ($= 1 - 0.717$); while this is not dramatically rapid, it is certainly more plausible than the slow 0–10 percent estimates that some writers have reported.[11] The point estimate of the long-run income elasticity is 0.68 and a 95 percent confidence interval for the income elasticity, derived by a method due to Fieller,[12] turns out to be (0.60, 0.82). Consequently, the income elasticity appears to be significantly less than unity.[13]

Besides yielding plausible parameter values, equation (4) also fits the data quite well. This can be seen in Figure 1, which depicts the actual values of the real money stock along with the values predicted by equation (4).

INCOME ELASTICITY: A CLOSER LOOK

While equation (4) seems to be a satisfactory first approximation to a money demand function, the results need closer scrutiny.

Billions of dollars

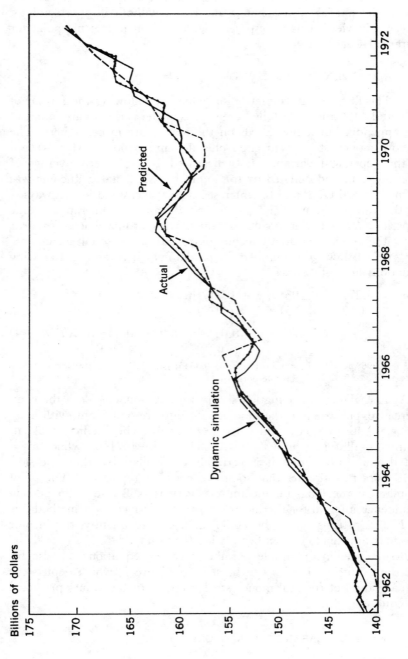

Figure 1. *Actual and Predicted Values of Real Money Stock, Quarterly, 1962–72*

One aspect that deserves additional attention is the estimate of the long-run income elasticity. Judged by the size of the confidence interval reported above, the estimate of this important parameter appears to be fairly precise. On the other hand, William Poole [27] has suggested that the income elasticity estimated from quarterly postwar data really cannot be pinned down accurately. Since it will shed some further light on the quality of the estimates in (4), a brief exploration of Poole's argument will be worthwhile.

Suppose an estimating equation takes the form

$$\ln m_t = a + b \ln y_t + c \ln r_t + d \ln m_{t-1} \tag{5}$$

The short-run income elasticity is b while the long-run elasticity is $b/(1-d)$. Suppose the long-run elasticity is constrained to be some number e. Equation (5) then becomes

$$\ln m_t - e \ln y_t = a + c \ln r_t + d(\ln m_{t-1} - e \ln y_t), \tag{6}$$

which for a given e could then be simply estimated. A comparison of the properties of (6) for alternative values of e could then be made. Poole tried values of e ranging from 0.5 to 3.0 and emphasized two properties of the resulting estimates He found that the estimated interest elasticity steadily increased with e, rising to 2.5–2.7 for $e = 3.0$; and the R^2 of the estimated equation was essentially flat for values of e from 1 to 3. It was this latter finding that led Poole to suggest the impossibility of obtaining a firm estimate of the income elasticity.

The equation Poole primarily focused on had one interest rate variable and no lagged dependent variable; it was, that is, like (6) with $d = 0$. It is consequently of some interest to see how equation (4) behaves for alternative values of e. Table 1 reports the relevant results, giving long-run interest elasticities for RTD and RCP, the speed-of-adjustment parameter, γ, and the R^2 and standard error. The interest elasticities display a clear tendency to increase with e, but the rise is not nearly as pronounced as Poole found.[14] The table also shows a systematic decline in the speed of adjustment as e increases.

As for the relative explanatory power of the equation as e increases, the table points to uniformly high R^2s, which rise steadily with e. That this is misleading, however, is plain in the second row of the table, which was obtained by constraining e to be the value implied by equation (4). This procedure naturally reproduced the results of that equation except for the R^2. The trouble is that the dependent variable in (6) changes as e changes and consequently the R^2 is not strictly comparable across rows of the table.[15] The standard error of the regression, which is comparable, tells a different story. It clearly is lowest for the equation reported in the second row, as it should be. As e rises so does the standard error, although the deterioration is mild.

TABLE 1 *Effects of Alternative Long-run Income Elasticity Constraints on Money Demand Equation*

Constrained elasticity	Interest elasticities		Speed-of-adjustment parameter	R^2	Standard error	Root mean-squared error		
	Time deposits	Commercial paper				Sample period		Ex post to 1972,[b] dollar level[a]
						Log	Dollar level[a]	
0.6	0.135	0.049	0.325	0.9976	0.00441	0.0105	1.29	3.65
0.68[c]	0.160	0.066	0.283	0.9984	0.00432	0.0093	1.11	1.65
0.8	0.177	0.101	0.192	0.9989	0.00441	0.0099	1.29	2.71
0.9	0.186	0.136	0.140	0.9991	0.00450	0.0106	1.51	5.28
1.0	0.193	0.178	0.107	0.9993	0.00457	0.0112	1.68	7.90
1.1	0.194	0.222	0.086	0.9995	0.00462	0.0128	1.79	10.46
1.5	0.193	0.400	0.046	0.9997	0.00472	0.0150	2.03	19.81
2.0	0.184	0.633	0.028	0.9999	0.00477	0.0154	2.11	29.58

Sources: Derived from equation (4), as discussed in the text. For data sources and definitions, see appendix.

a. In billions of 1958 dollars.

b. Obtained by estimating equation (4) through 1961 and extrapolating forward by dynamic simulation to the end of 1972.

c. Full sample constraint.

Another, perhaps more useful, way of looking at the overall performance of equation (4) for alternative values of e relies on dynamic simulation. In a dynamic simulation the lagged values of the dependent variable that are fed into the equation are those that are generated by the equation itself, not the historical values.[16] This is in general a more stringent test of an estimated equation than something like the R^2, and indeed is probably a more relevant test from a forecasting point of view. In this vein, I dynamically simulated the basic equation over the full sample period for each value of e. Table 1 also reports the root mean-squared error (RMSE) of the simulated around the true values. The first RMSE column is in the same units as the standard error while the second converts the logarithmic equation to dollar levels so that the units are in billions of 1958 dollars.[17] Equation (4) (the second row of Table 1) yielded an RMSE of $1.1 billion. Alternative values of e led to a deterioration of the RMSE much more marked than the corresponding worsening of the standard error of the regression, pointing up the more discriminating nature of this technique.[18]

An even more vivid illustration of this point arises from the ex post performance of the basic equation. The last column of Table 1 reports for alternative values of e the root mean-squared errors obtained from estimating the equation through 1961 and extrapolating forward by dynamic simulation to the end of 1972. The quality of these extrapolations deteriorates dramatically for high values of e.[19]

On balance, then, the specific estimates of equation (4) still seem satisfactory, both in terms of absolute performance and relative to the equations obtained for alternative income elasticities. Taken as a whole, the results seem to suggest that the relevant income elasticity can be pinned down within a reasonable range of accuracy, and that it is significantly less than unity, reflecting economies of scale.

SHORT-TERM INSTABILITIES?

The tentative conclusion just reached—that an equation like (4) does a satisfactory job of tracking money demand—was based on summary statistics derived from the within-sample performance of the equation. However, one of the primary concerns is the potential for short-run instability in the demand function for money. This problem can be attacked in a variety of ways, but one straightforward way is to ascertain the quality of the short-term ex post forecasts generated by this specification. To do this the specification in (4) was estimated over twelve sample periods, each starting in 1952:2 and differing in that the terminal point was systematically moved from the end of 1961 to the end of 1972, in steps of four quarters. Based on the estimates

obtained for each sample period, the equation was dynamically simulated for the next four quarters.

A number of features of the estimated equations are contained in
columns 1 through 6 of Table 2. Columns 1 through 4 list the individual coefficient estimates, which on casual inspection do appear to
shift around somewhat. Columns 5 and 6 give the standard error of
the regression and the RMSE (in billions of dollars) from within-
sample dynamic simulations. Both these numbers tend to rise as the
end point is extended, in part because the mean of the dependent
variable is also increasing.

Columns 7 and 8 assess the out-of-sample forecasting performance,
giving both the RMSE of a four-quarter forecast and the mean error.
The data underlying these calculations are plotted in Figure 1. The
four-quarter forecast is for the year *following* the end point for a particular row. For example, the worst forecasting error occurred in 1966
with an RMSE of $2.3 billion and this appears in the 1965 row. In
five of the twelve years the ex post forecast was no worse than the
within-sample RMSE, which seems a creditable performance. Furthermore, this was true in 1971, a year reputed to be one of instability,[20]
as well as in 1972. The forecasts for 1973 appear to be a bit wide of
the mark but this judgment is based on only two observations—of
preliminary data, at that—so one should not make too much of it.

On the whole, the money demand function does not exhibit marked
short-run instability. However, this is only one chapter of the short-
term forecasting story. For one thing, the analysis has assumed both
known interest rates and real GNP. In addition, it explains money
demand in real terms so that to forecast nominal money demand
would require a price forecast, which would introduce further error.[21]
Given these caveats, however, it is reassuring to find a reasonable
degree of short-run stability.

LONG-TERM STABILITY

The companion question to the one just considered is whether
the money demand function is stable in the long run. This question is
usually addressed with annual data, often covering a span of seventy or
so years; sometimes the focus is on whether the same money demand
function held both in the 1930s and in the rest of the period.[22] The
concern here is solely with whether quarterly data from the postwar
period can be used homogeneously in face of a number of institutional
developments (such as the certificate of deposit and Eurodollar markets) that at least suggest the possibility of shifts in the demand for
money.[23]

Long-run stability can be examined in a variety of ways. The data sample can be split up at a priori chosen points[24] and the resulting estimates for the subperiods can be compared, either formally—say, via the Chow test—or informally. One useful informal comparison is to simulate dynamically the equation based on the first part of the period over the second part, thus extending the technique used in the previous section to a longer forecasting period.

The last column of Table 2 reports the root mean-squared errors for a number of such simulations. In each case, the money demand equation was estimated through the indicated end point and simulated from the following quarter through the end of 1972. The RMSEs are thus based on observations over varying periods, the longest being forty-four quarters. As could be expected, these RMSEs are generally larger than the four-quarter RMSEs, although markedly so only for the equations reported in the first two rows of the table. Moreover, these equations display coefficients that differ substantially from subsequent entries. This in turn is consistent with the Slovin-Sushka finding cited earlier and argues for a more careful examination of the pre- and post-1961 periods. Equations (4′) and (4″) report the estimates of equation (4) obtained by breaking the sample at the end of 1961.

$$\ln m = \underset{(1.9)}{0.699} + \underset{(4.6)}{0.216} \ln y + \underset{(6.4)}{0.604} \ln m_{-1}$$

$$- \underset{(5.4)}{0.019} \ln RCP - \underset{(4.1)}{0.060} \ln RTD \quad (4')$$

$R^2 = 0.978$; standard error $= 0.0036$.
Sample period: 1952:2–1961:4.

$$\ln m = \underset{(1.8)}{0.657} + \underset{(3.3)}{0.191} \ln y + \underset{(4.8)}{0.632} \ln m_{-1}$$

$$- \underset{(2.4)}{0.014} \ln RCP - \underset{(0.3)}{0.010} \ln RTD. \quad (4'')$$

$R^2 = 0.992$; standard error $= 0.0050$.
Sample period: 1962:1–1972:4.

The biggest difference between these two equations appears in the coefficient of RTD and it is largely attributable to the sizable jump in RTD that occurred precisely at the breaking point.[25] A formal test of stability, carried out by applying a Chow test to this sample split, resulted in an F statistic of 0.84, which does not allow one to reject the hypothesis of stability.[26]

On balance, then, the evidence does not seem to suggest any need to estimate the money demand equation over separate subsamples of the postwar period.

TABLE 2 *Summary Statistics for Money Demand Equation, and Ex Post Forecasts for Alternative Sample Periods Ending with 1961 through 1972*

| End point[a] | Coefficient | | | | Standard error (5) | Root mean-squared error | | Four-quarter mean error (8) | Full ex post root mean-squared error[d] (9) |
| | Income (1) | Interest rate | | Money lagged (4) | | Sample period[b] (6) | Four-quarter ex post forecast[e] (7) | | |
		Time deposits (2)	Commercial paper (3)						
1961	0.216	-0.060	-0.019	0.605	0.0036	0.80	1.42	0.01	5.22
1962	0.183	-0.046	-0.020	0.687	0.0036	0.85	1.60	1.43	4.08
1963	0.196	-0.045	-0.021	0.718	0.0036	0.96	0.65	0.30	1.24
1964	0.203	-0.046	-0.021	0.728	0.0035	0.99	0.88	-0.86	2.57
1965	0.205	-0.047	-0.021	0.719	0.0035	0.93	2.33	-1.69	2.19
1966	0.187	-0.042	-0.022	0.703	0.0038	1.08	1.14	1.04	2.71
1967	0.199	-0.045	-0.022	0.691	0.0037	1.02	1.48	1.24	2.21
1968	0.204	-0.046	-0.022	0.702	0.0037	1.05	0.70	0.27	1.13
1969	0.204	-0.046	-0.023	0.702	0.0037	1.08	2.05	1.84	1.53
1970	0.201	-0.045	-0.022	0.702	0.0038	1.10	0.86	-0.14	1.23
1971	0.193	-0.044	-0.020	0.718	0.0041	1.10	1.10	-0.47	1.10
1972	0.193	-0.045	-0.019	0.717	0.0043	1.12	1.56[e]	-1.57	...

Source: Derived from equation (4), dynamically simulated as described in the text. For data sources and definitions, see appendix.

a. Each sample period begins with 1952:2 and has a terminal point that systematically moves from the end of 1961 to the end of each succeeding year in steps of four quarters.

b. In billions of 1958 dollars.

c. This column gives the RMSE (of the level in billions of 1958 dollars) for the year following the end point in the corresponding row.

d. This column gives the RMSE (of the level in billions of 1958 dollars) for all quarters following the end point up until the end of 1972.

e. For 1972, the RMSE is for the first two quarters of 1973 only instead of the full year following the terminal point.

Alternative Specifications of the Basic Equation

Up to this point I have analyzed extensively the properties of essentially one specification—that embodied in equation (4). As the first section made clear, however, many questions concerning specification can only be resolved empirically. The purpose of the present section is to shed some light on these issues.

AGGREGATION AND DISAGGREGATION IN THE DEFINITION OF MONEY

Aggregation. To this point I have used the most common definition of money—M_1, which is the sum of currency and demand deposits. Other writers, however, have preferred a broader definition, such as M_2, which includes time deposits at commercial banks. This choice seems questionable on a variety of grounds since it constrains the specification, including the adjustment pattern, of M_1 and time deposits to be the same. Furthermore, since RTD should positively affect time deposit holdings and should negatively influence M_1 holdings, aggregation may badly muddy interest rate effects. On the other hand, an argument sometimes advanced in favor of M_2 is that it yields a more stable demand function.[27] In fact, according to evidence developed later, this is definitely not the case.

The tabulation below contains the results of estimating equation (4) with the M_2 definition and with time deposits alone, and, for comparison, repeats the equation (4) estimates:

Definition of money	Income	Money variable lagged	RTD	RCP	R^2	Standard error
M_2	0.119 (2.6)	0.948 (33.4)	0.006 (0.8)	−0.030 (7.7)	0.9987	0.0044
Time deposits	0.255 (3.0)	0.847 (18.7)	0.062 (4.7)	−0.051 (7.2)	0.9997	0.0075
M_1	0.193 (5.3)	0.717 (11.5)	−0.045 (4.0)	−0.019 (6.0)	0.9953	0.0043

It is evident from these numbers that the use of M_2 produces an equation with properties quite different from those of either of the component equations. First, the speed of adjustment is an unreasonably slow 5 percent per quarter as compared with 15 percent for time deposits and 28 percent for M_1. Second, RTD, as expected, has a negligible and insignificant impact on M_2, reflecting the offsetting

TABLE 3   Root Mean-Squared Errors for M_2 and Time Deposits,
and Income Coefficients, Alternative Sample Periods Ending
with 1961 through 1971

	Root mean-squared error						
	Currency plus demand and time deposits, M_2			Time deposits			
		Ex post			Ex post		
End point[a]	Sample period (1)	Four-quarter (2)	Full (3)	Sample period (4)	Four-quarter (5)	Full (6)	Income co-efficient (7)
1961	1.74	1.54	71.46	0.94	1.52	46.76	−0.011
1962	1.70	5.05	71.55	0.96	3.22	43.37	0.026
1963	2.12	2.30	54.64	1.30	2.52	37.61	0.039
1964	2.39	3.56	39.57	1.60	5.04	28.58	0.072
1965	2.80	3.25	18.71	2.27	0.57	10.86	0.156
1966	2.78	7.84	34.98	2.35	4.18	10.80	0.154
1967	2.76	3.09	18.83	2.52	1.38	4.87	0.169
1968	3.02	7.00	6.81	2.32	3.99	3.68	0.177
1969	3.38	9.81	24.08	2.98	2.93	6.64	0.191[b]
1970	4.14	5.11	4.94	2.29	2.02	1.73	0.248[b]
1971	4.81	1.10	1.10	2.18	2.60	2.60	0.267[b]

Source: Same as Table 2.
a. See Table 2, note a.
b. Coefficient significant at 5 percent level.

effects of the component equations. Finally, the long-run income elas-ticity of M_2 is a huge 2.3, which exceeds both the 1.7 for time de-posits and the 0.7 for M_1.

The only redeeming feature of the M_2 equation is that its standard error is only a smidgeon more than the M_1 equation, while that of the time deposit equation alone is substantially higher. This, however, is illusory as can be seen by dynamic simulations. Table 3 reports the results of both four-quarter ex post forecasts and longer-term ex post forecasts obtained by systematically changing the sample period as before. These are in columns 2 and 3 while the within-sample RMSE appears in column 1. Judged on the basis of these results, the equa-tion for M_2 is extremely inadequate. As compared with the results in Table 2, the RMSEs of the four-quarter ex post forecast are both large and variable—ludicrously so in the longer-run extrapolations. From these results one would expect the equation for M_2 to fail any formal test for stability and, indeed, it does. Splitting the sample at the end of 1961 and applying a Chow test yields an F statistic of 3.53; the corresponding likelihood ratio test yields a χ^2 of 18.6. Both of these are significant at the 1 percent level, allowing one easily to reject the hypothesis that the equation for M_2 is stable over the sample period.

Since the M_1 equation was previously found to be stable, the suspicion is that the difficulty lies with the time deposit component, because that component is itself unstable or because of the aggregation process or both. Superficially, the time deposit equation based on the full sample appears quite reasonable. When subjected to the kind of dynamic simulation tests just described, however, this equation also appears questionable. The results are reported in columns 4 through 7 of Table 3. The three sets of RMSEs for time deposits are superior to the corresponding RMSEs for M_2. When judged by an absolute standard, the within-sample and four-quarter RMSEs might be acceptable but the full-period RMSEs remain distinctly unreasonable. The source of the difficulty is indicated in the last column of Table 3, which reports the estimated income coefficient for alternative sample periods. That coefficient rises steadily over the period and does not achieve statistical significance until the sample period runs through 1969. One would expect, as with M_2, that the time deposit equation would fail a formal stability test. The appropriate Chow F statistic is 4.25 and the corresponding χ^2 is 22.1, allowing one to reject stability by either test at the 1 percent level.

This finding suggests, at the very least, that the simple specification used for M_1 will not work for time deposits and therefore should not be implicitly so used by estimating a similar equation for M_2.[28] The situation is, however, worse than that, since even given the questionable time deposit equation, the ex post forecasts of M_2 obtained from the aggregate equation are inferior to those obtained from adding together the separate component forecasts, thus suggesting that aggregation is inflicting some positive harm in the present context.[29]

In summary, for both theoretical and empirical reasons, aggregation to the level of M_2 seems to be a distinctly inferior procedure.

Disaggregation. Although these findings confirm that greater aggregation in the estimation of the demand for money is not called for, there remains the question of whether some disaggregation would be appropriate. The most obvious type of disaggregation would be to estimate separate equations for currency and demand deposits,[30] as is done in many macroeconometric models for a variety of reasons. For one, disaggregation permits greater flexibility in the choice of variables and specification of adjustment patterns. Second, and perhaps of more practical importance, currency is needed as an endogenous variable for analyzing monetary policy. In particular, a means of splitting up high-powered money (a variant of which is usually taken as a policy instrument) into reserves and currency may be needed to trace out the money supply mechanism. In any event, there are good precedents for attempting to explain currency and demand deposits separately.

The tabulation below reports the results of estimating separate equations for currency and demand deposits along the lines of equation (4).

Dependent variable	Income	Consumer expenditures	Money variable lagged	RTD	RCP	R^2	Standard error
Demand deposits	0.181 (5.2)	...	0.693 (9.9)	−0.040 (3.7)	−0.021 (6.0)	0.992	0.0049
Currency	0.190 (5.3)	...	0.804 (19.0)	−0.046 (3.9)	−0.007 (2.0)	0.998	0.0042
Currency	...	0.279 (6.2)	0.591 (8.3)	−0.025 (1.7)	−0.001 (0.2)	0.998	0.0043

The first two equations use exactly the same specification and sample period as equation (4). Both seem relatively satisfactory, and surprisingly enough, both interest rate variables show up in the currency equation. The long-run income elasticity of the demand deposit equation is 0.59, while that of the currency equation is 0.97. These bracket the 0.68 elasticity found for M_1. The speed-of-adjustment coefficients also bracket the M_1 result with demand deposits adjusting somewhat more rapidly than currency.

The final row of the tabulation contains the results of one minor modification in the currency equation, the substitution of consumer expenditures for GNP as the transactions variable and the corresponding use of the consumption deflator.[31] This procedure has pronounced effects on the equation: first, it renders both interest variables statistically insignificant; and second, it considerably speeds up the adjustment of currency holdings.[32]

How do the component equations stand up when subjected to dynamic simulation? The relevant results are reported in Table 4. The two versions of the currency equation perform comparably on the four-quarter simulations, producing only small forecasting errors. The demand deposit equation, as expected, yields smaller RMSEs than the aggregate equation although it still makes a sizable error in forecasting 1966. The long-term extrapolations for all three equations also perform creditably. As between specifications of the currency equation, the GNP formulation does better in the early part of the period but the consumption specification does better at the end of the period.

Comparing the RMSEs in Table 4 with those in Table 2 suggests that extrapolation of M_1 might be accomplished better with the component equations, especially since any offsetting errors in the component equations should help in forecasting. To assess this possibility,

TABLE 4   Root Mean-Squared Errors for Extrapolations of
Demand Deposit and Currency Equations, Sample Periods
Ending with 1961 through 1971

| | Four-quarter extrapolation | | | Full ex post extrapolation | | |
| | | Currency, by transactions variable | | | Currency, by transactions variable | |
End point[a]	Demand deposits	Consumer expenditures	Gross national product	Demand deposits	Consumer expenditures	Gross national product
1961	0.59	0.10	0.09	2.07	2.64	0.45
1962	0.44	0.61	0.68	1.25	0.61	1.59
1963	0.42	0.30	0.05	1.94	3.83	1.17
1964	0.84	0.23	0.22	2.27	1.26	0.77
1965	2.06	0.34	0.45	1.78	1.37	0.87
1966	0.92	0.13	0.25	2.21	0.47	0.69
1967	1.40	0.17	0.34	1.79	0.23	0.84
1968	0.75	0.25	0.10	0.90	0.36	0.43
1969	1.43	0.09	0.23	1.15	0.14	0.29
1970	0.78	0.19	0.22	1.14	0.16	0.20
1971	0.97	0.35	0.37	0.97	0.35	0.37

Source: Same as Table 2.
a. See Table 2, note a.

I summed the separate forecasts for currency and demand deposits and then computed the appropriate RMSEs. These are reported in Table 5, which also includes for convenience the corresponding results from Table 2 (labeled "aggregate").

On the whole the ex post forecasts from the component equations do extremely well. In particular, they improve markedly the extrapolations of M_1 relatively far into the future (see the first two rows of the table). Overall, the most successful formulation is that which used consumer expenditures as the transactions variable in the currency equation. In the eleven cases considered it yields an RMSE lower than the aggregate equation eight times for long-term extrapolations and six times for short-period projections. This evidence provides some independent support for model builders who choose to use separate currency and demand deposit equations and who include consumption in the currency equation.[33]

On balance, the message of this section should be clear: as far as the money demand equation is concerned, more rather than less disaggregation appears to be desirable.

PARTIAL ADJUSTMENT, EXPECTATIONS, AND LAGS

So far, the analysis has relied on a very simple form of dynamic adjustment, a Koyck-type equation that uses a single lagged depen-

TABLE 5   *Root Mean-Squared Errors for Aggregate and Disaggregate Forecasts of M_1, Sample Periods Ending with 1961-1971*

	Four-quarter forecast			Full ex post forecast		
	Disaggregate, by transactions variable			Disaggregate, by transactions variable		
End point[a]	Gross national product	Consumer expenditures	Aggregate	Gross national product	Consumer expenditures	Aggregate
1961	0.64	0.64	1.42	1.87	4.48	5.22
1962	1.13	1.05	1.60	1.56	1.37	4.08
1963	0.41	0.53	0.65	2.97	5.47	1.24
1964	1.04	1.06	0.88	2.95	3.35	2.57
1965	2.49	2.53	2.33	2.48	2.84	2.19
1966	1.10	0.97	1.14	2.82	1.93	2.71
1967	1.72	1.54	1.48	2.50	1.75	2.21
1968	0.73	0.77	0.70	1.04	1.02	1.13
1969	1.64	1.40	2.05	1.28	1.19	1.53
1970	0.88	0.87	0.86	1.15	1.15	1.23
1971	1.12	1.09	1.10	1.12	1.09	1.10

Source: Aggregate columns are from Table 2; disaggregate data are derived from separate forecasts for currency and demand deposits, the components of M_1.
 a. See Table 2, note *a*.

dent variable. While this is a convenient specification, it has the questionable feature of restricting the adjustment pattern of money holdings to be the same with respect to both income and interest rates. Careful consideration of the source of lagged adjustments in money holdings is thus in order.

The justification offered above for the form of equation (4) rested on a vague appeal to the partial adjustment mechanism. Despite the superficial plausibility of this mechanism, its theoretical foundation in the context of the demand for money is unclear. For capital stock accumulation the mechanism is satisfactory, but the analogy between money holdings and capital equipment is far from perfect for many reasons. One is that the exact nature of the costs involved is much less clear in adjusting financial portfolios than in the case of adjusting stocks of machinery and plant. Second, the lags that result statistically for money adjustment appear too long to be explained on grounds of adjustment costs. Finally, even if the analogy is granted, it does not necessarily imply the simple formulation of (3) or (3') and indeed does so only under very special assumptions.[34]

This unsatisfactory state of affairs can be partially remedied by reliance on a different rationale for the lagged adjustment. Pushed back one step, the adjustment can be conceived as a slow response of desired stock itself to actual current values of income and interest rates, rather than a gradual shift in money holdings to meet a promptly adopted new level of desired holdings. The response could be slow because of inertia or because individuals respond to expected values that are in turn a function of past values.[35] Of course, expectational and partial adjustment lags may exist in combination.

The workings of a pure expectations influence may be examined in a demand function of the form

$$m = a + by^e + cr^e, \tag{7}$$

where y^e and r^e are expected (or, if one prefers, "permanent") measures.[36] Since y^e and r^e are unobservable, they must be replaced by measured variables. One common device for doing so is to assume that expectations are "adaptive," that is,

$$y_t^e - y_{t-1}^e = \lambda(y_t - y_{t-1}^e) \tag{8}$$

$$r_t^e - r_{t-1}^e = \lambda(r_t - r_{t-1}^e). \tag{9}$$

This device implies that y_t^e is a geometric distributed lag of current and past values of y; that is,

$$y_t^e = \lambda \sum_{i=0}^{\infty} (1 - \lambda)^i y_{t-i}. \tag{8'}$$

Equations (8) and (9) may then be combined with (7) to yield

$$m_t = a + b\lambda y_t + c\lambda r_t + (1 - \lambda)m_{t-1}. \tag{10}$$

Equation (10) obviously has the same form as the equations estimated above, such as (4), but λ has a different interpretation.[37] Equations (8) and (9) have the same λ, implying the restrictive assumption that expectations of y and r are formed analogously. A more natural specification in place of (9) would be

$$r_t^e - r_{-1}^e = \delta(r_t - r_{t-1}^e), \tag{11}$$

where δ may be different from λ. Combining (7), (8), and (11) produces a considerably more complicated estimating equation:

$$m_t = c_0 + c_1 y_t + c_2 y_{t-1} + c_3 r_t + c_4 r_{t-1} + c_5 m_{t-1} + c_6 m_{t-2}, \tag{10'}$$

where the cs are nonlinear functions of the respective original parameters.

This version of the adaptive expectations model leads to a considerably richer lag structure. In fact, even greater generality may be obtained by allowing expectations to adjust in different proportions to two or more of the previously observed forecasting errors, as in[38]

$$y_t^e - y_{t-1}^e = \lambda_1(y - y_{t-1}^e) + \lambda_2(y_{t-1} - y_{t-2}^e). \tag{12}$$

Another extension of the formulation is accomplished by combining the adaptive expectations and partial adjustment models. This procedure introduces another lag in all the variables and some further nonlinear restrictions.[39]

TABLE 6 *Estimates of Alternative Forms of Lagged Adjustments in Demand-for-Money Equations*

Regression	Income	Money lagged	Interest rate		Income lagged	Interest rate lagged		Money lagged twice	ρ	R^2
			Commercial paper	Time deposits		Commercial paper	Time deposits			
A	0.193 (5.3)	0.717 (11.5)	−0.019 (6.0)	−0.045 (4.0)	...	...	...	...	0.41 (4.1)	0.995
B	0.168 (3.0)	0.657 (8.9)	−0.011 (2.5)	−0.029 (1.8)	0.064 (1.0)	−0.014 (2.9)	−0.025 (1.5)	...	0.47 (4.8)	0.996
C	0.181 (6.2)	1.105 (12.4)	−0.015 (6.6)	−0.044 (4.9)	...	...	...	−0.382 (4.8)	0.09 (0.8)	0.996
D	0.178 (3.2)	0.977 (9.2)	−0.013 (3.1)	−0.036 (2.2)	0.028 (0.4)	−0.005 (1.0)	−0.014 (0.8)	−0.289 (2.9)	0.20 (1.9)	0.996

Source: Derived from equations (4) and (10′) and two modifications of (10′), discussed in the text. For data sources and definitions, see appendix. The numbers in parentheses here and in all the following tables are *t*-statistics.

TABLE 7   *Comparison of Cumulative Percentage Responses of Regressions A and B of Table 6 after Selected Numbers of Quarters*

Number of quarters	Regression A (text equation 4)	Regression B (text equation 10')		
		Income	Interest rate on time deposits	Interest rate on commercial paper
1	28.3	24.7	18.1	15.7
2	48.6	50.3	45.6	45.7
3	63.0	67.2	63.8	65.7
4	73.5	78.2	75.6	78.6
7	90.2	93.2	91.3	96.6

Source: Same as Table 6.

Table 6 reports the results of estimating a relatively simple version of these alternatives, equation (10'), as well as two modified versions that either omit the second-order lag in the dependent variable or the lagged variables for income and interest rates. For comparison, equation (4) is reported as regression A in Table 6.

Several features of the results are worth noting. First, the long-run income and interest rate elasticities are virtually identical for all four equations. There are, however, differences in the timing of the responses among the four equations. These differences are illustrated for two of the equations in Table 7, which gives the fraction of the total response to a change in income or interest rates that has occurred after a given number of quarters. For the simple Koyck equation this response is identical for all variables, but this is clearly not the case for the second equation in Table 6.

A second feature is that the three lagged variables for income and interest rates are collectively significant when used without m lagged twice but not when it is included.[40] Finally, m lagged twice appears significant whether or not these other variables are included.[41]

In my judgment, these results leave open the question of whether a specification more complicated than the original Koyck model is appropriate. Clearly, however, satisfactory estimation of equation (10') is impeded by pronounced multicollinearity. Consequently, unless the nonlinear restrictions underlying such an equation are taken into account properly, it seems pointless to estimate a more sophisticated version.[42] An alternative and potentially more promising route is to rely on Almon distributed lags.

The basic estimating equation for this technique is given by

$$\ln m_t = c + \sum_{i=0}^{n_1} w_i \ln y_{t-i}$$

$$+ \sum_{i=0}^{n_2} w_i' \ln RTD_{t-i} + \sum_{i=0}^{n_3} w_i'' \ln RCP_{t-i}. \quad (13)$$

TABLE 8 *Estimates of Income and Interest Elasticity Coefficients Using Almon Distributed Lags in the Demand-for-Money Equations*[a]

Currency plus demand deposits, M_1			Demand deposits		
Income	RTD	RCP	Income	RTD	RCP
0.146	−0.028	−0.014	0.131	−0.024	−0.014
(3.6)	(2.1)	(3.7)	(3.1)	(1.67)	(3.4)
0.119	−0.033	−0.014	0.105	−0.031	−0.014
(4.8)	(4.9)	(6.7)	(4.3)	(4.7)	(7.2)
0.094	−0.034	−0.012	0.082	−0.032	−0.013
(6.9)	(4.7)	(5.7)	(6.5)	(4.2)	(6.1)
0.073	−0.030	−0.011	0.063	−0.028	−0.012
(6.5)	(3.7)	(3.9)	(5.9)	(3.2)	(4.2)
0.056	−0.021	−0.009	0.047	−0.019	−0.010
(3.7)	(3.2)	(3.0)	(3.0)	(2.6)	(3.3)
0.041	−0.009	−0.006	0.034	−0.004	−0.007
(2.2)	(1.3)	(2.0)	(1.7)	(0.6)	(2.2)
0.030	0.009	−0.003	0.024	0.017	−0.003
(1.5)	(0.6)	(0.7)	(1.2)	(1.1)	(0.7)
0.022	...	...	0.018	...	...
(1.2)			(0.9)		
0.017	...	...	0.015	...	...
(1.1)			(0.9)		
0.016	...	...	0.015	...	...
(1.2)			(1.2)		
0.018	...	...	0.019	...	...
(1.1)			(1.2)		
0.023	...	...	0.025	...	...
(0.9)			(0.9)		
...	...	...	...	...	...
...	...	...	...	...	...
Σ = 0.656	Σ = −0.145	Σ = −0.068	Σ = 0.577	Σ = −0.121	Σ = −0.073
(17.3)	(8.8)	(5.4)	(19.4)	(10.3)	(5.8)
$R^2 = 0.995$, standard error = 0.0046, $\rho = 0.82$			$R^2 = 0.992$, standard error = 0.0051, $\rho = 0.69$		

Source: Derived from text equation (13). The sample period is 1952:2 through 1972:4. For data sources and definitions, see appendix.
RTD and RCP are the interest rates on time deposits and commercial paper, respectively.
a. The summations are calculated from data before rounding.

This equation can be rationalized in a number of ways.[43] For example, the form of its composite variables is simply a generalization of equation (8′) with a finite horizon. Alternatively, one may simply regard (13) as a convenient and flexible equation for approximating a rather complicated underlying process.

A number of a priori expectations surround the coefficients in (13). The w_is, representing the lag distribution for income, should all be positive and should probably decline monotonically. The corresponding interest rate coefficients should be negative; they might well exhibit a humped pattern, especially for RTD, because RCP is likely to affect primarily large transactors, who are less subject to a learning delay.[44]

Equation (13) was estimated over the same sample period as equation (4)—1952:2 through 1972:4—by the Almon technique, with an adjustment for serial correlation. The individual lag coefficients variable

	Currency with income as transactions variable			Currency with consumer expenditures as transactions variable		
	Income	RTD	RCP	Consumer expenditures	RTD	RCP
	0.153	−0.020	−0.0045	0.247	−0.028	−0.0050
	(5.4)	(1.3)	(1.2)	(3.8)	(1.6)	(1.1)
	0.126	−0.018	−0.0047	0.261	−0.012	−0.0036
	(6.2)	(2.0)	(2.1)	(5.4)	(0.9)	(1.3)
	0.103	−0.017	−0.0047	0.191	−0.009	−0.0023
	(7.2)	(1.5)	(2.0)	(3.9)	(0.7)	(0.8)
	0.082	−0.016	−0.0044	0.036	−0.020	−0.0010
	(7.4)	(1.8)	(2.1)	(0.5)	(1.1)	(0.2)
	0.065	−0.016	−0.0039	...	...	...
	(6.1)	(1.0)	(1.1)			
	0.051	...	...	...	...	...
	(4.4)					
	0.041	...	...	...	...	...
	(3.2)					
	0.033	...	...	...	...	...
	(2.5)					
	0.029	...	...	...	...	...
	(2.3)					
	0.028	...	...	...	...	...
	(2.3)					
	0.031	...	...	...	...	...
	(2.6)					
	0.037	...	...	...	...	...
	(2.8)					
	0.046	...	...	...	...	...
	(2.6)					
	0.058	...	...	...	...	...
	(2.4)					
	Σ = 0.883	Σ = −0.086	Σ = −0.022	Σ = 0.734	Σ = −0.069	Σ = −0.012
	(13.4)	(2.8)	(2.7)	(12.5)	(2.4)	(1.5)
	R^2 = 0.998, standard error = 0.0045, ρ = 0.97			R^2 = 0.997, standard error = 0.0048, ρ = 0.97		

were assumed to lie on a third-degree polynomial and no end-point constraints were imposed. The length of each lag (n_1, n_2, and n_3) was determined empirically with the rough aid of the information on speed of adjustment from the stock adjustment equations.

The results reported in Table 8 agree remarkably well with those obtained earlier. For the long-run income and interest elasticities, which are reported in Table 9, the Koyck and Almon estimates do not differ by more than 0.02. The equations do differ, of course, in the pattern of lagged response, and on this score, the results of equation (13) seem sensible. The length of the lag on income is substantially longer than that of the corresponding lag for interest rates, a finding that is roughly supported by some previous work.[45] Furthermore, the peak impact of RTD occurs after two quarters, so the interest rate response does exhibit the humped pattern posited above.

More details on the exact timing of responses are given in Table

TABLE 9   *Comparison of Long-run Income and Interest Elasticities from Koyck and Almon Estimates, for Money and Components*

Dependent variable	Koyck			Almon		
	Income	RTD[a]	RCP[a]	Income	RTD[a]	RCP[a]
Money, M_1	0.68	0.16	0.07	0.66	0.15	0.07
Demand deposits	0.59	0.13	0.07	0.58	0.12	0.07
Currency	0.97	0.23	0.04	0.88	0.09	0.02
Currency[b]	0.68	0.06	0.00	0.73	0.07	0.01

Sources: Koyck. equation (4); Almon, equation (13). *RTD* and *RCP* are the interest rates on time deposits and commercial paper, respectively.
a. All interest elasticities are negative.
b. Currency equation using consumer expenditures as a transactions variable.

10, which reports the fraction of the total response to changes in income and interest rates that has occurred after a given number of quarters.[46] The Koyck version—equation (4)—necessarily has only one pattern of response while the Almon equation has three separate patterns. The Almon responses to income changes are uniformly slower than the Koyck responses. For interest rates, the Almon response is slower for several quarters but then overtakes the Koyck response.

TABLE 10   *Comparison of Cumulative Percentage Responses, after Selected Numbers of Quarters, of Koyck and Almon Equations, for Money and Components*

	Dependent variable							
	Currency plus demand deposits, M_1				Demand deposits			
Number of quarters	Koyck	Almon			Koyck	Almon		
		Income	RTD	RCP		Income	RTD	RCP
1	28.3	22.2	19.3	20.5	30.7	22.7	19.8	19.2
2	48.6	40.3	42.1	41.2	51.9	40.9	45.4	38.4
3	63.0	54.6	65.5	58.8	66.7	55.1	71.9	56.2
4	73.5	65.7	86.2	75.0	76.9	66.0	95.0	72.6
7	90.2	85.1	100.0	100.0	92.3	84.2	100.0	100.0
10	96.3	93.5	100.0	100.0	97.3	92.5	100.0	100.0

	Dependent variable							
	Currency with income as transactions variable				Currency with consumer expenditures as transactions variable			
		Almon				Almon		
	Koyck	Income	RTD	RCP	Koyck	Consumer expenditures	RTD	RCP
1	19.6	17.3	23.2	20.5	40.9	33.7	40.6	41.7
2	35.3	31.6	44.2	41.8	65.1	69.2	58.0	71.7
3	48.0	43.3	70.0	62.2	79.4	95.2	71.0	90.9
4	58.2	52.6	82.6	82.2	87.4	100.0	100.0	100.0
7	78.2	70.4	100.0	100.0	97.5	100.0	100.0	100.0
10	88.7	80.6	100.0	100.0	99.5	100.0	100.0	100.0

Sources: Same as Table 9. *RTD* and *RCP* are the interest rates on time deposits and commercial paper, respectively.

Evidently, constraining all the responses to the same shape in the Koyck version produces an inappropriate average response which masks individual differences.

In addition to the results for M_1, Tables 8, 9, and 10 report the findings of Almon versions of separate equations for estimated demand deposits and currency. The results for demand deposits are, not surprisingly, quite comparable to those for M_1 both in terms of absolute performance and in comparison with the Koyck version presented above. Somewhat larger differences emerge between the Koyck and Almon versions of the two currency equations; but on the whole the Almon currency equation performs creditably.

In summary, a modest amount of evidence suggests that the Koyck formulation of equation (4) is a bit too restrictive.[47] The price paid for this simplification does not seem severe but it deserves additional research—for example, to examine the comparative performance of alternative lag structures in such simulation experiments as those reported earlier.

INFLATIONARY EXPECTATIONS

The discussion of lags and expectation formation in the previous section was restricted to income and interest rate variables. This section explores another variable—prices—and particularly investigates whether inflationary expectations have an independent role to play in the demand-for-money function.

Even at the theoretical level, this question is controversial. On a strict transactions view of the demand for money, a variable measuring anticipated inflation seems to have no place.[48] On the other hand, in theoretical writings on demand-for-money functions in the Chicago tradition, money serves as an alternative for physical goods, and the expected rate of price change is given a prominent role.[49] This approach has been buttressed by empirical evidence from hyperinflations abroad. In view of these latter findings, Harry Johnson [20] calls the absence of "American evidence that the expected rate of change of prices enters the demand for money function . . . something of a puzzle. He tentatively attributes it to the relative mildness of U.S. inflations and to the possible presence of threshold effects.[50]

In the spirit of empiricism of this paper and in light of the divergence of opinion just cited, the performance of expected inflation variables in money demand equations will be given a brief look. Following one of many possible routes, I shall modify equation (7) to include an expected rate of inflation, ρ^e:

$$m = a + by^e + cr^e + d\rho^e. \qquad (7')$$

TABLE 11   Coefficients of Variables in Demand-for-Money Equations, for Three Measures of Price Expectations

| | | | Interest rate | | | | |
| | | | | | | | |
Measure	Income	Money lagged	Time deposits	Commercial paper	Price variable	R^2	ρ
Equation (14)	0.166	0.782	−0.038	−0.015	−0.657	0.996	0.46
	(4.9)	(13.1)	(3.6)	(5.0)	(4.2)		
de Menil I	0.200	0.698	−0.046	−0.016	−0.143	0.996	0.41
	(5.6)	(11.3)	(4.1)	(4.9)	(1.9)		
de Menil II	0.200	0.693	−0.044	−0.016	−0.211	0.996	0.41
	(5.6)	(11.1)	(4.0)	(4.8)	(1.8)		

Sources: Row 1 gives the results of estimating equation (14) as derived in the text, defining the expected rate of inflation by an adaptive expectations mechanism. In rows 2 and 3, direct measures of price expectations from series constructed from surveys of expected price performance are substituted in equation (14). The series are from G. de Menil, "Rationality in Popular Price Expectations" (Princeton University, August 1973; processed). For other data sources, see appendix.

If the expected rate of inflation is defined by an adaptive expectations mechanism as in (8) or (9), the resulting equation takes the form[51]

$$\ln m_t = a + b \ln y_t + c \ln m_{t-1} + d \ln RTD_t$$
$$+ e \ln RCP_t + f \ln (P_t/P_{t-1}). \quad (14)$$

The results of estimating equation (14) are given in the first row of Table 11. The price variable is quite significantly negative and its inclusion raises the elasticity for income and lowers the speed of adjustment as compared with equation (4). The elasticities for the interest rate variables remain virtually the same. (The measures in rows 2 and 3 are considered after the discussion of Table 12.)

The impact of the price variable on the money demand equation can be assessed by a simple conceptual experiment. In an equilibrium situation that has persisted long enough, and in which interest rates are constant, real income is growing at 4 percent and the actual rate of inflation is 2 percent, equation (14) states that real money stock should grow at 3 percent and the nominal money stock at 5 percent. Now imagine a once-and-for-all change in the rate of inflation from 2 percent to 6 percent that leaves interest rates and the rate of growth of real GNP unchanged. In the long run, the rate of growth of the real money stock will remain 3 percent, though the nominal money stock will grow at 9 percent. In the short run, however, substantial deviations from these rates of growth will occur if income growth and interest rates are to remain unchanged. I used the estimates of equation (14) to compute these short-run deviations, with the results reported in Table 12.

The largest effect occurs in the initial quarter and after eight quarters the growth rates have nearly reached their equilibrium values. At that point the real money stock is $2\frac{1}{2}$ percent below where it would have been had the rate of inflation remained unchanged. The nomi-

TABLE 12   *Short-run Rates of Growth of the Money Stock in Transition from 2 Percent to 6 Percent Inflation, with Fixed and Variable Interest Rates*

Percent

	Interest rates fixed		Interest rates variable	
Quarter	Real	Nominal	Real	Nominal
1	0.4	6.4	−5.7	0.3
2	1.0	7.0	−3.8	2.2
3	1.4	7.4	−2.3	3.7
4	1.8	7.8	−1.1	4.9
5	2.1	8.1	−0.2	5.8
6	2.3	8.3	0.5	6.5
7	2.5	8.5	1.0	7.0
8	2.6	8.6	1.5	7.5

Source: Computed from estimates of equation (14). For the variable interest rate columns, the interest rate on time deposits is assumed to rise from 5 percent to 6 percent, and that on commercial paper from 6 percent to 9 percent.

nal money stock (given the assumed super-accommodating behavior of the Federal Reserve) is $5\frac{1}{2}$ percent higher.

It is, of course, unrealistic to assume that nominal interest rates will be unchanged in the face of this higher rate of inflation. For illustrative purposes, assume that *RTD* would rise from 5 percent to 6 percent and *RCP* from 6 percent to 9 percent as a result of the higher inflation. The resulting money growth rates are given in the final two columns of Table 12, and reveal more dramatic variations. At the end of eight quarters the real money stock is about $8\frac{1}{2}$ percent lower than it otherwise would have been and the nominal money stock is $\frac{1}{2}$ percent lower.

While the specific inflationary assumptions and calculations are unrealistic, the results in Table 12 indicate that substantial short-run variations in the growth of money demand may accompany changes in inflationary expectations and these in turn may immensely complicate the job of the monetary authorities.

It is also possible to interpret equation (14) as arising from a partial adjustment model rather than from expectational lags. To do this requires modifying the equation defining the desired stock of money— for example, (2) above—to include the anticipated rate of inflation:

$$m^* = f(y, r, \rho^e). \tag{2'}$$

Under this interpretation, however, equation (14) results only in the unlikely event that expectations are perfectly accurate—that is, only if $\rho^e = \Delta P_t / P_{t-1}$. Fortunately, some alternative measures for ρ^e yield a more satisfactory interpretation. In particular, George de Menil has constructed two series of expected price performance from the annual surveys of inflationary expectations conducted by the Survey Research

Center of the University of Michigan, that can be used to give a direct measure of expectations.[52] Substituting these in equation (14) leads to substantially smaller price coefficients (see Table 11), which barely border on statistical significance and do not provide strong support for the anticipated inflation variable.

In fact, an alternative view of the stock adjustment process suggests that (14) is misspecified regardless of how ρ^e is measured. In particular, it may be more plausible to combine (2) or (2') with an adjustment equation specified in nominal terms:

$$\ln M_t - \ln M_{t-1} = \gamma(\ln M_t^* - \ln M_{t-1}), \tag{3''}$$

where $M_t^* = P_t m_t^*$. If this is done the following equation results:

$$\ln (M_t/P_t) = a + b \ln y_t + c \ln (M_{t-1}/P_t) \\ + d \ln RTD_t + e \ln RCP_t + f\rho^e. \tag{15}$$

The major difference between (14) and (15) is the deflator for the lagged nominal stock of money. Equation (15) uses the current price level while (14) uses the lagged price level. Within the context of the stock adjustment model, equation (14) thus implies that any reduction of the real value of the lagged nominal money stock due to rising prices is subject to immediate adjustment, while equation (15) views it as subject to partial or lagged adjustment.

When (15) was estimated with each of the three possible measures for ρ^e, it never yielded a significant coefficient for the ρ^e.[53] At least under the stock adjustment interpretation, then, this suggests that misspecification of equation (14) led to a spurious effect of ρ^e.[54] Under the expectational lag hypothesis, (14) is the proper specification.[55]

The expectational version can be investigated further with Almon distributed lags. Among other things, this technique has the virtue of getting the lagged money stock out of the equation and removing the possible statistical artifact just cited. The relevant estimating equation is

$$(\ln m_t = k + \sum_{i=0}^{n_1} w_i \ln y_{t-i} + \sum_{i=0}^{n_2} w_i' \ln RTD_{t-i}$$

$$+ \sum_{i=0}^{n_3} w_i'' \ln RCP_{t-i} + b\rho^e \tag{16}$$

in which expected inflation can be expressed by either of the de Menil measures or by

$$\rho^e = \sum_{i=0}^{n_4} w_i''' \ln (P_{t-i}/P_{t-i-1}). \tag{17}$$

The various results are given in Table 13.[56] Only one of the two equations using the direct measures has a statistically significant price effect, and even that effect is much smaller than that yielded by the distributed lag proxy—that is, equation (17). This latter variable seems to

TABLE 13   *Coefficients Showing Effect on Equation (16) of*
Three Alternative Measures of Price Expectations

Measure	Income	Interest rate		Price level	R^2	Standard error	ρ
		Time deposits	Commercial paper				
Equation (17)	0.693 (16.7)	−0.157 (8.9)	−0.062 (4.8)	−1.911[a] (2.1)	0.996	0.0044	0.84
de Menil I	0.652 (17.6)	−0.144 (9.1)	−0.066 (5.1)	−0.088 (1.1)	0.995	0.0046	0.81
de Menil II	0.641 (17.9)	−0.138 (8.9)	−0.064 (5.2)	−0.257 (2.1)	0.995	0.0045	0.80

Sources: Row 1 gives the results of estimating equation (16), as derived in the text, with Almon distributed lags (equation 17). In rows 2 and 3, direct measures of price expectations from de Menil (cited in Table 11), are substituted in equation (16). For other data sources and definitions, see appendix.

a. Individual coefficients are as follows:

	Lag					
	0	1	2	3	4	5
Coefficient	−0.607 (3.2)	−0.440 (2.2)	−0.311 (1.4)	−0.222 (1.0)	−0.172 (1.0)	−0.160 (1.1)

work reasonably well; it produces a sensible dynamic adjustment pattern (shown in Table 13, note *a*) in which the length of the lag for past rates of inflation is slightly shorter than that for interest rates and considerably shorter than the income lag.[57]

Taken together, these results are a mixed bag. Under the expectations view, some case emerges for including a measure of expected inflation in the demand for money. On the other hand the partial adjustment view, at least as amended, suggests that this case may rest merely on a statistical curiosity. The reader should feel free to indulge his own prejudices.

THE APPROPRIATE SCALE VARIABLE:
INCOME OR WEALTH?

An issue that has been extensively examined in the literature is whether income or wealth (or perhaps permanent income) is the appropriate scale variable. Laidler [21] has reviewed this literature and concludes that the evidence favors wealth. Citing work of Meltzer, he suggests that once wealth is included, income has little to explain. Furthermore, he reports work of Brunner and Meltzer that suggests that the wealth variable has superior predictive ability. Nonetheless, numerous writers continue to follow the transactions approach, which focuses on income as the primary scale variable.

The evidence cited by Laidler is based on long-term annual data while recent writings following the transactions approach have tended to be concerned with a shorter term. Whatever the merits of Laidler's evidence in the long-term context, the conclusions do not necessarily apply in explaining the short-run demand for money with quarterly data, and their robustness should be examined.

TABLE 14   *Estimates of the Money Demand Equation with Alternative Wealth and Income Variables*

Equation (4) variant	Money lagged	Interest rate Time deposits	Interest rate Commercial paper	Income	Wealth	Change in wealth	ρ	R^2
1	0.920 (25.4)	−0.027 (2.5)	−0.015 (4.2)	...	0.104 (3.9)	...	0.52	0.995
2	0.986 (30.7)	−0.005 (0.5)	−0.010 (2.9)	...	0.040 (1.5)	0.201 (3.2)	0.39	0.995
3	0.801 (12.5)	−0.031 (2.7)	−0.014 (4.1)	0.139 (3.6)	...	0.160 (2.9)	0.35	0.996
4	0.729 (11.4)	−0.049 (4.2)	−0.018 (5.7)	0.165 (3.8)	0.032 (1.1)	...	0.43	0.995
5	0.801 (12.5)	−0.031 (2.5)	−0.014 (4.1)	0.140 (3.3)	−0.001 (0.04)	0.161 (2.7)	0.35	0.996

Source: Derived from variants of the basic money demand equation (4). For data sources and definitions, see appendix.

While the transactions approach emphasizes income, it allows room for a wealth variable since some transactions are obviously associated with portfolio shifts related to total wealth. Unfortunately, a good measure of such transactions is difficult to obtain. An attempt to use the value of stock (equity) transactions had only limited success.[58] Another possibility is to add the change in net worth to the variables in the demand for money, thus allowing money holdings to absorb an arbitrary fraction of initial allocations of new wealth.[59]

Table 14 reports the results of estimating several variants of the basic equation. The first substitutes a measure of net worth for the income variable while the second uses both net worth and its change. The next two equations use the income variable and one of the net worth measures while the last equation utilizes all three. Several findings are worth emphasizing.

First, without an income variable the speed of adjustment becomes unreasonably low. Second, income and the change in net worth both achieve statistical significance when they appear in the same equation, suggesting that transactions on wealth account may well be important. Finally, unlike the results cited above, the level of net worth is unimportant when used with income alone while the latter retains its significance. When all three variables are used, the level effect of net worth is obliterated.

The predictive ability of the various equations is reported in Table 15, reflecting the results of dynamic simulations of the specifications embodied in equations (1) and (3) of Table 14. The results of using the wealth variable alone in level form are distinctly inferior to the original equation (4) (see Table 2) both for extrapolations and within the sample period. When the variable reflecting change in wealth is

TABLE 15   Root Mean-Squared Errors for Extrapolations with
Wealth Variables, Alternative Sample Periods Ending with
1961 through 1971

End point[a]	Income and change in wealth			Wealth only		
	Ex post			*Ex post*		
	Full	*Four-quarter*	*Sample period*	*Full*	*Four-quarter*	*Sample period*
1961	9.84	2.75	0.49	17.57	3.53	0.93
1962	5.89	0.96	0.85	16.38	2.42	1.40
1963	2.68	0.84	0.95	11.00	1.17	1.95
1964	1.53	0.72	0.99	8.21	0.65	2.16
1965	1.67	1.10	0.94	5.47	0.73	2.24
1966	1.95	0.41	1.02	7.10	2.36	2.19
1967	2.35	0.94	1.03	5.77	2.16	2.32
1968	1.67	1.04	1.00	3.49	0.50	2.34
1969	1.81	2.35	1.03	4.67	4.57	2.38
1970	1.81	0.90	1.08	1.57	0.81	2.50
1971	1.62	1.62	1.10	1.30	1.30	2.53

Source: Equations 1 and 3 of Table 14, dynamically simulated.
a. See Table 2, note *a*.

added in equation (4), the results are somewhat more mixed, but the original equation is still to be preferred on its ex post performance.

On balance, then, at least for quarterly data, use of an income variable in the demand-for-money equation seems eminently sensible. A variable reflecting the change in wealth slightly improves the explanatory power of the equation but slightly worsens its predictive ability.[60]

Some Econometric Issues

The previous two sections considered a number of basic problems in the specification of the money demand function. The present section focuses on a somewhat narrower and more technical set of issues and considers in sequence questions (7) through (10) posed at the beginning of the paper.

ALTERNATIVE INTEREST RATES

The original debate over interest rates initially centered on whether *any* interest rate mattered. In more recent years, with this question settled, discussion has turned to the appropriate rate or rates to include the money demand function.[61] The major dispute has concerned short rates (on commercial paper, Treasury bills, and the like) versus longer rates[62] (on corporate bonds, U.S. government obligations, or even equities), although the importance of various types of saving deposit rates (at savings and loan associations, mutual savings banks, and commercial banks) has also been an issue. Most researchers do not confront the question directly, however; they simply use whatever set of interest rates is consistent with the rationale offered for the demand for money. In the context of the transactions approach such a set typically means something like the two rates (RCP and RTD) used in equation (4) but there are other choices. Table 16 reports the results of some alternative specifications.

The rates considered, in addition to RCP and RTD, were the Treasury bill rate, RTB, a weighted-average saving rate, $RAVG$ (combining RTD, a savings and loan, and a mutual savings bank rate), and, for completeness, the corporate bond rate (RCB). Generally speaking, RCP and RTB appear interchangeable as do RTD and $RAVG$. Although the results are not shown in the table, a weighted average of the savings and loan and mutual savings bank rates, and a separate rate on certificates of deposit, were also tried. The former worked, although it did not do as well as RTD or $RAVG$ and was not significant when used in conjunction with RTD. The certificate rate was quite insignificant.

Table 16 makes clear that including a saving deposit rate of any sort increases the speed of adjustment, from much less than 10 percent per quarter to about 20 percent. The corporate bond rate does not work nearly as well as these others, never achieving statistical significance and in some unreported combinations actually yielding a positive coefficient.

On balance then, the specification in (4) seems to work about as well as any other. One potential problem with this for extrapolation purposes is that RTD (or $RAVG$) has become more difficult to measure in view of the widespread importance of consumer-type certificates.

TIME UNIT OF MEASUREMENT

The quarterly money series used thus far was obtained by averaging the officially reported monthly data for the three months of the quarter. These monthly data are in turn produced by averaging daily data. Gibson [14] has argued that this procedure is the proper way of characterizing the behavior of the money series over a quarter, and that it provides a reasonable correspondence with the GNP data from the national income accounts. But the money stock series has been measured in many other ways in empirical research on the demand for money: by an average of two months' data centered on the end

TABLE 16 *Coefficients for Alternative Interest Rate Variables in the Money Demand Equation*

| Equation | Income | Money lagged | Interest rate | | | | | ρ | R^2 |
			Time deposits	Commercial paper	Treasury bills	Saving, weighted average	Corporate bonds		
1	0.200 (5.1)	0.691 (10.1)	−0.049 (4.0)	...	−0.012 (4.3)	...	...	0.51 (5.4)	0.995
2	0.193 (5.3)	0.717 (11.5)	−0.045 (4.0)	−0.019 (6.0)	...	...	...	0.41 (4.1)	0.995
3	0.192 (5.5)	0.756 (14.5)	...	−0.020 (6.5)	...	−0.068 (4.1)	...	0.39 (3.8)	0.995
4	0.214 (5.3)	0.713 (11.9)	...	...	−0.014 (4.9)	−0.080 (4.2)	...	0.49 (5.1)	0.995
5	0.049 (4.2)	0.929 (26.4)	...	...	−0.012 (3.8)	...	...	0.49 (5.2)	0.994
6	0.053 (5.4)	0.942 (32.5)	...	−0.018 (5.4)	...	...	...	0.41 (4.1)	0.994
7	0.189 (4.4)	0.663 (8.6)	−0.051 (3.7)	...	...	...	...	0.69 (8.6)	0.994
8	0.210 (4.4)	0.656 (8.6)	...	...	...	−0.086 (3.6)	...	0.74 (9.9)	0.994
9	0.061 (2.8)	0.901 (18.9)	...	...	...	...	−0.021 (1.7)	0.63 (7.4)	0.993
10	0.205 (4.6)	0.674 (8.9)	−0.049 (3.6)	...	...	...	−0.017 (1.4)	0.66 (8.1)	0.994

Source: Derived by estimating equations in log linear form over the sample period 1952:2 to 1972:4 by the Cochrane-Orcutt technique. For specific definitions of the variables, see appendix.

TABLE 17 *Coefficients for Alternative Measures of the Money Stock in the Money Demand Equation*

| Measure | Income | Money lagged | Interest rate | | R^2 | Standard error | ρ |
			Time deposits	Commercial paper			
Last month of quarter	0.207 (5.6)	0.706 (11.4)	−0.047 (4.1)	−0.023 (7.6)	0.996	0.0043	0.38
Two-month average centered on end of quarter	0.226 (6.0)	0.677 (10.9)	−0.051 (4.5)	−0.024 (7.8)	0.996	0.0044	0.36
Point estimate (flow of funds)	0.224 (4.7)	0.690 (9.3)	−0.047 (3.5)	−0.022 (7.2)	0.992	0.0068	−0.12
Quarterly average (equation 4)	0.193 (5.3)	0.717 (11.5)	−0.045 (4.0)	−0.019 (6.0)	0.995	0.0043	0.41

Source: Derived from estimating equation (4) with each of the alternative measures.

of the quarter, by data for the last month of the quarter, and by end-of-quarter point estimates (for example, from call report data).

Would substituting one of these definitions change any of the basic results? This question is of particular interest, because Gibson has found that, for the early postwar period, the time unit of measurement may have a pronounced impact on the coefficient of the speed of adjustment.

The results obtained from estimating equation (4) with each of the three alternative measures just noted are reported in Table 17. (The point estimate of the money stock is taken from the flow of funds data, which will be utilized more extensively below.)

The three results reported in Table 17 and the results of the original equation (4) are obviously all quite similar to one another.[63] Consequently, Gibson's finding that use of quarterly average data led to a much more rapid speed of adjustment is not borne out when the sample period is extended to the later part of the postwar period.

SERIAL CORRELATION AND SIMULTANEITY

All of the estimates reported so far have been obtained by applying the Cochrane-Orcutt technique for correction of serial correlation in conjunction with ordinary least squares. Thus, problems of simultaneous equation bias have been ignored. In the absence of a complete model, the choice of means to carry out simultaneous equation estimation is somewhat arbitrary. Moreover, a casual interpretation of the evidence suggested that simultaneity bias was not likely to be important but that serial correlation was. These rough impressions were checked by choosing a plausible set of instruments and reestimating equation (4) by ordinary least squares (OLSQ) and by two-stage least squares, both corrected (TSCORC) and not corrected (TSLS) for serial correlation.[64] The results are reported in Table 18.

The results obtained by OLSQ and TSLS are fairly similar to each other and to the estimates given in equation (4). Correcting for both simultaneity and serial correlation (TSCORC) yields a considerably faster speed of adjustment but the long-run elasticities are essentially the same as in equation (4).[65] To see whether this faster speed of adjustment would improve the tracking ability of the equation, I performed the standard set of dynamic simulations described above. I also computed these simulations based on the estimates obtained by OLSQ, with the results reported in Table 19.

For OLSQ, the within-sample RMSEs are all about 40 percent larger than the corresponding results in Table 2, thus pointing up the benefits of correcting for serial correlation.[66] The ex post results also favor the original estimates, but by a smaller margin. In six out of the eleven cases, the within-sample results with TSCORC are actually

TABLE 18 *Effect of Alternative Estimating Techniques on Basic Money Demand Equation*

| | | | Interest rate | | | | |
Estimation technique	Income	Money lagged	Time deposits	Commercial paper	R^2	Standard error	ρ
Ordinary least squares	0.177	0.751	−0.041	−0.019	0.994	0.0048	...
	(5.4)	(13.6)	(4.1)	(8.2)			
Two-stage least squares	0.216	0.690	−0.052	−0.021	0.994	0.0048	...
	(4.7)	(9.1)	(3.7)	(8.0)			
Two-stage corrected least squares	0.350	0.466	−0.094	−0.021	0.994	0.0048	0.51
	(4.4)	(3.6)	(3.7)	(4.4)			

Source: Same as Table 17.

TABLE 19   Root Mean-Squared Errors for Ordinary and Two-Stage
Corrected Least Squares Estimating Techniques, Alternative
Sample Periods Ending with 1961 through 1971

End points[a]	Ordinary least squares			Two-stage corrected least squares		
		Ex post			Ex post	
	Sample period	Four-quarter	Full	Sample period	Four-quarter	Full
1961	1.12	1.33	6.37	0.81	1.87	3.32
1962	1.19	1.98	5.39	0.86	1.21	1.57
1963	1.35	1.86	2.12	0.91	0.45	2.61
1964	1.46	0.90	1.61	0.92	1.54	3.25
1965	1.44	1.92	1.48	0.85	2.16	1.95
1966	1.50	0.60	2.33	1.11	1.20	2.93
1967	1.47	1.85	2.61	0.99	1.44	2.22
1968	1.46	1.36	1.84	0.99	0.79	1.32
1969	1.46	1.48	1.77	1.03	2.18	1.61
1970	1.48	1.21	0.91	1.11	1.08	1.44
1971	1.52	0.60	0.60	1.11	1.38	1.38

Source: Derived from dynamic simulations using the techniques of Table 18.
a. See Table 2, note *a*.

better than the original. However, the ex post extrapolations distinctly favor the original estimates on balance.

An alternative specification of the money demand function also sheds some light on the simultaneity question. The money demand function can be inverted to put an interest rate on the left-hand side, relegating the money variable to the right-hand side.[67] Among the interest rates used above, the commercial paper rate seems to be the more natural candidate. The result of inverting equation (4) and estimating by ordinary least squares corrected for serial correlation is as follows:

$$\ln RCP = -6.75 - 9.128 \ln m + 7.319 \ln m_{-1}$$
$$(1.1) \quad (3.5) \quad (3.0)$$

$$+ 2.761 \ln y - 0.280 \ln RTD. \quad (18)$$
$$(2.5) \quad (0.8)$$

$R^2 = 0.928$; standard error $= 0.116$; $\rho = 0.82$.

If one reinverts (18), an equation rather different from (4) results.[68] In particular, the elasticities are 1.53 for income, 0.55 for RCP, and 0.15 for RTD. Only the last estimate is even close to what was previously obtained.

Surprisingly enough, given the results of Table 18, the source of the discrepancy turns out to be the existence of rather strong simultaneous equations bias in (18). That this is the case can be seen by reestimating (18) by TSCORC, which yields[69]

$$\ln RCP = 17.77 - 30.338 \ln m + 12.329 \ln m_{-1}$$
$$ (2.1) (4.7) (2.2)$$

$$+ 12.197 \ln y - 3.135 \ln RTD. \quad (19)$$
$$(3.7) (3.0)$$

$$R^2 = 0.853; \text{ standard error} = 0.165; \rho = 0.54.$$

The results of (19) are dramatically different from (18) and in fact much more in line with (4). The implied elasticities are 0.68 for income, 0.17 for RTD, and 0.06 for RCP, virtually identical to those obtained initially. The major difference between (19) and (4) is that the speed of adjustment of (19) is considerably faster—roughly 60 percent per quarter, which is even faster than the corresponding result in Table 18.

On balance, it appears important to correct for serial correlation and probably for simultaneous equations bias as well, especially if an interest rate is the dependent variable. One virtue of the TSCORC estimates is that they produce substantially faster speeds of adjustment. On a partial adjustment view, this result seems desirable, but it did not appear particularly to improve the tracking ability of the equation. It might, however, make a greater difference in the context of a complete econometric model. Finally, while it might have been desirable to use simultaneous equations techniques throughout this analysis, the generally comparable performance of the original and TSCORC estimates suggests that the results would not be qualitatively affected by such a procedure.

HOMOGENEITY WITH RESPECT TO PRICES AND POPULATION

In the demand functions considered throughout this paper real money holdings have been assumed to be a function of real GNP. Although some writers have used nominal magnitudes, the specification in real terms is the most common form used in empirical research and is the one suggested by economic theory. For example, under the simplest Baumol-Tobin formulation, money holdings are given by

$$M = (kY/2r)^{\frac{1}{2}}, \quad (20)$$

where k is a fixed charge per transaction. Dividing both sides of (20) by the price level yields

$$\frac{M}{P} = \left[\frac{k}{P} \cdot \frac{Y}{P} / 2r \right]^{\frac{1}{2}}, \quad (21)$$

or

$$m = (k'y/2r)^{\frac{1}{2}}, \tag{22}$$

where k' is a transactions cost in real terms. Assuming k' is constant yields the type of specification employed in this paper—that is, an equation of the form

$$\ln m = a + b \ln y + c \ln r. \tag{23}$$

While (20) implies that the appropriate specification is in real terms, it says less about whether deflation by population is required. Indeed, strictly speaking, one cannot aggregate (20) in any simple way. Rather, the distribution of income needs to be taken into account, which suggests that some features of the income distribution might be important variables in the money demand function and that in the aggregate either real income or real income per capita may not be strictly appropriate variables. However, in the simplified situation in which each individual has the same income, aggregation of (20) is possible, and that case does imply that real per capita money holdings become a function of real per capita income.

As an empirical matter, the appropriateness of each type of deflation can be tested simply. For prices one should estimate an equation of the form

$$\ln m = a + b \ln y + c \ln r + d \ln P, \tag{24}$$

and test the hypothesis that $d = 0$. For population, one estimates

$$\ln m = a + b \ln y + c \ln r + d \ln (POP). \tag{25}$$

If per capita deflation is appropriate one should be able to accept the hypothesis that $\hat{d} = 1 - \hat{b}$ and that $\hat{d}$ is significantly different from zero. It should be noted that these latter tests ignore the problem of income distribution and simply compare the merits of two approximations—using real income or real income per capita.

Versions of equations (24) and (25) based on the detailed specification of equation (4) are reported below.

$$\ln m = 0.272 + 0.193 \ln y - 0.019 \ln RCP - 0.045 \ln RTD$$
$$\quad (1.6) \quad (5.3) \qquad\quad (5.9) \qquad\qquad (3.8)$$
$$+ 0.717 \ln m_{-1} + 0.0017 \ln P \quad (24')$$
$$\qquad (11.0) \qquad\qquad (0.008)$$

$$\ln m = 0.820 + 0.222 \ln y - 0.019 \ln RCP - 0.033 \ln RTD$$
$$\quad (1.8) \quad (5.1) \qquad\quad (6.2) \qquad\qquad (2.3)$$
$$+ 0.707 \ln m_{-1} - 0.133 \ln (POP). \quad (25')$$
$$\qquad (11.3) \qquad\qquad (1.2)$$

In (24′) the coefficient of ln P is insignificantly different from zero so that one cannot reject the hypothesis of unitary price elasticity.[70] In equation (25′), the coefficient of population is insignificantly differ-ent from zero. Consequently, unlike deflation by the price level, defla-tion by population does not seem to be called for.[71]

Disaggregation Using Flow of Funds Data

A number of results reported in the last two sections suggested the desirability of greater disaggregation of money holdings by type of asset (such as currency and demand deposits). I shall now explore disaggregation with respect to type of holder, using flow of funds data, compiled by the Federal Reserve, that disaggregate money holdings into the following broad categories: households; business; state and local governments; financial sectors; rest of the world; and mail float.

Ideally, each of these components should be analyzed in the context of a complete model of the determination of assets and liabilities for each type of holder, so as to yield a clear picture of the appropriate explanatory variables and permit systematic use of balance sheet con-straints. This, however, is a task for an army of econometricians (one has already been mobilized, in fact). Within the scope of this paper, it is possible merely to explore component money holdings with some rough and ready adhockery.

The nature of the venture is clarified by the basic data on money holdings at the end of 1972:

Sector	Dollars (billions)	Percent of total	Percent change, 1952–72
Business (including float)	72.3	27.0	36.6
Household	156.5	58.3	152.3
State and local government	14.6	5.4	102.8
Financial	17.0	6.3	151.5
Rest of the world	7.8	2.9	309.0
All sectors	268.3	100.0	105.0

Source: Board of Governors of the Federal Reserve System, *Flow of Funds Accounts, 1945–1972* (August 1973) (see appendix at the end of this paper). Figures are based on data before rounding.

At that time, 15 percent of money holdings were accounted for by groups other than business and households; for these groups the vari-ables conventionally used in money demand equations may not be appropriate. Furthermore, the composition by sector has changed greatly in the past twenty years. In particular, the share of business holdings of money has declined from 40 percent in 1952, while households have steadily increased their share from 48 percent. The remaining components have risen in the aggregate but have also exhibited substantial fluctuations.

Money holdings of the different sectors have also moved in diverse ways in the short run as evidenced by the very low and frequently negative simple correlation coefficients for the seasonally adjusted quarterly flows of the different sectors over the period 1952:2 to 1972:4:

Business	Household	State and local government	Financial	Rest of the world
	-0.11	-0.03	-0.06	-0.09
		-0.14	0.25	-0.05
			-0.19	0.09
				0.06

This result again suggests that disaggregating by holder should pay off.

Dissaggregation will not be a simple matter, however. The first problem lies in the quality of the data. In recent years the Federal Reserve has conducted a survey on the ownership of demand deposits by the type of holder.[72] Attempts to reconcile these data with the flow of funds data have revealed a number of discrepancies that raise serious questions about the quality of the flow of funds data in general and the allocation between business and households in particular. Judging by the survey, the flow of funds data understate business holdings and overstate household holdings of money.

Even taking the data at face value, a number of other clues warn that the analysis of sectoral money holdings may be complicated. When the total percentage growth in the various components from the end of 1952 to the end of 1972 is compared with the growth in the transactions variables relevant for each sector, some marked differences emerge. For example, business transactions are nearly three times their 1972 level (if measured by business sales) or three and one-half times (if measured by business output), but business money holdings have increased by less than one-half. Similarly, state and local government spending is ten times what it was twenty years earlier, while money holdings have just doubled. For households, transactions as measured by consumption have quadrupled and money holdings are two and one-half times the earlier level. At the very least these numbers suggest that "income" elasticities are dramatically different across sectors. In principle, allowing for such differences is one of the virtues of disaggregating. More importantly, however, this evidence suggests that a simple transactions model (especially if couched in real terms) will have a hard time explaining money holding by business and by state and local governments. With these caveats, I turn to some results.

The sample period for all the estimates to be presented is identical to the one used above—1952:2 to 1972:4. All estimates were obtained by ordinary least squares with a correction for serial correlation, although this was not much of a problem. The equations were estimated in logarithmic form and the lag specification was limited to the Koyck form.[73]

HOUSEHOLD SECTOR

The household sector has the largest share of total money holdings and in many ways is the easiest to explain. Essentially the same type of specification used for aggregate money demand works equally well for the household sector. Some representative results are contained in Table 20.

The first equation is identical in specification to equation (4). Both income and interest elasticities for the household sector exceed those found for total money holdings, with the long-run income elasticity exceeding unity. The change in net worth, as before, also achieves statistical significance. An equally sensible equation is obtained if one substitutes consumption for GNP as the scale variable.[74] On the whole, the results for the household sector are reasonable.

BUSINESS SECTOR

The business sector comes next in the size order of money holdings but here, as anticipated, I met with considerably less success. One typically unsatisfactory result follows:

$$\ln mb = 0.359 + 0.010 \ln SALE + 0.905 \ln mb_{-1}$$
$$(1.4) \quad (0.5) \quad\quad\quad (18.9)$$

$$- 0.016 \ln RCP. \quad (26)$$
$$(2.3)$$

$$R^2 = 0.948; \text{ standard error} = 0.014; \rho = 0.02.$$

This equation is in real terms, deflated by the business deflator of the national income accounts; *SALE* is manufacturing and trade sales.

Unfortunately, the equation produces a transactions variable that is not significant and a speed of adjustment that is unreasonably slow. A number of attempts were made to improve this equation. In particular, I tried a business GNP measure, a certificate of deposit rate, a measure of cash flow, and inventory investment, but none of these variables

TABLE 20 Coefficients for Household Demand for Money[a]

Lagged money	Interest rate		GNP	Consumer expendi- tures	Change in net worth	R^2	Standard error	ρ
	Time deposits	Commercial paper						
0.736 (11.5)	−0.055 (3.3)	−0.025 (4.5)	0.312 (4.4)	...	...	0.991	0.013	−0.20
0.784 (12.6)	−0.044 (2.7)	−0.017 (2.7)	0.251 (3.6)	...	0.230 (2.0)	0.992	0.012	−0.27
0.796 (12.3)	−0.045 (2.5)	−0.021 (3.7)	...	0.249 (3.5)	...	0.992	0.013	−0 15
0.844 (13.8)	−0.033 (2.0)	−0.013 (2.1)	...	0.187 (3.7)	0.260 (2.2)	0.993	0.013	−0.24

Sources: Based on flow of funds data from the Board of Governors of the Federal Reserve System. See the appendix for specific information on data used.

a. The period of fit is 1952:2 to 1972:4. The equations are estimated in logarithmic form by ordinary least squares, with a correction for serial correlation, and use the Koyck lag specification.

achieved statistical significance. I also tried a linear functional form but this did not help either. On balance I can only conclude either that the quality of the data makes this a futile exercise or that considerably more ingenuity is needed to explain aggregate business money holdings.[75]

FINANCIAL SECTOR

Next in importance in volume of money holdings comes the financial sector (savings and loan associations, mutual savings banks, and so on). For this sector, the appropriate scale variable is a measure of deposit activity. The level of deposits and the change in deposits used jointly worked relatively well. Two such equations using these variables are given in Table 21. The first employs these variables in conjunction with the Treasury bill rate while the second adds a variable designed to capture the anticipated outflow of deposits due to disintermediation. This variable is defined as the ratio of the Treasury bill rate to the saving deposit rate after 1968:3 and zero before. The higher this variable the more financial institutions expect to lose funds

TABLE 21 Coefficients for Financial Sector Demand for Money[a]

Lagged money	Treasury bill rate	Deposits	Change in deposits	Proxy for outflow of deposits[b]	R^2	Standard error	ρ
0.698 (8.5)	−0.014 (1.6)	0.154 (4.0)	0.514 (1.6)	...	0.995	0.018	0.12
0.659 (8.1)	−0.016 (1.9)	0.179 (4.5)	1.429 (2.9)	0.066 (2.2)	0.995	0.018	0.04

a. See sources and note for Table 20. The equations are in undeflated form.

b. Ratio of the Treasury bill rate to the saving deposit rate after 1968:3, and zero before.

through disintermediation and the more liquid they therefore wish to be. This variable obtains the expected positive sign and is statistically significant at the 5 percent level. On the whole, then, money holdings by the financial sector appear to lend themselves to a reasonably straight-forward explanation.[76]

STATE AND LOCAL GOVERNMENT SECTOR

The final equation to be considered is for the state and local government sector. From initial examination of the data, this was expected to be a troublesome sector, and indeed it was. As with the business sector, a number of specifications were tried, including several interest rate variables and a budget surplus variable. No fully satisfactory equation ever emerged. A typical equation is

$$\ln msl = 0.092 + 0.946 \ln msl_{-1} + 0.011 \ln gsl$$
$$(0.6) \quad (22.1) \quad\quad\quad (0.4)$$

$$- 0.022 \ln RCP, \quad (27)$$
$$(1.0)$$

$$R^2 = 0.867; \text{ standard error} = 0.047; \rho = -0.10.$$

where *gsl* is state and local government expenditures.[77] Quite evidently I am unable to provide anything close to a satisfactory explanation for this sector.

OVERVIEW

Taken as a whole, the batting average on disaggregation by holder is .500. Two of the four categories, households and the financial sector, are reasonably well explained; two others, business and state and local government, are not. One would expect that the first two would behave reasonably well in the simulation exercises I have performed, and—sparing the reader the details—this was the case. The remaining two sectors, not surprisingly, did relatively poorly. Table 22 summarizes the performance in the aggregate with the relevant root mean-squared errors for total money holdings. The left half of the table corresponds to the aggregate flow of funds equation reported in Table 17, while the right half extrapolates aggregate money holdings based on the equations for the individual components.[78] While the aggregate equation does not uniformly dominate the individual equations, one plainly would not forecast total money holdings by separate use of this particular set of component equations. Nevertheless, despite this tentatively pessimistic finding, the results hold enough promise to warrant withholding a final verdict on this issue. Further research along these lines is clearly in order.

TABLE 22 Root Mean-Squared Errors for Aggregate and
Component Money Holding Equations, Alternative Sample
Periods Ending with 1961 through 1971

End point[a]	Aggregate equation			Component equations		
	Ex post		Within-sample	Ex post		Within-sample
	Full	Four-quarter		Full	Four-quarter	
1961	7.21	2.07	0.73	18.71	2.60	1.19
1962	4.54	1.28	0.87	17.41	1.03	1.20
1963	2.33	2.04	0.95	14.95	3.03	1.32
1964	3.70	0.67	1.06	3.59	1.03	1.66
1965	3.50	2.93	0.99	2.96	1.15	1.60
1966	2.15	1.08	1.15	3.44	2.03	1.65
1967	2.23	1.80	1.09	4.51	1.40	1.55
1968	2.82	1.59	1.12	6.77	1.98	1.51
1969	2.94	1.86	1.13	5.11	1.54	1.69
1970	3.83	1.99	1.17	6.29	3.20	1.69
1971	3.30	3.30	1.18	3.84	3.84	1.89

Sources: See sources and note for Table 20. The aggregate equation corresponds to the aggregate flow of funds equation in Table 17. The component equations used are (26) for the business sector, (27) for the state and local government sector, the first equation in Table 21 for the financial sector, and the fourth in Table 20 for the household sector. Money holdings for the rest of the world were considered exogenous.

a. See Table 2, note *a*.

Concluding Remarks

In the process of sequentially examining each of the questions set forth at the beginning of this paper, a considerable amount of information has emerged concerning the nature of the demand for money. This section enumerates the highlights of the findings, attempts to illustrate them by examining velocity, both actual and simulated, under a variety of assumptions, and briefly assesses the demand for money through 1974.

Perhaps most interesting is the apparent sturdiness of a quite conventional formulation of the money demand function, however scrutinized. More particularly, such a function yields sensible interest and income elasticities. The income elasticity appears to be significantly less than unity and can be pinned down reasonably well on the basis of quarterly data. In addition, the conventional equation exhibits no marked instabilities, in either the short run or the long run. Finally, the conventional equation yields a reasonable speed of adjustment to changes in income or interest rates, with patterns and magnitudes of adjustment that are generally similar in the Koyck and Almon specifications.

While the conventional equation performs well, it is nevertheless possible to improve on it in a number of ways. In the first instance disaggregation of M_1 into currency and demand deposits appears desirable from both a structural and a forecasting point of view. Aggregation to the level of M_2, however, is definitely counterproductive. Furthermore, the addition of a number of variables appears to improve the performance of the standard formulation. These include the change in wealth and, possibly, a variable measuring inflation expectations. On the other hand, substitution of wealth for income imposes a marked deterioration in the performance of the equation.

Finally, while the diverse sectoral pattern of movements in money holdings exhibited by the flow of funds data implied some payoff to greater disaggregation, efforts in this direction were only partially successful. The tentative nature of the results suggests that this remains an open issue.

THE BEHAVIOR OF VELOCITY

An empirical money demand function has implications about the behavior of the income velocity of money, $v = y/m$. One important implication, long debated by economists, concerns the sensitivity of v to interest rate changes, which is simply the other side of the coin of the debate concerning the interest elasticity of the demand for money. The results here have reconfirmed the importance of interest rate variables in explaining the demand for money, and their implications for the behavior of velocity help to put their importance in perspective.

The basic money demand function estimated above can be written (in nonlogarithmic form) as

$$m = Ay^a r^b,$$

which yields

$$v = y/m = y^{1-a}/Ar^b.$$

This equation implies that, with a constant interest rate, velocity will increase at the fraction $(1 - a)$ of the growth rate of y. With a value of a of about 0.7, annual growth in y of 4 percent would lead to a 1.2 percent growth in v. Since 1952, v has actually increased at about $2\frac{1}{2}$ percent per year; the excess over 1.2 reflects the upward trend in interest rates.[79]

While velocity has trended upward, its path has hardly been steady, as the series labeled "actual v" in Figure 2 readily demonstrates for the period 1968:1 to 1973:2. To assess the sensitivity of velocity to alternative paths for income and interest rates, I dynamically simulated a version of equation (4) estimated through 1973:2 with four alternative paths. These four paths resulted from combining two assumptions for interest rates with two assumptions for GNP. In particular, interest

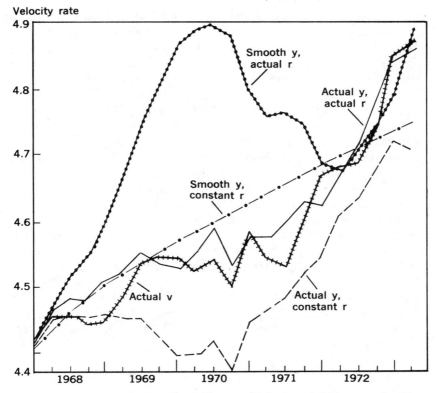

Figure 2. *Actual and Simulated Income Velocity of Money under Four Assumptions, Quarterly, 1968–73*

rates were either assumed to take on their historical values ("actual *r*" in Figure 2) or to remain constant at their 1967:4 values ("constant *r*"). Similarly, for income I either used actual values ("actual *y*") or let it grow smoothly ("smooth *y*") over the period (ending up at the actual value in 1973:2). In each case the dynamic simulation was started in 1968:1.

In comparison with the series labeled "actual *v*," the one labeled "actual *y*, actual *r*" in Figure 2 indicates the tracking ability of the equation with historical data. On the whole, that ability is reasonably satisfactory, but the pattern of errors is interesting.[80] When actual velocity is below that predicted by the equation, some interest rates must be higher and GNP lower than would otherwise be the case, given the money supply. The precise impact on interest rates and GNP depends on the relationship of investment and consumer demand to interest rates and income—the shape of the *IS* curve, a set of vital issues outside the scope of this paper. Nonetheless, to some extent, unusually low velocity is a drag on aggregate economic activity, while unusually high velocity is a stimulus, so long as the Federal Reserve does not fully offset the surprise by changing the stock of money.

By this standard, the low value of velocity early in 1969, a period of excess demand, exerted some anti-inflationary influence. On the other hand, the low velocity readings in the second and third quarters of 1971 could be a factor in the rather weak start of the economic recovery after the 1969-70 recession. In 1971:4 and 1972:1, velocity swung sharply upward and crossed its predicted value; that movement may have reinforced the acceleration of economic activity.

The series "smooth y, constant r" demonstrates, as indicated above, that velocity will steadily increase with continued growth in income. This latter curve can be compared with the remaining two curves—"smooth y, actual r" and "actual y, constant r"—to isolate the impact of fluctuations in interest rates and income, respectively. The historical movement of interest rates produces a strikingly different pattern from the constant interest rate assumption. Similarly, the actual pattern of income yields a velocity series that is markedly different from the steady growth assumption.

In short, velocity can be extremely variable in the short run (quite apart from the residuals in the money demand function) and any policy prescription that does not take this into account may be very misleading.

SOME ILLUSTRATIVE PROJECTIONS

In earlier parts of this paper, I made extensive use of dynamic simulations to examine the forecasting performance of various specifications. In view of the reasonably good performance, what can be said about the future behavior of money demand in 1974? One sensible way to approach this problem is to take as given forecasts for real GNP and for the GNP deflator and examine the behavior of money demand for alternative patterns of interest rates. For this purpose I chose the forecast produced by the Michigan quarterly model, which foresees real growth of about $2\frac{1}{2}$ percent and price inflation of 6 percent for the year 1974.[81]

Table 23 sets out the annual percentage rates of growth of the money stock (both in nominal and in real terms) consistent with three alternative patterns for the commercial paper rate.[82] The first panel shows a moderate decline in interest rates, the next a very mild decline in short rates, and the last a more substantial decline. It should be emphasized that these are not forecasts of actual money growth, but rather of the rates of monetary expansion consistent with the assumed values for interest rates.[83] Over the six quarters taken as a whole the three interest rate patterns imply nominal monetary growth rates of from 6 to $6\frac{3}{4}$ percent, with not much quarter-to-quarter variability

TABLE 23 *Real and Nominal Monetary Growth Required under Three Patterns for Interest Rates on Commercial Paper, 1973:3 through 1974:4*

Year and quarter	Pattern 1: moderate decline in interest rates			Pattern 2: mild decline in interest rates			Pattern 3: substantial decline in interest rates		
	Interest rate (percent)	Monetary growth rate (annual percentage)		Interest rate (percent)	Monetary growth rate (annual percentage)		Interest rate (percent)	Monetary growth rate (annual percentage)	
		Real	Nominal		Real	Nominal		Real	Nominal
1973:3	9.6	−2.3	5.1	9.6	−2.3	5.1	9.6	−2.3	5.1
4	9.0	−0.2	7.1	9.3	−0.4	6.9	9.0	−0.2	7.1
1974:1	8.5	0.8	7.0	9.0	0.4	6.6	8.3	0.9	7.1
2	8.0	1.3	6.4	8.7	0.8	5.9	7.6	1.6	6.7
3	7.5	1.7	6.6	8.4	1.2	6.1	6.9	2.2	7.1
4	7.0	2.4	7.0	8.1	1.7	6.3	6.2	3.0	7.6

Sources: Extrapolated from a version of text equation (4). The time deposit rate is held constant at its 1973:3 level. See the appendix for specific sources.

after 1973:3.[84] While this finding in no way offers a prescription for monetary policy, it does suggest that extremely low nominal growth rates are not consistent with any plausible expansion of the economy through 1974.

Appendix

DATA SOURCES

All dollar data used in this paper are in billions and are seasonally adjusted. The flow data are at annual rates. The interest rate variables are in percentage points and are not seasonally adjusted. Gross national product and related variables are based on the July 1973 revisions of the national income accounts (published in the *Survey of Current Business*) while the flow of funds data are based on the August 1973 revisions. Although readily available in published sources, many of the series used were actually taken from the data deck of the Federal Reserve-MIT-Pennsylvania (FMP) Econometric Model. This was generously supplied by Jared Enzler of the Board of Governors, Federal Reserve System. The flow of funds data needed for this study and helpful comments about their use were supplied by Stephen T. Taylor, also of the Board of Governors.

Currency, demand deposits, time deposits. Taken primarily from the February 1973 issue of the *Federal Reserve Bulletin*. The time deposits series excludes large negotiable certificates of deposit. Except as noted in the text these were measured as quarterly averages of monthly data.

Interest rates. The rates on Treasury bills, commercial paper, corporate bonds, time deposits, savings and loan deposits, and mutual savings bank shares were all taken from the FMP deck. The latter three variables were combined into the averaged variable used in Table 16 by weighting the individual rates. The weights summed to one and are proportional to the quantity of deposits associated with each rate in the previous period. These quantity variables were also used directly in Table 21.

Price indexes. Unless indicated, the nominal money stock is put in real terms by use of the implicit GNP deflator. The exceptions are in the cases where consumption is the scale variable, when the consumption deflator is used; in equation (26), when the business output deflator is used; and (27), where the implicit deflator for state and local government spending is used.

Flow of funds. Seasonally adjusted quarterly flows were cumulated (both forward and backward) starting from the 1970 stock data, to yield adjusted series for the various stocks used.

NOTES

1. The recent interest within the Federal Reserve System in monthly and even weekly models suggests that an even shorter-run focus might be appropriate.

2. See, for example, Laidler [21] and Boorman [4].

3. This is certainly true of the research reviewed, for example, in Laidler [21].

4. In fact, much of the short-term analysis seems to contradict many aspects of the received wisdom. For example, the evidence from the annual data tends to favor M_2 over M_1, long-term over short-term interest rates, and wealth over current income. Practitioners working with quarterly data tend to the opposite.

5. Whatever problems it may have caused money holders and policy makers, the behavior of interest rates in the last four years—historic peaks at the end of 1969, followed by pronounced cyclical behavior and ending with current near-record levels—is an econometrician's delight.

6. Although interest payments on demand deposits have been prohibited, the existence of service charges may produce an implicit yield on demand deposits. Some writers have used service charges as a measure of negative interest payment but this practice suffers from rather serious conceptual problems. Recently, Barro and Santomero [3] have constructed an explicit marginal return on deposits based on remission of service charges. Unfortunately, the series is annual and stops in 1968. It does, however, vary substantially in the late 1960s, suggesting that this may be an important omitted variable in demand-for-money equations.

7. One assumption necessary to produce (1′) is that real transactions costs have remained essentially constant. This is an assumption of doubtful validity and also may systematically bias standard estimates of the demand for money. For one lighthearted attempt to correct for this bias, see Telphlluch [30].

8. See, for example, Tobin [31] and Patinkin [26].

9. The ideal would be a theory that simultaneously treats the various considerations cited above. Such a fully general theory has yet to be produced but a number of promising starts have been made. For example, Ando and Shell have recently analyzed a model in which risk and transactions costs are handled simultaneously. They consider three assets: equities, saving deposits, and money. The rate of return on equities and the rate of change of the price level were considered to be random variables while the nominal rates of return on saving deposits and money were taken as known with certainty. Adopting an expected utility framework but allowing for transactions costs, they were able to show that the demand for money becomes a function of the volume of transactions and the interest rate differential between saving deposits and money. Assuming the latter is zero leads to a formulation like (1). In particular, money holdings do not depend on an expected return on equities, on wealth, or on anticipated inflation. I shall return to this below. See Ando and Shell [2].

10. This sample period was used in most of the equations that follow, primarily for ease of comparison with equations based on the flow of funds data, which are available only from 1952. Equation (4), run over the longer sample period, 1949:2 to 1973:2, resulted in the following:

$$\ln m = 0.286 + 0.179 \ln y + 0.731 \ln m_{-1} - 0.020 \ln RCP$$
$$(3.2) \quad (4.9) \qquad (12.0) \qquad\qquad (4.6)$$
$$- 0.040 \ln RTD.$$
$$(3.6)$$

$R^2 = 0.988$; $\rho = 0.217$; standard error $= 0.0073$;

Durbin-Watson statistic $= 2.08$.

The point estimates in the above equation and in (4) are quite similar although there are some indications of a difference with respect to the error structure (for example, the estimated ρ and standard error).

11. See, for example, the logarithmic specification in Modigliani, Rasche, and Cooper [25].

12. Fieller's method is needed since the long-run elasticity is a ratio derived from two estimated coefficients. The resulting interval will, in general, not be symmetric around the point estimate. This is true here since the midpoint of the interval is 0.71 while the point estimate of the elasticity is 0.68. Furthermore, in the present context, since the underlying estimates are not unbiased, I have only an approximate confidence interval. For a discussion of the Fieller technique, see Fuller [13].

13. This is usually an implication of the transactions approach to the demand for money. A problem arises in a concrete application of this approach, however, because it is not clear that real GNP is a good measure of transactions or that real transactions costs are constant.

14. Although it is not indicated, the t-statistic for RTD declined to about 0.5 as e increased.

15. Poole's results partly reflect this R^2 illusion but he has a number of specifications that do not suffer from this difficulty (for example, the one using the interest rate as the dependent variable).

16. Dynamic simulations in the presence of serially correlated errors also involve an additional correction for the lagged disturbance term.

17. The simulated values of the level were obtained simply by taking antilogs. In fact, this is not the best way to obtain them, but rough calculations suggested that the proper correction was small. On this see Goldberger [15].

18. The RMSE in row 2 of Table 1 is roughly twice the standard error but rises to over three times for $e = 2.0$.

19. The estimate of the long-run income elasticity obtained from data through 1961 is lower than the full-sample estimate of 0.68. Consequently, a more realistic estimate of an attainable RMSE is higher than the $1.65 billion reported in Table 1 (see Table 2). Nevertheless, the more realistic estimate of roughly $2 billion to $5 billion in Table 2 is distinctly lower than all the high e entries in Table 1.

20. See, for example, the discussion of this issue in Hamburger [18].

21. One other technical point should be noted. Table 2 is based on

estimates with the latest and therefore fully revised data (except for 1973). In practice, these data would not be available.

22. See, for example, Laidler [21].

23. Slovin and Sushka [29] have reported some evidence that the period 1955:1 to 1962:1 may be different from 1962:2 to 1968:4. This interval roughly coincides with the start of the market for certificates of deposit.

24. Rather than split the sample at some given point, one may use techniques for testing the hypothesis that a split occurred at some arbitrary point in the period. A number of these techniques are described in Goldfeld and Quandt [16], Chap. 9.

25. The time deposit rate, *RTD,* jumped from 2.9 to 3.5 percent at this point. This was the largest quarterly change in the sample and obviously is an important influence both on the variance of *RTD* and, consequently, on the precision with which its coefficient can be estimated. Extending the sample period in (4′) to include this observation reduces the RMSE corresponding to the last column in Table 2 to 2.8. Furthermore, including this observation in (4″) as well makes the coefficients of *RTD* in the two equations considerably more alike.

26. The Chow test is, strictly speaking, not quite valid here because of the use of the lagged dependent variables and the serial correlation correction. A more appropriate test, at least asymptotically, is the likelihood ratio test. This yielded a χ^2 statistic of 9.1. The appropriate critical value is 12.6 so this gives the same result as the *F* test.

27. See Laidler [21], p. 108.

28. I briefly experimented with several other interest rates in both the time deposit and M_2 equations but these never achieved statistical significance.

29. I spare the reader the additional numbers. However, the remark in the text is based on adding together the separate extrapolations for M_1 and time deposits and then comparing the RMSEs with those in Table 3.

30. Disaggregating by type of holder is considered below. To some extent, separation into currency and demand deposits is also a partial step in this direction.

31. This, for example, was used in Modigliani, Rasche, and Cooper [25].

32. There is some question, however, about the generality of this second finding. In particular, the lagged stock coefficients with GNP and consumption were virtually identical for all the equations underlying Table 4 below. Only when 1971 (or 1971 and 1972) was included in the sample did the difference cited in the text emerge.

33. This is the strategy followed in the FMP model. See Modigliani, Rasche, and Cooper [25].

34. On this, see Gould [17], pp. 47–55. Another problem with the partial adjustment mechanism in the present context is that the transactions approach may easily lead to "corner" solutions for an individual. That is, he may not respond at all unless some critical condition is met (say, the interest rate changes by more than a certain amount). This suggests the need to pay considerable attention to the details of aggregating over individuals to obtain a macro equation.

For a discussion of this point, see Breen [7].

35. On this, see Modigliani [24].

36. To simplify notation I have omitted "In," although the specification continues to be logarithmic.

37. The disturbance term in (10), which is not shown, is actually of a different form from the one implicit in (4).

38. This has been suggested in Carlson and Parkin [8]. Using (12) instead of (8) and a corresponding replacement for (9) yields a version of (10′) with three lags for y and r and four lags for m.

39. It also permits a test of the hypothesis that either the expectations mechanism or the partial adjustment mechanism is absent. See, for example, Feige [11].

40. The relevant F statistic for these variables is 3.5, which is significant at the 5 percent level, when the comparison is between B and A in Table 6. The corresponding F statistic for comparing D and C is an insignificant 0.4.

41. The equations reported in Table 6 were all estimated assuming first-order serial correlation. Allowing for second-order effects did not qualitatively change the results.

42. It should be noted that I have ignored such restrictions in estimating (10′). Basically, my energy deteriorated at this point.

43. See, for example, Dickson and Starleaf [10], or Modigliani, Rasche, and Cooper [25].

44. On this, see Modigliani, Rasche, and Cooper [25].

45. See, for example, Shapiro [28] and Feige [11].

46. It should be recalled that the dependent variable is measured in logarithms.

47. There appears to be some serial correlation left in the Almon equations even after correcting for first-order correlation. However, Dickson and Starleaf [10] perform a second-order correction in a somewhat analogous M_1 equation and get essentially the same kind of results as I did. For example, their income elasticity is identical to the one in Table 9 and the interest elasticities are quite close.

48. Under suitable assumptions this can be formally shown, as in Ando and Shell [2]. Inflationary expectations will be reflected to some extent in nominal interest rates and thus will indirectly affect the demand for money.

49. See, for example, the various studies in Friedman [12].

50. Also relevant here is the notion of Allais [1] that people will pay more attention to current and less to past events the more rapidly the current situation is changing. This suggests that one needs more than a simple distributed lag of past rates of inflation to measure expected inflation.

51. The functional form for the expected inflation term in (14) is equivalent to using $\Delta P_t/P_{t-1}$ directly without logarithms. This is so since

$$\ln (P_t/P_{t-1}) = \ln \left(1 + \frac{\Delta P_t}{P_{t-1}}\right) \doteq \Delta P_t/P_{t-1}.$$

The regressions reported below were, in fact, estimated both as shown and with $\Delta P_t/P_{t-1}$ as a variable and the results were identical to three decimal places.

52. The series are denoted de Menil I and de Menil II here, and their construction is described in Menil [23].

53. Equation (15) without ρ^e yielded essentially the same results as equation (4).

54. If the correct hypothesis is (15) with $f = 0$ and one estimates (14), one would expect to find the coefficient f in (14) to be roughly equal and opposite in magnitude to the coefficient c. This is so since $c \ln M_{t-1}/P_t = c \ln M_{t-1}/P_{t-1} - c \ln P_t/P_{t-1}$. Row 1 in Table 11 suggests that this is indeed the case.

55. One finding that is invariant to whether (14) or (15) is correct is the result contained in Table 12. While the numbers are slightly different for (15), the basic story told by that table holds.

56. To conserve space, except for the price variable from (17), I have reported only the sum of the lag coefficients. The individual coefficients, however, were extremely close to those reported in Table 8. The same lag lengths and polynomial degrees were used in Tables 8 and 13.

57. At least one vaguely similar equation that has been reported in the literature has the same feature. See Shapiro [28].

58. See Modigliani, Rasche, and Cooper [25].

59. This suggestion has been made by Brainard and Tobin [6]. Brainard and Tobin actually specify a demand-for-money equation in the context of a complete balance sheet, so they express money as a fraction of wealth as a function of interest rates and income. Furthermore, they suggest decomposing the change in net worth into new saving and capital gains since the source of the change in wealth may affect asset choice.

60. This conclusion should be tempered for two reasons. For one, the quality of the quarterly net worth data is suspect. In addition, as defined, net worth includes capital gains on equities that should probably be excluded or at least separated out. Along these lines Bosworth and Duesenberry [5] have successfully used a variable defined as net acquisition of financial assets in equations explaining household liquid assets of various types.

61. See, for example, Laidler [21]; Lee [22], pp. 1168–81; and comments by Harvey Galper and Michael J. Hamburger, *American Economic Review*, Vol. 59 (June 1969), pp. 401–07, and 407–12, respectively.

62. Hamburger [18] has been one main proponent of the longer rates, while Laidler [21] has suggested that the appropriate rate may depend on the definition of money.

63. The only difference of any note is that the residuals based on the point estimate definition do not seem to be serially correlated (all the other estimates of ρ are statistically significantly different from zero).

64. In carrying out the two-stage procedures, income and both interest rate variables were treated as endogenous. For TSLS the instruments used were population, the discount rate, state and local government spending, and the lagged money stock. To ensure consistency for TSCORC, four additional instruments were used—income lagged, both interest rates lagged, and money lagged twice.

65. The original estimates of elasticities for income and for interest rates on time deposits and commercial paper were 0.68, 0.16, and 0.07, respectively, while they are 0.66, 0.18, and 0.04 for the TSCORC equation.

66. A comparison of equation (4) to the OLSQ result in Table 18 indicates that the standard errors tend to be understated if serial correlation is ignored. The original standard errors are themselves somewhat understated since I have not accounted for the presence of the lagged dependent variable. See Cooper [9]. Cooper presents some formulas for making the appropriate correction, which for equation (4) yields roughly a 30 percent increase in all standard errors.

67. This procedure was used in Poole [27].

68. Poole [27] found a similar discrepancy.

69. The instruments are the same as described in note 64 above.

70. There is an alternative but not quite identical test which involves estimating (24) in nominal terms and testing whether $\hat{d} = 1 - \hat{b}$. When this was done, the hypothesis was accepted, confirming the appropriateness of deflating by the price level.

71. In addition to statistical insignificance of the coefficient of population, one can reject the hypothesis that its coefficient is equal to unity less the coefficient of y and the coefficient of m_{-1}. This latter test is the analog of the test for $\hat{d} = 1 - \hat{b}$ referred to in the text.

72. For a good description of the survey and a reconciliation with both the conventional money stock data and the flow of funds data, see "Survey of Demand Deposit Ownership," *Federal Reserve Bulletin*, Vol. 57 (June 1971), pp. 456–67.

73. Estimation of Almon distributed lags would have required sacrificing a substantial number of initial observations and would have made comparisons with earlier results difficult.

74. In this instance the consumption deflator is used to deflate all nominal magnitudes.

75. One direction for possible improvement would be to integrate the money holding and trade credit variables. Another problem of unknown proportions is created by the absence of any reliable information on compensating balances. Development of such information would also be a step in the right direction. Finally, the mail float item is included with the business sector. While this is approximately correct, some further work could be done. See the article cited in note 78 above.

76. The equations in Table 21 were run in undeflated form.

77. Equation (27) is in real terms, all nominal variables having been deflated by the state and local expenditure deflator. Estimation without deflation produced slightly better but still unsatisfactory results.

78. The equations used in these calculations were (26) and (27), the first equation in Table 21, and the fourth in Table 20. Money holdings of the rest of the world were taken as exogenous. Furthermore, the results were made comparable with those reported earlier by reinflating the component forecasts (where necessary) and then deflating by the GNP deflator.

79. Velocity (defined on the basis of M_1) has risen from about $2\frac{3}{4}$ in 1952 to nearly 5 in 1973.

80. The residuals depend on the starting point of the dynamic simulations, and hence the pattern discussed here could be different for other starting points.

81. See Hymans and Shapiro [19]. This forecast preceded the Arab oil embargo. The quarterly pattern of changes (at annual rates) produced by the model is as follows:

	Quarter					
	1973:3	*1973:4*	*1974:1*	*1974:2*	*1974:3*	*1974:4*
Real GNP	5.0	2.7	1.8	1.3	1.6	3.1
GNP deflator	7.4	7.3	6.2	5.1	4.9	4.6

82. The results are based on extrapolating a version of equation (4) estimated through 1973:2 where the time deposit rate is held at its level for 1973:3 through all succeeding quarters. While this is a convenient assumption, it is also in the nature of a forecast consistent with the assumed patterns of behavior for the commercial paper rate and the impact of interest rate ceilings.

83. The Michigan forecast of interest rates is essentially like the first panel in Table 23. Consequently, any major deviations from this pattern will not be consistent (as far as the Michigan model is concerned) with the assumed price and output behavior.

84. Extrapolations based on the equation including the price expectation term show roughly the same growth over the period as a whole but more quarter-to-quarter variability. For example, the growth rates of money corresponding to panel 1 in the table (in real terms) are as follows: —3.5; —0.8; 0.8; 1.9; 2.3; and 3.0.

REFERENCES

1. Allais, Maurice, "A Restatement of the Quantity Theory of Money," *American Economic Review,* 56: 1123–57 (December 1966).

2. Ando, Albert, and Karl Shell, "Demand for Money in a General Portfolio Model in the Presence of an Asset that Dominates Money," appendix to paper presented to Brookings Conference on Model Building, June 1972.

3. Barro, Robert, and Anthony M. Santomero, "Household Money Holdings and the Demand Deposit Rate," *Journal of Money, Credit and Banking,* 4: 397–413 (May 1972).

4. Boorman, John J., "The Evidence of the Demand for Money: Theoretical Formulation and Empirical Results," in John T. Boorman and Thomas M. Havrilesky (eds.), *Money Supply, Money Demand and Macroeconomic Models* (Boston: Allyn and Bacon, 1972).

5. Bosworth, Barry, and James Duesenberry, "A Flow-of-Funds Model and Its Implications," in *Federal Reserve Bank of Boston, Proceedings of the Monetary Conference,* 1973.

6. Brainard, William C., and James Tobin, "Pitfalls in Financial Model Building," *American Economic Review*, 58: 99–122 (May 1968).

7. Breen, William, "A Note on the Demand for Cash Balances and the Stock-Adjustment Hypothesis," *International Economic Review*, 12: 147–51 (February 1971).

8. Carlson, J. A., and M. Parkin, "Inflation Expectations" (Purdue University and the University of Manchester, May 1973).

9. Cooper, J. P., "Asymptotic Covariance Matrix of Procedures for Linear Regression in the Presence of First Order Autoregressive Disturbances," *Econometrica*, 40: 305–10 (March 1940).

10. Dickson, Harold D., and Dennis A. Starleaf, "Polynomial Distributed Lags-Structures in the Demand Function for Money," *Journal of Finance*, 27: 1035–43 (December 1972).

11. Feige, Edgar L., "Expectations and Adjustments in the Monetary Sector," *American Economic Review*, 57: 462–73 (May 1967).

12. Friedman, Milton (ed.), *Studies in the Quantity Theory of Money* (Chicago: University of Chicago Press, 1956).

13. Fuller, Wayne A., "Estimating the Reliability of Quantities Derived from Empirical Production Functions," *Journal of Farm Economics*, 44: 82–99 (February 1962).

14. Gibson, W. E., "Demand and Supply Functions for Money in the United States: Theory and Measurement," *Econometrica*, 40: 361–70 (March 1972).

15. Goldberger, Arthur S., "The Interpretation and Estimate of Cobbs-Douglas Functions," *Econometrica*, 36: 464–72 (July-October 1968).

16. Goldfield, Stephen E., and Richard E. Quandt, *Nonlinear Methods in Economics* (Amsterdam: North-Holland, 1972).

17. Gould, J. P., "Adjustment Cost in the Theory of Investment of the Firm," *Review of Economic Studies*, 35: 47–55 (January 1968).

18. Hamburger, Michael J., "The Demand for Money in 1971: Was There a Shift?" *Journal of Money, Credit and Banking*, 5: 720–25 (May 1973).

19. Hymans, Saul A., and H. J. Shapiro, "The Economic Outlook at Mid-Year" (University of Michigan, August 1973).

20. Johnson, Harry G., *Macroeconomics and Monetary Theory* (London: Aldine, 1972).

21. Laidler, David, *The Demand for Money: Theories and Evidence*, (Scranton, Pa.: International Textbook, 1969).

22. Lee, Tong H., "Alternative Interest Rates and the Demand for Money: The Empirical Evidence," *American Economic Review*, 57: 1168–81 (December 1967).

23. Menil, G. de, "Rationality in Popular Price Expectations" (Princeton, N.J.: Princeton University, 1973).

24. Modigliani, Franco, "The Dynamics of Portfolio Adjustment and the Flow of Savings through Financial Intermediaries," in Edward M. Gramlich and Dwight M. Jafee (eds.), *Savings, Deposits, Mortgages and Housing* (Lexington, Mass.: Heath, 1972).

25. Modigliani, Franco, Robert Rasche, and J. Philip Cooper, "Central

Banking Policy, the Money Supply and the Short-Term Rate of Interest," *Journal of Money, Credit and Banking,* 2: 166–218 (May 1970).

26. Patinkin, Don, *Money, Interest, and Prices: An Integration of Monetary and Value Theory,* 2nd ed. (New York: Harper & Row, 1965).

27. Poole, William, "Whither Money Demand?" *Brookings Papers on Economic Activity,* 3: 485–500 (1970).

28. Shapiro, A. A., "Inflation, Lags, and the Demand for Money," *International Economic Review,* 14: 81–96 (February 1972).

29. Slovin, M. B., and M. E. Sushka, "A Financial Market Approach to the Demand for Money" (Board of Governors of the Federal Reserve System, 1972).

30. Telphllunch, Saschba, "A Remark on the Transaction Demand for Money," Core Discussion Paper 7034 (Catholic University, Louvain, Belgium, 1970).

31. Tobin, James, "Liquidity Preference as Behavior Toward Risk," *Review of Economic Studies,* 25: 65–68 (February 1958) [reprinted in this volume—Ed.].

C. Quantity Theory

9 The Quantity Theory of Money— A Restatement

Milton Friedman *University of Chicago and National Bureau of Economic Research*

The quantity theory of money is a term evocative of a general approach rather than a label for a well-defined theory. The exact content of the approach varies from a truism defining the term "velocity" to an allegedly rigid and unchanging ratio between the quantity of money—defined in one way or another—and the price level—also defined in one way or another. Whatever its precise meaning, it is clear that the general approach fell into disrepute after the crash of 1929 and the subsequent Great Depression and only recently has been slowly re-emerging into professional respectability.

The present study is partly a symptom of this re-emergence and partly a continuance of an aberrant tradition. Chicago was one of the few academic centers at which the quantity theory continued to be a central and vigorous part of the oral tradition throughout the 1930's and 1940's, where students continued to study monetary theory and to write theses on monetary problems. The quantity theory that retained this role differed sharply from the atrophied and rigid caricature that is so frequently described by the proponents of the new income-expenditure approach—and with some justice, to judge by much of the literature on policy that was spawned by quantity theorists. At Chicago, Henry Simons and

Reprinted from Milton Friedman, ed., *Studies in the Quantity Theory of Money* (Chicago: University of Chicago Press, 1956). Chapter 1, pp. 3–21, by permission of the author and The University of Chicago Press. Copyright 1956 by The University of Chicago Press.

Lloyd Mints directly, Frank Knight and Jacob Viner at one remove, taught and developed a more subtle and relevant version, one in which the quantity theory was connected and integrated with general price theory and became a flexible and sensitive tool for interpreting movements in aggregate economic activity and for developing relevant policy prescriptions.

To the best of my knowledge, no systematic statement of this theory as developed at Chicago exists, though much can be read between the lines of Simons' and Mints's writings. And this is as it should be, for the Chicago tradition was not a rigid system, an unchangeable orthodoxy, but a way of looking at things. It was a theoretical approach that insisted that money does matter—that any interpretation of short-term movements in economic activity is likely to be seriously at fault if it neglects monetary changes and repercussions and if it leaves unexplained why people are willing to hold the particular nominal quantity of money in existence.

The purpose of this introduction is not to enshrine—or, should I say, inter—a definitive version of the Chicago tradition. To suppose that one could do so would be inconsistent with that tradition itself. The purpose is rather to set down a particular "model" of a quantity theory in an attempt to convey the flavor of the oral tradition which nurtured the remaining essays in this volume. In consonance with this purpose, I shall not attempt to be exhaustive or to give a full justification for every assertion.

1. The quantity theory is in the first instance a theory of the *demand* for money. It is not a theory of output, or of money income, or of the price level. Any statement about these variables requires combining the quantity theory with some specifications about the conditions of supply of money and perhaps about other variables as well.

2. To the ultimate wealth-owning units in the economy, money is one kind of asset, one way of holding wealth. To the productive enterprise, money is a capital good, a source of productive services that are combined with other productive services to yield the products that the enterprise sells. Thus the theory of the demand for money is a special topic in the theory of capital; as such, it has the rather unusual feature of combining a piece from each side of the capital market, the supply of capital (points 3 through 8 that follow), and the demand for capital (points 9 through 12).

3. The analysis of the demand for money on the part of the ultimate wealth-owning units in the society can be made formally identical with that of the demand for a consumption service. As in the usual theory of consumer choice, the demand for money (or any other particular asset) depends on three major sets of factors:

(*a*) the total wealth to be held in various forms—the analogue of the budget restraint; (*b*) the price of and return on this form of wealth and alternative forms; and (*c*) the tastes and preferences of the wealth-owning units. The substantive differences from the analysis of the demand for a consumption service are the necessity of taking account of intertemporal rates of substitution in (*b*) and (*c*) and of casting the budget restraint in terms of wealth.

4. From the broadest and most general point of view, total wealth includes all sources of "income" or consumable services. One such source is the productive capacity of human beings, and accordingly this is one form in which wealth can be held. From this point of view, "the" rate of interest expresses the relation between the stock which is wealth and the flow which is income, so if Y be the total flow of income, and r, "the" interest rate, total wealth is

$$W = \frac{Y}{r}. \tag{1}$$

Income in this broadest sense should not be identified with income as it is ordinarily measured. The latter is generally a "gross" stream with respect to human beings, since no deduction is made for the expense of maintaining human productive capacity intact; in addition, it is affected by transitory elements that make it depart more or less widely from the theoretical concept of the stable level of consumption of services that could be maintained indefinitely.

5. Wealth can be held in numerous forms, and the ultimate wealth-owning unit is to be regarded as dividing his wealth among them (point [*a*] of 3), so as to maximize "utility" (point [*c*] of 3), subject to whatever restrictions affect the possibility of converting one form of wealth into another (point [*b*] of 3). As usual, this implies that he will seek an apportionment of his wealth such that the rate at which he *can* substitute one form of wealth for another is equal to the rate at which he is just willing to do so. But this general proposition has some special features in the present instance because of the necessity of considering flows as well as stocks. We can suppose all wealth (except wealth in the form of the productive capacity of human beings) to be expressed in terms of monetary units at the prices of the point of time in question. The rate at which one form can be substituted for another is then simply $1.00 worth for $1.00 worth, regardless of the forms involved. But this is clearly not a complete description, because the holding of one form of wealth instead of another involves a difference in the composition of the income stream, and it is essentially these differences that are fundamental to the "utility" of a particular structure of wealth. In consequence, to describe fully the alternative com-

binations of forms of wealth that are available to an individual, we must take account not only of their market prices—which except for human wealth can be done simply by expressing them in units worth $1.00—but also of the form and size of the income streams they yield.

It will suffice to bring out the major issues that these considerations raise to consider five different forms in which wealth can be held: (i) money (M), interpreted as claims or commodity units that are generally accepted in payment of debts at a fixed nominal value; (ii) bonds (B), interpreted as claims to time streams of payments that are fixed in nominal units; (iii) equities (E), interpreted as claims to stated pro-rata shares of the returns of enterprises; (iv) physical non-human goods (G); and (v) human capital (H). Consider now the yield of each.

(i) Money may yield a return in the form of money, for example, interest on demand deposits. It will simplify matters, however, and entail no essential loss of generality, to suppose that money yields its return solely in kind, in the usual form of convenience, security, etc. The magnitude of this return in "real" terms per nominal unit of money clearly depends on the volume of goods that unit corresponds to, or on the general price level, which we may designate by P. Since we have decided to take $1.00 worth as the unit for each form of wealth, this will be equally true for other forms of wealth as well, so P is a variable affecting the "real" yield of each.

(ii) If we take the "standard" bond to be a claim to a perpetual income stream of constant nominal amount, then the return to a holder of the bond can take two forms: one, the annual sum he receives—the "coupon"; the other, any change in the price of the bond over time, a return which may of course be positive or negative. If the price is expected to remain constant, then $1.00 worth of a bond yields r_b per year, where r_b is simply the "coupon" sum divided by the market price of the bond, so $1/r_b$ is the price of a bond promising to pay $1.00 per year. We shall call r_b the market bond interest rate. If the price is expected to change, then the yield cannot be calculated so simply, since it must take account of the return in the form of expected appreciation or depreciation of the bond, and it cannot, like r_b, be calculated directly from market prices (so long, at least, as the "standard" bond is the only one traded in).

The nominal income stream purchased for $1.00 at time zero then consists of

$$r_b(0) + r_b(0) \, d \frac{\left(\dfrac{1}{r_b(t)}\right)}{dt} = r_b(0) - \frac{r_b(0)}{r_b^2(t)} \cdot \frac{dr_b(t)}{dt}, \qquad (2)$$

where t stands for time. For simplicity, we can approximate this functional by its value at time zero, which is

$$r_b - \frac{1}{r_b} \frac{dr_b}{dt}. \tag{3}$$

This sum, together with P already introduced, defines the real return from holding \$1.00 of wealth in the form of bonds.

(iii) Analogously to our treatment of bonds, we may take the "standard" unit of equity to be a claim to a perpetual income stream of constant "real" amount; that is, to be a standard bond with a purchasing-power escalator clause, so that it promises a perpetual income stream equal in nominal units to a constant number times a price index, which we may, for convenience, take to be the same price index P introduced in (i).[1] The nominal return to the holder of the equity can then be regarded as taking three forms: the constant nominal amount he would receive per year in the absence of any change in P; the increment or decrement to this nominal amount to adjust for changes in P; and any change in the nominal price of the equity over time, which may of course arise from changes either in interest rates or in price levels. Let r_e be the market interest rate on equities defined analogously to r_b, namely, as the ratio of the "coupon" sum at any time (the first two items above) to the price of the equity, so $1/r_e$ is the price of an equity promising to pay \$1.00 per year if the price level does not change, or to pay

$$\frac{P(t)}{P(0)} \cdot 1$$

if the price level varies according to $P(t)$. If $r_e(t)$ is defined analogously, the price of the bond selling for $1/r_e(0)$ at time 0 will be

$$\frac{P(t)}{P(0)r_e(t)}$$

at time t, where the ratio of prices is required to adjust for any change in the price level. The nominal stream purchased for \$1.00 at time zero then consists of

$$r_e(0) \cdot \frac{P(t)}{P(0)} + \frac{r_e(0)}{P(0)} \cdot d \frac{\left[\frac{P(t)}{r_e(t)}\right]}{dt} = r_e(0) \cdot \frac{P(t)}{P(0)}$$

$$+ \frac{r_e(0)}{r_e(t)} \cdot \frac{1}{P(0)} \cdot \frac{dP(t)}{dt} - \frac{P(t)}{P(0)} \cdot \frac{r_e(0)}{r_e^2(t)} \cdot \frac{dr_e(t)}{dt}. \tag{4}$$

Once again we can approximate this functional by its value at time zero, which is

$$r_e + \frac{1}{P}\frac{dP}{dt} - \frac{1}{r_e}\frac{dr_e}{dt}. \tag{5}$$

This sum, together with P already introduced, defines the "real" return from holding \$1.00 of wealth in the form of equities.

(iv) Physical goods held by ultimate wealth-owning units are similar to equities except that the annual stream they yield is in kind rather than in money. In terms of nominal units, this return, like that from equities, depends on the behavior of prices. In addition, like equities, physical goods must be regarded as yielding a nominal return in the form of appreciation or depreciation in money value. If we suppose the price level P, introduced earlier, to apply equally to the value of these physical goods, then, at time zero,

$$\frac{1}{P}\frac{dP}{dt} \tag{6}$$

is the size of this nominal return per \$1.00 of physical goods.[2] Together with P, it defines the "real" return from holding \$1.00 in the form of physical goods.

(v) Since there is only a limited market in human capital, at least in modern non-slave societies, we cannot very well define in market prices the terms of substitution of human capital for other forms of capital and so cannot define at any time the physical unit of capital corresponding to \$1.00 of human capital. There are some possibilities of substituting non-human capital for human capital in an individual's wealth holdings, as, for example, when he enters into a contract to render personal services for a specified period in return for a definitely specified number of periodic payments, the number not depending on his being physically capable of rendering the services. But, in the main, shifts between human capital and other forms must take place through direct investment and disinvestment in the human agent, and we may as well treat this as if it were the only way. With respect to this form of capital, therefore, the restriction or obstacles affecting the alternative compositions of wealth available to the individual cannot be expressed in terms of market prices or rates of return. At any one point in time there is some division between human and non-human wealth in his portfolio of assets; he may be able to change this over time, but we shall treat it as given at a point in time. Let w be the ratio of non-human to human wealth or, equivalently, of income from non-human wealth to income from human wealth, which means that it is closely allied to what is usually defined as the ratio of wealth to income. This is, then, the variable that needs to be taken into account so far as human wealth is concerned.

6. The tastes and preferences of wealth-owning units for the service streams arising from different forms of wealth must in general simply be taken for granted as determining the form of the demand function. In order to give the theory empirical content, it will generally have to be supposed that tastes are constant over significant stretches of space and time. However, explicit allowance can be made for some changes in tastes in so far as such changes are linked with objective circumstances. For example, it seems reasonable that, other things the same, individuals want to hold a larger fraction of their wealth in the form of money when they are moving around geographically or are subject to unusual uncertainty than otherwise. This is probably one of the major factors explaining a frequent tendency for money holdings to rise relative to income during wartime. But the extent of geographic movement, and perhaps of other kinds of uncertainty, can be represented by objective indexes, such as indexes of migration, miles of railroad travel, and the like. Let u stand for any such variables that can be expected to affect tastes and preferences (for "utility" determining variables).

7. Combining 4, 5, and 6 along the lines suggested by 3 yields the following demand function for money:

$$M = f\left(P, r_b - \frac{1}{r_b}\frac{dr_b}{dt}, r_e + \frac{1}{P}\frac{dP}{dt} - \frac{1}{r_e}\frac{dr_e}{dt}, \frac{1}{P}\frac{dP}{dt}; w; \frac{Y}{r}; u\right). \quad (7)$$

A number of observations are in order about this function.

(i) Even if we suppose prices and rates of interest unchanged, the function contains three rates of interest: two for specific types of assets, r_b and r_e, and one intended to apply to all types of assets, r. This general rate, r, is to be interpreted as something of a weighted average of the two special rates plus the rates applicable to human wealth and to physical goods. Since the latter two cannot be observed directly, it is perhaps best to regard them as varying in some systematic way with r_b and r_e. On this assumption, we can drop r as an additional explicit variable, treating its influence as fully taken into account by the inclusion of r_b and r_e.

(ii) If there were no differences of opinion about price movements and interest-rate movements, and bonds and equities were equivalent except that the former are expressed in nominal units, arbitrage would of course make

$$r_b - \frac{1}{r_b}\frac{dr_b}{dt} = r_e + \frac{1}{P}\frac{dP}{dt} - \frac{1}{r_e}\frac{dr_e}{dt}, \quad (8)$$

or, if we suppose rates of interest either stable or changing at the same percentage rate,

$$r_b = r_e + \frac{1}{P}\frac{dP}{dt}, \tag{9}$$

that is, the "money" interest rate equal to the "real" rate plus the percentage rate of change of prices. In application the rate of change of prices must be interpreted as an "expected" rate of change and differences of opinion cannot be neglected, so we cannot suppose (9) to hold; indeed, one of the most consistent features of inflation seems to be that it does not.[3]

(iii) If the range of assets were to be widened to include promises to pay specified sums for a finite number of time units—"short-term" securities as well as "consols"—the rates of change of r_b and r_e would be reflected in the difference between long and short rates of interest. Since at some stage it will doubtless be desirable to introduce securities of different time duration (see point 23 below), we may simplify the present exposition by restricting it to the case in which r_b and r_e are taken to be stable over time. Since the rate of change in prices is required separately in any event, this means that we can replace the cumbrous variables introduced to designate the nominal return on bonds and equities simply by r_b and r_e.

(iv) Y can be interpreted as including the return to all forms of wealth, including money and physical capital goods owned and held directly by ultimate wealth-owning units, and so Y/r can be interpreted as an estimate of total wealth, only if Y is regarded as including some imputed income from the stock of money and directly owned physical capital goods. For monetary analysis the simplest procedure is perhaps to regard Y as referring to the return to all forms of wealth other than the money held directly by ultimate wealth-owning units, and so Y/r as referring to total remaining wealth.

8. A more fundamental point is that, as in all demand analyses resting on maximization of a utility function defined in terms of "real" magnitudes, this demand equation must be considered independent in any essential way of the nominal units used to measure money variables. If the unit in which prices and money income are expressed is changed, the amount of money demanded should change proportionately. More technically, equation (7) must be regarded as homogeneous of the first degree in P and Y, so that

$$f\left(\lambda P, r_b, r_e, \frac{1}{P}\frac{dP}{dt}; w; \lambda Y; u\right)$$

$$= \lambda f\left(P, r_b, r_e, \frac{1}{P}\frac{dP}{dt}; w; Y; u\right) \tag{10}$$

where the variables within the parentheses have been rewritten in simpler form in accordance with comments 7 (i) and 7 (iii).

This characteristic of the function enables us to rewrite it in two alternative and more familiar ways.

(i) Let $\lambda = 1/P$. Equation (7) can then be written

$$\frac{M}{P} = f\left(r_b, r_e, \frac{1}{P}\frac{dP}{dt}; w; \frac{Y}{P}; u\right). \tag{11}$$

In this form the equation expresses the demand for real balances as a function of "real" variables independent of nominal monetary values.

(ii) Let $\lambda = 1/Y$. Equation (7) can then be written

$$\frac{M}{Y} = f\left(r_b, r_e, \frac{1}{P}\frac{dP}{dt}, w, \frac{P}{Y}, u\right)$$

$$= \frac{1}{v\left(r_b, r_e, \frac{1}{P}\frac{dP}{dt}, w, \frac{Y}{P}, u\right)}, \tag{12}$$

or

$$Y = v\left(r_b, r_e, \frac{1}{P}\frac{dP}{dt}, w, \frac{Y}{P}, u\right) \cdot M. \tag{13}$$

In this form the equation is in the usual quantity theory form, where v is income velocity.

9. These equations are, to this point, solely for money held directly by ultimate wealth-owning units. As noted, money is also held by business enterprises as a productive resource. The counterpart to this business asset in the balance sheet of an ultimate wealth-owning unit is a claim other than money. For example, an individual may buy bonds from a corporation, and the corporation use the proceeds to finance the money holdings which it needs for its operations. Of course, the usual difficulties of separating the accounts of the business and its owner arise with unincorporated enterprises.

10. The amount of money that it pays business enterprises to hold depends, as for any other source of productive services, on the cost of the productive services, the cost of substitute productive services, and the value product yielded by the productive service. Per dollar of money held, the cost depends on how the corresponding capital is raised—whether by raising additional capital in the form of bonds or equities, by substituting cash for real capital goods, etc. These ways of financing money holdings are much the same as the alternative forms in which the ultimate wealth-owning

unit can hold its non-human wealth, so that the variables r_b, r_e, P, and $(1/P)(dP/dt)$ introduced into (7) can be taken to represent the cost to the business enterprise of holding money. For some purposes, however, it may be desirable to distinguish between the rate of return received by the lender and the rate paid by the borrower; in which case it would be necessary to introduce an additional set of variables.

Substitutes for money as a productive service are numerous and varied, including all ways of economizing on money holdings by using other resources to synchronize more closely payments and receipts, reduce payment periods, extend use of book credit, establish clearing arrangements, and so on in infinite variety. There seem no particularly close substitutes whose prices deserve to be singled out for inclusion in the business demand for money.

The value product yielded by the productive services of money per unit of output depends on production conditions: the production function. It is likely to be especially dependent on features of production conditions affecting the smoothness and regularity of operations as well as on those determining the size and scope of enterprises, degree of vertical integration, etc. Again there seem no variables that deserve to be singled out on the present level of abstraction for special attention; these factors can be taken into account by interpreting u as including variables affecting not only the tastes of wealth-owners but also the relevant technological conditions of production. Given the amount of money demanded per unit of output, the total amount demanded is proportional to total output, which can be represented by Y.

11. One variable that has traditionally been singled out in considering the demand for money on the part of business enterprises is the volume of transactions, or of transactions per dollar of final products; and, of course, emphasis on transactions has been carried over to the ultimate wealth-owning unit as well as to the business enterprise. The idea that renders this approach attractive is that there is a mechanical link between a dollar of payments per unit time and the average stock of money required to effect it—a fixed technical coefficient of production, as it were. It is clear that this mechanical approach is very different in spirit from the one we have been following. On our approach, the average amount of money held per dollar of transactions is itself to be regarded as a resultant of an economic equilibrating process, not as a physical datum. If, for whatever reason, it becomes more expensive to hold money, then it is worth devoting resources to effecting money transactions in less expensive ways or to reducing the volume of transactions per dollar of final output. In consequence, our ultimate demand function for money in its most general form does not con-

tain as a variable the volume of transactions or of transactions per dollar of final output; it contains rather those more basic technical and cost conditions that affect the costs of conserving money, be it by changing the average amount of money held per dollar of transactions per unit time or by changing the number of dollars of transactions per dollar of final output. This does not, of course, exclude the possibility that, for a particular problem, it may be useful to regard the transactions variables as given and not to dig beneath them and so to include the volume of transactions per dollar of final output as an explicit variable in a special variant of the demand function.

Similar remarks are relevant to various features of payment conditions, frequently described as "institutional conditions," affecting the velocity of circulation of money and taken as somehow mechanically determined—such items as whether workers are paid by the day, or week, or month; the use of book credit; and so on. On our approach these, too, are to be regarded as resultants of an economic equilibrating process, not as physical data. Lengthening the pay period, for example, may save bookkeeping and other costs to the employer, who is therefore willing to pay somewhat more than in proportion for a longer than a shorter pay period; on the other hand, it imposes on employees the cost of holding larger cash balances or providing substitutes for cash, and they therefore want to be paid more than in proportion for a longer pay period. Where these will balance depends on how costs vary with length of pay period. The cost to the employee depends in considerable part on the factors entering into his demand curve for money for a fixed pay period. If he would in any event be holding relatively large average balances, the additional costs imposed by a lengthened pay period tend to be less than if he would be holding relatively small average balances, and so it will take less of an inducement to get him to accept a longer pay period. For given cost savings to the employer, therefore, the pay period can be expected to be longer in the first case than in the second. Surely, the increase in the average cash balance over the past century in this country that has occurred for other reasons has been a factor producing a lengthening of pay periods and not the other way around. Or, again, experience in hyperinflations shows how rapidly payment practices change under the impact of drastic changes in the cost of holding money.

12. The upshot of these considerations is that the demand for money on the part of business enterprises can be regarded as expressed by a function of the same kind as equation (7), with the same variables on the right-hand side. And, like (7), since the analysis is based on informed maximization of returns by enter-

prises, only "real" quantities matter, so it must be homogeneous of the first degree in Y and P. In consequence, we can interpret (7) and its variants (11) and (13) as describing the demand for money on the part of a business enterprise as well as on the part of an ultimate wealth-owning unit, provided only that we broaden our interpretation of u.

13. Strictly speaking, the equations (7), (11), and (13) are for an individual wealth-owning unit or business enterprise. If we aggregate (7) for all wealth-owning units and business enterprises in the society, the result, in principle, depends on the distribution of the units by the several variables. This raises no serious problem about P, r_b, and r_e, for these can be taken as the same for all, or about u, for this is an unspecified portmanteau variable to be filled in as the occasion demands. We have been interpreting $(1/P)(dP/dt)$ as the expected rate of price rise, so there is no reason why this variable should be the same for all, and w and Y clearly differ substantially among units. An approximation is to neglect these difficulties and take (7) and the associated (11) and (13) as applying to the aggregate demand for money, with $(1/P)(dP/dt)$ interpreted as some kind of average expected rate of change of prices, w as the ratio of total income from non-human wealth to income from human wealth, and Y as aggregate income. This is the procedure that has generally been followed, and it seems the right one until serious departures between this linear approximation and experience make it necessary to introduce measures of dispersion with respect to one or more of the variables.

14. It is perhaps worth noting explicitly that the model does not use the distinction between "active balances" and "idle balances" or the closely allied distinction between "transaction balances" and "speculative balances" that is so widely used in the literature. The distinction between money holdings of ultimate wealth-owners and of business enterprises is related to this distinction but only distantly so. Each of these categories of money-holders can be said to demand money partly from "transaction" motives, partly from "speculative" or "asset" motives, but dollars of money are not distinguished according as they are said to be held for one or the other purpose. Rather, each dollar is, as it were, regarded as rendering a variety of services, and the holder of money as altering his money holdings until the value to him of the addition to the total flow of services produced by adding a dollar to his money stock is equal to the reduction in the flow of services produced by subtracting a dollar from each of the other forms in which he holds assets.

15. Nothing has been said above about "banks" or producers of money. This is because their main role is in connection with the

supply of money rather than the demand for it. Their introduction does, however, blur some of the points in the above analysis: the existence of banks enables productive enterprises to acquire money balances without raising capital from ultimate wealth-owners. Instead of selling claims (bonds or equities) to them, it can sell its claims to banks, getting "money" in exchange: in the phrase that was once so common in textbooks on money, the bank coins specific liabilities into generally acceptable liabilities. But this possibility does not alter the preceding analysis in any essential way.

16. Suppose the supply of money in nominal units is regarded as fixed or more generally autonomously determined. Equation (13) then defines the conditions under which this nominal stock of money will be the amount demanded. Even under these conditions, equation (13) alone is not sufficient to determine money income. In order to have a complete model for the determination of money income, it would be necessary to specify the determinants of the structure of interest rates, of real income, and of the path of adjustment in the price level. Even if we suppose interest rates determined independently—by productivity, thrift, and the like—and real income as also given by other forces, equation (13) only determines a unique equilibrium level of money income if we mean by this the level at which prices are stable. More generally, it determines a time path of money income for given initial values of money income.

In order to convert equation (13) into a "complete" model of income determination, therefore, it is necessary to suppose either that the demand for money is highly inelastic with respect to the variables in v or that all these variables are to be taken as rigid and fixed.

17. Even under the most favorable conditions, for example, that the demand for money is quite inelastic with respect to the variables in v, equation (13) gives at most a theory of money income: it then says that changes in money income mirror changes in the nominal quantity of money. But it tells nothing about how much of any change in Y is reflected in real output and how much in prices. To infer this requires bringing in outside information, as, for example, that real output is at its feasible maximum, in which case any increase in money would produce the same or a larger percentage increase in prices; and so on.

18. In light of the preceding exposition, the question arises what it means to say that someone is or is not a "quantity theorist." Almost every economist will accept the general lines of the preceding analysis on a purely formal and abstract level, although each would doubtless choose to express it differently in detail. Yet there clearly are deep and fundamental differences about the im-

portance of this analysis for the understanding of short- and long-term movements in general economic activity. This difference of opinion arises with respect to three different issues: (i) the stability and importance of the demand function for money; (ii) the independence of the factors affecting demand and supply; and (iii) the form of the demand function or related functions.

(i) The quantity theorist accepts the empirical hypothesis that the demand for money is highly stable—more stable than functions such as the consumption function that are offered as alternative key relations. This hypothesis needs to be hedged on both sides. On the one side, the quantity theorist need not, and generally does not, mean that the real quantity of money demanded per unit of output, or the velocity of circulation of money, is to be regarded as numerically constant over time; he does not, for example, regard it as a contradiction to the stability of the demand for money that the velocity of circulation of money rises drastically during hyperinflations. For the stability he expects is in the functional relation between the quantity of money demanded and the variables that determine it, and the sharp rise in the velocity of circulation of money during hyperinflations is entirely consistent with a stable functional relation, as Cagan so clearly demonstrates in his essay.[4] On the other side, the quantity theorist must sharply limit, and be prepared to specify explicitly, the variables that it is empirically important to include in the function. For to expand the number of variables regarded as significant is to empty the hypothesis of its empirical content; there is indeed little if any difference between asserting that the demand for money is highly unstable and asserting that it is a perfectly stable function of an indefinitely large number of variables.

The quantity theorist not only regards the demand function for money as stable; he also regards it as playing a vital role in determining variables that he regards as of great importance for the analysis of the economy as a whole, such as the level of money income or of prices. It is this that leads him to put greater emphasis on the demand for money than on, let us say, the demand for pins, even though the latter might be as stable as the former. It is not easy to state this point precisely, and I cannot pretend to have done so. (See item [iii] below for an example of an argument against the quantity theorist along these lines.)

The reaction against the quantity theory in the 1930's came largely, I believe, under this head. The demand for money, it was asserted, is a will-o'-the-wisp, shifting erratically and unpredictably with every rumor and expectation; one cannot, it was asserted, reliably specify a limited number of variables on which it depends. However, although the reaction came under this head, it was largely rationalized under the two succeeding heads.

(ii) The quantity theorist also holds that there are important factors affecting the supply of money that do not affect the demand for money. Under some circumstances these are technical conditions affecting the supply of specie; under others, political or psychological conditions determining the policies of monetary authorities and the banking system. A stable demand function is useful precisely in order to trace out the effects of changes in supply, which means that it is useful only if supply is affected by at least some factors other than those regarded as affecting demand.

The classical version of the objection under this head to the quantity theory is the so-called real-bills doctrine: that changes in the demand for money call forth corresponding changes in supply and that supply cannot change otherwise, or at least cannot do so under specified institutional arrangements. The forms which this argument takes are legion and are still widespread. Another version is the argument that the "quantity theory" cannot "explain" large price rises, because the price rise produced both the increase in demand for nominal money holdings and the increase in supply of money to meet it; that is, implicitly that the same forces affect both the demand for and the supply of money, and in the same way.

(iii) The attack on the quantity theory associated with the Keynesian underemployment analysis is based primarily on an assertion about the form of (7) or (11). The demand for money, it is said, is infinitely elastic at a "small" positive interest rate. At this interest rate, which can be expected to prevail under underemployment conditions, changes in the real supply of money, whether produced by changes in prices or in the nominal stock of money, have no effect on anything. This is the famous "liquidity trap." A rather more complex version involves the shape of other functions as well: the magnitudes in (7) other than "the" interest rate, it is argued, enter into other relations in the economic system and can be regarded as determined there; the interest rate does not enter into these other functions; it can therefore be regarded as determined by this equation. So the only role of the stock of money and the demand for money is to determine the interest rate.

19. The proof of this pudding is in the eating; and the essays in this book contain much relevant food, of which I may perhaps mention three particularly juicy items.

One cannot read Lerner's description of the effects of monetary reform in the Confederacy in 1864 without recognizing that at least on occasion the supply of money can be a largely autonomous factor and the demand for money highly stable even under extraordinarily unstable circumstances. After three years of war, after widespread destruction and military reverses, in the face of impending defeat, a monetary reform that succeeded in reducing the stock of money halted and reversed for some months a rise in prices that had been going on at the rate of 10 per cent a month most of the war! It would be hard to construct a better controlled experiment to demonstrate the critical importance of the supply of money.

On the other hand, Klein's examination of German experience in World War II is much less favorable to the stability and importance of the demand for money. Though he shows that defects in the figures account for a sizable part of the crude discrepancy between changes in the recorded stock of money and in recorded prices, correction of these defects still leaves a puzzlingly large discrepancy that it does not seem possible to account for in terms of the variables introduced into the above exposition of the theory. Klein examined German experience precisely because it seemed the most deviant on a casual examination. Both it and other wartime experience will clearly repay further examination.

Cagan's examination of hyperinflations is another important piece of evidence on the stability of the demand for money under highly unstable conditions. It is also an interesting example of the difference between a numerically stable velocity and a stable functional relation: the numerical value of the velocity varied enormously during the hyperinflations, but this was a predictable response to the changes in the expected rate of changes of prices.

20. Though the essays in this book contain evidence relevant to the issues discussed in point 18, this is a by-product rather than their main purpose, which is rather to add to our tested knowledge about the characteristics of the demand function for money. In the process of doing so, they also raise some questions about the theoretical formulation and suggest some modifications it might be desirable to introduce. I shall comment on a few of those without attempting to summarize at all fully the essays themselves.

21. Selden's material covers the longest period of time and the most "normal" conditions. This is at once a virtue and a vice—a virtue, because it means that his results may be applicable most directly to ordinary peacetime experience; a vice, because "normality" is likely to spell little variation in the fundamental variables and hence a small base from which to judge their effect. The one variable that covers a rather broad range is real income, thanks to the length of the period. The secular rise in real income has been accompanied by a rise in real cash balances per unit of output—a decline in velocity—from which Selden concludes that the income elasticity of the demand for real balances is greater than unity—cash balances are a "luxury" in the terminology generally adopted. This entirely plausible result seems to be confirmed by evidence for other countries as well.

22. Selden finds that for cyclical periods velocity rises during expansions and falls during contractions, a result that at first glance

seems to contradict the secular result just cited. However, there is an alternative explanation entirely consistent with the secular result. It will be recalled that Y was introduced into equation (7) as an index of wealth. This has important implications for the measure or concept of income that is relevant. What is required by the theoretical analysis is not usual measured income—which in the main corresponds to current receipts corrected for double counting—but a longer term concept, "expected income," or what I have elsewhere called "permanent income."[5] Now suppose that the variables in the v function of (13) are unchanged for a period. The ratio of Y to M would then be unchanged, provided Y is *permanent* income. Velocity as Selden computes it is the ratio of *measured* income to the stock of money and would not be unchanged. When measured income was above permanent income, measured velocity would be relatively high, and conversely. Now measured income is presumably above permanent income at cyclical peaks and below permanent income at cyclical troughs. The observed positive conformity of measured velocity to cyclical changes of income may therefore reflect simply the difference between measured income and the concept relevant to equation (13).

23. Another point that is raised by Selden's work is the appropriate division of wealth into forms of assets. The division suggested above is, of course, only suggestive. Selden finds more useful the distinction between "short-term" and "long-term" bonds; he treats the former as "substitutes for money" and calls the return on the latter "the cost of holding money." He finds both to be significantly related to the quantity of money demanded. It was suggested above that this is also a way to take into account expectations about changes in interest rates.

Similarly, there is no hard-and-fast line between "money" and other assets, and for some purposes it may be desirable to distinguish between different forms of "money" (e.g., between currency and deposits). Some of these forms of money may pay interest or may involve service charges, in which case the positive or negative return will be a relevant variable in determining the division of money holdings among various forms.

24. By concentrating on hyperinflations, Cagan was able to bring into sharp relief a variable whose effect is generally hard to evaluate, namely, the rate of change of prices. The other side of this coin is the necessity of neglecting practically all the remaining variables. His device for estimating expected rates of change of prices from actual rates of change, which works so well for his data, can be carried over to other variables as well and so is likely to be important in fields other than money. I have already used it to estimate "expected income" as a determinant of consumption,[6]

and Gary Becker has experimented with using this "expected income" series in a demand function for money along the lines suggested above (in point 22).

Cagan's results make it clear that changes in the rate of change of prices, or in the return to an alternative form of holding wealth, have the expected effect on the quantity of money demanded: the higher the rate of change of prices, and thus the more attractive the alternative, the less the quantity of money demanded. This result is important not only directly but also because it is indirectly relevant to the effect of changes in the returns to other alternatives, such as rates of interest on various kinds of bonds. Our evidence on these is in some way less satisfactory because they have varied over so much smaller a range; tentative findings that the effect of changes in them is in the expected direction are greatly strengthened by Cagan's results.

One point which is suggested by the inapplicability of Cagan's relations to the final stages of the hyperinflations he studies is that it may at times be undesirable to replace the whole expected pattern of price movements by the rate of change expected at the moment, as Cagan does and as is done in point 5 above. For example, a given rate of price rise, expected to continue, say, for only a day, and to be followed by price stability, will clearly mean a higher (real) demand for money than the same rate of price rise expected to continue indefinitely; it will be worth incurring greater costs to avoid paying the latter than the former price. This is the same complication as occurs in demand analysis for a consumer good when it is necessary to include not only the present price but also past prices or future expected prices. This point may help explain not only Cagan's findings for the terminal stages but also Selden's findings that the inclusion of the rate of change of prices as part of the cost of holding money worsened rather than improved his estimated relations, though it may be that this result arises from a different source, namely, that it takes substantial actual rates of price change to produce firm enough and uniform enough expectations about price behavior for this variable to play a crucial role.

Similar comments are clearly relevant for expected changes in interest rates.

25. One of the chief reproaches directed at economics as an allegedly empirical science is that it can offer so few numerical "constants," that it has isolated so few fundamental regularities. The field of money is the chief example one can offer in rebuttal: there is perhaps no other empirical relation in economics that has been observed to recur so uniformly under so wide a variety of circumstances as the relation between substantial changes over short periods in the stock of money and in prices; the one is in-

variably linked with the other and is in the same direction; this uniformity is, I suspect, of the same order as many of the uniformities that form the basis of the physical sciences. And the uniformity is in more than direction. There is an extraordinary empirical stability and regularity to such magnitudes as income velocity that cannot but impress anyone who works extensively with monetary data. This very stability and regularity contributed to the downfall of the quantity theory, for it was overstated and expressed in unduly simple form; the numerical value of the velocity itself, whether income or transactions, was treated as a natural "constant." Now this it is not; and its failure to be so, first during and after World War I and then, to a lesser extent, after the crash of 1929, helped greatly to foster the reaction against the quantity theory. The studies in this volume are premised on a stability and regularity in monetary relations of a more sophisticated form than a numerically constant velocity. And they make, I believe, an important contribution toward extracting this stability and regularity, toward isolating the numerical "constants" of monetary behavior. It is by this criterion at any rate that I, and I believe also their authors, would wish them to be judged.*

NOTES

1. This is an oversimplification, because it neglects "leverage" and therefore supposes that any monetary liabilities of an enterprise are balanced by monetary assets.

2. In principle, it might be better to let P refer solely to the value of the services of physical goods, which is essentially what it refers to in the preceding cases, and to allow for the fact that the prices of the capital goods themselves must vary also with the rate of capitalization, so that the prices of services and their sources vary at the same rate only if the relevant interest rate is constant. I have neglected this refinement for simplicity; the neglect can perhaps be justified by the rapid depreciation of many of the physical goods held by final wealth-owning units.

3. See Reuben Kessel, "Inflation: Theory of Wealth Distribution and Application in Private Investment Policy" (unpublished doctoral dissertation, University of Chicago).

4. See Phillip Cagan, "The Monetary Dynamics of Hyperinflation," in Milton Friedman (ed.), *Studies in the Quantity Theory of Money* (Chicago: University of Chicago Press, 1956).

5. See Milton Friedman, *A Theory of the Consumption Function*, National Bureau of Economic Research (Princeton, N.J.: Princeton University Press, 1957).

6. See *ibid*.

* A concluding paragraph containing acknowledgments has been omitted. [Editor]

10 The State of the Monetarist Debate

Leonall C. Andersen *Federal Reserve Bank of St. Louis*

For over thirty-five years there has been continuing debate between two prominent schools of economic thought. In recent years these two schools have been characterized by the labels "monetarist" and "post-Keynesian" economics. The monetarist–post-Keynesian debate has ranged over three major fields of interest to economists. These are macro-economic theory, economic stabilization policy, and economic research methodology. I will concentrate primarily on the stabilization aspects of the debate, although I will of necessity bring in some discussion of the other two.

For purposes of this discussion, I will focus on six topics of the economic stabilization aspect of the debate. These are: the impact of monetary actions, the impact of fiscal actions, the trade-off between inflation and unemployment, the factors influencing interest rates, the degree of stability inherent in the economy, and the appropriate time horizon for stabilization policy. In discussing each of these topics, I will first summarize the contending views in the last half of the 1960s. Then, I will summarize the progress made in reconciling these views up to the present time.

I want to point out that my analysis of these topics is from the point of view of an active participant on the monetarist side of the debate. The analysis reflects my view of the debate and may not agree, in all aspects, with the views of other participants—monetarists or post-

Reprinted from the Federal Reserve Bank of St. Louis, *Review* (September 1973) by permission of the publisher.

Keynesians. In addition, for purposes of this discussion, I will contrast two polar positions. It must be recognized, however, that there are many who consider themselves to be in some middle-of-the-road position on many of the issues.

The Impact of Money

A POST-KEYNESIAN VIEW

Let us now examine the first issue—the role of money as an important driving force in the economy. Paul Samuelson [5], in commenting on the debate, has provided an excellent summary of the post-Keynesian view regarding money.

> As a limit upon the stimulus stemming from money creation by orthodox open-market operations, must be reckoned the fact that as the central bank pumps new money into the system, it is in return taking from the system *an almost equal quantum of money substitutes* in the form of government securities.

> What needs to be stressed is the fact that one cannot expect money created by this process *alone* . . . to have at all the same functional relationship to the level of the GNP and of the price index as could be the case for money created by gold mining or money created by the printing press of national governments or the Fed and used to finance public expenditures in excess of tax receipts.

Samuelson continues this analysis by pointing out that money creation in today's economy does not necessarily reflect creation of wealth, and thereby exerts no direct influence on aggregate demand. Creation of money, however, does change interest rates which in turn influence aggregate demand. He then points out that research of the late 1930s and 1940s led economists to reject money because interest rates were found to exert little influence on aggregate demand.

Samuelson [5] then presents his view of recent economic history by stating that Pigou's real balance effect of money on consumption served to reconcile the deep cleavage between neo-classical theory and the Keynesian revolution. He then contends that

> . . . by the 1950's and 1960's an accumulating body of analysis and data had led to a strong belief that open-market and discount operations by the central bank could have *pronounced macroeconomic effects upon investment and consumption spending in the succeeding several months and quarters.*

Despite this strong contention regarding the influence of monetary actions, post-Keynesian analysis, until recently, has persisted in denigrating the influence of money because of the rather weak, or long delayed, response of aggregate demand to changes in interest rates. Econometric models continued to stress the interest rate channel and shied away from incorporating any influence of real money balances. For example, when simulations of the original Klein-Goldberger [4] model of the late 1950s showed that the real balance effect swamped all other influences, the monetary sector was dropped from the model because such a result was deemed "unrealistic" and "implausible."

A MONETARIST VIEW

Now for the other side of this issue. The monetarists contend that changes in money exert a strong force on aggregate demand (measured in nominal terms), the price level, and output. In determining the impact of money, it is further contended that a distinction must be made between nominal and real economic magnitudes and between the short run and the long run.

Changes in the trend growth of money are considered the dominant, not the exclusive, determinant of the trend of nominal GNP and the price level. Long-run movements in output are little influenced by changes in the growth rate of money. Trend movements in output are essentially determined by the growth of such factors as the labor force, natural resources, capital stock, and technology. In the short run, however, changes in the trend growth of money or pronounced variations around a given trend exert a significant, but temporary, impact on output. The timing and magnitude of such impact depends on initial conditions at the time of a change in money growth. Two major indicators of initial conditions are the level of resource utilization and the expected rate of inflation.

Monetarists do not maintain, as asserted by many post-Keynesians, that money is the only influence on either nominal or real economic magnitudes. Other factors which exert a significant influence are factors which change the demand for money, productivity, and factor endowment. There is even room in this analysis for Keynes' "animal spirits" on the part of businessmen. The key proposition is that changes in money dominate other short-run influences on output and other long-run influences on the price level and nominal aggregate demand. I will have more to say later in this regard.

RECENT DEVELOPMENTS IN THE DEBATE

An integral part of the debate regarding the influence of money on economic activity is the different views held regarding the economic function of money. Some who denigrate the importance of money point out that it is one asset which carries no monetary yield. Others stress that money in today's economy is not wealth and conclude that changes in money have little direct influence on spending decisions. Some post-Keynesians view money as only one of a virtually continuing spectrum of financial assets and thus believe it to be of only secondary importance.

A further argument advanced about the role of money has been based upon the lack of synchronization between transactors' receipts and expenditures. In such a case, it is desirable for market participants to hold an inventory of money balances. This argument can be used to develop a model which delegates a powerful role for money in influencing economic activity. The post-Keynesians, however, have not produced such a model.

On the other side of the debate, empirical evidence has been presented to support the view that money matters to a considerable degree; but, until recently, little attention has been given to producing a rigorous analysis of the role that money plays in a market economy. In recent years, the view has been growing that money does have an extremely important influence because it is the asset used by society which minimizes the economic costs associated with collecting market information and conducting market transactions.

Brunner and Meltzer [2], using this cost of information and transactions argument, have presented an extended analysis of the emergence of money in a market economy. Their view of the role of money is the following:

> Our analysis extends the theory of exchange to include the cost of acquiring information about market arrangements, relative prices, or exchange ratios. Individuals search for those sequences of transactions, called transaction chains, that minimize the cost of acquiring information and transacting. The use of assets with peculiar technical properties and low marginal cost of acquiring information reduces these costs. Money is such an asset, and the private and social productivity of money are a direct consequence of the saving in resources that the use of money permits and of the extension of the market system that occurs because of the reduction in the cost of making exchanges.

> Thus, money as a medium of exchange, as a transaction dominating asset, results from the opportunities offered by the distribution of incomplete information and the search by potential transactors to develop transaction chains that save resources.

What has been the outcome of the debate thus far on the issue of the role of money in economic stabilization? There is no doubt that money has been assigned a more prominent role in recent years, but not to the extent advocated by monetarists. Econometric model builders have begun to give greater recognition to money. For example, Lawrence

Klein has reported that the Wharton model now has a real money balance effect and that now the model predicts better. Simulations of the MIT-FRB model, which had Franco Modigliani as one of the principal architects, demonstrate the long-run properties of money as stressed by monetarists; namely, changes in money, in the long run, influence mainly the price level.

In recent years, money has also received more attention in the conduct of economic stabilization. For years, post-Keynesians recommended that market interest rates be the strategic variable to be controlled in stabilization efforts. Policymakers tended to follow this recommendation almost exclusively until late in the 1960s.

Attention has gradually shifted in recent years toward more emphasis on money and less on interest rates. From 1951 to 1966, the Federal Open Market Committee stressed only market interest rates and other measures of money market conditions. From 1966 to 1970, money or other monetary aggregates served as a minor constraint on actions regarding interest rates. In 1971, interest rates were manipulated in an attempt to produce desired movements in money. Finally in 1972, changes in reserves available for private deposits were formally set forth as a means of controlling money. Such actions, however, were constrained to a considerable degree by interest rate considerations. Since 1969 the President's Council of Economic Advisers has recommended changes in money and credit as a better guide for monetary actions than market interest rates.

Although the debate regarding money is less acrimonious today, some important areas of contention remain. A foremost one is in regard to the speed of response of output, prices, and nominal GNP to a change in money. Monetarist theories and empirical studies point to a relatively quick, but short-lived, response of output to a change in money growth, with a longer time period required for prices to respond fully. Post-Keynesian econometric models, on the other hand, produce an impact of money changes only over a much longer period.

Many economists now agree with the proposition of monetarists that the long-run influence of money is only on the price level, with no lasting impact on output. Some, however, have distorted the monetarist view by asserting that monetarists believe that these long-run propositions also hold in the short run. For example, Governor Andrew Brimmer [1] of the Federal Reserve System, in commenting on the debate, concluded that ". . . there really is no difference between modern monetarists and modern Keynesians with respect to the long-run implications of their theory." But, he then asserts, "Monetarists appear to argue that the reactions expected in the long-run can also be expected to hold even in the short-run." This is simply incorrect.

Another major point of contention is the nature of the monetary transmission mechanism. Post-Keynesians have advanced their views of this mechanism and have built empirical models based on their views. On the other hand, monetarists, until recently, have not developed such empirical models. Brunner and Meltzer have now developed a theoretical model of the transmission mechanism, which is based on relative price theory, and plan to make empirical tests of its implications. At the Federal Reserve Bank of St. Louis, we are in the process of spelling out our theory of the channels by which changes in money influence nominal GNP, the price level, and output. Along with the theoretical work, we are attempting to estimate the parameters of these channels of monetary influence.

The Impact of Fiscal Actions

Let us now turn our attention to the second issue—the role of fiscal actions in economic stabilization. The generally accepted view is that changes in Federal Government expenditures and tax rates exert a strong and rapid force on aggregate demand. Most monetarists, but not all, contend that the influence of such actions is transitory.

Post-Keynesians advance three main arguments for the primacy of fiscal actions. Increases in Government spending add directly to aggregate demand, and reductions in tax rates increase disposable income, thereby increasing aggregate demand. Both of these actions are held to have a multiplier effect. Government borrowing adds to wealth which increases spending. With a constant money stock, higher interest rates result which, in turn, reduce the quantity of money demanded. To the extent that the velocity of circulation increases, there is a fiscal impact on aggregate demand.

Monetarists point out empirical evidence that the Government expenditure multiplier, with a constant money stock, is positive for a few quarters, but in the long run it is zero. The argument frequently advanced in support of such a response is the so-called "crowding-out" effect. In the absence of accompanying monetary expansion, Government expenditures must be financed by taxes or borrowing from the public. In either case, command over resources is transferred from the private sector to the Government, with the result that there is no net addition to purchases. Only in the case of a deficit financed by the monetary sector does Government spending exert more than a short-run positive influence on aggregate demand.

Such a response carries an implication opposite to that postulated by Samuelson regarding money. According to Samuelson, money has an important influence only when it is created to finance Government expenditures. Monetarists contend that Government expenditures increase aggregate demand permanently only if they are continually financed by creating money. Monetarists recognize, however, that

Government spending financed by borrowing can have an important indirect effect on spending because deficits tend to induce central banks to increase money.

The fiscal aspect of the debate is far from being resolved. The post-Keynesian view has continued to be the dominant one in both macroeconomic theory and in stabilization policy. Monetarists, however, have caused both theorists and model builders once again to take specifically into consideration the financing aspects of Government spending. These financing aspects, for the most part, had been dropped from both these endeavors in the early 1950s when the crude fiscal multiplier analysis came into vogue.

The general rejection of the challenging view has been mainly the result of its failure to specify the transmission mechanism whereby crowding-out occurs. Economists such as Brunner and Meltzer and Carl Christ have developed theoretical structures in which the Government's budget constraint plays an important role. Such structures will be useful in identifying the conditions under which crowding-out occurs. Monetarists continue to be skeptical regarding the influence of fiscal actions when such influence is measured without due regard given to financing considerations.

One final point. Just as in the case of the role of money, the debate over fiscal actions may be largely one of timing. Both the MIT-FRB model and the Data Resources model, which are built along post-Keynesian lines, have a zero Government spending multiplier with regard to real output. But this result takes a fairly long period of time to accrue. On the other hand, monetarists generally believe this same result occurs within a much shorter time interval.

The Inflation-Unemployment Trade-off

I am sure you are familiar with the argument that an economy must accept a high unemployment rate in order to have a low rate of inflation, or that a low unemployment rate can only be achieved at the cost of a high rate of inflation. Monetarists, as well as many other economists, reject this argument, contending that in the long run the "normal" or "natural" unemployment rate will eventually evolve regardless of the rate of inflation.

With regard to this issue, post-Keynesians have generally relied more on empirical evidence, while proponents of the alternative view have relied more on theoretical arguments. This is an interesting reversal of approaches from those used in the two previous issues.

In simple form, most empirical studies of the inflation-unemployment trade-off have proceeded in the following manner. The price level is said to be a markup of labor costs, which depend on wage rates and

productivity. Wage rate changes, in turn, are postulated to be negatively related to the degree of slack in the labor market, measured by
the unemployment rate. Empirical studies have found it possible to
measure such relationships; thus, post-Keynesians conclude that the
above mentioned trade-off exists.

Monetarists have developed mostly theoretical arguments in support
of the "no trade-off" proposition. It is not denied that a short-run
trade-off exists, but it is denied that such a trade-off exists in the long
run. The crucial consideration involves the formation of price expectations, a variable generally neglected until recently in post-Keynesian
analysis.

I will not go through this very complicated analysis. Instead, I will
merely point out the conclusion that when prices rise at a constant rate,
and if the expected rate of price change is the same, the unemployment
rate will be at its normal rate and will remain there until a shock
occurs. This normal unemployment rate is determined by such factors
as cost of labor market information, labor mobility, job discrimination,
and laws and organizations which impede the free functioning of the
labor market.

This trade-off issue is far from being settled. It is quite generally
agreed that the crucial consideration is the manner in which price
expectations are formed. No trade-off exists unless price expectations
are formed in such a manner that in the long run expected price
changes fully reflect actual price changes. Empirical evidence presented
to date has proven to be inconclusive—there is support for both sides
of the debate.

In one respect, some post-Keynesians have moved closer, but not
completely, to accepting the no trade-off view. Simulations of several
prominent econometric models give results which show a very sharp
trade-off relationship (that is, a large change in inflation, but a very
small change in the unemployment rate) instead of the comparatively
less sharp trade-off suggested in earlier empirical studies.

Both sides, however, are in quite general agreement regarding the
desirability of actions to improve the functioning of our labor and
commodity markets. Be there no trade-off, a sharp one, or a relatively
mild one, it is agreed that less restricted markets would tend to reduce
the rate of unemployment associated with any given rate of inflation.

Factors Influencing Market Interest Rates

The next issue in the debate which I will discuss is the one regarding the factors influencing market interest rates. This issue has
basically revolved around the distinction between real and nominal

interest rates. Another important point of difference has been the market in which interest rates are determined.

Post-Keynesians have advanced the view that the short-term interest rate is basically determined by the demand for and the supply of money balances in what they call the "money market." The short-term rate is then postulated to influence the long-term via a term structure relationship. Finally, there is a response of interest-sensitive components of aggregate demand, followed by an aggregate demand feedback on the interest rate.

For years, the price level was held constant in a large body of post-Keynesian analyses, with the result that all variables were in real terms, including interest rates. Monetarists have revived the much earlier view of Irving Fisher regarding interest rates. They focus on the nominal rate of interest, which is determined by factors influencing the real rate of interest, and takes into consideration the expected rate of inflation. According to this analysis, the real interest rate is determined by a multiplicity of factors traditionally summarized in the phrase "productivity and thrift." The nominal interest rate, in equilibrium, is equal to the real interest rate plus the expected rate of inflation.

This analysis has led monetarists to summarize the factors which influence market interest rates as the liquidity or money effect, the output effect, and the expected rate of inflation. An increase in the rate of money growth first decreases market interest rates, but then output rises in response to the faster money growth. This results in an increase in the demand for credit and interest rates rise. Finally, inflation increases, and, to the extent that this is reflected in expectations of inflation, an inflation premium is incorporated into market interest rates.

Experience with inflation since the mid-1960s has led most economists to incorporate price expectations into their interest rate analysis. Econometric model builders found it necessary to introduce this factor because, prior to doing so, their models had forecast interest rate movements rather badly in the inflationary period of the late 1960s. Outside of this change, however, their interest rate mechanism has remained essentially as outlined earlier.

A sharp controversy has existed regarding the appropriate role of interest rates in monetary policy. The conventional view has stressed interest rates as the key variable to be manipulated by the central bank in seeking to achieve its stabilization goals. High and rising interest rates have been interpreted as indicating monetary restraint. The opposing view insists that the central bank has very imperfect control over market interest rates in any period other than a very short one, and that a prolonged period of high and rising rates indicates monetary ease.

Even though some policy advisers, such as the Council of Economic Advisers and some members of the Federal Open Market Committee, have accepted the view that interest rates contain a price expectations component, interest rates still play an important role in stabilization policy. In addition, there has been almost a complete lack of understanding on the part of Congress both in regarding the modern view of interest rates and in applying this view to stabilization policy prescriptions.

Degree of Inherent Economic Stability

I now turn to the next issue—the dispute regarding the monetarist contention that the economy is inherently stable. Post-Keynesians contend otherwise. Samuelson [5] has summarized a few factors which he believes affect money GNP even if money is held constant:

> (1) . . . any significant changes in thriftiness and the propensity to consume . . . . (2) . . . an exogenous burst of investment opportunities or animal spirits. . . .

The alternative view does not deny that such factors exert a significant influence on GNP, output, and the price level. But it does challenge the conventional view that these factors lead necessarily to recurring fluctuations in output and prices which are of a cyclical nature or that there does not exist a self-correction mechanism. Monetarists contend that our economic system is such that disturbing forces, including even changes in money growth, are rather rapidly absorbed and that output will naturally revert to its long-run growth path following a disturbance.

Little empirical evidence has been produced in support of either view. Post-Keynesians offer simulations of the response of their models to shocks, while the challengers have appealed more to casual empiricism. Moreover, monetarists have not been convinced by post-Keynesian evidence which does not involve holding the growth of money constant.

This issue is also far from being resolved, but one significant step has been taken toward resolution. There is quite general agreement that the role of price expectations is very important. One crucial condition necessary to yield monetarists' results is that the current rate of inflation should respond to the expected rate of inflation, however the expectation is formed, with a coefficient of one.

As in the case of several of the other issues in the debate, the central point of contention of the inherent stability issue appears to be a matter of timing. Several econometric models built along post-Keynesian lines show, by simulation experiments, that shocks are absorbed over a fairly long period of time and do not produce cycles. On the other hand, monetarists postulate a shorter period for adjustment.

Appropriate Time Horizon for Stabilization Policy

Let us now turn to the final issue—the appropriate time horizon for stabilization policy. Post-Keynesians, with their view that the economy is basically unstable, have advocated very active stabilization actions in the short run. Even if a disturbance is absorbed, the time interval is considered to be so long that economic welfare will be greatly reduced if short-run stabilization actions are not taken. Some have expressed the belief that the economy can be turned around on a dime; therefore, in the case of high unemployment, stimulus can be applied until inflation rears its ugly head and then restraint can be applied to curb inflation. The term "fine-tuning" has been applied to this view. Since they hold that fiscal actions are powerful and have a relatively quick effect, and that changes in money have a very slow effect, the former tool of economic stabilization is preferred.

Monetarists, on the other hand, prefer a relatively stable growth of money over fairly long intervals of time. This position is based on the view that changes in money exert a strong, short-run effect on output, but little influence in the longer run. It is also based on the belief that the economy is inherently stable, thereby requiring no off-setting actions. Furthermore, it is contended that short-run stabilization actions have, in the past, been exercised in such a manner as to create economic instability, and thereby have reduced economic welfare.

This issue is far from being resolved, if it ever can be, because it involves one's notion of economic welfare. It will persist even if there is conclusive evidence of a short-run, but short-lived impact of stabilization actions on output and employment and a long-run impact on the price level.

According to Robert Solow [6], a prominent post-Keynesian,

> . . . there is a trade-off between the speed of price increase and the real state of the economy. It is less favorable in the long run than it is at first. It may not be "permanent"; but it lasts long enough for me.

Monetarists contend, on the other hand, that failure to take into consideration the long-run price level implications of stabilization actions in seeking short-run output and employment objectives seriously threatens economic welfare because the long run may very well be much shorter than usually believed. If such is the case, stabilization actions based on Keynes' dictum, "In the long-run we are all dead," may lead to a serious loss of economic welfare for those living today.

Present State of the Debate

I will now conclude by summarizing the changes in views regarding economic stabilization that have occurred over recent years. Then, I will present my views regarding some steps which are needed to be taken if the debate is to be resolved.

I believe that most observers will agree that money is now receiving more attention in economic theory, econometric model building, and stabilization policy than it did just five years ago. In addition, greater consideration is given to financing considerations in discussions regarding the influence of fiscal actions. The influence of price expectations on market interest rates is almost universally accepted, and the primacy of interest rates as a tool of economic stabilization has been seriously challenged. Although the stable monetary growth rule has not been generally accepted, there is a quite general acceptance of the proposition that money growth should be less variable than in the 1950s and 1960s. The proposition that inflation is primarily a monetary phenomenon, however, has not generally been accepted in stabilization policy.

Two main developments are desirable if this debate is to be resolved. The first involves monetarists and the second, post-Keynesians. Monetarists must spell out, in greater detail than up to now, the channels by which money influences nominal GNP, the price level, and output. Lawrence Klein [4], in commenting on the Wharton model and the academic version of the MIT-FRB model, has laid down this challenge to the monetarists:

> Each combines fiscal with monetary analysis; each has the usual kind of fiscal multiplier; each can measure up to any purely monetarist model yet conceived as far as accuracy of performance is concerned; and each is explicit about the channels of monetary influence in a structural way. They stand as challenges to the monetarist points of view.

As I mentioned several times, monetarists are rising to this challenge. However, if the debate is to be resolved, post-Keynesians must be willing to examine a different approach to macro-economics from their own and to consider different types of evidence. Some monetarists have rejected the traditional static IS-LM paradigm as an adequate framework for presenting their views. They are investigating alternatives based on relative price theory. Furthermore, they believe that explicitly dynamic analysis will be more useful than static analysis. Costs of information, adjustment, and transactions play a central role in this theorizing. With regard to evidence, the testing of simple hypotheses is deemed to be more useful than the building of elaborate structural models.

In conclusion, I am heartened that progress has been made in recent years in delineating the main issues of the debate and in resolving some of them. Moreover, the debate is less acrimonious than earlier. It is my expectation that great strides will be made in resolving the remaining issues in the near future.

Pro Keynesian*

Lawrence R. Klein *University of Pennsylvania*

Leonall C. Andersen's account of the issues is stated so well that I was immediately drawn into a detailed reading of this fascinating material. Of course, since I stand on the "other side" of the debate, I felt compelled to take issue with specific points although I found the piece, as a whole, very attractive.

> *Econometric models continued to stress the interest rate channel and shied away from incorporating any influence of real money balances. For example, when simulations of the original Klein-Goldberger model of the late 1950s showed that the real balance effect swamped all other influences, the monetary sector was dropped from the model because such a result was deemed "unrealistic" and "implausible."*

It is true that Arthur Goldberger found that "money market effects swamped all other effects . . . in an implausible way" when he computed dynamic multipliers for the model. It is also the case that results that looked implausible in 1959 may not appear to be so today. This does not mean, however, that the monetary sector was dropped from the model, as Andersen asserts. It merely means that this sector was dropped for Goldberger's method of evaluation of dynamic multipliers from a linear approximation to the model. They were not otherwise dropped.

With today's technology for digital evaluation of multipliers, we do not make linear approximations. Also, we do not necessarily make *ceteris paribus* calculations of dynamic multipliers. More often, we make *mutatis mutandis* evaluations of dynamic multipliers; that is,

---

* The relevant passage from Andersen's remarks appears in italics preceding each of Professor Klein's comments.

we compute deviations from an "equilibrium" (or "control" or "baseline") dynamic path. Along such a path reserves can grow in an accommodating fashion, and other exogenous variables can also change as they will. In a generalized approach to dynamic multiplier analysis, we would not necessarily find that monetary effects swamp all other effects.

> *Changes in the trend growth of money are considered the dominant, not the exclusive, determinant of the trend of nominal GNP and the price level. Long-run movements in output are little influenced by changes in the growth rate of money. Trend movements in output are essentially determined by the growth of such factors as the labor force, natural resources, capital stock, and technology.*

The claim here is that the trend growth of money is the dominant determinant of both nominal GNP and the price level. This is an imputation of remarkable power to money. If the economy is at full capacity or full employment real GNP and if it is asserted that money determines price level, then it is trivial to say that it also determines nominal GNP. If the economy is not necessarily at full equilibrium, then it is remarkable, indeed, that money is such a powerful variable that it is predominant in the determination of both nominal GNP and price level. I don't believe a word of it.

> *There is no doubt that money has been assigned a more prominent role in recent years, but not to the extent advocated by monetarists. Econometric model builders have begun to give greater recognition to money. For example, Lawrence Klein has reported that the Wharton model now has a real money balance effect and that now the model predicts better. Simulations of the MIT-FRB model, which had Franco Modigliani as one of the principal architects, demonstrate the long-run properties of money as stressed by monetarists; namely, changes in money, in the long run, influence mainly the price level.*

It is true that econometric model builders are now giving greater recognition to money, but I don't think the right reasons are conveyed to the reader.

(i) It should be remembered that Tinbergen devoted a great deal of attention to the money market in trying to interpret the 1920s in his celebrated League of Nations study. In my own work, I have studied real balance effects since early model building efforts at the Cowles Commission in the late 1940s (*Economic Fluctuations in the United States, 1921–1941*). I took up the problem again in micro econometric studies of the Surveys of Consumer Finances (*Contributions of Survey Methods to Economics*) and introduced real balance effects in the original formulations of the Klein-Goldberger Model in the early 1950s. There is nothing unusual about the fact that such effects appear again in the new Wharton Model (Mark III). It is just a continuation of research started more than 25 years ago and quite unrelated to today's monetarist debate.

(ii) As early as 1960, when a planning committee was outlining work for the SSRC model project (later the Brookings Model), the executive allocated responsibility to Daniel Brill and associates of the Federal Reserve Board for the development of a monetary sector, on a par with all other sectors. We recognized the importance of monetary factors from the start, but not along the lines now pursued by the monetarist school.

(iii) The reason why more attention is now being paid to monetary aspects in econometric model construction is that present samples of data cover a richer experience that was not previously available. The wartime accumulation of liquid assets first stimulated our curiosity, but it was not until the mid-1950s that interest rates showed appreciable variance. The monetary crises of 1966 and 1969–70 again enriched our data experience. The whole history of macro-econometric model building has been one of expansion through system enlargements, inclusion of more detail, and direction of added attention to specific sectors. It is no surprise that increased attention to the monetary sector should be taken up now, especially as flow-of-funds data become more accessible. In a similar way, increasing attention is being paid to the international sector, as the United States has more trade and payments crises. Gradually, model builders will cover all sectors of contemporary interest.

> *Both the MIT-FRB model and the Data Resources model, which are built along post-Keynesian lines, have a zero Government spending multiplier with regard to real output.*

Most American models, other than the St. Louis model, imply fiscal multipliers that rise fairly quickly to values between 2.0 and 3.0. They fluctuate in a narrow range for a number of years and then decline. This is brought out clearly in the analysis of the NBER/NSF Seminar on Model Comparison [G. Fromm and L. R. Klein, *American Economic Review* (May 1973)]. For the only period of policy relevance (before many other changes, besides the original fiscal policy change, have taken place) the fiscal multipliers are estimated to be substantial by a broad consensus. In a practical sense, for purposes of economic policy formulation, the latest results seem to cause no change in the standard analysis of the fiscal school.

> *Monetarists have developed mostly theoretical arguments in support of the "no trade-off" [inflation-unemployment] proposition. It is not denied that a short-run trade-off exists, but it is denied that such a trade-off exists in the long run. The crucial consideration in-*

*volves the formation of price expectations, a variable generally ne-
glected until recently in post-Keynesian analysis.*

Surely, it is not right to say that the post-Keynesian analysis has
neglected, until fairly recently, price expectations. A variable representing such expectations has always been in the theoretical and the
associated econometric analyses. I would say that careful analysis of
this variable has a thirty-five year history. In some cases price expectations were empirically represented by distributed lags of prices and
in other cases by direct measurement in sample surveys. It is a difficult
variable to measure properly, and the surrogates have not always been
good, but it has never been neglected. One might criticize the simple
approximations to anticipated prices that I used in *Economic Fluctuations*, but the recognition of the significance of expectations was quite
explicit.

> . . . *when prices rise at a constant rate, and if the expected rate of
> price change is the same, the unemployment rate will be at its normal
> rate and will remain there until a shock occurs. This normal unem-
> ployment rate is determined by such factors as cost of labor market
> information, labor mobility, job discrimination, and laws and organi-
> zations which impede the free functioning of the labor market.*

The concept of a "normal unemployment rate" as it is used in
modern macro-analysis does not seem to me to be very useful. To a
large extent, it is used euphemistically to cover up real problems in
achieving what is easily measurable as a broadly accepted statistical
target of full employment at 4.0 percent. For my own tastes, I think
that 4.0 percent is a pretty poor performance target for a modern
industrial state and would prefer the range of 3.0–3.5 percent. In any
event, I think that it would be unfortunate if the monetarist-fiscalist
debate got locked into assumed agreement on the so-called "normal
unemployment rate" as a target.

> *I now turn to the next issue—the dispute regarding the monetarist
> contention that the economy is inherently stable. Post-Keynesians
> contend otherwise. Samuelson has summarized a few factors which
> he believes affect money GNP even if money is held constant:*
>
> "(1) . . . *any significant changes in thriftiness and the propensity
> to consume . . . . (2) . . . an exogenous burst of investment op-
> portunities or animal spirits . . . ."*

I don't think that it is correct to say that Post-Keynesians contend
that the economy is inherently unstable. They may contend that it is
oscillatory or subject to fluctuations and that it has a tendency to
move about a position of underemployment equilibrium, but this is
far different from saying that the economy is unstable. The quotation
cited from Paul Samuelson is one that I would commonly associate

with a theory of the business cycle that he taught me three decades ago, with an ancestry related to Spiethoff, Tougan Baranovsky, Schumpetter, and Hansen. Their views can be superimposed on the Keynesian system, to derive a formally stable cyclical process.

> *Little empirical evidence has been produced in support of either view* [degree of economic stability]. *Post-Keynesians offer simulations of the response of their models to shocks, while the challengers appeal more to casual empiricism.*

The Wharton Model (*Econometric Models of Cyclical Behavior*) and the Klein-Goldberger Model ("The Dynamic Properties of the Klein-Goldberger Model," Adelman and Adelman; "On The Possibility of Another '29") have been shocked in many separate studies. A number of these have been published. They consider both once-and-for-all exogenous and repeated stochastic shocks. A persistent finding is that the models of the underlying dynamic economic system are quite stable. In the case of once-and-for-all shocks, there is a strong tendency for the system to return to a long-run growth path after a severely damped oscillatory movement. In the cases of stochastic shocks, a stable oscillatory movement occurs. A. L. Nagar's stochastic simulations of the Brookings Model (*The Brookings Model: Some Further Results*) appear also to be stable.

> *As in the case of several of the other issues in the debate, the central point of contention of the inherent stability issue appears to be a matter of timing. Several econometric models built along post-Keynesian lines show, by simulation experiments, that shocks are absorbed over a fairly long period of time and do not produce cycles. On the other hand, monetarists postulate a shorter period for adjustment.*

As noted in the preceding comment, simulations of econometric models built along post-Keynesian lines do show important business cycle characteristics. It is a strong claim on the part of such model builders that these systems are capable of generating the cycle, as it has been historically measured, when the models are subjected to repeated shocks in stochastic simulations. I regard this as a basic validation feature of contemporary econometric model building research, and this is an integral part of my challenge to the monetarists, to see whether they can do as well in reproducing accepted measures of cyclical characteristics from simulations of their models. I am disappointed in their not following this line of econometric research.

> *Let us now turn to the final issue—the appropriate time horizon for stabilization policy. Post-Keynesians, with their view that the economy is basically unstable, have advocated very active stabilization actions in the short run.*

At this point, I repeat earlier comments that post-Keynesians do not hold the ". . . view that the economy is basically unstable . . . ."

(Section entitled "Present State of the Debate")

Andersen sums up the debate nicely in these concluding paragraphs. Without accepting his view about the workings of the economy, I find that I can accept his view of the issues and procedures for continuing research on resolving some of the main issues. Careful statistical study of the evidence following best econometric practice can probably do much to settle some of the debatable issues. It is extremely healthy and welcome to see the debate shift from speculative theorizing, casual empirical referencing, and unsupported asserting, to serious work in applied econometrics. We may not resolve matters, but we shall learn more about the crucial issues and know where each side stands. We shall probably find out what would be needed in order to convince both sides of the correctness or incorrectness of their positions.

Pro Monetarist

Karl Brunner *University of Rochester*

Leonall C. Andersen notes correctly that theoretical issues, policy problems, and research strategy have been closely related in recent controversies. This interrelation may be recognized by rearranging the issues covered by Andersen into four broad groups which summarize the central contentions of the controversies. An explicit restatement of the nature of the issues seems useful in order to remove irrelevant contentions or misconceptions concerning the propositions involved. My summary is guided by the four questions entered at the head of each section below.

(1) HOW DO MONEY AND FISCAL POLICY INFLUENCE ECONOMIC ACTIVITY?

The orthodox Keynesian view contends that all information bearing on the transmission of monetary impulses is contained in the slope properties of the IS-LM diagram. A Pigovian modification includes shifts in the IS curve associated with the real balance effect. The evolution of the neo-Keynesian views flattened the slope of the IS curve. Keynesian analysis thus gradually reassessed the influence of money and monetary policy.

These changes in the perspective concerning the relative strength of monetary impulses did not modify the comparative role of fiscal and monetary policy in a stabilization program. The primary role was still designed to fiscal policy with monetary policy confined to a "passively permissive" role. This concept of policy is a consequence of the Keynesian interpretation of the transmission mechanism which persists independently of the changes noted above. Apart from a more or less significant real balance effect, monetary impulses are conveyed in the usual Keynesian view by the play of interest rates on financial assets. Thus, the transmission of monetary impulses depends on the responses of the small proportion of expenditure categories with comparatively high borrowing costs. The Keynesian view therefore implies that applications of monetary policy burden a comparatively small sector with the task of swinging the whole economy in the desired direction. This means that this view of the transmission mechanism assigns substantial social costs to the use of monetary policy. In contrast, stabilization programs based on fiscal adjustments apparently impose lower social costs for similar social benefits.

It is commonly known that monetarist analysis rejects the assessment of monetary and fiscal policies offered by the Keynesian view. It is not commonly understood, however, that the conflicting views bearing on policy programs follow from a fundamental difference in the conceptions governing the substitution relations of money. Keynesians constrain the substitution to money and financial assets of a similar risk class. On the other hand, monetarists postulate that transactions dominating assets (that is, money) substitute in all directions over the whole array of other assets. This difference implies that monetarist analysis rejects the IS-LM framework as an adequate representation of monetary processes.

Also, monetarist analysis does not accept the idea that the slope properties of such diagrams contain all the relevant information pertaining to the transmission of monetary impulses. In contrast, the credit market, usually dismissed or disregarded in Keynesian analysis, emerges with an important function in monetarist analysis. It follows that the impact of monetary actions on interest rates cannot be interpreted simply as a "liquidity effect" resulting from the interaction between money demand and money stock.

Furthermore, the role of the government sector's budget position and its impact on the economy via asset markets are thus accessible to monetarist analysis, but not to Keynesian analysis. Also, the Keynesian distinction between the "direct effects" of fiscal policy and the "indirect effects" of monetary policy are recognizably conditioned by the peculiarities of the Keynesian transmission mechanism. Once the nature of the contending views is properly understood, we may hopefully move in our empirical research beyond Samuelson's attempt to force the issue into the Keynesian strait jacket by trying to reduce it to conflicting propositions about the interest elasticity of money.

(2) DOES THE ECONOMY PRODUCE SELF-SUSTAINING FLUCTUATIONS OF MAJOR MAGNITUDES?

Keynesians usually answer this question in the affirmative. The *General Theory* contains several passages emphasizing the tenuous nature of long-run expectations and the unreliable gyrations of the marginal efficiency of investment. On the other hand, monetarists stress the shock absorbing capacity of the market process and the load factors usually produced by an unstable government and policy process. It is noteworthy that some of the exemplifications offered in Keynes' work, in spite of the general passages mentioned, actually support the monetarist thesis.

The contentions swirling around the stability of the economic process certainly require substantial further examination. Keynesians usually postulate that interaction between economic and political processes stabilize and at least do not destabilize the economy. Monetarists, on the other side, argue that such interaction operates more frequently in a destabilizing and welfare-reducing direction. It should be noted that Keynesians offer little evidence supporting their views. It is particularly noteworthy that all econometric models cast in a Keynesian mold, and examined in detail thus far, imply the monetarist stability thesis and reject the Keynesian thesis of an unstable process generating self-sustaining fluctuations of substantial magnitudes. But the monetarist case is not yet firmly established and the issue will persist.

(3) APART FROM AN UNSTABLE PROCESS, WHAT FORCES PRODUCE ECONOMIC FLUCTUATIONS?

Fiscalist Keynesians answer with a description of fiscal policy and stress the crucial significance of information about fiscal policy in order to appraise future economic trends. Others emphasize the role of a Wicksell-Keynes process and offer quotes about the autonomous operation of "animal spirits" affecting the anticipated real net yield on real capital. Monetarists, of course, stress the role of monetary impulses approximated by *relative* changes of some measure of the money stock. These differences in the views about the driving impulse forces should not be misconstrued into absolute categories. They involve statements asserting the *comparative* dominance and persistence of specific impulses. Moreover, the monetarist thesis does not require termination of empirical research with a beautiful time series exhibiting accelerations and decelerations of the money stock. Some monetarists penetrated substantially "behind" this phenomenon to establish a link between a country's financial institutions and the nature of the policy process. It follows, therefore, that the question of exogeneity or endogeneity of the money stock attracts only a mild interest for the resolution of our major issues.

(4) DO WE NEED THE ALLOCATIVE (SECTORAL) DETAILS FOR THE UNDERSTANDING OF AN ECONOMY'S MACRO-BEHAVIOR?

Many, but not necessarily all, Keynesians will answer affirmatively. On the other hand, monetarists emphasize the approximate separation of allocative and aggregative processes. They assert that *one* set of forces explains the position of relative price changes under a given distribution of such changes, and an essentially *different* set of forces explains the *position* of the *whole* distribution. They contend, therefore, that a detailed description of *which* relative price changes are located *where* under the distribution, yields no relevant information about the inflationary thrust of an economy. Some aggregative significance is, however, recognized for specific allocative patterns (currency ratio, time deposit ratio, investment ratio for the long-run resource effect but not for the short-run demand effect).

There remains a fundamental conflict on this issue which has molded substantial differences in research strategy. The producers of large scale econometric models are motivated by a denial of the monetarist thesis, and the latter implies a research strategy addressed to small models, partial hypotheses, and a gradual build-up of theories by combining relatively "simple" building blocks. Monetarists would also claim that they are less interested in technical sophistication *per se*, and assign more weight to economic content.

CONCLUDING OBSERVATIONS

Keynesian analysis usually resolves the problem of interpreting monetary trends by relying on interest rates. This decision is justified by references to the central role of interest rates in the transmission mechanism of their models.

Monetarists claim, on the other hand, that Keynesians have adopted, without analytic reasons, the central bank tradition of gauging the tightness or ease of monetary policy by the level of, or movements in, market interest rates. The IS-LM diagram implies that changes in interest rates would serve as a reliable indicator of monetary events if the IS curve is rigidly fixed and money demand is stable (ignoring the effects of changing price expectations on interest rates). Monetarists, however, contend that in a world in which the IS curve is changing and perhaps money demand is shifting, interest rate movements do not give reliable signals as to the tightness or ease of monetary policy. Unfortunately, the nature of the interpretation problem does not seem to be well understood, and an ossified inheritance persists in the literature. On the other hand, some progress can be noted in the determination of suitable policies and policy procedures. Both analytic examinations and simulations of econometric models have opened avenues for exploration to resolve the issues of policy strategy which should be acceptable to all parties in the controversy. The progress made in the analysis of the determination problem of monetary policy eventually may be matched by similar progress in the interpretation problem.

And so, where do we stand? Surely, the questions and positions have changed over the past twenty years. Beyond the noise of the ongoing debate, the gradual effect of searching examination was bound to modify subtly the views of Keynesians and monetarists. Moreover, the four major issues allow a variety of combinations. Some economists may reject the monetarist impulse hypothesis, but accept the monetarist view of the transmission mechanism. The evolution of such a spectrum with a "middleground" should enrich our future research activities. Such activities should yield substantive results over the years to the extent that economists successfully avoid the "media propensity" of equating all issues with ideological positions.

REFERENCES

1. Brimmer, Andrew F., "Monetarist Criticism and the Conduct of Flexible Monetary Policy in United States," Paper presented at the Institute of Economics and Statistics (Oxford University, April 24, 1972).

2. Brunner, Karl, and Alan H. Meltzer, "The Uses of Money: Money in the Theory of an Exchange Economy," *American Economic Review,* 61: 784–805 (December 1971).

3. Goldberger, Arthur S., *Impact Multipliers and Dynamic Properties of the Klein-Goldberger Model* (Amsterdam: North-Holland Publishing Company, 1959).

4. Klein, Lawrence R., "Empirical Evidence on Fiscal and Monetary Models," in James J. Diemond (ed.), *Issues in Fiscal and Monetary Policy—The Eclectic Economist Views the Controversy* (Chicago: De-Paul University, 1971).

5. Samuelson, Paul A., "Reflections on the Merits and Demands of Monetarism," in James J. Diemond (ed.), *Issues in Fiscal and Monetary Policy—The Eclectic Economist Views the Controversy* (Chicago: De-Paul University, 1971).

6. Solow, M. Robert, "Price Expectations and the Behavior of the Price Level" (Manchester University Press, 1969).

Part **III**

The Integration of Monetary and Value Theory

Keynes in the *General Theory* attacked what he called the traditional separation of monetary and value theory, what Patinkin was later to call the "classical dichotomy." Keynes' answer to the classical dichotomy was his asset preference theory embodied in his concept of "liquidity preference." He employed a two-stage theory of wealth accumulation; first, individuals decided how much they wished to save of their income after which they decided how their savings should be divided between monetary and non-monetary assets. In Keynes' theory of liquidity preference, the rate of interest determined the distribution of individuals' assets between money and income-earning assets, given their level of wealth. Thus the four basic functions in the Keynesian system are the supply of money, the liquidity preference schedule, the marginal propensity to consume, and the marginal efficiency of capital which together with a given wage unit determines the level of output and employment.

Hicks attempted to demonstrate that the principal novelty of Keynes was his liquidity preference theory and that with the exception of this, the economic system of Keynes was compatible with the classical model and might even be regarded as an extension of it. Furthermore, Hicks demonstrated that at full employment the Keynesian model was identical with the classical model. This reconciliation was not accepted by Lange, who claimed there was a fundamental "inconsistency" in the classical economic system which, furthermore, was not removed by the Keynesian analysis. Lange maintained that Say's Law (which he interpreted as meaning that people only produce goods in order to buy other goods) in combination with Walras' Law (that at some set of *relative* prices there would be no excess demand for goods or money) precluded any monetary theory since the excess demand for money in the market is equal to zero at some set of relative prices regardless of the absolute price level. Patinkin restated Lange's criticism by saying these two laws were inconsistent with the quantity theory of money. He pointed out that if the demand for commodities was not affected by changes in the absolute price level at full employment, it was difficult to understand the concern with the effects of inflation generated by an increase in the supply of money as postulated by the quantity theory. Patinkin challenged a "classical" system which said that the demand for commodities was determined by relative prices only, and the function of money was only to determine the absolute price level (although it may have been more the proponents of the classical system rather than the classical economists themselves who were guilty of this type of statement). In particular, Patinkin challenged the classical assumption that the doubling of all commodity prices would leave supply and demand for goods unchanged (i.e., the supply and demand functions of commodities were homogeneous of zero order in commodity prices).

This latter point of Patinkin's argument may be illustrated by rewriting the cash balance equation of the demand for money as an excess (or deficit) demand equation:

$$kpY - \hat{M} = X_m \qquad (1)$$

where kpY, the demand for nominal cash balances, less the money supply determined by the monetary authorities, $\hat{M}$, defines the excess (or deficit) demand for money, X_m. If the price level and the supply of money are increased in the same proportion, the excess demand for money will be increased by the same proportion:

$$kp(1 + \alpha)Y - M(1 + \alpha) = X_m(1 + \alpha) \qquad (2)$$

If, however, the money supply is increased exogenously by the monetary authority, then the excess demand for money will not increase proportionately to the increase in the supply of money:

$$kpY - M(1 + \alpha) = X_m - \alpha M \qquad (3)$$

However, assuming individuals possess no "money illusion," and find that at the existing price level they are holding more "real" balances, M/p, than they wish, they would then plan an increase in expenditures for goods and services which would lead to a rise in prices proportional to the increase in money supply, thus restoring the relationship in equation (2). A similar result would be obtained from an exogenous rise in the price level. The "real balance effect" is the change in the purchase of commodities and services required to restore the "real value" of cash balances upset by an initial rise in the price level, or change in the money supply. The spelling out of this "real balance" or "Pigou" effect, Patinkin argues, is necessary in order to establish a valid classical model where money is "neutral," which means that changes in the money supply affect only absolute prices and not relative prices or the rate of interest. The real balance effect provides an explicit bridge between the world of "real" economics and that of "monetary" economics. Patinkin's formal solution is that if

money, defined as real balances, is introduced like another commodity
into the Walrasian demand and supply functions along with some
additional assumptions (more of this in Part IV) then the dichotomy
between real and monetary markets is removed and the classical economic system is consistent. Patinkin explains the failure of the classical
economists to introduce explicitly the real balance effect, which they
recognized, as due to the fact that in the quantity equation they regarded the level of output as fixed by the size of the labor force and
independent of the price level.

Patinkin, in part, created some of his own problems by the manner
in which he introduced changes in the supply of money. Money is
created like "manna" from heaven outside the economic system which
he is analyzing. In two of the important methods by which the money
supply is normally increased, that is by an expansion of assets of the
banking system, or by government deficits financed at the central
bank, an excess demand *precedes* an increase in the money supply
rather than the reverse. In the case where money supply is increased
through open market operations the interest rate mechanism operates
to increase the demand for goods since, as Patinkin has pointed out,
the Keynesian "liquidity trap" is an institutional, not a theoretical,
restraint. If the monetary authority wished to become the sole holder
of debt in the economy, it could force the interest rate down to any
level it wished through further increases in the money supply, but the
consequence of this would be the destruction of the financial system.[1]
None of these methods excludes the operation of the "Pigou Effect"
but each minimizes the central importance Patinkin attaches to it.

Archibald and Lipsey in replying to Patinkin argued that if one
regards classical theory as employing the method of comparing one
equilibrium position with another (comparative statics), then the
classical theory is consistent and the general price level is determinate
without reference to Patinkin's "real balance" effect. This is illustrated
by equation (3). If the initial excess demand for money, X_m, is zero,
then the excess demand for money will change proportionally with
changes in the money supply. The importance of the "real balance"
effect, they claim, is in explaining how the system behaves in disequilibrium, that is, when Walras' Law does not apply.

The ultimate contribution of the "dichotomy" controversy appears
to be the rigorous demonstration by Patinkin that it is not possible to
divide the pricing process between a real market where relative prices
are determined and a monetary market where absolute prices are
determined. The equilibrium value of relative and absolute prices and

[1] See the interesting exchange between Hicks and Patinkin where they ap-
parently are in agreement on this point: J. R. Hicks, "A Rehabilitation of
'Classical' Economics?" *Economic Journal*, Vol. 67 (June 1957), 278–89, and
D. Patinkin's "Rejoinder," *Economic Journal*, Vol. 69 (September 1959), 582–87.

the rate of interest are determined simultaneously by the interaction of both markets, a result also arrived at by Hicks, although without specifying the behavioral link provided by the "real balance effect."

Lange and Patinkin concentrated their attack on the "neutrality" of money principally on the classical idea that a change in the money supply would leave relative prices unchanged. Metzler questioned whether the interest rate at full employment would remain unchanged (homogeneous in degree zero) in the face of changes in the supply of money. Neoclassical economists such as Wicksell believed that at full employment there existed a unique "natural" rate of interest. Keynes' analysis also implied that the rate of interest was uniquely determined at full employment.

Metzler's position was that whether or not the classical view was correct depended on how the money supply was changed. He demonstrated, by applying the "Pigou Effect," that if the money supply at full employment is changed by the monetary authorities through a purchase of securities which changes the stock of private financial assets, the results will differ from those when the money supply is varied without changing the stock of private financial assets (for example, by government deficit financing through the central bank). The latter method of changing the money supply yields results in conformity with the classical model while the former method does not, if one accepts the Pigouvian idea that consumption is not only a function of income but also of wealth.

In the case of an open market purchase of securities by the monetary authorities, the rate of interest will initially decline, increasing investment so that total demand exceeds full employment output, causing prices to rise. Metzler demonstrated that this increase in prices would leave the community with a smaller stock of *real* assets and a consequently greater desire to save so that the new equilibrium rate of interest would not return it to its former level. Metzler's wealth effect is the complement of Keynes' liquidity preference; just as changes in one form of wealth, the stock of money, may change the rate of interest, so can changes in the stock of other forms of wealth, securities, for example, change the rate of interest. Metzler's conclusion had important implications for growth theory since if it was possible for the monetary authority to affect changes in the rate of savings and interest at full employment, it opened the door to the possibility that the full employment rate of growth may be influenced by monetary policy.

11 Mr. Keynes and the "Classics": A Suggested Interpretation

John R. Hicks *Cambridge University*

I

It will be admitted by the least charitable reader that the entertainment value of Mr. Keynes' *General Theory of Employment* is considerably enhanced by its satiric aspect. But it is also clear that many readers have been left very bewildered by this Dunciad. Even if they are convinced by Mr. Keynes' arguments and humbly acknowledge themselves to have been "classical economists" in the past, they find it hard to remember that they believed in their unregenerate days the things Mr. Keynes says they believed. And there are no doubt others who find their historic doubts a stumbling block, which prevents them from getting as much illumination from the positive theory as they might otherwise have got.

One of the main reasons for this situation is undoubtedly to be found in the fact that Mr. Keynes takes as typical of "Classical economics" the later writings of Professor Pigou, particularly *The Theory of Unemployment*. Now *The Theory of Unemployment* is a fairly new book, and an exceedingly difficult book; so that it is safe to say that it has not yet made much impression on the ordinary

Reprinted from *Econometrica*, New Series, Vol. 5 (April 1937), 147–59, by permission of the author and publisher.

Professor Hicks discussed this subject again in his book *A Contribution to the Theory of the Trade Cycle* (Oxford 1950), Chapters 11 and 12, and in a later article, "A Rehabilitation of 'Classical' Economics?" *Economic Journal*, Vol. 67 (June 1957), 278–89.

teaching of economics. To most people its doctrines seem quite as strange and novel as the doctrines of Mr. Keynes himself; so that to be told that he has believed these things himself leaves the ordinary economist quite bewildered.

For example, Professor Pigou's theory runs, to a quite amazing extent, in real terms. Not only is his theory a theory of real wages and unemployment; but numbers of problems which anyone else would have preferred to investigate in money terms are investigated by Professor Pigou in terms of "wage-goods." The ordinary classical economist has no part in this *tour de force*.

But if, on behalf of the ordinary classical economist, we declare that he would have preferred to investigate many of those problems in money terms, Mr. Keynes will reply that there is no classical theory of money wages and employment. It is quite true that such a theory cannot easily be found in the textbooks. But this is only because most of the textbooks were written at a time when general changes in money wages in a closed system did not present an important problem. There can be little doubt that most economists have thought that they had a pretty fair idea of what the relation between money wages and employment actually was.

In these circumstances, it seems worth while to try to construct a typical "classical" theory, built on an earlier and cruder model than Professor Pigou's. If we can construct such a theory, and show that it does give results which have in fact been commonly taken for granted, but which do not agree with Mr. Keynes' conclusions, then we shall at last have a satisfactory basis of comparison. We may hope to be able to isolate Mr. Keynes' innovations, and so to discover what are the real issues in dispute.

Since our purpose is comparison, I shall try to set out my typical classical theory in a form similar to that in which Mr. Keynes sets out his own theory; and I shall leave out of account all secondary complications which do not bear closely upon this special question in hand. Thus I assume that I am dealing with a short period in which the quantity of physical equipment of all kinds available can be taken as fixed. I assume homogeneous labour. I assume further that depreciation can be neglected, so that the output of investment goods corresponds to new investment. This is a dangerous simplification, but the important issues raised by Mr. Keynes in his chapter on user cost are irrelevant for our purposes.

Let us begin by assuming that w, the rate of money wages per head, can be taken as given.

Let x, y, be the outputs of investment goods and consumption goods respectively, and N_x, N_y, be the numbers of men employed in producing them. Since the amount of physical equipment specialised to each industry is given, $x = f_x(N_x)$ and $y = f_y(N_y)$, where f_x, f_y, are *given* functions.

Let M be the *given* quantity of money.

It is desired to determine N_x and N_y.

First, the price-level of investment goods = their marginal cost = $w(dN_x/dx)$. And the price-level of consumption goods = their marginal cost = $w(dN_y/dy)$.

Income earned in investment trades (value of investment, or simply Investment) = $wx(dN_x/dx)$. Call this I_x.

Income earned in consumption trades = $wy(dN_y/dy)$.

Total Income = $wx(dN_x/dx) + wy(dN_y/dy)$. Call this I.

I_x is therefore a given function of N_x, I of N_x and N_y. Once I and I_x are determined, N_x and N_y can be determined.

Now let us assume the "Cambridge Quantity Equation"—that there is some definite relation between Income and the demand for money. Then, approximately, and apart from the fact that the demand for money may depend not only upon total Income, but also upon its distribution between people with relatively large and relatively small demands for balances, we can write

$$M = kI.$$

As soon as k is given, total Income is therefore determined.

In order to determine I_x, we need two equations. One tells us that the amount of investment (looked at as demand for capital) depends upon the rate of interest:

$$I_x = C(i).$$

This is what becomes the marginal-efficiency-of-capital schedule in Mr. Keynes' work.

Further, Investment = Saving. And saving depends upon the rate of interest and, if you like, Income. $\therefore I_x = S(i, I)$. (Since, however, Income is already determined, we do not need to bother about inserting Income here unless we choose.)

Taking them as a system, however, we have three fundamental equations,

$$M = kI, \quad I_x = C(i), \quad I_x = S(i, I),$$

to determine three unknowns, I, I_x, i. As we have found earlier, N_x and N_y can be determined from I and I_x. Total employment, $N_x + N_y$, is therefore determined.

Let us consider some properties of this system. It follows directly from the first equation that as soon as k and M are given, I is completely determined; that is to say, total income depends directly upon the quantity of money. Total employment, however, is not necessarily determined at once from income, since it will usually depend to some extent upon the proportion of income saved, and thus upon the way production is divided between investment and consumption-goods trades. (If it so happened that the elasticities of supply were the same in each of these trades, then a shifting of demand between them would produce compensating movements in N_x and N_y, and consequently no change in total employment.)

An increase in the inducement to invest (i.e., a rightward movement of the schedule of the marginal efficiency of capital, which we have written as $C(i)$) will tend to raise the rate of interest, and so to affect saving. If the amount of saving rises, the amount of investment will rise too; labour will be employed more in the investment trades, less in the consumption trades; this will increase total employment if the elasticity of supply in the investment trades is greater than that in the consumption-goods trades—diminish it if *vice versa*.

An increase in the supply of money will necessarily raise total income, for people will increase their spending and lending until incomes have risen sufficiently to restore k to its former level. The rise in income will tend to increase employment, both in making consumption goods and in making investment goods. The total effect on employment depends upon the ratio between the expansions of these industries; and that depends upon the proportion of their increased incomes which people desire to save, which also governs the rate of interest.

So far we have assumed the rate of money wages to be given; but so long as we assume that k is independent of the level of wages, there is no difficulty about this problem either. A rise in the rate of money wages will necessarily diminish employment and raise real wages. For an unchanged money income cannot continue to buy an unchanged quantity of goods at a higher price-level; and, unless the price-level rises, the prices of goods will not cover their marginal costs. There must therefore be a fall in employment; as employment falls, marginal costs in terms of labour will diminish and therefore real wages rise. (Since a change in money wages is always accompanied by a change in real wages in the same direction, if not in the same proportion, no harm will be done, and some advantage will perhaps be secured, if one prefers to work in terms of real wages. Naturally most "classical economists" have taken this line.)

I think it will be agreed that we have here a quite reasonably consistent theory, and a theory which is also consistent with the pronouncements of a recognizable group of economists. Admittedly it follows from this theory that you may be able to increase employment by direct inflation; but whether or not you decide to favour that policy still depends upon your judgment about the probable reaction on wages, and also—in a national area—upon your views about the international standard.

Historically, this theory descends from Ricardo, though it is not actually Ricardian; it is probably more or less the theory that was held by Marshall. But with Marshall it was already beginning to be qualified in important ways; his successors have qualified it still further. What Mr. Keynes has done is to lay enormous emphasis on the qualifications, so that they almost blot out the original theory. Let us follow out this process of development.

II

When a theory like the "classical" theory we have just described is applied to the analysis of industrial fluctuations, it gets into difficulties in several ways. It is evident that total money income experiences great variations in the course of a trade cycle, and the classical theory can only explain these by variations in M or in k, or, as a third and last alternative, by changes in distribution.

(1) Variation in M is simplest and most obvious, and has been relied on to a large extent. But the variations in M that are traceable during a trade cycle are variations that take place through the banks—they are variations in bank loans; if we are to rely on them it is urgently necessary for us to explain the connection between the supply of bank money and the rate of interest. This can be done roughly by thinking of banks as persons who are strongly inclined to pass on money by lending rather than spending it. Their action therefore tends at first to lower interest rates, and only afterwards, when the money passes into the hands of spenders, to raise prices and incomes. "The new currency, or the increase of currency, goes, not to private persons, but to the banking centers; and therefore, it increases the willingness of lenders to lend in the first instance, and lowers the rate of discount. But it afterwards raises prices; and therefore it tends to increase discount."[1] This is superficially satisfactory; but if we endeavoured to give a more precise account of this process we should soon get into difficulties. What determines the amount of money needed to produce a given fall in the rate of interest? What determines the length of time for which the low rate will last? These are not easy questions to answer.

(2) In so far as we rely upon changes in k, we can also do well enough up to a point. Changes in k can be related to changes in confidence, and it is realistic to hold that the rising prices of a boom occur because optimism encourages a reduction in balances; the falling prices of a slump because pessimism and uncertainty dictate an increase. But as soon as we take this step it becomes natural to ask whether k has not abdicated its status as an independent variable, and has not become liable to be influenced by others among the variables in our fundamental equations.

(3) This last consideration is powerfully supported by another, of more purely theoretical character. On grounds of pure value theory, it is evident that the direct sacrifice made by a person who holds a stock of money is a sacrifice of interest; and it is hard to believe that the marginal principle does not operate at all in this field. As Lavington put it: "The quantity of resources which (an individual) holds in the form of money will be such that the unit of money which is just and only just worth while holding in this form yields him a return of convenience and security equal to the yield of satisfaction derived from the marginal unit spent on consumables, and equal also to the net rate of interest."[2] The demand for money depends upon the rate of interest! The stage is set for Mr. Keynes.

As against the three equations of the classical theory,

$$M = kI, \quad I_x = C(i), \quad I_x = S(i, I),$$

Mr. Keynes begins with three equations,

$$M = L(i), \quad I_x = C(i), \quad I_x = S(I).$$

These differ from the classical equations in two ways. On the one hand, the demand for money is conceived as depending upon the rate of interest (Liquidity Preference). On the other hand, any possible influence of the rate of interest on the amount saved out of a given income is neglected. Although it means that the third equation becomes the multiplier equation, which performs such queer tricks, nevertheless this second amendment is a mere simplification, and ultimately insignificant.[3] It is the liquidity preference doctrine which is vital.

For it is now the rate of interest, not income, which is determined by the quantity of money. The rate of interest set against the schedule of the marginal efficiency of capital determines the value of investment; that determines income by the multiplier. Then the volume of employment (at given wage-rates) is determined by the value of investment and of income which is not saved but spent upon consumption goods.

It is this system of equations which yields the startling conclusion, that an increase in the inducement to invest, or in the propensity to consume, will not tend to raise the rate of interest, but only to increase employment. In spite of this, however, and in spite of the fact that quite a large part of the argument runs in terms of this system, and this system alone, *it is not the General Theory*. We may call it, if we like, Mr. Keynes' *special theory*. The General Theory is something appreciably more orthodox.

Like Lavington and Professor Pigou, Mr. Keynes does not in the end believe that the demand for money can be determined by one variable alone—not even the rate of interest. He lays more stress on it than they did, but neither for him nor for them can it be the only variable to be considered. The dependence of the demand for money on interest does not, in the end, do more than qualify the old dependence on income. However much stress we lay upon the "speculative motive," the "transactions" motive must always come in as well.

Consequently we have for the General Theory

$$M = L(I, i), \quad I_x = C(i), \quad I_x = S(I).$$

With this revision, Mr. Keynes takes a big step back to Marshallian orthodoxy, and his theory becomes hard to distinguish from the revised and qualified Marshallian theories, which, as we have seen, are not new. Is there really any difference between them, or is the whole thing a sham fight? Let us have recourse to a diagram (Figure 1).

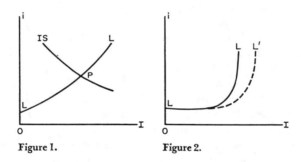

Figure 1.   **Figure 2.**

Against a given quantity of money, the first equation, $M = L(I, i)$, gives us a relation between Income (I) and the rate of interest (i). This can be drawn out as a curve (LL) which will slope upwards, since an increase in income tends to raise the demand for money, and an increase in the rate of interest tends to lower it. Further, the second two equations taken together give us another relation between Income and interest. (The marginal-efficiency-of-capital schedule determines the value of investment at any given rate of interest, and the multiplier tells us what level of income will be necessary to make savings equal to that value of investment.) The curve IS can therefore be drawn showing the relation between Income and interest which must be maintained in order to make saving equal to investment.

Income and the rate of interest are now determined together at P, the point of intersection of the curves LL and IS. They are determined together; just as price and output are determined together in the modern theory of demand and supply. Indeed, Mr. Keynes' innovation is closely parallel, in this respect, to the innovation of the marginalists. The quantity theory tries to determine income without interest, just as the labour theory of value tried to determine price without output; each has to give place to a theory recognising a higher degree of interdependence.

III

But if this is the real "General Theory," how does Mr. Keynes come to make his remarks about an increase in the inducement to invest not raising the rate of interest? It would appear from our diagram that a rise in the marginal-efficiency-of-capital schedule must raise the curve *IS*; and, therefore, although it will raise Income and employment, it will also raise the rate of interest.

This brings us to what, from many points of view, is the most important thing in Mr. Keynes' book. It is not only possible to show that a given supply of money determines a certain relation between Income and interest (which we have expressed by the curve *LL*); it is also possible to say something about the shape of the curve. It will probably tend to be nearly horizontal on the left, and nearly vertical on the right. This is because there is (1) some minimum below which the rate of interest is unlikely to go, and (though Mr. Keynes does not stress this) there is (2) a maximum to the level of income which can possibly be financed with a given amount of money. If we like we can think of the curve as approaching these limits asymptotically (Figure 2).

Therefore, if the curve *IS* lies well to the right (either because of a strong inducement to invest or a strong propensity to consume), *P* will lie upon that part of the curve which is decidedly upward sloping, and the classical theory will be a good approximation, needing no more than the qualification which it has in fact received at the hands of the later Marshallians. An increase in the inducement to invest will raise the rate of interest, as in the classical theory, but it will also have some subsidiary effect in raising income, and therefore employment as well. (Mr. Keynes in 1936 is not the first Cambridge economist to have a temperate faith in Public Works.) But if the point *P* lies to the left of the *LL* curve, then the *special* form of Mr. Keynes' theory becomes valid. A rise in the schedule of the marginal efficiency of capital only increases employment, and does not raise the rate of interest at all. We are completely out of touch with the classical world.

The demonstration of this minimum is thus of central importance. It is so important that I shall venture to paraphrase the proof, setting it out in a rather different way from that adopted by Mr. Keynes.[4]

If the costs of holding money can be neglected, it will always be profitable to hold money rather than lend it out, if the rate of interest is not greater than zero. Consequently the rate of interest must always be positive. In an extreme case, the shortest short-term rate may perhaps be nearly zero. But if so, the long-term rate must lie above it, for the long rate has to allow for the risk that the short rate may rise during the currency of the loan, and it should be observed that the short rate can only rise, it cannot fall.[5] This does not only mean that the long rate must be a sort of average of the probable short rates over its duration, and that this average must lie above the current short rate. There is also the more important risk to be considered, that the lender on long term may desire to have cash before the agreed date of repayment, and then, if the short rate has risen meanwhile, he may be involved in a substantial capital loss. It is this last risk which provides Mr. Keynes' "speculative motive" and which ensures that the rate for loans of indefinite duration (which he always has in mind as *the* rate of interest) cannot fall very near zero.[6]

It should be observed that this minimum to the rate of interest applies not only to one curve *LL* (drawn to correspond to a particular quantity of money) but to any such curve. If the supply of money is increased, the curve *LL* moves to the right (as the dotted curve in Figure 2), but the horizontal parts of the curve are almost the same. Therefore, again, it is this doldrum to the left of the diagram which upsets the classical theory. If *IS* lies to the right, then we can indeed increase employment by increasing the quantity of money; but if *IS* lies to the left, we cannot do so; merely monetary means will not force down the rate of interest any further.

So the General Theory of Employment is the Economics of Depression.

IV

In order to elucidate the relation between Mr. Keynes and the "Classics," we have invented a little apparatus. It does not appear that we have exhausted the uses of that apparatus, so let us conclude by giving it a little run on its own.

With that apparatus at our disposal, we are no longer obliged to make certain simplifications which Mr. Keynes makes in his exposition. We can reinsert the missing i in the third equation, and allow for any possible effect of the rate of interest upon saving; and, what is much more important, we can call in question the sole dependence of investment upon the rate of interest, which looks rather suspicious in the second equation. Mathematical elegance would suggest that we ought to have I and i in all three equations, if the theory is to be really General. Why not have them there like this:

$$M = L(I, i), \quad I_x = C(I, i), \quad I_x = S(I, i)$$

Once we raise the question of Income in the second equation, it is clear that it has a very good claim to be inserted. Mr. Keynes is in fact only enabled to leave it out at all plausibly by his device of measuring everything in "wage-units," which means that he allows for changes in the marginal-efficiency-of-capital schedule when there is a change in the level of money wages, but that other changes in Income are deemed not to affect the curve, or at least not in the same immediate manner. But why draw this distinction? Surely there is every reason to suppose that an increase in the demand for consumers' goods, arising from an increase in employment, will often directly stimulate an increase in investment, at least as soon as an expectation develops that the increased demand will continue. If this is so, we ought to include I in the second equation, though it must be confessed that the effect of I on the marginal efficiency of capital will be fitful and irregular.

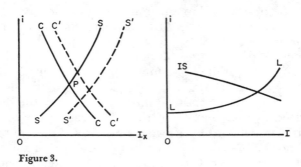

Figure 3.

The Generalized General Theory can then be set out in this way. Assume first of all a given total money Income. Draw a curve CC showing the marginal efficiency of capital (in money terms) at that given Income; a curve SS showing the supply curve of saving at that *given* Income (Figure 3). Their intersection will determine the rate of interest which makes savings equal to investment at that level of income. This we may call the "investment rate."

If Income rises, the curve SS will move to the right; probably CC will move to the right too. If SS moves more than CC, the investment rate of interest will fall; if CC more than SS, it will rise. (How much it rises and falls, however, depends upon the elasticities of the CC and SS curves.)

The IS curve (drawn on a separate diagram) now shows the relation between Income and the corresponding investment rate of interest. It has to be confronted (as in our earlier constructions) with an LL curve showing the relation between Income and the "money" rate of interest; only we can now generalize our LL curve a little. Instead of assuming, as before, that the supply of money is given, we can assume that there is a given monetary system—that up to a point, but only up to a point, monetary authorities will prefer to create new money rather than allow interest rates to rise. Such a generalized *LL* curve will then slope upwards only gradually—the elasticity of the curve depending on the elasticity of the monetary system (in the ordinary monetary sense).

As before, Income and interest are determined where the *IS* and *LL* curves intersect—where the investment rate of interest equals the money rate. Any change in the inducement to invest or the propensity to consume will shift the *IS* curve; any change in liquidity preference or monetary policy will shift the *LL* curve. If, as the result of such a change, the investment rate is raised above the money rate, Income will tend to rise; in the opposite case, Income will tend to fall; the extent to which Income rises or falls depends on the elasticities of the curves.[7]

When generalized in this way, Mr. Keynes' theory begins to look very like Wicksell's; this is of course hardly surprising.[8] There is indeed one special case where it fits Wicksell's construction absolutely. If there is "full employment" in the sense that any rise in Income immediately calls forth a rise in money wage rates, then it is *possible* that the *CC* and *SS* curves may be moved to the right to exactly the same extent, so that *IS* is horizontal. (I say possible, because it is not unlikely, in fact, that the rise in the wage level may create a presumption that wages will rise again later on; if so, *CC* will probably be shifted more than *SS*, so that *IS* will be upward sloping.) However that may be, if *IS* is horizontal, we do have a perfectly Wicksellian construction;[9] the investment rate becomes Wicksell's *natural rate*, for in this case it may be thought of as determined by real causes; if there is a perfectly elastic monetary system, and the money rate is fixed below the natural rate, there is cumulative inflation; cumulative deflation if it is fixed above.

This, however, is now seen to be only one special case; we can use our construction to harbour much wider possibilities. If there is a great deal of unemployment, it is very likely that $\partial C/\partial I$ will be quite small; in that case *IS* can be relied upon to slope downwards. This is the sort of Slump Economics with which Mr. Keynes is largely concerned. But one cannot escape the impression that there may be other conditions when expectations are tinder, when a slight inflationary tendency lights them up very easily. Then $\partial C/\partial I$ may be large and an increase in Income tend to *raise* the investment rate of interest. In these circumstances, the situation is unstable at *any* given money rate; it is only an imperfectly elastic monetary system—a rising *LL* curve—that can prevent the situation getting out of hand altogether.

These, then, are a few of the things we can get out of our skeleton apparatus. But even if it may claim to be a slight extension of Mr. Keynes' similar skeleton, it remains a terribly rough and ready sort of affair. In particular, the concept of "Income" is worked monstrously hard; most of our curves are not really determinate unless something is said about the distribution of Income as well as its magnitude. Indeed, what they express is something like a relation between the price-system and the system of interest rates; and you cannot get that into a curve. Further, all sorts of questions about depreciation have been neglected; and all sorts of questions about the timing of the processes under consideration.

The *General Theory of Employment* is a useful book; but it is neither the beginning nor the end of Dynamic Economics.

NOTES

1. Marshall, *Money, Credit and Commerce* (London 1923), p. 257.
2. Lavington, *English Capital Market* (London 1921), p. 30. See also Pigou, "The Exchange-value of Legal-tender Money," in *Essays in Applied Economics* (London 1922), pp. 179–81.
3. This can be readily seen if we consider the equations

$$M = kI, \quad I_x = C(i), \quad I_x = S(I),$$

which embody Mr. Keynes' second amendment without his first. The third equation is already the multiplier equation, but the multiplier is shorn of its wings. For since I still depends only on M, I_x now depends only on M, and it is impossible to increase investment without increasing the willingness to save or the quantity of money. The system thus generated is therefore identical with that which, a few years ago, used to be called the "Treasury View." But Liquidity Preference transports us from the "Treasury View" to the "General Theory of Employment."
4. Keynes, *General Theory* (New York 1936), pp. 201–2.
5. It is just conceivable that people might become so used to the idea of very low short rates that they would not be much impressed by this risk; but it is very unlikely. For the short rate may rise, either because trade improves, and income expands; or because trade gets worse, and the desire for liquidity increases. I doubt whether a monetary system so elastic as to rule out both of these possibilities is really thinkable.
6. Nevertheless something more than the "speculative motive" is needed to account for the system of interest rates. The shortest of all short rates must equal the relative valuation, at the margin, of money and such a bill; and the bill stands at a discount mainly because of the "convenience and security" of holding money—the inconvenience which may possibly be caused by not having cash immediately available. It is the chance that you may want to discount the bill which matters, not the chance that you will then have to discount it on unfavourable terms. The "precaution-

---

ary motive," not the "speculative motive," is here dominant. But the prospective terms of rediscounting are vital, when it comes to the *difference* between short and long rates.

7. Since $C(I, i) = S(I, i)$,

$$\frac{dI}{di} = -\frac{\partial S/\partial i - \partial C/\partial i}{\partial S/\partial I - \partial C/\partial I}.$$

The savings investment market will not be stable unless $\partial S/\partial i + (-\partial C/\partial i)$ is positive. I think we may assume that this condition is fulfilled.

If $\partial S/\partial i$ is positive, $\partial C/\partial i$ negative, $\partial S/\partial I$ and $\partial C/\partial I$ positive (the most probable state of affairs), we can say that the *IS* curve will be more elastic, the greater the elasticities of the *CC* and *SS* curves, and the larger is $\partial C/\partial I$ relatively to $\partial S/\partial I$. When $\partial C/\partial I > \partial S/\partial I$, the *IS* curve is upward sloping.

8. Cf. Keynes, *General Theory*, p. 242.

9. Cf. Myrdal, "Gleichgewichtsbegriff," in Hayek (ed.) *Beiträge zur Geldtheorie* (Vienna 1933).

12 *A Critique of Neoclassical Monetary Theory*

Don Patinkin *Hebrew University, Jerusalem*

Introduction. The Deficiencies of the Traditional Transactions and Cash-Balance Approaches in Analyzing the Effects of a Change in M. The Failure to Test the Stability of the Equilibrium Absolute Price Level and the Significance Thereof

Terminological disputes are rather sterile. Hence it is best to preclude them by making clear at the outset that "neoclassical" is being used here as a shorthand designation for the once widely accepted body of thought which organized monetary theory around a transactions or cash-balance type of equation, and which then used these equations to validate the classical quantity theory of money. Subsidiary—though, as we shall see, persistently recurring—components of this body of thought were a certain description of the demand function for money and a certain conception of the role of monetary theory *vis-à-vis* value theory.

Reprinted from *Money, Interest, and Prices*, second edition, by Don Patinkin, by permission of the author and Harper & Row, Publishers. Copyright © 1965 by Don Patinkin.

The footnotes that make reference to the series of historical notes included at the end of the original work have been deleted along with several cross references to other parts of the book. The Notes provide documentation from the literature in support of the interpretation presented in the text.

In its cash-balance version—associated primarily with the names of Walras, Marshall, Wicksell, and Pigou—neoclassical theory assumed that, for their convenience, individuals wish to hold a certain proportion, K, of the real volume of their planned transactions, T, in the form of real money balances. The demand for these balances thus equals KT. Correspondingly, the demand for nominal money balances is KPT, where P is the price level of the commodities transacted. The equating of this demand to the supply of money, M, then produced the famous Cambridge equation, $M = KPT$. In the transactions version—associated primarily with the names of Newcomb and Fisher—the velocity of circulation, V, replaced its reciprocal, K, to produce the equally famous equation of exchange, $MV = PT$. These equations were the parade-grounds on which neoclassical economists then put the classical quantity theory of money through its paces.[1]

The most persuasive formulations of this theory were developments of the following tripartite thesis: an increase in the quantity of money disturbs the optimum relation between the level of money balances and the individual's expenditures; this disturbance generates an increase in the planned volume of these expenditures (the real-balance effect); and this increase creates pressures on the price level which push it upwards until it has risen in the same proportion as the quantity of money. Among the writers mentioned above, only Wicksell[2] and Fisher[3] provided complete, systematic statements of this thesis. Nevertheless, the other writers made sufficient—if unintegrated—use of its individual components to justify our identifying these components with the general analytic background of neoclassical monetary theory.

Indeed, the basic fact underlined by the foregoing thesis—that the causal relationship between money and prices is not at all a mechanical one, but is instead the economic consequence of the prior effect of changes in the quantity of money on the demand for commodities—was already a commonplace of the classical quantity-theory tradition of Cantillon, Thornton, Ricardo, and Mill,[4] and was particularly vivid in the expositions of those writers who emphasized that the effects of an increase in the quantity of money on prices could not in general be said to be equiproportionate, but depended instead on whose money holdings, and hence whose demands, were increased.[5] This, after all, was the consideration which brought both classical and neoclassical economists to the recognition that a change in the quantity of money could generate "forced savings" and need not therefore always be neutral in its effects.

On the other hand, it must be emphasized that, in contrast to the neoclassical ones, none of these earlier expositions of the quantity theory should be regarded as having recognized the real-balance effect in the fullest sense of the term; for none of them brought out the crucial intermediary stage of the foregoing thesis in which people increase their *flow* of expenditures because they feel that their *stock* of money is too large for their needs. Instead, in a Keynesian-like fashion, these expositions more or less directly connected the increased *outflow* of money expenditures with the increased *inflow* of money receipts: people spend more money because they receive more money, not because their real cash balances as such have been augmented beyond the amount "which their convenience had taught them to keep on hand."[6] But it is precisely this augmentation—and the real-balance effect which it engenders—which helps explain why demand, and hence prices, remain at a higher level even in periods subsequent to the one in which the injection of new money into the economy takes place.

* * *

. . . [T]he neoclassical equations suffer from the obvious disability that they assign no explicit role to the rate of interest and hence cannot deal with that whole body of theory which analyzes this rate. In particular, they cannot serve to validate the classical proposition that a change in the quantity of money leaves the rate of interest unaffected. Indeed, not only can they not help, they hinder. For the omission of the rate of interest from the cash-balance equation creates the misleading impression that the classical invariance of this rate holds only in the special case where it does not affect the demand for money. No such restriction is necessary. This is not to deny that in other contexts neoclassical economists did recognize the influence of the rate of interest on the demand for money, and did make other significant extensions of classical interest theory. But it is to stress that these contributions found no place in those fundamental equations which, more than anything else, are the hallmarks of neoclassical monetary theory.

Again, our approach does not depend on the use of the cumbersome and frequently criticized aggregates K, V, P, T, but instead builds only on individual demands for individual commodities with their individual prices. And even when presented in an aggregative form—as it will be on pp. 273–84—it does not needlessly cripple the quantity theory by implying—as does the MV of the transactions equation—that the validity of this theory holds only in the obviously unrealistic case where the aggregate demand for commodities is directly proportionate to the quantity of money. The preceding approach insists only that the demand functions be free of money illusion; otherwise it leaves them free to reflect the full range and variety of individual reactions to changes in the level of initial money balances.

The cash-balance equation frequently replaced these unnecessary and vitiating restrictions on the commodity functions with equally unnecessary—and possibly invalid—restrictions on the money function. Since the details of these restrictions will be described on pp. 273–84, there is no need to discuss them further here. Aside from this substantive criticism, the neoclassical cash-balance approach is subject to the more general, pragmatic criticism that has already been voiced in the Introduction. In its neat description of the factors which lead individuals to hold money balances, this approach certainly accomplished its proclaimed objective of bringing these holdings "into relation with volition."[7] But all too often this "humanizing" of the demand for money led to an undue concentration on the money market, a corresponding neglect of the commodity markets, and a resulting "dehumanizing" of the analysis of the effects of monetary changes.

What we are saying is that despite the already emphasized fact that adherents of the cash-balance approach recognized the real-balance effect, . . . they frequently failed to provide a systematic dynamic analysis of the way in which the monetary increase generated real-balance effects in the commodity markets which propelled the economy from its original equilibrium position to its new one. Now, as the incisive counterexample of Wicksell proves, such an omission is *not* a necessary consequence of this approach. Nevertheless, it cannot be mere coincidence that it is precisely this dynamic analysis which was *not* integrated into the Cambridge cash-balance tradition of Marshall, Pigou, Keynes, and Robertson, with its deliberate emphasis on the money market. It thus appears that, in its analysis of the inflationary impact of a monetary increase, the Cambridge theory was actually less illumed by the spark of "volition" and individual behavior than the Fisherine transactions theory whose "mechanicalism" it was designed to correct![8]

As emphasized sufficiently above, it is one of the specific objectives of the alternative approach developed in this book to avoid this pitfall by taking the analysis directly into the commodity markets. A corollary advantage of this approach is that it enables a precise economic explanation of why, say, a doubling of the quantity of money causes a doubling—and just a doubling, neither more nor less—of the price level. It shows the essence of the quantity theory to lie in the automatic, corrective market forces which continue to operate through the real-balance effect until this doubled price level is attained. Once again, there is no logical reason why these forces could not have been developed as a standard component of neoclassical monetary theory. Nevertheless, the stubborn fact seems to be that only Wicksell bestirred himself to ask what would happen if prices deviated from the equilibrium level called for by the quantity of money, and to describe how the dynamic forces thereby generated would return them to this level.

The essence of the three preceding paragraphs can be summed up in one sentence: There is a basic chapter missing in practically all neoclassical monetary theory—the chapter which presents a precise dynamic analysis of the determination of the equilibrium absolute level of money prices through the workings of the real-balance effect. This is said, not for that aspect of dynamic analysis which describes the forces propelling the economy toward its new equilibrium position after an initial monetary increase—a problem adequately discussed by many neoclassical economists[9]—but for that aspect which describes the forces stabilizing the economy at this new position once it is reached—a problem separated by just a nuance from the preceding one, but nevertheless discussed only by Wicksell.

It would be a serious error to underestimate the significance of this nuance. The easiest way of convincing the reader of this is to bring him up sharply against the following facts: Walras was a man who never tired of establishing the stability of his system by elaborating on the corrective forces of excess supply that would be called into play should the price lie above its equilibrium value, and the forces of excess demand that would be called into play should it lie below. He did it when he explained how the market determines the equilibrium prices of commodities; he did it again when he explained how the market determines the equilibrium prices of productive services; and he did it a third time when he explained how the market determines the equilibrium prices of capital goods. But he did not do it when he attempted to explain how the market determines the equilibrium "price" of paper money. And Walras is the rule, not the exception. Precisely the same asymmetry recurs among writers of the Cambridge tradition—with their standard supply-and-demand exercise of testing the stability of the equilibrium price in value theory and their standard omission of a corresponding exercise for testing the equilibrium absolute price level in monetary theory![10]

Thus in back of this nuance is the persistent failure of these economists to carry over to their monetary theory a simple, familiar technique of their value theory—and this despite their declared intention of integrating these two theories. We shall return to the significance of this fact on pp. 284–91.

The Cash-Balance Equation and the "Uniform Unitary Elasticity of Demand for Money"

Another familiar proposition of the neoclassical cash-balance approach—one already alluded to in the preceding section—is that the demand for paper money has "uniform unitary elasticity" and is accordingly represented by a rectangular hyperbola. This theme recurs specifically in the writings of Walras, Marshall, and Pigou. In the case of the latter it is clear that it was considered to be a necessary condition for the validity of the quantity theory of money. In Pigou's words, "an increase in the supply of legal tender ought always, since the elasticity of demand [for legal tender] is equal to unity, to raise prices in the proportion in which the supply has increased." And there is the strong impression that this was also the intended context in which this proposition was advanced by other writers as well. Indeed, it is probably this assumed causal relationship which explains the importance that was attached to it.[11]

This makes it all the more essential to recall that not only is this proposition not necessary for the quantity theory, it is not even generally true. [T]he real-balance effect makes it generally impossible for the demand for money to be of uniform unitary elasticity, but that nevertheless an increase in the quantity of money causes a proportionate increase in prices. It should, however, be clear that the neoclassical contention about unitary elasticity is not inherent in the Cambridge function as such. Thus, if KPT is the demand for money and M its supply, the excess demand for money, $KPT - M$, correctly reflects the by-now familiar property than an equiproportionate change in P *and* in M causes a proportionate change in the excess amount of money demanded. On the other hand, a change in P alone generates a real-balance effect, hence a change in the planned volume of transactions, T, and hence a *non*proportionate change in the amount of money demanded, KPT. Thus, if properly interpreted, the Cambridge function does *not* imply uniform unitary elasticity.

There are two possible explanations for the failure of neoclassical economists to see this. First, they apparently never realized the need to pin down the meaning of T. Only occasionally did they give it the volitional connotation on which the argument of the preceding paragraph depends. At other times they treated it as something beyond the will of individuals—as the fixed "total resources . . . enjoyed by the community." And at still other times they shifted unawares from one connotation to the next. Second, even when they used T in its volitional sense—which is, of course, the only one that is consonant with the *raison d'être* of the cash-balance approach—they never realized that the real-balance effect precludes T from remaining constant in the face of a change in P. Indeed, a standard lemma of the neoclassical proof of the quantity theory of money was that P and T were independent!

The force of the foregoing criticism is, however, highly attenuated by two considerations. First, if the Marshallian demand curve of value theory is interpreted as one from which the income effect has been eliminated; and if this interpretation is also extended to the Marshallian demand curve of monetary theory[12]— then the appropriate form of this curve is indeed the rectangular hyperbola, generated by confronting individuals with an equi-proportionate change in both P and M. Second, even if this interpretation is not accepted, it should in all fairness be said that some exponents of the cash-balance approach merely used "unitary elasticity of demand" as a complicated way of stating that an increase in the quantity of money causes a proportionate increase in prices. In other words, they had in mind the elasticity of the market-equilibrium curve, not that of the demand curve, so that they were not really referring to what Marshall denoted by "elasticity of demand." This, however, should not be taken as implying that these writers indicated any awareness of the existence of two conceptually distinct curves. Indeed, they shifted uninhibitedly from one meaning of elasticity to the other—sometimes even within the same sentence. This points up the general fuzziness from which neoclassical monetary theory suffered as a result of its failure to draw the fundamental distinction between individual-experiments, on the one hand, and market-experiments, on the other.[13]

Valid and Invalid Dichotomies of the Pricing Process. The Proper Relation Between Monetary Theory and Value Theory

Let us return to the analysis of the effects of a change in the quantity of money. Instead of carrying out this analysis in terms of the absolute level of money prices—which is, of course, the usual approach—we can do it equivalently in terms of the *real* quantity of money; for once the nominal quantity of money is fixed, its real value varies in inverse proportion to the absolute level of money prices—or, in short, to the absolute price level. Such an approach can then proceed as follows: In the initial equilibrium position of our economy, the real quantity of money is just at that level which satisfies its transactions and precautionary needs. An exogenous increase in the nominal quantity of money then pushes the real quantity above this equilibrium value and thereby creates inflationary pressures in the various markets. The resulting price rise then reduces this real quantity and thereby lessens the disequilibrating inflationary pressures themselves. Now, by assumption, the initial monetary increase has not affected the economy's "taste" for real balances—that is, its desire to hold such balances in order to avoid the inconveniences, costs, and/or embarrassment of default. Hence the economy cannot achieve a new equilibrium position until the absolute price level has risen sufficiently to reduce the real quantity of money to its initial level once again.[14]

Let us now separate into two categories the given conditions (independent variables) which determine the nature of our exchange economy's equilibrium position. First, there are those which describe the economy's "real framework": namely, tastes (including those for *real* money balances) and initial holdings of commodities. Second, there are the conditions which describe its "monetary framework": namely, initial nominal holdings of money. Correspondingly, let us also separate the dependent variables of the analysis into two categories: "real variables," namely, the equilibrium values of relative prices, the rate of interest, and the real quantity of money; and the "monetary variable," namely, the equilibrium value of the absolute price level.[15]

Consider now the classical proposition that a change in the quantity of money merely causes an equiproportionate change in equilibrium money prices. The opening paragraph of this section enables us to replace this proposition by the equivalent one that such a change has no effect on the equilibrium values of relative prices, the rate of interest, and the real quantity of money. Now, to say that these values are independent of the nominal quantity of money is to say that they can be determined even without knowing this quantity. This permits us to conceive of the pricing process of our exchange economy as being divided into two successive stages: In the first one, specification of the real framework determines the equilibrium values of the real variables of the system. In the second, specification of the monetary framework then determines the equilibrium value of the monetary variable—for this value is simply the ratio between the specified nominal quantity of money and the equilibrium real quantity.

It should be clear that this arbitrary and mechanical act of specifying the nominal quantity of money has nothing whatsoever to do with monetary theory. For, as we shall argue below, this theory is concerned, at the individual level, with the relation between commodity demands and real balances and, at the market level, with the causes of changes in the equilibrium value of these balances. And both of these problems are fully analyzed in the first stage of the foregoing dichotomy. Thus this stage is coterminous with economic analysis: it comprises both value theory and monetary theory. Correspondingly, the second stage of this dichotomy is beyond the pale of economic analysis: it deals with a completely adventitious act.

It should also be clear that the foregoing dichotomy is purely a conceptual one. The real and monetary frameworks of the actual market place are obviously "specified" simultaneously. Similarly, there are only money prices in this market, and these are simultaneously determined. In brief, our dichotomy has no operational significance other than that of the basic quantity-theory proposition from which it is derived.

This dichotomy between relative and money prices must be sharply distinguished from that between money and accounting prices. First of all, there is the obvious difference in the nature of the prices involved. Parallel to this difference is the one between the data respectively specified at the second stages of these dichotomies. In the latter dichotomy this consists of the accounting price of one of the goods; in the present one it consists of the nominal quantity of money. Correspondingly, a change in the value of the supplementary datum in the present dichotomy affects money prices, whereas between money and accounting prices it does not. Finally, the dichotomy between money and accounting prices can have direct operational significance: there can be actual economics in which first money prices and then accounting prices are determined. Clearly, this additional set of prices is of no economic significance; but, in the present context, this is irrelevant.

Both of these dichotomies must be even more sharply distinguished from yet a third one which, though it has neoclassical roots in the works of Walras, Fisher, Pigou, and Cassel, did not achieve its most explicit form until the later expositions of Divisia, Lange, Modigliani, Schneider, and others. In this form it became undisputedly accepted as a statement of the proper relation between monetary theory, on the one hand, and value theory, on the other.

The point of departure of this familiar dichotomy (in practically every case in which it appears in the literature) is a pure outside-money economy consisting of commodities and money, but not bonds. The dichotomy then begins by dividing the economy into two sectors: a real sector, described by the excess-demand functions for commodities, and a monetary sector, described by the excess-demand function for money. The former functions are assumed to depend only on relative prices; the latter, on these variables and the absolute price level as well. This assumed insensitivity of the demand functions of the real sector to changes in the absolute level of money prices is referred to as the "homogeneity postulate"[16] and is said to denote absence of "money illusion."[17]

In a corresponding way, the market excess-demand equations corresponding to these functions are also separated into two groups. The equations of the real sector taken by themselves are then able to determine the equilibrium values of the only variables which appear in them—relative prices. These equations and the variables they determine thus constitute the domain of value theory. The equation of the monetary sector then determines the equilibrium value of the remaining variable—the absolute price level. And this equation and the variable it determines thus constitute the domain of monetary theory.

As with the "unitary elasticity of demand," much of the attractiveness of this dichotomy lay in the belief that it was a necessary condition for the validity of the quantity theory of money.[18] It was felt that unless the demand functions were independent of the absolute price level, monetary increases—which necessarily affect this level—could not preserve their classical neutrality with respect to the real phenomena of the economy. But once again the truth of the matter is that not only is this dichotomy not necessary, not only is it not valid, but its basic assumption is even a denial of the quantity theory itself! For to say that the demand functions of the real sector are not affected by changes in the absolute price level—that is, to assert that they satisfy the "homogeneity postulate"—is to imply that they are not affected by changes in the real value of cash balances. But it is precisely on this real-balance effect that the quantity theory in our present model depends for the inflationary impact of a monetary increase! On the other hand, this dependence in no way violates the *final* neutrality of, say, a doubling of the quantity of money. For in the new equilibrium position the individual is confronted not only with a doubled price level, but also with a doubled initial holding of money. Hence— as compared with the initial equilibrium position—there is no real-balance effect; hence there is no change in behavior; and hence the classical neutrality of money is reaffirmed.

More generally, if the function of monetary theory is to explain the determination of the absolute price level, then the "homogeneity postulate"—or, equivalently, absence of "money illusion" in the sense of the foregoing dichotomy—is the antithesis of all monetary theory within the simple model considered by the foregoing writers. For let the assumptions of the dichotomy obtain. Assume now that an initial position of equilibrium is disturbed in such a way as to cause an equiproportionate change in all money prices. Since this does not change relative prices, the "homogeneity postulate" implies that none of the demand functions in the real sector are thereby affected. Hence, since the commodity markets of this sector were initially in equilibrium, they must continue to be so. By Walras' Law, so must the money market. Thus the equiproportionate departure of money prices from any given equilibrium level creates no market forces—that is, creates no amounts of excess demand anywhere in the system—which might cause money prices to return to their initial level. Hence if any set of money prices is an equilibrium set, any multiple of this set must also be an equilibrium set. The absolute price level is indeterminate.

It follows that the foregoing dichotomy is involved in a basic internal contradiction. For if the demand functions of the real sector have the property it attributes to them, there cannot possibly be a "second stage" in which the absolute price level is determined.

Since the foregoing argument has on occasion been misunderstood, it may be worth while elaborating upon it. The first thing that should be noted is that the contradiction with which it is concerned has nothing to do with the possible inconsistency of a system of static excess-demand equations in the sense that such a system may not have a formal mathematical solution;[19] indeed, as has been emphasized, this type of question lies outside the interests of this book. Instead the notion of inconsistency with which the foregoing argument is concerned is the standard (and general) one of formal logic that a set of propositions is inconsistent if it simultaneously implies a proposition and its negative.[20]

The details of the foregoing argument can now be spelled out as follows: We start with the following three fairly reasonable assumptions: (1) Market forces will be generated to increase (decrease) the price of any given commodity if, and only if, there exists an excess demand (supply) for that commodity. (2) Market forces will be generated to increase (decrease) the absolute price level if, and only if, there exists an excess supply (demand) for money. (3) The absolute price level can change only if at least one commodity price changes.

Let the assumptions of the foregoing dichotomy now hold. For simplicity—and in accordance with the usual presentation of the dichotomy—assume also that the money equation is of the Cambridge form

$$KPT - M = 0.$$

Assume finally that the system is in an initial state of equilibrium which is disturbed in such a way as to cause a chance equiproportionate departure of commodity prices (and hence the absolute price level) from their equilibrium levels. As we have already seen, this does not generate any excess demands in any of the commodity markets. Hence by assumptions (1) and (3) above, there *will not* be generated market forces to cause a corrective change in the absolute price level; that is, this level is indeterminate.

Consider now the foregoing Cambridge equation—under the usual assumption that K, T, and M are kept constant during the discussion. Assume that the initial equiproportionate disturbance in commodity prices causes P to rise. It is then clear from the foregoing equation and assumption (3) that an excess demand for money is generated which *will* cause a corrective downward movement in the absolute price level; that is, this level is determinate. Hence a contradiction.

This contradiction can be expressed alternatively—and equivalently—in terms of an inconsistent system of *dynamic* market-adjustment equations. Graphically, the argument is as follows: Consider first the assumptions of the traditional dichotomy. These imply that the demand function for commodities is independent of real balances and hence the price level, and should therefore be represented by a vertical line. Now, if this vertical line does not coincide with the vertical supply curve, the *static* system of equations would be inconsistent: that is, it would have no equilibrium solution for a price level greater than zero. This, however, is *not* the inconsistency described in the three preceding paragraphs: for this continues to obtain even if the vertical commodity demand curve should coincide with the commodity supply curve as in Figure 1a, so that the *static* system of equilibrium equations would have a (indeed, an infinite number of) positive solution(s).[21] In particular, the foregoing argument states that even in this case there would remain the inconsistency that Figure 1a would show us that the system is in a state of *neutral* or *unstable* equilibrium, whereas Figure 1b (which depicts the Cambridge equation, and which must logically

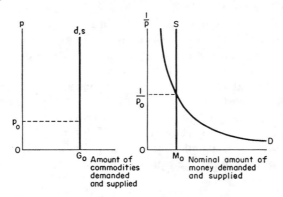

Figure 1a.   Figure 1b.

represent the obverse side of Figure 1a) would show us that it is in a state of *stable* equilibrium.

Yet another expression of this contradiction is the following: Start once again from a position of equilibrium, and assume that the quantity of money is doubled. Since the commodity equations of the foregoing dichotomy are assumed to be independent of real balances, this does not disturb the initial equilibrium in these markets. Hence—by assumptions (1) and (3)—no market forces are generated by this monetary increase to push the price level upwards. From the Cambridge equation and assumption (2), on the other hand, we see that such market forces are created. Hence a contradiction.

Actually, a much simpler way of dealing with this dichotomy is to note that it provides an operationally significant hypothesis—one capable of being tested by the facts of the real world. In particular, its basic "homogeneity postulate" implies that the behavior of consumers in commodity markets can never be affected by the real value of their money balances. But . . . there is considerable empirical evidence that this behavior has been so affected. Hence this evidence alone suffices to refute this dichotomy. In brief, reality shows that there cannot be a money economy without a "money illusion."[22]

This empirical approach enables us to dispose of a certain variation of the foregoing dichotomy which—though it has never been advanced as such in the literature—can pass the test of internal consistency. Specifically, though continuing to consider an outside-money economy, we now assume the existence of bonds as well as commodities and money. We assume further that though the commodity equations continue to be independent of real balances, the bond equation is not. In such a Keynesian system, relative prices and the rate of interest can be determined in the commodity markets and the absolute price level in the bond or money market. In particular, the argument by which we previously established the indeterminacy of the absolute price level no longer holds. For an equiproportionate departure of money prices from their equilibrium level now disturbs the equilibrium of the bond market, and the resulting excess demand then acts through the rate of interest to force prices back to their original level. Nevertheless, this variation of the dichotomy is also unacceptable. For it implies that the real-balance effect never manifests itself in the commodity markets. Once again, this implication is refuted by the aforementioned empirical studies of the consumption function.[23]

It should also be noted that if the bond market, too, is assumed to be independent of real balances, then the resulting model is not even internally consistent. In particular, it is involved in exactly the same type of indeterminacy already shown to hold for the invalid dichotomy. For once again an equiproportionate departure of money prices from an initial equilibrium position, the rate of interest being held constant, does not create any excess demands anywhere in the system. Hence no force is generated to bring prices back to their initial position.

The conclusion to be drawn from the foregoing discussion is that, once the real and monetary data of an economy with outside money are specified, the equilibrium values of relative prices, the rate of interest, and the absolute price level are simultaneously determined by all the markets of the economy. It is generally impossible to isolate a subset of markets which can determine the equilibrium values of a subset of prices. In the true spirit of general-equilibrium economics, "everything depends on everything else."

In particular, as we have seen, it is fatal to succumb to the temptation to say that relative prices are determined in the commodity markets and absolute prices in the money market. This does not mean that value theory cannot be distinguished from monetary theory. Obviously, there is a distinction; but it is based on a dichotomization of *effects*, not on a dichotomization of *markets*. More specifically, both monetary theory and value theory consider *all* markets of the economy simultaneously. But, in each of these markets, value theory analyzes individual-experiments which measure the substitution effect and that part of the wealth effect which does not stem from changes in real balances; and monetary theory, individual-experiments which measure the real-balance effect. Correspondingly, value theory analyzes market-experiments which do not (significantly) affect the absolute price level and hence do not generate real-balance effects; and monetary theory, market-experiments which do not (significantly) affect relative prices and hence do not generate substitution and nonmonetary wealth effects. Thus shifts in tastes, changes in technology, and the like are in the domain of value theory. Changes in the quantity of money and—as we shall see—shifts in liquidity preference are in the domain of monetary theory.

If we now examine this classificatory scheme, we will discover the grain of truth in the intuitive feeling that in some sense value theory is connected with the determination of relative prices and monetary theory with the determination of absolute prices. In particular, assume that by a *tâtonnement* involving all prices and all markets the equilibrium values of money prices have been reached. We can now make use of this information to take a step backwards and approach the equilibrium position once again—but this time by a restricted *tâtonnement*. For example, holding the absolute price level constant at its already determined *equilibrium* value, we can arbitrarily shift relative prices from theirs, and then study the nature of the dynamic forces that—working simultaneously in *all* markets —return the economy to its original equilibrium position. By the very definition of this procedure, such a return can be accomplished without any change in the absolute price level. Hence the restricted *tâtonnement* by which equilibrium relative prices are thus redetermined need involve only these prices, need accordingly generate only substitution and nonmonetary wealth ' effects, and can therefore be studied entirely within the confines of value theory.

Similarly, we can define a restricted *tâtonnement* which—starting from a knowledge of the *equilibrium* values of relative prices and interest—works simultaneously through *all* the markets of the economy to redetermine the equilibrium value of the absolute price level. Such a *tâtonnement* can clearly succeed without requiring any changes in relative prices and interest; that is, it need generate only real-balance effects. Hence it can be studied entirely within the confines of monetary theory.

This decomposition of the overall *tâtonnement* into two components is a convenient expository device. It can be used safely provided we are clear in our own minds that it separates out effects and not markets. In particular, we must guard against the apparent tendency to slip over from this valid device into the invalid proposition of the false dichotomy that, starting with an absolute price level held constant at an *arbitrary* level, a *tâtonnement* on relative prices in the *commodity markets alone* can determine these prices; that, holding these relative prices constant at the values so determined, a *tâtonnement* on the absolute price level in the *money market alone* can then determine this level; and that the absolute price level so determined, together with the relative prices determined by the first *tâtonnement* in the commodity markets, must *necessarily* preserve the equilibrium initially achieved in these markets. Clearly, this last statement will generally *not* be true unless the excess-demand equations of the commodity markets are actually independent of the absolute price level.

This is the crucial point. The dynamic groping of the absolute price level towards its equilibrium value will—through the real-balance effect—react back on the commodity markets and hence on relative prices. And it is precisely the constant failure to find this point explicitly recognized—and, indeed, the constant sensation of being just on the verge of having it explicitly contradicted— that is the basis of our original contention that the roots of the invalid dichotomy are to be found in the neoclassical analyses of Walras, Fisher, Pigou, and Cassel.[24]

The preceding discussion not only analyzes the invalid dichotomy, but also brings out the many deceptive similarities between it and the valid ones. That these similarities have played a significant role in the etiology and persistence of the dichotomy is suggested by several instances in the literature. Thus there is at least one explicit example of the way in which the valid insensitivity of demand to equiproportionate changes in *accounting* prices shifts undetected into the invalid insensitivity to equiproportionate changes in *money* prices. That is, the valid dependence of demand solely on the ratios of accounting prices is confused with the invalid dependence solely on the ratios of money prices. Indeed, this example considers this dependence to be a direct consequence of the "postulate . . . that the consumer's behavior is independent of the units in which prices are expressed. . . ." But here again the same confusion is at work. For after a change in the monetary unit has worked itself out, the individual is confronted with an equiproportionate change in money prices *and* in his money holdings. Thus if the dollar is replaced by the half dollar as the unit of measure, all money prices will eventually double; but—as the very first result of this conversion itself—so will halve the initial money holdings of each and every individual. Hence the proper analog of a change in the monetary unit is an equiproportionate change in *accounting* prices (which leaves the real value of initial money balances intact), not an equiproportionate change in *money* prices (which does not).[25]

Similarly, there are instances in which the valid dichotomy between accounting and money prices is confused with the invalid dichotomy between money and relative prices. Thus, in order to prove that *money* prices cannot be determined unless a special equation is added, it is argued that: "There are always just one *too few equations* to determine the unknown quantities involved. The equation of exchange $[MV = PT]$ is needed in each case to supplement the equations of supply and demand"—and the first sentence is supported by an explicit reference to a mathematical development by the same author which, in order to determine *accounting* prices, adds an equation arbitrarily setting the accounting price of one of the goods equal to unity![26]

Examples in the literature of an alleged connection between the invalid dichotomy and the quantity theory of money have already been noted above.[27] As will be recalled, these allegations were based on a misunderstanding of the nature of the neutrality of money. It remains now to suggest that in its more sophisticated form this may have expressed itself as a confusion between the invalid dichotomy and the first dichotomy described above (p. 276)—the one which is essentially a restatement of the quantity theory and which shows the valid sense in which relative and absolute prices are independently determined. In particular, we can find an example which states that "the proposition that the material set-up of our economic system determines only the *relative* and not the absolute prices of all commodities is so familiar that it hardly deserves further discussion"—and then justifies this statement with an implicit reference to the "homogeneity postulate" that demand remains unaffected by an equiproportionate change in money prices. Here we can almost see the exact point at which the line of reasoning slips off the correct path: Relative prices are determined independently of the absolute price level by the "material set-up of our economic system"—the valid dichotomy; "material set-up" means the conditions of demand in the commodity markets—the invalid dichotomy; but if these conditions alone determine relative prices, they can depend only on these prices—the "homogeneity postulate."[28]

Finally, we can find an example which—though not as clear as the preceding ones—seems to show how the valid intuitive feeling that different forces determine absolute and relative prices slips imperceptibly into the invalid identification of these forces with separate equations. How else can we interpret the train of thought revealed by the following passage: ". . . it is important to distinguish between the influences determining the general price level and the influences determining an individual price. The price level is determined by a comparatively simple mechanism, that of the equation of exchange. It is the result of the quantity of money and deposits, the velocities of their circulation, and the volume of trade. The general price level then helps to fix individual prices, although not interfering with relative variations among them. . . ."[29]

This is admittedly a small number of examples. Nevertheless, the stature of the economists who provide them, the definitive aura of received doctrine that they all gave to the reasoning by which they justified their statements, and the fact that this reasoning was never challenged—all this endows these few examples with a weight far out of proportion to their number. All this permits us to suggest that the explicit reasoning of these examples is representative of the general intellectual process that gave rise to the invalid dichotomy.

Conclusion: The Failure of Neoclassical Monetary Theory to Fully Understand the Real-Balance Effect

In view of the continued discussion of the foregoing issues in the recent literature, it is worthwhile—even at the cost of some repetition—to summarize the argument of this chapter until this point. We must first of all emphasize that we are dealing with an *empirical* question: namely, the role of the real-balance effect in neoclassical monetary theory. Correspondingly, the universe from which our observations must be, and have been, drawn is the relevant body of neoclassical literature.

The specific empirical findings that have emerged from our study can be set out as follows:

1. In their discussion of value theory, neoclassical economists generally included an analysis of the stability of equilibrium. By this is meant nothing more complicated than the usual simple graphical exposition by which neoclassical economists showed that if the price of any given commodity were above (below) the intersection of the demand and supply curves, then there would exist an excess supply (demand) to drive it down (up) again.

2. Neoclassical economists consistently proclaimed their objective of integrating their monetary theory with their value theory; that is, of analyzing the former in the same manner as they had analyzed the latter.

3. Nevertheless, with one or two exceptions, neoclassical economists did not include a stability analysis in their monetary theory. That is, they did not explain the nature of the corrective market forces that would be brought into play should the absolute price level deviate from its equilibrium value.

4. Therefore, the omission of this analysis cannot be explained away as being the result of either a chance oversight, on the one hand, or a conscious lack of interest in monetary stability analysis, on the other.

5. An alternative hypothesis to explain this phenomenon is that though the neoclassical economists did recognize the real-balance effect, they did not achieve a full understanding of it and therefore did not carry out the monetary stability analysis which is so vitally dependent upon it.

6. Like any other empirical hypothesis, this one too achieves additional credibility from the fact that it explains some additional phenomena: namely, the fact that neoclassical economists supported both the rectangular-hyperbola demand curve for money and—in all probability—the invalid dichotomy.

a. The evidence from the form of the demand curve is the weakest link in the chain. For it is not absolutely clear if neoclassical economists assumed the demand curve to have the form of a rectangular hyperbola because they failed to take into account the real-balance effect—or whether they did so because they assumed this effect to be eliminated as a result of compensating variations in initial money balances, or, alternatively, because they did not have in mind a demand curve at all, but instead a market-equilibrium curve. It is also possible that they had in mind [a] long-run rectangular hyperbola.

b. On the other hand, to the extent that we find indications of the invalid dichotomy in the neoclassical literature, the implications are straightforward. For this dichotomy reflects a failure to realize the direct contradiction between the real-balance effect, on the one hand, and the "homogeneity postulate" on the other; or, from an alternative viewpoint, a failure to realize the complete inappropriateness of denoting sensitivity of the individual to a change in the absolute price level by the term "money illusion," when in fact it is precisely this sensitivity which demonstrates the existence of a rational concern on the part of the individual with the surely nonillusory impact of such a change on the real value of his money holdings.

7. The foregoing hypothesis is on even stronger grounds with reference to the later literature, and this for two reasons. First, this literature explicitly accepts the invalid dichotomy as the undisputed statement of the relationship between monetary and value theory in an economy with outside money;[30] indeed, this view has persisted in some of the most recent writings. Second, this literature provides yet another phenomenon which accords with our hypothesis: namely, the failure to see the equilibrating role that the real-balance effect can play in eliminating an inflationary gap.

8. With reference to this later literature we might also note that the approach of Keynesian economics, with its emphasis on analyzing the demand for commodities as a function of the flow of income instead of the stock of assets, was hardly conducive to breaking down a mental block whose essence was the failure to see the significance of the effect of a change in the absolute price level on the real value of the *stock* of money.

In concluding this critique of neoclassical monetary theory, I would like to emphasize once again[31] that not only does it not require the abandonment of any significant aspect of this theory, but it actually rigorizes and completes it. Correspondingly, to the extent that it is meaningful to speculate about such matters, I have no doubt that neoclassical economists would have readily accepted the criticisms involved; would have declared the explicit introduction of the real-balance effect into the commodity demand functions to be a more precise reflection of their thinking on this matter all along and, indeed, a modification that could only strengthen their quantity-theory conclusions; and would accordingly have rejected the implication of some of their recent would-be defenders that they (neoclassical economists) had a vested intellectual interest in the "homogeneity postulate" and its related dichotomy.[32]

The Effects of a Change in K

Let us now leave doctrinal history and return to analytical questions proper. Until now, this chapter has essentially been concerned with the relation between the quantity of money and the level of prices—that is, with the relation between M and P in the Cambridge equation $M = KPT$. But neoclassical monetary theory also used this equation to analyze the relation between K and P, on the one hand, and T and P, on the other. Since, unlike changes in M, the exact translation of changes in K and T into terms of our model is difficult to determine, the exact bearing of the following argument on the neoclassical one must also remain slightly unclear. Nevertheless, as the reader will see, the economic forces that appear in this argument have a distinctly neoclassical character.

We begin with the effects of a change in K. (Obviously, whatever will be said for these effects holds in the inverse for those of a change in the V of $MV = PT$.) Consider, in particular, an economy whose equilibrium is disturbed by a sudden increase in K. This is represented in our model by an increased desire for liquidity resulting from an increase in the probability of running out of cash, or an increase in the inconvenience or penalty costs of so doing. More specifically, this "change in tastes" reflects itself as an increase in the amount of money individuals demand at a given set of prices, interest, and initial endowments. By the budget restraint, this upward shift in the demand for money implies a simultaneous downward shift in the demand for commodities and real bond holdings. That is, because of their given incomes, individuals cannot demand more of one good unless they give up something of another. As a result of this latter shift, equilibrium prices will fall. The interesting question which now confronts us is whether the equilibrium rate of interest must also change.

There is a simple, intuitive answer that can be given at this point. To say that there has been an increase in the individuals' liquidity preferences is analytically equivalent to saying that the liquidity convenience of one dollar of cash balances is now less than it was before. And this, in turn, is equivalent to saying that the "subjective quantity" of money in the hands of individuals has decreased. Hence it seems only natural to argue that the conditions under which the rate of interest remains constant after an increase in liquidity preference are precisely those under which it remains constant after a decrease in the quantity of money.

Let us state this somewhat more exactly. As in the case of a decrease in the quantity of money, we abstract from distribution effects. We also assume the increase in liquidity preferences to be "uniformly distributed"; that is, the liquidity preference of each and every individual is assumed to change with the same "intensity." As explained above, this increase causes downward shifts in the demands of all markets and hence replaces their original state of equilibrium by one of excess supply. Consider now any one market. Clearly, the excess supply in this market can now be removed by an equiproportionate decline in prices, while the rate of interest remains constant. Specifically, this decline will continue until the real value of cash balances has increased sufficiently to satisfy the individuals' increased liquidity preferences and hence restore their demand in this market to its original level. Thus, in some subjective sense, the real quantity of money that influences this market is the same as it originally was. Now, by assumption, the initial shift in liquidity preferences is a "neutral" one: it changes only the relative desirability of money *vis-à-vis* all other goods, not the relative desirabilities of these other goods amongst themselves. Hence if this subjective quantity of money is "the same" with respect to the market for one of these goods, it must be "the same" with respect to that for any other. That is, the equiproportionate price decline needed to equilibrate one market must be equal to that needed to equilibrate any other. Hence equilibrium can be restored to the economy as a whole at a lowered price level and an unchanged rate of interest.

Thus under these assumptions we obtain a reaffirmation of the classical position: An increase in K causes a decrease in P but leaves T and the rate of interest unaffected. By resorting to the device of carrying out the analysis in terms of changes in the real quantity of money instead of changes in P,[33] we can bring out the deeper connotation that neoclassical economists ascribed to this proposition: An increase in K creates automatic market forces which themselves generate the increased equilibrium quantity of real balances desired by the community. The wonders of the "invisible hand" never cease.

The Effects of a Change in T

Consider now an economy whose equilibrium is disturbed by a sudden increase in T. Let this be represented in our model by an exogenous doubling, say, of the individuals' initial commodity endowments. Such a change creates two opposing forces. On the one hand, there is, of course, an increase in the fixed supply of every commodity. On the other hand, there is an increase in wealth and a consequent increase in demand. If it should so happen that the increased demand for each and every commodity exactly offsets its increased supply, no further changes will occur, and the economy will remain in equilibrium at its original set of prices and interest rate. Clearly, this latter case implies a unitary marginal propensity to spend on commodities out of wealth. In general, however, this propensity can be assumed to be less than unity, for part of the increased wealth will be devoted to increasing the demand for money balances. Hence it can be expected that the increases in the amounts of commodities demanded will be less than in the respective amounts supplied, thus generating a downward pressure on prices.

Let us now see if an equiproportionate decline in prices can return the economy as a whole to a position of equilibrium. Consider first the market for one particular commodity. Clearly, it is possible to conceive of the price decline continuing until the resulting positive real-balance effect together with the original positive wealth effect suffice to increase the amount demanded to the same extent that the amount supplied was originally increased. That is, it is possible that by an equiproportionate decline in prices, the rate of interest being held constant, the market for *any one* particular commodity can be brought back into equilibrium.

But the economy consists of many commodity markets, and each of them has been disturbed by the original increase in endowments. In general, the resulting wealth effect will not be the same in all markets. Hence, in contrast with the preceding section, there is no reason why the equiproportionate decline in prices needed to bring one of these markets into equilibrium should be the same as that needed for any other one. That is, there is no reason why a given equiproportionate decline in prices should succeed in equilibrating all markets simultaneously. Hence, in order for such an over-all equilibrium to be restored, relative prices and interest will, in general, also have to change.

Assume now that the exceptional occurs and that an equiproportionate decline in prices—interest constant—does succeed in restoring the economy as a whole to equilibrium. Clearly, even in this case there is no reason why this decline should be in inverse proportion to the original increase in commodity endowments. For the necessary magnitude of this decline depends on the strength of the wealth effect, as well as on the size of the increase in endowments.

Thus we can confirm the neoclassical position that an increase in T decreases P. Furthermore, we also confirm the neoclassical contention that (even when there is no change in the rate of interest) this decrease will, in general, *not* be an inversely proportionate one. In terms of the Cambridge equation, this contention rests on the assumption that K and T are *not* independent; that a change in the latter will affect the former. In particular, it assumes that an increase in the volume of transactions creates the possibility of economies in the relative magnitude of money balances necessary for a given level of security against insolvency. That is, it implies that an increase in T decreases K. Hence, $M = KPT$ can continue to be satisfied even though P does not change in inverse proportion to T.[34]

The Implications of Say's Identity

We conclude this chapter with a discussion of Say's Identity. My own sympathies are with those who deny that this identity is a basic component of the classical and neoclassical position. Nevertheless, there are certain passages which can be cited in support of the opposite contention. Furthermore, whatever the proper interpretation, the attention that has been given to the identity since Keynes makes it desirable to analyze it in detail—particularly since some of its logical implications have not been correctly understood.[35]

Following Lange, we define Say's Identity as stating that—regardless of the prices and interest with which they are confronted—individuals always plan to use all of their proceeds from the sale of commodities and bonds for the purpose of purchasing other commodities and bonds. In other words, they never plan to change the amount of money they hold: its amount of excess demand is identically zero. In still other words—and as a direct consequence of the budget restraint—the aggregate value of the amounts of excess *supply* of commodities must always equal the value of the amount of *demand* for bonds: people divert any reduced expenditures on commodities to the purchase of bonds, never to the building up of money balances.[36]

It can readily be seen that this assumption implies that equilibrium money prices are indeterminate. For consider an economy with n goods: $n-2$ commodities, bonds, and money. Assume that this economy is in equilibrium at a certain set of values for the rate of interest and for the $n-2$ money prices. Let us now arbitrarily change one of these prices. Consider first the $n-2$ commodity markets. In general, it will be possible to find another set of $n-2$ values for the rate of interest and for the remaining $n-3$ money prices which will again equilibrate these $n-2$ markets. But, by Say's Identity, any set of prices and interest which equilibrates these markets must also equilibrate the bond market, for, under this assumption, if the excess supplies of commodities are zero, so is the demand for bonds.[37] Finally, since the excess demand for money is identically zero, this market too is obviously in equilibrium. Thus the economy as a whole can be in equilibrium at an infinite number of sets of money prices. In mathematical terms, Say's Identity reduces the number of independent market excess-demand equations to $n-2$, and these do not suffice to determine the equilibrium values of the $n-1$ price and interest variables.[38]

Thus Say's Identity is inconsistent with the existence of a money economy with determinate prices. But this is the only type of money economy that has any economic meaning. Hence we can say that the existence of Say's Identity implies the existence of a barter economy. Conversely, the existence of a barter economy implies the existence of Say's Identity. For in such an economy it is physically impossible to "sell" one commodity or bond without "buying" another; thus Say's Identity in this economy is nothing but a statement of the budget restraint. In other words, people never plan to change their level of money balances in a barter economy, because, by definition, such balances are always zero.

Let us now return for a moment to the "homogeneity postulate." As was demonstrated above,[39] this postulate implies the absence of a real-balance effect and the consequent indeterminacy of money prices. By the same argument as in the preceding paragraph, we can then say that the existence of the "homogeneity postulate" implies the existence of a barter economy. Conversely, the existence of a barter economy implies the existence of the "homogeneity postulate." For in such an economy there are no money holdings, the "absolute price level" has no meaning, and hence there can be no real-balance effect.

Thus, contrary to the accepted opinion, Say's Identity and the "homogeneity postulate" are logically equivalent properties: both are necessarily present in a barter economy; both are necessarily absent from a money economy. Thus the existence of the one implies the coexistence of the other.[40]

With this we have also said all that need be said for our purpose about a barter economy. Such an economy is the home—the necessary and only home—of the "homogeneity postulate" and Say's Identity. Prices in this economy can be measured either in terms of one of the commodities or—as in a Wicksellian "pure credit economy"—in terms of an abstract unit of account. Thus, at most, only relative and accounting prices are defined. The former are determined by the workings of market forces, the latter—as always—by arbitrary decree. Money prices not even being defined, their determinacy or indeterminacy cannot be meaningfully discussed.[41]

NOTES

1. The reader will observe that $M = KPT$ and $MV = PT$ are treated here as *equations*, and not as *identities*. It will also be observed that these two equations have been treated as analytically equivalent. Without committing ourselves on the attempts that have sometimes been made to distinguish substantively between them, we merely note that for our present purposes any such distinction can be disregarded. Cf. J. M. Keynes, *Treatise on Money* (London 1930), Vol. 1, pp. 237–39; Marget, *Theory of Prices*, Vol. 1 (New York 1938), pp. 424–33.

For good recent accounts of the two neoclassical equations and their respectively associated theories, see L. V. Chandler, *The Economics of Money and Banking*, rev. ed. (New York 1953), Chapters XXIII–XXV; A. G. Hart, *Money, Debt, and Economic Activity*, rev. ed. (New York 1953), Chapters 10 and 12.

2. K. Wicksell, *Interest and Prices*, trans. R. F. Kahn (London 1936), pp. 39–41.

3. I. Fisher, *Purchasing Power of Money* (New York 1911), pp. 153–54.

4. This is one of the central themes of Marget's study; see, in particular, *Theory of Prices*, Vol. 1, pp. 307, 345 ff., and 500 ff. It also seems to me that a good part of H. Hegeland's monograph on the *Quantity Theory of Money* (Göteborg 1951) suffers from the failure to recognize this fact; see *ibid.*, especially pp. 38–9, 57, 87–92.

5. Cf., e.g., R. Cantillon, *Essay on the Nature of Trade* (1755), trans. and ed. H. Higgs (London 1931), p. 179; Mill, *Principles*, pp. 491–92. Marget (*Theory of Prices*, Vol. 1, p. 502) cites similar passages from Lubbock and Cairnes.

For this emphasis in later writers, see Walras, *Eléments d'économie politique pure*, first ed. (Lausanne 1874), p. 181, who essentially repeats Mill; see also the definitive ed. of the *Eléments*, ed. Jaffé (London 1954), p. 328. See also Wicksell, *Interest and Prices*, p. 40; Schumpeter, "Money and the Social Product," *op. cit.*, pp. 191–92, 204–6; and Mises, *op. cit.*, pp. 139–40. But Mises carries himself away to an invalid extreme when he attempts to prove that even in the case of an equiproportionate increase in initial individual money balances, prices will not rise equiproportionately (*ibid.*, pp. 141–42).

6. Fisher, *Purchasing Power of Money*, p. 153, with "his" changed to "their," and "him" to "them."

7. Pigou, "The Value of Money," *Quarterly Journal of Economics* (November 1917); reprinted in *Readings in Monetary Theory*, eds. F. A. Lutz and L. W. Mints (Philadelphia 1951), p. 174.

8. It is for this reason that the foregoing Cambridge economists are not listed together with Wicksell and Fisher on p. 269 as having presented a full statement of the tripartite quantity-theory thesis. In order to evaluate the validity of this criticism, the reader must himself compare the expositions of the Cambridge school with those of Wicksell and Fisher. It is similarly instructive to contrast the Cambridge expositions with those of such cash-balance theorists as Mises (*op. cit.*, pp. 132–35, 138–40, 147–49) and R. G. Hawtrey [*Currency and Credit*, 3rd ed. (London

1927), Chapters 3–4, especially pp. 35, 59–60; as can be seen from p. 35, Hawtrey's "unspent margin" is identical with what is usually referred to as a cash balance].

9. Cf. the references to Fisher, Wicksell, Mises, and Hawtrey in note 8 above.

10. That the asymmetry just described has persisted down to the present can be seen by examining the more recent literature from the same viewpoint that has just been used for the neoclassical. On the other hand, there is not much point in trying to trace this inconsistency back to the classical literature: its value-theory discussions are of too different a nature.

11. Pigou, *Essays in Applied Economics* (London 1923), p. 195.

12. The foregoing interpretation is, of course, that of Milton Friedman, who argues that Marshall assumed movements along his demand curve to be accompanied by compensating variations which keep real income constant ["The Marshallian Demand Curve," *Journal of Political Economy*, Vol. 57 (1949), as reprinted in *Essays in Positive Economics* (Chicago 1953), pp. 50–53]. While not accepting the specifics of this argument, I do agree that Marshall's demand curve does not reflect the income effect; see my "Demand Curves and Consumer's Surplus," in Carl Christ, *et al.*, *Measurement in Economics: Studies in Mathematical Economics and Econometrics in Memory of Yehuda Grunfeld* (Stanford 1963), pp. 104–8.

13. Once again Wicksell is an exception. For he makes it clear that the rectangular hyperbola he draws in his monetary theory is a market-equilibrium curve.

14. Compare this with the change in the equilibrium real quantity of money that characterizes a shift in liquidity preference; see below, pp. 287–88.

15. Throughout the following analysis we abstract from distribution effects. This enables us to consider the total of initial nominal—and hence real—bond holdings as identically zero. Accordingly, neither one of these holdings appears in the preceding classificatory scheme.

16. This term was first used by W. Leontief, "The Fundamental Assumption of Mr. Keynes' Monetary Theory of Unemployment," *Quarterly Journal of Economics*, Vol. 51 (1936–37), p. 193. It originates in the fact that, in mathematical terms, demand functions which are not affected by an equiproportionate change in money prices are said to be "homogeneous of degree zero" in these prices.

17. It should be clear to the reader that this does *not* correspond to our use of this term, which defines absence of money illusion as insensitivity to changes in the absolute level of *accounting*—and not *money*—prices.

In order to avoid any possible confusion, we might repeat that throughout this discussion "absolute price level" is a shorthand expression for "absolute level of *money* prices."

18. This was explicitly claimed by, for example, Leontief, "The Fundamental Assumption of Mr. Keynes," *op. cit.*, p. 193, and Modigliani, "Liquidity Preference," *op. cit.*, p. 217.

19. A fact that has been duly noted by various commentators on the dichotomy discussion; thus see Assar Lindbeck, "Den Klassiska 'Dichoto-

mien,' " *Ekonomisk Tidskrift*, Vol. 63 (1961), pp. 32, 35, and 39; and H. G. Bieri, "Der Streit um die 'klassische Dichotomie,' " *Schweizerische Zeitschrift für Volkswirtschaft und Statistik*, Vol. 2 (1963), pp. 177–78.

On the other hand—and as has already been indicated in a symposium participated in by Baumol ("Monetary and Value Theory," *Review of Economic Studies* [October 1960], section I and p. 31, final paragraph), Hahn (*op. cit.*, p. 42), and Ball and Bodkin (*op. cit.*, p. 49, footnote 4)— the recent criticism of the foregoing argument by Archibald and Lipsey (*Review of Economic Studies* [October 1958], pp. 9–17) stems from a failure to see this fact and is therefore beside the point.

Though relying on this symposium for his summing-up of the dichotomy discussion, Harry Johnson's recent survey also incorrectly implies that the foregoing argument deals with the inconsistency of a system of static equations ("Monetary Theory and Policy," *op. cit.*, p. 340, lines 13–20) [reprinted in this volume—Ed.].

20. Cf., e.g., M. R. Cohen and E. Nagel, *An Introduction to Logic and the Scientific Method* (New York 1934), p. 144; Patrick Suppes, *Introduction to Logic* (Princeton 1957), pp. 36–7.

21. It is this coincidence of the demand and supply curves which is assured by the assumption of Say's Identity (cf. pp. 290–91 above) made by Hickman, Archibald and Lipsey, and the other writers.

22. Once again, the reader is warned that this is *not* being used here in our sense of the term.

23. For a more precise statement of the argument see my "Indeterminacy of Absolute Prices in Classical Economic Theory," *Econometrica*, Vol. 17 (1949), p. 22.

24. It should be clear that the criticism of these paragraphs is *not* directed against the frequent neoclassical practice of taking the absolute price level as given in the partial-equilibrium analysis of value theory. The same methodological considerations which permit this analysis to hold constant certain relative prices also permit it to do the same for the absolute price level. The purpose of this assumption is simply to enable the money price of a commodity to serve as a perfect index of its relative price. Cf. Marshall, *Principles*, eighth ed., p. 62. This practice goes back at least to Mill, *Principles*, p. 439; cf. Marget, *Theory of Prices*, Vol. 2, (New York 1942), p. 281, footnote 128.

25. The example referred to here is that of Samuelson; the quotation is also his.

The line of reasoning in the second half of this paragraph is one that I have frequently heard—though I have not succeeded in finding any additional example of it in the literature. Cf., however, Boulding, *Economic Analysis*, p. 320.

26. Cf. above, pp. 276 f.

The passage cited is from Fisher, italics in original. Precisely the same confusion can be found in Cassel.

27. See the references to Leontief and Modigliani above, p. 293, note 18.

28. The example referred to is that of Leontief, italics in original.

29. The example is that of Fisher.

30. On an outside-money economy, see note 23 above.

31. Cf. my "Indeterminacy of Absolute Prices in Classical Monetary Theory," *Econometrica*, XVII (1949), pp. 23–7. Cf. also pp. 271–72 and 277–78 above.

32. On these speculations, see again the reference cited in note 31.

It should also be clear from all this that there is no logical connection between the dichotomy issue and the classical-Keynesian controversy.

It might also be noted that the explicit use of the real-balance effect helps tie together other loose ends of the traditional theory. Thus see Amotz Morag's use of the real-balance effect in public finance theory to prove the long-debated equivalence of an income tax and a uniform sales tax ["Deflationary Effects of Outlay and Income Taxes," *Journal of Political Economy*, Vol. 67 (1959), pp. 266–74]. See also Michael Michaely's use of the real-balance effect in international trade theory to resolve the apparent contradiction between the "relative-price" and "absorption" approaches to the analysis of devaluation ["Relative-Prices and Income-Absorption Approaches to Devaluation: A Partial Reconciliation," *American Economic Review*, Vol. 50 (1960), pp. 144–47].

33. See above, pp. 271–72.

34. On these economies, cf. the reference to Fisher, *Purchasing Power of Money*, pp. 153–54.

35. "Say's Identity" is the useful term suggested by G. S. Becker and W. J. Baumol in order to emphasize that it may not really represent "Say's Law" in its classical and neoclassical meaning. But Becker and Baumol's attempt to give a classical connotation to the concept they call "Say's Equality" can only mislead.

36. The budget restraint is

the amount of market excess demand for current money holdings
 = the aggregate value of the amounts of market excess supplies
   of current commodities
 — the (discounted) value of the amount of market demand for
   current bond holdings.

By Say's Identity, the left-hand side of this equation is identically zero, so that this yields the conclusion just stated in the text.

37. The demand and *excess* demand for bonds are identical, so that equilibrium exists in this market when either is zero.

38. For a graphical analysis of the indeterminacy generated by Say's Identity in the case of an economy consisting only of commodities, see Figure 1a and its related discussion on pp. 270–72 above.

39. Page 280 f. Note that the extension of the present argument to an economy with bonds has caused us to make a corresponding extension of the "homogeneity postulate" to include the bond market. However, the reader who prefers to retain the original sense of this term as applying only to the commodity markets can simply ignore all references here to the bond market and the rate of interest and follow the analysis as if it applied to an economy with only commodities and money. This does not change the argument in any significant way. At the same time, this modification brings us back to the framework actually considered by Lange and Modigliani.

40. Note that the proof of this proposition rests on the basic assumption that—from the viewpoint of meaningful economic analysis—the class of monetary economies with indeterminate price levels is an empty one. This fact has been overlooked in Archibald and Lipsey's recent criticism (*op. cit.*, p. 14, footnote 2).

41. As the reader has undoubtedly realized, here is another (cf. pp. 282 ff. above) deceptive similarity which may have helped give rise to the invalid dichotomy: the "homogeneity postulate" *is* a correct description of rational behavior in a barter economy—but not in a money economy.

13 *Monetary and Value Theory: A Critique of Lange and Patinkin*

G. C. Archibald *University of British Columbia*
and Richard G. Lipsey *Queen's University*

A change in the price level which causes a departure of desired from actual real balances may lead to a change in individuals' spending. The object of this paper is to enquire into the operation and significance of this real-balance effect in classical value and monetary theory, about which there has for some time been controversy. Lange argued that the classical dichotomy between the real and monetary sectors of the economy is invalid, and that an integration of value and monetary theory is required. Patinkin has attempted this integration in his book *Money, Interest, and Prices*, arguing that the real-balance effect provides the necessary link between the two parts of the system. In this paper we argue that the classical dichotomy is valid, and that the integration undertaken by Patinkin is therefore unnecessary. In part one we enquire into the operation of the real-balance effect in a classical exchange model. This is necessary because Patinkin's analysis is incomplete and leaves many important points obscure. We find that, while the price level is of course determined by the desire to hold balances together with the stock of money, the role of the real-balance effect is *only* to provide an explanation of how the system behaves in disequilibrium. Thus the real-balance effect is irrelevant to those

Reprinted from *Review of Economic Studies*, Vol. 26 (October 1958), 1–22, by permission of the authors and publisher.

famous propositions of the quantity theory which are the result of comparative static analysis. In part two we enquire into the formal consistency of the classical model, a question which is given great importance by the fact that nearly all modern value theory presupposes the validity of the classical dichotomy. We find that the model has a consistent solution which does not depend in any way on the presence in the model of the real-balance effect. We find, however, that the model offers no explanation of behaviour out of equilibrium, and that the role of the real-balance effect is again to provide an explanation of disequilibrium behaviour. We see that it is the absence of such an explanation from the formal classical model that has led to the persistent and erroneous view that the system is inconsistent. We also see in what way Lange's original argument was mistaken.

In part three we investigate the role of the real-balance effect in a classical model with production and saving as well as exchange. We find once again that the role of this effect is to explain how this system behaves out of equilibrium, but that the equilibrium level of employment is independent of its operation in the model. We argue that Patinkin's claim, that his analysis "invalidates" the Keynesian theory of employment, is completely unfounded.

The Real Balance Effect in a Classical Exchange Model

We start by considering the exchange model of the first part of Patinkin's book. In this model, in which time is divided into discrete contracting periods called weeks, it is important to distinguish between equilibrium at a point of time and equilibrium over time. As Hicks has put it, a stationary economy ". . . is in full equilibrium, not merely when demands equal supplies at the currently established prices, but also when the same prices continue to rule at all dates . . ."[1] Patinkin apparently overlooks this distinction; his analysis never goes beyond the conditions for equilibrium in one week. It is, as we shall see in (7) below, for this reason that he is forced to make some unusual assumptions to obtain the classical results. Our investigation of the properties of the model in full, as well as in weekly, equilibrium is necessary in order to understand how Patinkin arrives at his results, how the classical results may in fact be obtained directly from the comparative static analysis of the model in full equilibrium, and what role is played by the real-balance effect in the many cases that may be studied.

The individual is assumed to have a given real income paid in goods,[2] and a given initial stock of money. We assume for the moment that relative prices do not vary so that goods may be treated as a single composite (G) with a single price (p). The individual's stock of money divided by p is his real balance H. We assume an indifference system between *holding* real balances for the week and *consuming* goods. The demand for balances is assumed to be purely a transactions demand.[3] The market opens every Monday, and a process of *tâtonnement* and recontract continues until equilibrium prices are reached. The market then closes, all contracts become binding, and trade takes place. The *tâtonnement*, in which equilibrium prices are found, is quite distinct from the actual trading, which takes place afterwards. The conditions for *weekly* equilibrium are, for the individual, that he has achieved the preferred division of his total resources between consumption and holding balances for the week, and, for the market, that supplies of and demands for goods are equal. It is consistent with these conditions, however, that the individual shall have added to or subtracted from his balances. If this is the case, he will begin the following week with a different total of resources, and his behaviour will be different. *Full* equilibrium obtains when market prices are unchanged from week to week. This requires that each individual's behaviour be unchanged from week to week, that is, that his consumption be constant. Since in this model an individual must divide the whole of his resources between consumption and balances it follows that, when his consumption is constant, so also are his balances (i.e., he consumes a bundle of goods equal in value to the bundle with which he was endowed at the beginning of the week). Thus the full equilibrium level of consumption is necessarily equal to total income, and independent of the desire to hold balances, the stock of money, and the equilibrium level of prices.

In order to understand how this model works, it is necessary to analyse:

(1) the individual's weekly equilibrium;
(2) how he reaches full equilibrium;
(3) how this full equilibrium is altered by a changed desire for balances;
(4) how it is altered by a change in the price level;
(5) how the market reaches full equilibrium;
(6) how full equilibrium in the market is altered by a change in the money stock;
(7) how weekly market equilibrium is altered by a change in the money stock which takes place when full equilibrium does not obtain;
(8) the effects on the market of a non-proportional change in individuals' stocks of money;
(9) the bearing of the above on the demand for money; and

(10) the part played in the above by the real-balance effect. Since Patinkin neglects the conditions for full equilibrium, his analysis is devoted mainly to (1), (7), (8) and (9).

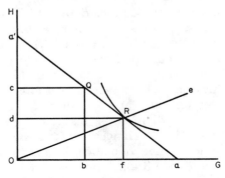

Figure 1.

(1) The individual's behaviour in this model may now be analysed with the aid of Patinkin's diagram. In Figure 1, units of the composite good are measured along the G axis and of *real* balances along the H axis. The budget line relating real goods to real balances must have an invariant slope of 135°; in Patinkin's words, "The unitary negative slope of this line reflects the fact that, by definition, one unit of liquid command over commod- ities-in-general [real balances] can always be exchanged for one unit of actual commodities-in-general" (*op. cit. ibid.*, p. 69). At the beginning of any week the individual's total resources consist of his income for that week *plus* his stock of real balances (money balances held over from the previous week divided by the price level which, for the moment, we assume to remain constant). If this total equals Oa in goods, it is necessarily also Oa' in balances, where $Oa = Oa'$, and the budget line is aa'. The individual is in equilibrium for the week when he is at a point of tangency between his budget line and an indifference curve. The locus of such points of tangency defines an expansion path Oe.

(2) We now come to the essential part of the argument that Patinkin overlooked. Intersection of the budget line and the ex- pansion path only provides an equilibrium for the week in question. Suppose that the individual, in the diagram just considered, starts the week in the position Q. This means that he has received income equal to Ob, and has retained balances equal to Oc (= ba). To attain his preferred position, R, he spends cd (= bf of goods) from his balances, in addition to spending his whole income. Thus his balances carried over to next week will be only Od. Hence, even if he receives the same income next week, he starts the period

with a different (smaller) total of resources. The budget line the following Monday will be closer to the origin by the distance $bf = cd$, and the individual's market behaviour will therefore be changed. Full (stock) equilibrium, which is only attained when his behaviour is repeated each week, requires that the division of his resources between goods and balances with which he starts the week is the preferred division for that total of resources. We now amend Patinkin's diagram to make explicit the distinction between expenditure out of income and expenditure out of balances. Consider Figure 2. The individual has a constant real income OY. Erect a perpendicular YY' which intersects the expansion path Oe at i. If his initial real balances are Ya, his budget line is aa', his initial position S_1, at the intersection of aa' with YY', and his preferred position P_1. In the first week he therefore consumes Og goods, running down his balances by Yg. It follows that next period his budget line will be $jj'(ja = Yg)$, and his initial position S_2. The preferred position is now P_2, obtained by spending S_3P_2 from balances; and the starting point for the next period is in turn S_3. It is clear that this process continues, with ever smaller adjustments, as the individual approaches ever closer to i (which cannot be attained in a finite number of periods). Only when the individual is at i is he in full stock equilibrium; that is to say, at i he spends the whole of his income OY, while maintaining his stock of balances unchanged. (This analysis can obviously be repeated

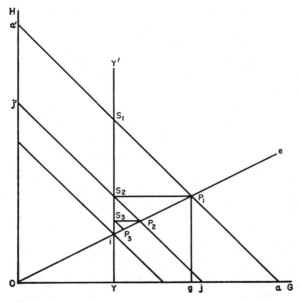

Figure 2.

for the case in which the individual starts with too low a level of real balances.)

(3) Suppose that a change in tastes were to alter the expansion path in Figure 3 from Oe to Oe', indicating an increase in the desire to hold balances. The position of stock equilibrium is given by the intersection of YY' with the new expansion path at k. The equilibrium level of real balances is increased by ik; the equilibrium level of consumption is unchanged at OY, i.e., is independent of the desired level of balances, although, in the weeks in which balances are being built up, consumption is less than income.

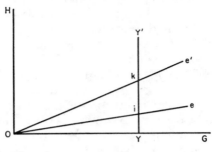

Figure 3.

(4) Suppose that the individual is in a position of full equilibrium, i in Figure 2, where with income OY his balances are constant at Yi. Now, if the price level changes, his stock of real balances (nominal money balances divided by the price level) changes in proportion. A change in the price level therefore has the effect of moving his budget line.[4] If the price level is halved, his real balances are doubled, and the budget line moves to $jj'(Yi = iS_2)$. His preferred position the following week is P_2, and, if the price level remains constant at the new level, he will return to i, by weekly steps, in the fashion already analysed. Thus the full-equilibrium levels of consumption and real balances are independent of the price level.

(5) For the market to be in weekly equilibrium, it is necessary that the demand for and supply of each good be equal. Individuals may, however, consume more or less than their income by running down or adding to their balances. The equality of demand for and supply of goods implies that, if any individuals are running down balances, others are increasing theirs by exactly the same amount. Thus if all individuals are not in stock equilibrium, balances change hands each period. *Full stock equilibrium thus requires a unique distribution of balances* among the individuals in the market. Except in a special case, the process of redistributing balances by trade will cause the price level to vary from week to

week.[5] Apart from this special case, a constant price level requires full equilibrium for each consumer.

Let us take a simple example, illustrated in Figure 4, in which there are only two individuals with identical incomes of OY, identical non-linear expansion paths Oe, but different initial balances. Individual I has balances Yc and budget line cc'; individual II has balances Yf and budget line ff'. I now wishes to add Yv to his balances, and is therefore an excess supplier of goods by the same amount. II wishes to spend Yd out of his balances, and is therefore an excess demander of goods by the same amount. Equilibrium in the market this week requires that $Yv = Yd$. Assume that this is the case, and that the *tâtonnement* is therefore concluded and trade takes place. Next week I's budget line, which has moved out by $Yv = Yd$, passes through Z; and II's, which has moved in by $Yd = Yv$, passes through W. I wishes to move to L, and II to M. Given the shape of Oe, the horizontal distance of L from YY' exceeds that of M from YY'. Hence I's excess supply of goods exceeds II's excess demand, and trade cannot take place at last week's price level. Prices are therefore bid down. This, however, increases the real balances of both individuals, and therefore moves both budget lines to the right. As the budget lines move to the right, I's excess supply of goods diminishes, and II's excess demand increases. When the two have been brought into equality the *tâtonnement* ends, and the market is in equilibrium this week.

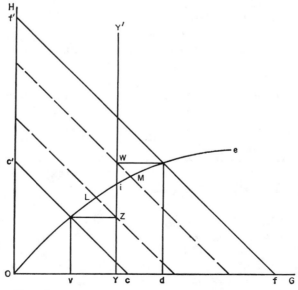

Figure 4.

The process of adjustment is therefore as follows:[6] trade each week moves the two budget lines closer together; the price reduction required to equilibrate the market the following week moves them both to the right; the week's trade then again brings them closer together. Ultimately the two budget lines coincide, passing through *i*, the position of full equilibrium for each individual. Only then will the price level cease to vary. (This analysis can obviously be repeated for the case in which the price level increases from week to week.)

(6) Now suppose that each individual in the market is in a position of full equilibrium, such as point *i* in Figure 2, when the stock of money is doubled. In order to avoid distribution effects we shall assume for the present that each individual simply wakes up on Monday morning to find his nominal money balances doubled. At the prevailing price level each individual's budget line therefore moves out, e.g., to *jj'* in Figure 2. Now *each* individual wishes to spend out of balances. When the market opens there is therefore an excess demand for goods (equal to S_3P_2 for the individual in Figure 2). This excess demand causes a rise in the price level, which continues, through the process of *tâtonnement*, until supply of and demand for goods are restored to equality. The rising price level *during* the *tâtonnement* reduces each individual's real balances, and therefore moves his budget line inwards *without trade taking place*. The *tâtonnement* must continue, with the price level rising, until the excess demand for goods has been removed. This requires that individuals cease to attempt to alter their balances. This in turn requires that the price level rise until balances are restored to their original real worth, i.e., that the price level is doubled. In terms of Figure 2, the individual endeavouring to spend S_3P_2 of his newly increased balances finds that the efforts of others to do likewise are increasing the price level. The increase moves his budget line closer to the origin, and continues until the budget line is restored to its original position. Thus a doubling of each individual's stock of cash leads to a doubling of the price level on the first occasion that the market opens. When the whole market starts from full equilibrium, full equilibrium is restored by the *tâtonnement alone*, there being no actual expenditure out of balances and no week-by-week adjustment.

(7) In (6) above we saw that a change in the stock of money leads to a proportionate change in the full equilibrium price level. Patinkin, however, does not analyse the model in full equilibrium: he considers a change in the stock of money which takes place during a process of adjustment such as that analysed in (5) above. We may now see how he obtains his results. Suppose that the *tâtonnement* has just ended, *but that no goods have yet changed hands*.

The price level is therefore such as would clear the market this week, i.e., the excess supply of goods offered by some individuals is equal to the excess demanded by the others (the price level is not, however, one which will necessarily be repeated the following week, nor the same as that which prevailed in the preceding week). Now we follow Patinkin in doubling the stock of money by doubling the balances of each individual. We cancel all the contracts of the previous *tâtonnement*, and start a new *tâtonnement*. Those individuals who had contracted to reduce their balances will now wish to make a larger reduction, and will therefore increase their excess demand for goods; those who had contracted to add to their balances will now wish to make a smaller addition, and will therefore decrease their excess supply of goods. Thus the price level must rise, and must continue to rise until excess supplies and demands for goods are again equal. This requires that the budget lines be restored to the position they occupied at the close of the previous *tâtonnement*, i.e., that the price level double. The price level that is doubled is not, however, that of the previous week: it is the price level at which trade *would* have taken place this week had the stock of money not doubled. If, in the absence of a change in the stock of money, this week's price level would not have been equal to last week's, a doubling of the stock of money which doubles this week's price level does not cause it to be double last week's. Thus Patinkin obtains conclusions which appear to agree with those of the quantity theory only by comparing prices at which trade takes place (after the second of the week's two *tâtonnements*) with prices at which it would have taken place (after the first).[7] To obtain the result that doubling the quantity of money doubles actual market prices, we must compare positions of full equilibrium as in (6) above.

(8) The analysis has so far been conducted on Patinkin's assumption that, when the stock of money is increased, there are no distribution effects. Patinkin argues that the absence of distribution effects is a necessary condition for the result that doubling the money stock doubles the price level.[8] If the doubling is conducted in the fashion analysed in (7) above, this is true. In the usual case, in which positions of full equilibrium are compared, it is not true. Let us now consider the consequences of an increase in the stock of money which is not distributed in such a fashion as to cause an equi-proportionate increase in the money balances of all individuals. Since each individual's final equilibrium is fully defined by his expansion path and his real income, any given increase in the stock of money has the same effect on the position of final equilibrium as that of any other equal increase however it may be initially distributed. In the case of a non-proportionate distribution

the equilibrium cannot, of course, be reached *merely* by a change in the price level, but will require a redistribution of balances by the process of adjustment through trade already analysed. The path of adjustment, but not, of course, the final equilibrium, depends on the actual distribution of the increase in the money stock. We must notice that the conclusion obtained in (7) above, that a doubling of the money stock causes the price level at which trade next takes place to be double what it otherwise would have been, depends on the absence of distribution effects. The conclusion that doubling the stock of money doubles the full equilibrium price level does not depend on this assumption.

(9) The equilibrium level of real balances is uniquely determined by tastes and incomes, and invariant to the money stock. Hence the total market demand for nominal money with respect to the reciprocal of the price level is the rectangular hyperbola of the classical writers. Consider, however, the case of an individual who is in full equilibrium when the price level is halved. Since, by assumption, he does not spend the whole increase in his real balances in the first week, his nominal balances are not at once halved. Hence his immediate demand curve for money is of less than unit elasticity. Each week, however, he reduces his balances until, when full equilibrium is restored, his nominal balances are half their original amount. The inelastic individual demand curve discussed by Patinkin[9] therefore belongs solely to weeks in which full equilibrium has not been attained. The individual's curve relating the full equilibrium demand for money to the price level is, of course, always, like the market curve, a rectangular hyperbola.

(10) Patinkin defines the real-balance effect as ". . . the influence on demand of a change in real balances, other things being held constant" (*ibid.*, p. 21). Since in full equilibrium consumption is equal to income, a change in real balances can only change real consumption during a process of adjustment. Thus the real-balance effect is a transitory phenomenon, which is operative only in some disequilibrium situations.[10] Its role is to provide a possible *dynamic* explanation of how the economy moves from one position of static equilibrium to another. Thus, if we are interested in those well-known propositions of the quantity theory which are propositions in comparative statics, the real-balance effect is irrelevant.[11]

The Consistency of the Classical Exchange Model

In the traditional classical system it was assumed that the demand and supply functions for goods were homogeneous of degree zero in absolute prices; relative prices and equilibrium quantities were uniquely determined in the "real" sector of the economy, and the absolute price level by a demand function for money to hold of the Cambridge type and a given stock of money. Lange opened the modern controversy by arguing that this model is necessarily inconsistent.[12] Patinkin then took up and elaborated Lange's argument. Patinkin's position has been criticised,[13] but the authors of the main summaries of the controversy have found substantially in his favour.[14] The opinion that the classical system is inconsistent has led Patinkin to the view, already expressed by Lange, that relative and absolute prices cannot be separately determined, and hence to the attempt to combine their determination with the aid of the real-balance effect. This question of the consistency of the classical system is of considerable importance. In the first place, it is fundamental to real static theory. Patinkin writes that ". . . once the real and monetary data of the economy are specified, the equilibrium values of relative prices, the rate of interest, and the absolute price level are simultaneously determined by all the markets of economy. It is generally impossible to isolate a subset of markets which can determine the equilibrium values of a subset of prices."[15] If this is correct, then most existing real static theory, e.g., of international trade, must be radically at fault. In the second place, if we are to understand the proper role of the real-balance effect in economics, we must know whether it is required to restore consistency to the otherwise inconsistent classical model, or has some other function. In this section, therefore, we shall enquire into the question of consistency (which has been much confused by the fact that different authors appear to have used the term in different senses).

(1) The view that the classical system is inconsistent appears to rest mainly on the argument that it contains two excess demand functions for money. One excess demand function is obtained from the supply and demand functions for goods. The excess demand for money is equal to the total amount of money demanded in exchange for goods *minus* the total amount supplied in exchange for goods. Since the physical volume of transactions is independent of the absolute price level in this model, the money value of transactions varies in proportion to the price level. Thus this excess demand function for money is homogeneous of degree one in absolute prices. The second excess demand function is for money to hold. It is obtained from the Cambridge equation where the demand for money (K times the money value of transactions) is homogeneous of degree one in absolute prices, and the stock supply of money is an institutionally determined constant (i.e., homogeneous of degree zero in the prices). The excess demand function,

which is the difference between the demand (homogeneous of degree one) and the supply (homogeneous of degree zero) is therefore non-homogeneous. It is alleged that the existence of these two functions makes the model inconsistent.[16] The usual demonstration runs as follows: assume that the system is in equilibrium; double all money prices; since relative prices are unaffected, the goods markets are still in equilibrium; hence, by Walras' Law, the money market is in equilibrium; thus either the system leaves money prices undetermined, in the absence of a stock demand for money, or, if there is a stock demand, there are two inconsistent excess demand functions.[17]

The existence of these two excess demand functions raises two separate questions which have been much confused during the controversy. These are:

1. Has the model, in general, a solution, i.e., is it formally consistent?
2. Does it make economic sense?

It has been demonstrated, by both Hickman and Valavanis, that the model is not, in general, formally inconsistent. We shall present Hickman's example of a classical model here and, for convenience, provide a numerical example. The fact that this example has a consistent solution answers the first question. The second question is more difficult. If non-equilibrium values of some of the variables are substituted into the model, the results appear to be, in some sense, "self-contradictory." That is to say, if the price level is arbitrarily doubled, there is an excess demand for money to hold but no excess supply of goods. The answer to the question is that the model has no economic interpretation when it is out of equilibrium. Some writers have apparently inferred from this that the answer to the first question is also no. This is not a valid inference.[18] The fact that the model has no interpretation out of equilibrium, however, presents problems which we must consider. Before doing so, we shall show that, although Hickman's example is formally consistent, it does not conform to *all* the requirements of a static economic model. We shall accordingly modify it and present a second numerical example. We shall then show what significance is to be attached to the difficulties which occur out of equilibrium. Finally, we shall consider what modifications are made to the model by the inclusion of a real-balance term.

(2) Now let us consider the example of the classical model set out by Hickman, in which there are only two goods and money (d_1, d_2, s_1, and s_2 are the parameters). The monetary equation is linearly dependent on the goods equations; when X_1 and X_2 equal zero, X_3 must equal zero and is, therefore, redundant as an equilibrium condition. We have two commodity equations, but only

TABLE 1

	DEMAND	SUPPLY	EXCESS DEMAND
Good I	$D_1 \equiv d_1 \dfrac{p_2}{p_1}$	$S_1 \equiv s_1 \dfrac{p_1}{p_2}$	$X_1 \equiv d_1 \dfrac{p_2}{p_1} - s_1 \dfrac{p_1}{p_2} = 0$
Good II	$D_2 \equiv d_2 \dfrac{p_1}{p_2}$	$S_2 \equiv s_2 \dfrac{p_2}{p_1}$	$X_2 \equiv d_2 \dfrac{p_1}{p_2} - s_2 \dfrac{p_2}{p_1} = 0$
Money	$D_3 \equiv p_1 S_1 + p_2 S_2$	$S_3 \equiv p_1 D_1 + p_2 D_2$	$X_3 \equiv -p_1 X_1 - p_2 X_2 = 0$

one relative price. If the two equations were independent they would in general solve for different relative prices, hence consistency in the model requires that the commodity equations be dependent. "A necessary and sufficient condition [for dependence] is that . . . the determinant of the matrix of the coefficients of X_1 and X_2 vanishes, i.e., that $s_2 = d_1(d_2/s_1)$."[19] If this condition is satisfied, then by solving either of the commodity equations we obtain the relative price which may be substituted into the supply or demand functions to obtain equilibrium quantities. We may now complete the system by adding a Cambridge equation

$$K(p_1 D_1 + p_2 D_2) = M_0$$

where K and M_0 are constants. The values of D_1, D_2, and p_1/p_2 are already known $\left(\dfrac{p_1}{p_2} = \sqrt{(d_1/s_1)} = \sqrt{(s_2/d_2)} \right)$, and the money prices can now be obtained.

Let us now take a numerical example by giving specific values to the parameters of the system, and show that it has a solution. If we put $d_1 = 4$ and $s_1 = 16$ into the excess demand equation for Good I, we obtain $\dfrac{p_1}{p_2} = \tfrac{1}{2}$ and $D_1 = S_1 = 8$. Consistency requires that $\dfrac{d_1}{s_1} = \dfrac{s_2}{d_2}$; hence, if we arbitrarily put $d_2 = 4$, we must have $s_2 = 1$. Putting these values into the second commodity equation, we have

$$4 \frac{p_1}{p_2} - \frac{p_2}{p_1} = 0$$

which gives $\dfrac{p_1}{p_2} = \tfrac{1}{2}$, the value which satisfied the first equation. We also have $D_2 = S_2 = 2$. Now, having determined relative prices and equilibrium quantities, we may determine money prices. If we take $K = \tfrac{1}{3}$ and the supply of money as \$10, we have

$$\tfrac{1}{3}(8p_1 + 2p_2) = \$10.$$

With $\dfrac{p_1}{p_2} = \frac{1}{2}$, this yields $p_1 = \$2.50$ and $p_2 = \$5.00$.

This example is a sufficient refutation of the charge that the system of homogeneous goods equations, together with the Cambridge equation, can have no solution, i.e., is formally inconsistent.

(3) There remains the question of the economic interpretation which is to be put on this model when it is not in equilibrium. Before we can discuss this, however, there is a problem about the equilibrium properties of the model which we must take up, and which will necessitate some modifications. Let us again consider the numerical example. Its solution was

$$D_1 = S_1 = 8 \qquad\qquad p_1 = \$2.50$$
$$D_2 = S_2 = 2 \qquad\qquad p_2 = \$5.00.$$

If we substitute these values into the money equations (third row of the table above) we obtain

$$D_3 = S_3 = 8 \times \$2.50 + 2 \times \$5.00 = \$30,$$

the money value of transactions. The money value of trade in Good I is \$20.00, and in Good II \$10.00. Since, however, one good can only be purchased by selling the other good or by running down balances, it follows that, in the aggregate, purchasers of Good I are running down their balances, while suppliers of that good are adding to theirs; and that purchasers of Good II are adding to their balances while suppliers are reducing theirs. Hence this model, while mathematically consistent, does not yield a full static equilibrium solution. In the solution obtained there is a continuous flow of balances from one set of individuals to another. One of the conditions of full equilibrium described in part one was that each individual be satisfied with his balances, i.e., a unique distribution of balances is one of the conditions of full equilibrium. This condition is simply not to be found in the model just examined. There is no equilibrium distribution of balances, and cannot be unless behaviour is altered. The alteration of behaviour, however, requires that we alter the supply and demand functions.

We must now modify the model to allow for an equilibrium distribution of balances. We must therefore select forms of the supply and demand functions which are not merely consistent but which also conform to this condition. We now require that in equilibrium the money value of the goods supplied by each individual equal the money value of the goods demanded by him. Now any individual can, in general, reach balance equilibrium at any set of relative prices with which he is faced. Hence we have, for any set of relative prices, a set of demands and supplies for each individual which describes his desired sales and purchases if he is in balance equilibrium at that set of prices. This is the set which must be described by the functions used for full-equilibrium static analysis. Thus the supply and demand functions we now require will have the property that the flow demand will equal the flow supply of goods for each individual at each set of relative prices, i.e., will give supply and demand when balances are in equilibrium. If this is not the case, then either (a), as in the example above, we never reach balance equilibrium, or (b), the analysis must include the process of adjustment described in part one. If we want balance equilibrium, and propose to consider only positions of full equilibrium (if, that is, the analysis is static, and omits the process of adjustment), then the supply and demand functions must be appropriately written. The selection of the set of functions appropriate to comparative statics, however, has the effect of writing Say's Identity into the model—if the functions give balance equilibrium at every set of relative prices for all individuals, then the aggregate excess demand for goods in general is zero at every set of relative prices, which is Say's Identity.[20] This is necessary if the solution is to be consistent with balance equilibrium.[21] In the models considered here, in which we are concerned only with trade in two goods, Say's Identity requires that the value of trade in the two goods be identical.[22] In a multi-good exchange model in which Say's Identity held for each individual, and so for the goods market as a whole, we should not, of course, have this simple relationship between pairs of goods.

The example may now be modified to conform with this requirement. First, we notice that the two excess demand functions were, to meet the requirements of consistency, made linearly dependent. That is, we had

$$X_1 \equiv 4\frac{p_2}{p_1} - 16\frac{p_1}{p_2} = 0,$$

and

$$X_2 \equiv 4\frac{p_1}{p_2} - 1\frac{p_2}{p_1} = 0.$$

The second is obtained when the first is multiplied by $-\frac{1}{4}$. The two are, of course, consistent whenever one can be obtained by multiplying the other by any constant λ. Our new requirement, however, is that money receipts from the sale of the first good equal money expenditure on the purchase of the second.[23] Hence

D_1p_1 must equal S_2p_2, i.e., S_2 must equal $\frac{p_1}{p_2} D_1$. Similarly D_2 must

equal $S_1 \frac{p_1}{p_2}$. Hence the second equation is obtained from the first by multiplying by $-\dfrac{p_1}{p_2}$. Say's Identity is therefore equivalent in the two-good model to restricting the choice of the constant λ to the particular value $-\dfrac{p_1}{p_2}$.

Let us now alter our numerical example to illustrate these requirements. We had

$$D_1 \equiv 4\,\frac{p_2}{p_1}, \quad S_1 \equiv 16\,\frac{p_1}{p_2}, \quad \text{and} \quad X_1 \equiv 4\,\frac{p_2}{p_1} - 16\,\frac{p_1}{p_2} = 0,$$

which gave $\dfrac{p_1}{p_2} = \tfrac{1}{2}$ and $D_1 = S_1 = 8$.

Now taking as our constant $\lambda = -\dfrac{p_1}{p_2} = -\tfrac{1}{2}$, we obtain

$$X_2 \equiv 8\,\frac{p_1}{p_2} - 2\,\frac{p_2}{p_1} = 0,$$

that is,

$$D_2 \equiv 8\,\frac{p_1}{p_2} \quad \text{and} \quad S_2 \equiv 2\,\frac{p_2}{p_1},$$

which gives $D_2 = S_2 = 4$ and $\dfrac{p_1}{p_2} = \tfrac{1}{2}$.

Taking $K = \tfrac{1}{3}$ and $M_0 = \$10.00$ as before, we have

$$\tfrac{1}{3}(8p_1 + 4p_2) = \$10.00$$

which, with $\dfrac{p_1}{p_2} = \tfrac{1}{2}$, gives $p_1 = \$1.875$ and $p_2 = \$3.75$. Since, by construction, $p_1D_1 = p_2S_2$ and $p_2D_2 = p_1S_1$, we obviously have $D_3 \equiv S_3$.[24] The value of trade in Good I is $8 \times \$1.875 = \$15.00$, and in Good II is $4 \times \$3.75 = \$15.00$.

(4) We have now seen, following Hickman, that the classical system is not necessarily inconsistent. We have also demonstrated that we must have Say's Identity to obtain full static equilibrium, but that this does not prevent us from solving the Cambridge equation to obtain money prices. We must now return to the second of our two original questions: what happens to this model in disequilibrium? Suppose that, in the numerical example above, we double money prices. As we leave relative prices unaltered, equilibrium in the goods markets is undisturbed, and the physical volume of transactions is unchanged although its money value has doubled, i.e., the value of trade in each good has increased from $15.00 to $30.00, so that $D_3 \equiv S_3$ now equal $60.00. Substituting these values into the Cambridge equation, however, we find an excess demand for money equal to K times the value of

trade *minus* the stock of money, here $(\frac{1}{3} \times 60) - 10$, which gives an excess demand of $10.00. Now the problem is to reconcile this with the identity $D_3 \equiv S_3$.

There are three points to consider here.

(i) Whatever interpretation may be put on the fact that $D_3 \equiv S_3$ while the Cambridge equation shows an excess demand, it is invalid to conclude from this that the model is formally inconsistent. The fact that the model has an equilibrium solution from which we can depart in the first place is sufficient to rule out this argument.

(ii) The example above, in which we doubled prices, is in denial of Walras' Law. Although there is an excess demand for money to hold, there is no excess supply of goods. In fact, Walras' Law does not hold in this model at all. This raises a problem of interpretation which we shall consider in (iii) below. The absence of Walras' Law, however, follows directly from the division of the system into two subsections, the real and the monetary, which can be solved separately. If we assume that the quantities of goods traded depend *only* on relative prices, and that the money price level can be determined independently, then we cannot expect to find the Walrasian relation between the goods equations and the Cambridge money equation. *Thus the classical dichotomy consists in building a model in which Walras' Law does not hold.* Now we can understand the error in Lange's original argument. He wrote (*op. cit.*, p. 52)

$$D_n - S_n \equiv \Delta M,$$

that is, the excess of the flow demand for money over the flow supply is identical with the desired change in money balances (Walras' Law). In our example this would be

$$D_3 - S_3 \equiv K(p_1 D_1 + p_2 D_2) - M_0,$$

which is not true. He then argued that if $D_n \equiv S_n$ (Say's Identity) there could be no monetary theory, because ΔM would be identical with zero. The error lies simply in identifying $D_n - S_n$ with ΔM in the classical model.[25] The dichotomy precludes this relationship between the two parts of the system—Walras' Law does not hold. If Lange's identification were valid, then the rest of his argument would follow. Thus Lange's criticism of the classical model depends on his assuming that Walras' Law holds whereas, as we have seen, the classical dichotomy precludes Walras' Law.

(iii) Now we have the problem of interpretation. Walras' Law says that goods can only be demanded if goods or money are offered in exchange. It is therefore a relationship which must obtain if a model is to make economic sense. When the classical model is in equilibrium the relation does obtain, i.e., the excess demands for both goods and money to hold are zero. Hence the equilibrium solution to the system makes sense. The relationship does not, however, hold out of equilibrium, i.e., is not an identity in this model. Hence, out of equilibrium, the system does not make economic sense. It does not describe a possible form of disequilibrium behaviour. Formally, what this means is that, in the classical model, the Cambridge equation is an independent *constraint*.[26] The model, although it has a determinate static solution, does not display any *market* mechanism that we can look to to correct a disequilibrium. If we want the system to do this, we may abandon the homogeneity assumption, and insert the real-balance terms into the supply and demand functions. Now, if there is an excess supply of, or demand for, money to hold, we shall find a corresponding excess demand for or supply of goods which will explain the revision of the price level. Thus Walras' Law will hold, and Say's Identity will not. The real-balance effect provides an *explanation* of the price level adjustment by which equilibrium is achieved which is not to be found in the classical model. It is not, however, required to obtain consistency in the model.

(5) Suppose, then, that we do insert the real-balance term into the demand and supply functions for goods. As we have repeatedly emphasized, expenditure out of balances must be zero in full equilibrium. Hence, in comparative statics, the real-balance term may immediately be removed from the functions without making any difference whatever to the *solution* of the system. It follows that the functions into which it is inserted must be such that, in its absence, they would not only be consistent but would also be free of the problem of the distribution of real balances. To obtain full static equilibrium without the real-balance effect, we require Say's Identity. To obtain full static equilibrium with the real-balance effect, we require a form of the functions such that, when the real-balance term is removed, Say's Identity holds.[27]

Thus if, for example, we attempt to insert the real-balance term into the functions of our first numerical example, in (2) above, we are at once involved in a genuine contradiction. It will be remembered that the solution of the example involved an endless redistribution of balances. To obtain a stable distribution of balances, it would be necessary to insert the real-balance terms into the functions in such a fashion that desired and actual balances were *never* equal. Indeed, it would be necessary to provide for a permanent discrepancy between desired and actual balances which exactly counterbalanced, in each case, the changes in balances which would otherwise be made. We should thus be attributing to the individuals the following behaviour: the equilibrium level of relative prices would always induce them to spend more (less) than they received, but the non-equilibrium level of their real balances would always exactly prevent them. Thus a system which does not have a full static equilibrium solution cannot be given one by the insertion of the real-balance term.

We may conclude, therefore, that the real-balance effect can usefully be inserted to provide an explanation, absent from the formal classical model, of the market process which leads to monetary equilibrium. If, however, we are concerned only with the full static equilibrium solution of the model, then we do not require the real-balance term.[28]

The Real-Balance Effect in a Classical Production Model[29]

(1) We shall now investigate the model of Part II of Patinkin's book in which there is production as well as exchange. We have already shown, in part one of this paper, how equilibrium in the goods market, the equilibrium level of real balances, and the price level are determined. So far, however, real income has been taken as given. It is now determined in accordance with purely classical assumptions. Patinkin assumes an upward sloping curve of labour as a function of *real* wages, and a downward sloping demand curve for labour, also as a function of *real* wages. As the stock of capital is fixed,[30] and perfect competition is assumed, the demand curve is the real marginal product curve of labour. The equilibrium levels of employment and real income are *uniquely* determined by the intersection of these two curves. A bond market is now added to the model. Individuals may now divide their resources between spending on consumption (a flow), buying bonds (a flow), and holding real balances (a stock). The bonds are supplied by firms which are also assumed to have a transactions demand for balances. The proceeds of the sale of bonds may be used either to increase balances or to finance new investment. The rate of interest equates the demand for with the supply of bonds.

We now come to a source of considerable confusion. In full equilibrium, as before, individuals must be neither adding to, nor subtracting from, their balances. In full equilibrium, therefore, income is divided only between consumption and purchases of new bonds, i.e., the whole of current saving is necessarily devoted to the purchase of bonds.[31] Similarly, if the balances of firms are in equilibrium, the whole proceeds of the sale of bonds must be devoted to investment. It follows that, if balance equilibrium obtains, i.e., if the price level is in equilibrium, equality of saving and investment, and equality of supply of and demand for bonds, are alternative statements of the same equilibrium condition. Patinkin, however, writes (*Money, Interest, and Prices*, p. 188):

> It must finally be emphasized that the savings-investment condition is *not* an alternative statement of the equilibrium condition in the bond market. In particular, an act of saving is not necessarily an act of demanding bonds; for the funds withdrawn from consumption might be added instead to cash balances. Conversely, the demand for bonds might be at the expense of cash balances, instead of at the expense of consumption. Similarly, an act of investment is not necessarily an act of supplying bonds; for the funds for the investment program might be forthcoming instead from cash balances. Conversely, the supply of bonds might be for the purpose of adding to cash balances and not for financing investment.

It seems that Patinkin is again thinking only in terms of a weekly equilibrium.

The main characteristics of the model are now apparent: since, in full equilibrium, income is divided between consumption and the purchase of bonds, and since expenditure on bonds flows entirely into investment, equilibrium expenditure cannot diverge from the full-employment level of income determined in the labour market. Consider what happens in this model if people wish to reduce their present level of consumption. They may either buy more bonds or endeavour to add to their real balances. In the first case, the increased supply of saving flows into investment, and there cannot be any change in equilibrium total real expenditure. In the second case, the reduced demand for goods simply reduces the price level until the real value of the nominal balances is raised to the desired level. There is no change in real consumption or saving: again the equilibrium level of total real expenditure is unchanged. Thus the crucial assumptions in Patinkin's model are that the levels of income and employment are uniquely determined by the real forces in the labour market, and that the rate of interest is free to equate saving and investment at any level of income so determined. If a unique equilibrium condition is specified for the labour market, and if the equilibrium level of employment is defined as full employment, it follows tautologically[32] that equilibrium in the model requires full employment.

Let us consider how the full equilibrium conditions of Patinkin's model may be illustrated in a 45° diagram. In Figure 5 the *C* curve relating households' consumption to their income is drawn on the assumption that their balances are fully adjusted to each level of income. The vertical distance between the *C* curve and the 45° line then measures their desired bond purchases. When real balances held by firms are in full equilibrium, equilibrium in the bond market requires that firms spend on investment exactly the amount

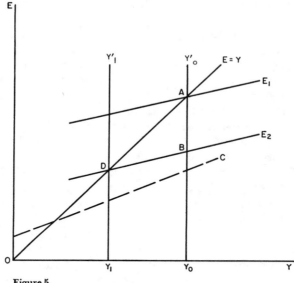

Figure 5.

saved by households. It follows that, when balances are fully adjusted and the bond market is in equilibrium, the addition of the firms' demand curve for investment goods to the households' demand curve yields an aggregate demand curve which coincides throughout with the 45° line. The equilibrium level of income is determined in the labour market; and *any* level of income determined in the labour market (such as OY_0) yields an equilibrium here (where the perpendicular to $Y°$ intersects the 45° line). This construction is used by Patinkin (*ibid.*, p. 249) to illustrate a classical model in which ". . . regardless of the rate of interest and level of prices, the total demand of households and firms for commodities is always equal to the total income of the economy" (Say's Identity). He then argues that, if account is taken of the real-balance effect and the "aggregate supply curve," the classical position is seen to depend ". . . *not* on any special form of the aggregate demand function, but on the assumption that this function—whatever its form—is sufficiently sensitive to price and interest variations . . ." to ensure full employment (pp. 249–50, our italics). He accordingly draws an aggregate demand function, Keynesian in appearance, of less than unit slope.[33] Since this differs from the presentation of the model which we gave above, we must see how it is in fact obtained.

Suppose that we start from a position of full equilibrium, such as A in Figure 5, and that the level of income is then varied. Then the curve E_1 traces desired aggregate expenditure when the rate of interest and the price level, and therefore real balances, are held constant. On the assumptions that, when income rises, neither household consumption nor bond purchases rise to the equilibrium level appropriate to the new level of income until balances have been adjusted, and that firms' investment does not rise to the new equilibrium level until their balances have been adjusted, the E_1 curve has a slope of less than unity. There is, of course, an E curve through every point on the 45° line. Each curve shows how desired aggregate expenditure would vary if income varied while interest and prices were held constant at the equilibrium level appropriate to the level of income at which the E curve cuts the 45° line. The distance between the E curve and the 45° line measures the gap between desired and actual balances *plus* the gap between desired saving and investment. Suppose that we start from a position of full equilibrium at D on Y_1Y_1', and increase income to OY_0 by assuming, e.g., a suitable change in the labour market. The desired level of real balances now exceeds the actual level, hence to restore equilibrium prices must fall as income rises, and *vice versa*. Both desired saving and desired investment also rise, so that the gap between the two may be positive or negative, and the change in the rate of interest required to restore equilibrium may be in either direction.[34] The distance AB measures the amount by which desired expenditure falls short of the new level of income. The disequilibrium is corrected *not* by moving along the "aggregate demand curve" with changing income until the 45° line is reached, but by moving along the income line Y_0Y_0' by changing the price level and the rate of interest until the position A is reached.

(2) Patinkin attempts many comparisons with, and criticisms of, Keynesian analysis. It will be apparent that his model cannot be used to "validate" or "invalidate" the Keynesian model, which is simply different. Patinkin, however, argues that his analysis

> . . . forces upon Keynesian economics the abandonment of the once-revolutionary "diagonal-cross" diagram [the familiar 45° diagram] with which it swept its way into the textbooks. It compels it to realize that this diagram takes account neither of the supply side of the commodity market nor of the real-balance effect which its excess over the demand side generates. It therefore compels it to concede that . . . the intersection of the aggregate demand curve . . . with the 45° diagonal . . . does not imply that there exist no automatic market forces to push real income up from the unemployment level . . . Indeed, it compels it to accept the classical contention that such forces not only exist, but even succeed eventually in raising income to the full-employment level . . . [35]

So far as we know, a model can be usefully criticised on only two grounds, its consistency and its empirical relevance. A model can of course be constructed that includes features omitted from the Keynesian model. Which model is to be used, and for what problems, is then a matter for empirical investigation: no conclusion can be reached *a priori* that one model is "better" than another or "forces the abandonment" of another.

Patinkin actually appears to rest this conclusion on three particular arguments.[36]

(i) The effect on "the" aggregate demand function of the real-balance effect. This has been extensively explored. What has not been explored is the result of inserting the real-balance effect into a (Keynesian) model from which unemployment equilibrium was not *already* excluded by the assumptions about the labour market.

(ii) An argument about the Keynesian labour market which we must now consider. Patinkin argues that, since unemployment in his model can occur if the equilibrium conditions in the labour market are not satisfied, unemployment could occur in a Keynesian model for the same reason (pp. 237–39). Hence, he argues, the Keynesian labour supply function (perfectly elastic over a range at the ruling money wage rate) can be replaced by the classical labour supply function (upward sloping against real wages). If this is done it follows, as is well known, that equilibrium involved full employment.[37] The argument that this shows that the Keynesian analysis (for the case of fixed money wages) should be *abandoned* is a *non sequitur*.

(iii) That ". . . Keynesian economics is the economics of un-employment *dis*equilibrium" (p. 235, italics in original). Let us see what this might mean.

(*a*) That the Keynesian model has been misunderstood, and that unemployment equilibrium cannot in fact be obtained in it. This does not appear to be Patinkin's case.

(*b*) That, since unemployment can occur only in disequilibrium in the classical model, it can occur only in disequilibrium in any model. This is a *non sequitur*.

(*c*) That, in Patinkin's opinion, unemployment could not be permanent in the real world. This, whether or not it is true, can establish nothing about either the consistency of a short-run static model or its usefulness in explaining unemployment when unemployment does occur.

(*d*) That a dynamic model might be constructed in which unemployment was not permanent. Again, this establishes nothing about the consistency or relevance of a static model.

The claim that Keynesian economics is the economics of "unemployment *dis*equilibrium" cannot be established on any of these interpretations. "Equilibrium" is, in any case, nothing but the short-hand for the set of values of the variables that satisfies the equations of the given model.

There are many strands to Patinkin's argument,[38] some of which have doubtless eluded us. It is certain, however, that one model cannot be used to invalidate another. A consistent model may be constructed in which equilibrium can obtain with fixed money wages and unemployment. Another consistent model may be constructed in which fixed money wages lead to disequilibrium and unemployment. The question of which model is to be preferred, and in what circumstances, is one for empirical rather than *a priori* investigation.

NOTES

1. J. R. Hicks, *Value and Capital*, 2nd ed. (London 1939), p. 132.
2. Each individual is assumed throughout the analysis to receive the same bundle of goods at the beginning of each week. The total income of the community is consumed each week, i.e., no stocks of goods are carried forward from week to week.
3. It is always necessary, but not always easy, to provide a motive for the stock demand for money without which its marginal utility and hence its price would be zero. Patinkin endeavours to solve this problem by constructing an elaborate system of random payments in which a balance is required to provide security against the risk of default caused by the lack of synchronization between payments and receipts. There are some awkward problems involved: it is difficult to make the transition from a demand for security in Patinkin's model, in which the security provided by balances of given size depends non-linearly upon the volume of the individual's transactions, to a unique relationship between total resources and desired balances. These problems were the subject of a paper circulated to the members of Professor Robbins' seminar by G. C. Archibald in January 1957. In the present paper we merely assume that the individual's tastes are such that the allocation of his total resources between consumption and balances depends uniquely on the amount of his total resources. This means that the demand for balances depends on income *and* existing balances. It is one of the purposes of this section to show that a model based on this assumption produces, in full equilibrium, results identical with those which follow from the more usual assumption that the demand for balances is a function of income only.
4. It will be noticed that, if real income is constant, the budget line can move only if real balances change, while real balances change either if consumption is not equal to income or if the price level changes.
5. If all individuals have identical linear expansion paths, then balances can be redistributed until full stock equilibrium is reached without variation in the price level.

6. We cannot assume that relative prices are constant in this process. We are therefore involved in an index number problem in measuring G and H. The argument of the text, however, does not depend on the assumption of constant relative prices, although, strictly speaking, the graphical illustration does.

7. Don Patinkin, *Money, Interest, and Prices: An Integration of Monetary and Value Theory*, 1st ed. (Illinois 1956), Chapter 3, section 4.

8. Cf. *ibid.*, p. 41.

9. See particularly *ibid.*, Chapter 3, sections 5 and 6.

10. If the individual is not in full equilibrium, he changes his consumption from week to week as his balances change. Similarly if the market is not in full equilibrium, balances and expenditure change from week to week. If, however, real balances are changed by a change in the money stock without distribution effects when the market is in full equilibrium, equilibrium is restored by the *tâtonnement alone*. Thus correction of a disequilibrium in balances only requires a change in individuals' real consumption when it is necessary to redistribute balances among the individuals in the market. When the disequilibrium can be corrected by a change in the price level alone, then no one in fact alters consumption.

11. Thus we cannot accept Patinkin's claim that the real-balance effect ". . . is the *sine qua non* of monetary theory" (*op. cit.*, p. 22).

12. O. Lange, "Say's Law: A Restatement and a Criticism," in *Studies in Mathematical Economics and Econometrics* (Chicago 1942), pp. 49–68.

13. Patinkin, "The Indeterminacy of Absolute Prices in Classical Economic Theory," *Econometrica*, Vol. 17 (January 1949), and "The Invalidity of Classical Monetary Theory," *Econometrica*, Vol. 19 (April 1951). For criticism see W. Braddock Hickman, "The Determinacy of Absolute Prices in Classical Economic Theory," Wassily Leontief, "The Consistency of the Classical Theory of Money and Prices," and Cecil G. Phipps, "A Note on Patinkin's 'Relative Prices,'" all in *Econometrica*, Vol. 18 (January 1950). See also the later article by S. Valavanis, "A Denial of Patinkin's Contradiction," *Kyklos*, Fasc. 4 (1955).

14. Karl Brunner, "Inconsistency and Indeterminacy in Classical Economics," *Econometrica*, Vol. 19 (April 1951), and G. S. Becker and W. J. Baumol, "The Classical Monetary Theory: The Outcome of the Discussion," *Economica*, Vol. 19 (November 1952). For a full bibliography of the controversy see Patinkin, *Money, Interest, and Prices*, 1st ed., pp. 454–59 note 1; and for a critical bibliography see Valavanis, *op. cit.*

15. Patinkin, *Money, Interest, and Prices*, 1st ed., p. 110.

16. Cf. Patinkin, Mathematical Appendix 7a to *Money, Interest, and Prices*, 1st ed., pp. 333–35, and "The Invalidity of Classical Monetary Theory," p. 138.

17. Cf. Patinkin, *Money, Interest, and Prices*, 1st ed., pp. 108–9. These arguments for inconsistency are accepted by Becker and Baumol, *op. cit.*, sections II and III.

18. See Becker and Baumol, *op. cit.*, note 1, p. 360, where, after repeating the argument for inconsistency outlined above, they merely assert that "Hickman's system . . . must be in error."

19. Hickman, *op. cit.*, p. 14.

20. We follow Lange, *op. cit.*, in our use of the terms Walras' Law and Say's Law. Consider an economy with $n - 1$ goods and money. Walras' Law is the identity $\sum_{i=1}^{n-1} p_i S_i + p_n S_n \equiv \sum_{i=1}^{n-1} p_i D_i + p_n D_n$, i.e., total supply of goods and money is identical with total demand for goods and money. Say's Law is the identity $\sum_{i=1}^{n-1} p_i S_i \equiv \sum_{i=1}^{n-1} p_i D_i$, i.e., total supply of goods is identical with total demand for goods. In the text we call this relation Say's Identity.

21. Patinkin, *Money, Interest, and Prices*, 1st ed., p. 121, writes that ". . . Say's Identity and the 'homogeneity postulate' are logically equivalent properties . . . " From the fact that, in the example discussed above, we had the latter without the former, it can be seen that this is mistaken.

22. This follows from the Say's Identity requirement that the value of Good I demanded by each individual equal the value of Good II supplied by him.

23. We may interpret this graphically as follows: consistency only requires that the two pairs of supply and demand curves intersect at the same relative price; thus if the curves D_1 and S_1 intersect at the price z, any pair D_2 and S_2 which intersect at the same price are consistent whatever the quantity traded at this price. By our new requirement, given the curves D_1 and S_1, we are restricted to the single pair D_2 and S_2, which not only intersect at the same price, but also satisfy the condition that the values of the quantities traded in each market be identical.

24.
$$X_1 \equiv d_1 \frac{p_2}{p_1} - s_1 \frac{p_1}{p_2} = 0;$$

$$X_2 \equiv s_1 \frac{p_1^2}{p_2} - d_1 = 0;$$

and

$$X_3 \equiv p_1 X_1 + p_2 X_2 \equiv d_1 p_2 - s_1 \frac{p_1^2}{p_2} + s_1 \frac{p_1^2}{p_2} - d_1 p_2 \equiv 0.$$

25. This point has been clearly argued by Valavanis, *op. cit.*

26. This point is made by both Hickman and Valavanis. To ask how the system *behaves* out of monetary equilibrium is to ask how a system behaves when a constraint is violated.

27. The real-balance term Patinkin inserts into his functions is $\dfrac{M_0}{p}$, where M_0 is the given stock of money and p the price level. Since, as we have shown, behaviour in equilibrium does not depend upon the level of $\dfrac{M_0}{p}$ in this model, this may be misleading. We should write the demands for goods

$$D_i \equiv f_i \left[p_1, \ldots, p_{n-1}, \left(\frac{M_0}{p} - B \right) \right],$$

and the supplies

$$S_i \equiv g_i \left[p_1, \ldots, p_{n-1}, \left(B - \frac{M_0}{p} \right) \right], \qquad (i = 1, \ldots, n - 1),$$

where B is the desired level of real balances and $\dfrac{M_0}{p}$ the actual level.

We now add the equilibrium condition $\dfrac{M_0}{p} - B = 0$. Hence, if we only require the static solution to the system, we may immediately remove the real-balance term from these functions. Thus any properties required in the static solution must be contained in the system when it is written without the real-balance term.

28. Thus we cannot accept Patinkin's claim that the analysis of the real-balance effect provides ". . . the ultimate rigorous validation of the classical theory of money itself" (*Money, Interest, and Prices*, 1st ed., p. 99).

29. Our analysis of the full equilibrium properties of the model described in this section was subsequently shown to contain certain inadequacies. None of these, however, affect the substance of our basic criticism of Patinkin. See R. J. Ball and R. Bodkin, "The Real Balance Effect and Orthodox Demand Theory: A Critique of Archibald and Lipsey," *Review of Economic Studies*, Vol. 28 (October 1960), 44–49, and our own comments in the same issue.

30. This is a short-run model in the sense that net investment has no discernible effect on the stock of capital nor, therefore, on the demand curve for labour.

31. We should notice that, just as there is a unique distribution of the stock of money in full equilibrium, so also is there a unique distribution of the stock of old bonds. Trading in this stock would involve a redistribution of balances among individuals incompatible with full equilibrium.

32. See Patinkin, *Money, Interest, and Prices*, 1st ed., pp. 213–14.

33. *Ibid.*, pp. 131–32 and Figure 11.

34. Patinkin, *ibid.*, p. 130, puts the level of income into the investment function. If it is omitted, then the rate of interest must fall as income rises unless a zero increase in saving is assumed.

35. *Ibid.*, p. 237. Words omitted refer only to a diagram in Patinkin's book.

36. The first is the subject of extensive discussion; the second directly follows this conclusion in Patinkin's text; and the third immediately precedes it.

37. If we alter an otherwise Keynesian model by specifying an upward-sloping supply curve of labour plotted against the real wage rate, we make underemployment equilibrium impossible. This is one of the models considered by F. Modigliani, "Liquidity Preference and the Theory of Interest and Money," *Econometrica* (1944), reprinted in *Readings in Monetary Theory* (American Economic Association, 1952).

38. See the whole of Patinkin's Chapters 13 and 14, *Money, Interest, and Prices*.

14 Wealth, Saving, and the Rate of Interest

Lloyd A. Metzler *University of Chicago*

I

The fundamental thesis of classical economics, that a free-market economy has an automatic tendency to approach a state of full employment, has been a subject of heated controversy in recent decades. Indeed, after the publication of Keynes's *General Theory* there were many economists who rejected the classical thesis completely on the ground that it contained internal inconsistencies. Today, however, we are witnessing a renaissance of the classical doctrines. In part, the renaissance is attributable to world-wide economic developments since the end of the war, which have been characterized by a high level of demand and by full employment in almost all industrial countries. But the rebirth of classical theory is also attributable, in part, to attempts to reconstruct the classical doctrines along lines which make them immune to the Keynesian criticisms.

The principal architect of the reconstruction is Pigou,[1] but the basic idea of the remodeled classical theory can be found in the works of other economists as well, particularly in the works of Scitovszky[2] and Haberler.[3] The innovation which these economists introduced was a reconsideration, or perhaps I should say an

Reprinted from *Journal of Political Economy*, Vol. 59 (April 1951), 93–116, by permission of the author and The University of Chicago Press. Copyright 1951 by The University of Chicago Press.

elaboration, of the forces determining the quantity of real saving. In the classical theory the amounts of saving and investment out of a full-employment level of income were regarded as functions of the interest rate alone, and the latter was thus the primary governing force of the economic system as a whole. Equilibrium was attained, according to the classical theory, only when the interest rate was such that the quantity of real saving out of a full-employment income was equal to the quantity of real investment.[4] Scitovszky, Pigou, and Haberler retained this basic concept of equilibrium but argued that saving depends upon the real value of privately held wealth as well as upon the interest rate. Other things remaining the same, they said, real saving tends to be smaller and real expenditure for consumption tends to be larger, the larger is the real value of private wealth. For convenience, I shall hereafter use the expression "saving-wealth relation" to designate such a functional connection between current saving and private wealth.

The saving-wealth relation was employed by Pigou and Haberler to defend the classical theory against the criticism of Keynesian economics. In particular, the relation was employed to show that a flexible-wage economy has an automatic tendency to approach a state of full employment, as postulated in the classical theory. On account of the special purpose which it originally served, the saving-wealth relation is now widely considered to be a modification, but not a fundamental change, in the classical theory. Indeed, Haberler even suggests that some sort of functional connection between saving and wealth is implicit in works on economics which preceded the explicit recognition of the saving-wealth relation.[5]

I do not share these views. In my opinion the saving-wealth relation is more nonclassical in its implications than any of the contributions to the subject would lead one to believe. Although the Scitovszky-Pigou-Haberler system resembles the classical system in its tendency toward a state of full employment, it is quite unlike the classical system in other respects, and these other respects have generally been overlooked. The most striking difference between the new system and the classical concerns the interest rate, and this is the subject which I wish to explore in the present paper.

The distinguishing feature of the classical theory of the interest rate is its emphasis upon so-called "real" conditions of demand and supply and its denial of the influence of monetary policy or banking policy. The classical economists believed that there exists a unique interest rate, or a unique pattern of long-term and short-term rates, at which the economic system is in equilibrium and that this unique interest rate cannot be influenced by changes in the quantity of money. The following quotation from Ricardo is representative of the classical opinion:

> Interest for money . . . is not regulated by the rate at which the bank will lend, whether it be 5, 4, or 3 per cent, but by the rate of profits which can be made by the employment of capital, and which is totally independent of the quantity or of the value of money. Whether a bank lent one million, ten million, or a hundred million, they would not permanently alter the market rate of interest; they would alter only the value of money which they thus issued. In one case, ten or twenty times more money might be required to carry on the same business than what might be required in the other.[6]

In contrast to the classical doctrine, the theory of the interest rate implicit in the Scitovszky-Pigou-Haberler system is at least partly a monetary theory, as I shall demonstrate below. In this system there is no single interest rate and no single pattern of rates at which the economy is in equilibrium. Rather, there are an infinite number of different rates capable of performing the equilibrating function, and the particular rate that prevails at any given time depends to a considerable extent upon the policy of the banking authorities. Thus, in salvaging one feature of classical economics—the automatic tendency of the system to approach a state of full employment—Pigou and Haberler have destroyed another feature, namely, the real theory of the interest rate. In this respect Pigou, the archdefender of classical economics, has deserted Mill and Marshall and joined Schumpeter and Keynes![7] Although remnants of the classical, real theory of the interest rate remain, these are over-shadowed, I believe, by the monetary feature which has been added. Moreover, the added feature which transforms the interest rate into a monetary rate is not liquidity preference, as in Keynesian economics, but the saving-wealth relation.

The subsequent analysis will be more understandable, I believe, if I digress from my principal theme long enough to indicate briefly the way in which the saving-wealth relation became prominent in economic theory. For this purpose consider an economic system in which the demand for investment is so low and the supply of saving so high that potential full-employment saving exceeds potential full-employment investment at all positive interest rates. In this event, there is no achievable interest rate which fulfils the classical condition of equilibrium. Whatever the interest rate may be, the demand for goods and services as a whole falls short of productive capacity. This is the Keynesian system in its simplest form. And the outcome of this situation, as envisaged by Keynes, is a cumulative reduction in output and employment, the reduction continuing until potential saving is reduced to the level of potential investment through a reduction in real income.

Suppose, however, that wages and other factor costs tend to fall when unemployment develops. To what extent will the reduction in costs stimulate output and move the system back toward full employment? Keynes argued that a general wage reduction affects output primarily through its influence on the interest rate. Any decline in wages and other costs is likely to result, he asserted, in a corresponding decline in other prices. In real terms, then, the only significant effect of the reduction in wages and other costs is an increase in the real value of money balances which tends, through liquidity preference, to reduce the interest rate. If full-employment saving exceeds full-employment investment at all possible interest rates, however, the reduction in the interest rate cannot conceivably eliminate all the deflationary gap and restore output to the full-employment level. Keynes's theory thus leads to the conclusion that wage-and-cost reductions are not an effective remedy for deficient demand.[8]

Pigou attempted to refute this Keynesian view concerning wage-and-cost reductions, and in doing so he introduced the saving-wealth relation. He suggested that, as wages and prices decline, the resulting increase in the real value of money balances will stimulate demand in a way which is independent of the change in the interest rate. Money balances constitute a part of private wealth, and the increase in the former accordingly implies an increase in the latter. As the real value of private wealth increases, the amount of saving out of a full-employment level of real income tends to decline. In this manner the excess of potential saving over potential investment which accounted for the initial unemployment is eventually eliminated. In the absence of barriers to price-and-cost reductions, the system thus has an automatic tendency to approach a state of full employment, as envisaged in the classical theory. Saving is brought into line with investment not primarily through a reduction of the interest rate but rather through a general deflation and a corresponding increase in the real value of the money supply.

I do not wish to discuss the relevance of the saving-wealth relation to the arguments frequently heard for a policy of over-all flexibility of wages and prices. Other economists have pointed out that the portion of cash balances whose real value is increased by a general deflation normally constitutes a relatively small part of total assets and that an enormous reduction of prices would therefore be required to increase the real value of a country's total wealth by any substantial amount. They have argued, further, that the general increases or decreases in prices and costs required for the successful operation of such a system might easily lead to expectations of additional price increases or decreases which would upset the stability of the whole system.[9] Such questions of economic policy, however, are not the immediate concern of this paper. I mention them here only to avoid a possible misunderstanding of what I shall say later. In what follows, I shall make the most favorable assumptions possible as to the effects of price movements upon the demand for goods and services; I shall ignore the adverse influence of fluctuating prices upon expectations and assume that there is a substantial tendency for saving to decline when the real value of private wealth rises. Given these favorable assumptions, I shall then ask how an economic system containing the saving-wealth relation is related to classical theory.

II

Before describing the theory of interest implicit in the Scitov-szky-Pigou-Haberler system, I wish to say something about the meaning of a "monetary" theory of interest rates. A theory is usually regarded as a monetary theory if the economic system envisaged is one in which the equilibrium interest rate, or the equilibrium pattern of rates, can be altered by a change in the quantity of money. Although this definition is satisfactory for most purposes, it is not sufficiently accurate to characterize an economic system containing the saving-wealth relation. It is inadequate, in particular, because it does not indicate the manner in which the quantity of money is altered. As I shall demonstrate below, the influence of a change in the quantity of money in the Scitovszky-Pigou-Haberler system depends not only upon the magnitude of the change but also upon the way in which it is brought about. Some changes in the quantity of money will alter the equilibrium interest rate while others will not.

We may distinguish, I believe, between two fundamentally different types of increase or decrease in the quantity of money. The first type is a change which takes place through open-market transactions of the central bank. The significant feature of this type of change is that it consists of an exchange of one form of asset for another. When money holdings are increased through central-bank purchase of securities, for example, holdings of securities outside the central bank are reduced by a corresponding amount. The second type of change consists of a direct increase or decrease in the money supply without any offsetting changes in private holdings of other assets. The supply of money may be reduced, for example, by a currency reform in which one unit of new money is exchanged for two units of old. Or the supply of money may be reduced by means of a governmental budgetary surplus, provided that the excess monetary receipts are im-pounded. In both these examples the supply of money is altered without altering private holdings of other assets, and it is this characteristic which distinguishes the second type of monetary change from the first.

I intend to show in subsequent parts of this paper that the theory of interest implicit in the Scitovszky-Pigou-Haberler system is a monetary theory if the change in the quantity of money is of the first type and a real theory if the change is of the second type. This means that open-market transactions of the central bank will have a *permanent* influence on the interest rate at which the system is in equilibrium, even after the bank has stopped its purchases or sales of securities. If the change in the quantity of money does not affect the private holdings of other assets, however, it will have no lasting influence on the interest rate. With respect to the rate of interest, the Scitovszky-Pigou-Haberler theory thus occupies an intermediate position between the classical theory and the Keynes-ian. The classical theory is a real theory of the interest rate from the point of view of both types of monetary change. According to the classical doctrine, neither a central-bank purchase or sale of securities nor an arbitrary increase or decrease in the quantity of money can have any effect upon the interest rate at which the economic system returns to equilibrium. As I have indicated above, the equilibrium interest rate of the classical theory is the rate at which full-employment potential saving is equal to full-employ-ment potential investment, and this equilibrium rate is inde-pendent of both the quantity of money and the policy of the central bank. The classical theory, then, is a nonmonetary or real theory of the interest rate, regardless of whether the monetary disturbance is of the first type or the second type.

At the other extreme is Keynes's theory, which is a purely mone-tary theory from the point of view of either type of monetary dis-turbance. According to Keynes, the rate of interest is governed largely by the decisions of asset-holders concerning the proportions in which they wish to hold money and securities; that is, in Keynes's terminology, the rate is determined by liquidity preference.[10] Other things remaining unchanged, the desired ratio between money and securities tends to rise with a fall in the interest rate, and the equilibrium interest rate is the one at which the desired ratio of money to securities corresponds to the actual ratio. From this it follows that any monetary or banking policy which increases the actual quantity of money relative to the actual quantity of securities will reduce the interest rate at which the system is in equilibrium. Thus, both an arbitrary increase in the quantity of money (a disturbance of the second type) and an increase in the quantity of money through a limited and temporary purchase of securities by the central bank (a disturbance of the first type) will reduce the equilibrium interest rate in Keynes's system.

This brief and somewhat elliptical summary of the Keynesian and classical theories of the interest rate is intended to emphasize the polar positions which the two theories occupy, relative to the theory implicit in the Scitovszky-Pigou-Haberler system. The equilibrium interest rate in the classical theory is independent of monetary disturbances, regardless of whether such disturbances are of the first type or the second type. The equilibrium interest rate in Keynes's theory, on the other hand, can be permanently altered by a monetary disturbance of either type. In short, the classical theory is a real theory from the point of view of either type of disturbance, while the Keynesian theory is a monetary theory from the point of view of either type. The polar positions of the two theories explain, I believe, why no distinction has been made in the past between the two types of monetary disturbance. As I shall demonstrate below, however, the theory of the interest rate implicit in the Scitovszky-Pigou-Haberler system is intermediate between the classical theory and the Keynesian theory. It is a monetary theory from the point of view of the first type of monetary disturbance and a real theory from the point of view of the second type. But all this will, I hope, become clear as we proceed.

III

The economic system which will be investigated below is one in which the capital market is subject to three main influences: (1) the influence of current saving and investment, as in the classical or neoclassical theory; (2) the influence of decisions concerning the holding of cash or securities, as in Keynes's doctrine of liquidity preference; and (3) the influence of wealth on current saving, as in the Scitovszky-Pigou-Haberler reconstruction of the classical theory. I assume that the equilibrium rate of interest, or the equilibrium pattern of rates, is determined by the interplay of these three influences.

At the outset I wish to make a number of simplifying assumptions. Although these assumptions are somewhat unrealistic, few of them are absolutely essential, and most of them could be substantially modified without altering any of my principal results. I assume, in the first place, that the economy with which we are dealing is a closed economy with a fixed amount of labor. Second, I assume that the wage rate tends to rise whenever the demand for labor is greater than the fixed supply and to fall whenever the demand is smaller than the fixed supply. Third, I assume that all agents of production except labor are produced means of production and that all production is carried on at constant returns to scale. Under these conditions the relative prices of all commodities and services are determinate and independent of the commodity composition of the national income. We can therefore speak unambiguously of a rate of total output, or of a level of national income, at which the economy's resources are fully employed. Fourth, I assume that owners of private wealth hold such wealth in only two forms, money (including demand deposits) and common stock, and that all common stock involves approximately the same degree of risk.[11] Fifth, I assume that the central bank is legally authorized to buy and sell the common stock held by the owners of private wealth and that this common stock constitutes the only non-monetary asset of the banking system.

Given these assumptions, one can readily construct a simple geometric interpretation of the forces governing the interest rate. These forces will operate in two different markets: a market for goods and services as a whole and a market for securities. Consider, first, the market for goods and services. Stability of the general price level in the goods-and-services market obviously requires that the total demand arising from a full-employment level of real income shall be equal to the economy's productive capacity; and this is equivalent to the requirement that potential saving out of a full-employment level of income shall be equal to potential investment. If potential investment at full employment exceeds potential saving, the demand for goods and services as a whole exceeds full-employment output; prices and costs accordingly tend to rise. If potential full-employment investment falls short of potential full-employment saving, on the other hand, this implies that the demand for goods and services as a whole falls short of full-employment output. Hence prices and costs tend to fall.

In the classical theory real saving and real investment were functions of a single variable—the interest rate—and the economy was assumed to be in equilibrium at only one rate. In the theory now being investigated, however, the amount of real saving at full employment is regarded as a function of two variables—the interest rate and the real value of wealth in the hands of the savers. As soon as the second variable is introduced, the concept of a single interest rate at which the goods-and-services market is in equilibrium loses its meaning. In place of the equilibrium rate of classical theory, we now have a schedule of rates, or a functional relation between the interest rate and the real value of private wealth.

In order to see how such a schedule can be derived, suppose that on a certain date the total of all privately held wealth—money and securities combined—has a certain real value. If the value of private wealth is fixed, saving may be regarded as a function of the rate of interest alone, and I shall assume that with this given saving schedule a rate of interest can be found at which full-employment saving is equal to full-employment investment. Consider, now, what would happen if the interest rate were arbitrarily increased above its equilibrium level. At the higher interest rate potential saving out of a full-employment income would exceed potential investment, which means that, other things remaining the same, the community's demand for goods and services would fall short of its capacity to produce. In other words, the increase in the rate of interest, taken by itself, would bring about a deflationary gap. But if the community's combined holdings of money and securities were increased in some manner at the same time that the rate of interest were raised, then the deflationary gap might be avoided. The increase in asset holdings would tend to reduce the amount of saving corresponding to any given rate of interest, thereby offsetting, or perhaps more than offsetting, the tendency toward excessive saving attributable to the rise in the rate of interest. The rise in the rate of interest would reduce investment, but the increase in the value of private wealth would reduce saving; and it is thus conceivable that full-employment potential saving might equal potential investment at the higher interest rate as well as at the lower rate.

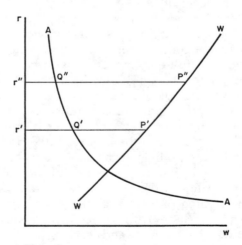

Figure 1.

Many other combinations of the interest rate and the real value of private wealth will fulfil the condition that full-employment saving equals full-employment investment, and we may accordingly conceive of a schedule or a functional relation indicating what the real value of private wealth would have to be, for many different interest rates, in order to make the community's demand for goods and services as a whole equal its capacity to produce. The real value of private wealth which fulfils this condition will be an increasing function of the rate of interest. Such a function is plotted as the line *WW* in Figure 1. For convenience, *WW* will be called the "wealth-requirements schedule." At any point on this line potential saving out of full-employment income is equal to potential investment. But, as we move upward and to the right along the line, both saving and investment decline. Investment declines because of the rise in the interest rate, while saving declines because of the increase in the real value of private wealth. Any point below *WW* in Figure 1 represents a point of inflationary potential. At such a point the rate of interest is too low, given the value of private wealth, to bring about an equality between full-employment saving and investment. The demand for goods and services thus exceeds capacity, and prices tend to rise. In the same way one can show that any point *above WW* represents a point of *de*flationary potential. It follows that the demand for goods and services is equal to the economy's productive capacity only for combinations of the interest rate and the value of private wealth lying on *WW*.

The wealth-requirements schedule has been developed, above, in terms of the real value of private wealth as a whole and no distinction has been made between private holdings of money and private holdings of securities. Such a distinction has thus far been unnecessary because saving was assumed to be a function of *total* asset holdings and not of the *composition* of these assets. When we later discuss the securities market, however, we shall find that the division of total assets between money and securities is the decisive factor in this market. Our later task will accordingly be simplified if the wealth-requirements schedule can be broken down into its two component parts, namely, money and common stock.

If the community holds a given amount of common stock, the real value of these stock holdings will obviously depend upon the interest rate. Indeed, the interest rate itself is nothing more than the yield of the stock, and this yield, in turn, is the ratio of the income earned by the stock to its market price. In the short run the income earned by the common stock is a given amount, determined by the fixed supplies of the various agents of production; and this means that the yield, or the rate of interest, varies inversely with the real value of the stock. To put the matter the other way round, we may say that the real value of the given common stock is inversely related to the prevailing rate of interest. The higher the rate of interest, the lower the real value of common-stock holdings and conversely. In Figure 1 the value of the community's security holdings is expressed as such a function of the interest rate by the line AA.

I wish to show, now, how the wealth-requirements schedule, WW, can be expressed in terms of money and interest rates rather than in terms of total wealth and interest rates. For this purpose, suppose that the interest rate is temporarily set at r'' in Figure 1. The wealth-requirements schedule tells us that, in order to prevent an excess or deficiency of demand from developing in the goods-and-services market at this interest rate, the community's holdings of money and securities combined will have to be $r''P''$. But the value of securities alone, at an interest rate of r'', is the distance $r''Q''$ in Figure 1. If the community is to have a sufficient amount of total assets to maintain a balance between demand and supply in the goods-and-services market, its holdings of money will therefore have to equal the difference between $r''P''$ and $r''Q''$, or $Q''P''$. This difference is plotted in Figure 2 as the line $r''T''$. A similar construction for a rate of interest r' carries over the distance $Q'P'$ of Figure 1 to $r'T'$ of Figure 2. The line MM of Figure 2 is the locus of all such points as T' and T''. Given the community's private holdings of securities, MM indicates the amount of money which will have to be held, at any particular interest rate, in order to keep the amount of saving out of full-employment income equal to the amount of investment. For brevity, MM will be called the "money-requirements schedule." The money-requirements schedule is thus the horizontal difference between the wealth-requirements schedule, WW, and the schedule of the real value of securities, AA.

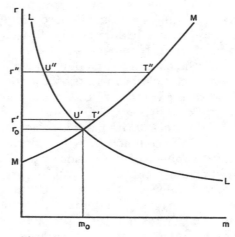

Figure 2.

IV

The line *MM* of Figure 2, like *WW* of Figure 1, indicates the conditions needed to maintain a balance between supply and demand in the market for currently produced goods and services. In addition to this goods-and-services market, the market for securities must also be taken into account. The entire economic system cannot be in equilibrium unless the latter market, as well as the former, has reached a balanced position. The market for *new* securities has already been allowed for, by implication, in the preceding discussion of saving and investment; in the absence of hoarding, equality between saving and investment implies equality between the supply of and the demand for new securities. But this new-securities market is usually a relatively small part of the total securities market; in many countries, indeed, the value of new securities offered on the market in a given year is an exceedingly small fraction of the value of previously issued, or old, securities. This means that decisions of asset-holders to augment or reduce their stocks of old securities will frequently exert a much greater influence on the rate of interest than will discrepancies between current saving and current investment. The old-securities market must therefore be taken into account, along with the market for goods and services as a whole, in order to complete the description of interest rates given by Figures 1 and 2.

The existing stock of securities will influence security prices and the rate of interest only if asset-holders, on balance, decide to increase or decrease their holdings of securities, that is, only if the typical asset-holder wishes to substitute additional money for part of his security holdings or additional securities for part of his money holdings. Decisions of this sort depend largely upon the *composition* rather than the size of asset portfolios. Thus, in deciding whether to buy or sell securities, the typical asset-holder compares the existing ratio between his money holdings and his security holdings with the ratio which he regards as satisfactory under the given economic conditions. The degree of his actual liquidity, compared with a sort of optimum liquidity, governs his actions in the securities market.

I shall follow Keynes in assuming that, other things remaining the same, the typical asset-holder wishes to increase his liquidity as the rate of interest falls. Unless the banking authorities intervene, however, private asset-holders cannot, on balance, increase or decrease their holdings of old securities; as of a given moment of time, both the number of shares of stock and the quantity of money in private hands are fixed quantities. This means that, if the prevailing money-securities ratio differs from the desired ratio, security prices and the rate of interest must continue to change until the desired ratio is brought into line with the prevailing ratio; in short, the demand must be adjusted to the existing supply through appropriate movements in the rate of interest.

The influence of liquidity preference may be examined from another direction, and for present purposes this alternative point of view is more convenient. Instead of starting with a fixed amount of securities and a fixed quantity of money and asking how the rate of interest will be adjusted so that demand will equal supply, we may start with a fixed amount of securities and a fixed interest rate and ask what the total money holdings would have to be in order to satisfy the typical asset-holder with his money-securities ratio. By assuming a number of different interest rates and making similar calculations for each, a liquidity-preference schedule, or a demand-for-money schedule, can thus be built up. Suppose, for example, that, at an interest rate of r'' (Figure 1), the typical asset-holder wishes to hold money in an amount equal to two-thirds the value of his security holdings. At this interest rate the security holdings of the community as a whole have a real value of $r''Q''$, as shown in Figure 1. It follows that asset-holders as a group will attempt to alter their security holdings and hence alter the rate of interest, unless the real value of money holdings amounts to two-thirds of $r''Q''$. Let the point U'' in Figure 2 be chosen so as to make $r''U''$ equal to two-thirds of $r''Q''$. Suppose, now, that, when the interest rate falls to r', the typical asset-holder wishes to hold money equal to the full value of his securities. The value of total securities at an interest rate of r' is $r'Q'$ (Figure 1), and the condition of equilibrium in the old-securities market requires that money holdings shall equal this same amount. We may therefore select a point, U', in Figure 2 such that $r'U'$ is equal to $r'Q'$. The liquidity-preference schedule, LL, in Figure 2 is the locus of all such points as U'' and U'; it shows what the community's holdings of money would have to be, at any given interest rate, in order to create a proper balance between cash and securities.

From the construction of the diagram it is apparent that there are two reasons why the demand for money, LL (Figure 2), tends to rise as the rate of interest falls. First, the typical asset-holder usually wants to hold a larger ratio of cash to securities at low interest rates than at high rates. And, second, the real value of securities, the denominator of the cash-securities ratio, is increased by a fall in the interest rate. In most discussions of liquidity preference only the first of these reasons is taken into account, but the second may be equally important.[12]

v

I have now discussed two different functional relations between the rate of interest and the real quantity of money; the first of these I called a money-requirements schedule, while the second is the usual liquidity-preference schedule. The money-requirements schedule represents all combinations of money balances and the rate of interest for which the community's demand for goods and services as a whole is exactly equal to its capacity to produce. At any point not on this schedule there is either an excess or a deficiency of demand and consequently a tendency for prices and costs to rise or fall. The money-requirements schedule, *MM*, thus indicates the possible combinations of the interest rate and the quantity of real cash balances which will maintain over-all price equilibrium in the goods-and-services market. The liquidity-preference schedule, on the other hand, describes the conditions of price equilibrium in the *securities* market. If the actual quantity of real cash balances lies on *LL*, there will be no tendency for asset-holders as a whole to attempt to shift from securities to cash or from cash to securities and, accordingly, no tendency for the price of securities or the rate of interest to change. At any point *not* on *LL*, however, the price of securities will either rise or fall, depending upon whether the demand for cash at the prevailing interest rate is smaller or greater than the actual amount.

From Figure 2 it is now apparent that only one combination of the interest rate and the real value of money balances will satisfy the conditions of equilibrium in both the goods-and-services market and the securities market. I have denoted this combination by the two letters r_0 and m_0. If all prices, including wages and the costs of other agents of production, tend to rise when demand exceeds supply and to fall when supply exceeds demand, the combination r_0 and m_0 is the one toward which the economic system will gravitate. The nature of this market mechanism will be clarified, I believe, if we consider what happens to the system when the interest rate and the real value of money balances differ from the equilibrium combination r_0 and m_0.

This is done in Figure 3, where I have reproduced the essential features of Figure 2. The points *B, C, D,* and *E* in Figure 3 represent four points which do not lie on either the liquidity-preference schedule or the money-requirements schedule. Suppose, first, that the actual situation with regard to the rate of interest and the real value of cash balances at a given moment of time can be represented by the point *B*. What happens, in this event, to the variables of our system? The liquidity-preference schedule shows that, at the rate of interest represented by *B*, the community's demand for real money balances falls short of actual money holdings. Asset-holders accordingly attempt to substitute securities for their excess cash holdings, thereby forcing up security prices and reducing the rate of interest. Moreover, in the situation *B* the goods-and-services market as well as the securities market is out of balance. The

diagram shows that, at the prevailing interest rate, money holdings are too large to bring about an equality between full-employment saving and full-employment investment. Saving is below the
equilibrium level because of the excessive cash holdings, and the
demand for goods and services thus exceeds the economy's capacity
to produce. As a result, prices tend to rise, and the real value of
money balances is reduced. The movements in the rate of interest
and in the real value of money balances are indicated by the short
arrows emanating from point B.

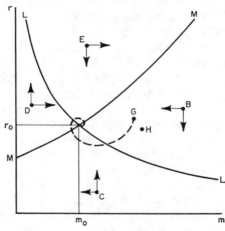

Figure 3.

By similar reasoning one can demonstrate that, at point C,
security prices tend to fall, and the interest rate is correspondingly
increased, while the prices of goods and services rise and the real
value of cash balances is reduced. Likewise, at D, security prices
fall, the rate of interest is increased, commodity prices and wages
fall, and the real value of cash balances tends to rise. Finally, if the
actual position of the variables is at E, security prices rise, the interest rate is reduced, commodity prices fall, and the real value
of cash balances is thus increased. Movements of the variables in
the neighborhood of the points C, D, and E have again been indicated by arrows.

Figure 3 demonstrates that when the economic system is out of
balance at least one force is always operating to bring the variables
of the system closer to the equilibrium point, r_0, m_0. The other
force, indicated by the second of the two arrows at each of the
points B, C, D, and E, operates in such a way as to impart a circular
or cyclical movement to the variables. This suggests that, if the rate
of interest and the quantity of real cash balances were initially at
some nonequilibrium point such as G, the approach to equilibrium

might be a spiral or damped cycle like the one depicted in Figure 3. Although such a damped cycle is possible, it is not inevitable, as I shall demonstrate in the Appendix. In any event, I believe it is highly unlikely that the cyclical movement implied by Figure 3 bears any close resemblance to the typical observed business cycle. Most observed cycles are cycles of output and employment, whereas the cycle depicted in Figure 3 is largely a cycle of prices and interest rates.[13] I have presented the dynamic problem concerning the movements of prices and interest rates merely to show the tendency of the system to approach an equilibrium position and not as a contribution to the theory of business cycles.

VI

I have now shown that the market for goods and services and the market for securities can be in equilibrium simultaneously only at the point r_0, m_0 and that the economic system has an automatic tendency to approach this equilibrium. Superficially, this suggests a close analogy between the rate of interest, r_0, and the classical concept of the equilibrium rate. Like the equilibrium rate of classical theory, the rate r_0 is the only one compatible, under the assumed conditions, with equilibrium of the economic system as a whole; that is, r_0 is the only rate which satisfies both the liquidity-preference requirement and the requirement that full-employment saving shall be equal to full-employment investment. Why, then, does r_0 not have as much claim to be regarded as a real rate as does the classical concept of the real rate of interest?

Whether the rate r_0 is a real rate or a monetary rate depends, as I have indicated earlier, upon the nature of the monetary disturbance. If the disturbance is of the first type—that is, if it is a change in the quantity of money associated with the purchase or sale of securities by the central bank—it will alter some of the functional relations of Figures 1 and 2 and will accordingly change the equilibrium interest rate. The rate r_0 must therefore be regarded as a monetary rate from the point of view of monetary disturbances of this sort. On the other hand, if the monetary disturbance is of the second type, which consists of an increase or decrease in the quantity of money without any offsetting changes in other assets, then it will not alter the functional relations of Figures 1, 2, and 3 and will not permanently change the interest rate. The rate r_0 is thus a real rate from the point of view of monetary disturbances of the second type. Because it is simple to describe, I shall first consider a monetary disturbance of the second type.

Suppose that the economic system is initially in equilibrium at a rate of interest r_0 and a quantity of real cash balances m_0. And suppose that, while other things initially remain unchanged, the quantity of money is arbitrarily doubled by giving to each holder of money an additional quantity equal to the amount he already holds. Temporarily, the variables of the system will then be at point H of Figure 3; except for the increase in the quantity of money, nothing in the system will have changed. As I have shown above, however, there will be an automatic tendency for the variables of the system to return eventually to the former equilibrium position, r_0 and m_0. At point H both the securities market and the goods-and-services market will be out of balance, and changes will therefore occur in the interest rate and in the level of prices. The changes in prices, in turn, will affect the real value of cash balances.

Consider, first, the securities market. After the initial monetary disturbance, the quantity of money held by the typical asset-holder is larger than he would like to hold at the prevailing interest rate, r_0. Asset-holders as a group therefore attempt to convert some of their excess cash into securities. As a result, security prices rise, which means that the interest rate falls. The fall in the interest rate increases investment, while the initial increase in the real value of cash balances reduces saving. The demand for goods and services as a whole thus exceeds productive capacity, so that commodity prices and costs begin to rise. The rise in prices tends to reduce the real value of cash balances and thereby initiates a movement of the variables back toward the original equilibrium position. The details of this dynamic process need not concern us here. Suffice it to say that the system as a whole will not be restored to equilibrium until the real value of cash balances is reduced to m_0 and the rate of interest is restored to its former level, r_0.

If the central bank does not acquire or dispose of any assets during the period of adjustment, the real value of money balances can be reduced only by an increase in the price level. Since the real value of cash balances is ultimately restored to its former level, m_0, we know that the increase in prices, in the final position of equilibrium, must be as large as the original increase in the quantity of money. In other words, doubling the nominal quantity of money must result eventually in doubling all money prices and costs, including the money prices of securities as well as the money prices of goods and services. The real variables of the system all return to their former equilibrium levels. The rate of interest, the real value of saving and investment, and the real value of securities, as well as the real value of cash balances, are all the same in the new equilibrium as before the monetary disturbance occurred. The only permanent effect of increasing the quantity of money is a proportionate increase in the general level of prices and costs.[14]

With respect to monetary disturbances of the second type, such as the one I have just described, the economic system embodying both a saving-wealth relation and a liquidity-preference schedule is evidently quite similar to the classical system. In both the classical system and the system depicted in Figure 3 the values of all real variables are independent of the quantity of money. But this is true of the system in Figure 3 only if the monetary disturbances are of the second type, whereas it is true of the classical system for both types of monetary disturbance. If the disturbance is of the first type, which consists of open-market transactions by the central bank, then the equilibrium interest rate will be altered, as I have suggested above. With respect to monetary disturbances of the first type, the equilibrium interest rate of Figure 3 is therefore a monetary rate, and in this regard it resembles the Keynesian interest rate more closely than it does the classical. In other words, by purchasing or selling securities, the banking authorities can alter not only the temporary interest rate which prevails while the open-market transactions are taking place but also the rate at which the system will return to equilibrium after the bank's transactions in securities have ceased.

The power of the banking authorities to alter the equilibrium interest rate is attributable not to their influence upon the nominal quantity of money but to their influence upon the quantity and value of privately held securities. A central-bank purchase of securities, for example, reduces the quantity of privately held securities. This means that the AA schedule of Figure 1 is shifted to the left. And since the liquidity-preference schedule, LL, and the money-requirements schedule, MM, were both derived, in part, from the AA schedule, a shift in the latter causes the former schedules to shift as well. The system as a whole therefore comes into balance, after the securities purchases have been made, at a different rate of interest.

The effect of open-market transactions upon the equilibrium of the system can be described in terms of a ratio indicating the proportion of the total supply of securities held in private hands. Let this ratio be represented by the letter λ. Consider, first, the situation in which λ has a value of 1.0. This means that the total available supply of securities is held by private asset-holders, so that the central bank's assets consist exclusively of currency. Given the holdings of securities by private asset-holders, the rate of interest at which the system is in equilibrium can be determined, as in our earlier illustration, by the intersection of a liquidity-preference schedule, LL, and a money-requirements schedule, MM. Assuming that the value of private asset holdings when λ = 1.0 is given in Figure 4 by the solid line AA and that the wealth-requirements schedule is WW, the liquidity-preference schedule and the money-requirements schedule can be derived as in my earlier illustration. These derived schedules, for $\lambda = 1.0$, are represented in Figure 5 by the solid lines LL and MM, respectively. Under the assumed conditions with respect to security holdings, the equilibrium rate of interest is r_0, and the equilibrium value of real cash balances is m_0, as shown in Figure 5.

Suppose that this equilibrium is disturbed by a substantial purchase of securities on the part of the central bank. The dynamic process by which the economy adapts itself to such open-market transactions will probably be highly complicated. The securities will be purchased at many different prices from the various asset-holders, and this means that we cannot predict exactly how the open-market transactions will affect the cash balances of all asset-holders together. In any event, the real value of cash balances will be influenced by price movements as well as by the central bank's dealings in securities, and it is the combined effect of both influences which ultimately governs the equilibrium value of the real money supply. In view of our interest in the equilibrium of the system, we may pass over the dynamic problems and investigate, instead, the influence of the central bank's security purchases upon the schedules in Figures 4 and 5 which determine the ultimate resting places of our variables.

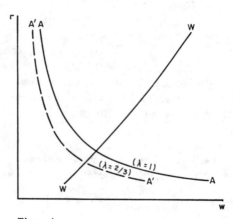

Figure 4.

Suppose that the central bank continues to purchase securities until it has acquired one-third of the common stock available to the economy as a whole and that all transactions between asset-holders and the central bank cease at this point. When the securities market and the goods-and-services market are once again in equilibrium, how will the rate of interest compare with the rate that prevailed before the open-market transactions began? According to the classical theory, the rate of interest should return to its former level as soon as the bank's security purchases have ceased. According to the system depicted in Figures 4 and 5, however, the security purchases by the central bank will permanently *lower* the equilibrium rate of interest.

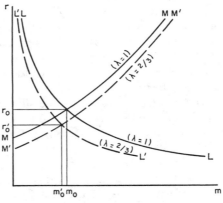

Figure 5.

If the bank acquires one-third of all available securities, the security holdings of private asset-holders will of course be only two-thirds as large as they formerly were, so that λ will have a value of $\frac{2}{3}$. This means that at any given interest rate the real value of private security holdings will be two-thirds of its former value. The broken line $A'A'$ of Figure 4 is drawn at two-thirds of the horizontal distance of the solid line AA from the vertical axis, and $A'A'$ thus represents the real value of private security holdings, expressed again as a function of the rate of interest, after the central bank has acquired its securities. The wealth-requirements schedule, WW, depends upon preferences and upon the savings and investment schedules and presumably will be unaffected by the open-market transactions. Since the money-requirements schedule, MM, depends upon the value of private security holdings as well as upon WW, however, the MM schedule will be shifted. At any given rate of interest, the total assets—money and securities combined—needed to maintain equality between full-employment saving and full-employment investment will be the same as before. But the value of private security holdings has been reduced by the central bank's purchases, and this means that total assets cannot be maintained at the level needed for full employment unless private money holdings are increased by a corresponding amount. In short, the money-requirements schedule, MM, is moved to the right by the same amount that the securities schedule, AA, is moved to the left.[15] The new money-requirements schedule corresponding to $\lambda = \frac{2}{3}$ is shown in Figure 5 as the broken line $M'M'$.

The liquidity-preference schedule, as well as the money-requirements schedule, is affected by the central bank's purchase of securities. At any given interest rate, the proportions in which the typical asset-holder wishes to hold money and securities are presumably the same as in the old equilibrium. The value of private security holdings, however, is now only two-thirds of the former value at the same interest rate. The desired ratio between money holdings and security holdings will thus not be maintained unless the real value of money balances is reduced to two-thirds of its former value. In other words, the LL schedule in Figure 5 is shifted to the left, the relative amount of the shift being the same as the leftward shift of the securities schedule, AA. The new liquidity-preference schedule, for $\lambda = \frac{2}{3}$, is represented in Figure 5 by the line $L'L'$.

The combined effect of the shift in the liquidity-preference schedule and of the shift in the money-requirements schedule is a reduction in the equilibrium rate of interest from r_0 to r_0', as indicated in Figure 5. Thus, the banking authorities by means of a limited purchase of securities have *permanently* reduced the interest rate at which the economic system is in equilibrium. The dynamic process of adjustment by which the equilibrium interest rate moves from r_0 to r_0' will probably be highly complex, as I have indicated earlier. Nevertheless, I believe that the influence of the central bank upon the equilibrium interest rate will stand out more clearly if we consider a greatly simplified dynamic sequence.

When the central bank begins to purchase securities, the first effect is a rise in security prices and a corresponding decline in the rate of interest. The actual security transactions themselves do not alter the total value of private asset holdings but merely change the form in which assets are held. The initial result of the bank's purchases, therefore, is a rise in the value of private asset holdings (capital gains) together with a reduction in the rate of interest and a shift on the part of asset-holders from securities to money. One may presume that at the new, lower rate of interest the asset-holders have exchanged securities for cash in such a way as to satisfy their demands for liquidity; for, if this were not true, the prices of securities would continue to rise, and the interest rate to fall, until the asset-holders were willing to part with the amount of securities that the central bank wanted to buy. Although the point representing the new quantity of private money holdings and the new, temporary rate of interest will thus lie somewhere on the liquidity-preference schedule $L'L'$, it cannot at the same time lie on the money-requirements schedule, $M'M'$, or the wealth-requirements schedule, WW. The fall in the interest rate, taken by itself, would normally lead to an excess of full-employment investment over full-employment saving and thus create an excess demand for goods and services. The inflationary pressure is further increased, however, by the capital gains, which increase the value of total private wealth holdings and thereby reduce current saving. As a result, prices and costs tend to rise, and the real value of the money supply is correspondingly reduced. The rise in prices and the reduction in the real value of private money holdings must continue until the real value of security-and-cash holdings combined is low enough to encourage a sufficient amount of saving to make full-employment saving once more equal to full-employment investment. The new equilibrium is finally achieved, as Figures 4 and 5 demonstrate, at a permanently lower rate of interest.

Now, since the new equilibrium must lie on the wealth-requirements schedule, WW, as well as on the money-requirements schedule, $M'M'$, it is obvious that, when prices have finally stopped rising and the rate of interest has reached its new and lower equilibrium, the value of total private wealth must be smaller than in the old equilibrium. In short, the final result of the open-market security purchases by the central bank is a reduction in the real value of the total wealth in private hands. This reduction has occurred in two stages: the liquidity of the typical asset-holder has first been increased through the central-bank purchase of securities; and the real value of the larger liquid balances has subsequently been reduced through inflation. Thus, under a regime of flexible prices, central-bank purchase of securities is an indirect means of reducing the real value of the total assets—cash and securities combined—in private hands. The reduction in the value of privately held wealth tends, in turn, to increase saving and thereby reduces the rate of interest at which full-employment saving is equal to full-employment investment. To summarize briefly, then, we may say that the central bank is able to alter the equilibrium rate of interest through its power to alter the real value of private wealth.

VII

Assuming that saving depends upon the real value of private wealth as well as upon the interest rate, I have now demonstrated that the equilibrium interest rate is partly a real rate, as in the classical theory, and partly a monetary rate, as in Keynes's theory. Monetary disturbances of one type affect the equilibrium interest rate of the system, while disturbances of another type do not. In general, any monetary disturbance which alters the amount of securities held by the typical asset-holder tends also to affect the interest rate at which the economic system as a whole is in equilibrium. On the other hand, any monetary disturbance which does not affect private security holdings will leave the equilibrium interest rate unchanged.

The distinction which I have made between the two types of monetary disturbance suggests that the true cause of a change in the interest rate is not a change in the quantity of money per se but a change in the amount of other assets held by the typical asset-holder. This conjecture is, indeed, correct. Open-market transactions of the central bank alter the equilibrium interest rate not because they affect the quantity of money but because they affect the quantity of privately held securities. Consider again, for example, the open-market transactions which I have described in Figures 4 and 5. In those illustrations the central bank is assumed to purchase one-third of all privately held securities. As a consequence, the level of prices is increased, the real value of private wealth declines, the propensity to save increases, and real saving finally comes into balance with real investment at a permanently lower interest rate.

Suppose, now, that the amount of privately held securities were reduced without any offsetting change in the quantity of money. Such a reduction could be brought about by a capital levy of one-third on all securities, payable only in kind. In other words, the government could require that one-third of all privately held securities be turned over to it. In what respects would the effects of such a policy differ from the effects of the open-market transactions described in Figures 4 and 5? Examination of the figures reveals that the interest rate, the volume of real investment, the real value of cash balances, and the other real variables of the system are affected in exactly the same way by a one-third levy in kind upon all securities as by a central-bank purchase of the same amount of securities. The nominal quantity of money is of course larger when the securities are acquired by purchase than when they are acquired by taxation. But the real value of bank balances is exactly the same, in the new position of equilibrium, in both cases. Thus, the only difference between the effects of the two means of acquiring the securities is a difference in the level of prices and costs. The price level is higher when the securities are acquired by purchase than when they are acquired by taxation. In all other respects the two situations are identical as far as the final results are concerned.

The foregoing example reveals the close analogy between central-bank security purchases and a capital levy on securities. In the system investigated above, a purchase of securities by the central bank is a means of reducing the real value of privately held wealth and operates just as effectively in this direction as a corresponding capital levy payable in kind. Indeed, the central bank's power to alter the equilibrium interest rate arises exclusively from its influence on the real value of privately held securities.

Through its power to change the interest rate, the central bank can also affect the rate of growth of the economy as a whole. At each different equilibrium interest rate full-employment saving is of course equal to full-employment investment, but the amount of real saving and investment varies with variations in the equilibrium interest rate. When the equilibrium rate is increased, the economic system comes into balance at a lower real value of investment and saving; and, when the equilibrium rate is reduced, the real value of saving and investment tends to increase. By purchasing securities, the central bank can reduce the real value of private wealth, thereby increasing the propensity to save and causing the system to attain a new equilibrium at a permanently lower interest rate and a permanently higher rate of capital accumulation. In a similar manner, the bank, through sales of securities, can increase the real value of private wealth, lower the propensity to save, raise the equilibrium rate of interest, and reduce the rate of capital accumulation.

Whether the bank has a substantial influence or only a negligible influence upon the rate of growth of the system depends upon its authority to buy and sell securities and upon the magnitude of the saving-wealth relation. If the saving-wealth relation is large, so that the propensity to save increases or decreases appreciably as the real value of private wealth falls or rises, and if the bank is authorized to buy and sell securities in large quantities, then the rate of growth may be affected to a considerable extent by central-bank policy. In practice, however, there will usually be an institutional barrier to the amount of securities the bank can sell; it cannot sell more securities than its owns. And this means that, when the bank has divested itself of all its securities, it has no further power to raise the equilibrium interest rate and lower the rate of growth. There may be a similar barrier to the amount of securities the bank can purchase, since only certain types of assets are eligible for the bank's portfolio. If the bank has acquired all the assets it is authorized to purchase, no further reduction of private wealth, and no further increase in private saving, can be accomplished by central-bank activity in the securities market.

In terms of the theory set out above, we may say that the central bank's power over the equilibrium interest rate and the equilibrium rate of growth will usually be determined by institutional arrangements which prevent it from purchasing more than a small fraction of private wealth or from selling more assets than it possesses. This might mean, for example, that the institutional arrangements were such that the value of λ would have to lie between 0.9 and 1.0. In most countries these institutional limits may well be so narrow that the actual power of the central bank to influence the equilibrium of the system is negligible. Nevertheless, if saving depends upon the real value of private wealth as described in the saving-wealth relation, the rate of interest must be regarded as partly a monetary rate. For, if the institutional limits to central-bank action were removed or reduced, the possible variation in the equilibrium interest rate which could be brought about by the central bank would be correspondingly increased.

Appendix

The geometrical methods employed in the text of this paper were not sufficiently powerful to deal with some of the more difficult problems encountered, particularly the dynamic problems. I am therefore adding an analytical appendix. The symbols used in this appendix have the following meanings:

r represents the rate of interest, or the yield on common stock
m represents the real value of private money holdings
a represents the real value of all common stock, whether held by private owners or by the central bank
λ represents the proportion of the total supply of common stock held by private owners
w represents the real value of all privately held wealth, including both money and common stock
S represents the real value of current saving
I represents the real value of current investment

The amount of real saving out of a full-employment income is assumed to depend upon the real value of private wealth as well as upon the rate of interest, and we may accordingly write $S = S(r, w)$. Investment, under conditions of full employment, is assumed to depend only upon the rate of interest, and the investment function may therefore be written as follows: $I = I(r)$. If real national income under conditions of full employment is y_0, and if a proportion, c, of this consists of business profits, the real value of all common stock will be the capitalized value of these profits, thus: $a = cy_0/r$. The only remaining functional relation to be defined is the liquidity-preference function. Let $L(r)$ be such a function, indicating the proportion in which asset-holders as a group wish to hold money and common stock. With the aid of these definitions we may now write down the following system of equations:

$$
\left.
\begin{aligned}
S(r, \dot{w}) &= I(r), \\
L(r) &= \frac{m}{\lambda a}, \\
w &= \lambda a + m, \\
a &= \frac{cy_0}{r}.
\end{aligned}
\right\}
\tag{1}
$$

The first of equations (1) expresses the condition that, in equilibrium, full-employment saving must equal full-employment investment. The second equation says that the rate of interest must be such that the desired proportion between money holdings and security holdings on the part of the owners of private wealth is equal to the actual proportion. The third equation is an identity, defining the real value of private wealth as the sum of private money holdings and private security holdings. Finally, the fourth of equations (1) says that the real value of all common stock is the capitalized value of business profits, where the capitalization is done at the prevailing rate of interest, r.

If the value of λ is given, equations (1) are sufficient to determine the equilibrium values of the four variables, r, w, m, and a; i.e., the equations determine the rate of interest, the total real value of privately held wealth, the real value of money balances, and the real value of all common stock. The price level does not enter explicitly in equations (1), since all variables are in real terms. Nevertheless, price movements are implicitly taken into account through movements of m, the real value of the money supply. In the absence of open-market transactions, indeed, m can change only by means of general inflation or deflation.

Security purchases or sales by the central bank are indicated in equations (1) by changes in the value of λ. An increase in λ, for example, indicates a larger proportion of total securities in private hands and hence signifies security sales by the central bank. Changes in λ will obviously alter the equilibrium values of all our variables. In order to see how a central-bank sale of securities affects these equilibrium values, we may differentiate (1) with respect to λ, as follows:

$$(S_r - I_r)\frac{dr}{d\lambda} + S_w\frac{dw}{d\lambda} = 0,$$

$$-\frac{1}{\lambda a}\frac{dm}{d\lambda} + L_r\frac{dr}{d\lambda} + \frac{m}{\lambda a^2}\frac{da}{d\lambda} = -\frac{m}{\lambda^2 a},$$

$$\frac{dm}{d\lambda} - \frac{dw}{d\lambda} + \lambda\frac{da}{d\lambda} = -a$$

$$-\frac{a}{r}\frac{dr}{d\lambda} - \frac{da}{d\lambda} = 0$$

$$\left.\begin{array}{c}\\ \\ \\ \\ \\ \\ \\ \\ \end{array}\right\} \quad (2)$$

Solving equations (2) for

$$\frac{dr}{d\lambda}, \quad \frac{dm}{d\lambda}, \quad \frac{dw}{d\lambda}, \quad \text{and} \quad \frac{da}{d\lambda},$$

we find

$$\frac{dr}{d\lambda} = -\frac{S_w}{\Delta}\left(\frac{1}{\lambda} + \frac{m}{\lambda^2 a}\right),$$

$$\frac{dm}{d\lambda} = \frac{1}{\Delta}\left\{(S_r - I_r)\frac{m}{\lambda^2 a} - aS_wL_r\right\},$$

$$\frac{dw}{d\lambda} = \frac{1}{\Delta}(S_r - I_r)\left(\frac{1}{\lambda} + \frac{m}{\lambda^2 a}\right),$$

$$\frac{da}{d\lambda} = \frac{1}{\Delta}\frac{aS_w}{r}\left(\frac{1}{\lambda} + \frac{m}{\lambda^2 a}\right).$$

$$\left.\begin{array}{c}\\ \\ \\ \\ \\ \\ \\ \end{array}\right\} \quad (3)$$

The symbol Δ in equations (3) represents the basic determinant of the system, i.e.,

$$\Delta \equiv \begin{vmatrix} 0 & S_r - I_r & S_w & 0 \\ -\dfrac{1}{\lambda a} & L_r & 0 & \dfrac{m}{\lambda a^2} \\ 1 & 0 & -1 & \lambda \\ 0 & -\dfrac{a}{r} & 0 & -1 \end{vmatrix},$$

$$\equiv (S_r - I_r)\frac{1}{\lambda a} + S_wL_r - \frac{S_w}{r} - \frac{mS_w}{\lambda ar}.$$

$$\left.\begin{array}{c}\\ \\ \\ \\ \\ \\ \\ \\ \\ \end{array}\right\} \quad (4)$$

The subscripts in equations (3) and (4) indicate differentiation of the S, I, and L functions with respect to the variable appearing in the subscript. I assume the system is stable in the classic sense that an increase in the rate of interest creates an excess of potential saving over potential investment; this implies that $S_r - I_r$ is positive. The saving-wealth relation is represented in (3) and (4) by S_w, which is negative, indicating that an increase in the real value of private wealth reduces real saving. The slope L_r of the liquidity-preference schedule is assumed to be negative, which implies that an increase in the rate of interest reduces the desired ratio between money and securities.

With the given signs of S_r, I_r, etc., one can see from (4) that Δ is a positive determinant. Moreover, the direction of change of most of the variables of the system can be readily determined. Thus, (3) shows that $dr/d\lambda$ is positive, $dw/d\lambda$ is positive, and $da/d\lambda$ is negative. This means that open-market sales of securities have increased the rate of interest, increased the real value of private wealth (cash and securities combined), and reduced the real value of the total supply of common stock. The only change whose sign is indeterminate is $dm/d\lambda$, the change in the real value of private money holdings. The reason for this indeterminacy is not far to seek: the central-bank sales of securities have reduced private money balances, but the real value of the remaining private balances have subsequently been increased through a general deflation. The final position of real money balances thus depends upon the relative strength of these opposing forces. But whatever happens to the real value of privately held money, equations (3) show that privately held wealth as a whole has been increased by the central bank's sales of securities. The increase in the real value of private wealth has reduced the rate of saving, and it is this reduction of saving which accounts for the permanent rise in the equilibrium rate of interest.

Thus far I have investigated the stationary or equilibrium values of the system without saying anything about the dynamic process of adjustment. I shall conclude this appendix with a few remarks concerning the behavior of the variables through time, during intervals when the system is not in equilibrium.

Consider, first, the behavior of prices when total demand is different from productive capacity. The difference between demand and productive capacity is measured, of course, by the difference between potential full-employment saving and potential full-employment investment. If the former exceeds the latter, demand for goods and services falls short of productive capacity, and prices and costs accordingly tend to decline. Conversely, if full-employment investment exceeds full-employment saving, total demand exceeds capacity, and both prices and costs rise. In the absence of new borrowing or lending by the banking system, however, an increase in prices is equivalent to a fall in the real value of money balances, and the time movement of the general price level may therefore be described in terms of movements in the value of money. As a first dynamic postulate, then, I write:

$$\frac{dm}{dt} = k_1[S(r, w) - I(r)]. \tag{5}$$

Equation (5) says that the price level tends to fall, and the real value of money balances tends to rise, whenever potential saving exceeds potential investment. Likewise, prices rise, and the real value of money balances falls, when potential saving falls short of potential investment. The speed of the price movement, in both cases, is assumed in (5) to be proportional to the size of the inflationary or deflationary gap, and the constant, k_1, represents this speed of adjustment.

So much for the general price level in the commodity-and-service market. Consider next the movement of prices in the securities market. I assume, as I indicated in the text, that the securities market is dominated by transactions in old securities rather than by supply-and-demand conditions in the new-securities market. Specifically, I assume that security prices tend to rise whenever asset-holders on balance attempt to shift from money to securities and that security prices fall when asset-holders attempt a shift in the opposite direction. The attempted shift, in turn, depends upon whether the actual ratio of cash to securities is higher or lower than the desired ratio, as indicated by the liquidity-preference function. Since a rise in security prices is equivalent to a fall in the rate of interest, our second dynamic postulate may be written

$$\frac{dr}{dt} = k_2\left[L(r) - \frac{m}{\lambda a}\right]. \tag{6}$$

In words, equation (6) says that the rate of interest rises, which means that security prices fall, when the desired ratio of money to securities exceeds the actual ratio. And, conversely, the rate of interest falls when the desired ratio is less than the actual ratio.

Equations (5) and (6) are the only equations of adjustment that we shall need. These two equations are the dynamic counterpart of the first two of equations (1). They do not form a complete system, however, since we have only two equations in four unknowns. Before we can solve our dynamic equations, we must have two more equations. The two missing equations are the third and fourth equations of our static system (1). These are merely definitional equations and are assumed to be satisfied at any moment of time, without lag. The third equation defines private wealth at a given moment as the sum of private security holdings and private money holdings, while the fourth equation defines the rate of interest as the yield on securities. The complete dynamic system is as follows:

$$
\left.
\begin{aligned}
\frac{dm}{dt} &= k_1[S(r, w) - I(r)], \\[1em]
\frac{dr}{dt} &= k_2\left[L(r) - \frac{m}{\lambda a}\right], \\[1em]
w &= \lambda a + m \\[1em]
a &= \frac{cy_0}{r}.
\end{aligned}
\right\}
\tag{7}
$$

Equations (7) cannot be explicitly solved, since we do not know the exact form of the functions S, I, and L. I shall therefore make a linear approximation of (7), which will be valid only for small deviations from the equilibrium values of the variables. If r_0, w_0, m_0, and a_0 represent the equilibrium values, we may write, as such a linear approximation,

$$
\left.
\begin{aligned}
\frac{dm}{dt} &= k_1(S_r - I_r)(r - r_0) + k_1 S_w(w - w_0), \\[1em]
\frac{dr}{dt} &= - k_2\frac{1}{\lambda a}(m - m_0) + k_2 L_r(r - r_0) + k_2\frac{m}{\lambda a^2}(a - a_0), \\[1em]
0 &= (m - m_0) - (w - w_0) + \lambda(a - a_0), \\[1em]
0 &= - \frac{a}{r}(r - r_0) - (a - a_0).
\end{aligned}
\right\}
\tag{8}
$$

The solution of (8) takes the form

$$
m = m_0 + A_1 e^{\rho_1 t} + A_2 e^{\rho_2 t_1},
\tag{9}
$$

with similar results for r, a, and w, where A_1 and A_2 depend upon the initial values of the variables, and where ρ_1 and ρ_2 are the roots of the following equation:

$$
\begin{vmatrix}
-\rho & k_1(S_r - I_r) & k_1 S_w & 0 \\[1em]
-\dfrac{k_2}{\lambda a} & k_2 L_r - \rho & 0 & \dfrac{k_2 m}{\lambda a^2} \\[1em]
1 & 0 & -1 & \lambda \\[1em]
0 & -\dfrac{a}{r} & 0 & -1
\end{vmatrix} = 0.
\tag{10}
$$

Equation (10) may be expended in powers of ρ as follows:

$$\rho^2 + \left(\frac{k_2 m}{\lambda ar} - k_2 L_r - k_1 S_w\right)\rho + k_1 k_2 \Delta = 0, \qquad (11)$$

where Δ is the basic determinant of the static system, (1).

The coefficients of the powers of ρ in equation (11) are positive, which means that the real parts of the roots of equation (11) are all negative. Thus the dynamic system is stable, for small deviations from equilibrium, regardless of the numerical values of L_r, S_w, etc. In other words, if the liquidity-preference function, the saving function, and the investment function do not alter their form or position as prices rise or fall, the dynamic system will eventually reach a stationary or static position. This does not mean, of course, that an economic system in which the saving-wealth relation is operative will always be a stable system in reality; for equations (7) and (8) have made no allowance for expectations, and such expectations may exert a strongly destabilizing influence on the system. If prices of commodities are rising, for example, consumers and producers may anticipate further price increases; if so, saving will probably decline and investment will increase, thereby widening the inflationary gap and accelerating the price rise. Likewise, if security prices are rising, asset-holders may revise downward their estimate of what constitutes a normal ratio between money and securities; and, if they do, the resulting attempt to shift from money to securities will cause a further rise in securities prices. These possibilities suggest that equations (7) and (8) are stable only in a narrow sense.

Assuming that the system is stable, we may inquire, in conclusion, about the nature of the approach toward equilibrium. Is the solution of equation (8) cyclical or noncyclical? The answer to this question depends upon the roots of equation (10) or (11). The dynamic system will not be cyclical unless these roots are complex numbers. This means that $b^2 - 4c$ is negative, where b is the coefficient of ρ in (11) and c is the constant term. I leave it to the reader to prove the following propositions: (1) the roots of equation (11) may be either real or complex, which means that the dynamic system may or may not have a cyclical solution. (2) If k_1 and k_2, the speeds of adjustment in the commodity market and the securities market, respectively, are decidedly different in magnitude, the roots are likely to be real and the dynamic system is thus likely to be a noncyclical system. (3) If $S_r - I_r$ is large, so that a small rise in the rate of interest creates a substantial deflationary gap, the system will probably be cyclical.

NOTES

1. A. C. Pigou, *Employment and Equilibrium* (London 1941), Chapter 7; "The Classical Stationary State," *Economic Journal*, Vol. 53 (December 1943), 342–52.

2. T. Scitovszky, "Capital Accumulation, Employment and Price Rigidity," *Review of Economic Studies*, Vol. 8 (1940–41), 69–88.

3. G. Haberler, *Prosperity and Depression*, 3d ed. (Geneva 1941), pp. 491–503.

4. Consider, for example, the following remark of J. S. Mill: "There must be, as in other cases of value, some rate [of interest] which . . . may be called the natural rate; some rate about which the market rate oscillates, and to which it always tends to return. This rate partly depends on the amount of accumulation going on in the hands of persons who cannot themselves attend to the employment of their savings, and partly on the comparative taste existing in the community for the active pursuits of industry, or for the leisure, ease, and independence of an annuitant" (*Principles* [5th ed.], Book 3, Chapter 23, § 1). Although Mill does not specify in this passage that the saving and investment which govern the interest rate are full-employment saving and full-employment investment, the tenor of his work strongly suggests that this is what he had in mind (see, e.g., *ibid.*, Book 3, Chapter 14).

5. Haberler, *op. cit.*, p. 499, note 2.

6. David Ricardo, *Principles of Political Economy* (London 1948), p. 246.

7. Although Pigou is usually considered to be a defender of classical or neoclassical economic theory, his ideas concerning the interest rate were somewhat nonclassical even before the publication of his *Employment and Equilibrium*. He believed, in particular, that the banking system has a limited influence upon the equilibrium interest rate as well as upon the market rate. If the banks establish a market rate below the equilibrium rate, for example, prices and costs tend to rise, and the real expenditures of fixed-income groups are reduced. The resources thus freed are available for capital development, and the increased supply of capital reduces the equilibrium interest rate. Apart from this reservation, Pigou's earlier conception of the interest rate seems to be largely classical in its implications (see A. C. Pigou, *Industrial Fluctuations*, 2d ed. [London 1929], *passim*, but esp. p. 277).

8. J. M. Keynes, *General Theory of Employment, Interest and Money* (New York 1936), Chapter 19. On p. 267 of this chapter, Keynes says: "There is, therefore, no ground for the belief that a flexible wage policy is capable of maintaining a state of continuous full employment; . . . The economic system cannot be made self-adjusting along these lines."

9. M. Kalecki, "Professor Pigou on 'The Classical Stationary State,' a Comment," *Economic Journal*, Vol. 54 (April 1944), 131–32; D. Patinkin, "Price Flexibility and Full Employment," *American Economic Review*, Vol. 38 (September 1948), 543–64.

10. Keynes, *op. cit.*, Chapters 13, 15, and 18.

11. Common stock has been selected as the typical security in order to avoid the difficulties associated with bonds during periods of inflation

or deflation. Throughout the paper I assume that, in the absence of movements in interest rates, common-stock prices rise or fall to the same extent that other prices rise or fall, so that a general inflation or deflation does not affect the real value of securities. This means that the real value of a given quantity of securities is a function of the rate of interest alone. (See below.) Although the theory is simplified in this respect by regarding common stock as the typical security, two new problems are thereby introduced, and these must not be overlooked. Perhaps most important, when all investment is financed by issuing common stock, the idea of a functional relation between the rate of interest and the real volume of investment becomes somewhat vague. Under these circumstances businessmen do not commit themselves, as they do when they issue bonds, to the payment of fixed capital charges. Saying that investment depends upon the rate of interest when all securities are common stocks is equivalent to saying that businessmen undertake more investment when stock prices are high than when they are low.

Apart from the problem of defining an investment function, the use of common stock in our argument presents the further problem of separating risk payments from interest payments per se. I have attempted to avoid this second problem by assuming that the degree or risk is about the same for one stock as for another. I realize, however, that such an assumption does not meet the basic difficulty and that, in a more extended treatment of the subject, allowance should be made for differences in risk.

12. The best account I have found of the second reason for the negative slope of the liquidity-preference schedule is by E. Solomon in "Money, Liquidity, and the Long-Term Rate of Interest: An Empirical Study, 1909–38" (University of Chicago dissertation, 1950).

13. Superficially, the cycle of interest rates and prices described above seems to be somewhat like the monetary part of Hicks's business-cycle theory. In reality, however, the two cyclical processes are quite different. The process envisaged by Hicks involves movements of output and employment rather than movements of prices and costs; and savings in Hicks's theory depend upon the rate of interest and real income, whereas savings in the present paper depend upon the rate of interest and the real value of private wealth (J. R. Hicks, *A Contribution to the Theory of Business Cycles* [London: Oxford University Press, 1949], Chapters 11 and 12).

14. Using a model more complex than the one I have been considering, D. Patinkin previously demonstrated that if both the saving-wealth relation and liquidity preference are active forces, monetary disturbances of the second type will not affect the equilibrium interest rate (see "The Indeterminacy of Absolute Prices in Classical Economic Theory," *Econometrica*, Vol. 17 [January 1949], 23–27). Patinkin did not examine the effects of monetary disturbances of the first type and accordingly concluded that the model he had constructed was closer to the classical model than to the Keynesian.

15. In describing the consequences of open-market transactions, I assume that the securities schedule, *AA*, is the only schedule of Figure 4 which is *directly* influenced by the central bank's purchase or sale o

securities; the other schedules (i.e., the wealth-requirements schedule, the money-requirements schedule, and the liquidity-preference schedule) are assumed to be affected only in so far as they are related to, or derived from, the securities schedule, AA. This implies that the income available to the typical asset-holder is not altered by the central bank's dealings in securities. If disposable income tended to fall or to rise with an increase or decrease in the central bank's holdings of securities, the saving and investment schedules would also be affected, and the wealth-requirements schedule, which is derived from the saving and investment schedules, would tend to shift.

Taken by themselves, however, open-market transactions may well have a slight influence on disposable income. If the central bank buys securities, for example, the income on these securities is transferred from the former owners to the bank. In the absence of offsetting transactions, the security purchases thus reduce the disposable income of private asset-holders and increase the profits of the central bank by a corresponding amount. I do not wish to discuss the complications introduced by this connection between open-market transactions and disposable income. I therefore assume throughout that any additional profits which the central bank earns by reason of its acquisition of securities are ultimately passed on to private hands in the form of reduced taxes. Under these circumstances, the security purchases by the bank will redistribute income between former asset owners and taxpayers but will not influence the total of disposable income.

Part **IV**

The Supply
of Money

Patinkin in his attempt to reformulate Keynesian theory on the basis of classical assumptions demonstrated that money would be "neutral" if one postulated wage and price flexibility, inelastic expectations, and the absence of money illusion, distribution effects and government debt operations. Many economists felt that the heart of several economic problems had been assumed away, and therefore sought to elaborate the conditions under which money might not be "neutral."

It has been pointed out that the development of the financial structure of a country might have significant effects on the supply of money and money substitutes. The net debtor position of a closed economy must be zero since for every debtor there must be a creditor. However, it has long been accepted that the behavior of the government as a debtor is not analogous to that of private debtors and that analytically it is not desirable to net out government debt which includes part of the money supply. The generalization of this idea that there might be differences in the behavior between various debtors and creditors in the private sector and that the financial structure might have some influence on the type of debt issued and held by various groups in the economy led to several attempts to develop monetary theory under more general assumptions. One well-known attempt was that of Gurley and Shaw in their book *Money in a Theory of Finance* (1960), where they examined situations where money was not "neutral."

Money is unique in that it is both a medium of exchange and a store of value. In its former function it has few close substitutes but in its latter capacity, there are many assets which provide similar services. Financial intermediaries, in particular, supply assets which provide a substitute store of value. To the extent that there are other substitute stores of value, the amount of money needed to maintain a certain level of income and prices may be economized upon by increasing the supply of substitute financial assets. Thus Gurley and Shaw examined the conditions under which these non-bank financial intermediaries supply substitute assets.

Gurley and Shaw argued that the rate of interest from the supply side is not determined only by the rate of growth of the money supply, as Keynes maintained, but also to a large extent by the rate of growth of non-bank financial intermediaries. The rate of growth of non-bank financial intermediaries may be an important factor in explaining the secular trend in the velocity of money. From the point of view of counter-cyclical policy the central concern is whether the rate of growth of financial intermediaries will be such as to produce destabilizing changes in velocity counter to the direction of government policy.[1] The answer to this question in turn depends on the short-run determinants of the rate of growth of non-bank financial intermediaries which issue money substitutes.

The traditional way of looking at the money supply was to consider it the result of government debt operations and the average reserve ratio of commercial banks. Tolley, along with others, pointed out that the reserve ratio may also be treated as a behavioral variable, determined jointly by the government—when it changes legal reserve requirements; the public—when it changes its division of assets between currency and deposits; and by banks—by their willingness to maintain excess reserves. It has been shown that changes in the supply of money by open market operations or by changes in legal reserve requirements will have different repercussions on the cost and size of the government debt and on resource allocation. The result of these developments has been to evolve a supply theory of money to complement the highly developed demand theory for money.[2]

More recently there has been renewed interest in the flow-of-funds approach developed by Morris Copeland in the early fifties. This approach analyzes the behavioral and institutional difference in the sources and uses of funds of individual sectors and the interaction among sectors subject to overall accounting identities. This approach tends to say that the way money supply is changed and structure of the federal debt have significant effects that are not caught by small aggregative models. The large-scale models of the economy, such as the MPS and the Wharton School models, have had until recently relatively primitive financial sectors.

[1] See Richard S. Thorn, "Non-Bank Financial Intermediaries, Credit Expansion and Monetary Policy," *IMF Staff Papers,* Vol. 6 (November 1958), 375–78.
[2] One interesting attempt of this type was Karl Brunner's "A Scheme for the Supply Theory of Money," *International Economic Review* (January 1961), pp. 79–109.

15 *Financial Intermediaries and the Saving-Investment Process*

John G. Gurley
and Edward S. Shaw *Stanford University*

It is fashionable these days to speak of the growing institutional-ization of saving and investment. Rapid advances in recent years by pension funds, open-end investment companies, credit unions, and savings and loan associations, among others, have caught our eye. But the advance has been going on at least since the Civil War, and, as Raymond Goldsmith has recently shown, it was quite pro-nounced during the first three decades of this century. It is with these three decades that our paper is primarily concerned. Our method of analyzing financial data, however, requires explanation since it is based on unconventional theory. Accordingly, the first portions of the paper are largely theoretical. After that, we get down to brass tacks.

Deficits, Security Issues, and GNP

It is easy to imagine a world in which there is a high level of saving and investment, but in which there is an unfavorable climate for financial intermediaries. At the extreme, each of the economy's spending units—whether of the household, business, or government

Reprinted from *Journal of Finance*, Vol. 11 (March 1956), 257–76, by permission of the authors and publisher.

variety—would have a balanced budget on income and product account. For each spending unit, current income would equal the sum of current and capital expenditures. There could still be saving and investment, but each spending unit's saving would be precisely matched by its investment in tangible assets. In a world of balanced budgets, security issues by spending units would be zero, or very close to zero.[1] The same would be true of the accumulation of financial assets. Consequently, this world would be a highly uncongenial one for financial intermediaries; the saving-investment process would grind away without them.

Financial intermediaries are likely to thrive best in a world of deficits and surpluses, in a world in which there is a significant division of labor between savers and investors. In the ideal world for financial intermediaries, all current and capital expenditures would be made by spending units that received no current income, and all current income would be received by spending units that spent nothing. One group of spending units would have a deficit equal to its expenditures, and the other group would have a surplus equal to its income. And, of course, the *ex post* deficit would necessarily be equal to the *ex post* surplus. In this setting, the deficit group would tend to issue securities equal to its deficit, and the other group would tend to accumulate financial assets equal to its surplus. Security issues and financial-asset accumulations, therefore, would tend to approximate GNP or the aggregate of expenditures. No more congenial world than this could exist for financial intermediaries.

Unfortunately for these intermediaries, our own economy has been much closer to the first than to the second world. With some exceptions during the past half-century, the annual security issues of spending units over complete cycles have averaged somewhat below 10 per cent of GNP in current prices. These issues include government securities, corporate and foreign bonds, common and preferred stock, farm and non-farm mortgages, and consumer and other short-term debt. We shall call these primary security issues. Thus, at the turn of the century when GNP was around $20 billion, primary security issues ran a bit less than $2 billion per annum. In the late 1940's, with a GNP of approximately $250 billion, primary issues hovered around $20 billion per annum. Dividing the half-century into thirteen complete cycles, we find that the average annual ratio of primary issues to GNP was between 7 and 10 per cent in nine of the cycles. The exceptional cases include World War I, when the ratio reached 20 per cent, the 1930's, when the ratio fell to 3 or 4 per cent, and World War II, when it climbed to 25 per cent. However, if we consider longer phases, 1897–1914, 1915–32, and 1933–49, the ratio was between 9 and 10 per cent in each phase. There is sufficient strength, then, in the link between borrowing and GNP to make the relationship useful for financial analysis. And while the ratio lies closer to zero than to 100 per cent, still it is high enough to permit financial intermediation to be a substantial business.

The Role of Financial Intermediaries

What is the business of financial intermediaries? They lend at one stratum of interest rates and borrow at a lower stratum. They relieve the market of some primary securities and substitute others—indirect securities or financial assets—whose qualities command a higher price. This margin between yields on primary and indirect securities is the intermediaries' compensation for the special services they supply.

The financial institutions that fit these specifications are savings and loan associations, insurance companies, mutual savings banks, Postal Savings banks, investment companies, common trust funds, pension funds, government lending agencies, and others. In addition, we count the monetary system, including commercial banks, as one among many intermediaries. It is a vitally important intermediary, in view of its functions and its size. But its elevated rank among intermediaries does not alter the principle that the monetary system, like other intermediaries, transmits loanable funds by issues of indirect financial assets to surplus units and purchases of primary securities from deficit units. The indirect financial assets, deposits and currency that it issues or creates, are, like the indirect financial assets issued or created by other intermediaries, substitutes for primary securities in the portfolios of spending units. We shall return to this point in a few moments.

Internal and External Finance of Expenditures

In a world of balanced budgets, each spending unit's current and capital expenditures would be financed entirely from its current income. Thus, aggregate expenditures in the economy would be self-financed or internally financed. Internal finance would be equal to GNP.

In a world of deficits and surpluses, some expenditures would be financed externally. The extent of such financing is measured by the sum of the deficits (or surpluses) run by spending units. If at a GNP of $400 billion, the sum of all spending units' deficits is $40 billion, then 10 per cent of GNP is financed externally and 90 per cent is financed internally.

External finance may take two forms: direct finance and indirect finance. The distinction is based on the changes that occur in the financial accounts of surplus units' balance sheets. The finance is indirect if the surplus units acquire claims on financial intermediaries.[2] It is direct if surplus units acquire claims on debtors that are not financial intermediaries.[3]

While the proportion of GNP that is externally financed has not changed much over the past half-century, the proportion that is indirectly financed has risen and, of course, the proportion that is directly financed has fallen. In short, a growing share of primary issues has been sold to financial intermediaries.[4] But the relative gainers have been the non-monetary intermediaries and the relative loser has been the monetary system. Now, if we look at these trends from the standpoint of surplus spenders, we have the following picture: the surplus units have accumulated financial assets in annual amounts that, over long periods, have been a fairly steady percentage of GNP. However, these accumulations have been relatively more and more in the form of indirect financial assets, and relatively less and less in the form of primary securities. Moreover, the accumulations of indirect financial assets have swung toward the non-monetary types and away from bank deposits and currency. Commercial banks and the monetary system have retrogressed relative to financial intermediaries generally.

A Reconsideration of Banking Theory

A traditional view of the monetary system is that it determines the supply of money: it determines its own size in terms of monetary debt and of the assets that are counterparts of this debt on the system's balance sheet. Other financial intermediaries transfer to investors any part of this money supply that may be deposited with them by savers. Their size is determined by the public's choice of saving media.

As we see it, on the contrary, the monetary system is in some significant degree competitive with other financial intermediaries. The growth of these intermediaries in terms of indirect debt and of primary security portfolios is alternative to monetary growth and inhibits it. Their issues of indirect debt displace money, and the primary securities that they hold are in some large degree a loss of assets to the banks.

Bank deposits and currency are unique in one respect: they are means of payment, and holders of money balances have immediate access to the payments mechanism of the banking system. If money were in demand only for immediate spending or for holding in transactions balances, and if no other financial asset could be substituted as a means of payment or displace money in transactions balances, the monetary system would be a monopolistic supplier exempt from competition by other financial intermediaries.

But money is not in demand exclusively as a means of payment. It is in demand as a financial asset to hold. As a component of balances, money does encounter competition. Other financial assets can be accumulated preparatory to money payments, as a precaution against contingencies, or as an alternative to primary securities. For any level of money payments, various levels of money balances will do and, hence, various sizes of money supply and monetary system.

The more adequate the non-monetary financial assets are as substitutes for money in transactions, precautionary, speculative, and—as we shall see—diversification balances, the smaller may be the money supply for any designated level of national income. For any level of income, the money supply is indeterminate until one knows the degree of substitutability between money created by banks and financial assets created by other intermediaries. How big the monetary system is depends in part on the intensity of competition from savings banks, life insurance companies, pension funds, and other intermediaries.

Financial competition may inhibit the growth of the monetary system in a number of ways. Given the level of national income, a gain in attractiveness of, say, savings and loan shares vis-à-vis money balances must result in an excess supply of money. The monetary authority may choose to remove this excess. Then bank reserves, earning assets, money issues, and profits are contracted. This implies that, at any level of income, the competition of non-monetary intermediaries may displace money balances, shift primary securities from banks to their competitors, and reduce the monetary system's requirement for reserves. In a trend context, bank reserves cannot be permitted to grow as rapidly as otherwise they might, if non-monetary intermediaries become more attractive channels for transmission of loanable funds.

Suppose that excess money balances, resulting from a shift in spending units' demand away from money balances to alternative forms of indirect financial assets, are not destroyed by central bank action. They may be used to repay bank loans or to buy other securities from banks, the result being excess bank reserves. At the prevailing level of security prices, spending units have rejected money balances. But cannot banks force these balances out again, resuming control of the money supply? They can do so by accepting a reduced margin between the yield of primary securities they buy and the cost to them of deposits and currency they create. But this option is not peculiar to banks: other intermediaries can stimulate demand for their debt if they stand ready to accept a reduced markup on the securities they create and sell relative to the securities they buy. The banks can restore the money supply, but the cost is both a decline in their status relative to other financial intermediaries and a reduction in earnings.

The banks may choose to live with excess reserves rather than pay higher prices on primary securities or higher yields on their own debt issues. In this case, as in the previous two, a lower volume of reserves is needed to sustain a given level of national income. With their competitive situation improved, non-monetary intermediaries have stolen away from the banking system a share of responsibility for sustaining the flow of money payments. They hold a larger share of outstanding primary securities; they owe a larger share of indirect financial assets. They have reduced the size of the banking system at the given income level, both absolutely and relatively to their own size, and their gain is at the expense of bank profits.[5]

A Reconsideration of Interest Theory

It is clear from the foregoing remarks that this way of looking at financial intermediaries leads to a reconsideration of interest theory. Yields on primary securities, the terms of borrowing available to deficit spenders, are influenced not only by the amount of primary securities in the monetary system—that is, by the supply of money—but also by the amount of these securities in non-monetary intermediaries—that is, by the supply of indirect financial assets created by these intermediaries. Suppose that savings and loan shares become more attractive relative to bank deposits, resulting in an excess supply of money. Now, if we suppose that the monetary system chooses and manages to keep the money supply constant under these circumstances, the excess supply of money will cause yields on primary securities to fall. The activities of non-monetary financial intermediaries, then, can affect primary yields. The same money supply and national income are compatible with various interest rate levels, depending upon the size of non-monetary intermediaries and upon the degree to which their issues are competitive with money.[6]

The analysis is only a bit more complicated when we allow for issues of primary securities and the growth of income. Let us take these one at a time. At any income level, some spending units will have deficits and others surpluses. During the income period, the deficit spenders will tend to issue primary securities in an amount equal to their aggregate deficits. Now, if the surplus spenders are willing to absorb all of the issues at current yields on these securities, there will be no tightening effect on security markets. Surplus spenders will accumulate financial assets, all in the form of primary securities, and financial intermediaries will purchase none of the issues.

But this is an unlikely outcome. Ordinarily, surplus spenders can be expected to reject some portion of the primary securities emerging at any level of income and demand indirect financial assets instead, unless their preference for the latter is suppressed by a fall in prices of primary securities and a corresponding rise in interest rates charged to deficit spenders. This incremental demand for indirect financial assets is in part a demand for portfolio diversification. The diversification demand exists because there is generally no feasible mixture of primary securities that provides adequately such distinctive qualities of indirect securities as stability of price and yield or divisibility. The incremental demand for indirect assets, however, reflects not only a negative response, a partial rejection of primary securities, but also a positive response, an attraction to the many services attached to indirect assets, such as insurance and pension services and convenience of accumulation. Part of the demand is linked to the flow of primary security issues, but another part is linked more closely to the level of income.

For these reasons, then, ordinarily some portion of the primary issues must be sold to financial intermediaries if present yields on these securities are to be defended. Assuming for the moment that the monetary system is the only financial intermediary, the increase in the money supply must be equal to the portion of primary issues that spending units choose not to accumulate at current yields. If the monetary system purchases less than this, spending units will accumulate the residual supply at rising interest rates to deficit spenders. The emergence of security issues and a diversification demand for money based on these issues means that the money supply must rise at a given income level to maintain current yields on primary securities.

Still retaining the assumption that the monetary system is the only financial intermediary, we now permit income to grow. As money income gains, spending units demand additions to their active or transactions balances of means of payment. An upward trend in money payments calls for an upward trend in balances too. The income effect also applies to contingency or precautionary balances. If spending units are increasingly prosperous in the present, they feel able to afford stronger defenses against the hazards of the future.[7]

The combination of the income and diversification effects simply means that, when income is rising, a larger share of the issues must be purchased by the monetary system to prevent a rise in primary yields. The system must supply money for both diversification and transactions, including contingency, balances.

We may now introduce non-monetary intermediaries. The growth of these intermediaries will ordinarily, to some extent, reduce the required growth of the monetary system. We have already presented the reasons for this, so it suffices to say that primary yields may be held steady under growth conditions even with a monetary system that is barely growing, provided other intermediaries take up the slack.

In summary, primary security issues depend on aggregate deficits, and the latter in turn are related to the income level. At any income level, the diversification effect of these issues means that financial intermediaries must grow to hold primary yields steady. If income is rising, too, there is an incremental demand for money and perhaps for other indirect assets for transactions and contingency balances, requiring additional intermediary growth. To the extent that the issues of non-monetary intermediaries are competitive with money balances of whatever type, the required growth of the monetary system is reduced by the expansion of other intermediaries.

Financial Aspects of Output Growth, 1898–1930

We turn now to the task of attaching empirical content to this theoretical structure.[8] Our period runs from about 1898 through 1930. It starts with an upturn in economic activity, following the depression of the 1890's. It then traces the especially high rate of growth in real output through 1906, the Panic of 1907 and the ensuing depression, and the continuance of output growth, at a reduced pace, from 1909 to World War I. It covers the accelerated activity of the war and postwar years and the sharp downturn in 1920–21. Finally, the homestretch of the period is characterized by fairly steady output growth, with minor setbacks in 1924 and 1927. Over the entire period, GNP in current prices rose by more than 500 per cent, while GNP in 1929 prices grew by almost 200 per cent, at an average annual rate of about 3.5 per cent.

PRIMARY SECURITY ISSUES

From 1898 to 1930, the annual ratio of primary security issues to GNP in current prices averaged just a bit more than 10 per cent.[9] However, the range of fluctuation in the annual ratios was large, from about 2 to 20 per cent. During years of rapid acceleration in GNP, the ratio was relatively high, and this was especially true during the war years. During years of retarded growth, the ratio dipped below its average value, but there was no year when primary security issues were negative.

A steadier picture, then, is obtained when the years are grouped into complete cycles, as Table 1 shows. Each of these subperiods, of which there are nine, commences with a recovery year and ends with either a recession or a depression year. These subperiods are: 1898–1900, 1901–4, 1905–8, 1909–11, 1912–14, 1915–21, 1922–24, 1925–27, and 1928–30. In this way, nine ratios are obtained, each of which is equal to the cumulated primary issues divided by cumulated GNP during a subperiod. Leaving aside the exceptional years from 1915 to 1921, the ratios fall within the range of 7.1 per cent and 10.0 per cent, with six of them between 8.8 per cent and 10.0 per cent. The "exceptional" ratio was 14.1 per cent. All in all, the series shows remarkable stability, with no evidence of an upward or downward trend.[10]

TABLE 1 *Primary Security Issues and GNP 1898–1930, by Subperiods*

(In Millions of Dollars; Percentages)

PERIOD	TOTAL NET ISSUES*	GNP	RATIO OF NET ISSUES TO GNP	ALTERNATIVE RATIO†
1898–1900	4,731	50,812	9.3	9.3
1901–04	8,603	86,174	10.0	10.0
1905–08	10,117	110,141	9.2	9.2
1909–11	9,126	98,081	9.3	9.3
1912–14	9,557	109,170	8.8	8.8
1915–21	67,595	479,394	14.1	14.1
1922–24	17,197	244,207	7.0	7.1
1925–27	26,497	282,652	9.4	9.5
1928–30	23,196	291,878	7.9	8.2

* Unadjusted for mortgage write-downs and foreclosures.
† Net issues adjusted for mortgage write-downs and foreclosures.

DIRECT AND INDIRECT FINANCE

The primary security issues were directly financed through spending units or indirectly financed through financial intermediaries. In terms of the nine cycles, the indirect finance ratio— the ratio of primary securities purchased by intermediaries to total primary issues—commenced at 56 per cent and then fell slowly and steadily, with a single interruption, until it reached 36 per cent in 1915–21. In the next phase, 1922–24, the ratio leaped to almost

80 per cent, and then fell to 65 per cent in 1925–27, and finally to 50 per cent in 1928–30. There were two downward sweeps in the series. The first covered the initial two decades of the period. The second, starting from a fantastically high level, covered most of the third decade. Because of this high starting-point, the indirect finance ratio was unusually high, on the average, during most of the 1920's. From 1922 to 1929, for example, the ratio averaged about 65 per cent. This compares to 47 per cent from 1898 to 1914, and 36 per cent from 1915 to 1921.

The direct finance ratio—the proportion of total issues purchased by non-financial spending units—naturally behaved in the opposite fashion. In 1898–1900 it began a long upward sweep, which carried to the subperiod 1915–21. In the following cycle, it fell to an extremely low level, and then rose during the remainder of the period. Table 2 records these trends.

The significant finding here is the steady retrogression of financial intermediation during the first two decades and its resurgence during the 1920's. The counterpart of the retrogression was the growing share of primary issues absorbed by spending units, and the counterpart of the resurgence was the relatively low share of issues absorbed by spending units.

TABLE 2   Direct and Indirect Finance Ratios 1898–1930, by Subperiods

(In Percentages)

	DIRECT FINANCE RATIOS			INDIRECT FINANCE RATIOS		
	I*	II†	III‡	I*	II†	III‡
1898–1900	43.7	43.7	45.2	56.3	56.3	54.8
1901–04	46.0	46.0	45.9	54.0	54.0	54.1
1905–08	56.7	56.7	55.0	43.3	43.3	45.0
1909–11	53.5	53.5	49.7	46.5	46.5	50.3
1912–14	58.5	58.5	58.3	41.5	41.5	41.7
1915–21	63.5	63.5	64.5	36.5	36.5	35.5
1922–24	20.7	21.2	18.8	79.3	78.8	81.2
1925–27	35.1	35.3	34.5	64.9	64.7	65.5
1928–30	49.7	49.4	47.5	50.3	50.6	52.5

* Unadjusted for mortgage write-downs and foreclosures.
† Adjusted for mortgage write-downs and foreclosures.
‡ Above adjustment plus adjustment for foreign purchases of primary securities.

INDIRECT FINANCE AND FINANCIAL INTERMEDIARIES

The principal intermediary during the period was the monetary system, including Federal Reserve Banks after 1914. Up to World War I, life insurance companies, mutual savings banks, and savings and loan associations dominated the non-monetary intermediary group. After the war, land banks, management investment companies, and federal agencies and trust funds became important.

The main responsibility for the retrogression of financial intermediation during the first two decades, or at least up to 1915, must be laid at the door of the monetary system, that is, commercial banks. In 1898–1900, the system absorbed over 40 per cent of the primary issues. By 1912–14, it was purchasing less than 25 per cent of the issues. This relatively low share was not raised during the subperiod 1915–21, even with the addition of the Federal Reserve Banks to the monetary system. However, this perhaps is not surprising in view of the abnormally heavy issues of securities during these years. But the performance of the system did not improve from 1922 to 1930, on the average, when security issues were normal relative to GNP. In fact, during these years, the average annual share of issues taken by the system fell to 21 per cent.[11]

The group of non-monetary intermediaries purchased 15 per cent of total issues in 1898–1900. The share rose very slowly to 17 per cent just before the war, and then fell to 11 per cent in the face of the heavy issues of the war period. After that, the activity of these intermediaries was phenomenal. During 1922–24, their share jumped to 40 per cent, remained at about this level in the following sub period, and then hit 50 per cent during the final three years of the period. The high indirect finance ratio during most of the 1920's, therefore, was due principally to the growth of non-monetary intermediation. These and the monetary trends are shown in Table 3.

In short, the monetary system retrogressed up to World War I and it participated very little in the resurgence of intermediation after that date.

TABLE 3   *Indirect Finance Ratios of Selected Intermediaries, 1898–1930, by Subperiods*

(In Percentages)

	MONETARY SYSTEM*	LIFE INSURANCE COMPANIES	MUTUAL SAVINGS BANKS	SAVINGS AND LOAN ASSN'S	MNGM'T INVEST. CO'S	ALL OTHERS
1898–1900	41.3	6.7	7.7	−0.8		1.4
1901–04	38.3	8.1	5.3	0.5		1.8
1905–08	25.6	9.7	4.2	1.6		2.2
1909–11	28.0	8.0	5.5	2.2		2.8
1912–14	24.4	8.2	4.0	2.7		2.2
1915–21	24.5	4.3	2.7	1.9	0.1	3.0
1922–24	39.3	12.8	7.8	8.0	0.1	11.3
1925–27	26.3	13.6	6.2	7.7	1.8	9.3
1928–30	0.2	17.2	5.0	4.7	17.1	6.1

* Includes Federal Reserve Banks after 1914.

DIRECT FINANCE RATIOS AND LONG-TERM YIELDS

Our theoretical framework suggests that there should be a positive relationship between the direct finance ratio and changes in interest rates on primary securities. We should expect interest rates to rise whenever a large share of primary issues is absorbed by spending units; in the opposite case, when intermediation is heavy, we should expect falling rates.

The direct finance ratio may be a crude indicator of changes in primary yields. This may be most easily seen in terms of a simple financial growth model. Assuming that non-monetary indirect assets are competitive only with money, spending units' incremental demand for primary securities is: $e(abY - tdY)$. [The term] abY is primary security issues, where a is the ratio of issues to aggregate deficits of spending units, b is the ratio of deficits to GNP in current prices, and Y is GNP in current prices. tdY expresses spending units' incremental demand for transactions and contingency balances. At given interest rates, spending units will desire to purchase the proportion, e, of the residual supply of primary securities. The remainder of the issues, $1 - e$, they will want sold to financial intermediaries so that an equivalent amount of indirect assets for diversification balances may be accumulated. Thus, $e(abY - tdY)$ is the desired incremental demand of spending units for primary securities. Interest rates will remain steady if the incremental realized supply of the securities to spending units is equal to this demand.

Now, dividing through by abY, we have:

$$\begin{pmatrix} \text{Realized Direct} \\ \text{Finance Ratio} \end{pmatrix} = \begin{pmatrix} \text{Desired Direct} \\ \text{Finance Ratio} \end{pmatrix} = e - g \, (et/ab),$$

where g is the annual growth rate of GNP. When the realized exceeds the desired ratio, interest rates will rise. When the desired ratio is the larger, interest rates will fall. If we assume that the desired ratio moves within relatively narrow limits, a high realized ratio will generally indicate upward pressure on yields, and a low realized ratio will generally mean downward pressure on yields. With this assumption, then, we can compare the realized ratio to changes in interest rates.

Before doing this, though, we should take a moment to comment on the last assumption. Is it likely that the desired ratio will move within narrow limits? The answer is almost certainly "no" when we are dealing with annual data. To begin with, as we have seen, ab fluctuated between 2 per cent and 20 per cent during the period. Second, the annual growth rate of GNP was highly unstable.[12] Third, speculative demand, reflected in e, was undoubtedly quite high in some years and quite low in others. Finally, even annual t may have been unstable. Consequently, a high realized ratio, for example, may not indicate upward pressure on interest rates because the desired ratio may be just as high or higher.

But, in some large degree, these problems disappear when we work with annual averages during complete cycles. We have previously observed that, in these terms, *ab* was remarkably stable. In addition, fluctuations in speculative demand are likely to be smoothed out when annual data are averaged over a cycle. Moreover, the growth rate of GNP is less unstable when it is expressed as an average annual rate during a cycle, and the same is probably true of *t*. The assumption, then, that the desired ratio fluctuates within relatively narrow limits would appear to be reasonable, provided that annual averages for our subperiods are used. Nevertheless, there is nothing to prevent the desired ratio from showing an upward or downward drift over long periods of time. Our results should be checked against this possibility.

There is one more problem to straighten out. The interest rate used in this paper is the long-term yield on high-grade corporate bonds. This series, extending from 1900 to 1950, was recently compiled by W. Braddock Hickman.[13] For our period, it is probably the best series available. However, we have experimented with other long-term yields and with unweighted averages of several, and the results are substantially the same in every case. On the other hand, our results are much less satisfactory when short-term rates are used. There are some obvious reasons for this, and probably others not so obvious, but there is no time to explore them here.

We may now return to the heart of the matter. We have seen that the (realized) direct finance ratio,[14] starting at 44 per cent, rose almost without interruption through the sixth subperiod, 1915–21, at which time it was 64 per cent. It then fell sharply to 20 per cent, moved up to the still relatively low level of 35 per cent, and ended the period a little below 50 per cent. On the basis of these movements, we should expect growing upward (or diminishing downward) pressures on the long rate lasting through the phase 1915–21. We should then expect the rate to fall sharply in 1922–24, fall again but less sharply in 1925–27, and perhaps rise a little (or fall a little) in 1928–30.

In a way it is embarrassing to find that the actual world is almost identical to this mental image of it. The average yearly changes in the long rate during the eight subperiods were as shown in Table 4. The sole interruption to the rise in the direct finance ratio during

TABLE 4

1901–04	+0.017	1915–21	+0.189
1905–08	+0.068	1922–24	−0.313
1909–11	−0.037	1925–27	−0.143
1912–14	+0.073	1928–30	+0.040

the first two decades came in the phase 1909–11. Over the same period, the only interruption to the upward trend of interest rates also came in this phase. With this exception, each increase in rates up to the 1920's was larger than the preceding one. This conforms exactly to movements in the direct finance ratio. The sharpest fall in rates came in 1922–24, and the next sharpest in the following subperiod. Again, this is in conformity with the ratio. Finally, there was a small upward movement in yields, as we would expect, during the final years of the period.

Using the direct finance ratio as the independent variable and the average annual change in bond yield as the dependent one, the coefficient of correlation is 97.5 per cent, with a standard error of about one-tenth of 1 per cent. A direct finance ratio of 48 per cent was sufficient to hold the yield almost constant. Anything higher raised it, and anything lower reduced it. A change in the ratio of 5 percentage points changed the yield by 0.05[15] (see Figure 1).

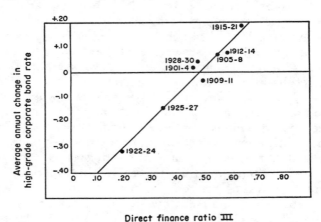

Direct finance ratio III

Figure 1.

SOME ALTERNATIVE MODELS

An alternative model frequently used is that which relates the income velocity of the money supply to interest rates. Aside from some basic difficulties with this model, which we have discussed elsewhere, it is not likely to be useful under growth conditions, especially when non-monetary intermediation is important. For one thing, under ordinary circumstances, the money supply has to grow relative to national income to keep interest rates stable. This is because primary security issues tend to force rates up unless a portion of the issues is sold to the monetary system. Moreover, the money supply growth required to stabilize interest rates depends on the growth of other indirect assets that are competitive with money. If non-monetary intermediaries are growing rapidly, it is perfectly possible for money supply growth to lag behind income growth without any adverse effects on security markets.

There is a good example of this in our period from 1922 to 1929 or 1930. In the subperiod, 1922–24, income velocity averaged 3.63. It was 3.67 in the next phase, and 3.74 from 1928 to 1930. Over these years, income velocity was higher than it was during any other phase of the full period with the exception of the war years. And yet these high and rising velocities were compatible with downward trends in interest rates over most of this decade. The reason is simply that non-monetary intermediaries grew so rapidly that the required growth of the monetary system was sharply reduced. Financial analysis cannot stop with the money supply when other indirect assets are of growing importance.

Nevertheless, as other investigators have discovered, there was a fairly good relationship between income velocity and interest rates during the period 1900 to 1930, in spite of the negative correlation between the two variables during most of the 1920's. But the relationship is much less impressive than the one presented above, especially when one views the 1920's as the crucial decade, the decade of rapid growth in non-monetary intermediation (see Figure 2).

The link between velocity and yields is weakened, moreover, when time deposits are included in the money supply. In fact, in this case, a negative correlation for most of the period is evident (see Figure 3). Finally, the relationship between marginal velocity and the change in yields is not very close, whether time deposits are included in or excluded from the money supply (see Figures 4 and 5).

Briefly, then, we have obtained the best results when account is taken of primary security issues and the growth of all intermediaries, including the monetary system. The two familiar variables, the money supply and national income, form only a part of the total picture.

NOTES

1. Securities might be issued by spending units to build up their financial assets or their holdings of existing real assets. However, in a world of balanced budgets, no spending unit would have a *net* accumulation of these assets, positive or negative.

2. In our empirical work, we exclude from indirect finance some kinds of claims on intermediaries, such as accrued expenses or even stockholder equities, that are essentially like debt issues of non-financial spending units.

3. It may help to illustrate these financing arrangements. Suppose that at a GNP of $400 billion the sum of all spending units' deficits is $40 billion. Suppose further that $40 billion of primary securities, such

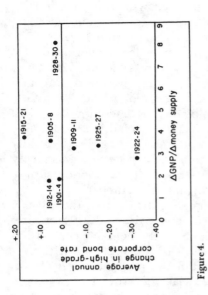

Figure 4.

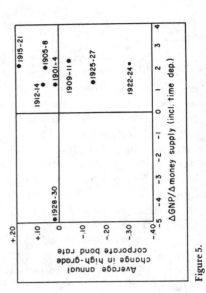

Figure 5.

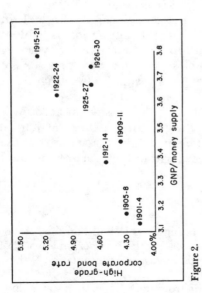

Figure 2.

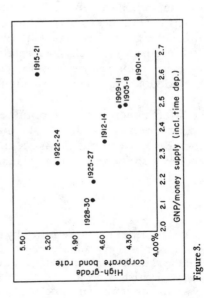

Figure 3.

as corporate bonds and mortgages, are issued to cover the deficits. The primary securities may be sold directly to surplus spending units whose aggregate surplus will also be equal to $40 billion, looking at it *ex post*. In this case direct finance will take place, with surplus spenders acquiring various types of primary securities. Alternatively, if the primary securities are sold to financial intermediaries, surplus spenders will accumulate claims on these intermediaries, indirect financial assets instead of primary securities. In this event we say that the expenditures represented by the primary securities have been indirectly financed. If indirect finance occurs through commercial banks, surplus spenders accumulate bank deposits; if through savings and loan associations, they acquire savings and loan shares; if through life insurance companies, policyholder equities; and so on.

4. This growth has not been steady. Indeed, it is shown later that there was retrogression in intermediation from 1898 to 1921. The share of issues going to intermediaries rose in the 1920's, rose further in the 1930's, and remained high in the 1940's.

5. We may mention a few additional issues in banking theory. As intermediaries, banks buy primary securities and issue, in payment for them, deposits and currency. As the payments mechanism, banks transfer title to means of payment on demand by customers. It has been pointed out before, especially by Henry Simons, that these two banking functions are at least incompatible. As managers of the payments mechanism, the banks cannot afford a shadow of insolvency. As intermediaries in a growing economy, the banks may rightly be tempted to wildcat. They must be solvent or the community will suffer; they must dare insolvency or the community will fail to realize its potentialities for growth.

All too often in American history energetic intermediation by banks has culminated in collapse of the payments mechanism. During some periods, especially cautious regard for solvency has resulted in collapse of bank intermediation. Each occasion that has demonstrated the incompatibility of the two principal banking functions has touched off a flood of financial reform. These reforms on balance have tended to emphasize bank solvency and the viability of the payments mechanism at the expense of bank participation in financial growth. They have by no means gone to the extreme that Simons proposed, of divorcing the two functions altogether, but they have tended in that direction rather than toward indorsement of wildcat banking. This bias in financial reform has improved the opportunities for non-monetary intermediaries. The relative retrogression in American banking seems to have resulted in part from regulatory suppression of the intermediary function.

Turning to another matter, it has seemed to be a distinctive, even magic, characteristic of the monetary system that it can create money, erecting a "multiple expansion" of debt in the form of deposits and currency on a limited base of reserves. Other financial institutions, conventional doctrine tells us, are denied this creative or multiplicative faculty. They are merely middlemen or brokers, not manufacturers of credit. Our own view is different. There is no denying, of course, that the monetary system creates debt in the special form of money: the monetary system can borrow by issue of instruments that are means of payment.

There is no denying, either, that non-monetary intermediaries cannot create this same form of debt. They would be monetary institutions if they could do so. It is granted, too, that non-monetary intermediaries receive money and pay it out, precisely as all of us do: they use the payments mechanism.

However, each kind of non-monetary intermediary can borrow, go into debt, issue its own characteristic obligations—in short, it can create credit, though not in monetary form. Moreover, the non-monetary intermediaries are less inhibited in their own style of credit creation than are the banks in creating money. Credit creation by non-monetary intermediaries is restricted by various qualitative rules. Aside from these, the main factor that limits credit creation is the profit calculus. Credit creation by banks also is subject to the profit condition. But the monetary system is subject not only to this restraint and to a complex of qualitative rules. It is committed to a policy restraint, of avoiding excessive expansion or contraction of credit for the community's welfare, that is not imposed explicitly on non-monetary intermediaries. It is also held in check by a system of reserve requirements. The legal reserve requirement on commercial banks is a "sharing ratio"; it apportions assets within the monetary system. The share of assets allocated to the commercial banks varies inversely with the reserve requirement. The proportion of the commercial banks' share to the share of the central bank and Treasury is the "multiple of expansion" for the commercial banking system. The "multiple of expansion" is a remarkable phenomenon not because of its inflationary implications, but because it means that bank expansion is anchored, as other financial expansion is not, to a regulated base. If credit creation by banks is miraculous, creation of credit by other financial institutions is still more a cause for exclamation.

6. We can reach the same conclusion by looking at the supply of and the demand for primary securities. The shift in demand to savings and loan shares reduces spending units' demand for bank deposits by, say, an equivalent amount. Consequently, the demand by spending units for primary securities is unchanged at current yields. Also, there is no change in this demand by the monetary system, since we have assumed the money supply constant. However, there is an increase in demand for primary securities by savings and loan associations. So, for the economy as a whole, there is an excess demand for primary securities at current yields, which is the counterpart of the excess supply of money.

Downward pressure on primary yields is exerted as long as the indirect debt of non-monetary intermediaries is to some degree competitive with money and as long as the additional demand for primary securities by these intermediaries is roughly equivalent to their creation of indirect debt.

7. For periods longer than the Keynesian short run, it is hardly safe to assume that transactions and contingency demands for additional money balances are proportional to increments in the level of money income. They may be elastic to interest rates on such primary securities as Treasury bills and brokers' loans. For any increment in money income, they may rise with real income. As a larger share of national income involves market transactions, as population moves from farms to cities, as a dollar of income is generated with more or fewer dollars of inter-

mediate payments, as credit practices change, as checks are collected more efficiently or as deposits cease to bear interest and bear service charges instead, one expects the marginal ratio of active balances to income to vary. And incremental demand for contingency balances must be sensitive not only to income, and perhaps to interest rates, but to the evolution of emergency credit facilities, to job security and social security, to an array of circumstances that is largely irrelevant in short-period analysis.

8. Our empirical work was made possible by Raymond W. Goldsmith's significant contributions, especially his *A Study of Saving in the United States* (Princeton, N.J.: Princeton University Press, 1955).

9. The flow of securities is measured in issue prices. The issues are net of retirements. The average for the full period is the cumulated flow of securities divided by cumulated GNP. For the entire period, this flow was about $180 billion. In 1898, the current value of outstanding primary securities was between $35 and $40 billion.

10. This is somewhat surprising in view of the large changes during the period in the proportion of total issues represented by each of the several types of issue. For example, at the turn of the century, mortgage issues were about 10 per cent of total issues, but the proportion grew rapidly to 25 per cent a decade later, and then to 35 per cent at the end of the period. On the other hand, consumer and other debt, mainly short-term consumer and business borrowing, moved in exactly the opposite way, from 35 per cent to about 10 per cent. United States government securities fluctuated widely as a percentage of total issues. Except for the first subperiod, the ratio was negligible to 1914. It was 33 per cent from 1915 to 1921, and then averaged over minus 10 per cent for the remainder of the period. Common and preferred stock issues, with two exceptions, were either a bit below or above 20 per cent of total issues during each subperiod. In the 1915–21 phase, the proportion was about 12 per cent, and it was 44 per cent from 1928 to 1930. State and local government securities gained relative to the others during the period while corporate and foreign bonds, if anything, lost some ground.

11. The share was a great deal higher than this though from 1922 to 1924 and somewhat higher from 1925 to 1927. The system purchased only 0.2 per cent of the issues from 1928 to 1930. However, excluding the "bad" years of 1929 and 1930, the system purchased only 29 per cent of the issues (from 1922 through 1928), which is much lower than its share from 1898 to 1904.

12. The first two factors may partly cancel. When g is high, ab tends to be high, too, and the reverse is also true.

13. W. Braddock Hickman, *Trends and Cycles in Corporate Bond Financing*, (Occasional Paper No. 37 [New York: National Bureau of Economic Research, 1952]), pp. 34–35. The use of the series carries a disadvantage, since our initial subperiod, 1898–1900, cannot be used in the correlation analysis.

14. The ratio used here is corrected for net foreign purchases of primary securities (see Table 2, ratio III).

15. The estimating equation is: average annual change in bond yield = −0.50 + 1.04049 (direct finance ratio).

16 *Providing for Growth of the Money Supply*

George S. Tolley *University of Chicago*

One often sees the observation that economic growth necessitates a continuing increase in the money supply. Some writers view the provision of this increase as the most important consideration of monetary policy. Others have taken account of it in formulating specific stabilization schemes for the economy, and still others feel that it offers a convenient way of helping to reduce the national debt. In spite of these views, there has been little explicit consideration of the alternative ways in which a given growth in the quantity of money might be achieved and even less consideration of the effects on policy goals of the various alternatives.

Decisions concerning the growth of the quantity of money may both affect and be affected by broader choices concerning the level of taxes and government expenditures and the management of the national debt. Moreover, the way in which increases in the quantity of money come about is closely related to the functioning of the banking system. This article considers the relevance of growth of the money supply for these matters.

Part one of the article identifies the reserve base of the money supply and the average reserve ratio for the money supply. The determinants of these two variables are discussed, and suggestions

Reprinted from *Journal of Political Economy*, Vol. 65 (December 1957), 465–85, by permission of the author and The University of Chicago Press. Copyright 1957 by The University of Chicago Press.

from previous literature as to their appropriate values are noted. Part two deals with the relation of choices of the reserve base and the average reserve ratio to the national debt. It makes explicit the sense in which growth of the money supply implies debt retirement and examines factors that have affected historical debt retirement associated with the money supply. Suggestions are made for predicting this debt retirement. The problem of how to relate choices of the reserve base and the average reserve ratio to debt policy is then discussed. Part three deals with the implications for resource allocation of the choice of the reserve base and the average reserve ratio. From this analysis emerges an estimate of the tax on deposits that is implied by the fact that no interest is paid on the reserve base. Finally, two specific programs are considered that are within the spirit of the present institutional framework and would take account of resource-allocation objectives in the choice of the reserve base and the average reserve ratio.

Framework for Analyzing Decisions Concerning the Money Supply

In the familiar consolidated statement published by the Federal Reserve Board called "Member-Bank Reserves, Reserve Bank Credit, and Related Items," the two terms "money in circulation" and "member bank reserve balances" are directly relevant to the money supply. I shall refer to the sum of the two terms as the "reserve base of the money supply." If we were interested only in the part of the money supply that is in the form of bank deposits, the reserve base would include member-bank reserves but not money in circulation. The latter is included because hand-to-hand currency forms part of the money supply.[1]

The reserve base, R, equals the money supply, M, multiplied by the average reserve ratio, ρ:

$$\rho M = R.$$

The average reserve ratio is jointly determined by government, banks, and the non-bank public. An important way in which the public may affect ρ is by changing the desired ratio of currency holdings to deposits. For example, a shift toward deposits away from currency decreases ρ, since every dollar of deposits requires only ten or fifteen cents of reserve base on the average, whereas a dollar of currency requires a full dollar of reserve base. One of several ways in which banks can influence ρ is through changes in excess reserves. In this paper we are particularly interested in government's influence on ρ. Government influences ρ via changes in required reserve ratios for deposits.[2]

From the equation in the preceding paragraph it is evident that there is a variety of reserves and reserve ratios that will result in a given stock of money. If we suppose that there will be a unique stock of money in some future year consistent with employment and price-level objectives, any change in the average reserve ratio implies a corresponding and proportionate change in the reserve base. For this reason, the reserve ratio affects the amount of debt retirement occurring as the quantity of money increases secularly. Moreover, the reserve ratio is an important variable in its own right, since it affects the functioning of the banking system. One part of monetary-fiscal management is thus the choice of a desirable combination of reserve ratios and reserves.

Aside from calling attention to this particular policy problem of the choice each year of one pair among the many possible pairs of values of ρ and R, the formulation that has been given helps to clarify the effects on government operations of growth in the money supply. The formulation might also be useful, even though no government action to influence ρ was contemplated in a particular year, in suggesting how to predict the debt retirement that would accompany growth of the money supply. One of the major purposes of this study is to clarify such effects so that they may be better predicted and planned for in monetary-fiscal management.

The main suggestions for an appropriate solution of the problem posed here come from writers who have not been directly concerned with growth of the money supply. We may distinguish four main types of suggested solutions. The solution that has perhaps received most attention is the 100 per cent reserve proposal. That is, in the terms used here, the reserve ratio would be (roughly) 1, and the amount of reserves would be equal to the quantity of money.[3] A second suggested solution has been that the creation of new money be backed by 100 per cent reserves. This implies (again, roughly) raising ρ gradually through time in such a way that R would increase by the same amount as the money supply.[4] A third solution does not lend itself readily to the present formulation, but it is so closely related to the others that it clearly deserves mention here. This solution is embodied in the various bond-reserve proposals for banks. These proposals differ from the others in having a somewhat more direct bearing on problems of debt management and bank earnings.[5] A fourth solution, namely, simply to maintain present arrangements, is implicit in most writings. Required reserve ratios would be maintained at present levels (or perhaps varied in connection with countercyclical actions), with ρ and R determined by the public and the banks given these required reserve ratios.

In expressed opinion we find no consensus as to whether ρ or R should largely guide our choice. Some of the proposals have been motivated by one and some by the other.[6] The tendency for debt rather than banking considerations to be more important in recent thinking is undoubtedly due in part to growth of the debt and in part to a loss of faith in the efficacy of monetary reform such as is embodied in the 100 per cent reserve plan.

National Debt Considerations

The statement was made earlier that increases in the money supply are a source of debt retirement. If this statement is true, where do we look in the government accounts to find this debt retirement? Debt retirement attributable to the money supply cannot be seen clearly in the budget surplus or deficit as usually defined, and a reinterpretation of government accounts is therefore desirable. One of the main manifestations of growth in the money supply is the increase at the Federal Reserve banks in member-bank reserve balances and in the item "currency in circulation," both of which tend to expand with growth of the money supply. These are liabilities, and their growth makes for a corresponding increase in assets. If we momentarily neglect changes in the gold stock, we see that the Federal Reserve banks in the normal course of their operations—open-market operations and the like—must find themselves accumulating earning assets, mainly government bonds.

Increases in earning assets of the Federal Reserve banks are a major part of the debt retirement associated with growth of the money supply. The view advanced here is that the holdings of securities of the Federal Reserve banks should be subtracted from the nominal national debt if we are to get a meaningful picture of the debt. Most of the earning assets of the Federal Reserve banks are, in any case, government bonds. The Federal Reserve banks might be viewed as repositories for fictitious federal debt. The fictitious nature of this debt is evidenced by the fact that, although interest is paid by the Treasury on this debt, a large portion of Federal Reserve bank earnings are transferred to the Treasury.

Like growth of the money supply, acquisitions or losses of gold do not appear in the budget as usually defined. In much the same way that the growth of the money supply represents debt retirement, an outflow of gold represents debt retirement. A normal effect of a gold outflow would be to deplete member-bank reserves, but Federal Reserve policy rightly aims at not allowing gold movements to affect the money supply. The ultimate effect of a gold outflow tends to be that the gold assets lost are replaced

TABLE 1   Yearly Changes Derived from "Member-Bank Reserves, Reserve Bank Credit, and Related Items"

(Millions of Dollars)[a]

| | SOURCES OF DEBT RETIREMENT | | DISPOSITION OF DEBT RETIREMENT | | |
| | Increase in reserve base, R^c | Decrease in gold stock | Increase in net Treasury currency[d] | Increase in reserve bank credit | Decrease in Federal Reserve liability items[e] |
Year[b]					
1921	− 775	− 410	99	−1247	− 39
1922	− 232	− 510	90	− 894	63
1923	392	− 265	124	0	3
1924	118	− 438	34	− 371	16
1925	190	128	− 7	313	12
1926	131	− 87	− 8	50	2
1927	− 14	− 140	7	− 112	− 48
1928	22	478	14	503	− 17
1929	− 20	− 215	9	− 185	− 60
1930	− 191	− 209	0	− 382	− 20
1931	292	− 421	− 17	− 75	− 37
1932	474	1037	41	1367	104
1933	336	− 399	183	− 90	− 156
1934	1487	−3825	−2607	252	18
1935	1334	−1260	225	8	− 159
1936	1327	−1492	361	− 7	− 521
1937	1473	−1710	− 896	89	571
1938	1138	− 645	1305	34	− 846
1939	2580	−3147	− 92	− 17	− 457
1940	4564	−3853	509	− 48	248
1941	1034	−2661	47	− 264	−1408
1942	2025	− 113	252	508	1152
1943	4818	349	683	4801	− 317
1944	5864	1215	− 1	7696	− 618
1945	6296	960	58	7032	167
1946	2702	− 57	422	2152	73
1947	41	− 996	950	−2286	378
1948	883	−2266	9	− 270	−1113
1949	68	− 934	52	−2204	1287
1950	−2270	235	19	− 993	−1060
1951	3739	2475	65	5340	808
1952	1578	−1590	97	− 492	382
1953	1279	883	124	1863	176
1954	− 753	536	553	228	− 999
1955	− 638	249	42	−1041	611
1956	863	− 121	74	618	50

[a] Sources: *Banking and Monetary Statistics* (Washington: Board of Governors of the Federal Reserve System, 1943), pp. 373–77, with more recent figures from *Federal Reserve Bulletin.*

by earning assets—probably government bonds—leaving member-bank reserves unaffected. The acquisition of earning assets by the Federal Reserve banks in response to the gold outflow is debt retirement in the same sense that acquisition of earning assets associated with growth of the money supply is debt retirement. Naturally, by the same line of reasoning, contractions in the money supply and inflows of gold can be considered to be debt-increasing.

It will be apparent that, in interpreting the government accounts, the Federal Reserve banks are being viewed in the present analysis as part of the government sector of the economy. This way of viewing them seems reasonable, since Federal Reserve banks are inseparably involved with the Treasury in buying and selling gold and in issuing money or the right to create money. The main determinant of Federal Reserve earnings is the extent of these transactions, and a large part of these earnings are transferred to the Treasury.

All this is made more explicit in Tables 1 and 2. In Table 1, yearly changes from the consolidated account "Member-Bank Reserves, Reserve Bank Credit, and Related Items" have been arranged to show how debt-retirement items have impinged on the government accounts. Debt retirement stems from increases in the reserve base, R, and decreases in the gold stock, which are shown in the first two columns. The sum of these two columns equals the sum of the remaining columns. Most of the debt retirement is reflected in increases in reserve bank credit, as suggested in the preceding discussion. However, because of institutional happenstance, which will not be considered here, the debt retirement may also be reflected in net Treasury currency and other Federal Reserve accounts.

"Member-Bank Reserves, Reserve Bank Credit, and Related Items" is a capital account or balance sheet. The interpretation just advanced can be extended to the current accounts by considering the earnings and expense statement of the Federal Reserve banks as summarized in Table 2. Since the bulk of the banks' earning assets are government securities, the banks receive few payments from the public. Treasury payments on these securities are "fictitious" government expenditures. That is, the government budget records them as expenditures, whereas in the present interpretation they are like an interagency transfer. Federal Reserve bank earnings other than on government securities are unrecorded

---

[b] End of June.

[c] Money in circulation plus member-bank reserve balances.

[d] Treasury currency outstanding minus Treasury cash holdings.

[e] Deposits other than member-bank reserve balances with Federal Reserve banks and other Federal Reserve accounts.

TABLE 2 Receipts and Disposition of Receipts of Federal Reserve Banks

(Millions of Dollars)*

	RECEIPTS		DISPOSITION OF RECEIPTS		
Year	From government securities	Other†	Paid to public‡	Paid to Treasury	Transferred to surplus
1920	7	174	38	61	83
1921	6	117	47	60	16
1922	17	34	40	11	− 1
1923	7	43	45	4	3
1924	15	24	41		− 3
1925	13	29	39		2
1926	13	35	38	1	8
1927	14	29	38		5
1928	11	53	40	3	21
1929	8	63	44	4	23
1930	17	19	39		− 2
1931	12	17	37		− 7
1932	27	23	37	2	11
1933	38	12	50		− 1
1934	46	3	42		6
1935	40	3	42		1
1936	35	3	37		
1937	39	2	38		3
1938	34	2	35		1
1939	37	2	34		4
1940	42	1	26		18
1941	40	1	41		1
1942	51	1	49		4
1943	68	1	29		40
1944	103	2	55		49
1945	140	3	60		82
1946	147	3	69		81
1947	156	3	75	75	8
1948	299	5	119	167	19
1949	312	4	102	193	21
1950	273	3	57	197	22
1951	389	6	111	255	28
1952	442	14	118	292	46
1953	497	16	130	343	40
1954	435	4	126	276	36
1955	399	14	128	252	33
1956	572	24	140	402	54

* Sources: *Banking and Monetary Statistics* (Washington: Board of Governors of the Federal Reserve System, 1943), p. 356, with more recent figures from *Federal Reserve Bulletin.*

† Total current earnings minus earnings from government securities.

‡ Total current earnings minus net current earnings before payments to the Treasury plus dividends paid.

government receipts. Federal Reserve receipts are offset in part by expenses of the Federal Reserve banks and by payments to the Treasury. The offset is not exact, however; the difference is equal to transfers to surplus. In consolidating the Federal Reserve banks into the government sector, these transfers to surplus should be added to the receipts of the government to arrive at the budget surplus or deficit.

Tables 1 and 2 have shown how, in the accounts, the effect of the money supply on the debt is obscured by the handling of gold under present arrangements and by the issuance of Treasury currency. Were it not for these two items, the effects of the money supply on debt could be directly related to holdings of securities by the Federal Reserve banks. These items have reduced the amount of debt accumulated by the Federal Reserve in connection with growth of the money supply. There has nevertheless been a substantial increase in Federal Reserve earnings because of increased holdings of government securities. The government budget surplus or deficit, as usually measured, has not been greatly affected by these intra-government payments because (1) the Federal Reserve has, in turn, made payments to the public and (2) it has made offsetting intra-government payments by transferring a large part of its unspent earnings to the Treasury.

Having considered how the money supply is a source of debt retirement, let us now consider factors that affect the extent of this debt retirement.

Because—as we saw on pages 83–85—the reserve base, R, is equal to the average reserve ratio, ρ, times the money supply, M, debt retirement may stem from increases both in the average reserve ratio and in the money supply. Moreover, the money supply can be related to variables that have considerable interest both analytically and from a policy point of view. Consider the Cambridge-type equation of exchange,

$$M = KPY,$$

where P is the price level, Y is real national income, and K is the reciprocal of the income velocity of money. If we substitute this in the fundamental relation from Part I (namely, $R = \rho M$), we have

$$R = \rho KPY.$$

Two different interpretations of this identity may be considered. First, it may be viewed as a way of predicting the effects of increases in the reserve base, R, which might be brought about through Federal Reserve open-market purchases. Viewed in this way, the identity delineates the possible effects of the increase. At one extreme, there might be a compensating increase in the average reserve ratio, ρ, perhaps due simply to an increase in excess reserves. In this event the money supply and hence the remaining variables, K, P, and Y, might not change. As we shall see shortly, however, the determinants of ρ are ordinarily rather stable, so that a compensating increase in ρ is unlikely.[7] Another possibility is that there would be a compensating decline in velocity (increase in K), in which case P and Y still might not be affected. If we could predict the extent of the change in velocity, then, depending on the state of full employment or unemployment in the economy, we could go about predicting the effect of the increase in the reserve base, R, on the price level, P, and real income, Y.

A second interpretation of the identity is of more interest for this discussion than the one just considered. This second interpretation is suggested by the observation that policy objectives pertaining to the price level and income are obviously of overriding importance in comparison with debt retirement. The identity allows one to see what the implications of price level and income changes are for debt retirement. A given set of values of the variables on the right-hand side is consistent with one and only one value for the reserve base R. Hence the identity enables us to see how debt retirement attributable to the money supply has been associated with the joint outcome of changes in the average reserve ratio, velocity, the price level, and real income.

With this second interpretation of the identity in mind, let us look at the historical data. Table 3 is derived by multiplying the percentage changes in ρ, K, P, and Y by the value of R in the previous year. Estimates are thus obtained of an amount of debt retirement associated with these variables each year. The sum of these changes is not exactly equal to the change in R, and the interaction effect of the variables is also presented.[8]

The figures in Table 3 suggest that all the factors shown have at times been significant. As we might expect, the growth of real income appears to be the most consistent factor making for debt retirement. The price-level column suggests very literally and dramatically how much debt was monetized through inflation in the 1940's. Changes associated with velocity have at times been substantial in both directions. The effects of the much-discussed secular decline in velocity, however, do not show through in these figures. Even in the relatively stable period of the 1920's, changes associated with velocity seem to be positive about as often as negative. Apparently, then, it is principally because of growth in real income and of inflation that increases in M have been a highly consistent and substantial source of debt retirement.

For ρ, the pattern is one of decreases in the 1920's, increases in the 1930's, and decreases in the 1940's and 1950's. For some years, such as 1922 and 1950, the decreases were big enough to outweigh

TABLE 3 Analysis of Yearly Changes in the Reserve Base, R

(Millions of Dollars)*

		ASSOCIATION OF CHANGE IN R WITH OTHER VARIABLES				
Year†	Change in R	ρ	K	P	Y	Interaction of ρ, K, P, Y
1921	− 775	− 409	1839	−1322	− 538	−344
1922	− 232	− 458	− 178	− 221	674	− 49
1923	392	− 149	− 319	170	732	− 42
1924	118	− 161	387	− 52	− 42	− 14
1925	190	− 341	− 150	202	506	− 28
1926	131	− 168	87	− 159	388	− 16
1927	− 14	− 232	357	− 139	12	− 12
1928	22	− 280	144	62	106	− 10
1929	− 20	− 68	− 346	− 39	458	− 25
1930	− 191	− 102	872	− 259	− 619	− 83
1931	292	506	1061	− 644	− 492	−140
1932	474	1697	805	− 711	− 995	−322
1933	336	1125	− 373	− 274	− 48	− 93
1934	1487	779	− 532	409	804	27
1935	1334	293	− 25	212	814	39
1936	1327	261	− 407	65	1427	− 19
1937	1473	1306	− 877	532	566	− 54
1938	1138	782	1226	− 234	− 592	− 44
1939	2580	1392	− 48	− 129	1259	106
1940	4564	2611	− 178	256	1626	249
1941	1034	−1213	−2362	1705	3352	−449
1942	2025	− 48	−3260	3125	2786	−579
1943	4818	−1535	1466	1744	3046	98
1944	5864	1452	1144	619	2268	381
1945	6296	− 247	6301	1065	− 789	− 33
1946	2702	−2757	6757	3653	−4074	−877
1947	41	−1668	−2592	4652	64	−416
1948	883	453	−4450	2403	2132	345
1949	68	86	127	303	− 448	0
1950	−2270	−3642	−3733	599	3974	532
1951	3739	2340	−5128	3042	2771	714
1952	1578	−1123	159	810	1662	70
1953	1279	− 707	− 286	445	2086	−259
1954	− 753	−2325	2022	94	− 994	450
1955	− 638	−2951	−1297	601	2809	200
1956	863	− 416	−1251	1474	1183	−127

* Sources: *Banking and Monetary Statistics* (Washington: Board of Governors of the Federal Reserve System, 1943), pp. 34–35, 373–77, with more recent figures from *Federal Reserve Bulletin;* U.S. Department of Commerce, *National Income and Product of the United States* (Washington: Government Printing Office, 1951), pp. 146 and 150, with more recent figures from *Survey of Current Business.*

† R and ρ, end of June.

the effects of increases in the money supply. The years 1931–33 are particularly interesting. Here the money supply was contracting. This was more than offset, however, by increases in ρ, so that the net effect was one of debt retirement. All the changes associated with ρ are sizable. Changes in this variable significantly increased debt retirement in the 1930's and decreased it in the rest of the period.

Table 4 shows the relative importance of the various determinants of ρ and suggests why it has changed.[9] Declines in the proportion of the money supply in the form of currency have been the chief source of changes in ρ in recent years. Over the longer run, increases in the average required reserve ratio for deposits have also been important.

Tables 3 and 4 suggest how the identity we have been considering might be used by policy-makers to predict future debt retirement associated with the growth of the money supply. The identity might be used in the following way. Trends for the variables on the right-hand side would be studied. Given that full employment is desirable and may ordinarily be achieved, a growth in real income, Y, of something like 3 per cent per year may be expected. Policy-makers may wish to plan for a stable level of prices, or, perhaps more realistically, for slightly rising prices. In a secular context, velocity as determined by behavior in the private sector appears to be rather stable—perhaps subject to slight decline over time. Aside from required reserve ratios, ρ is also largely determined in the private sector and appears to be subject to a rather smooth secular decrease. All these trends would be put into the identity so as to predict and plan for the debt retirement associated with the growth of the money supply. The effect of planned changes in ρ resulting from changes in required reserve ratios could obviously also be included in the scheme.[10]

Thus far we have been largely concerned with the mechanics of the debt retirement and its prediction. Let us now consider the central question of what light the debt effects of the money supply throw on choosing optimal values of ρ and R. In doing this, it may be well to emphasize that large sums are involved and that therefore the question appears to be important. The figures that have been presented indicate that, under present circumstances, with ρ in the neighborhood of 0.20 to 0.25, the growth of the money supply accounts for about one and a half billion dollars of debt retirement yearly.

The possibilities for debt retirement through changes in ρ are also great. As indicated in Table 3, the effects of changes in ρ have often been of the same order of magnitude as the effects of real income. Many of the changes in ρ have, of course, been the

TABLE 4 *Analysis of the Average Reserve Ratio, ρ**

		NON-BANK PUBLIC		BANKS			
		Currency	Deposits‡	Excess reserves‡	Currency	Deposits‡	Government deposits‡
Year†	ρ	$\rho_C \times M_C/M$	$\rho_M \times D/M \times M_M/D$	R_E/M	$\rho_C \times M'_C/M$	$\rho_M \times M'_M/M$	$\rho_M \times M'_M/M$
1920	0.177	1 × 0.104	× 0.896 × 0.609		1 × 0.027	× 0.087	× 0.009
1921	.167	1 × .098	× .902 × .600		1 × .026	× .072	× .012
1922	.154	1 × .086	× .914 × .626		1 × .021	× .080	× .005
1923	.151	1 × .088	× .912 × .609		1 × .019	× .075	× .008
1924	.147	1 × .082	× .918 × .626		1 × .021	× .086	× .006
1925	.139	1 × .074	× .926 × .633		1 × .020	× .083	× .006
1926	.137	1 × .072	× .928 × .631		1 × .020	× .078	× .006
1927	.131	1 × .068	× .932 × .640		1 × .019	× .078	× .006
1928	.126	1 × .067	× .933 × .627		1 × .016	× .071	× .007
1929	.124	1 × .066	0.065 × .934 × .620		1 × .015	0.065 × .067	0.065 × .008
1930	.123	1 × .062	× .938 × .651		1 × .016	× .086	× .008
1931	.132	1 × .070	× .930 × .628		1 × .017	× .091	× .013
1932	.164	1 × .103	.065 × .897 × .587	0.004	1 × .018	.065 × .069	.065 × .022
1933	.189	1 × .117	.068 × .883 × .601	.012	1 × .016	.068 × .081	.068 × .039
1934	.208	1 × .105	.068 × .895 × .617	.039	1 × .016	.068 × .098	.068 × .051
1935	.215	1 × .097	.073 × .903 × .643	.049	1 × .016	.073 × .110	.073 × .022
1936	.220	1 × .097	.072 × .903 × .676	.050	1 × .019	.072 × .123	.072 × .022
1937	.244	1 × .101	.145 × .900 × .707	.016	1 × .018	.145 × .111	.145 × .013
1938	.259	1 × .097	.125 × .903 × .675	.051	1 × .019	.125 × .117	.125 × .011
1939	.284	1 × .100	.128 × .900 × .688	.069	1 × .017	.128 × .130	.128 × .013

(*Continued*)

TABLE 4 (Continued)

		NON-BANK PUBLIC		BANKS			
		Currency	Deposits‡	Excess reserves‡	Currency	Deposits‡	Government deposits‡
Year†	ρ	$\rho_C \times M_C/M$	$\rho_M \times D/M \times M_M/D$	R_E/M	$\rho_C \times M'_C/M$	$\rho_M \times M'_M/M$	$\rho_M \times M'_M/M$
1940	.327	1 × .101	.134 × .899 × .694	.104	1 × .017	.134 × .147	.134 × .012
1941	.309	1 × .112	.134 × .888 × .727	.071	1 × .019	.134 × .142	.134 × .009
1942	.308	1 × .136	.151 × .863 × .747	.034	1 × .018	.151 × .124	.151 × .022
1943	.289	1 × .155	.126 × .845 × .767	.014	1 × .016	.126 × .103	.126 × .072
1944	.303	1 × .179	.113 × .821 × .758	.012	1 × .014	.113 × .093	.113 × .152
1945	.301	1 × .181	.113 × .819 × .742	.011	1 × .012	.113 × .088	.113 × .159
1946	.281	1 × .168	.123 × .832 × .751	.007	1 × .011	.123 × .075	.123 × .077
1947	.271	1 × .160	.133 × .840 × .749	.004	1 × .012	.133 × .067	.133 × .007
1948	.273	1 × .155	.142 × .846 × .747	.004	1 × .014	.142 × .065	.142 × .012
1949	.274	1 × .153	.145 × .847 × .744	.006	1 × .013	.145 × .063	.145 × .013
1950	.254	1 × .148	.126 × .852 × .748	.003	1 × .012	.126 × .064	.126 × .021
1951	.268	1 × .148	.143 × .852 × .755	.002	1 × .012	.143 × .065	.143 × .034
1952	.262	1 × .143	.141 × .857 × .759	.001	1 × .014	.141 × .069	.141 × .031
1953	.258	1 × .142	.138 × .858 × .752	.001	1 × .014	.138 × .067	.138 × .019
1954	.246	1 × .136	.124 × .863 × .749	0.003	1 × .014	.124 × .074	.124 × .028
1955	.232	1 × .132	.117 × .868 × .750		1 × .014	.117 × .069	.117 × .024
1956	0.230	1 × 0.132	0.116 × 0.868 × 0.750		1 × 0.011	0.116 × 0.068	0.116 × 0.022

* Sources: *Banking and Monetary Statistics* (Washington: Board of Governors of the Federal Reserve System, 1943), pp. 34–35, 72–75, and 373–77, with more recent figures from *Federal Reserve Bulletin*.
† End of June.
‡ Excess reserves not available for 1920–31; calculation of ρ_M for those years is prevented.

436

effect of private rather than government behavior. Many of the changes have been associated with shifts in the form in which the public holds money. For instance, a shift away from low-reserve-using money, such as time deposits, toward high-reserve-using money, such as demand deposits and currency, implies a rise in ρ. However, there have also been changes in required reserve ratios.

Two effects of a change in ρ on debt retirement may be noted. First, if there is a rise in ρ, the reserve base—for a given money supply—must increase proportionally. Second, in subsequent periods changes in the money supply will have a magnified influence on the reserve base.

As an example of possibilities at an extreme, suppose 100 per cent reserve requirements were introduced. Then ρ would be somewhat greater than 1.[11] The increase in the reserve base R would be something like $175 billion, given the present money supply. We may suppose that most of the assets acquired by the Federal Reserve banks would be government bonds. As noted previously, this may be considered to be debt retirement, since the interest on bonds held by the Federal Reserve tends not to be paid to the public but to revert to the Treasury or to some extent to be transferred to the surplus account of the Federal Reserve banks. With 100 per cent reserves, then, the federal debt held outside the Federal Reserve would be reduced to a small fraction of its present value.

A second result of 100 per cent reserves would be a magnified effect of future increases in the money supply. If we conservatively suppose that the money supply will grow at a rate of 3 per cent per year, the asset acquisitions of the Federal Reserve—if member banks were required to carry 100 per cent reserves—would be over $6 billion per year in view of the fact that the money supply is well over $200 billion. This would quadruple the debt retirement that is taking place under present arrangements.

The literature is not completely lacking in proposals motivated by the debt effects of the money supply. It has been suggested that we plan a yearly deficit equal to the debt retirement arising from increases in the money supply.[12] This would seem to imply that the present size of the debt, whatever it may happen to be, is optimal. It has also been suggested that, by maintaining a balanced budget, we allow the growth of the money supply gradually to retire the debt.[13] This would seem to imply that the optimal debt is zero and that the optimal rate of retirement is arbitrarily dictated by the growth of the money supply.

To relate the choice of ρ and R explicitly to debt policy might be more desirable than the two procedures just noted. We may conjecture that, even in the absence of any transition problems,

the optimal size of the debt is greater than zero and, further, that
it increases secularly, perhaps being some multiple of income.[14]
If we make these suppositions and abstract from transition problems, the optimal values of ρ and the debt, together with the increasing money supply, determine the optimal government deficit
in any year. This proposal, unlike the proposals mentioned above,
involves a deficit somewhat greater than the debt retirement associated with the growth of the money supply, in order to increase
the debt secularly.

The idea that it would be desirable to have a secularly increasing
debt arises from visualizing a moving equilibrium in which the
portfolio items of the banks and the non-bank public all grow
according to some secular pattern. Suppose, for instance, that the
optimal situation is one in which the quantities of all assets are
increasing at the same rate—say at 3 per cent per year. Then, in
order that the quantity of government securities may increase by
3 per cent, the required government deficit is 0.03 (public debt +
ρ_M). This is because the injection of new securities must allow for
the debt retirement that will be associated with growth.[15]

Since the present values of ρ and the debt are probably non-
optimal, both the optimal values and the rate of transition would
need to be determined. There is probably universal agreement
that we should not attempt very large changes in the debt in any
one year, and there is probably nearly as complete agreement
that the present debt is too large. These considerations suggest
that, for the years in the immediate future, declines in the quantity
of government securities are desirable.[16]

Resource-Allocation Considerations

Changes in ρ may affect bank service charges. This is because
such changes affect a main source of bank earnings, namely,
holdings of earning financial assets. This raises the suspicion that
we are involved in a resource-allocation problem. Variations in
service charges may be expected to influence the volume of deposits that people wish to hold, and thus we find that we are concerned with the question: What is the optimum volume of bank
deposits?[17]

The optimum quantity of commodity X, so the usual analysis
runs, is that which would prevail under perfect competition.
Applied to bank deposits, a *first* supposition might be that bank
charges corresponding to 100 per cent reserves would induce the
optimum volume of deposits. This would be supported by the

notion that the cost of producing money is the cost of mining gold, to which should be added the service costs associated with deposit procedures. However, the notion that the cost of producing money is the cost of mining gold is not tenable, as is perhaps most convincingly shown by the existence of fractional reserve banking. Put more strongly, the absurdity of foregoing the resources needed to mine an amount of gold equivalent to the entire money supply is apparent. Yet such a view is inherent in this first supposition. A *second* supposition might be at the opposite extreme that, in holding deposits, depositors should forego only service costs, since resources other than those used for servicing are not required to produce deposits. (The difference between the interest on securities and interest on deposits would just equal service costs.) Banking procedures indicate that this supposition is also wrong, at least if applied to a gold standard. As a practical matter, banks cannot function without some reserves. A *third* supposition is, then, that under a gold standard, with competition in banking, we might expect an optimal situation in which depositors' costs included both service charges and the cost of mining the fractional amount of gold behind each dollar. This supposition seems tenable, except that nations do not operate on a gold standard nowadays. Our final position is that without a gold standard, since reserves then cost nothing to produce, we revert to the second solution, in which depositors forego only service costs.

If this final position is valid—as I believe it to be—what are the indications for policy? Disregarding policy aims other than optimum resource allocation, ρ should be determined by competition in the banking system, which would almost certainly result in a lower ρ than now prevails. Alternatively, interest might be paid by the Federal Reserve banks on member-bank reserves. In this way banks would be enabled to pass on to depositors the savings from having fiat instead of gold reserves.

The preceding argument suggests that the acquisition of assets by the Federal Reserve in connection with the growth of deposit money constitutes the proceeds from a tax on deposits. Let us try to examine the way in which the tax manifests itself. To do this, assume that banking is a competitive industry, one of whose functions is to provide bank-account services. With fractional reserve banking, deposit creation enables banks to earn income other than from service charges. Competition keeps service charges below the cost of providing bank-account services by the amount of income associated with the asset holdings made possible by deposit creation. Service charges may then possibly be negative, taking the form of interest paid on deposits.

The following expression estimates the average rate of return on non-cash assets:

$$\frac{\text{Gross bank earnings minus service-charge income}}{\text{Total assets minus cash assets}}$$

The numerator of this expression is of particular interest. It is intended to approximate bank income associated with holdings of assets. Suppose that a part of this income can be attributed to deposit creation, as follows: (Average rate of return on non-cash assets) × (total deposits minus cash assets). The idea is that for all deposits in excess of reserves of cash assets there are corresponding holdings of earning assets yielding the average rate of return.[18] Our estimate of the cost per deposit dollar of providing bank-account service, then, is: (Average rate of return on non-cash assets) × (1 minus the ratio of cash assets to deposits) + (service-charge income per deposit dollar). This estimate is obtained by adding service-charge income to the component of asset earnings attributed to deposits and dividing the resulting expression by total deposits. The procedure arises from the assumption made in the preceding paragraph that competition will make the sum of these two kinds of income equal to the cost to banks of providing bank-account services.

For member banks, the 1951–54 average estimated cost of providing bank-account services is 2.44 per cent. The estimate results from multiplying the average rate of return on non-cash assets, 3.44 per cent, by the fraction of deposits not backed by cash, 0.748, and adding service charges of −0.13 per cent. The net negative service charge results from interest paid on time deposits, which is about twice as great as receipts of service charges on deposits.[19]

Let us pause to note that the preceding calculations permit us to conjecture what changes might take place with changes in required reserves for deposits. Perhaps the simplest way to state the conclusion is that, as cash assets are raised toward 100 per cent of deposits, service charges must approach about $2\frac{1}{2}$ per cent if bank earnings are not to change and if the composition of banks' remaining earning assets is not altered. Since required reserves are only part of cash assets, required ratios could actually be raised to a point at which service charges somewhat exceeded my estimate. The opinion may be ventured that the estimated maximum service charge is not so large as to cause great concern, given time for adjustments to take place; that is, no disaster seems to be implied by the adjustments in service charges that the alternative choices would involve.

We are now in a position to obtain a crude measure of the tax on deposits. Let us assume for a minute that cash assets are zero. Then, corresponding to every dollar of deposit liability, we could visualize a full dollar's worth of earning assets. This would contrast with the situation in 1951–54, when, because of cash assets, we find only $0.748 of non-cash assets for a dollar of deposit liability. Hence the estimate of the rate of return on non-cash assets is 3.44 per cent, we can visualize an increase in bank earnings for every deposit dollar of $(1 - 0.748) \times 3.44$ per cent, or 0.87 per cent. To estimate the tax, we need to consider required reserves and not simply total cash assets. During the period, required reserves were almost exactly half of total cash assets.[20] Applying this figure to total cash assets gives the estimate that earnings per deposit dollar would be increased 0.43 per cent if required reserves were zero.

This result may be incorporated into the previous analysis. Since banks' earning assets yield 3.44 per cent and banks pay (net) 0.13 per cent on deposits, we can call 3.31 per cent the charge for money. The latter is the return foregone in holding money, assuming that money-holders could choose the same average asset composition as banks if they substituted earning assets for money. It is supposed here that, of this charge, 2.44 per cent is paid to the productive factors (labor and capital) that provide bank-account services.[21] An additional cost is the return foregone by banks in holding non-reserve cash assets, amounting to 0.43 per cent, as derived in the preceding paragraph. If this reduction in asset earnings is added to the cost of bank-account services, the estimated total cost of providing a deposit dollar is 2.87 per cent. The remaining 0.43 per cent as we total to the 3.31 per cent charge for money is the return foregone in holding required reserves.[22] The 0.43 per cent is the estimate of the tax. Put in ad valorem terms, the estimate of the tax is about 15 per cent[23] of the cost of providing deposit money.[24]

Suppose one wished to alleviate the tax on deposits. This would require that service charges be reduced on deposits where these are now levied, and it would require that interest rates be increased on deposits that draw interest. Existing legal restrictions over banks in these matters might therefore need to be lifted or altered. As required reserves were lowered or—alternatively—as interest began to be paid on reserves, it would be desirable to watch banks' behavior to check on whether the increased earnings tended to be kept by banks or whether through competition they were passed along to depositors. If they were not passed along, the establishment of maximum service charges and minimum interest rates might be contemplated.

In the manner just described, the return foregone in holding deposits would be reduced. That is, the price of deposits would decline, and one would expect the demand for them to increase, with deposits being substituted for other assets. This conjecture stems from a belief that the demand for money—in real or deflated terms—depends on the return foregone in holding money. We would be moving along the demand schedule for (real) money and for this reason would expect the real quantity of money to increase. Other things being equal, this implies a decline in the velocity of circulation of money. Would there be undesirable disorganization in the financial markets because of the asset substitutions just referred to? My feeling is that the substitutions would not be large enough to cause disorganization. As a precautionary measure, however, the tax on deposits might be reduced only gradually. This would help to prevent disorganization that might be caused by sudden change, and it would enable one to see through experience the magnitude of the effects of reducing the tax on deposits.

Thus far, we have discussed taxation only on deposit money. What about the other part of the money supply—hand-to-hand currency? The tax on hand-to-hand currency consists of the earnings that holders of currency forego over and above the small costs of creating the currency. The revenue from the tax is the increased holding of earning assets by the Federal Reserve, made possible by the fact that currency is provided to the public at a price greater than its cost of production. The tax is much higher on currency than on deposits, since the Federal Reserve accumulates several fold more earnings assets for each dollar's growth in currency than for an equal growth in deposits.[25]

The tax on currency could be alleviated by paying interest on currency. This would be more novel than the previous proposal to pay interest on reserves, but it is suggested by the same logic.[26]

Resource-allocation considerations thus give us a very definite answer to the choice of ρ and R. It is important to note that this choice, if taken, would make unnecessary much of the analysis in the earlier parts of this paper. There would be no debt retirement associated with growth of the money supply, since earnings on securities deposited as reserves would not be retained by the government.

Are there policy desiderata that militate against the choice that is indicated by resource-allocation considerations? One argument against the choice might be that the contribution to *aggregate cyclical stability* of maintaining higher reserves than would prevail under banking competition is worth the cost in resource allocation. However, this argument seems weak for two reasons. First, other equally good (better?) counter cyclicaldevices are available. Second, regardless of the level of required reserves, interest could be paid on reserves so as to alleviate the tax on deposits.[27]

A second possible argument against the choice indicated by resource-allocation considerations might be that continued *purchases of gold are a cost of providing money*. It can be argued that, were it not for monetary arrangements, these purchases would be unnecessary and that they can be offset, roughly, by debt retirement associated with the growth in reserves. From our earlier consideration of the government accounts, it can be seen that debt retirement from reserves would exactly offset gold purchases under a gold standard. This argument condones the practice of having the government accumulate gold. The costs of this practice are hardly negligible, and it does not seem to be desirable to obscure these costs by pretending that there is a relation between the money supply and the stock of gold.[28]

A third argument might be that the *tax on deposits is a legitimate excise*. Obviously, however, the tax came about by historical accident. It is difficult to think of reasons for regarding it as a good tax in its own right.

A final argument might be that the *assumption of competition in banking is invalid*. This argument fails not because of any proof that competition is effective in banking but because forcing banks to forego interest on required reserves does not seem a sensible way to combat lapses from competition.

Aside from the policy desiderata that have been considered, are there serious practical problems of implementation that stand in the way of the resource-allocation choice? One problem in implementing the choice would be to specify the rate of interest to be paid by the Federal Reserve. Conceptually, we can visualize a rate such that the central bank pays out exactly the earnings on assets acquired in money creation. These assets may not be completely identifiable in practice, partly because the Federal Reserve acquires some assets not connected with money creation and partly because some non-Federal Reserve accounts (for example, Treasury currency) are connected with money creation. It is even more challenging to specify what form the Federal Reserve ought to give to the assets it holds, since this obviously affects the extent of its earnings. This article has not attempted to throw any light on the question of what is optimum portfolio composition for the central bank.

Other problems of implementation center around gold. We may accurately say that in the past the acquisition of the gold stock has been financed by the tax on money. As we saw in discussing national debt considerations, the *decrease* in earning assets that is implied by gold acquisition is the government payment for the gold. The *increase* in government earning assets implied by additions to member-bank reserves and to currency in circulation is the revenue from the tax on money. A principal reason for the historical net acquisition of earning assets by the Federal Reserve is that the revenue from the tax has been greater than the value of gold purchases.

Under the policy in question, that of eliminating the tax, there would be no increase in earnings from future additions to the money supply. The Federal Reserve would not have the means it has had in the past of offsetting its gold acquisitions and could thus look forward to a continuous decrease in earnings as assets were exchanged for gold. Other sources of revenue would become necessary to carry out this program.

Perhaps the worst difficulty of all is that the Federal Reserve might find itself insolvent immediately. Not only must additions to the gold stock be financed, but the existing stocks of gold and money must be considered. Because of past gold acquisitions, the offsetting asset to a large amount of member-bank reserves and currency in circulation is gold rather than earning assets. Consequently, the Federal Reserve does not have enough earnings to make the tax on the present money stock zero. To alleviate the tax on money completely, that is, to be able to pay interest on liabilities by having an amount of earning assets equal to them, it would be necessary not only to make provision for paying for continuing additions to the gold stock but also—in effect—to purchase the existing stock of gold. The purchase could be accomplished by issuing government securities to the Federal Reserve in an amount equal to the gold stock. This would obviously represent a sizable increase in the national debt and in concomitant payments of interest on the debt. These additional receipts of interest on the government bonds by the Federal Reserve are precisely what would enable it to pay the interest on its own liabilities.

Do these problems that would be encountered rule out any practical application of the conclusions reached in our earlier analysis? A negative answer to this question is indicated by two more restricted applications of the analysis that will be discussed in closing.

Most of the difficulties just mentioned could be circumvented by paying interest on member-bank reserves at the same rate as on government bonds. In fact, reserves might simply take the form of government bonds. Since government bonds are the type of security that has usually been acquired by the Federal Reserve, no drastic change from present portfolio behavior would be required of the Federal Reserve.

If interest were paid on member-bank reserves only, perhaps both the chief strength and the chief weakness would arise in refraining from paying interest on hand-to-hand currency. It would not then be necessary to make adjustments connected with the existing stock of gold because currency in circulation somewhat exceeds the gold stock. The Federal Reserve has enough earning assets to pay interest on bank reserves if it does not attempt to pay interest on currency. Future increases in the amount of hand-to-hand currency would provide some offset to possible future additions to the gold stock. However, it might still be necessary to find supplemental sources of revenue in order to finance gold acquisitions completely.[29]

While the pricing of deposits vis-à-vis non-money should be improved by paying interest on member-bank reserves, perhaps the main weakness of the scheme would be worse pricing of deposits vis-à-vis currency. The scheme aims at eliminating the tax on deposits but would not reduce the present high tax on currency that is implied in failure to pay interest on currency.

Now consider a second possible application of our conclusions. Though this proposal does not go so far as the scheme just considered, it might nonetheless represent a substantial improvement over present procedures. An explicit policy might be followed of making the proceeds of the tax on money equal to the value of additions to the gold stock. Central-bank operations, *including* gold acquisition, would then yield zero profit. From the point of view of welfare, we would have a situation resembling the gold standard.

This policy assumes that we should try to do at least as well as a gold standard in achieving welfare goals while providing the money supply. The historical net acquisition of earning assets by the Federal Reserve suggests that we may not now be meeting that norm. Under a gold standard, the charge for money tends to be just enough to cover costs of acquiring the gold that is concomitant to the money, while, under present arrangements, the charge for money more than covers gold costs.

The important difference between this policy and a gold standard as usually visualized is that the stock of money would not vary in response to changes in the gold stock. Rather, the average reserve ratio, ρ, would vary. The stock of money would be varied according to price level and employment objectives, as is clearly in line with present policy intent. That is, countercyclical action could continue to be taken independently of the gold stock, as it is at present, which is not possible under a gold standard as traditionally visualized. The contrast with present policy is that, at present, the earning assets of the Federal Reserve rather than ρ tend to vary with changes in the gold stock.

Under present procedure, when gold is acquired, the Federal Reserve loses earning assets. Depending on the rate of gold accumulation as compared with increases in the money supply, the Federal Reserve may have either a net gain or a net loss of earning assets over time.[30] Historically, as we have seen, it has had a net gain. Under the policy being considered, required reserve ratios would be varied in response to differing relative rates of gold accumulation and increases in the money supply, so that in the future there might be little or no net change in earning assets. Ideally, the policy would be started from a position of substantially no earning assets—a zero profit level—that would be unaltered as the policy operated through time. However, the policy would not necessarily have to be initiated at such a position. If initiated from the present level, the implication would be that the Federal Reserve would keep present earning assets but would look forward to acquiring—or losing—no more in the future.

Typically, under the suggested policy, there would be two responses to an inflow of gold. First, there would be sales of securities, in an amount equal to the gold inflow. In this way potential reserve funds would be kept from rising. Second—and this is the novel part of the policy—required reserve ratios would be raised so that reserve funds required for the existing quantity of money would rise by the amount of the gold inflow. The earning assets acquired as member banks increased their reserves would then just equal the amount lost through the open-market sale.

On the other hand, increases in the quantity of money would result in lower required reserve ratios. With no change in required reserve ratios, earning assets of the Federal Reserve normally tend to rise as the quantity of money increases. As this happened, the Federal Reserve would simply reduce required reserve ratios, so as to restore its original volume of earning assets.

Perhaps the most significant difference between present practice and the policy suggested here is that under the latter more frequent changes would be made in required reserve ratios. The Federal Reserve could thus begin following the policy immediately in its day-to-day operations if it so desired.[31] Unlike the possible policy discussed earlier, this policy does not involve any drastic change, such as paying interest on reserves or currency. It seems entirely consistent with the spirit of present arrangements. This is particularly true because present institutional arrangements obviously still have a strong gold-standard orientation. The policy may be viewed as an attempt to follow a gold standard as nearly as is feasible, given that internal monetary policies are to be pursued independently of the gold stock.

The possibility we have been discussing may also be viewed as providing a criterion for setting required reserve ratios. There has been a notable lack of criteria for desirable levels of reserve ratios. Although reserve ratios are often adjusted countercyclically, on an *ad hoc* basis, there appears to be no consensus that they provide a good countercyclical weapon. Meanwhile, the amount of earning assets of the Federal Reserve has tended to be a meaningless residual of effects of gold movements and changes connected with the money supply. The possibility we have discussed would eliminate these imprecisions. It would aim at a situation in which users of money bear neither more nor less than the cost of the gold stock, in place of a situation in which money is taxed capriciously.

Conclusion

The reserve base, R, of the money supply has been defined here to comprise currency in circulation plus member-bank reserves, and the average reserve ratio, ρ, has been defined as the ratio of the reserve base to the money supply. Determinants of the reserve base and the average reserve ratio are often considered as independent variables, whose net effect is to determine the money supply. For instance, under present arrangements, a shift of the public's desired ratio of currency to deposits would change the money supply—if there were no compensating change in the reserve base. That is, such a shift would change the average reserve ratio and, with a given reserve base, would change the money supply.

In the present analysis, however, compensating changes in the reserve base and the average reserve ratio have been realistically supposed to take place. The assumption has been that the Federal Reserve authorities will insure that adjustments between the reserve base and the average reserve ratio will result in a given money supply, dictated by price level and income objectives largely independent of the reserve base and the average reserve ratio.

An advantage of the framework used in this paper is that it permits a simple summary of the factors relating the money supply to government. Such a summary has been presented in Tables 1–4.

Two major conclusions about optimal values of the reserve base and the average reserve ratio have been reached: (1) interrelationships of variables influenced by government suggest that the choice of the reserve base and the average reserve ratio be related explicitly to debt policy; and (2) resource-allocation considerations suggest having lower required reserves or interest-bearing reserves or both. The same type of reasoning suggests paying interest on hand-to-hand currency. Guided by the second conclusion, the last part of the paper suggests two specific programs within the spirit of the present institutional framework that would take account of resource-allocation objectives in choosing values of the reserve base and the average reserve ratio.

There remains the question of how debt and resource-allocation objectives might be taken into account simultaneously. This question has not been dealt with in this article. Most of the debt could be eliminated by imposing high reserve requirements for commercial banks. This would imply a large, but hardly disastrous, tax. In order to maintain bank earnings, service charges on deposits would have to rise. At the other extreme—as was emphasized in part three—the tax on money could be completely eliminated, in which case there would be no debt retirement associated with the growth of the money supply.

The opinion may be ventured that, in the absence of some attempted balancing between the two types of objectives, even to pursue one to the complete exclusion of the other would represent an improvement over present practices. Until now decisions concerning the reserve base and the average reserve ratio do not seem to have been mobilized toward the accomplishment of any particular aim. Yet this paper has indicated that these decisions can make a significant contribution either to achieving an optimal size of the national debt or to achieving optimal arrangements from the standpoint of resource allocation in the use of money.

NOTES

1. Lloyd W. Mints has stated this point of view succinctly in observing that banks operate with a "mixture of 100 per cent and fractional reserve requirements. They may not issue notes to be used as hand-to-hand currency, which is equivalent to a right of note issue with a requirement of 100 per cent reserves; but against their deposits they are required to hold only fractional reserves" (*Monetary Policy for a Competitive Society* [New York: McGraw-Hill Book Co., Inc., 1950], p. 6).

2. I ignore some details concerning government deposits, whose influence is usually negligible. The various influences on ρ are reflected in this expression:

$$\rho = \rho_C \left[\frac{M_C}{M}\right] + \rho_M \left[\frac{D}{M}\right]\left[\frac{M_M}{D}\right] + \frac{R_E}{M}$$
$$+ \rho_C \left[\frac{M'_C}{M}\right] + \rho_M \left[\frac{M'_M}{M}\right] + \rho_M \left[\frac{M''_M}{M}\right].$$

The first term is the reserve ratio for currency multiplied by the proportion of the total stock of money which the public holds in the form of currency. Thus ρ_C is the required reserve ratio for currency, equal to 1 under present arrangements, and M_C is the amount of currency held outside banks. The second term is the required reserve ratio for deposits ρ_M, times the proportion of the total stock of money which the public holds in the form of deposits times the proportion of these deposits held in member banks. The ratio ρ_M is itself a weighted reserve ratio; that is, it is the average of required ratios for different kinds of deposits, weighted by the proportions of the kinds of deposits. The third term is excess reserves, R_E, divided by the stock of money. The remaining terms are the same as the first or second terms, except that they pertain to the banks and the government instead of the public. Thus, in the fourth term, M'_C is the amount of currency held by the banks; and, in the fifth term, M'_M is the amount of interbank deposits held in member banks. In the last term, M''_M is the amount of government deposits held in member banks.

The preceding expression is derived by considering the reserve base as equal to the sum of reserve-using magnitudes and dividing the resultant equality by the money supply. Table 4 presents values of ρ and reveals the importance of each of the components in this expression.

3. Among recent writers, Milton Friedman has advocated this proposal. See his "A Monetary and Fiscal Framework for Economic Stability," *American Economic Review*, Vol. 38 (June 1948), 245–64; and "Commodity Reserve Currency," *Journal of Political Economy*, Vol. 59 (June 1951), 203–32. Earlier literature includes Laughlin Currie, *Supply and Control of Money in the United States* (Cambridge: Harvard University Press, 1934); Irving Fisher, *100% Money* (New York: Adelphi Co., 1935); Albert G. Hart, "The Chicago Plan of Banking Reform," *Review of Economic Studies*, Vol. 2 (May 1935), 104–16; and Henry C. Simons, *A Positive Program for Laissez-faire: Some Proposals for a Liberal Economic Policy* (Chicago: University of Chicago Press, 1934).

4. See Mints, *op. cit.*, pp. 191–96.

5. Apparently, this type of proposal was originally made in L. H. Seltzer, "The Problem of Our Excessive Banking Reserves," *Journal of the American Statistical Association*, Vol. 35 (March 1940), 24–36.

6. All except the fourth, of course, might be taken to imply little conflict between ρ and R, since these proposals would result in higher values for both variables. Nevertheless, even among these, the specific choices are quite different.

7. Unless, of course, required reserve ratios were deliberately raised to induce a compensating increase.

8. The equation used in Table 3 is

$$\Delta R = R\frac{\Delta\rho}{\rho} + R\frac{\Delta K}{K} + R\frac{\Delta P}{P} + R\frac{\Delta Y}{Y} + I,$$

where I is the interaction term obtained as a residual. The measures used here have the advantage of being internally consistent; that is, the variables are defined so that the equation $R = \rho KPY$ is, in fact, fulfilled in any year. The measure of money income is gross national product, and this is separated into real income and price level by use of the implicit price deflator of the gross national product as prepared by the Department of Commerce. Velocity is gross national product divided by the same measure of the money supply as that used in obtaining ρ. The money supply is deposits adjusted, including both time and demand deposits, plus currency outside banks.

9. ρ is the sum of the remaining columns in Table 4. The table presents numerical values for terms in the expression given in note 2.

10. The formulation in this paragraph has much in common with that of Clark Warburton. An important difference, however, is that Warburton would use the increase in the money supply as a central criterion in pursuing stabilization objectives, whereas I am interested here only in the implications of increase in the money supply for fiscal planning. This paper is neutral on what the role of the quantity of money can or should be in achieving stabilization objectives (see Clark Warburton, "Monetary Theory, Full Production, and the Great Depression," *Econometrica*, Vol. 13 [April 1945], 74–84; "Volume of Savings, Quantity of Money, and Business Instability," *Journal of Political Economy*, Vol. 55 [June 1947], 222–33; "The Secular Trend in Monetary Velocity," *Quarterly Journal of Economics*, Vol. 63 [February 1949], 68–91; "Banks and Business Fluctuations," *Estadistica: Journal of the Inter-American States Institute*, Vol. 3 [March 1950], 59–68).

11. It is possible for ρ to be greater than 1 because the banks and government hold reserve-using currency and deposits not considered to be part of the money supply. To calculate ρ with 100 per cent reserves, let ρ_M equal 1 in Table 4.

12. See Friedman, "A Monetary and Fiscal Framework for Economic Stability," p. 251.

13. See Mints, *op. cit.*, pp. 191–96.

14. Two main lines of argument in favor of a positive government debt are that it is an instrument of stabilization and that taxpayers as a group may rationally wish to defer tax payments.

15. One can think of a variety of reasons, of course, why the quantities of all assets might not increase just at the same rate. Secular shifts in the supply and demand for different kinds of assets are to be expected. If we assume that capitalization influences the price of interest-bearing securities, their values will be affected by changes in the rate of interest.

16. In contemplating changes in ρ, we also need to take into account the ability of the banking system to adjust to portfolio changes in an orderly manner.

17. Curiously, the literature on 100 per cent reserves—where the bank earnings and hence the service-charge problem become most acute—does not seem to contain any meaningful consideration of this question.

18. The following important assumptions underlie this scheme: (1) that reserves for deposits may be taken to include all cash assets; (2) that income associated with asset holding may be attributed entirely to non-cash assets; and (3) that assets other than reserves may be viewed as if they were all earning the average return. Obviously, the scheme can be defended only as providing a first approximation.

19. The figures given in this paragraph are derived from *Federal Reserve Bulletin*, Vol. 41 (May 1955), 564.

20. From *Federal Reserve Bulletin*, Vol. 41 (May 1955), 508 and 517.

21. This was derived on p. 398.

22. The discrepancy of 0.01 was lost in rounding.

23. Very nearly the same estimate is obtained from using data for the latest year available, 1956.

24. To note only one of many possible qualifications, since banks probably reduce other cash assets to some extent because they hold required reserves, the charge for money may not be so greatly affected by required reserves as is assumed in the text. It may be emphasized that the admitted crudity of the estimates does not imply a corresponding lack of usefulness. For example, we can now assert that the tax in ad valorem terms must almost certainly lie somewhere between, say, 5 and 50 per cent; this was not obvious before.

25. To obtain an estimate of the tax on currency similar to that obtained above for deposits would require investigation of government expenses in providing hand-to-hand currency.

26. I believe that there would be no particular difficulty in paying interest on currency. However, no attempt has been made to explore this extreme kind of reform very deeply in this article.

27. If interest were paid on reserves, reserves might become such an attractive asset to banks that they would choose to hold substantially more than the present legal minimum reserves. For stabilization purposes, the Federal Reserve authorities might find it desirable for reserves to be near their minimum legal levels so that short-run changes in the money supply could be effected quickly if the need arose. If interest were paid on reserves, therefore, required reserve ratios might be raised to whatever level was needed to insure that banks had an incentive to stay near these ratios. The payment of interest would help to mitigate the undesirable resource-allocation effects of this procedure.

28. The accumulation of earning assets by the Federal Reserve indicates that there has in any case been more than enough debt retirement to offset gold purchases. The second alternative program discussed below seeks to make the tax on money exactly enough to cover gold acquisitions.

29. Would the best solution to this problem be to cease continuous accretions to the gold stock? Of course, another (bad?) solution to the problem would result from inflating the price level sufficiently so that increases in currency alone would be enough to offset increases in gold.

30. Other less important influences on the volume of earning assets are being neglected here.

31. This statement applies particularly to the variant in which earning assets would be left at current levels. If earning assets were to be zero, there might be a series of reductions in required reserve ratios.

Part **V**

The Rate
of Interest

The rate of interest is the link between the flow of income and the stock of capital and, as such, it is of central importance in the calculus of economics. This crucial role of the rate of interest has been long recognized and consequently has been subjected to searching analysis for several centuries. In spite of this prolonged examination, our knowledge of the nature of the rate of interest and its role in the economy is less developed than that of many other economic factors which have not had the benefits of as long, nor as intensive, an inquiry.

The modern discussion of the rate of interest has concentrated on five areas: (1) criticism of Keynes' theory of liquidity preference; (2) the relationship between stock and flow analyses; (3) the effect of inflation on interest rates; (4) the effectiveness of the rate of interest as a policy instrument; and (5) the term structure of interest rules.

Two general approaches have been followed in developing the modern monetary theory of the rate of interest. The first, the loanable funds approach developed by Wicksell and his followers, introduced financial considerations into the classical theory of the rate of interest in which the rate of interest depended essentially on the marginal productivity of capital and the time preference of income receivers. Wicksell treated the rate of interest as a price which would equate the supply of loanable funds (savings, S, and changes in the money supply, ΔM) with the demand for money (investment, I, and hoarding, H, i.e., the desired change in the community's stock of money and securities). The rate of interest would vary until it just equated the supply of and demand for loanable funds so that:

$$S + \Delta M = I + H$$

The various terms in the preceding equation were defined with differing degrees of netness and disaggregated for various sectors of the economy to produce a theory of varying degrees of complexity.[1]

---

[1] See Joseph W. Conard, *Introduction to the Theory of Interest* (Berkeley, 1963), Chapter 9, still the best review of interest rate theory available.

The liquidity preference theory of interest made the rate of interest equate individuals' desires to divide their wealth between money and securities with the actual stock of wealth and securities. In addition, Keynes made some special assumptions concerning the demand for money at very low interest rates. We have seen that Keynes assumed that a community's preferences to hold a certain proportion of its assets in the form of money was a function of the rate of interest and that this preference schedule was relatively constant in the short-run so that the money supply which was established by the monetary authority determined the equilibrium rate of interest in the short-run.

The loanable funds theory was expressed in terms of flow variables while the liquidity preference theory was expressed in terms of the willingness to hold a particular stock of money. The conditions under which these two theories are equivalent engendered a great deal of discussion during which many new facets of the role of the rate of interest were discovered, or rediscovered and made more precise.

Hicks made an early attempt to reconcile the two theories by applying Walras' Law. He pointed out that in a general equilibrium system the demand, D, and supply, S, of goods, g, securities, s, and money, m, depend on the price of goods, P, and the price of securities, which may be expressed as the rate of interest, i. In general equilibrium there can be no excess (or deficit) demand in any of these three markets, so that the demand and supply in each market must equal one another:

$$D_g(P, i) = S_g(P, i) \qquad \text{(goods market)} \qquad (1)$$
$$D_s(P, i) = S_s(P, i) \qquad \text{(securities market)} \qquad (2)$$
$$D_m(P, i) = S_m(P, i) \qquad \text{(money market)} \qquad (3)$$

Hicks explained that, as a consequence of Walras' Law, if two of the markets are in equilibrium, there must also be an equilibrium in the third market, so that one of the equations shown above is redundant and may be omitted. The loanable funds approach omits the equation for the money market while the liquidity preference approach omits the equation for the securities market. Hicks' analysis is formally correct in that it showed that the loanable funds approach was consistent with the liquidity preference approach in Walrasian general equilibrium. The exact relevance of this type of equilibrium, however, to the Keynesian equilibrium and that of other models, and the question of the determinacy of other variables such as the general price level has given monetary theorists much to think about in recent years.

A great deal of confusion is eliminated by recognizing the three types of equilibrium to be considered. One is short-run equilibrium, where the influence of the size of the flows on the level of stocks may be regarded as negligible. This is largely the type of equilibrium

Keynes had in mind (". . . in the long-run we are all dead"). The second type of equilibrium is where the flow variables have sufficient time to affect the level of stocks and vice versa but there is not sufficient time for stocks to attain equilibrium levels. This may be called the medium-run equilibrium and is largely the type of equilibrium that has caused the most problems. Last, there is the equilibrium where all the stocks and flows have attained their equilibrium levels; this may be called the classical long-run equilibrium.

Patinkin's criticism of Keynes is, in part, inappropriate in that he compares a theory which is a long-run equilibrium theory developed under the assumptions of perfect interest and price certainty with Keynes' short-run equilibrium theory in which uncertainty plays a central role. If there were no interest and price uncertainty there would be no speculative demand for money and one of the most significant differences between Keynesian and classical theory would disappear.

Although Keynes recognized the importance of changes in the stock of non-monetary financial assets on saving,[2] he chose to ignore these effects in his final analysis. From one point of view this was justified in that it was the short-run equilibrium that interested Keynes, where the magnitude of the flows was negligible relative to the stocks of existing assets (with the exception of the stock of money which was determined autonomously by the monetary authority), and the stocks of non-monetary assets could be treated as constant. However, from another viewpoint one may question this treatment of the stock problem, since the rate of interest is the yardstick by which the stock of capital is measured. Changes in the rate of interest result in changes in the real value of all income-yielding assets unless there are compensating changes in the price level to offset this effect. This effect requires little time to take place and one may question whether it is proper to ignore it, even in Keynes' short-run equilibrium. One may rationalize Keynes' position by saying that he did not feel this was important in the depression situation he was intent in analyzing, where the rate of interest was close to a minimum level set by the "liquidity trap" and the opportunity for capital gains would be small. The possibility of capital losses would only strengthen his major argument.[3] However, in growing and relatively prosperous economies, economists have asked what might be the effects of the rate of interest on the stock of assets and thus on consumption and investment decisions.[4]

[2] *General Theory of Employment, Interest and Money* (New York 1936), p. 92.
[3] The quotation of Fouraker, given by Shackle, on the Cambridge method is particularly relevant here.
[4] See Richard S. Thorn, "Long-Run Adjustments to Changes in the Capital-Output Ratio and the National Debt," *Yale Economic Essays,* Vol. 2 (Spring 1962), 247–99.

The flows may be in equilibrium in that wealthholders and investors do not wish to add to their stocks faster than they are presently adding to them though they are not satisfied with their present level. Thus it is a "desired level of stocks" only in the sense that, all other things taken into consideration, it is the highest level to which individuals believe they may raise their stocks at that moment. However, this obviously is not a stationary equilibrium since it is assumed that individuals will still add to their stocks. Only when the stocks of all assets have attained their desired levels and the levels of investment and saving have adjusted to this situation, will a stationary long-run equilibrium be attained. A good deal of controversy might have been avoided if these three equilibrium time periods were clearly distinguished and if the participants defined precisely what they meant by "stationary" and "dynamic equilibrium." It is possible in medium-run situations to have a stationary equilibrium in the flow variables and disequilibrium in the stock variables in a stationary sense, although in terms of a dynamic analysis both stock and flow variables may be in equilibrium. Much of the early discussion of the relationship between stocks and flows took place in the framework of models that did not specify the relationship between the level of stocks and the rate of saving which would make it possible to reconcile static and dynamic relationships.

The distinction between medium- and long-run equilibrium is very much like the distinction Wicksell made between medium-run situations where the money rate of interest differed from the "natural" rate of interest as determined by the marginal productivity of capital, and long-run situations where they were equal. In some respects the contemporary discussion of the stock and flow problem has taken on, in a highly formalized way, the problem that fascinated Wicksell more than a half century ago.

The contemporary discussion, besides attempting to define what is meant by equilibrium of stocks and flows in the medium-run, has raised several other important questions. Does Say's Law hold in the medium-run when there are stocks of money in existence which may be employed to alter the level of demand? Does the rate of interest affect the rate of saving in any significant manner in the medium- and long-run? Is the rate of saving linked to the level of permanent income or the level of wealth? All these questions still await definitive answers.

The term structure of interest rates attracted new attention in the postwar period. It first appeared in connection with the now discredited "bills only" doctrine of the Federal Reserve whereby monetary open market operations were confined primarily to Treasury bills in an effort to minimize the effects upon the rate of interest for long-term government debt. It was later discussed in connection with the Federal Reserve's attempt to raise short-term interest rates without substantially increasing long-term interest rates, in an attempt to reduce the strain on the balance of payments caused by the outflow of short-term funds without adversely affecting domestic investment.

Two conflicting theories of the term structure of interest rates have come into prominence. One is the "expectational theory," which maintains that the long-term interest rate is some weighted average of the expected short-term rates. The other approach may be called the "institutional theory," which maintains that institutional investors are, by and large, risk-averters and determine their holdings of debt of different maturities on the basis of liquidity, hedging, cost of acquiring and administering debt, and expectations. However, "institutional" theorists believe that the "behavior of borrowers and lenders is not ordinarily dominated by the last named factor."[5]

[5] J. M. Culbertson, "The Term Structure of Interest Rates," *Quarterly Journal of Economics,* Vol. 71 (November 1957), 490.

17 Recent Theories Concerning the Nature and Role of Interest

G. L. S. Shackle *British Academy*

Preface

The place of interest rates in the economic process has since 1945 been mainly discussed, within the literature in English, along three lines: first, criticism and defence of Keynes's position; secondly, advocacy of a stock or of a flow analysis, or of the need to combine them; thirdly, examination of the claim of interest to be a suitable and effective regulator of the pace of growth of the nation's wealth. The following survey tries to explain and criticise this debate and to interject some suggestions into it, without aiming at more than an illustrative coverage of the literature. It is earnestly hoped that the absence of a name from this article will not be taken to imply any judgment on the value and importance of any person's work.

Part I THE NATURE OF INTEREST

Types of Economic Theory

When we have no theory about economic affairs, no state of those affairs and no temporal succession of states seems inconceivable. A theory restricts the conceivable states and successions of states to those in which the relations between quantifiable things in the economy conform to some specified rules. Theories differ

Reprinted from *Economic Journal*, Vol. 71 (June 1961), 209–54, by permission of the author and the Royal Economic Society.

from each other in the list of quantifiable (not necessarily measurable) things to be considered, and in the precise character of the rules about their interrelations. This meaning of "economic theory" leaves unlimited the number of different theory-classifying schemes we can set up. But in historical fact the cleavages between groups of theories have run along a few clear lines, which can for practical purposes be easily defined. These lines, of course, intersect each other and yield cross-classifications.

One dichotomy is between *equilibrium* and *development* theories. Equilibrium is a test that selects for the economist one particular situation out of an infinity of situations and justifies his calling attention to it as something special. Judged by the smallness of the ratio of what it accepts to what it rejects, no other test seems able to rival its selective power. No other test, it may also be claimed, can state so sharply in what the accepted differs from the rejected situations. By contrast, no test of comparable power and conviction can be found for selecting among paths of development. On the most general grounds, equilibrium has great claims as an economiser of thought. To dispense with it has meant, in practice, to be reduced to mere factual enumeration. For ninety years few economists, save the German historical school, have based their theories upon any other principle. Even those most anxious to disparage it as a *description of what is* and, still more, of what ought to be, have nonetheless needed it as a means of understanding and of accounting for what is. Even Keynes's *General Theory of Employment, Interest and Money* [20], so strongly repudiating some of the conclusions of equilibrium theories, was itself an equilibrium theory in its method.

Theories may secondly be distinguished according to the mode of choice which faces their acting subjects. When a theory supposes the available alternatives to be perfectly known to these subjects in every respect which concerns them, I shall speak of a theory of *pure* choice. Under any other assumption the acting subject has, with greater or less freedom, to create his own list of alternatives before he can choose among them. If the alternatives are not *given* to him, or in so far as they are not given, he must necessarily produce them by his own thought, judgment and imagination. Choice of this two-stage kind I shall call *impure* choice.

A subject facing pure choice has no motive for not dealing at once with every question that arises concerning the details of the action he shall adopt. For he knows everything about the consequences of every available act. But a subject facing impure choice may elect a "simple" immediate act designed to secure freedom of deferred choice among more specialised alternatives. In fact, rather than decide what to buy, he may elect to retain money. In theories of pure choice there is thus room for money only as a unit of account and none for money as a store of value, an *asset*. But all the interesting properties of money arise from its use as an asset. Thus theories of pure choice are "non-monetary" theories.

Finally, we must make a subdivision within the equilibrium method. For this method can, paradoxically, be concerned either with *events* or with *states*. *Long-period* equilibrium is, of course, a state, and its meaning may even excuse us from asking whether it would, given stability of all the "non-economic governing conditions," eventually be attained or not. There are degrees of strictness with which long-period equilibrium may be interpreted. We may mean by it the perfect and complete adjustment of everything in the economy to everything else, a general equilibrium attained after no matter how long a time. Or we may have in mind a period sufficient for some particular impulse (such as an increase in the money stock) to have worked itself out through the system as it exists, even though that system itself may not be in complete long-period internal adjustment. Let us call this a "middle-period" equilibrium. Middle-period equilibrium is also, then, essentially a means of studying states.

When we seek to determine a state of affairs in which, if the economy ever arrived at that state, it could remain at rest, because this state is one of long-period general equilibrium, we are not concerned with the path from the existing to that ultimate state, we are not interested in the *event* or chain of events carrying the economy from one situation to the other. But in the short period the temporary and partial equilibrium, which defines as it were a gravitational force acting on the economy, serves rather to describe an event than a state. It answers the question "What will happen next to the economy?" The two meanings of equilibrium are thus rather sharply contrasted in regard to the part they play in analysis. In its short-period connotation, equilibrium can enable a dynamic tale to be told in static language.

Keynes and the Classics

If we have spent some time preparing the foregoing classificatory scheme, our reason is that theories can appear to be widely divergent and contradictory, while in fact, because they are answering different questions, they are perfectly harmonious. An example is provided by the first source we shall consider. Professor Patinkin [35] finds Keynes's interest theory wrong on almost all counts. In this criticism, however, Patinkin is setting a long-period equilibrium analysis of almost pure choice, which therefore is in vital respects non-monetary, against Keynes's short-period equilibrium analysis of impure choice treating money in its full-blooded sense. No reader of Keynes's article "The General Theory of Employment" [21], published in February 1937 in answer to critics, will be in doubt that Keynes looking back saw as the main theme of his book the commanding importance of uncertainty and of the conventions by which the insoluble problems it poses, and the nonsense it makes of pure "rational calculation," can be shelved in order to make life possible at all. Professor Patinkin, by contrast, says: "the limited objective of this [Patinkin's] book . . . is to understand the functioning of a money economy under perfect interest and price certainty." And a little earlier: "Once the Pandora box of expectations and interest and price uncertainty is opened upon the world of economic analysis, anything can happen." Patinkin's analysis, worked out with watch-like precision, is concerned with money as a means, merely, of meeting random demands for payment, and not as a means of speculation or of deferring specialised decisions.

Patinkin, then, quite excludes those Bulls and Bears who would otherwise smash up the china shop of rational economics. They are, to a degree which Patinkin, despite an incomparable scrupulousness towards his reader, does not perhaps sufficiently make clear, the heart of Keynes's liquidity preference theory. Once the transactions motive is satisfied, all the rest of the existing money must be held by Bears (or at least, non-Bulls), of whom there have got to be enough for this purpose. The business of the interest rate, *qua* equilibrator of liquidity preference, is to move to such a level as will create these necessary Bears, or eliminate some of them if there are too many. Nor are we, in this dynamic world of speculation, free to think of the speculative demand for money as depending solely on the *level* of the interest rate. At any moment this demand may be powerfully influenced by the most recent *movement* of the interest rate, its extent and speed. We may go farther. People who are holding money because they think the interest rate will rise may decide to hold it no longer if they observe the interest rate to remain where it is. For at a constant interest rate (that is, constant prices of bonds) they are missing an income (namely receipt of interest) which they could have with no offsetting capital loss. Thus if the constancy of the interest rate has been due to a force of non-Bulls just brought to sufficiency by the presence in it of some Bears who count on a rising rate, this constancy will soon destroy itself by disillusioning these Bears, who will buy bonds, and cause the rate to fall. Interest may be *inherently restless*. All this is outside the limits of Professor Patinkin's concerns. It is, indeed, beyond the range of the equilibrium method.

His main contention is a simple and compelling one. Money's usefulness, no matter in what context, derives ultimately from its exchangeability for goods (including factors of production) of those kinds which are wanted for their own sake or for their *technical* transformability into goods wanted for their own sake. Money by definition cannot be enjoyed, consumed or made a physical tool of; it can, ultimately, only be exchanged. It can be stored, but even then only with a view to its being in the end, at some time or other, exchanged. It can be lent, but only with the result of promising more money later on, which money will then be serviceable only by being exchanged. If you are holding money with a view to paying for things the quantity of money you need depends on the prices of the things you have contracted to pay for. The marginal utility of a given stock of money thus depends on the price level. This is true whatever the *proximate* motive for holding the money, whether it be to bridge the unforeseeable time-gap between receipts and spendings or to make the time-shape of spending different from the time-shape of income by the issue or purchase of bonds, or even (so Patinkin says, and here we are not quite so readily convinced) to make a capital gain in the bond market.

If, by government decree, the British unit of currency were altered overnight from the pound to the florin, everyone whose bank had owed him £100 would now owe him 1,000 florins. Everyone who had owed his tailor £20 would now owe him 200 florins. Everyone who had yesterday purchased a bond for £1,000 due to be redeemed in one year's time for £1,050, would now own a bond due to be redeemed in one year's time for 10,500 florins. If, in the familiar way, tastes, techniques and real resources were the same to-day as yesterday, nothing that mattered to anyone would have changed. In France the transition to the "new franc" is almost an example, in reverse, of the very thing we have supposed. Why, in either of these cases, should the interest rate change? There is no reason.

Change of the currency unit and re-expression of all prices, debts and money stocks in terms of the new unit is, in comparative statics terms, the same thing as a change in the quantity of *each person's* money and of all prices, all incomes and all debts in one and the same proportion. Can it be claimed that this is what an increase in the total money stock will in the long period achieve? If all prices and wages were flexible; if the extra money were introduced in such a manner that everybody's holdings (positive or negative) of bonds and holdings of money were increased in one and the same proportion; if expectations were inelastic; if there were nowhere any money illusion (no tendency to regard a ten-shilling note as something in itself and not merely as ten shillings' worth of purchasing power at the prices happening at any moment to prevail); then an increase in the economy's total stock of money would leave the rate of interest unchanged for the same reason that a change in the currency unit would do so. Professor Patinkin is scrupulous to point out how far from practical reality some of these necessary conditions are. But he does believe that those which are least easily accepted are also the least harmful to the long-period neutrality of money. Equi-proportionate changes in every item of a list in which every individual's money holding is an item, his bond holding is an item and his debt on bonds he has issued is an item are wildly unlikely; but if tastes are not too dissimilar this may not make much difference. Elastic expectations he dismisses as incompatible with meaningful economic analysis. And as to absence of money illusion, he seems to be in two minds whether to make it an assumption or to claim it as a consequence of rationality.

Many who have spoken of money as a veil have failed to make explicit the conditions on which this neutrality will be achieved, and have not, in particular, insisted that money balances as well as money incomes must be supposed to be multiplied by the same factor as prices. Turning this necessary condition round, Patinkin shows that money balances cannot be increased without bringing into play forces, of that utterly familiar kind consisting in the observance of the equi-marginal utility principle, which will in the long run, and unless obstructed by law or human perversity, push prices up in the same proportion as the balances have been increased. These forces will at the same time, given this price flexibility, cause the quantities of bonds issued and held by firms and individuals to be increased in yet again this same proportion. All these consequences together constitute what he calls the "real balance effect." Time will, indeed, be needed for all these changes to work themselves out through the system, and while they are doing so the rate of interest will be lower than before. But when they have done so, an increase in the stock of money will, as Ricardo [42] and Wicksell [49] said, leave the interest rate unchanged.

Keynes must be supposed, according to Patinkin, to have thought that an increase in the stock of money would permanently oversatisfy liquidity preference at the former interest rate, and would therefore lower the rate to that level where the increased transactions balances required by the increased general output or the higher prices (or both) due to the increased investment flow at the lower interest rate would soak up such of the extra money as was not wanted by the lower rate's newly created Bears. How could he believe this? By believing that asset holders as well as wage-earners were money illusioned. We may well think it natural for those who had experienced the gentle deflation of 1920–35 to be very differently conditioned towards money from those who, in 1956, had suffered fifteen years of continuous quite rapid *in*flation. Circumstances alter cases. But there is more than this. Keynes saw economic life as made up of events and not of states. His method only was an equilibrium one, the picture he sought to explain was of booms and depressions, inflations and crises, continual challenge and change. "Equilibrium is blither," he (orally) said.

Patinkin draws from his model the following conclusions on interest:

(i) In a world where each individual feels certain that he knows, for each future date within his horizon, what interest rate, what price of each good and what level of his own income will prevail (that is, a world of "interest, price and income certainty"), a greater than zero interest rate could exist, and would be accounted for by the desire of people to consume according to a different time-shape from their incomes, and by the desire of entrepreneurs to make profits by investing in equipment. (We may note that a world of "interest, price and income certainty" is by no means the same as a world of perfect foresight. In Patinkin's model expectations are held with certainty, but are in general not correct.) Not only does interest belong to a world of certainty as well as to one of uncertainty, but "a proper approach to interest differentials begins in the classical manner with the determination of the rate on long-term bonds by the basic forces of thrift and productivity, and goes down from this rate to the shorter-term ones." (The latter part of this sentence is disturbing to a reader who is basically willing to see in Patinkin's work, not a competitor to the liquidity preference or Bulls and Bears theory, but a solution of a quite different problem. That problem is indeed the "long-period" one. But what has this to do with "long-term bonds"? They are the objects of day-to-day and hour-to-hour speculation like any Stock Exchange security.)

(ii) The threefold role of the interest rate is to equalise for every individual (in his private or his entrepreneurial capacity) the utility of consuming a marginal amount now with the utility of having the prospect of consuming the compound-interest-increased equivalent of this amount in the future; to equalise for him the utility which his marginal unit of money holdings affords by its liquidity with the utility which a bond, purchased with it, would afford by promising interest; and to equalise for him the interest he could obtain (or avoid paying) on the marginal bond with the rate of profit promised by the equipment purchasable with the price of this bond. This "threefold margin" was so named by Sir Dennis Robertson [38].

(iii) An increase in the economy's total money stock does not inevitably or essentially entail a change in the long-period equilibrium rate of interest. Any such change will arise from the special *distribution* of the extra money, and not from its coming into existence. To believe otherwise it is necessary to believe in money illusion on the part of asset owners.

(iv) "The amount of money demanded depends upon the rate of interest, the rate of interest does not depend upon the amount of money." This merely means that the rate of interest does not depend only on the amount of money but also, among other things, on prices, which when time has been given following an increase in the economy's stock of money, will increase in the same proportion as the stock, thus leaving the "real" situation and the equilibrium rate of interest unchanged. When we add that the amount of money demanded also depends on prices as well as interest, the paradox vanishes.

The facts support Professor Patinkin in his chosen context. Huge increases in the British quantity of money have been accompanied over the past twenty years, not by a fall but a rise in the long-term and, far more dramatically, in the short-term interest rates. But this long period context is nothing that Keynes ever had in mind.

In his review article in the *Economic Journal* [18], Professor Hicks applies his incisive diagrammatic tests to reach much the same understanding of Professor Patinkin's book as our broader approach above had led us to. That book is concerned, Professor Hicks says, with "full equilibrium" (this appears to us identical with "long-period" equilibrium). Full or long-period equilibrium assumes that money wages, along with all other prices, are perfectly flexible downwards as well as upwards. (The question whether this flexibility requires time or not is, let us interject, inapplicable to long-period equilibrium, for whose purposes time is not scarce.) It is in assuming this downward flexibility that the full equilibrium theory, which is the "classical" theory as Keynes meant that term, differs from Keynes's theory, whose primary assumption (realistic for the 1930's but not for the early nineteenth century) is that the money wage is given and, for institutional reasons, will not fall and, for reasons of abundant unemployed resources, will not rise as employment changes. With perfect upward and downward wage flexibility, Professor Hicks shows that real income (measured in wage units) can stand at one level, and one only, given the community's income-and-consumption schedule, the marginal efficiency of capital, the quantity of money and the absence of any speculative motive for holding money. For only at one level of real income will the amount that people wish to save out of that income be equal to the investment which, given the interest rate corresponding to the given quantity of money *and that level of real income*, the entrepreneurs are willing to do. If the entrepreneurs, all taken together, tried to have a larger investment flow than this the result would be a rise of prices and money wages without any increase of employment or output, for the unique real-income point is a point both of full employment and "full unemployment." This rise in prices, in face of the fixed quantity of money, would shift the income-interest-rate schedule towards the interest-rate axis, and thus, by raising the interest rate corresponding to a given real income, drive investment down to its former level. Similarly, a too-small investment flow would lower wages and prices and reduce the interest rate corresponding to any given real income, and so push investment and income back to their former levels. In this model it is the "real" factors of productivity and thrift which determine the interest rate. If thrift were weaker the "saving gap" between production (that is, income) and consumption would be smaller, a smaller investment flow would suffice to fill it, this small investment flow (given the schedule of the marginal efficiency of capital) could be induced by a higher interest rate and prices, given the quantity of money, would adjust themselves upwards so that this quantity of money only just sufficed for the transactions and precautions needs at this higher interest rate. Or if the marginal efficiency schedule (productivity of capital) were to shift, again a different interest rate would arise just sufficient to induce the investment necessary to fill but not over-fill the saving gap. In this model it is the level of money prices and so, given real income, the level of money income, which is altered if the quantity of money is altered. In terms of Dr. Hahn's analysis, which we shall discuss below, the classical full-equilibrium economy was effectively "decomposed" into two independent sub-systems, the "real" system, which determined *everything* "real," including the rate of exchange between present and future goods, and the "money" system, which determined only the arbitrary monetary name (measure) of the real income, *etcetera*, determined elsewhere, which it was powerless to influence in any other respect.

In pointing to the absence of downward flexibility of wages as the essential difference between the full-equilibrium model and Keynes's model, Hicks neglects in the early part of his discussion, as Patinkin does throughout, a feature which is even more characteristically Keynesian, namely, the speculative motive for liquidity. For in this neglect there is involved, given the de-natured marginal efficiency schedule which in the full-equilibrium model is no more than a physical productivity schedule, the neglect of the whole matter of uncertainty of expectation. Hicks does insist, however, on the third vital difference between Keynes and all the classics, including Patinkin: the classics were concerned with the full long period, which is the same as to say, with full flexibility. Keynes was concerned with the short period, in which some things are stickier than others.

Quite at the end of his article (superb in its clarity and penetration) Hicks brings up reluctantly the speculative motive like a shameful atom bomb to settle the matter. He has shown that the question whether unemployment can be cured by monetary expansion turns on whether we assume full flexibility of the interest rate so that it can fall to whatever level may be needed for the stimulation of a full-employment-giving level of investment, or whether we assume that there is a "floor" to the interest rate, below which it cannot be forced by any ordinary expansion of the money stock:

> In order to show that we get a better understanding of these problems by considering effects [of shifts of the marginal efficiency schedule or the income-consumption schedule.—G.L.S.S.] on employment and income first, and then correcting by possible repercussions through interest, all that is necessary is to maintain that there are ranges over which the repercussions through interest will be rather insignificant. To do that no more is necessary than to emphasise the ability of speculative funds to stabilise the rate of interest against considerable disturbances. Which is effectively what Keynes did.

To treat the transactions motive as central and the speculative motive as incidental or peripheral is as though an oceanographer should study the inflow from rivers but neglect the tide. Professor Hicks has, however, preferred to defend Keynes with classical and not with Keynesian weapons, for even he, it seems, is not willing to give Keynes full applause for his great *tour de force*: the writing of *earthquake economics* within a framework of comparative statics. One more remark seems here permissible. The theory against which Keynes has to be defended is the classical theory, which shows interest to be determined by the "real forces," productivity and thrift. That theory also shows that there can be no such thing as unemployment. It was this sort of approach which, seen from the standpoint, say, of 1933, aroused his formidable contempt.

Professor Patinkin's "Rejoinder" [37] to Professor Hicks was concerned only with insisting again on the "real balance" or "Pigou" effect, whereby, it is claimed, a fall of prices, by increasing the purchasing power of people's stocks of money, will induce them to spend more (when? over how long a period? in how thin a life-long trickle? or [abandoning Patinkin's unswerving assumption of "rationality"] in how disturbing a burst of extravagance?) on commodities. The question in this regard is whether people who are saving out of income take *income* or *assets* as the proper measure of the basis of their spending power. But this whole question and Patinkin's "Rejoinder" bear on the theory of employment rather than on that of interest.

The classical case is the long-period case. In terms of comparative statics we ideally compare, not the states of one economy at two different dates, however remote from each other in time, since then one state must precede and "lead to" the other, and we are always tempted to ask about "flexibility" and other things strictly irrelevant; but we compare two structurally identical and atemporal economies (with tastes, techniques and nearly all resources identical between the two) in one of which the quantity of money, say, is larger than in the other; and we observe what other things must then also be different.

The same "classical" conclusions for the long-period (or as we should say, atemporal) case, at which Professor Hicks arrives diagrammatically, had been put forward in 1944 by Dr. Franco Modigliani [30] in an argument which, however, Dr. F. H. Hahn in 1955 [16] found self-contradictory. Dr. Hahn reports as follows Modigliani's conclusions:

> if the supply function of labour is homogeneous of degree zero in all prices including money wages [that is, if equi-proportionate changes in all prices leave unchanged the quantity of labour supplied], then
>   (i) the rate of interest is determined by investment and savings [saving?] and
>   (ii) liquidity preference determines the level of prices and *not* the rate of interest.

If, says Dr. Hahn in effect, the "real" variables (that is, relative prices, the rate of interest and the size of the general output of all goods together) form a self-contained system sufficient to determine all its own variables and impervious to any and all other influences, while the quantity of money and the level of absolute (*i.e.*, money) prices form a separate and independently self-determining system, then, if we reject Say's Law, we might have a situation where the "real" system was in disequilibrium, with total demand for commodities exceeding total supply, and yet where the "money" system was in equilibrium, with the demand for and supply of money equal to each other. But this, says Dr. Hahn, would contradict Walras's Law, according to which the total demand for all goods, *including money*, cannot fail to be (is iden-

tically) equal to the total supply, since "all goods" includes everything in terms of which demand can be exercised and likewise
everything comprised in "supply." However, if we assume Say's
Law, that is, *identical* (unconditional and logically inevitable)
equality between total demand and total supply of all goods *other
than* money, then by Walras's Law there must also be identical
equality between the quantity demanded and the quantity supplied of money, so that, since this equality holds regardless of any
change in the size of the money stock (the supply of money), no
such change can serve to determine the absolute price level; there
is no need for any particular price level to equalise the demand for
and the supply of money. By this dilemma, between a contradiction if we reject Say's Law and the indeterminacy of absolute
(that is, money) prices if we accept Say's Law, Dr. Hahn holds
Modigliani's argument condemned.

We think that in this part of a highly ingenious article Dr. Hahn
is over-subtle. No doubt it is true that unless *both* systems, real and
monetary, are in equilibrium, both must be in disequilibrium:
there must be excess demand in both (numerically equal and of
opposite sign) or in neither; but when the "real" system is in
equilibrium, this equilibrium includes a determinate interest rate,
to which the given *nominal* money stock must accommodate itself
by appropriate change of the absolute price level and so of the real
purchasing power represented by the given nominal money stock.
There is, we are assuming, equilibrium in the "real" system and so,
by Walras's Law, there must be equilibrium in the money system;
and this latter equilibrium can be attained because by assumption
changes of the price *level* do not disturb the equilibrium of the
real system.

This is the escape from Dr. Hahn's two-pronged fork, if we are
prepared to reject Say's Law; and surely Say's Law, true in a
non-monetary economy, can find no logical basis in an economy which
uses money. If goods are in fact bought and sold for money, and a
money stock exists in the economy, it seems plain that money can
be withdrawn from the stock and used on the commodity market,
thus upsetting Say's Law. But suppose, against all reason, we
insist on believing in Say's Law in the "real" part of a money
economy? Then surely we must ask for a *complete* money economy.
What is wrong with Dr. Modigliani's model is that it makes no
mention of bonds. How can money be lent except in exchange for
bonds? If, then, the money system in Dr. Modigliani's model
comprises money *and bonds* it can obey a "Say's Law" of its own in
the sense that the total demand and supply of monetary assets
(money *and* bonds) must be identically equal, and still determine
the interest rate by an equilibrium money price of bonds.

Dismissing theories which make interest to depend only on productivity and thrift, or on the *ex ante* equality of saving and investment, because such theories take no account of people's decisions of what to do with their accumulations of *past* saving, which exist at all moments in various forms exchangeable for each other at prices which express the interest rate, Dr. Hahn turns to theories which do concern themselves with the prices of *old*, as well as those of *new*, bonds. These other theories are, first, the loanable-funds theory, which says that the interest rate will change unless the excess demand for bonds is zero, and secondly, the liquidity preference theory, which some have interpreted as saying that the interest rate will change unless the excess demand for money is zero. Dr. Hahn, however, rejects this latter interpretation. For people can add to their money balances by supplying, in any interval, productive services in excess of the value of goods they demand for consumption in that interval. But Keynes explained that liquidity preference enters only at the second of two decision-stages involved in the satisfaction of people's time-preferences. At the first of these stages the individual must decide how much of his income to consume or how much to save, and here there is no question of liquidity preference. At the second stage, however, he must decide in what kind of assets he shall hold the results of saving, and here alone liquidity preference is involved. A theory which says that the interest rate is what equilibrates the demand and supply of money can, therefore, in particular circumstances imply that the interest rate equilibrates *reluctance to save* with desire for liquidity. The next step of Dr. Hahn's reasoning from this consideration is not quite easy to follow. For he is not satisfied simply to accept the consideration as a necessary consequence of discussing the interest rate in terms of a model of general interdependence. On these latter lines we might be inclined to dismiss this objection against regarding the interest rate as the price which eliminates an excess demand for money. For on what *general* ground can we elect the rate of exchange between one pair of mutually exchangeable things as worthy of attention and ignore that between another pair? Sir Dennis Robertson's threefold frontier between consumption, the purchase of earning assets and the accumulation of liquid ones, and indeed the general interdependence conception as a whole, require us to look upon the desire to consume, and the desire to accumulate liquid assets, as possible direct rivals of each other. In particular circumstances the motive to save may be the desire not for wealth in general but for the security or manoeuvring power conferred by *liquid* wealth. I may be willing to forgo wine for a year in order to have one hundred pounds in the bank, but not in order to pay off one-tenth of my mortgage debt. Apparently accepting such a view, Dr. Hahn nevertheless argues that "liquidity preference must be taken as determining the *ratio* ("form") in which assets are demanded, and *not* the total quantity of assets demanded or supplied" [16]. The argument which he builds on this leads us, by an interesting fresh route, to that question and difficulty which in my own view are the supreme enigma of interest theory and the real source of all its troubles.

Let us suppose, then, (Dr. Hahn says), that at some date *ex ante* saving is less than *ex ante* investment, and that accordingly there is an excess supply[1] of bonds. Suppose also that the *ratio* in which money and bonds are demanded is the same as that in which they are supplied. In this case the loanable-funds theory predicts a rise in the interest rate, but Dr. Hahn's interpretation of the liquidity preference theory predicts no change in the interest rate. Dr. Hahn none the less reconciles the two theories. Excess demand equations, he says, are to be understood as holding *ex ante*; that is to say, the equality of the two sides is looked to be attained at the end of some still-future "planning period" (which we may distinguish as the investment planning period). His model assumes that investment plans are (objectively; presumably within the knowledge of some super-human observer) certain to be fulfilled. This in turn implies that investors will during the (investment) planning period obtain the necessary finance. Thus within that period two transactions must take place: first, bonds must be sold for money, and then this money must be used to buy investment goods (machines, etc.). Extending from the investor's "present" to some interior date of the investment planning period, therefore, there is a second and shorter period which we might call the finance planning period. There are in fact two planning periods, a shorter one concerned with obtaining finance and a longer one concerned with using it. Corresponding to *each* of these there is a pair of ratios, the ratio in which money and bonds are demanded and the ratio in which they are supplied. Between the members of one of these pairs (in particular, the one referring to the end of the investment planning period) there can be equality notwithstanding that between the members of the other pair there is inequality, an inequality caused by the intending investors' temporary need to accumulate funds ready to spend on investment goods. As soon as this spending actually takes place the equilibrium of the investment planning period will re-assert itself over the disequilibrium of the finance planning period. Both theories are right: the loanable funds theory, which says that there will be disequilibrium in the finance planning period, and the liquidity preference theory, which says that there will be equilibrium in the investment planning period (in the circumstances assumed, viz., a ratio between the supply of money and that of bonds which is correct provided demand is not distorted by the need for "finance" for investment schemes).

If, in thus reconstructing Dr. Hahn's argument, I have preserved its essence, we have, I think, to recognise two very important questions which it raises. The first is whether it is useful or appropriate to think of finance and investment not merely as distinct stages in each separate equipment-augmenting operation by each individual business-man but also as *observable* stages in the economy's aggregate flow of equipment augmentation. For surely the release of finance which occurs when one firm spends its hoard can supply the need of another firm to build up its hoard? To say this is not in the least to deny that when a *given* aggregate national income contains a large investment component there may be required a different ratio of money to bonds from what is required when the income consists wholly of consumption. For when all transactions are small no marshalling of great sums may be needed. It will also be true that when the investment flow is planned to increase, the interest rate will tend to rise because the necessary extra finance will have first to be marshalled and then later released. But, secondly, a much more interesting and radical difficulty confronts us. The length, in calendar terms, of the planning periods is not a matter of indifference, for the relative quantities of new and old bonds offered for sale during such a period will depend on it. More fundamentally, what is the meaning, in the theory, of the length of the planning period and what determines it? These questions raise a basic theoretical and methodological issue, that of the co-existence in some markets, and pre-eminently in the bond market, of two separate possible equilibria, an equilibrium of stocks and an equilibrium of flows, and that of the relation between these two and the question whether one or other is dominant or by what process they influence each other and can both be satisfied at once.

Stock Analysis or Flow Analysis?

An essential step towards answering these questions resulted from a debate in 1950 among Professors Klein [23; 24], Fellner and Somers [13; 14] and Brunner [6]. Klein sought to show that Fellner and Somers in an earlier article [12] had been wrong to treat stock analysis and flow analysis in monetary interest theory as equivalent. He asked whether they deemed the interest rate to depend, in effect, on the whole history of the demand and supply relation for securities since time was, or only on that relation in some current period. They replied that if the whole history up to the beginning of the current period had resulted, at that beginning, in an equilibrium, then any divergence from equilibrium in the current period must result from the events of that period. This answer was rejected by Klein as question-begging. Karl Brunner, however, carried the whole matter forward by showing that if we opt for a stock rather than a flow theory, we have then to choose between a liquidity preference and a securities theory, and that different behaviour in the securities market is implied by these two theories.

Brunner considers first whether a stock or a flow theory is appropriate to the securities market. The contrast, we may interpolate, is between a market such as that for electricity or fresh milk, where what is demanded from moment to moment or from day to day must, in so far as demand is met, be produced from moment to moment or from day to day, and a market such as that for antique furniture, where supply is an existing and non-augmentable quantity existing at all times. The market for securities is evidently nearer to the antique furniture than the electricity end of the scale. Moreover, it is one where "the decision to hold the stock is continuously appraised in the light of current market situations." On the implied ground that the market is dominated by the effect of price changes in releasing a large volume of orders to sell *from stock* or to buy from stock, a volume which is large, that is to say, in relation to the orders which can arise from new issues, Professor Brunner simply declares that except in a stationary state where new issues are zero and where, accordingly, both stock equilibrium and flow equilibrium are achieved together, we shall find the "momentary" price to be determined by the stock relation. In the stationary state both stock and flow relations must be simultaneously satisfied, since the stationary state is one where the stock relation is satisfied subject to a special condition, viz., that flows be zero. The non-stationary heading covers the case of stock equilibrium combined with flow disequilibrium and the case of stock disequilibrium combined with flow equilibrium.

It is not easy to tell from what Professor Brunner writes whether he regards the stationary state, with zero new issues of bonds per unit of time, as the only possible double equilibrium, that is, simultaneous equilibrium of both stock desired to be held with stock existing, and flow desired to be issued with flow desired to be absorbed. When I am in a moving vehicle I am at each instant at some particular place (my "stock" situation) and moving at a certain speed (my "flow" situation). The combination of these two circumstances may be exactly what I desire for that instant. Were I not moving, I might wish to be in a different place; or were I at that instant in a different place I might desire to be moving at a different speed. Thus, it does not seem inconceivable that a particular stock of bonds and a particular pace of new issue of bonds may both be compatible with one and the same interest rate and that the combination of all three of these values of variables may satisfy everybody. In terms of our analogy, I may be moving, not because I would have preferred to be in a different place *at the given instant*, but because I aim to be in a different place at a later instant. In economic terms, wealth owners all taken together may be willing, at some particular interest rate, to increase their holding of bonds at just the pace at which borrowers wish, at that interest rate, to issue new bonds. I think that Professor Brunner does envisage this as a possible situation, since he seems in one passage to insist that, *even* in such a situation, the stock position is dominant. We must here interpolate a further passage of our own to ask whether in such a situation the stock position is indeed dominant.

The case for saying that wealth owners' and income-earners' attitude to existing stocks of "old" bonds is dominant, as compared with would-be lenders' and borrowers' attitude to new issues, rests in our judgment on the idea that *the quantity released on to the market* (by any considerable change in the interest rate) of old bonds *could* be much larger than that of new issues. A trespasser hesitates to walk through the farm-yard at night, not because he is menaced by one dog awake, but because that dog may wake the whole hostile household. But whether this will be so or not depends on how sound the household sleeps; or in our own terms, on how sensitive bond-holders, actual or potential, are to changes of price. This sensitiveness in its turn depends, we now assert, on the *uncertainty* of their price expectations. For let us consider an economy where there are no new issues or fresh borrowing nor redemption of debt, but merely a constant stock of bonds. Let us suppose that each wealth owner has in mind some specific future date (not necessarily the same for everyone) which is the nearest he cares to look to for capital gain or loss, and that each has in mind a particular price of bonds, which price he treats as *certain* to be attained on that date. Then, with due allowance for impending payments of coupon interest, any bond-holder whose expected price is higher than the current market price will be willing to hold bonds, anyone whose expected price is below the current market price will be unwilling to hold them. Using the horizontal axis of a Cartesian diagram for numbers of bonds, and the vertical axis for bond prices, we could draw a curve connecting with each present market bond price the number of bonds which, with a given set of bond price expectations (one price for each person), wealth owners would be willing to hold at that price. It would, of course, be downward sloping towards the right, since in order to find additional willing holders of bonds we should have to lower the present market price so that it sank below the expected prices of a further section of wealth owners, or in market terminology, so that it turned some more Bears into Bulls.

Now unless this curve had some actually horizontal segments, any change in the existing quantity of bonds would, so long as expectations of bond prices remained unchanged, require some change of the interest rate (that is, of the current market price of bonds). If expectations of all actual or potential bond-holders, or of all those within some range of expected bond prices, changed, the "shape and position" of the curve would change bodily, and again there would have to be some change of the current market price of bonds; that is, of the interest rate. But now let us suppose that instead of each wealth owner entertaining with certainty a unique expected bond price, he had in mind a range of prices, all of which he regarded as possible. It might then be a reasonable first-approximation hypothesis that a bond-holder would not wish to be rid of his bonds in exchange for money unless the current market price rose above the upper limit of his range of (subjectively) possible future prices, and would not wish to acquire more bonds in exchange for money unless the current market price fell below the lower limit of the range. This supposition would require us to draw two curves, one showing, for each hypothetical existing number of bonds, the price above which the current market price must not rise if that number of bonds is to find willing holders, the other showing, for each hypothetical size of the stock of bonds existing, the price below which the current market price must not fall if that number of bonds is not to fall short of the desired number. In this case the number of bonds existing could be changed within some range without necessitating a change in the interest rate (see Figure 1a) or expectations could change to some extent without necessitating such a change (see Figure 1b).

Let us turn to a more formal aspect of the determination of price in a market which can be supplied from an existing stock as well as from new production. Suppose that output of the good in question, measured as so-and-so many units of the good per unit of time, can be at all times differentiated with respect to time so that, in ordinary language, changes in its size are "smooth" and do not include jump-discontinuities. Then the quantity of the good coming on to the market from new production will, *in zero time at any instant*, be zero. Since in a market supplied *only* from new production we can suppose demand also to vanish to the same order as supply, when shorter and shorter intervals tending to zero were considered, a balance between demand and supply in every interval can be

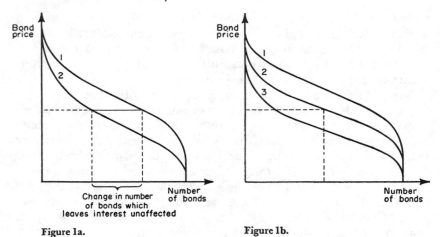

Figure 1a.

Figure 1b.

Curve 1: each ordinate shows highest bond price which will limit desired stock of bonds to that represented by the abscissa.

Curve 2: each ordinate shows lowest bond price which will make desired stock of bonds not less than that represented by the abscissa.

Curves 1 and 2: higher range of bond prices compatible with given bond stock.

Curves 2 and 3: lower range of bond prices compatible with given bond stock.

conceived, and we can perhaps further, with some artificiality, suppose such an equality *at all moments* between the demand-flow and the supply-flow to be brought about by price changes. But supply *from pre-existing stock* can be of finite amount in a zero interval of time. It is this circumstance which, in the less extreme form which it would take in reality, where flows are not "smooth" in the sense we have assumed, compels us to say that at any instant the price in such a market is dominated to some extent by the stock position. How great is this extent?

We know that except for some so-called "tap" issues of British Government securities, and any similar arrangements elsewhere, new bond issues do not conform to the smooth-stream model, but are made in large blocks by means of subscription lists which remain open for a few days, hours or minutes. There is thus much more in common between the mechanism and market impact of a new issue and that of a sale of a block of existing ("old") securities than the extreme analogy of electricity versus antique furniture would suggest. It thus appears that the most convenient way of combining the two sources of supply in one analysis is simply to regard the interest rate, in the way we were doing a few pages earlier, as the price which must stand at or move to that level at which all existing bonds, no matter whether they have existed for a century or have only this moment been put upon the market, can find willing holders. A new issue is thus incorporated into the analysis, not as something separate which influences matters *qua* "flow," but simply as what brings about a change in stocks and requires additional willing bond-holders to be found.

This leads to one final aspect of our interpolation. An equilibrium in the bond market may be looked on as having, possibly, two stages. There may at some instant, and some interest rate, be equality between the number of bonds requiring to be held and the number for which there exist willing holders. But the bonds existing may not be all in the hands of those willing to hold them. Thus sales must, or can, take place *at the current interest rate (i.e.,* bond price inverted) in order to bring about a complete matching of desired with actual individual holdings, this state of affairs being the second stage to which we referred above. It thus follows that the occurrence of bond sales and purchases is not an infallible sign of stock disequilibrium in the aggregative sense.

In the second part of his article Professor Brunner shows that even when we have accepted the appropriateness of a "stock" approach to the bond market, we have still to choose between a "liquidity" theory and a "securities" theory. The former declares that the rate of interest will change unless the existing stock of *money* is equal to the desired stock of money; the latter declares that the rate of interest will change unless the existing stock of *bonds* is equal to the desired stock of bonds. Further, the liquidity theory makes the speed of change of the interest rate to depend on the size of the difference between the existing and the desired stock of money, while the securities theory makes the speed of change of interest to depend on the size of the difference between the existing and the desired stock of bonds. The securities theory embodies Professors Fellner and Somer's belief that "in a multidimensional system there are a great many factors which affect the interest rate. However, in *any* system, these factors can affect the market rate of interest only through their effect on the demand and supply of interest-bearing securities." One thing, it appears, Professors Fellner and Somers have overlooked, although it fits without difficulty into their formula just quoted. Anything which affects *equally and simultaneously* the stock of bonds desired and the stock existing, and which *also* at the same time has its own independent effect on the thoughts, feelings or mental attitudes which underlie the desire for a given stock of bonds, so as to make this desire compatible with a different interest rate, can cause the rate to change *without* upsetting the equality of the desired and the existing stock of bonds. Indeed, what economist would not be willing to draw a diagram in which the demand and the supply curve of some commodity had each shifted in just such a way as to intersect at a different price but an unchanged quantity?

What thoughts, feelings or attitudes could change in such a way as to lead to such a shift? Professor Brunner's equations of the liquidity theory include among the independent variables, on which the speed of change of the interest rate might be supposed to depend, the speed of change of other prices in the system. We should ourselves prefer to say that the most relevant such influences are plainly *expectations* of price changes rather than observed, that is, *ex post* changes. Professor Brunner, however, does not refer, in his article, to expectations. In the specific mathematical form which Professor Brunner gives to it the securities theory gives no explicit place to the influence of any thoughts except those which can be resolved into functions of public *ex post* quantities.

The dilemma we found in Professor Brunner's article, which he himself seems to sweep aside, the dilemma that if there are two distinct mechanisms or sets of influences bearing on the interest rate, each by itself capable of attaining an equilibrium of its own, these two must in some way be mutually reconciled if they both bear on one and the same rate, may find a solution along lines which, for a different purpose, Mr. A. Llewellyn Wright [50] has most ingeniously suggested. The essence of Mr. Wright's proposal is that in an economy with *changing* income, and so with changing amounts per unit of time by which equipment and aggregate idle balances ("reserve," "speculative" or "pure liquidity" balances, as they might alternatively be called) are being augmented, the requirement of equality between the number of dependent variables and the number of mutually independent equations (which equality Mr. Wright, reasonably as we think, seems still prepared to accept as the equivalent of determinateness in many circumstances) allows *two* interest rates to operate simultaneously and separately on the market, the essential explanation being that their respective levels control the speeds of growth, respectively, of the saving-investment flow and of the hoarding or dishoarding flow. This, if in presenting it I have properly interpreted Mr. Wright, seems a most fertile suggestion. It means that a person's or a firm's affairs can be in equilibrium even when, for example, he is paying one rate of interest to borrow money and receiving a different one for lending it, not essentially because of any differences in risk or other such circumstances, but because he thus achieves the desired changes in the respective speeds of growth of his accumulated stocks of assets of different kinds. He ought, according to static analysis, to borrow just so much at any time that the rate of interest he pays on his marginal borrowing equals the rate he receives on his marginal lending. In a dynamic system the loss he appears to suffer by this failure to observe an equi-marginal rule may be the price he pays for, or the loss which is compensated by, the desired changes between one period and the next of the amounts added per period to his stocks, respectively, of equipment and of money.

The foregoing is my own statement of what Mr. Wright's article suggests to me. He, at least, proposes that there are two interest rates differing in their role and in the influences determining them; differing, that is to say, more essentially than in merely being "short-term" and "long-term" rates, although they may fall under these respective headings. One of these rates, called the "money rate of interest," is determined on a market which is almost literally the money market: "It can be regarded as the average rate of interest charged on bank overdrafts in any period; or, better still, it can be regarded as the Bank Rate." The other, called the "investment rate of interest," is "the rate which rules in the investment market proper, the market where the demand for investible funds is brought into equality with the supply of investible funds." His purpose in distinguishing, even in fundamental theory, two interest rates is to find for his lagged Keynesian model an extra variable unencumbered by an extra equation, since he believes the model otherwise to be over-determinate. As to the fitness of his device for its purpose, we are bound to ask whether this is not an example of that very disaggregation which Mr. Wright in his article recognises as ineffective, and Professor Brian Tew [45] has put forward the objection which must occur to every reader: can we conceptually split the loan market into halves so independent of each other that we need not have any equation connecting the prices which reign in them? We think, nonetheless, that Mr. Wright's work may yet be found to bear usefully upon our own problem, which, if the rate of interest has really to equilibrate both stock held with stock existing, and the *time-constricted* acts of offering bonds and money for mutual exchange, is also one of over-determinateness.

The problem of how "stock" influences and "flow" influences upon bond prices are related to each other can perhaps be put as follows. At any instant a stock of bonds exists. The change in the size of this stock in a short enough time interval is negligible, and thus, it appears, the bond price at any instant must be determined by those influences which make people willing or unwilling to hold a stock of bonds. Against this argument, however, the following may occur to us: in the market for such a good as electricity there is at no time any stock. The *quantity existing* at any instant is zero. Yet there is a price, validly looked upon as depending on the confrontation of supply conditions and demand conditions. Evidently a price can be determined by the comparison of the potential sizes of two flows, each depending on this price, which must be such as to equalise them. Yet is it not true that the quantity supplied in any interval tends to zero with that interval, just as the growth of a stock in some time interval becomes negligible if that interval is taken short enough? The answer plainly is, that when we are simply concerned with two flows, both the quantity supplied and the quantity demanded vanish to the same order, and thus, in a familiar way, we can think of the ratio of these two flows as remaining finite while we carry to the limit the shortening of the interval of measurement. In the measurement of a stock, of course, no time interval is in any way relevant, and thus a flow which requires some finite lapse of time to be accumulated into some finite quantity cannot influence the size or price of a stock *at some instant*.

It is an argument of this sort which I take to underlie Mr. R. W. Clower's [8] disposal of the problem:

> The aggregate quantities of various assets existing in an economy in any given period of time are inherited from the past. These quantities can be altered only gradually as a result of future economy decisions, so that if we consider appropriately short time periods, current additions to (or depletions of) aggregate asset stocks can be ignored.

Mr. Clower's purpose is to show that productivity and thrift do play an essential role in the interest rate's historical course. By regarding the rate at any moment as depending purely on the stock situation at that moment, namely the size of the bond stock, the expectations of individuals about future bond prices, the current prices of other assets, Mr. Clower can maintain that new issues of bonds, and retirements of existing bonds, occurring to-day, do not affect the rate to-day, unless they alter expectations. But when we look at two dates separated in time, the interest rate at the later date will be what it proves to be partly because of the change in size of the bond stock which new issues and retirements in the interval have brought about. The time rate at which such new issues and retirements will have taken place will be influenced by changes in productivity and thrift.

Changes in productivity may arise, as Mr. Clower points out, from inventions or other sources, and thrift also is subject to many influences. Indeed, we may say that these are in a sense only names for certain superficial aspects of the whole complex course of economic history, and Mr. Clower's aim is not, I think, to isolate productivity and thrift because they are more important than other strands in that skein, but because he wishes to get these recurrently self-assertive explanations of interest permanently filed away in the right box.

Despite the solutions to which we may resort for a practical means of handling, in our theoretical discussions, the co-existence of a "stock" mechanism and a "flow" mechanism in the market where money and bonds are exchanged for each other, this co-existence remains the most serious theoretical problem concerning the interest rate. In his article "The Equivalence of the Liquidity Preference and Loanable Funds Theories and the *New* [italics in original] Stock-flow Analysis" [27], Mr. Cliff Lloyd concludes that it is at present unsolved. He presents the matter formally, in the frame of Professor Hicks's demonstration that the liquidity preference and loanable funds theories are equivalent:

> In a consistent *n*-good system, two of the goods being bonds and money, if any $n - 1$ excess demand equations are satisfied, the *n*th must also be satisfied, thus the *n*th may be dropped .... The loanable funds theory drops the money equation, the liquidity preference theory drops the bond equation, but the two are equivalent .... This is quite a simple and clear-cut proof, provided that each of the goods in the system is represented by only one excess demand equation, but ... in an explicit stock-flow theory any stock-flow good will be represented by two excess demand equations [27].

A stock-flow good is one whose quantity, existing as a stock at each instant, can be different at different instants because a flow of the good is produced and another flow consumed, and because these flows, each measured as so-and-so many units per time-unit, can differ from each other. By equilibrium in respect of such a good, Mr. Cliff Lloyd means constancy of the stock. However, a price for the good which makes equal the stock existing and the stock desired to be held is not necessarily the same as the price which makes equal the flow produced and the flow consumed. The difference between the desired and existing stocks, considered as a function of price, gives as an excess stock demand equation, the difference between desired consumption flow and flow of production forthcoming, considered as a function of price, gives us the excess flow demand equation. Unless the difference between production and consumption is zero, the stock will be changing; that is to say, the market for the good will not be in equilibrium. The converse, however, is not true. Equality between the flows of production and consumption does not imply equality between the desired and the existing stocks. "Thus according to the 'new' stock-flow economics a stock-flow good, that is, one which is produced, consumed and held, must be represented in a general equilibrium system not with one but with two excess demand equations" [27].

Hence Mr. Cliff Lloyd infers that, whether or not in fact the liquidity preference and loanable funds theories are one and the same, Professor Hicks's proof that they are so does not hold in regard to a good which is produced and consumed as well as being held in stock. He is careful *not* to infer that no proof can ever be found.

Mr. Cliff Lloyd's argument calls for one or two comments. He does not appear to be justified in saying that Clower and Bushaw [9] were the first to study the equilibrium of a good which is produced and consumed as well as held in stock. Contrary to his assertion, Karl Brunner's article [6] referred to above deals with this case. Mr. Cliff Lloyd's particular problem is the same as that posed by Mr. Llewellyn Wright [50], but Mr. Cliff Lloyd sees no *general* solution. He shows that special assumptions will give us a model where the two excess demand equations are in effect one and the same, so that Professor Hicks's proof would apply. His way of specifying the two excess demand equations of the general case appears to us to be open to criticism. In our paraphrase of his argument we have been speaking, first, of an excess flow demand equation (as he does), but secondly, of an excess stock demand equation (as he does not). He prefers to add together the stock and flow demands and so define his second equation as "the market excess demand equation which shows the total market demand, both stock and flow, for the good." All the difficulties we have referred to in earlier pages, of justifying any particular choice of the length of the period of measurement of the flow, and, more fundamentally, the doubtful propriety of adding together two quantities of different dimension, a stock with no time-denominator and a flow which is necessarily expressed as so much per unit of time, are involved in Mr. Cliff Lloyd's method, which we have therefore chosen to re-express.

In an article [36] later than his book Professor Patinkin has argued as follows: each individual has some stock of money "now," and desires the prospect of having some particular stock at the "next" date when the matter will arise, which date we may (by a usual convention) take to be the same for everyone. Thus each individual's attitude may be *alternatively* expressed, either as a desire for some future *stock* or as a desire for some particular *change*, between now and then, in his existing stock. Dividing this change by the number of time units in the interval, we have a flow. (Professor Patinkin in this particular article does not make explicit the need for this latter step.) Thus, says Professor Patinkin, stock analysis and flow analysis are alternative ways of looking at the matter, and we have not two equations, but one.

This argument seems to us fallacious. The size which a thing has at some instant and its speed of change at that instant are two distinct things, each separately subject to choice. If Professor Patinkin prefers to regard the individual as choosing the size that his money stock shall have at the "next" date rather than "now" he must allow him to choose *also* the speed at which that money stock shall be growing, or about to grow (or decline) at that next date. However, he writes:

> Before concluding this part of the paper, I should like to re-state its general argument in the following way: Stock analysis, as well as flow analysis, pre-supposes a period of time: namely the period between the moment *at* which the individual is making his plans, and the moment *for* which he is making them. Hence if the periods pre-supposed by the analysis are the same, the excess-demand function of stock analysis must be identical with that of flow analysis. This proposition holds also in the limiting case where the period is an instantaneous one.

Why does Professor Patinkin think that the individual, in making his plans *for* a particular moment, must only concern himself with the change which will then *have occurred* and not with the one which will then be about to occur? Why, in other words, should the individual concern himself only with *one* future moment? Is it because Professor Patinkin is in this passage concerned only with "static equilibrium"? But in static equilibrium analysis do we speak of plans and distinguish the moment when they are made from the moment when they apply? The really essential point, however, is that stock equilibrium can be achieved *instantaneously* by *price changes*, *e.g.*, of bonds, without the price which effects this equality between desired and *existing* stocks necessarily bringing about an equality between the stocks desired for the "next" relevant date and the stocks which, comprising existing stock and impending "production," will exist on that next date.

Patinkin's position of 1958 [36] has been criticised by Mr. Hugh Rose [41], who refers in a short note published in 1959 to a 1957 article [40] of his own. In that earlier article Mr. Rose interprets and contrasts the Keynesian and loanable funds theories of interest. Professor H. G. Johnson [19] had suggested that the Keynesian theory is "static," seeking only to explain the state of affairs in a short-period equilibrium and how changes in circumstances will alter the equilibrium values, while the loanable funds theory is dynamic and seeks to explain precisely how interest and income move from one equilibrium to another when circumstances have changed. In contrast with this position of Professor Johnson's, Mr. Rose sees Keynes's theory also as dynamic.

In Mr. Rose's general dynamic model (providing a formal frame within which both Keynesian and loanable funds theories can be dynamically interpreted) it is assumed that the expenditure plans of both households and business are always realised, any discrepancy between the total of these plans, on one hand, and current production, on the other, falling on the buffer stocks of finished goods held by producers. Such a discrepancy is the excess demand (positive or negative) for goods. The excess demand for money is the difference between the stock of money which the public desires to hold and the stock which exists. The loanable funds theory says that the interest rate will change if the sum of the two excess demands is other than zero. The Keynesian theory (in Mr. Rose's view) says that the interest rate will change if, and only if, the excess demand for money is other than zero. If then, we believe that the excess demand for loans is the sum of the excess demands for goods and for money, Keynes appears to be maintaining that the interest rate can change even if the excess demand for loans (the excess supply of securities) is zero, and remain constant even when the excess demand for loans is not zero. Mr. Rose's solution of this dilemma is two-fold. First, he rejects "Walras's Law" that the algebraic sum of the excess demands for goods, money and securities is zero. Secondly, he shows that in Keynes's construction the excess demand for loans is always equal to the excess demand for money.

This latter result arises in the simplest fashion. Producers finance the whole of their production (of consumption goods and investment goods taken together) by sales, made concurrently with the production itself, of consumers' goods and securities. If the total of consumers' goods and securities which income receivers want to buy is smaller than the total that producers want to sell the difference is plainly an excess demand for money, and this excess demand for money is exactly the excess of the securities offered by producers over the securities demanded by income receivers: the excess demand for money and the

$$\begin{pmatrix} \text{excess supply of securities} \\ \text{excess demand for loans} \end{pmatrix}$$

are equal. An even simpler statement of the matter is as follows: In the Keynesian system the excess demand for goods *in any one period* is identically zero; for we are to conceive of decisions how much of this and that good to produce within, say, the coming month being taken at the beginning of that month and always adhered to. When goods have been produced someone has in a sense bought them, whether they wanted to or not; for someone has done the work and has a claim to the result. The lack of sufficient effective demand shows itself, in the minds of enterprisers, *before* they make their decisions as to how much to produce in the coming month; and naturally they are much influenced in their production decisions by reflecting on how much of last month's production has been left, contrary to their plans, on their own hands and been "bought" by themselves.

There is no doubt in the present writer's mind that Keynes thought of the interest rate as adjusting itself to the nut-cracker squeeze of the quantity of money existing and the quantity desired, by changes in the price of fixed-interest securities, as these were offered or demanded by those who wished for extra money or had more money than they wanted. Liquidity preference can, of course, be influenced by very many circumstances and considerations, including the prices and price changes of consumers' goods or producers' goods: all markets are in some degree inter-dependent. But it is on the securities market that the interest rate actually *emerges* as, *e.g.*, the quotient of Consol coupon rate over Consol market price.

None the less, we must maintain that it is an essential part of Keynes's vision that the interest rate *can* change without any transactions in bonds at all, and without any emergence on the Stock Market of an excess demand or supply of bonds. If it happened that every holder of bonds or money said to himself at some moment: "If the rate of interest were one point higher, my present holding would be just what I should choose to have" and if a testing of the market revealed this consensus of opinion, then the rate might be found to have moved up one point without any transactions. That is made virtually explicit in the *Treatise on Money*.

Professor H. G. Johnson's highly condensed and wide-ranging survey article on "Some Cambridge Controversies in Monetary Theory" [19] is remarkable for the contrast between the ease with which he is able, on Keynesian lines largely made explicit by Mrs. Joan Robinson, to handle every kind of shift in the macro-economic situation and show what sequence of changes will be undergone by the interest rate, the net investment flow, income and the rest, when some autonomous psychological, technical or political transition disturbs an equilibrium, on one hand; and on the other, the awkward and artificial air of his account of them in terms of a Robertsonian dynamics. Professor Johnson says that "The Keynesian theory . . . is a static theory; it is not concerned with the succession of changing [partial] equilibrium positions but only with the position which represents an equilibrium of all the forces at work." This may be formally true; I am sure it does not represent the spirit or purpose of Keynes's thought. To be formally correct, Keynes ought, no doubt, to have carefully specified the precise character and mode of operation of the influence exerted by prosperous conditions on the inducement to invest, and to have pointed out in so many words that prosperous conditions arise when, for any reason, employment, output and income are increased; and so on. He did not do so. The accelerator, the "investment coefficient" and all such are markedly absent from the *General Theory* (though not, in substance, from the *Treatise on Money*). In Chapter 22 of the *General Theory*, however, Keynes indicates plainly his conception of the way in which wide shifts of the *schedule* or curve of the marginal efficiency of capital induce abrupt and great changes in investment and hence in all its dependent variables.

Is it then better to have highly special, arbitrary and clanking mechanical systems, in which our assumptions single out one or two variables, make expectations, confidence and the whole gossamer fabric of investment-incentive to depend on these alone, and tell us precisely what effect a change in these variables will have on investment; or is it better to recognise that the inducement to invest is influenced by countless subtle aspects of the recent past and the "news" (all taking colour and meaning, of course, from the historical background which has conditioned men's minds and bequeathed them their resources) and leave ourselves freedom to analyse these from case to case as best we may by *formally* treating (as Keynes did in effect) the inducement to invest as autonomous or exogenous? Again, when we try to understand the effects of changes in the quantity of money, is it better to chase packets of money in and out of the labyrinth of balances held or spent at different times for different kinds of purposes, at the greatest risk of muddling the identities of the various packets and the dates of the various transactions, or is it better to consider a *stock* of money, existing at a particular moment and matching or failing to match the stock desired at that moment; desired for a list of motives which we can make short or long at convenience: payments reserve, speculative asset, "finance" marshalled for impending investment or what you will; and thus to show what market forces, at that same moment, will bear on the prices of bonds and thus push up or down the rate of interest? Keynes's critics have discussed whether his system is static or dynamic: they have not seen that it is *dramatic*, and that this quality arises from his method of cornering many problems and complications in one concept and dealing with them by a radical simplification. That this is the true Cambridge secret has been well understood by Mr. Lawrence E. Fouraker [15]. Writing of Marshall and Keynes he says:

> Their intellects were too proud, resourceful and thorough to go on with the thesis without firmly establishing the connections. Having satisfied themselves, however, they employed a curious

device when it came to recording the results of their pursuits. Instead of leading the reader through the intricate analytical processes that their own minds had recently traversed, they would provide a short cut, in the form of an assumption whose purpose was to eliminate consideration of the difficult problem they had faced and solved.

If all Keynes's critics had possessed Mr Fouraker's insight, what seas of ink could have been saved.

The Classical System: Incomplete or Over-determined?

The question "What determines the interest rate?" has been in postwar years one of a group of intimately linked problems which in the course of debate have seemed to swing round each other continually in a sort of whirlpool, now one, now another becoming central as article succeeds article from writers with different viewpoints. Among these problems is the question, discussed with brilliant clarity by Becker and Baumol [1], whether, as Lange [26] and Patinkin [31, 32, 33, 34] have maintained, the Lausanne School and other neo-classicals so defined their systems that *either* these systems were incomplete through asserting the *identical* equality of total commodity demand and supply (Say's *identity*) and thus being able to show only how inter-commodity exchange rates are determined and unable to show how absolute money prices are determined, or *else* that they were self-contradictory through assuming, in addition to Say's identity, that stocks of money are wanted for their own sake, so that the total stock of money can be other than just what, at given money prices of commodities, is desired, and can thus affect the demand for these commodities and make it other than equal to the supply. In brief, are the commodity market and the money market entirely separate from each other, so that the one determines in a wholly self-contained manner the *relative* prices of commodities and the other determines nothing because there is in it only one good, and this is always available (being not a real money but a mere *numéraire*) in just the quantity required, just as runs in cricket are available to the man in the scorer's box in just the quantity he requires for recording the events in the field of play? Or, on the contrary, are the markets connected so that when there is an excess supply of money there is *ipso facto* an equal excess demand for goods?

Becker and Baumol argue (with the support of much evidence by quotation) that what the classicals had in mind was not Say's identity but Say's *equality*. At first sight we might be inclined to think that Say's equality is a mere definitional truism to the effect that in equilibrium demand and supply are equal. But Becker and

Baumol mean by it the assertion that if an equilibrium is disturbed, as by an arbitrary increase or reduction in the existing quantity of money, a new equilibrium will be found through such changes in the price level as will make the new quantity of money just sufficient. For if the desired and existing money stock are unequal, people will offer a greater, or smaller, total money value of commodities than they demand, in order to acquire, or dispose of, stocks of money. When money prices of commodities have been given time to adjust themselves to this pressure the desired stock of money, which depends on the prices of commodities, will have adjusted itself to the quantity existing.

The question which here interpolates itself is this: If we add to the assumed system a bond market, will a change in the price of bonds, that is, a change of the interest rate, help to adjust the desired to the existing money stock? From Ricardo to Patinkin, some have said that the long-period *equilibrium* interest rate will be unaffected, and will therefore have no effect on the equilibrium of the rest of the system. Keynes, being uninterested in the long period (in which, by definition, all prices including those of productive factors are perfectly flexible), said nothing about long-period equilibrium, but said instead, like Ricardo, that in the short period the interest rate will be different and will affect other things.

Becker and Baumol do not themselves consider any role of an interest rate, but conclude that the neo-classicals did not treat the economic system as divided into two entirely separate enclaves, the non-monetary and the monetary, but instead believed, as Becker and Baumol express it, that "money derives a 'utility' from the goods it can buy, it is true, but because it can buy them at the moment the buyer considers convenient."

From a conventionally simplified frame for the question whether or not an economic system, given time, will adjust itself to any change in the size of its money stock so as to reach a new equilibrium not differing in essentials from the old, the ripples have spread out towards answers based on more and more subtle and complex assumptions. Mr. E. J. Mishan [29] distinguishes between a "cash balance effect" and an "asset-expenditure effect," and charges Patinkin with having treated them as one, at first under the name "Pigou effect" and later as "real balance effect." When the price level falls, even a person who happens at that moment to have no cash balance may feel a desire or a freedom, because his assets are now worth more in terms of the kinds of goods he desires, to spend more per time-unit on such goods. If, however, his assets consist partly in cash, he will have an additional incentive to increase his expenditure per time-unit. For now he has in hand a larger stock of cash than is needed for convenience in bridging the time gap between receipts and outgoings of cash, and so it will be natural to get rid of some of the surplus cash. Once we introduce bonds and a bond market into our system, it is plain that surplus cash may be spent either on commodities (encouraging their output and raising their prices directly) or on bonds (lowering the interest rate and encouraging investment, and so other output, *indirectly*). Because of such considerations, it is exceedingly difficult to justify any particular line of separation between monetary theory and interest theory.

In the brilliant article of 1956 by S. C. Tsiang [46] we find carried a stage further the policy of generalising the analysis so as to embrace the mutual influence of interest, employment, output, income and velocity of circulation. Mr. Tsiang's first purpose is to show, in a manner quite different from that of Walras's Law, that the liquidity preference and loanable funds theories of the determination of interest are identical "in the sense that the two sets of demand and supply functions, *i.e.*, the demand for and the supply of loanable funds, and the demand for money to hold and the stock of money in existence, would determine the same rate of interest in all circumstances, if both sets of demand and supply functions are formulated correctly in the *ex ante* sense."

Mr. Tsiang rejects the approach via Walras's Law on the ground that it links interest no more intimately with money than with any of the other multifarious goods of the general equilibrium system. Walras's Law, which simply says that the demand for everything, including money, is necessarily identical with the supply of everything, including money, shows that in the general equilibrium system we have one redundant demand and supply equation which follows from all the rest, and that accordingly some one equation, *no matter which*, may be dropped. Such an argument leads to no more explicit theory of interest than the mere statement that interest is included in the general determinate equilibrium. To invoke the Law is, says Mr. Tsiang, to use an *ex post* definition of the demand and supply of money.

Mr. Tsiang's criticism of Fellner and Somers [12] concerns the very fundamental question of how to combine stock and flow demand in one analysis. Fellner and Somers, he says, define the total supply of money as total money expenditures on goods and services as well as on the purchases of "claims" plus the amount of money held unspent.

> This total of the so-called "supply of money," the main components of which are flows over time, does not necessarily equal the total stock of money in existence (which is the usual meaning of the supply of money in the liquidity preference theory) unless the period of time over which the flows of money expenditures are measured is so defined as to make them equal.

Mr. Tsiang in his positive analysis does in fact define a "period" with this special purpose in view. But his "period" is in effect an instant, his payments are merely the allocation to various uses, by each holder of money, of all the money he possesses at that instant. In fact, Mr. Tsiang is simply adopting that definition [22] of the total quantity of money in existence, which says that it equals the total of all payments that can be made by all money holders *simultaneously*. By compelling all the economic subjects in his system to make payments at such discrete instants, Mr. Tsiang combines the notion of stock of money existing *at* an instant, with flow of payments made during some time *interval*, viz., the interval separating two of his discrete instants. Thus he shows that when people want to hold money, *for whatever reason*, and there is in total only just so and so much money for them all to hold, something must adjust their desires to this circumstance. That something is the rate of interest, and it is a matter of indifference whether we call his system a liquidity preference or a loanable funds system.

We said, however, that Mr. Tsiang's construction allows people to desire to hold money "for any reason." This, in his view, is the crux of the matter and the point on which he thinks liquidity preference theorists took a distorted view. Perhaps he is doing them an injustice. His starting-point (where surely everyone can agree) is that demand and supply schedules are *ex ante* concepts. It is indeed obvious that, since they express potential reactions, conditional decisions as to what will be done should this or that circumstance arise, they must refer to intended, future action; they are descriptions of people's forward-looking states of mind, even if we happen to be studying those states of mind from a viewpoint which places them in our past. Now Mr. Tsiang fastens upon Keynes's admission, in his article called "Alternative Theories of the Rate of Interest" [22], that intended acts of large-scale investment may provide a special motive for liquidity preference, that is, for desiring to accumulate or marshall large money balances ready for the execution of these investment schemes. Such mobilising of money "at the ready" for investment, Keynes called the motive of "finance." It was, in his view, just one more source of a desire to hold money rather than to be the possessor of someone else's I.O.U.s. Now Mr. Tsiang says that this "finance" motive is merely a part of the ordinary "transactions demand" for money. We can wholeheartedly agree with him, and so would Keynes have done, and so does Professor Hicks in his famous "Suggestion for Simplifying the Theory of Money." Professor Hicks says, in effect, that when your desire for money arises from the transactions motive, it is a desire to have money *ready* to make payments, because the time which will elapse between your receipt of the money and the need to pay it out is, or may be, too short to make the lending of a small sum worth while. Of course, the transactions motive is an *ex ante* motive. Whoever said it was not? Only proponents of a mechanical quantity theory of money.

Mr. Tsiang concludes his sections on interest with these words:

> All the disagreements between the loanable funds and liquidity preference theories on practical issues seem to arise from the failure on the part of liquidity preference theorists themselves to perceive the dependence of the aggregate liquidity preference (or demand for money) function upon the consumption and investment functions.

We feel bound to say that this statement betrays a misunderstanding of the *methodology* of the liquidity preference theory. That theory elects to concentrate on the question: Given the expectations, plans, uncertainties, hopes and fears, as well as the distribution of resources, which exist *at some moment*, where must the price of bonds stand to equilibrate the resulting market impulses? Those expectations and plans have been shaped by past history and by the most recent "news," but they have been so shaped by an inter-play so complex and subtle as to defy explicit analysis. We can, if we wish (and Mr. Tsiang is one among many who have wished), make assumptions which will enable us to trace explicitly the emergence of to-day's market situation from yesterday's. Such a model will be a mind-clearing stereotype of certain aspects of how things happen in the economic world. But in what sense, or under what conditions, can they serve as predictive models?

Mrs. Joan Robinson introduces her article on "The Rate of Interest" [39] with a definition of "a dynamic analysis" which will surely never be bettered. Its characteristic is, she says, "that it cannot explain how an economy behaves, in given conditions, without reference to past history; while static analysis purports to describe a position of equilibrium which the system will reach no matter where it started from." She further explains the paradox of Keynes's *General Theory*: "Short-period analysis is concerned with the equilibrium of a system with a given stock of capital and with given expectations about the future. Past history is thus put into the initial conditions, so that the analysis is static in itself, and yet is part of a dynamic theory." Thus we have, from Cambridge itself, a sanction and confirmation of Mr. Fouraker's thesis [15].

Disposing first of the role of productivity and thrift, Mrs. Robinson shows that these govern the answer to the question "What rate of interest will bring about full employment?" For a fall of the interest rate stimulates investment, and the degree to which investment needs stimulation, in order to make employment full, depends on the size of the saving-gap to be filled, and this gap itself is, if anything, made smaller by a fall in the interest rate. If the market rate of interest ever stands below the full-employment rate there will be inflation which will drive the market rate up to equality with the full-employment rate. The latter thus provides a "floor" for the market rate.

Turning to the short period, Mrs. Robinson ascribes the relation between the income expected from each kind of asset, and the price of that kind, to the varying types and degrees of illiquidity which those kinds involve. These types of illiquidity she distinguishes as *inconvenience, capital uncertainty, lender's risk* and *income uncertainty*. Inconvenience is the lack of a perfect market, depriving the asset-holder of "the power to realise its value in cash, whatever the value may be at the moment." Here we have perhaps some ambiguity about the meaning of "the" value. This sounds like "market value"; but the market value *at any moment* is what can *immediately* be obtained, and if the market is limited and imperfect this may be nothing. It might be better to define inconvenience as the asset-holder's lack of assurance that whatever (now unknown) value he shall attach to his asset at some future moment he will be able at that moment without delay or cost to sell it for that price. Uncertainty concerning future capital value can be otherwise expressed as uncertainty about what rate of interest will rule at future moments. Keynes, Mrs. Robinson says, "regards the rate of interest primarily as a premium against the possible loss of capital if an asset has to be realised before its redemption date." Lender's risk is the fear of the borrower's default. Income uncertainty exists for the lender when he lends on short term and will have soon to relend at he knows not what rate of interest.

Different assets, Mrs. Robinson says, are affected in different degrees by each of these qualities. Bills are very little, and bonds very much, subject to capital uncertainty, while the case is reversed for income uncertainty. Thus the relative prices and yields of bills and bonds will depend, given the supply of each, on the relative (weighted) number of "widows and orphans" who desire certainty of *income* and financial institutions who set great store by their balance sheets and desire certainty of capital values. "The general pattern of interest rates depends on the distribution of wealth between owners with different tastes, relatively to the supplies of the various kinds of assets."

On this basis Mrs. Robinson discusses the kinds of ripples or of permanent changes of level which will occur in the interest-rate pond when various disturbing events, such as changes in the quantity of money, in expectations, in thriftiness, in the size of the investment flow, and such as the adoption of a cheap-money policy, are thrown into it. Far the most intractable of these influences is expectations, and these she treats by a masterly and highly realistic *tour de force*, that of assuming that at all times, with greater or less conviction, people assume that interest rates will sooner or later return to some "normal" level which more or less recent experience has established in their minds. This accepted "norm" can itself be changed, and a cheap-money policy ill-timed or too recklessly pursued, which has therefore to be abandoned, may strengthen the general belief in a norm which is higher than the one that might have been established by a more canny approach.

There was, until 1930 or thereabouts, a "Cambridge" approach to monetary theory, in which the names of Marshall, Lavington, Robertson and Keynes suggested distinct but harmonious variants. In 1926, indeed, Sir Dennis Robertson's *Banking Policy and the Price Level* lit up the horizon of professional economics and heralded the great era of monetary theory that lasted until the War. The generous acknowledgment it made of suggestive discussions with Keynes promised a Cambridge school as closely knit as the Vienna or the Stockholm school. Unhappily the cave was not big enough to hold two giants. Sir Dennis's apparatus, with its refreshing terminology of "splashing," "lacking" and so forth, was aimed at a careful unravelling of the monetary skein. It has its lasting place in the history of thought, it typically illustrates its inventor's ingenious power to match the closest analysis with the freest fancy, and it explains the delight which his style has given to thousands of hearers and readers. Keynes's ultimate method, by contrast, was the sword of Alexander. He cut, not unravelled, the monetary tangle of ideas.

The Cambridge concert of ideas was split by the *General Theory*, and even Professor Hicks's powerful synthesising habit of mind has been unable to close the gap. That gap, we are therefore entitled to assume, is unclosable. We cannot here avoid an expression of view. The Keynesian whale under Mrs. Robinson's management can swallow with ease all fish which come to its jaws. To play them with Robertsonian hook and line, with no matter what ingenious shifts and stratagems, is much more laborious.

In his review [2] of Maurice Allais' *Economie et Intérêt*, Professor Kenneth Boulding has shown with what brevity and verve the heart of interest may be penetrated:

> What is determined in the market [he writes] is not strictly the rate of interest but the price of certain "property rights" . . . stocks, bonds or items of physical property. Each of these . . . represents to an individual an expected series of future values, which may be both positive and negative. If this expected series of values can be given some "certainty equivalent" . . . then the market price of

the property determines a rate of interest on the investment. This rate of interest, however is essentially subjective and depends on the expectations of the individual; the objective phenomenon is the present market price of the property.

As basic theory this, we think, is irreproachable. It is true too, as Boulding later hints, that nothing in life can in strictness be justifiably taken as certain: for what sort of guarantees does the human situation offer? None the less, we must qualify Boulding's position, for the practical necessities of life drive us to accept some things as unquestionable: sunrise and sunset, eventual personal dissolution and the payment of due interest by the British Government! The series of future payments to which a gilt-edged security gives the right is still, and with entire good sense, *treated in practice* as certain, even though the whole civilised fabric to which such arrangements belong is now destructible. Thus the yields of gilt-edged securities of various terms, short, medium or long, come very near to being "objective" interest rates. Professor Boulding has, strangely, omitted to mention the basic uncertainty which afflicts even the holder of gilt-edged securities, and which ultimately explains the very need for positive interest, namely, the impossibility of knowing *when and at what price* he will be driven by circumstances to sell his security. His main contention surely is invincible: the search for a "pure" interest rate in abstraction from "risk, liquidity, convenience, etc." is meaningless, "a search [in a dark room] for a black cat that isn't there."

In the foregoing we have tried to illustrate, by a commentary on selections from the post-1945 literature, those of the central problems in the determination of interest which have mainly engrossed attention since wartime preoccupations receded. In addition to this debate on fundamentals, there have been a number of more special contributions. Mr. F. P. R. Brechling [3], Dr. Börje Kragh [25] and Mr. Ralph Turvey [47], to mention them in alphabetical order, have pointed out that "the amount of money which people desire to hold as a store of wealth depends not only on the rate of interest but also on the *total* amount of wealth available." Thus in order to describe the effect of an increase in the existing quantity of money, two kinds of "reaction curves" are needed, one showing the reaction of the rate of interest to increases in the money stock effected by open-market operations which merely *exchange bonds for money* and leave the total stock of wealth unchanged, and the other showing the reaction of the rate of interest to *ceteris paribus* changes in the money stock. "The two curves will co-incide if the marginal propensity to hold money is zero."

Upon the results of his skilful empirical research into the finance of small businesses, Mr. N. J. Cunningham [10] has built a theoretical analysis of great ingenuity. His first basic finding is that the opportunity cost to a firm of investing its own ploughed-back reserves in the purchase of equipment is, for a variety of reasons, less than the cost of borrowing funds for the purpose. The most important of these reasons is that, by borrowing, an entrepreneur endangers his firm in a manner, and to a degree, which does not arise when he lays out his own undistributed profits which have been held in the form of cash or easily marketable securities. It is impossible in a few lines to do justice to Mr. Cunningham's subtle and thoroughgoing discussion, but he points mainly to the fact that, so far from being able to borrow unlimited funds at a constant market interest rate, the entrepreneur is acutely aware that the cost per unit of his borrowings will increase with the size of his total debt and that these borrowings will eventually reach an absolute limit, which will, moreover, become narrower at those very times of difficulty for the firm when borrowing may be most necessary to it. This power to borrow, Mr. Cunningham urges, is looked upon by the business-man, and should be treated by the economist, as a form of liquid reserve, a means of satisfying his precautionary and speculative motives for desiring liquidity. The "subjective" cost to the entrepreneur of using borrowed funds for the purchase of durable equipment must therefore reflect a *double illiquidity*. It requires the lender to substitute an illiquid asset (viz., an I.O.U.) in his portfolio, for a liquid asset, viz., cash; and it deprives the borrower of one possible source of liquid funds which he could otherwise resort to in emergency or in face of an unforeseen profit opportunity. The consequence of this difference of implication between owned and borrowed funds is that the curve of *marginal cost of funds for investment* is likely to have a step or jump-discontinuity at the point where "owned" funds are exhausted and resort must be had to borrowing. This vertical segment of the curve is the most striking of several features of the situation, all of which lead, in one set of circumstances or another, to the conclusion that changes of the market interest rate may quite visibly leave the firm's inducement to invest in equipment unaffected. These considerations are an important theoretical complement to the argument advanced on pages 419-21 of this article.

Mr. George Clayton [7] has considered the very interesting problem of the *velocity of circulation of real balances*. When the velocity of circulation of money is slow, as in a business depression, can the banking system of its own power do anything to increase the frequency with which given quantities of *real purchasing power* change hands? His article points out how in some circumstances the public's desire for larger nominal balances regardless of the loss of income involved, with the resulting divorce of the long-term from the short-term interest rate, added to the insensitiveness of investment to any fall of the long-term rate which may be achieved, can frustrate the speeding up of the "real" velocity of circulation even in a depression with heavy unemployment of resources. When there is full employment the banks' attempt to increase their outstanding loans merely results in higher prices. One way of expressing these well-recognised facts is to say that the banking system's power to increase the nation's nominal stock of money is by no means necessarily a power to increase the nation's money income, still less its real income. In introducing the notion of "real velocity of circulation" Mr. Clayton has, we think, greatly contributed to ease of discourse on these matters.

Mr. J. K. Eastham, in a very valuable article [11], has traced the fluctuating historic distinctions between the interest and the profit components of the earnings of "capital," and has shown the importance, for a theory of accumulation, of keeping interest among the obstacles and profit among the inducements to investment, that is, to the construction of specialised, concrete equipment.

From this survey of recent tendencies in the theory of how interest is determined, we turn now to consider the state of opinion, and to make some suggestions of our own, about the role of interest in the theory of the inducement to invest.

Part II THE ROLE OF INTEREST

The Investment Horizon

A change in an interest rate can, like a change in any other economic variable, transmit with more or less effect, and more or less delay, an impulse from one part of the economic system to another. Theory suggests that its more powerful effects are likely to be upon the demand for durable goods and upon the balance of payments. Demand for durable goods, whether by producers or householders, is investment, and the question whether interest-rate changes do or do not appreciably affect investment has been actively studied by observation, question and analysis from the 1938 attempt by the Oxford Economists' Research Group onwards.

A necessary tool for any such study is a clear conception of the *formal* role of the interest rate in the *formal* structure of a profitability calculation. Since money in hand can be lent at positive interest wherever an organised loan market exists, money in hand is equivalent on to-day's market to a larger sum of deferred money. Expected instalments of profit, or of services (such as enjoyment of a house) having a market value, are deferred money, and in order to find to-day's market worth of a series of such instalments, each must be adjusted for its deferment and, in some cases, also for its uncertainty. Any such instalment which is treated as free from uncertainty must accordingly be divided by: one plus the annual interest rate: and must be thus divided once for each year of deferment.

Since the interest rate thus occurs in the denominator of a fraction, this fraction, which is the "present" or "discounted" value of a deferred, but certain, unit instalment, will be smaller, the larger the interest rate. Thus to-day's demand price for any asset or object which is counted upon with certainty to yield specified deferred instalments will be lower, the higher the interest rate. If other relevant circumstances are unchanged, and if in particular the cost of production of such an asset is independent of the interest rate, fewer such assets will be demanded in each time-unit after than before a rise of the interest rate.

This scheme of analysis can be refined. We can suppose that the supply price of any type of equipment (any "machines") rises as the number of units ordered per time-unit increases. We can suppose that the series of deferred instalments attributed to the asset is a different one in the minds of different individuals, each relying upon some information, and some interpretive background of experience, private to himself. Each will then have his own demand price and, we may suppose, his own convenient number of machines which he will order per time-unit provided the supply price is less than his demand price. When the number of machines being supplied per time-unit is such that the corresponding supply price is just low enough to evoke that number of orders per time-unit we have an equilibrium.

But suppose that we wish to express such an equilibrium as consisting in the equality of a "rate of return," on one hand, and the loan interest rate, on the other? The appropriate formal algebraic equation looks exactly like the one by which, given the loan interest rate, we calculate the present value of a given series of annual deferred instalments. The meaning of the letters in this equation, however, is different. Instead of a present value or *demand price* we now have on the left-hand side a *supply price*, and instead of the loan interest rate prevailing in the market, we have on the right-hand side an *unknown* whose numerical value is to be determined by solving the equation. This unknown percentage, or, if we prefer, vulgar fraction or decimal fraction, is the marginal efficiency of capital. In equilibrium, the marginal (or "lowest effective") demand price of each sort of machines, and their supply price, will have been driven to equality by the search for profit. In equilibrium, therefore, the marginal efficiency of capital will have been driven, by rising supply price, to equality with the interest rate on loans. This means that, in equilibrium, the personal demand price entertained by the least sanguine of those business-men from whom an order for machines is actually elicited, will be equal to the supply price, and that therefore the percentage per annum at which this marginally sanguine placer of orders must discount his expected profits, to make their present value equal to the supply price of machines, is equal to the loan rate he must pay on money borrowed to buy these machines.

We need not, however, suppose that there are any intra-marginal investors. If we assume that the series of deferred instalments, which a machine is counted on, by the potential investor, to yield to him if he buys it, depends itself upon the number of machines ordered, and that each of these instalments is a decreasing function of that number, we can suppose *each* business-man to carry the number of orders he gives per unit of time up to that level where his own ("personal") demand price for machines is no greater than their supply price. Thus a much more interesting sense is given to the word "marginal" when we speak of the marginal efficiency of capital. If, in this case, we cease to assume implicitly that loans of no matter what term carry one and the same rate of interest, and suppose instead that each deferred instalment of profit or service is discounted at the particular rate appropriate to its own deferment, then we can accommodate in our scheme of thought the idea that some business-men will value more highly than others the prospect of recovering relatively early the money they propose to invest in machines. Such men will direct their orders to machines of types which offer an *early* concentration of instalments, each large relatively to the total amount of the whole series of instalments promised by such a machine.

In all this there has been no mention of depreciation or amortisation. Have those notions any relevance for investment decisions? Depreciation is loss of value or prospective earning power by a durable good. When a potential buyer of such a machine looks forward to a date at which some particular set or portion of the deferred instalments which it promises will have been obtained from it he will see it as destined to have, at that future date, a lesser value than it has now, and a value which he can reckon on the basis of the deferred instalments lying *beyond* that date and the interest rates which, by inference from the rates prevailing *now* for loans of various terms, he can reckon to prevail on that future date. This gradual ebb of value, as it occurs, will have to be somehow reflected in the book-keeping of his business and in the published condensations of those accounts, and for this purpose it may suit him to represent this decay by a conventional "depreciation allowance" whose annual amount may be a constant or a term of a geometric series or what not. What has this convention of book-keeping to do with the basic profitability or non-profitability of the investment? Nothing.

It is a pity that a number of writers on the question whether the size of the investment-flow is responsive to changes of interest rates, or not, still feel it necessary to encumber their analyses with irrelevant discussions of amortisation. An interesting debate followed the publication of the evidence obtained on that question by Professors M. D. Brockie and A. L. Grey [4], who had concluded therefrom that the interest-elasticity of firms' demand for equipment was low. Dr. W. H. White [48] interpreted their figures differently, but failed to convince them, and the debate must be called inconclusive. It did, however, raise the exceedingly interesting question of the lengthening which Brockie and Grey [5] believe to have occurred in the "pay-off period." If the yearly profit which a proposed investment is counted upon to earn is taken as constant for all years there will be some number of years such that the total profits of those years equals the first cost (construction cost) of the investment. As a more refined definition, we may take the pay-off period to be that number of years whose total *discounted* profits equal the construction cost of the investment. In the Oxford Economists' 1938 study [28] business-men were often heard to say that they would not order equipment unless it promised to "pay for itself in 3 (sometimes even 2) years." Grey and Brockie [4] found that 85% of their respondents used either the "pay-out period" method or "an alternative formulation amounting to virtually the same thing (the percentage of initial cost of the investment recovered out of earnings each year) . . . for evaluating prospective investments." White [48] comments upon this:

> Because the pay-out-period method requires that initial cost be recovered during a very small number of years, it connotes very short economic horizons, very high required rates of return and unscientific investment planning; consequently, the investment plans of 85% of large firms may be assumed unaffected by the cost of capital.

Any economic theoretician will readily sympathise with Dr. White's attitude. Nevertheless, we must beware here of letting pure theory kick aside too much of practical realism. Can it be truly called scientific to base profitability estimates on years too far ahead for knowledge about the observable *present* to throw any light upon their circumstances? Dr. White is correct, as we showed many years ago [43], in saying that interest-rate changes will be almost powerless to change the inducement to invest, when the planning horizon is only two or three years into the future. But this is not a reason for pretending that we can see beyond the horizon.

Why do [43, 44] business-men place their horizon at only two or three years ahead, and *ignore* deliberately the possibility that their proposed equipment may still, in the years beyond that horizon, prove capable of making goods which will sell for more than the running-costs of the machines? It is because they cannot be *sure* that these profits will be earned, they cannot brush aside the threat that newer inventions will enable their rivals to undercut them or to oust their product with a better one. The present throws light on the immediate future, but that light dims rapidly as we peer farther ahead. The business-men are not "unscientific," they are cautious. Now plainly no equipment is worth buying if the money to be spent on it will not be recovered, let alone any return for "enterprise," "decision-making," "risk-taking" or the general services of the enterpriser. If only three years' profit can be counted on, that profit must be at a rate equal to one-third, at the very least, of the first cost of the machine. A minimum requirement of 34% per annum may seem, at first glance, to be a deliberate rejection of countless profit opportunities which might yield, say, 20 or 15%, still much in excess of the *loan interest rate*. In such an argument two wholly different ideas are being utterly confused. To spend £1 million and to get back £150,000 in each of three years, and then nothing, is not to make a profit.

The true relation between the crude annual profit, assumed to be the same from year to year and to be earned for just so-and-so many years and then to relapse to nothing, and treated as a proportion of the first cost of the equipment, on the one hand; and the rate of return which can be legitimately compared with the loan rate of interest, on the other; is simply the following. Each year's assumed profit is to be divided by: one plus an "unknown" fraction: divided once, for each year of deferment; the answers thus obtained are to be summed, and their sum is to be set equal to the machine's first cost. The resulting equation is then to be solved for the "unknown" fraction, and the numerical value obtained is the "marginal efficiency of capital" which can be compared *meaningfully* with the interest rate. There is still no mention of amortisation. An example [43] will illustrate the matter. Let the first cost of a machine be 100, and the assumed earnings (excess of sale proceeds of product over *running* costs, no mention of amortisation) in each of the next three years be 40, with nothing thereafter. Then the marginal efficiency of capital is 10% per annum, and it *will not pay* to buy this machine with loaned money on which a rate of interest of more than 10% per annum has to be paid, notwithstanding the appearance that the machine is going to earn "40% per annum" of its first cost.

In any such calculation the air of precision and certainty are entirely bogus. We have deliberately spoken of "assumed" profits.

What is in question here is the need for some basis of argument, something to be set against the background of fact, news, experience and technical knowledge which the business-man has at command. We have avoided speaking of expected profits, for the reason that "expected" can cover everything from a feeling of conviction to the merest toying with a wild hope. The business-man who resolves to count on nothing beyond three years ahead is well aware of the open door to good fortune which he will thus offer. If all goes well, the machine which has earned 40% of its first cost in each of the first three years of its life may continue to do so, thus realising a larger overall gain.

By contrast with these uncertainties, the powerlessness [43] of interest rates, within the ordinary range of 2–8% per annum, to influence the demand price of *near horizon* equipment by undergoing any change of a size which may be supposed to occur within months, is a matter of plain arithmetic. It is plain for anyone to see what kind of difference is involved when we divide the supposed profit of three years hence by $\left(\dfrac{104}{100}\right)^3$ instead of by $\left(\dfrac{105}{100}\right)^3$, that is by $\dfrac{225}{200}$ instead of by $\dfrac{232}{200}$. This is the sort of difference made when the interest rate changes by a whole percentage point, from 5 to 4% per annum.

The ineradicable uncertainty of enterprise, the nearness of the horizon thus imposed, the powerlessness of interest rate changes, are all intimately bound together. Where this uncertainty is less (it is, of course, a subjective thing, a judgment or a state of mind, we are not called upon to justify a feeling that some forms of durable goods are more confidently counted on then others to yield profits in the distant future) the interest rate may have a powerful leverage. A house which is counted on to yield £100 per annum for eighty years has, at an interest rate of 4% per annum, a present value of £2,400; at 2% per annum it has a present value of £4,000. Upon which of the equal annual instalments, counted upon with certainty to be received from some durable good, does a small change of the interest rate used for discounting have the largest *absolute* effect in altering the present value of that instalment? The answer [43] may at first surprise a reader who has not come across it. The greatest absolute change in the present value of any one equal instalment affects that instalment whose deferment, in years, is equal to the reciprocal of the annual interest rate. Thus if that rate is 3% per annum the largest gain in present value, due to a change to $2\frac{7}{8}$% per annum, will be achieved by the instalment due in thirty-three years' time. It would be for our children or our children's children to say whether or not we should allow a change in the yield of Consols to tempt us to build houses for them, could we but consult their future knowledge now!

Harrodian Dynamics

We turn to a broader canvas. Sir Roy Harrod's *Towards a Dynamic Economics* [17] reverts in its broad style and spirit to the classic models, where the whole darkling plain of human affairs was in view, but its economic features were emphasised by the lamps of settlement. A different metaphor suggests its character in detail.

Rivers, tides and ocean currents irresistibly present themselves as an image and analogy of the economic process. There are the short-period waves and the idiosyncratic storms, there are tides and more constant, oneway currents acting slowly over great stretches of time. This picture is brought to mind by the view of interest which underlies Sir Roy's economics of long-period growth or decline. No one better understands Keynes's short-period pre-occupations or his view of interest as the hourly and momently fluctuating equilibrator of Bull and Bear expectations. Yet in his *Towards a Dynamic Economics*, written immediately after the War, Harrod is concerned with the slowest, most deep-seated and steady forces which bear upon, and are transmitted by, the rate of interest. The view that liquidity preference and expectations (the specula-tive motive), however important and spectacular their effects, are waves on the surface of a deep tide representing the "real" forces of thrift and productivity, is one shared in some degree by writers as widely separated as Sir Dennis Robertson and Mrs. Joan Robinson. Like Mrs. Robinson, Harrod in discussing the long-term forces, reverts in effect to the older usage whereby "interest" covered any gain due to the possession of a stock of wealth, other than the market appreciation of the assets themselves. Saving is the continual or repetitive act by which wealth is permitted to ac-cumulate. What considerations in the income-receiver's mind must be overcome by a positive interest rate, in this older sense, if he is ever to save?

> There are two quite distinct reasons for spending now rather than waiting for a larger sum later. One is that the larger sum may veritably have less utility than the smaller sum now, the other the lack of telescopic faculty whereby we fail to estimate justly the utility that the larger sum will have.

In the secure and virtually tax-less Victorian world the well-to-do no doubt looked upon "the family" and its "fortune" as ever-lasting, only provided each successive generation took seriously its duty of maintenance and improvement. But can we, even so, argue as though life were a space within which there is free movement for the human individual; as though he were provided with some sort of fix-point and a mental theodolite, by which he can survey the country of life and make some objective comparison of the utility a given expenditure would give him at different parts of that life?

> A man may choose to sacrifice 2 units of utility—of utility not money—in 20 years from now for the sake of 1 unit now; but in 20 years' time he will presumably regret having done so.

At the later date, we might by this reasoning equally well argue, he will regret not having lived for twenty years at subsistence level in order at last to be rich. In so far as *any* current consumption impoverishes my later years, I ought to live in a garret in order to be buried in a Pharaoh's tomb. But in what sense can the actual, experienced and not merely imagined utility of one moment be compared with that of a different moment? What common ground, what fix-point is there, in the time not of the sophisticated outsider but of the living individual in his moment-to-moment experience? Every comparison of *my own* utility (not that of the "economic subject" under my microscope) which I can *in fact* make is inevitably made at some one moment. Who has the right to tell me that this comparison is ill-judged? What sense will it make, in forty years' time, if my then self says, "That young man ought to have saved for my old age instead of spending to enjoy his youth"?

These are intensely difficult matters and we may perhaps be forgiven for taking an unusual view of them. In doubting the meaningfulness of that sort of inter-temporal comparisons which underly Böhm-Bawerk's "first ground" for the existence of interest we are saying only that a man cannot stand outside of time and of his own immediate present, and weigh the relative expediency, by some objective, impersonal, omni-temporal standard, of this act or that. Comparisons of "then" and "now" are made *now*. There is no "third point" in time, no neutral, a-temporal common ground, from which the comparison can be made so as to leave the individual still free to act "now" in whatever way that comparison suggests.

The central and continuous theme of *Towards a Dynamic Economics* is the search for those various sets of circumstances, any one set among which, once attained, would carry the economy on a path of steady enrichment of each and all of its subjects; and if such circumstances seem too precarious or elusive, then a search for the policy and means by which the economy can be consciously held to such a path. Sir Roy looks upon a steady, slow secular fall of the interest rate as able, to some extent, to take the place of the accelerator in providing an inducement to invest strong enough to keep the economy at full employment along a rising ceiling of output. The accelerator, if relied upon alone to maintain full employment, might require a pace of growth of output *greater* than the upward slope of the ceiling; a pace of growth, that is to say, which it would be impossible to maintain. Therefore the rate of interest must be pushed ever downward in order that a steady *deepening* of the structure of capital equipment may reinforce the *widening* induced by the growth of output. Besides the problem of a chronic tendency to under-employment equilibrium there is, however, a second problem, that of the business cycle, and here Sir Roy regards the interest rate as wholly ineffective. He compares as follows the two problems:

> While the fall in the long-term rate may not produce any strong immediate effect by making entrepreneurs reconsider their productive methods or by making durable goods more attractive to the consumer, it is not inconsistent with this to hold that in due time, that is after there has been time for the lower rate to sink in and become part of the furniture of the mind of entrepreneurs and others, the various adjustments consequent upon it may add up to a sizeable amount.

But—

> This does not help us with our trade cycle problem. What we there want is responsiveness preferably within a few months, but, at the very worst, within a year or two. . . . I am inclined to attach great weight to the views of those who urge us not to expect a very great increase of capital outlay in the period immediately following a change in the long-term rate of interest.

Interest is the most paradoxical of all economic quantities. At first sight it seems to present us with the opportunity of doing calculations, and of obtaining in this way results which are at once quantitatively exact, logically inescapable and theoretically interesting. It is one of the main pillars of the claim of economics to be Queen of the Social Sciences, the only one of those sciences reducible to mathematical statement and analysis. It runs in an unbroken thread through the whole theory of accumulation of wealth, both on the saving and on the investment side, and thus seems to reign over the theories of employment, of money, of growth, of the general price level and of the balance of payments. It can appear, from this viewpoint of pure theory, as the pivot of the entire system, the sun in the midst of its planets. Yet when examined closely, these claims dissolve. It has been admitted from Marshall's time at least that the influence of the interest rate on saving is doubtful even as to its algebraic sign. More recently its influence on investment has been denied on the basis of businessmen's own testimony. Bank rate is still nominally the Bank of England's leading-rein for the commercial banking system, but it has had to be reinforced by "directives," special deposits, hire-purchase regulations and what not. It seems likely that the interest rate, or the system of rates, will continue to receive from theoreticians the homage due to a ceremonial monarch, without in fact counting for more than such a monarch in the real affairs of western nations.

NOTE

1. By a slip Dr. Hahn's article refers to an excess *demand* for bonds.

REFERENCES

1. Becker, G. S., and W. J. Baumol, "The Classical Monetary Theory: The Outcome of the Discussion," *Economica*, 19 (November 1952).
2. Boulding, K. E., "M. Allais' Theory of Interest," *Journal of Political Economics*, 59 (February 1951).
3. Brechling, F. P. R., "A Note on Bond Holding and the Liquidity Preference Theory of Interest," *Review of Economic Studies*, 24 (1956–57).
4. Brockie, M. D., and A. L. Grey, "The Marginal Efficiency of Capital and Investment Programming," *Economic Journal*, 66 (December 1956).
5. ———, "The Rate of Interest, the Marginal Efficiency of Capital and Investment Programming—A Rejoinder," *Economic Journal*, 69 (June 1959).
6. Brunner, K., "Stock and Flow Analysis: Discussion," *Econometrica*, 18 (July 1950).
7. Clayton, G., "A Note on the Banking System's Power to Lend," *Metroeconomica*, 7 (1955).
8. Clower, R. W., "Productivity, Thrift and the Rate of Interest," *Economic Journal*, 64 (March 1954).
9. ———, and D. W. Bushaw, "Price Determination in a Stock-flow Economy," *Econometrica*, 22 (July 1954).
10. Cunningham, N. J., "Business Investment and the Marginal Cost of Funds," *Metroeconomica*, 10 (1958).
11. Eastham, J. K., "A Redefinition of the Boundary between Interest and Profit Theories," in J. K. Eastham (ed.), *Dundee Economic Essays* (Dundee, 1955).
12. Fellner, W., and H. M. Somers, "Note on 'Stocks' and 'Flows' in Monetary Interest Theory," *Review of Economics and Statistics*, 31 (May 1949).
13. ——— "Stock and Flow Analysis: Comment," *Econometrica*, 18 (July 1950).
14. ——— "Stock and Flow Analysis: Note on the Discussion," *Econometrica*, 18 (July 1950).

15. Fouraker, L. E., "The Cambridge Didactic Style," *Journal of Political Economy*, 66 (February 1958).

16. Hahn, F. H., "The Rate of Interest and General Equilibrium Analysis," *Economic Journal*, 65 (March 1955).

17. Harrod, Sir Roy, *Towards a Dynamic Economics* (London, 1948).

18. Hicks, J. R., "A Rehabilitation of 'Classical' Economics?" *Economic Journal*, 67 (June 1957).

19. Johnson, H. G., "Some Cambridge Controversies in Monetary Theory," *Review of Economic Studies*, 19 (1951–52).

20. Keynes, J. M., *The General Theory of Employment, Interest and Money* (London, 1936).

21. ———, "The General Theory of Employment," *Quarterly Journal of Economics*, 51 (February 1937).

22. ———, "Alternative Theories of the Rate of Interest," *Economic Journal*, 47 (June 1937).

23. Klein, L. R., "Stock and Flow Analysis in Economics," *Econometrica*, 18 (July 1950).

24. ———, "Stock and Flow Analysis: Further Comment," *Econometrica*, 18 (July 1950).

25. Kragh, B., "Two Liquidity Functions and the Rate of Interest: A Simple Dynamic Model," *Review of Economic Studies*, 17 (1949–50).

26. Lange, O., "Say's Law: A Restatement and a Criticism," in O. Lange, F. McIntyre, and T. O. Yntema (eds.), *Studies in Mathematical Economics and Econometrics*, in memory of Henry Schultz (Chicago 1942).

27. Lloyd, C. L., "The Equivalence of the Liquidity Preference and Loanable Funds Theories and the *New* Stock-flow Analysis," *Review of Economic Studies*, 27 (June 1960).

28. Meade, J. E., and P. W. S. Andrews, "Summary of Replies to Questions on Effects of Interest Rates," *Oxford Economic Papers*, No. 1 (October 1938).

29. Mishan, E. J., "A Fallacy in the Interpretation of the Cash Balance Effect," *Economica*, 25 (May 1958).

30. Modigliani, F., "Liquidity Preference and the Theory of Interest and Money," *Econometrica*, 12 (1944).

31. Patinkin, D., "Relative Prices, Say's Law and the Demand for Money," *Econometrica*, 16 (April 1948).

32. ———, "The Indeterminacy of Absolute Prices in Classical Economic Theory," *Econometrica*, 17 (January 1949).

33. ———, "A Reconsideration of the General Equilibrium Theory of Money," *Review of Economic Studies*, 18 (1949–50).

34. ———, "The Invalidity of Classical Monetary Theory," *Econometrica*, 19 (April 1951).

35. ———, *Money, Interest and Prices* (Evanston, Ill., 1956).

36. ———, "Liquidity Preference and Loanable Funds: Stock and Flow Analysis," *Economica*, 25 (November 1958).

37. ———, "Keynesian Economics Rehabilitated: A Rejoinder to Professor Hicks," *Economic Journal*, 69 (September 1959).

38. Robertson, Sir D., "Mr. Keynes and the Rate of Interest," in *Essays in Monetary Theory* (London, 1940).

39. Robinson, J., *The Rate of Interest and Other Essays* (London, 1952).

40. Rose, H., "Liquidity Preference and Loanable Funds," *Review of Economic Studies*, 24 (February 1957).

41. ———, "The Rate of Interest and Walras's Law," *Economica*, 26 (August 1959).

42. Sayers, R. S., "Ricardo's Views on Monetary Questions," *Quarterly Journal of Economics*, 67 (February 1953).

43. Shackle, G. L. S., "Interest-rates and the Pace of Investment," *Economic Journal*, 56 (March 1946).

44. ———, "Business and Uncertainty," *Bankers' Magazine*, 189 (March 1960).

45. Tew, B., "Sequence Analysis and the Theory of the Rate of Interest," *Economic Journal*, 66 (September 1956).

46. Tsiang, S. C., "Liquidity Preference and Loanable Funds Theories, Multiplier and Velocity Analyses: A Synthesis," *American Economic Review*, 46 (September 1956).

47. Turvey, R., "Consistency and Consolidation in the Theory of Interest," *Economica*, 21 (November 1954).

48. White, W. H., "The Rate of Interest, the Marginal Efficiency of Capital and Investment Programming," *Economic Journal*, 68 (March 1958).

49. Knut Wicksell, *Interest and Prices*, trans. R. F. Kahn (London 1936).

50. Wright, A. L., "Sequence Analysis and the Theory of the Rate of Interest," *Economic Journal*, 65 (December 1955).

18 *The Term Structure of Interest Rates*

Douglas Fisher *Concordia University*

This chapter surveys one of the more perplexing subjects in monetary economics—the theory of the term structure of interest rates. The general approach is to trace the development of term structure theory from Hicks to the present in a manner which emphasizes its relation to the mainstream of thinking on monetary problems. There are two problems with the existing literature which have perplexed the uninitiated. One is simply that the results have been given in a particularly arid way, emphasizing numerical examples; this is not easily remedied. The second problem is that it is often not easy to discern the theoretical structure of each situation, as the unstated assumptions seem particularly numerous in term structure theory.

The chapter is divided into three main sections. The first and longest section presents a discussion of the term structure literature which developed around the J. R. Hicks [12]-F. A. Lutz [16] formulation of the problem and continued, with a large quantity of empirical work, into the 1960s. Here, the argument is advanced that while Hicks' (and Lutz') original formulation has some potential for a more general solution to the problem of the term structure, he, in fact, defined the "term structure problem" to be distinct from the "interest rate problem." This definition has plagued his lineal descendants in the debate. The second part of the paper discusses the literature pursuing empirically the original line of Hicks and Lutz; this literature concentrates on yields relative to maturity, holding the level of interest rates constant. In the third section of the paper two strands of the recent literature are examined. One strand attempts to

510

study the term structure as a "capital asset" problem by either portfolio or random walk methods. The other, at once more appealing and less amenable to empirical study, marries the term structure literature with that of the "dynamic consumption plan." It will be seen that this gives a better feel for the *holding period,* an important underlying concept often not worked explicitly into the analysis of the term structure.

I. *The Traditional Literature*

A. HICKS' CLASSIC STATEMENT OF THE EXPECTATIONS HYPOTHESIS

It is important to an understanding of Hicks' formulation of the Expectations Hypothesis to note that he is discussing dynamics. In Hicksian dynamics the concern is with a system in which every quantity is dated; it is a short step from such distinction to the formulation of the problem of the term structure of interest rates in terms of spot and future (forward) transactions and, in particular, in terms of the date of settlement of the contract.

> A fundamental approach to the problem of interest suggests itself naturally, after the discussions of the preceding chapter. We have learnt to distinguish transactions according to the date at which they are due to be executed. Spot transactions are due to be executed currently—that is to say, in the current week in which they are drawn up. Forward transactions are due to be executed entirely at a future date—both sides of the bargain in the same future week. But there is no reason why the two sides of a bargain should be due to be executed at the same date. Thus we get a third type, loan transactions, which are such that only one side of the bargain is executed currently, the other being due to be executed at some future date, or perhaps a series of future dates. The essential characteristic of a loan transaction is that its execution is divided in time. (Hicks [12])

A loan by Hicks' system, then, consists of two one-sided transactions, one a loan transaction in which a bond is exchanged for money and one or more forward transactions which "undo" the loan arrangement. Indeed, while Hicks carefully distinguished among: (a) the money loan, (b) the spot transaction, and (c) the forward transaction, in his own description of the process, only (b) and (c) emerge clearly:

> Looking at it this way, the rate of interest for loans of two weeks, running from our first Monday, is compounded out of the "spot" rate of interest for loans of one week and the "forward" rate of interest,

also for one week loans, but for loans to be executed in the second week. (Hicks [12])

Thus at a critical point an analogy with spot and future commodity prices (or spot and forward exchange rates) is effected, but an analogy which is misleading, since the spot deal in the bond market already contains an element of future delivery, as this is usually defined.

One might press this important point a little further since it helps explain why "the" interest rate has dropped out of the formal term structure literature. Hicks notes, in building his analogy, that

(A) . . . it is possible to lend coffee for one year by selling coffee spot, lending the money proceeds, and covering the sale by a purchase on the forward market. (Hicks [12])

If he were to stick strictly to the analogy, he might have said that

(B) . . . it is possible to lend commodities in general for one period by selling commodities, and lending the money proceeds by purchasing a one-period bond.

If the analogy is constructed in this way, the spot price becomes the price level and the forward price becomes the one-period interest rate. The two arrangements are perfectly symmetrical in this construction since in the one case one gets back the original amount of coffee and in the other one gets back his money and can get back his commodities if

(a) he purchases the commodities specifically on some forward market, or if
(b) the market money rate of interest reflects perfectly and accurately the rate of inflation (that is, if expectations about the price level are accurate and are reflected perfectly in interest rates).

The net advantage, then, of (b) is that the purchasing power of money is linked into the term structure in a formal way and, consequently, so can a good deal of monetary theory. In contrast, the Hicksian approach as stated must work with "the" interest rate (short term) as a predetermined variable in both theoretical and empirical studies.

It is inconvenient to have a theory behind one-period interest rates which is separate, in all but special cases, from the theory for 2 to n period interest rates. Setting this reservation aside for the moment, let us accept Hicks' framework and consider his pure Expectations Hypothesis. One-period interest rates are determined in a general equilibrium framework in which either a long or short term interest rate, but not both, is included; indeed, interest itself is justified in terms of the trouble (cost) of transactions:

> Under the conditions of our model, it must be the trouble of mak-
> ing transactions which explains the short rate of interest . . . thus
> the imperfect "moneyness" of those bills which are not money is due
> to their lack of general acceptability; it is this lack of general accept-
> ability which causes the trouble of investing them, and causes them
> to stand at a discount. So far as our model economy is concerned,
> that is really all that needs to be said about the relation between
> money and interest. We have now seen how there comes to be a
> short rate of interest. Long rates have been explained in Chapter
> XI in terms of speculation on the future course of the short rate.
> (Hicks [12])

These comments, he feels, keep the theory from being a bootstrap
theory but, at the same time, leave it arid in the quality of its empirical
implications.

To begin with, it is not clear what sort of speculator Hicks had in
mind. He seems best described as anyone who is uncovered in the
bond market rather than, as in Keynes, someone who acts on his
belief that he knows better than other participants in the market what
the market is going to do. While the betting in the Hicksian casino
is from now to infinity, it is the sort of betting which everyone does
who undertakes a risky contract. This definition has the undesirable
property (since forward rates are assumed to be determined by speculators) that it is hard to conceive of effective empirical tests of the
hypothesis. Evidence that forward rates predict badly is of no use, once
we assume speculation. It only implies that speculators predicted
badly, not that they do not determine interest rates. Even the finding
of successful expectations-generating mechanisms is frustrated by the
fact that more successful methods of speculation are always likely to
be found. The best way out of the dilemma is a model which puts
speculation in opposition to its natural antithesis—hedging—but to do
this the antithesis itself needs to be given full scope.

Hicks certainly recognized other than speculative behavior, and his
formulation of the "liquidity preference" hypothesis is a clear case in
point. Hicks argues that "if no extra return is offered for long lending,
most people would prefer to lend short" [12]. Since borrowers (presumably) have no such qualms, the forward market for loans has a
"constitutional weakness on one side, a weakness which offers an opportunity for speculation" [12]. This means that

> The forward rate of interest for a particular future week . . . is
> thus determined, like the future price of a commodity, at that level
> which just tempts a sufficient number of speculators to undertake
> the forward contract [12].

That is, the actual forward rate exceeds the expected short rate by a
risk-premium: one must pay people to get them to gamble in the

Hicksian casino. Furthermore, these premiums ought to rise mono-tonically with maturity as described in equation (1).

$$_tr_{t+k} = E_t(R_{t+k}) + L_k \qquad 0 < L_1 < L_2 < \ldots \qquad (1)$$

In this formulation, the observed forward rate $_tr_{t+k}$, referring to period $t + k$ and observed at time period t, is argued as consisting of an expected interest rate (for period $t + k$) and a liquidity premium (L_k).

Since this last proposition of Hicks is essentially empirical in nature, it is easy to think of exceptions. It is not correct, of course, to say that all people would prefer to lend short unless a special premium is offered because it essentially depends on people's planned holding periods (in this case the length of time that they wish to lend). That is, optimal holding periods do indeed depend on attitudes toward interest rate risk but they also depend on the expected patterns of receipts and expenditures of the lenders and borrowers. With regard to the former, I can be bribed, since I am a rational mean-variance man, to undertake a loan longer than my original plans. This last is the case of the risk premium, but it should also be clear that my planned holding period may be longer than the maturity of any asset available, in which case we would deduce risk discounts.[1] So a firm a priori case cannot be established.

In a paper devoted to the cyclical behavior of the term structure of interest rates, Reuben Kessel [14] attempted to employ the Hicksian monotonicity directly on the data. Observing that

> If forward rates are not expected rates, but expected rates plus a liquidity premium, one should expect these time series to show that yields of short-term governments are usually less than long-term governments.

Kessel goes on to study the variations in this premium, variations that he feels generally have a positive relationship with the level of interest rates (and with the cycle in general).

If one is to interpret the average differences between long and short rates as a liquidity premium, then other causes of the "bias" must be eliminated. The most obvious bias is in the expected rate itself (for example, for excessive optimism or the like). But there can also arise technical problems, having to do with differences in bond cou-pons (a bond with a higher coupon will generally have a higher yield), or with serial correlation in the interest rate series. In particu-lar, if there is some positive autocorrelation (for whatever reason) in short term interest rates, then tests such as Kessel's will tend to over-state the liquidity premium.[2] Consider, for example, an equation describing the yield of an n-period bond, measured at time t.

$$\text{Price}_t = \frac{C}{(1 + R_{n,t})} + \frac{C}{(1 + R_{n,t})^2} + \cdots + \frac{C + F}{(1 + R_{n,t})^n} \quad (2)$$

Here C represents the coupon and F the face value of the bond. When one compares successive values of these yields (for different securities), one can transform the set of yields into a set of forward rates.

$$1 + R_{1,t} = 1 + r_{1,t}$$
$$\begin{array}{cc} \cdot & \cdot \\ \cdot & \cdot \\ \cdot & \cdot \end{array}$$
$$1 + R_{n,t} = \sqrt[n]{(1 + r_{1,t})(1 + r_{2,t}) \cdots (1 + r_{n,t})} \quad (3)$$

Then, one can directly calculate forward rates by comparing successive pairs of yields from equations (3):[3]

$$1 + r_{n,t} = \frac{(1 + R_{n,t})^n}{(1 + R_{n-1,t})^{n-1}} \quad (4)$$

We may approach the serial correlation problem as follows. With the value of $R_{1,t}$ taken as a "certainty equivalent" in the fashion of Hicks, we can describe the second year of a two-year contract (i.e., describe the discounting factor) as two one-year contracts, *ex post*:

$$(1 + R_{2,t})^2 = (1 + R_{1,t})(1 + R_{1,t+1}) \quad (5)$$

where t identifies the present. A *measured* forward rate for this second period hence is given by $_t r_{1,t+1}$ and is the result of a single contract, *ex ante*.

$$(1 + R_{2,t})^2 = (1 + R_{1,t})(1 + {_t r_{1,t+1}}) \quad (6)$$

The expectations hypothesis asserts that $_t r_{1,t+1} = E_t(R_{1,t+1})$, that is, that the forward rate is an expected rate, without bias. In such a case we can see, taking expectations of equation (5), that (5) and (6) give the same answer. That is, if expectations are unbiased, measured forward rates (or measured yields) will be unbiased.

But for three periods ahead, the procedure produces an additional bias (which gets worse for longer periods). We may express the discounting of the third period alone $(1 + R_{3,t})^3$, *ex post* for three one-year contracts, as:

$$(1 + R_{1,t})(1 + R_{1,t+1})(1 + R_{1,t+2})$$

If we take expectations of this expression we get

$$K_1 = (1 + R_{1,t})[1 + E_t(R_{1,t+1}) + E_t(R_{1,t+2})$$
$$+ E_t(R_{1,t+1}, R_{1,t+2})] \quad (7)$$

We may also express $(1 + R_{3,t})^3$ in terms of forward rates from a single *ex ante* contract as:

$$(1 + R_{1,t})(1 + {}_tr_{1,t+1})(1 + {}_tr_{1,t+2})$$

If we then assume Hicksian unbiasedness, in which case ${}_tr_{1,t+1} = E_t(R_{1,t+1})$ and ${}_tr_{1,t+2} = E_t(R_{1,t+2})$, we may rewrite the second expression as:

$$(1 + R_{1,t})[1 + E_t(R_{1,t+1})][1 + E_t(R_{1+2})]$$

Multiplying this expression out, we get:

$$K_2 = (1 + R_{1,t})[(1 + E_t(R_{1,t+1}) + E_t(R_{1,t+2})$$
$$+ E_t(R_{1,t+1})E_t(R_{1,t+2})] \quad (8)$$

It is not that expectations are biased in this case, but that when one formulates a problem with unbiased expectations one gets biased estimates. We can see this by comparing the two approaches by subtracting K_2 from K_1; to be unbiased, this difference should be zero, as it was between equations (5) and (6). Here, the result is:

$$E_t(R_{1,t+1}, R_{1,t+2}) - E_t(R_{1,t+1})E_t(R_{1,t+2}) = \frac{Cov_t(R_{1,t+1}, R_{1,t+2})}{(1 + R_{1,t})} \quad (9)$$

Thus, when there is positive autocorrelation in actual yields [so that the covariance in equation (9) is positive], then the *ex post* increment in equation (7) is larger than the expected increment predicted by the expectations hypothesis in equation (8). Even without direct biases in expectations, forward rates may be biased estimates of expected rates and hence averaging procedures like that of Kessel will not do; that is, an average positive slope in the yield curve (over a long period of time) would result from positive autocorrelation in interest rates themselves. Fortunately, there are other approaches which get at the liquidity premium problem.[4]

B. LUTZ' RESTATEMENT OF THE PROBLEM

Lutz [16], in his early paper on the term structure problem, lays out the assumptions needed to validate the extreme Expectations Hypothesis. The assumptions are that

(1) there is certain and accurate forecasting in the market
(2) there are no transactions costs
(3) individuals have identical expectations
(4) there is complete shiftability for lenders and borrowers

The last condition means that there are no restrictions on, and no prejudices against, e.g., holding 10 one-year contracts covering the life of a loan of ten years or 1 ten-year contract, covering the same period. It follows immediately, for all conceivable periods, that

(a) holding period yields are equal.

It is also true that (which was implicit in the discussion of Hicks)

(b) the long-term rate can be conceived of as an average of future short rates.

Lutz also deduces three important propositions about the term structure:

(c) the long rate can never fluctuate as widely as the short rate
(d) it is possible that the long rate may move temporarily contrariwise to the short rate
(e) a rising yield structure indicates that
  (i) future interest rates are above the one-period rate
  (ii) the long term rate will rise later on

Proposition (c) depends directly on proposition (b); the influence of a given fluctuation in the short rate on the long rate is modified by the averaging of all future (expected) short rates which are assumed to be components of the long rate. Since these rates are accurately foreseen, the only adjustment needed for the long rate is the adjustment for the one rate dropped from the series and the one added at the other end. The short rate changes by the full amount, while the long rate changes by the contribution of the short rate to the average, and by the addition of the new rate at the end, also averaged. It is possible for this addition to be in a different direction and larger than the change in the short rate (as both are averaged)—hence proposition (d). Propositions (e) also follow directly; since interest rates are determined by expectations and expectations are accurate, the events forecast in the structure inevitably come to pass.

The theory just described is empty if interpreted as an equilibrium theory; that is, there is no conceivable pattern of term-differentiated yields which it could not explain. On the other hand, it is also unclear in the theory what actually determines the holdings of the various maturities. Wood [36] has recently tried to recast the theory into disequilibrium decision rules and has discovered that with no transactions costs, perfect certainty, and perfect accuracy, the Lutz theory is not a long horizon theory at all, but that the optimal investment strategy is to plan from period to period; the further assumption, that bonds must be held to maturity, restores the Lutzian clarity.

In fact, any departure from the overly restrictive Lutzian assumptions requires some sort of adjustment. For example, if forecasts are accurate but not certain, individuals will, with no transactions costs, always prefer to forecast all rates for the shortest period of time possible (and hold bonds in this way), costlessly revamping their portfolios at the end of each short period, with the benefit of a lowered uncertainty. Here, too, one could usefully employ the assumption that bonds must be held to maturity to convert the theory into a "long view" theory. One must make a similar adjustment if one has certainty but not accuracy, in which case individuals will stay short in order to benefit from their errors. It is important to recognize that all maturities are held in any case; what is at question, when the short versus long view is in debate, is whether the theory in question implies one or the other (or, for that matter, both). Increasing the reality of the assumptions tends to force one into favoring the short view hypothesis, as discussed in detail in Malkiel's [17] study.

Lutz also considers the rationale of a liquidity premium. In Hicks the liquidity premium arose because of a "constitutional weakness" on one side of the market; in Lutz it is clear that this weakness has to do with uncertainty. I have just argued that with accurate forecasting and uncertainty we needed to assume that bonds must be held to maturity to generate the "long horizon" hypothesis. Thus, even if all interest rates fluctuated to the same degree, the increasing haziness about long-term rates would suggest a risk premium. Further, if one's holding period is itself a stochastic concept, with the possibility of needing one's cash an increasing function of time, some increasing insurance will be required to force one to go long. On the other hand, if the holding period is known for certain, and a suitable bond is available, no risk premium is required, no matter how fuzzy the view of rates before or after that maturity.[5]

But the introduction of uncertainty raises a more fundamental problem: whether there is a liquidity "premium" or a liquidity "discount" actually depends on the specification of the utility function and its arguments (Green [10]). Consider a case in which there is one consumption good (C), three periods $(0, 1, 2)$, and two states of the world (A, B), with the latter describing two different endowments (the same for all individuals) as:

$$A: C_0, C_{1a}, C_{2a}$$
$$B: C_0, C_{1b}, C_{2b}$$

where A and B are expected to occur with equal probability. One may suppose that each identical individual will seek to maximize the expected value of his intertemporal consumption (via his intertemporal utility function $U(C_0, C_1, C_2)$), subject to an intertemporal budget constraint, which contains the intertemporal prices P_a and P_b.

These intertemporal prices can be expressed as discounts (D) which give the present value of future consumption or as "increments" (N) which give the future value of present consumption. Let D_{01} indicate the "price" of period 1 consumption expressed in terms of period 0 consumption and D_{02} the price of period 2 consumption in terms of period 0 consumption. Since in equilibrium these prices will be equal to the ratios of expected utilities $E(U)$, we have:

$$D_{01} = \frac{E(U_1)}{E(U_0)} = \frac{E(U_1)}{U_0}$$

$$D_{02} = \frac{E(U_2)}{E(U_0)} = \frac{E(U_2)}{U_0}$$

(10a)

Note that $E(U) = U_0$ since there is no uncertainty about the base period in this model. We can construct a similar set for the future base (increment) prices, as well:

$$N_{01} = \frac{U_0}{E(U_1)}$$

$$N_{02} = \frac{U_0}{E(U_2)}$$

(10b)

When one compares the forward prices applied to the consumption streams by the individual consumer one can deduce an implicit forward rate (D_f), which is described in the following set of relations:

$$D_f = \frac{D_{02}}{D_{01}} = \frac{E(U_2)}{E(U_1)} = \frac{1}{N_f} = \frac{1}{E(U_1)/E(U_2)}$$

(11)

There will be an actual forward rate D_{12} (and an actual backward rate N_{12}) which is equal to U_2/U_1 (or $N_{12} = 1/D_{12}$). Thus one may, as before, compare the expectation of this forward rate with the expectations described in Equation (11). Thus, if

$$N_f = \frac{E(U_1)}{E(U_2)} > E(N_{12})$$

(12)

a liquidity premium is implied since the implied rate (expressed as an increment) is greater than the mathematical expectation $E(N_{12})$. If the ratio of the expected utilities is greater than the expectation of the actual forward ratio, using base 0 weights, then the forward rate reflects a discount:

$$D_f = \frac{E(U_2)}{E(U_1)} > E(D_{12})$$

(13)

No generalization will hold, however, because formal consumer theory does not contain a presumption that uncertain future consumption is more or less valuable than present; indeed, future income may be so uncertain and so desirable that it seems likely that the further we look ahead the more one will find relatively safe bonds preferred to the extent of commanding a risk discount, rather than a risk premium.[6] Consider Christmas clubs.

Lutz analyzes the effect of his other assumptions as well. Removing the assumption of identical expectations makes the results indeterminate unless individual wealth is bounded. Further, Lutz examines transactions costs and concludes that they will lead to a rising yield structure. But here one must again enter a qualification on account of the holding period, as follows.

It is useful to compare Lutz' treatment with that of Kessel [14] of a much later vintage; in fact, Kessel arrives at much the same conclusion as Lutz [16]. To begin with, let us assume that brokerage fees are $.50 per $100 for a 1-year bond and $3 per $100 for a 30-year bond, held to maturity.[7] The appropriate first comparison, if we stick to pure brokerage costs, is between the 30-year bond and the 1-year bond, renegotiated 29 times; in this case, the cost of the renegotiated route is $15 in comparison with $3.[8] We can conclude, then, that on these grounds, assuming holding period yields must be equal (for expected = actual yields and expected = actual costs) long term bonds will yield less than short term bonds, since brokerage costs will decline per unit of time. The result is a downsloping yield curve. This is about all one can say in the Lutzian world, where all securities are required to be held until maturity.

According to Kessel, in contrast to Lutz, the holding period is at most one year. In this case the conclusions we just arrived at are reversed. That is, holding a 30-year bond for one year implies a cost of $3 in comparison to the cost of $.50 for holding a one-year bond for one year. Further, one would thereby expect long term yields to be above short term yields. There is, however, no contradiction in these two cases since each was taken assuming a different holding period. It is natural that a ten-period bond is best for someone who wishes to lend for ten periods; indeed, a cusped shape might describe the configuration of average (per unit time) brokerage costs around a ten-year holding period. Even a model of the term structure which is built only on transactions costs can generate any shape of yield curve imaginable. Further, the existence of brokerage fees gives us one reason for expecting investors to hold securities of their desired length (in terms of their holding period).

C. THE DEVELOPMENT OF THE ALTERNATIVE HYPOTHESIS

The expectations hypothesis has remained in a shadow with regard to its empirical verification because it was never obvious that it had a converse. While from the beginning hedging had been mentioned, it has not had a formal place in much of the literature because the holding period itself has not had such a place. With the introduction of the concept of the holding period a confusion has arisen in the discussion concerning the *ex post* and the *ex ante* holding periods.

The holding period, as partially described above, is an idea which can arise from the theory of consumer choice over time. An individual saving unit (or its agent) would form a plan of its ideal consumption stream and allocate its assets accordingly. Given a distaste for risk (and no risk premiums), positive transactions costs, and perfect certainty (whether accurate or not), it would tend to align the actual maturity of its assets with the expected maturity of its obligations (or planned needs). If its needs were uncertain for some reason and if it were risk aversive, the unit might even tend to hold assets shorter in maturity than its expected obligations, planning to fill in the intervening period with an asset of shorter term (or no term) which earns a certain return less (by a liquidity premium) than that which could have been obtained by the unit otherwise.

This way of constructing a life-time consumption plan implies a view, however cautious, of all forward interest rates from now until the end of the individual's planning horizon. The unit is assumed to be in equilibrium at each point in time, continuously feeding in information and revising its lifetime plan when appropriate, as the data change.[9] The converse to the life-time view, of course, is the short-period view already discussed in connection with Hicks. Joan Robinson [27] actually put it more forcefully and it is here that the worry about forecasting rates until infinity first appeared in the literature.[10]

J. M. Culbertson's [7] contribution to the discussion (aside from stating the opposite hypothesis to the Hicks-Lutz theory) was to provide explicit use of the holding period in an attempt to refute the earlier theory. Culbertson frames the expectations hypothesis in a narrow way, in order to subject it to an empirical test.

> As developed by John R. Hicks and Friedrich A. Lutz, the theory argues that the interest rate on a long-term debt tends to equal the average of short-term rates expected over the duration of the long-term debt. [7]

This proposition was called Lutz' first deduction above. It follows almost immediately that "holding period yields will be equal" for the average holding periods in the market.

Referring to the segmentation hypothesis as belonging more to practical men, Culbertson [7] argues that the rate structure can be altered by open market operations differentiated by term-to-maturity and that this influence of "relative quantities" is the dominant factor determining the structure. Expectations are important "mainly as a factor determining very short-run movements in long-term rates." Culbertson puts his faith in four major, essentially empirical arguments:

(1) That with regard to the liquidity difference between short and long term debt, that "short-term debt is more liquid than long-term debt."[11]

(2) That while expectations are a factor, "the behavior of most borrowers and lenders is not ordinarily governed by such expectations."[12]

(3) That there are substantial changes in the maturity structure of the supply of debt and this fact, coupled with the fact that demand is somewhat slow to respond, implies considerable segmentation effects.[13]

(4) That the differences in lending rates related to debt maturity is complicated, for example, by the size of the operation and, for that matter, by the size of the operator, so that prediction is extremely hazardous.

When he looks at the evidence, however, Culbertson fails to present effective tests of his propositions. Concerning liquidity premiums, he notes a point which while once widely accepted, is now in doubt, that

> in the absence of offsetting forces yields on short-term debt would be expected to average lower than those on long-term debt because of liquidity premiums [7],

a point which follows directly since he refers to it as a "fact" that short term debt is more liquid than long term debt. More helpfully, he notes that

> the rate difference arising out of liquidity differences should tend to be widened, for example, during periods in which other factors operate to increase demands for liquidity or to reduce the availability of liquid investment assets. [7]

But his example, the liquid 1920s, when curves were (he says) flatter than the illiquid 1930s, does not convince one since the difficult task of testing the influence of "demand which is strong relative to supply" is not undertaken, nor are the data purged of expectations, which could easily explain the same pattern.

With regard to expectations, Culbertson argues that the planning period for active speculators is obviously very short for two reasons:

(1) because one can form more precise expectations about events in the near future

(2) quite adequate fluctuations (that is, quite adequate enough for sizable gains) for short periods are averaged out (normalized) over longer periods of time

The second point is buttressed by noting that not only does the financial press appear to think in these terms, but the relatively high leverage available in bond markets makes life as exciting as one could wish at the short end of the market. On the other hand, ordinary investors will not plan for quick gains and their conservative behavior, Culbertson says, will dominate in the market. This empirical proposition is further strengthened by some allegations about how institutions will behave.

> The maintenance of relatively constant portfolio structure insures the institution that its earnings will not turn out disastrously lower (or embarrassingly larger) [!!] than those of competitors.[14]

Culbertson, it would seem, is also pessimistic about the application of profit-maximizing models to institutions' behavior.

To test for speculation, Culbertson looks at the data to see "the nature of the opportunities for successful speculation which were not taken."[15] In particular, he looks at holding period yields to see if one could have profited, but didn't. The *holding period yield* is "defined as that annual rate of return at which the discounted value of interest payments and the sale price of the debt is equal to the initial price."[16] Culbertson's definition is analogous to Irving Fisher's marginal efficiency of capital. Thus, if rates are determined by speculators (and, perforce, a known market holding period equal to the planning period) we should observe equal holding period yields; that is, we should observe that "holding period yields on debts of all maturities should be equal for any and all holding periods."

The first thing one must do here is to distinguish between the *ex post* and the *ex ante* holding period. It is the latter, the planned holding period, to which the theory refers. It is the consistency of plans which is relevant rather than the consistency of the results of the plans, even assuming perfect certainty. Culbertson notes this, but yet observes:

> Study of the behavior of actual holding-period yields permits the drawing of some important conclusions about speculation in debt markets, for it indicates in clear terms the nature of the opportunities for successful speculation which were not taken. It indicates the extent to which speculation of the market was imperfect, because speculative activity was insufficient in scope or incorrect in form and did not succeed in bringing to equality the rates of return earned on different debts. [7]

Any test of this proposition, since it involves the assumption that the observed holding period was the same as the planned holding period, is basically a test of the proposition that forecasting is accurate.

II. *Tests of the Expectations Hypothesis*

Recent work has taken three general directions: Meiselman's empirical work is in the Hicks-Lutz tradition; Malkiel [17] pursues Joan Robinson's [27] line of attack; while Modigliani and Sutch [23] grafted Culbertson's segmentation hypothesis onto an expectations model. Meiselman's study stimulated a great deal of derivative work since he seemed to have found a way around the "expectations must be accurate to be tested" dilemma. Joseph Conard [6] had previously discussed this problem, observing that while the perfect-foresight model could be tested in this vein, it fails in his opinion. Even a version with uncertainty has some empirical problems:

> The problem of verification here arises from the impossibility of dogmatizing about what expectations are or have been at any time; without knowing these, disproof of the neoclassical theory is not possible. (Conard [6])

The basic problem is that "it is necessary in empirical work to specify how expectations are revised or formed" (Telser [32]). Thus, one must always test a particular model which can then never claim to represent "the" hypothesis, but only a particular researcher's hypothesis. One must also account for differences in individual expectations and for the fact that expectations change over time. (Even the actual expectations-generating mechanism may change over time.)

A. THE MEISELMAN TEST

Meiselman's contribution consists of the formulation of a successful "error-learning" test of the expectations hypothesis. In Equation (4), the forward rate was defined. Meiselman argues that this rate, calculated from a set of actual market yields, is determined by speculators. Further, he argues, this forward rate reflects expectations without bias (such as liquidity premiums), leaving us in the awkward position of having to model expectations before we can test the expectations hypothesis. Meiselman then proposes that changes of forward rates applying to any particular (future) period can be interpreted as revisions of forecasts (under the expectations hypothesis) and can be confronted with specific hypotheses.[17] His particular hypothesis is that these forward rates are revised on the basis of errors in prediction of the one year rate. Thus, in Equation (14), the one-period forward rate applying to period $t + n$ is observed at two points in time, t and $t - 1$; this revision is then hypothesized to be a function of the error in prediction of the one year rate (E_t).

$$_t r_{1,t+n} - _{t-1} r_{1,t+n} = a_n + b_n E_t + _t u_{1,t+n}$$
$$n = 1, \ldots, T \quad (14)$$

The error term here, reflecting Meiselman's particular hypothesis, is calculated as the difference between the observed one year rate for time t (often referred to as the "spot rate") and the shortest forward rate from time $t - 1$.

$$E_t = {}_t R_{1,t} - {}_{t-1} r_{1,t}$$

TABLE 1 *American and British Tests of the Meiselman Hypothesis (Standard Errors in Parentheses)*

n	American			British		
	CONST.	b	R²	CONST.	b	R²
1.	.00 (.02)	.703	.906	.033 (.036)	.834	.931
2.	.00 (.03)	.526	.867	.007 (.033)	.735	.880
3.	−.01 (.04)	.403	.768	.011 (.050)	.647	.810
4.	−.03 (.04)	.326	.682	.018 (.058)	.566	.706
5.	−.02 (.04)	.277	.412	.028 (.067)	.490	.576
6.	−.01 (.03)	.233	.391	.041 (.075)	.420	.440
7.	−.02 (.03)	.239	.398	.057 (.084)	.358	.313
8.	.01 (.03)	.208	.348	.076 (.095)	.304	.206

Source: D. Meiselman, *The Term Structure of Interest Rates* (Englewood Cliffs, N.J.: Prentice-Hall, 1962), p. 22; D. Fisher, "Expectations, the Term Structure of Interest Rates, and Recent British Experience," *Economica* (August 1966) p. 324.

Equation (14) expresses the Meiselman hypothesis in the form of a linear regression, with the u term representing the residuals. In the following table two tests of this model are compared; the independent variable in each case is the error in prediction of the one year rate while the dependent variable is changed from regression to regression and refers to revisions of forward rates progressively further along the yield curve.

In the American test, considerable interest has been expressed in the fact that the constant term was zero—attributed incorrectly by Meiselman to the lack of a risk premium[18]—and to the steady decline of the slope coefficients with maturity. In general, following Telser [32], there is the following set of relationships between the estimated coefficients and the theoretical parameters in Table 1.

(a) $\hat{a}_n = \dfrac{a_1(1 - b_1^n)}{1 - b_1}$

(b) $\hat{b}_n = b_1^n$ (15)

(c) $_t\hat{U}_{t+n} = {_t}U_{t+n} + (b_1)_t U_{t+n-1} + \cdots + (b_1^n)_t U_{t+1}$

For $b_1 < 1$, the statement (a) requires that the intercepts should increase and approach $\dfrac{a_1}{1 - b_1}$, as n increases; they are zero in the American case while they increase in the British case (although somewhat too rapidly). Statement (b) requires a geometric decline in the slopes, which both sets of data exhibit; and (c) suggests that the variances of the residuals should increase (if there is no serial correlation). As judged by the R^2 the United States case does not provide a uniform increase in the unexplained variance, while the British case does. Taken together however, these tests provide strong support for Meiselman's model.

The main problem with the Meiselman formulation is that the attempt to separate the expectations hypothesis from its rivals is not that convincing. Adolf Buse [2] argues the case when he notes that:

> the discriminatory power of the model with respect to alternative hypotheses is shown to be very low,[19]

and in particular, that:

> such results are implied by any set of smoothed yield curves in which short-term interest rates have a greater variability than long-term rates. [2]

While it is a fact that short term interest rates fluctuate more than long, it is also an economic fact which should be explained in the context of one's theory of the term structure of interest rates. This Buse does not do; instead he proposes as a test of his smoothness hypothesis the following:

> To test the hypothesis that [the] Meiselman results are implied by any set of [smoothed] yield curves whose variance diminishes with maturity, the two sets of available data . . . were ordered randomly, and the new orders were used to test the Meiselman model. [2]

The test employed was that of whether or not the regression coefficients and the coefficients of determination declined with the period to which the forward rate applied—the same test just described as part of the arithmetic of the relationship; not surprisingly, the random orderings were as convincing as the natural orderings.

It is not clear in Buse's work why the observation about declining variance is needed. Indeed, it had been concluded earlier that Meiselman's model could not be effectively distinguished from a naive extrapolative model (which was referred to as the "inertia" hypothesis) and this is about as much as one need say about its weakness to discriminate (Kessel [14]; Fisher [8]). Further, while the scrambling of the underlying data does seem to make nonsense of the idea that yield curves are tied together by expectations from period to period, it is itself counterproductive in that the scrambled data are also nonsense. In Meiselman's defense it could be noted that in any event his estimating equation is based on the "random walk" model; that is, a one-period forward rate, referring to time t, would be described as an unbiased random walk if

$$_t r_{t+1} = {_{t-1}} r_{t+1} + W_t \tag{16}$$

where W_t is a random error.[20] Recognizing Meiselman's dependent variable as $_t r_{t+1} - {_{t-1}} r_{t-1}$, we note that Meiselman successfully introduces an element (the error in prediction of the one year rate) in addition to the random error. Buse's comments seem beside the point; the successful introduction of an "inertia" term of equal power establishes that Meiselman's model does not discriminate between rival hypotheses about the formation of expectations, but it sheds no light on the "segmentation" or "liquidity preference" theories which are the main rivals of the speculative view because these items are given no formal role in the theory, not because long term rates fluctuate less than short, an essentially adventitious detail here.

B. A LONG HORIZON OR A SHORT HORIZON?

From Joan Robinson's [27] paper onward, the view that market forecasts were over short periods rather than over all conceivable future periods was popular with those who seemed closer to actual market practices. The essential difficulty has turned out to be that of framing the short view hypothesis in such a way as to provide an effective contradiction to the long period hypothesis. Around the edges, one comes across the argument that the so-called "long horizon" views of Hicks and Lutz (and subsequently Meiselman) are so only by the unstated assumption that the securities considered must be held until maturity. Without this assumption, the Hicks-Lutz theory collapses to the short-period case.

Malkiel [17] has argued persuasively for the superior effectiveness of the short period expectations view. Most earlier and later writers have not been able to tear themselves free of this assumption. Malkiel, in particular, relies on the "expected normal range of interest rate expectations," which he argues implies a yield curve with substantial movement around the short end, leveling off quite rapidly as the perception of the future fades into the (sometimes shifting) normal range. Earlier, something like this view had been promoted in the *Radcliffe Report*,[21] itself written in the Keynesian tradition. Malkiel explicitly introduces the "planning horizon" to motivate his perception here; indeed, along with Jacob Michaelsen, Malkiel in essence rejects the fixed liquidation date for the portfolio, common in the Hicks-Lutz theory, in favor of a horizon running ahead at most one year.

> Especially those close to the actual investment process of financial institutions doubted that expectations were held and acted upon for any but a very short horizon. (Malkiel [17]; Michaelsen [22])

It should have been pointed out though that whether or not this view has any important role to play depends on giving it a life independent of the rival (long period) hypothesis. Malkiel [17], indeed points out that his model has the same implications:

> We have seen that our alternative formulation of the expectations theory has relied on behavioral postulates which differ widely from those of the traditional theory. In this section, we shall show that, despite these differences, the alternative model of the theory gives precisely the same implications as does the traditional analysis. [17]

At this point, Malkiel's proposition runs into a theoretical problem raised by Luckett [15]; that is, notwithstanding the apparent contrast in horizons, the two exhibit identical predictions about forward rates because they both imply equal holding period yields. One can derive the Malkiel theory as follows: Define the expected "holding period" yield for the maturity $t + n$ as $_tH_{t+n}$ with the presubscript denoting the single period horizon for which the expectation is taken. The condition that holding period yields are equal is:

$$_tH_{t+1} = {_tH_{t+n}} \qquad n = 1, 2, \ldots \tag{17}$$

In this case, no matter how the investment is sliced up into one-period loans, all ways of getting to the period $t + n$ provide an equivalent amount, along the expected short period yield curve at time t.

We can define the price of this $t + n^{\text{th}}$ maturity as $_tP_{t+n}$ using a known price at the *beginning* of t; then $_{t+1}P_{t+n-1}$ will denote the expected price of that security for the next period (the security will be one period shorter in maturity). Assuming all interest payments are made at the maturity $t + n$ we can ignore them; the expected yield then for this $t + n^{\text{th}}$ security is:

$$\frac{_{t+1}P_{t+n-1} - {_tP_{t+n}}}{_tP_{t+n}} = {_tH_{t+n}} \tag{18}$$

which, as noted, is the holding period yield for the one-period horizon entirely in terms of a capital gain.

The terminal value of the bond is known, of course, and is $_tP_{t+n}$ $(1 + {_tR_{t+n}})^{t+n}$ where the interest rate reflects the expansion of the capital value. We may compare this certain value with the expected price one period hence $(_{t+1}P_{t+n-1})$ to deduce an expected long term interest rate:

$$(1 + {}_{t+1}r_{t+n-1,t})^{t+n-1} = \frac{{}_{t}P_{t+n}(1 + {}_{t}R_{t+n})^{t+n}}{{}_{t+1}P_{t+n-1}} \qquad (19)$$

This is not a forward rate but one can arrive at a set of forward rates directly, by application of Equation (4) to Equation (19).

$$(1 + {}_{t+n}r_{1,t}) = \frac{(1 + {}_{t+1}r_{t+n,t})^{t+n}}{(1 + {}_{t+1}r_{t+n-1,t})^{t+n-1}} \qquad (20)$$

Since the long term interest rates on the right hand side are analogous to the yields of Equations (3), the formal equivalence of the Hicks and Malkiel models is readily established; Luckett [15] presents a formal proof.

The important point, of course, is that under such conditions one must seek a theoretical structure which permits a testable difference to exist between these two disparate views of the world. It might be thought, for example, that the Meiselman model effects such a discrimination, but we have already seen, in Equations (15), that Meiselman's test collapses into a two-parameter (a_1 and b_1) model, so it should come as no surprise that it too fails to offer any help on this important question.

C. MODIGLIANI AND SUTCH AND THE PREFERRED HABITAT

Turning to the more recent work on an alternative hypothesis, we may consider a paper by Modigliani and Sutch [23] updated later by Modigliani and Shiller [24]. In the earlier of these papers, the theoretical structure is described by the following assumptions: (1) individual investors are uncertain about future rates; (2) transactions have definite holding (or borrowing) periods (the "preferred habitat" for their funds); (3) transactors exhibit risk aversion; and (4) there are speculators operating in the market who simultaneously borrow and lend in different maturities whenever the expected return dominates the risk. While hedgers, inactive speculators, and active speculators operate side-by-side in the market, it is the hedger who presumably dominates, with his risk-averse profile and, in an uncertain world, his preferred habitat equal to the actual period of liability. Under hedgers' influence, the market for each security would then clear depending on the relative quantities of securities available; ignoring the speculators entirely, if the supply of funds to the n-period market were greater than the supply of securities of that maturity, then a kind of risk discount, sufficient to drive out the suppliers of funds (if securities were fixed in quantity) would develop.

This risk discount, or in the converse case, risk premium, to induce the speculators and speculative investors to hold the security in question, will not be a monotonic function of term-to-maturity unless (in aggregation) the gap between demand and supply widens with maturity, and there is no a priori reason for that to happen. Hicks, we can recall, had taken the opposite viewpoint. Modigliani and Sutch [23] propose that:

> The habitat theory, on the other hand, asserts that there is little we can say a priori about the behavior of P_m [the risk premium] except on the basis of definite knowledge of prevailing habitats of both lenders and borrowers, for which we have in fact not much usable information.

One problem with this approach is that it supposes that an active speculator has a fixed habitat *ex ante*. It seems more likely that the active speculator commits funds to the market for a minimum period which depends on such considerations as tax laws, among others. He reviews his financial portfolio from day to day and only reacts when his expectations about other securities are on net out of line (by sufficiently more than the transactions costs) with the prospects his current portfolio presents to him. It is the essence of his activity that he has no fixed "habitat" and it is probably better for empirical purposes to assume that he is hoping for transitory income rather than that he is organizing his future consumption. The latter is a natural way to motivate the preferred habitat for "inactive" speculators. There is surely a distinction here which ought to be modeled.

The Modigliani-Sutch empirical test is not able to confirm the existence of a cyclically related term premium.[22] They begin by defining the difference between the yield on a long-term bond R_{mt} and that on the certainty-equivalent R_{1t} (in Hicks the latter is a one-year rate) as consisting of an expected capital gains component $\Delta R^*_{m-1,t}$ modified by a variable proportionality factor (to deal with the discounting of future gains) and a term-premium P_{mt} relating to periods m and 1.

$$\Delta R^*_{m-1,t} - R_{1t} = \gamma \Delta R^*_{m-1,t} + P_{mt} \qquad (21)$$

The particular hypothesis about $\Delta R^*_{m-1,t}$ is that it is determined by the course of short-term interest rates over the recent past (e.g., by the random walk model). This permits Modigliani and Sutch to describe their hypothesis by an Almon polynomial (quite arbitrarily they chose a fourth degree polynomial) which proved to have its lowest standard error of estimate at 16 quarters. The actual model tested was a reduced form of Equation (21) and the

Almon hypothesis was:

$$R_{m,t} - R_{1,t} = \alpha + \sum_{i=0}^{n} \beta_i R_{1,t-i} + P_{m,t} + \eta_t \qquad (22)$$

with the error term being η_t. The equation actually estimated merges $P_{m,t}$ with the constant and the error and transposes $R_{1,t}$ to the right hand side with a theoretical coefficient; it appears to fit the data closely, leaving little room for debt-management and variable liquidity premium hypotheses. The residuals, however, exhibit serial correlation ($DW = .582$). When we look at portfolio models below, we will see an explanation of the serial correlation in interest rates in terms of the "market segmentation hypothesis."

To test the hypothesis that lengthening of the debt (e.g.) should increase the gap between the short- and long-term premium, the technique employed is to put measures of the maturity composition of the debt into equations derived from (22). Five of the 16 measures tested were successful (in the sense of providing a t-value greater than 2); the measures included the average length to maturity of the total debt and the proportion of the total which was short, in level and first difference form, but for some reason no Almon format was attempted on these variables. Of the five "successful" tests, three had incorrect signs, leading the authors to conclude against the hedging hypothesis.

Some statistical problems with their test have already been noted; most important was the arbitrary use of the Almon scheme. But there is a theoretical objection to their measures of "relative quantities" which was raised by Wallace [33]. That is, the proportion of the federal debt with m years to maturity implicitly ignores (for example) the fact that a rise in the proportion of debt of m years can be achieved by either

(1) issuing m period debt and retiring debt 1 to m - 1 years to maturity, which implies a rise of (for example) the spread between long and short rates, where the long rate is more than m periods to maturity, or
(2) issuing m period debt and retiring debt of L (longer) periods to maturity, which implies a fall of the spread between long and short rates, generally.

III. *Recent Developments in Term Structure Theory*

A. PORTFOLIO MODELS

Actually, the tests of the preceding section can be interpreted by a portfolio model, although the formal methods of portfolio theory promise more than is usually delivered empirically on the term structure problem. There have been many portfolio studies employing both long-term and short-term securities, but generally the formal propositions of the term structure literature have not been part of the specification of the problem. One of the reasons portfolio models do not adapt themselves readily to the problem is that the most popular versions are generally single-decision period models—this is a methodology which best models short-horizon hypotheses like the Malkiel model. A second problem is that as we aggregate we lose much of the flavor of the portfolio model.

The Bierwag and Grove [1] application of the Tobin model to the Meiselman problem attempts to do much more:

> The assumption of single-valued expectations means that investors in Meiselman's world will never diversify among securities—they will always be "plungers." It is difficult indeed to see how an equilibrium structure of interest rates could be determined in a world populated with plungers with identical single-valued expectations. [1]

In the Bierwag-Grove model, the consumer constructs a portfolio which has weights $(a_1 + a_2 = 1)$ assigned to two bonds, a long one (a_1) and a short one (a_2), and maximizes a utility function which has as arguments the expected return and the variance of the expected return of the portfolio. In fact, Bierwag and Grove could have solved for a portfolio with three securities in it but, instead, they elected to permit the investor to borrow (there was no *absolute* wealth constraint in the individual maximizing problem): this, in turn, enabled them to obtain a measure of risk aversion or, when negative, risk-love.

The function actually maximized is $U(\bar{p}, S^2)$ in a Lagrangean form

$$z = U(\bar{p}, S^2) - \lambda(a_1 + a_2 - 1) \qquad (23)$$

with the expected value of $\bar{p}$ for the second period given by

$$\bar{p} = a_1(1 + R_{1,t})r_{2,t} + a_2(1 + R_{1,t})E[R_{1,t+1}] \qquad (24)$$

and with $r_{2,t}$ as the only forward rate in the problem.[23] What prevents our speculator from being a plunger is his uncertainty which, in turn, is a result of variation in the spot rate. All of this variation comes from the second term in (24) because $R_{1,t}$ is a "certainty equivalent"; thus the expected variance is

$$S^2 = a_2^2(1 + R_{1,t})^2 \, Var(R_{1,t+1}) = a_2^2(1 + R_{1,t})^2\sigma^2 \qquad (25)$$

Further note that a_1 or a_2 can be negative; if a_1 is negative, the investor will be levered, in effect borrowing in the long-term market to lend in the short. The first order conditions for the three variables $(a_1, a_2,$

and λ) in the model are:

$$\frac{\partial U}{\partial a_1} = \frac{\partial U}{\partial \bar{p}} (1 + R_{1,t}) r_{2,t} - \lambda = 0$$

$$\frac{\partial U}{\partial a_2} = \frac{\partial U}{\partial \bar{p}} (1 + R_{1,t}) E(R_{1,t+1}) + \frac{2\partial U}{\partial S^2} a_2 (1 + R_{1,t})^2 \sigma^2 - \lambda = 0 \quad (26)$$

and

$$\frac{\partial U}{\partial \lambda} = a_1 + a_2 - 1 = 0$$

Given the value of λ in the first equation, we can solve for a_2 explicitly from the second; this yields

$$a_2^* = \frac{\mu[E(R_{1,t+1}) - r_{2,t}]}{(1 + R_{1,t})\sigma^2} \quad (27)$$

μ (which contains the parameters from the utility function) is "an index of audacity" and is given by Equation (28).

$$\mu = -\frac{1}{2} \frac{\partial U/\partial \bar{p}}{\partial U/\partial S^2} \quad (28)$$

If $\mu > 0$, the investor is a risk-averter. We note that in (27), the "equilibrium" condition, the proportion of funds invested in short-term securities, varies directly

   (i) with audacity (μ),
   (ii) with the difference between the investors expectation and the forward rate,

$$[E(R_{1,t+1}) - r_{2,t}], \text{ and}$$

   (iii) with the variance of the expected return (σ^2).

If the investor invests in long-term securities, with a two-period horizon to the problem, he is simply a pure risk-averter; that is, one notes that if (i) or (ii) is zero he invests all his funds in long securities; if σ^2 is zero he will plunge, as noted before, since a_2 will be either $-\infty$ or $+\infty$.

If all individuals are alike, then all will have identical expectations and identical values of μ; this will make it impossible to achieve any results in a market situation [since it will make it unreasonable to assert any difference between $E(R_{1,t+1})$ and $(r_{2,t})$]. We can, of course, employ this model directly in a disaggregated context, although its usefulness will probably vary inversely with the degree of aggregation.

Bierwag and Grove [1] produce some further results when individuals are not identical: if both sides of Equation (27) are multiplied by the wealth of investor i (V_i), we get

$$V_i a_2 = X_{2i} = \frac{\mu V_i[E(R_{1,t+1}) - r_{2,t}]}{(1 + R_{1,t})\sigma^2} \qquad (29)$$

X_{2i}^* is now the amount invested in short-term bonds. If the investor holds X_{2i}^0 short bonds anyway, his excess demand is given by

$$X_{2i} - X_{2i}^0$$

Market equilibrium requires that

$$\sum_{i=1}^{n} (X_{2i}^* - X_{2i}^0) = 0 \qquad (30)$$

Since $\sum_{i=1}^{n} X_{2i}^0 \equiv 0$ (i.e., assets $\equiv$ liabilities of inside bonds), this market condition reduces to

$$\sum_{i=1}^{n} X_{2i}^* = \frac{\sum_{i=1}^{n} \mu_i V_i[E(R_{1,t+1}) - r_{2,t}]}{(1 + R_{1,t})\sigma_i^2} = 0 \qquad (31)$$

We may then solve explicitly for the equilibrium forward rate $r_{2,t}^*$ to get a weighted average of forward rates (note that we cannot solve for $R_{1,t}$ and $R_{2,t}$ but only their ratio):

$$r_{2,t} = \sum_{i=1}^{n} E_i(R_{1,t+1})v_i \qquad (32)$$

with the weights (v_i) defined to be

$$v_i = \frac{\mu_i V_i/\sigma_i^2}{\sum_{i=1}^{n} (\mu_i V_i/\sigma_i^2)} \qquad (33)$$

The ith investor, then, influences this forward rate directly with (i) his investment fund (v_i); (ii) his audacity (μ_i); and (iii) the confidence of his prediction $\left(-\frac{1}{\sigma_i^2}\right)$. We see, clearly, how important these elements are, since some diversity in opinions is required for a sensible solution.

There are further studies by Richard Roll [28] and by Thomas Cargill [4] which apply the "efficient markets model" explicitly to the term structure problem. Roll doubts that tests such as that just presented will show statistical effectiveness because the past price of a stock is the cheapest and most obvious variable to monitor; that is, such results as those just exhibited cannot easily be distinguished from random walk models which would also test a reduced form of the type given in Equation (32). Roll's theoretical structure is an elaboration of the Bierwag-Grove model which also includes a maturity preference variable, but his actual empirical tests rely essentially on a higher degree of serial correlation to find against a "pure expectations model" and in favor of two versions of the market segmentation hypothesis. But Roll's work is by far the most convincing support for the segmentation hypothesis that exists.

Cargill [4], extending the work of Sargent [30], points out that unless one tests the expectations hypothesis as a joint hypothesis, one may not find effective tests of the proposition. That is, in addition to the condition that forward rates be expected rates, the hypothesis also requires that expectations be formed in the manner suggested as appropriate for an efficient market. With regard to efficiency, Cargill notes that:

> The efficiency of the bond market is dependent on the existence of large numbers of competitive market participants motivated by profit maximization who have more or less equal access to the emerging market information. Randomly emerging information, competitive behavior on the part of market participants, and the uncertainty as to the exact equilibrium future interest rates imparts a random movement to increments in forward rates on successive calendar dates. [4]

Then, Cargill (like Roll) argues that the presence of serial correlation in revisions in forward rates implies segmentation.

B. THE HOLDING PERIOD IN THE DYNAMIC CONSUMPTION MODEL

In some ways, the main problem with the two main traditional theories of the term structure is that they explain too much: any conceivable shape of the yield curve can be attributed to the actions of speculators or of hedgers, particularly if one takes the position either that speculators do not have to forecast correctly or that the preferred habitat is anywhere along the yield structure. It seems that in a situation like this, the natural thing to do is to see if the effect of speculation or hedging can be discerned in some other context than in the bond market.[24] A case in point is the dynamic consumption problem, in which the individual wealth holder is given a motive, that of reconciling his lifetime consumpton plan with the expected configuration of his income stream, to take up a particular pattern of bond holdings.

Let us attempt a generalization before turning to some of the more specific cases in the literature.

Assume that each individual maximizes an intertemporal utility function (34), where the (C_i) represents

$$U = U(C_t, \ldots, C_L) \tag{34}$$

a lifetime $(t, \ldots, L)$ consumption plan, with $L - t$ being the number of remaining years one expects to live (t being one's age). An individual will expect to earn income until year N, in which case the present value of his expected earned income is given by:

$$\sum_{i=t}^{N} \left(\frac{Y_i}{(1 + r_{i+1-t})^{i+1-t}} \right) = Y_t$$

where the interest rate is the yield appropriate to the period at which the income is to be received. We could expect this income stream to have a humped shape, reaching a peak at some age prior to retirement; if we include pensions in this component, then the curve might reasonably be expected to decline continuously from the peak until expected death, in which case $N = L$.

If we suppose the individual employs exogenously issued bonds to do the job of straightening out his consumption stream, then we can suppose a stream of coupon payments will be received, which must be discounted as well.

$$\sum_{i=t}^{L-1} \frac{X_i}{(1 + r_{i+1-t})^{i+1-t}} = X_t$$

Further, let us suppose that there is some initial wealth left over from previous periods $(= a_t)$.

On the disbursement side, the individual will have a life-time consumption plan given by

$$\sum_{i=t}^{L-1} \frac{C_i}{(1 + r_{i+1-t})^{i+1-t}}$$

and will plan to purchase bonds up until one period prior to his expected demise; B_i is the purchase price of a bond maturing at period i.

$$\sum_{i=t}^{L-1} \frac{B_i}{(1 + r_{i+1-t})^{i+1-t}}$$

It may differ from F_i, the similarly discounted issue price of the bond (face value), in which case an expected capital gain is built into the problem.

If we assume, to the contrary, that bonds are issued at par and held to maturity at which time they are cashed at par, then there still re-

mains an interesting term structure problem; the budget constraint
becomes

$$a_t + \sum_{i=t}^{L-1} \frac{X_i}{(1 + r_{i+1-t})^{i+1-t}} + \sum_{i=t}^{N} \frac{Y_i}{(1 + r_{i+1-t})^{i+1-t}}$$

$$= \sum_{i=t}^{L} \frac{C_i}{(1 + r_{i+1-t})^{i+1-t}} \quad (35)$$

We could derive first order conditions here, with the term differentiated
interest rates as arguments, but of more interest is the fact that there
are some direct empirical implications in an aggregate context; the
aggregation leaves us with bond holders of different ages, who are
otherwise alike. Thus, given the exogenously determined stock of bonds
of the relevant maturities, if the income stream and the consumption
stream do not coincide over time, the relative interest rates and the
planned consumption stream will have to (jointly) adjust until the
bond market clears.

The following situation might represent a consumption income profile
for a society; if individuals are spread evenly along the time axis and

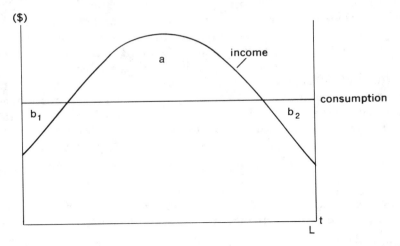

with $b_1 + b_2 = a$ (no estate motive), a flat yield curve may be predicted. But suppose as a result of a baby boom some 40 years ago that
the larger proportion of wage earners are in the net savings area (a),
at the peak; it is easy to see that the theory suggests that there will be
a relatively large supply of savings and that this supply will be seeking
long-term securities (of over 25 years to maturity). This motivates
higher prices and lower yields for long-term securities; indeed, something like a humped curve (since 40-year-olds are probably supporting
a larger number of children) will develop. A direct empirical test suggests itself.

· Joseph E. Stiglitz [31], building on some earlier work of H. A. J. Green [10], has attacked the problem in a more conventional way. Aside from offering a more general solution to the term structure problem (to be discussed below) he notes that there is even a payoff for the conventional theory of liquidity preference:

> If our hypothesis that individuals desire wealth for the consumption it provides is accepted, then it is not correct, in spite of common usage in economics dating at least back to Keynes, to consider long-term bonds as riskier than short-term bonds, and a theory of the demand for short-term bonds based on those considerations . . . may be misleading. [31]

This occurs simply because the "risk" is not defined to be the risk of a fluctuation in the interest rates from now until next period but instead to be the "risk" of not achieving a target consumption, in which case the risk averter may react differently in the two situations. To put it succinctly, he may prefer long-term bonds because his consumption stream is thereby less uncertain. He may also diversify. Stiglitz's paper is at root based on a very simple model. Assuming an initial wealth of W_o, a two-period model with one- and two-year bonds and similar expectations held with certainty, Stiglitz shows that an individual maximizing expected utility over the two periods, but consuming "nothing" in the present period, will not necessarily specialize in the holding of either a short or a long asset as has been argued in the literature since at least Hicks; this result obtains because the individual's choice is a blend of his expectations and his attitude toward risk.

The two-period wealth constraint for a given wealth (W_o) is

$$W_1 = W_o \left[\frac{a}{P_1} + \frac{(1-a)}{P} P_2 \right] \tag{36}$$

where P is the price of a two-year bond, P_1 the price of a one-year bond, and a is the percentage of W_o invested in one-year bonds. Since $P_1 = \frac{1}{1+r_1}$, if we let $g_1 = 1 + r_2$, and $G = g_1 g_2$, we can write Equation (37)

$$W_1 = W_o \left[a g_1 + \frac{(1-a)}{g_2} G \right] \tag{37}$$

g_2, measuring the yield on a one-period bond one period hence, is, of course, unknown. In the general case offered by Stiglitz, the consumer maximizes

$$U(C_1, C_2)$$

subject to

$$C_1 + \frac{C_2}{g_2} = W_1$$

The necessary (and assumed to be sufficient) condition for an optimum, then, is

$$U_1 = g_2 U_2 \tag{38}$$

so that in the final analysis, our results depend on expectations about forward rates (g_2).[25]

The problem, then, becomes that of finding the optimal value of a which maximizes

$$EU[C_1, (W_1 - C_1)g_2]$$

and this simply requires that

$$EU_2[g_1 g_2 - G] = EU_1 \left[\frac{1}{P_1} - \frac{P_2}{P} \right] = 0 \tag{39}$$

from Equation (38). Then, the following deductions about the term structure can be derived directly from Equation (39).

(1) If the individual is risk neutral (that is, if he does not care in which period he consumes), then the long rate will be the product of the short rates $(g_1 g_2 = G)$; Hicks' "normal backwardation" follows immediately.

(2) But this is not general. If consumers are risk aversive, as g_2 varies consumers will vary their consumption plan (C_1, C_2) in different ways.[26] Further, with less general utility functions, Stiglitz shows that individuals will not necessarily specialize in one or the other security, but may hold both; in fact, the amount (but not the existence) of speculation depends on relative risk aversion. The results differ from the traditional analysis on three accounts.

(1) Stiglitz has capital gains in the problem.

(2) Short-term bonds have a negative covariance with long-term bonds, suggesting by standard portfolio theory that some diversification will occur.

(3) Stiglitz abandons the artificial distinction between the savings decision and the portfolio allocation problem.[27] It may also be pointed out that these considerations are fundamental to a coherent statement of a number of problems in monetary economics.

Aside from this challenge to the conventional liquidity preference theory, Stiglitz also argues that the traditional view about the effect of relative quantities is incomplete. In particular, earlier writers had concluded that the monetary authorities could not affect the term structure without affecting expectations. Stiglitz shows that in his simplest case, even when expectations are unchanged, the term structure can change; but this result becomes less surprising when one realizes that his study is in many ways better specified, in particular in having a budget constraint.

In general, Stiglitz advanced the discussion in two main ways. Most importantly, he carried along the more general term structure theory as a part of the problem of intertemporal maximization of expected utility. Like Roll, who generalized the "equilibrium asset price" models to show that much of the standard theory consists of special cases, Stiglitz establishes that the restrictions on utility functions one would have to employ to get these same results are unthinkable. Further, of course, Stiglitz's model is open to testing in the usual "demand system" fashion. On the other hand, Stiglitz still has an overly simple two-period model and a model in which bonds are held to maturity, begging the fundamental question of maturity preference.

Green [11] pursues Stiglitz's line explicitly, and offers firmer support to the former's contention that open market operations can change the term structure without changing expectations. While Green's results are roughly the same as Stiglitz's, his methods are more general. Green begins by pointing out that a collection of Stiglitz-type individuals will not have demand functions which are in general equilibrium because current consumption is not the problem; in other words, Stiglitz, like Hicks at the beginning of the era, effectively divides the savings decision from the portfolio decision; it will be recalled that Stiglitz claimed differently.

The second major difference in Green's model is the inclusion of a known-with-certainty stream of future additions to wealth; Stiglitz only had current wealth. One immediate consequence is that the possibility of selling a two-year bond after one year takes on more meaning in Green's model although it is still there only as an *ex-post* reaction to the market solution. These two adjustments are bought at the cost of increasing the complexity of Green's model beyond the point of simple summarization. Suffice it to point out that all of the things we are interested in—especially the strength of "preferred habitat"—make more sense in models in which the holding period is motivated in some way—here by reference to a lifetime reconciliation between income and consumption. This accounts for individual behavior—and is very likely to have some useful empirical implications—but it doesn't, of course, help much with the problem of the financial institutions which dominate the maturity-differentiated market. We do, however, have the possibility of work by analogy in that direction. Green, indeed, helps by producing explicit demand functions for the two types of bonds he considers, following the assumption of a quadratic utility function.

NOTES

1. See, for example, comments in Wehrle [34] and in Conard [6].

2. A condition under which this formula holds is stated by Hicks as follows:

> If no interest is to be paid until the conclusion of the whole transaction, then the same capital sum must be arrived at by accumulating for two weeks at the two-week rate of interest, as alternatively by accumulating for one week at the one-week rate, and then accumulating for a second week at the "forward" rate. ([12], p. 145)

We may arrive at the formula in the text by noting that Equation (2) can be written as a set of forward rates as follows:

$$\text{Price}_t = \frac{C}{(1 + r_{1,t})} + \cdots + \frac{C + F}{(1 + r_{1,t})(1 + r_{2,t}) \cdots (1 + r_{n,t})}$$

Then, for $C = 0$ and $F = 1$, we may equate Equation (3) with the expression just derived to produce

$$(1 + R_{n,t})^n = (1 + r_{1,t})(1 + r_{2,t}) \cdots (1 + r_{n,t}) \quad .$$

3. It is worth pointing out that while the calculation of R_n in Equation (2) utilizes only one particular security, that of r_n in Equation (4) involves more than one, as the note makes clear. Thus, forward rates may differ because the bonds differ in coupon, face value, number of interest payments per year, and even issue price. This problem has produced a literature, notably that by Malkiel [17], McCulloch [21], and Buse [2].

4. Nelson [25] considers some. An updating appears in McCulloch [20]; McCulloch concludes his empirical work thusly:

> Without imposing any particular form on the liquidity premium, we were able to demonstrate the following: there is a liquidity premium, significantly greater than zero. This premium has been large enough since the Accord to imply that for some maturities, borrowers or lenders who desire one borrowing or lending period would do better in a different maturity in spite of the extra costs incurred. (p. 116)

5. Recall the argument above, as well, that liquidity premiums may decline if holding periods exceed the maturities available, as they may for life insurance companies.

6. McCulloch [20], whose analysis this is, considers a particular example using a simple Bernoulli utility function; he concludes that the result depends on whether the coefficient of variation of marginal utility decreases (risk premium) or increases (risk discount) with distance into the future. There is, similarly, no theoretical reason for the monotonic behavior to approach an asymptote, although in practice it may very well do so.

7. Generally, we might expect costs to be the same, but dealing in a thin market, such as the long-term bond market, imposes larger inventory costs (per dollar of transactions) on brokers.

8. These costs are differently discounted, of course. That is, there is an opportunity cost to dealing with brokers, since one can always hold a time deposit at essentially no brokerage cost. Relative to the long contract, the short contract provides the opportunity for ducking some of these implied costs; this is one of the reasons a person with a ten-period horizon might prefer to stay short.

9. Then, on account of the cost of adjusting or acquiring information and on account of lags in acquiring the skills necessary to manage a portfolio and the like, the individual unit may re-examine its position periodically, perhaps every six months. This might produce observable lags in behavior although, in practice, this sort of behavior applies more to small than to large units and is something which one would expect to disappear with aggregation. In any event the "plan" is long-period, but the data are revised periodically, to see whether or not an adjustment to the plan is necessary.

10. Joan Robinson pointed out that:

> In real life it would be perfectly rational for a man to expect (on the basis of experience) that, for example, over the next year or two the bill rate will continue to be held steady at a low value while the bond rate fluctuates round, say 3%. But it would not be rational for him to think that he knows exactly what the rates of interest will be every day from to-day till Kingdom Come. ([27], p. 102)

Her view, essentially, is an empirical generalization. Some years later a more specific statement of the Robinson position was put forward by Dudley G. Luckett [15].

11. Culbertson [7] refers to this as a fact. Some qualification such as "government" is clearly in order, at the least; it is also not quite clear how liquidity is to be defined here.

12. Culbertson [7], p. 490. Here he also notes what was later argued out in the literature that the "short-run view of long-term rates" does not also imply "equal holding period yields," as discussed below.

13. This, then, suggests that an empirical test, in which one has forward rates as the dependent variable and an appropriate measure of relative quantities, lagged forward rates, and a trend factor on the other side, may show some influence of segmentation. The effect, of course, could disappear quickly, so the implied "run" may have to be shorter than a quarter. It is, of course, fairly difficult to test a theory which is couched in terms of the "speeds of adjustment" of part of the market.

14. Culbertson [7], p. 499. It is worth pointing out here that there are two ways institutions might match up their assets and liabilities, as emphasized by Richard Roll [28] much later. Depending on the nature of the business, an institution might effect a "time dependent" hedge in which case it would hold a bond whose maturity declines year by year with a liability of a similar nature, or it might effect a "maturity dependent" hedge because its (expected) liability is always of the same duration (for example, one might guess, the life insurance company).

15. Culbertson [7], p. 500. From this point we must be careful to distinguish arbitrage from speculation. It is often not clear in Culbertson's

discussion that it is not the former (where speculators can be accused of missing the obvious) that underlies his formulation of the problem.

16. Culbertson [7], p. 500. This is also the definition of a yield.

17. Telser [32] notes that since the Meiselman model refers to changes in interest rates, it is consistent with any shape of the yield curve conceivable.

18. While a positive coefficient may be evidence of a premium, a zero is not. Basically this is because a model in first differences is being tested; both Kessel [14] and John Wood [35] show the algebra.

19. These expressions are proved in Telser's paper; they are the result of the overlapping of interest rates in the Meiselman equation.

20. Actually, Buse [2] seems to establish that Meiselman's results are not due to serial correlation in the usual sense, since Buse has scrambled the data by date. The underlying problem is mainly a conceptual one: the influence of "the" interest rate swamps the adjustments along the structure. "The" interest rate has been given no place in the theory, yet it figures in the regressions. What one really wants to do is see if Meiselman's error term adds anything to the inertia hypothesis, for example.

21. *Report* of the Committee on the Working of the Monetary System (London: Her Majesty's Stationery Office, Cmnd. 827, 1959).

22. Reuben Kessel [14] had earlier argued that there was a cyclical pattern to liquidity premiums but that it was positively related to changes in the level of interest rates rather than to the cycle itself. Nelson [25] got the opposite sign on the same relationship, while J. H. McCulloch [20] was unable to confirm that there was any relation between the level of interest rates and the liquidity premium.

23. We can rearrange this term, making use of the budget constraint, to get an expression which exhibits the difference of opinion between the investor's expectation $E(R_{1,t+1})$ and the market forward rate $(r_{2,t})$:

$$\bar{p} = (1 + R_{1,t})(r_{2,t} + a_2[E(R_{1,t+1}) - r_{2,t}])$$

24. In a recent paper (Fisher [9]), I have employed the speculative variables suggested by this literature in short-run demand-for-money functions, with some success.

25. That is, since W_1 is only a function of g_2,

$$C_1 = C_1(g_2; ag_1, G) \text{ and}$$
$$C_2 = (W_1 - C_1)g_2$$

26. If

$$G/g_1 > Eg_2 \text{ he will specialize}$$
$$G/g_1 < 1/E(1/g_2) \text{ he will specialize in shorts,}$$

and if

$$1/E(1/g_2) < G/g_1 < Eg_2 \text{ some will go long, some short and some not at all, depending on their expectations and their utility functions.}$$

That is, the first term merely states that the known forward rate between period 1 and period 2 is greater than the forward rate expected. Thus, the third condition represents something of a knife-edge; we have no idea of its empirical significance, of course.

27. There is a connection between the two in Stiglitz's [31] analysis, but he can hardly claim a large advance in this area, since his stock of initial wealth is fixed; the savings decision has already occurred, except for the possibility of not spending everything in the second period.

REFERENCES

1. Bierwag, G. S., and M. Grove, "A Model of the Term Structure of Interest Rates," *Review of Economics and Statistics,* 49: 50–62 (February 1967).

2. Buse, A., "Interest Rates, the Meiselman Model, and Random Numbers," *Journal of Political Economy,* 75: 49–62 (February 1967).

3. Buse, A., "Expectations, Prices, Coupons, and Yields," *Journal of Finance,* 25: 809–18 (September 1970).

4. Cargill, T. F., "The Term Structure of Interest Rates: A Test of the Expectations Hypothesis," *Journal of Finance,* 30: 761–77 (June 1975).

5. Cargill, T. F., and R. Meyer, "Estimating Term Structure Phenomena from Data Aggregated over Time," *Journal of Money, Credit and Banking,* 6: 503–16 (November 1974).

6. Conard, J., *An Introduction to the Theory of Interest* (Berkeley: University of California Press, 1959).

7. Culbertson, J. M., "The Term Structure of Interest Rates," *Quarterly Journal of Economics,* 71:485–517 (November 1957).

8. Fisher, Douglas, "Expectations, the Term Structure of Interest Rates, and Recent British Experience," *Economica,* 33: 319–29 (August 1966).

9. Fisher, Douglas, "The Speculative Demand for Money: An Empirical Test," *Economica,* 40: 174–79 (May 1973).

10. Green, H. A. John, "Uncertainty and the Expectation Hypothesis," *Review of Economic Studies,* 34: 387–98 (October 1967).

11. Green, Jerry, "A Simple General Equilibrium Model of the Term Structure of Interest Rates," Harvard Institute of Economic Research Discussion Paper (1971).

12. Hicks, J. R., *Value and Capital,* 2nd ed. (Oxford: Oxford University Press, 1946).

13. Johnson, Harry G., and A. R. Nobay (eds.), *Issues in Monetary Economics* (Oxford: Oxford University Press, 1973).

14. Kessel, Reuben, *The Cyclical Behavior of the Term Structure of Interest Rates* (New York: Columbia University Press, 1966).

15. Luckett, Dudley G., "Multiperiod Expectation and the Term Structure of Interest Rates," *Quarterly Journal of Economics,* 81: 327–29 (May 1967).

16. Lutz, Friederick A., "The Structure of Interest Rates," *Quarterly Journal of Economics,* 55: 36–63 (November 1940).

17. Malkiel, Burton, *The Term Structure of Interest Rates* (Princeton, N.J.: Princeton University Press, 1966).

18. McCulloch, J. H., "Measuring the Term Structure of Interest Rates," *Journal of Business,* 44: 19–31 (January 1971).

19. McCulloch, J. H., "An Estimate of the Liquidity Premium" (Chicago: University of Chicago Press, Ph.D. Dissertation, June 1973).

20. McCulloch, J. H., "An Estimate of the Liquidity Premium," *Journal of Political Economy,* 83: 95–120 (February 1975).

21. McCulloch, J. H., "The Tax-Adjusted Yield Curve," *Journal of Finance,* 30: 811–30 (June 1975).

22. Michaelsen, Jacob, "The Term Structure of Interest Rates and Holding-Period Yields on Government Securities," *Journal of Finance,* 20: 444–63 (September 1965).

23. Modigliani, Franco, and R. Sutch, "Debt Management and the Term Structure of Interest Rates: An Empirical Analysis of Recent Experience," *Journal of the Political Economy,* 75: 569–89 (August 1967).

24. Modigliani, Franco, and R. Shiller, "Inflation, Rational Expectations and the Term Structure of Interest Rates," *Economica,* 40: 12–43 (February 1973).

25. Nelson, Charles R., *The Term Structure of Interest Rates* (New York: Basic Books, 1972).

26. Norizoe, Kotaro, *Selection of Optimum Bond Portfolio,* Claremont Graduate Center, Unpublished Ph.D. thesis, June 1974.

27. Robinson, Joan, "The Rate of Interest," *Econometrica,* 19: 92–111 (April 1951).

28. Roll, Richard, *The Behavior of Interest Rates* (New York: Basic Books, 1970).

29. Rowan, D. C., and R. J. O'Brien, "Expectations, the Interest Rate Structure and Debt Policy," in K. Hilton and D. Heathfield, *The Economic Study of the United Kingdom* (London: Macmillan, 1970).

30. Sargent, T. J., "Rational Expectations and the Term Structure of Interest Rates," *Journal of Money, Credit and Banking,* 4: 74–97 (February 1972).

31. Stiglitz, Joseph E., "A Consumption Oriented Theory of the Demand for Financial Assets and the Term Structure of Interest Rates," *Review of Economic Studies,* 37: 321–52 (July 1970).

32. Telser, Lester, "A Critique of Some Recent Empirical Research on the Explanations of the Term Structure of Interest Rates," *Journal of Political Economy,* 75: 546–61 (August 1967).

33. Wallace, Neil, "Comment on Debt Management and the Term Structure of Interest Rates," *Journal of Political Economy,* 75: 590–92 (August 1967).

34. Wehrle, Leroy S., "Life Insurance Investment: The Experience of Four Companies," in J. Tobin and D. Hester (eds.), *Studies in Portfolio Behavior* (New York: Columbia University Press, 1966).

35. Wood, John, "The Expectation Hypothesis: The Yield Curve and Monetary Policy," *Quarterly Journal of Economics,* 78: 457–70 (August 1964).

36. Wood, John, "Expectation and the Demand for Bonds," *American Economic Review,* 59: 522–30 (September 1969).

Part **VI**

Monetary Policy

The conduct of monetary policy and the development of monetary theory followed largely independent paths in the immediate prewar and postwar periods. The theorists directed their energies toward developing Keynesian analysis leaving monetary policymakers for the most part to their own devices in solving the monetary problems of the wartime and immediate postwar periods, or, in many cases, became policymakers themselves. This situation was reversed first by the Patman Hearings in 1951 and later as the result of the two major inquiries into the operation of the monetary system on both sides of the Atlantic, conducted by the Radcliffe Committee, which published its findings in 1959, and the Commission on Money and Credit, which issued its report in 1961.

The three groups conducted a sweeping inquiry into the goals of monetary policy, the institutional arrangements employed in monetary decision-making, the effectiveness of existing institutions in the choice of policy instruments and in the diagnosis of the economic situation, and the possible need for new policy instruments. The two latter reports received poor marks at the hands of the academicians which, in a way, was inevitable since they were grading the unsettled state of monetary theory and policy according to standards upon which they themselves hardly agreed even with regard to fundamental issues. Under these conditions it was unreasonable to expect the two broadly composed inquiring groups to resolve the wide range of open issues. In one way, however, the inquiries were a success. They confronted policymakers with the theoretical issues that were involved in their decision-making and theoreticians with the practical issues that their theories had to answer if they were to affect policy. This confrontation gave a new impetus to the study of monetary problems. But what was, perhaps, most important of all, these inquiries gave rise to the extensive empirical testing of theoretical and pragmatic hypotheses concerning the operation of the monetary system.

Tinbergen, in his pioneering work on the theory of economic policy, noted that in a determinate economic model with a fixed number of goals (targets) to be achieved by controlling policy variables (instruments), the specification of feasible goals is dependent on the number and type of instruments.[1] He established the necessary and sufficient conditions for the number of policy instruments relative to the number of independent targets. Tinbergen's analysis was extended by Theil who introduced the notion of "optimal" policy.[2] Using a quadratic utility function Theil was able to generalize Tinbergen's analysis to the case where the targets were flexible rather than predetermined and tradeoffs were permitted.

The traditional objective of monetary policy was to maintain the internal and external value of the currency. The policy instruments placed at the disposal of the monetary authority were adequate to achieve these objectives. In recent years, however, the number of objectives the monetary authority has been asked to take into consideration, among them full employment and an adequate rate of growth, has increased considerably. The responsibility for achieving these objectives is shared with other branches of government and new policy instruments have been devised, most importantly, fiscal policy. It appears likely, however, that the policy objectives of British and American governments exceed the number of feasible policy instruments at their disposal, and, consequently, economic authorities are forced to maintain a changing hierarchy of objectives. Which economic objectives are to be assigned to the monetary authority and how the priorities assigned to these goals are to be revised is still an unsolved problem.

Mundell suggested that the principle of Tinbergen needed to be supplemented for policy purposes by what he called the principle of effective market classification whereby policy instruments are paired with the objectives upon which they have the most influence.[3] If this principle is violated, Mundell cautioned, what may appear to be stabilizing policies may actually have the contrary effect.

Aside from these general problems, there exists the question of whether instruments of monetary policy can significantly influence the course of the economy in a desired direction. This problem is discussed in several of the selections. The question may be broken down into three parts: (1) diagnosis—can the economic situation be determined early and with sufficient reliability to employ discretionary policies; (2) selection and use of policy instruments—which existing or new policy instruments should be applied and in what magnitude in order to achieve desired objectives in particular economic situations; (3)

---

[1] Jan Tinbergen, *On the Theory of Economic Policy* (Amsterdam, 1952). The objectives must be consistent and independent, as well as meet other conditions, for the statement to be generally true.

[2] Henry Theil, *Economic Forecasts and Policy* (Amsterdam, 1961) and *Optimal Decision Rules for Government and Industry* (Amsterdam, 1964).

[3] Robert Mundell, "The Appropriate Use of Monetary and Fiscal Policy for Internal and External Stability," *IMF Staff Papers* (March 1962), pp. 70–77. Also reprinted in the first edition of this book.

effectiveness—assuming the correct policy instruments are applied to achieve their maximum effectiveness, will they be able to make a significant contribution toward achieving the desired objectives.

Hamburger surveys the literature in an attempt to answer the questions of whether the lags in monetary policy may be so great and variable as to cast a serious doubt on discretionary monetary policy.

Benjamin Friedman examines whether the question of monetary indicators has any value for the conduct of monetary policy in an uncertain world with significant lags between changes in monetary variables and their effect on ultimate policy goals and whether a single indicator can be relied upon as an accurate guide to policy.

The article by Smith is an introduction into the control theory literature. Control theory seems to be an answer to a policymaker's prayer, at least in its formulation of the policy problem. Its weakness is that in its present state of mathematical development it does not provide easy, or in some cases any, answers to problems where there is significant uncertainty both in the specification of the model and in the length of the lags between the instrumental and target variables. Nevertheless control theory portends to be a promising avenue of attack on the policy problem.

The monetary authorities on both sides of the Atlantic, although placed on the defensive largely as a result of the critical nature of contemporary analysis of monetary policy, have not let the developments of recent years go unheeded. In a slow, deliberate manner many basic changes are being wrought in the operations of the central bank. One of the most important is the gradual integration of monetary policy into the total framework of economic policy, including fiscal policy, with an improved coordination between the central bank and other branches of government. One of the most pressing general issues yet to be resolved is whether monetary rules, discretionary policy, or some mix of the two would be the best possible course for future monetary policy.

The current worldwide experience of inflation with unemployment —stagflation—has presented monetary policymakers with a thorny dilemma for which economists have offered little assistance in providing a satisfactory policy resolution.

19 The Radcliffe Report and Evidence

John G. Gurley *Stanford University*

A drama critic recently wrote of an evanescent Broadway play: "It was paved with good intentions, and, like most pavements, it was trodden underfoot." While for myself, I hesitate to call this an epitaph to the Radcliffe *Report*, it describes pretty well the initial responses of the *Report's* horde of critics, some of whom judged it the most monumental flop of the 1959 season, and most of whom felt that it had nice stage settings and all that, but was terribly weak in the theme.

These judgments are understandable and probably not grossly unfair. Nevertheless, I believe that they are based on the worst the *Report* has to offer and not on the best. At its worst, the *Report* is full of exaggerations, errors, confusions, conflicting statements, and careless writing. These no doubt represent, as the critics suggest, the "real" *Report*. But, if one attributes the exaggerations to a desire to escape the conventional, the conflicting and hazy statements to the task of achieving unanimity among diverse committee members, the confusions and errors to deadlines—if, in short, one excuses the weaknesses—and chooses the very best from its pages, the *Report* has much to recommend it.

In this idealized form, the *Report* presents a pioneering analysis of Britain's financial system, in which the monetary system and money are considered as only part of a complex, but integrated,

Reprinted from *American Economic Review*, Vol. 50 (September 1960), 672–700, by permission of the author and the American Economic Association.

structure of financial institutions, assets, and markets, and in which monetary policy, debt management, and fiscal policy are treated as coordinating techniques of a general financial policy aimed at regulating spending through this financial structure. In the underlying theme of the *Report*, all issuers of financial assets are relevant to financial policy; the private sectors issuing their debts and equities; the Treasury issuing various forms of government securities; the monetary system creating money and other claims; and nonbank intermediaries creating liquid claims. The idealized *Report* sees the level and structure of interest rates, which are the immediate targets of financial policy, determined partly by the whole range of financial assets—the level by the relation of liquid assets, including money, to holdings of financial and physical assets, and the structure to the composition of financial assets and demands for these components, with expectations playing their role in both cases. It sees money as only one asset among many, banks as only one type of institution among many, and the control of money as only one aspect of an over-all financial policy. This is the *Report* at its best.

The Committee on the Working of the Monetary System, known as the Radcliffe Committee, was appointed by the Chancellor of the Exchequer in May 1957 "to inquire into the working of [Britain's] monetary and credit system, and to make recommendations." The Committee was composed of the chairman, Lord Radcliffe, two businessmen, two bankers, two trade union leaders, and two academic economists, the latter being Professors A. K. Cairncross and R. S. Sayers. During the fifty-nine days of hearings, scattered from July 1957 to April 1959, evidence was obtained from the Treasury, the Bank of England, clearing banks and other financial institutions, dozens of trade associations, business leaders, and many economists. In addition, the Committee received memoranda from many of these witnesses and from others, including the National Institute of Economic and Social Research, the Central Statistical Office, and, inevitably, a few monetary cranks.

The unanimous *Report* of the Committee was published in August 1959. This was followed in March 1960 by four volumes of evidence.[1] The first of these, *Minutes of Evidence*, is a huge, 980-page, double-column tome of the hearings. The other three volumes—*Memoranda 1, 2*, and *3*—contain 142 papers submitted by various groups and individuals. As a rough guess, the *Report* and four volumes of evidence are packed with upwards of $3\frac{1}{2}$ million words, a fact that I must note because it is possible that I have inadvertently slid over a hundred thousand or so here or there, and by so doing have done less than full justice either to the Committee or to some of its contributors.

I begin with a brief outline of the Committee's principal views on monetary theory and policy. I shall then discuss these views, in about the same order, supplementing the discussion with material from the oral and written evidence.[2] Since this procedure misses three areas that occupied much of the Committee's time—international finance, the status of the Bank of England, and financial statistics—I touch upon these briefly at the end.

The Report's Monetary Theory and Policy: An Outline

The following appear to qualify as the Committee's dominant views on monetary theory and policy:

1. The money supply has been largely uncontrolled during the postwar period; neither the banks' cash ratio nor their liquidity ratio has placed an effective upper limit on monetary growth.

2. But the money supply is of no great concern. First, it is incidental to the level of interest rates. These rates, though affected by liquidity, are determined largely by the expectations and confidence of the public, which in turn are determined by what the monetary authorities say. Second, there is virtually no direct relationship between the money supply and spending.

3. Interest rates, in and of themselves, have had little or no direct effect on spending decisions.

4. While spending is not directly affected by interest rates, it is affected by liquidity, which is composed of the money supply and the money people can get hold of. The private sector's liquidity is increased by the lending of commercial banks and other financial intermediaries, because such lending increases the supply of loanable funds ("the money people can get hold of"), and the growth of liquidity stimulates spending. The important thing about financial institutions is not the liquid liabilities (monetary or otherwise) they create but the lending they do—the assets they purchase.

5. The lending of all financial institutions can be indirectly controlled through changes in the level and structure of interest rates. A rise in interest rates will slow down their lending by imposing capital losses on their security holdings. Thus, while a rise in interest rates has little direct effect on spending, it depresses spending indirectly by reducing the lending of financial institutions and so the public's liquidity.

6. This means that the "centre-piece" of monetary action is the level and structure of interest rates, and not the money supply. The structure of rates can best be influenced by debt management policy working on the composition of the national debt. Since, however, it is not a good thing to have highly fluctuating interest

rates, and since the lending of financial institutions in ordinary times should not be directly controlled, more emphasis should be placed on fiscal policy as a short-run stabilizer, leaving monetary policy to set the tone of longer-run developments.

7. But, during emergency situations, when runaway inflation threatens, monetary policy should be used vigorously. In these cases, lending should be restricted directly, by controls on commercial-bank lending, perhaps by the extension of such controls to other intermediaries, by consumer credit regulations, and by restrictions on issues of long-term securities.

Control of the Money Supply

DEFINITION OF MONEY

The Committee regards the money supply as consisting of notes[3] (but evidently not coins!) outside of banks plus net deposits, the latter being liabilities of London clearing banks and of Scottish and Northern Irish banks.[4] However, nowhere in the *Report*—and, indeed, nowhere in the *Minutes of Evidence* or the three volumes of *Memoranda*—is there an extended series of the money supply in accordance with this definition.[5] Bank deposits comprise not only current accounts, which earn no interest and are repayable on demand, but also deposit accounts, which are similar to our time deposits, not subject to check, and hence, strictly speaking, not used as money by the public.[6] The Committee recognizes that deposit accounts are not quite the same as current accounts, but nevertheless they are counted as money. The reason seems to be that they are easily exchangeable for money.[7] The inclusion of these accounts raises the question of why other highly liquid claims, such as deposits in acceptance houses, in hire-purchase companies, in Trustee Savings Banks, and so on, are excluded.[8] While the Committee does lay down an explicit definition of money, at other times it goes out of its way to "fuzz up" the concept, by placing the supply of money in quotation marks, followed by "however that is defined," "whatever that may be made to mean," and similar derogations.[9]

CASH AND LIQUIDITY RATIOS OF BANKS

The Bank of England normally attempts to control the volume of bank deposits in the traditional way—by controlling the supply of certain bank assets which are held, by convention and not by statute, in fairly constant proportions to deposit liabilities. The conventional cash ratio is 8 per cent, with cash consisting of vault cash and deposits at the Bank of England. Deposit expansion is also limited potentially by a conventional 30 per cent liquidity ratio, where liquid assets for this purpose include cash, Treasury bills, call loans, and commercial bills.[10] There has been a spirited debate in recent years concerning which ratio, if either, is the effective one.

To reduce bank deposits, the Bank of England can decrease the banks' cash and thus their liquid assets by selling securities in the market. To regain liquidity, the banks can sell short-dated bonds, which do not count as liquid assets, to the discount houses, the latter financing the bonds by borrowing at call from the banks, with call loans counting as liquid assets. Or the banks may sell bonds and buy Treasury bills or commercial bills. It has been easy enough for banks to get liquid assets, but none of these operations replenishes their cash. For this purpose the banks must borrow from (or sell something to) the central bank. In the United States, borrowing is done directly; in Britain it is done indirectly through the discount houses. These houses hold Treasury bills, short-dated government bonds, and commercial bills, and they borrow at call from London clearing banks and other banks. In addition, they and not the clearing banks are permitted to borrow from the Bank of England. When the clearing banks lose cash, therefore, they may call some loans from the discount houses. Under pressure, these houses may then either sell Treasury bills to or borrow from the Bank of England, and in these ways restore to the clearing banks the cash initially lost.[11] But, as the Bank explained to the Committee:

> It should be noted that the creation of a cash shortage is not without effect. For, particularly, if it is such as to compel borrowing from the Bank of England, which is relatively expensive to the Discount Houses, they will try to reduce such borrowing so far as possible by raising their bids for money [that is, selling bills or short bonds], thus causing short-term interest rates to rise.[12]

This was further explained, in response to a question from the Committee, as follows:

> If we wanted to raise interest rates, then we would give less or possibly no help in the ordinary way [by purchasing bills from the discount houses], and we would say: "If you want cash you must come to the Discount Office for it." And moreover we could if need be so arrange things that the market needed a great deal of cash. . . .[13]

This is the familiar process by which open-market sales of a central bank reduce the "cash" of commercial banks and force them to reduce earning assets and the money supply, raising market rates of interest. Commercial banks can get more cash from the central bank any time they want to, but they presumably have a demand schedule for cash that is negatively related to its price. Hence, if the central bank raises the price, the banks will demand less cash, and so less earning assets and less monetary liabilities.

The Committee seems to have misunderstood this evidence, taking it to mean that, since banks could get more cash at any time, the cash ratio was therefore ineffective in limiting the money supply. This confusion appeared several months later when the Committee was again questioning spokesmen for the Bank. The latter stated that during times of inflationary pressure it would be better for the government to finance a deficit by selling Treasury bills to the market than by borrowing from the central bank (by Ways and Means advances), inasmuch as, though either measure could increase the liquid assets of banks, the latter would raise their cash base. This prompted the following exchange:[14]

> I understood their policy of increasing deposit liabilities would be determined by their total of liquid assets, not the amount of cash? ——The two things come out to the same, in the sense that the total of liquid assets in either case is affected in the same way; but the composition of their liquid assets would be different. With the Bank of England making Ways and Means Advances, their cash would be inflated. It would be inflated to a point beyond the 8 per cent they require, and to that extent they would be looking round for earning assets. . . .
>
> Is not this a different doctrine from what we have been told hitherto?——I do not think so. . . .
>
> We are now back on the question of the whole control of the volume of bank deposits; we have been taught hitherto that it is the liquid assets ratio that matters?——Surely we have said there are two aspects of this control. . . .[15]

Passing over this and other evidence, the Committee in its *Report* states that the cash ratio was ineffective.[16] Nevertheless, at other times, the Committee seems to recognize that this is incorrect, for it is stated, in substance, that the cash ratio would be ineffective only if the Bank of England set out to stabilize the Bill rate (which it generally has not done); otherwise, it would be effective.[17] But it is the former view that carries the day. In the Committee's eyes, the more effective ratio is the liquidity ratio, though it is stressed that banks have found it comparatively easy to evade this, through the mechanism described above, and that it has been thirty years since bank lending has been restrained by liquidity considerations.[18] In the end, one gathers that the Committee believes that the money supply has been largely uncontrolled.

These views are not easily reconciled with the fact that interest rates have increased sharply during the last decade in Britain, unless of course it is held that the money supply has nothing to do

with the level of interest rates, a proposition I turn to in a moment.
The banks have been subject, it is true, to requests to hold the line
on or to reduce their advances (loans and overdrafts), but these
restrictions have been short-lived, and in any case the banks could
always purchase other earning assets and so increase their deposit
liabilities.[19] In view of all the evidence, it seems more reasonable to
conclude that there has been more or less effective control of the
money supply, at least since 1951, and that this control has probably
operated primarily through the cash base of the banks, as described
by Bank officials.

Interest Rate Determination

At one point in its *Report*, the Committee presents an admir-
able account of the determination of the level of interest rates.
After extolling the role of liquidity in economic analysis, the statement continues:

> We would nevertheless emphasize that the amount of money . . . is
> of considerable significance. The other classes of liquid assets . . . are
> inferior, in convenience to the holders, and this inferiority has to
> be compensated by the payment of interest. If there is less money
> to go round, in relation to the other assets (both physical and
> financial), it will be held only by people willing to make a greater
> sacrifice in order to hold it: that is to say, rates of interest will rise.
> But they will not, unaided, rise by much, because in a highly de-
> veloped financial system . . . there are many highly liquid assets
> which are close substitutes for money, as good to hold and only
> inferior when the actual moment for a payment arrives . . . (i.e.,
> the more efficient the financial structure, the more can the velocity
> of circulation be stretched without serious inconvenience being
> caused).[20]

Unfortunately, this statement is in sharp conflict with what
appears to be the Committee's principal view of this subject. While
it can be reasonably argued that the *Report* does not in fact present
a theory of interest rate determination—or, perhaps better, that it
obliquely presents several—it is fair to say, I think, that the
Committee looks upon "expectations and confidence" of the public
as the chief determinant of rate levels—though lip service is paid
now and then to the role of liquidity. And these expectations are
greatly affected by what the authorities say, by the public's interpretation of their mood. That is, expectations are molded by the
"faces" made by the authorities; presumably, a squinty-eyed look
might raise interest rates, a vapid stare maintain them, and an
ebullient expression lower them. When this theory takes over, the

authorities never change interest rates by operating on the money supply or on liquidity generally; rather: "The authorities must seek . . . to influence the general liquidity situation by operating on rates of interest."[21] It is even stated that the money supply is incidental to interest rate policy.[22] It is for this reason that the Committee can properly hold the view that the money supply has been largely uncontrolled in the face of sharp changes in levels of interest rates; for after all money has little or nothing to do with interest rates.[23]

The theory that interest rates are determined by words and faces is indicated repeatedly in the *Minutes of Evidence*.[24] As an example, consider this exchange with Winfield Riefler, then assistant to the chairman of the Board of Governors of the Federal Reserve System:

> Then is not much the most important thing you do not the buying and selling of Bills, not the raising or lowering of [discount] rates, but what you *say*?——No.
>
> Why do you have to operate in the market as well as telling the market what you think about things?——Our operations in the market actually determine the funds available.[25]

This evidently left the Committee incredulous. Though there are some indications that it was not willing to accept wholeheartedly the dominance of expectations in interest rate determination,[26] the truth is that this factor, by elimination, becomes the only solid explanation of rate movements in the *Report*, a theory which suggests that bond markets in Britain are peopled by a lot of nervous wrecks. The Committee was also influenced in this view by R. F. Kahn,[27] to whom I shall return later.

The Committee landed in this position despite the fact that F. W. Paish and others presented data to show the very close postwar relationship between the ratio of money to national income and bond rates,[28] and despite Paish's excellent testimony about this relationship. Here is a sample of it:

> During the period up to 1956 during which there was this tremendous drop in the ratio of bank deposits to national income, was there not considerable liquidity in business?——If there is so much liquidity, why are firms willing to pay very high rates of interest for raising long-term loans on the London market?
>
> They may expect prices to rise?——It is liquidity in relation to what they want to do. I would say that the long-term rate of interest is the inverse of liquidity.
>
> Would this mean that you would feel that if you knew the ratio of bank deposits to net national money income you could predict what the rate of interest would be?——So long as the conditions remain, I would say almost exactly.

The point you are putting to us is that there is an inverse relationship between the liquidity of the system and the rate of interest,
liquidity being defined not just in the terms of the money supply,
but to include near-money?——I would put it in terms of the
money supply. One would expect the amount of near-money to
affect the shape of the curve. . . .

The issue is whether the relationship is sufficiently close and the
lags sufficiently limited to allow of operational application?——I
would say that in the short run one can get it down to pure expectations if one can persuade people that long-term rates are going to
fall and that they will have a heavy capital appreciation. There
could be very marked temporary shifts on those expectations; but
if the authorities wanted to stabilize the long-term rate round about
$4\frac{1}{2}$ per cent, they would have to allow the ratio of bank deposits to
national income to rise to more nearly 40 per cent than 35 per cent.[29]

And in response to an additional question about the effects of
near-money, he answered:

I would say that whereas they could get a given rate of interest
with a 40 per cent ratio of bank deposits to national income if there
was not very much near-money in the system, they might need
35 per cent to get the same rate if there was a lot of near-money
in the system. They would have to set off the increased liquidity
due to large holdings of near-money by having less real money,
in order to get the same effect on total liquidity.[30]

Excellent memoranda and testimony were also submitted on
this question by many others. Altogether, there seems to be an impressive body of evidence to support the view that the money-
income ratio, modified by the presence of other liquid assets, and
within the context of "real" variables, was the principal determinant of the level of interest rates in Britain during the postwar
period.[31] But, for some reason, the Committee chose to ignore this
evidence.[32]

The Direct Effects of Interest Rates on Spending

The Committee adopts a "three-gears" view of interest rates.
At any time, people believe that interest rates are either in low,
middle, or high gear. Any play of rates within a given gear is not
likely to have much, if any, direct effect on spending. If people
"are to be shaken into some change of course, the gear must be
changed."[33] A rise in the Bank Rate from $4\frac{1}{2}$ per cent to 7 per cent,
for example, would generally be regarded as a shift from middle
to high gear.

Nevertheless, though such upward shifts have occurred in postwar Britain, and so might have produced downward pressure on

spending through the "interest rate effect," the Committee states that it found very little evidence that this has in fact happened.[34] According to the Committee, it found no evidence that higher interest rates, in and of themselves, reduced consumption; there was practically no indication that interest rates were important to large firms with respect to investment in either inventories or fixed capital; expenditures of the nationalized industries were also largely impervious to changes in interest rates; the same was true for local authorities' expenditures; and spokesmen for the smaller firms treated the interest rate effect with general skepticism.[35] "It has become clear that, as the system works at present, changes in rates of interest only very exceptionally have direct effects on the level of demand. . . ."[36] If we accept these statements, they would seem to dispose once and for all of the subject, as it relates to postwar Britain up to 1959.

But, from other material presented to the Committee by witnesses and others,[37] it is doubtful that the statements can be accepted in their present extreme form. When this evidence is compared with the conclusions of the Committee, it is hard to escape the feeling that its final appraisal should have been more guarded.

There is, first of all, the survey made by the Federation of British Industries of its manufacturing members with respect to the impact of higher interest rates in early 1955 on their investment decisions. Among the questions, was: "Was the rise in Bank Rate from 3 to $4\frac{1}{2}\%$ during January and February, 1955 a *major* factor in taking your business decisions?" (Their italics.) Almost 12 per cent (179) of the firms answering (1526) said that it was. Of these 179 firms, 40 per cent were in the engineering, shipbuilding, electrical, and textile industries. The rest were found among more than a dozen other industries. These firms reported deferment or reduction of investment projects, or reduction or deferment of inventory purchases, or other action.[38]

The Committee, in commenting on this survey in its *Report*, states:

> The response rate . . . was relatively low, and it may well be that answers came for the most part from those who had some positive reaction to report . . . in discussions with us representatives of the Federation were not confident that these figures could be regarded as firm enough to be the basis for general conclusions.[39]

The first part of this statement suggests that those who did not answer the survey may have had a lower ratio of yes-to-no answers than those who did. This may well be: but it should be noted that the questionnaire contained dozens of questions on other subjects, so that the nonrespondents could have had many other reasons for not participating.

As to the second part of the statement, I can find nothing in the *Minutes of Evidence* to support it. What I do find is a continual "hounding" of the witnesses, a barrage of counterarguments and suggestions from the Committee, until finally the witnesses wilt under extreme pressure and state that "it might not be so." First of all, the Committee made it quite clear to the witnesses that it considered the figure of 179 out of 1595 "astonishingly high" and "most surprising," especially in view of the fact that the firms at the time probably anticipated inflation. The witnesses, after some hesitation, finally agreed that the figure might indeed be surprising. The Committee then asked them whether such expectations of inflation might not swamp the effect of higher rates [yes], whether other measures that accompany the higher rates might not be responsible for reduced spending [very likely], whether the interest rate can be isolated from other influences [yes], and whether the interest rate is really a factor taken into account before investment is made [not a principal factor]. Having prodded the witnesses into saying that interest rates are relatively unimportant, the Committee next asked them how, in view of that, the interest rate came to be a major factor with 179 firms. The answer and the Committee's response to it follow:

> [First witness:] I am becoming nervous about how well the question was understood by these 179 people. [Second witness:] I do not think the 179 merely took account of the rise in interest rates alone; they took it in the context of the other measures. It is not explicit in the answers. [First witness:] We could go back to these 179 firms, and cross question them about this, and perhaps get more information.
>
> It is rather vital to our discussions. We have had so many people tell us over so many years that, at any rate in the manufacturing industries, the rate of interest hardly affects these decisions at all, and one has come to think that whatever else Bank Rate changes can do they cannot do anything much about investment in the manufacturing industries.——[Answer not relevant.]

And, finally, after the witnesses agreed that the factor of uncertainty in investment projects diminished the importance of interest rates—still another observation having nothing directly to do with the survey results—we find:

> That is exactly what the university lecturer says when he is lecturing. He is describing the position correctly when he says that?——
> In my limited experience, yes.

You will see why, after having had years of that, one finds these figures so surprising?——It is a complex of factors, and this expectation of inflation has, I am sure, been a very prominent consideration in that complex.

My experience as a partner in an issuing house is relevant [to what has just been said]. I cannot remember a case where a company has come to my firm, and asked what the cost of money would be.——[Answer not relevant.]

Is there not another aspect to this? A great deal of capital expenditure so classified is in fact a total of a very large number of small decisions taken throughout the period; in relation to those decisions all sorts of practical considerations of the market such as have been mentioned are really far more relevant and major considerations than the cost of money?——Yes.[40]

Well, the theory of the university lecturer won out over the facts. "In discussions with us," the Committee said—and I come back to this without further comment—"representatives of the Federation were not confident that these figures could be regarded as firm enough to be the basis for general conclusions."

Another survey in March 1958 was taken by The Association of British Chambers of Commerce, inquiring about the effects of the credit squeeze after September 1957 on a wide range of companies. 16,000 questionnaires were sent out, but there were only 3404 usable responses. Of those stating that they had, since September 1957, experienced reductions in their turnover or in investment programs, only 4 per cent said they were due to the higher cost of borrowing, though 20 per cent attributed them to that plus tight money and restrictions of bank credit. And 30 per cent of those firms said that they had taken steps to reduce or pay off their bank borrowing because of increased costs.[41] After noting this, the Committee throws doubt on the results in this way:

... but it may well be that the dramatic rise in cost, which certainly attracted much attention, was being blamed for reductions many of which were in fact dictated much more by expectations of a decline in the level of activity than by the rise in the rate of interest.[42]

Its concluding remarks about these two surveys are also interesting:

The results of these questionnaires add up to substantial evidence that a proportion, big enough to be relevant to policy, of business firms were vaguely discomforted by the changes in monetary conditions in 1955–57, and especially in September 1957; but we have not found sufficient evidence to justify a conclusion that in the conditions of the 1950s the rise in interest rates would by itself have directly provoked a worthwhile curtailment of demand.[43]

Aside from what is "worthwhile," the last part of this statement is necessarily true because the surveys did not seek to determine the amount of reduction in demand due to higher interest rates but only the number of firms reporting such a reduction.

A third survey was carried out, in October 1957, by the Birmingham Chamber of Commerce; questionnaires were sent to 3,400 member firms, and 610 responded. 185 firms reported that they had postponed or cancelled plans after 1955 for new factory or office buildings, extensions to existing buildings, replacement of machinery or equipment, or orders for new machinery or equipment. Of these, almost 40 per cent attributed such reductions to the increase in interest rates on borrowed capital.[44]

During the hearings with the representatives of The Association of British Chambers of Commerce, this was brushed aside rapidly, in the following way:

> In the Birmingham inquiry about 40 per cent of those who postponed or cancelled plans attributed this to an increase in interest rates. That is a very high proportion. Did it not surprise you?——
> I have no explanation of the results. It may be something that was peculiar to Birmingham. I wonder whether this may have had something to do with the recession in the motor industry.
>
> If we leave the Birmingham inquiry aside for the moment, and concentrate on your own much more elaborate inquiry. . . .[45]

As it turned out, the "moment" proved to be of infinite duration.

That is by no means all of the evidence submitted to the Committee that ran contrary to its general conclusions. Not all of the following evidence is clear-cut; in fact, much of it is at best sketchy, but all of it stood up under sharp questioning.

For example, representatives of the British Engineers' Association stated that higher interest rates increased their costs and so hurt their business;[46] those of the Country Landowners' Association testified that higher interest rates had cut back farm improvement projects substantially;[47] The Scottish Landowners' Federation had essentially the same story, claiming that capital expenditures in agriculture and forestry had been reduced by higher interest rates and would almost certainly be stimulated if credit became easier;[48] for this reason capital expenditures were also reduced by wholesalers, and their demand for inventories was curtailed;[49] it was the opinion of representatives of The Association of Investment Trusts that higher rates had cut back business spending all along the line;[50] a furniture dealer said that the rise in rates in September 1957 caused him to reduce capital expenditures, and that an increase in the Bank Rate "does come very much into our planning for the present and for the future";[51] a dealer in wine and spirits offered similar testimony;[52] witnesses for the Association of Municipal Corporations knew of several instances, involving water projects, housing programs, and so on, where expenditures were cut back because of higher interest rates;[53] a small amount of local authority's expenditures was said to be affected by a change in rates;[54] there is some evidence, though not much, that rubber merchants reduced inventories because of higher rates;[55] a survey carried out by the Council of Scottish Chambers of Commerce found that one-third of those firms replying stated that they had taken steps after September 1957 to reduce bank loans because of the higher cost;[56] the Committee heard that the high cost of money was a factor in reducing inventories of automobile dealers;[57] it also heard that retail chemists reduced or postponed capital expenditures and inventory purchases partly because of higher borrowing costs, though this was qualified in response to questioning;[58] a representative of the North of Scotland Hydro-Electric Board stated that higher rates undoubtedly slowed down their program for distributing electricity;[59] the building of a hotel was deferred partly because of higher borrowing costs;[60] evidence was put forth that some wholesale tobacconists, timber people, and others reduced inventories because rates went up;[61] two bankers stated that the higher rates after September 1957 caused some businesses to reduce overdrafts;[62] the same was reported by other bankers, who further claimed that merchants, and to a lesser extent, industrial concerns reduced inventories and that some capital expenditures were curtailed for interest-rate considerations, though this view was modified under questioning;[63] London clearing bankers, too, reported that bank loans probably fell after September 1957 due to higher borrowing rates.[64] The Committee also had the opinions of several economists that a change in interest rates was effective in altering spending throughout the economy;[65] and the Bank of England concurred with this.[66]

It is far from certain, of course, what all this adds up to, especially since an equally impressive list could be produced for the other side. But, as a minimum, it would seem that the Committee's extreme conclusions are presumptuous in view of the evidence it heard.

Liquidity and Financial Institutions

As I have noted, the Committee all but eliminates the money supply as a factor in the determination of interest rate levels; it believes that changes in these rates have had little direct effect on spending; and it does not think that there is any direct, close connection between the money supply and spending. But, while money is shoved out of the house through the front door, for all to see, it does make its reappearance surreptitiously through the back as a part of general liquidity: and the most important source of liquidity is the large group of financial institutions.[67]

This is the reason the Committee devotes much space in its *Report* not only to the monetary system but also to the large number of nonbank financial intermediaries. The more important of these intermediaries are the discount houses, hire-purchase companies, insurance companies, superannuation and pension funds, Post Office Savings Bank, building societies, and investment trusts. At the end of 1958 the assets of this group exceeded those of the monetary system by about 60 per cent.[68]

It is no simple matter to discover in the *Report* by what process the intermediaries alter liquidity, for the Committee shifts around from one point of view to another and never does get down to definitions. But its principal view seems to be that the public's liquidity is composed not only of the money supply but of the amount of money it can get hold of; at one point, the matter is put in even vaguer terms when it is stated that liquidity in the broad sense depends on "the amount of money people *think* they can get hold of."[69] Since people can get hold of money from financial institutions, liquidity is increased when such additional borrowing sources become available: the greater the number of potential lenders, especially institutional lenders, the greater is the public's potential liquidity, because it is then easier to raise funds.[70]

Put somewhat differently, the notion is that the proliferation and growth of financial intermediaries increase the demand for "bonds," which "makes money more available" and stimulates spending for current output, even though the banking system is tightly controlled. With one possible exception, nowhere in the *Report* is there a statement as explicit as that, and nowhere does the Committee attempt to explain the process just described.[71] The reader is simply left with the thought that if a new intermediary comes along, or if an old one grows, the aggregate demand for "bonds" is somehow increased—there is an increase in the supply of loanable funds, and more money is made available to potential spenders.

The Committee fails to note that the extent to which this is true depends on whether the growth of intermediaires reduces the public's demand for money—and so money becomes vital to the analysis. This may be illustrated as follows. Assume that there are three financial assets—bonds, money, and savings deposits—which are liabilities of the public, the monetary system, and nonbank intermediaries, respectively. Assume, further, for simplification, that the assets of all financial institutions consist only of bonds. Then, in the usual definition, the supply of loanable funds is defined:

(1) Supply of Loanable Funds $=\begin{cases} \text{Planned saving by public} \\ +\ \text{Increase in stock of money} \\ -\ \text{Increase in demand for money} \\ \quad\ \text{(hoarding).} \end{cases}$

To simplify further, assume that saving and investment are done by different groups and that savers do not repay debts. Then planned saving is equal to the public's increase in demand for bonds, money, and savings deposits; the public's increase in demand for savings deposits is equal to nonbank intermediaries' increase in demand for bonds; and the increase in the stock of money is equal to the monetary system's increase in demand for bonds. Hence,

(2) Supply of Loanable Funds $=\begin{cases} \text{Increase in demand for bonds by} \\ \text{the public, nonbank intermediaries,} \\ \text{and the monetary system.} \end{cases}$

It may be seen, then, that an increase in demand for bonds by nonbank intermediaries will increase the supply of loanable funds only if it is not accompanied by an equivalent or greater decrease in demand for bonds by the public and the monetary system. Suppose the public increases its demand for savings deposits, enabling nonbank intermediaries to increase their demand for bonds. Given the public's propensity to save, this means that there is a reduction in the public's demand for either money or bonds. If bonds, then the reduction in demand for bonds by the public is exactly offset by the increase in demand for bonds by nonbank intermediaries, and so the supply of loanable funds remains the same. On the other hand, if the shift is away from money, then the public does not reduce its demand for bonds, and neither does the monetary system reduce its demand for bonds (because a decrease in demand for bank liabilities will not alter the monetary system's outstanding liabilities and so will not change its bond assets). Hence, in this case, there is a net increase in the supply of loanable funds.

It is possible, therefore, that the purchase of bonds (lending) by nonbank intermediaries will not increase the supply of loanable funds. If it does not, then the public's increase in demand for money and savings deposits is matched exactly by the increase in the stock of these assets. There are more "liquid assets" in the economy, but there is also an equivalent increase in demand for them. The amount of funds made available to the public, at given interest rates and other terms of lending, is exactly the same as before; the growth of nonbank intermediaries has not changed the over-all situation.

It follows that the extent to which the growth of nonbank intermediaries will increase the supply of loanable funds (or "liquidity"
in the Committee's terms, i.e., the excess stock of liquid assets) depends on the degree of substitutability between savings deposits
and money, so that an answer to this question requires an analysis
of the types of claims issued by the intermediaries. By concentrating
on the asset side of the intermediaries' balance sheet, and neglecting the liability side, the Committee fails to come to grips with the
problem. Its failure to compare what is being withdrawn from the
market with what is being issued to the market—or, put another
way, its failure to consider the demand for liquid assets as well as
the supply of them—is at the heart of the difficulty. This one-sided
view is reflected in many conclusions in the *Report:* that nonbank
intermediaries are important only because they lend; that banks are
important not because they create money but because they make
loans; that it is not the money supply that should be controlled but
bank advances; and so on.[72]

I cannot say that the Committee is wrong in stating that nonbank
intermediaries have increased liquidity and the supply of loanable
funds, and have done this in such a way as to exert a destabilizing
influence on spending. These views may well be correct as applied
to postwar Britain. The point is that the analysis leading to these
conclusions is faulty, which not only leaves the reader unconvinced
of them but leads the Committee down some wrong policy paths.

The Committee raises the question of whether the destabilizing
activities of nonbank intermediaries should be controlled as the
banks' are. On this it states:

> If we are right in believing that the level of total demand is in-
> fluenced by the lending behaviour [the asset side again!] of an in-
> definitely wide range of financial institutions, and not just by the
> supply of money, it might be supposed that we should substitute
> for the traditional control of the supply of money a complex of
> controls of that wide range of financial institutions. Such a prospect
> would be unwelcome except as a last resort, not mainly because of
> its administrative burdens, but because the further growth of new
> financial institutions would allow the situation continually to slip
> from under the grip of the authorities.[73]

The *Report* later adds that:

> Any severely restrictive control of [bank] operations is certain, over
> a period of time, to be defeated by the development of rival insti-
> tutions; during the interim, the community will have suffered loss
> by interference with the most efficient channels of lending. We
> therefore begin with some presumption against discriminatory con-
> trol of banks, at any rate in ordinary times.[74]

In principle, then, there should be no discriminatory controls on
banks in ordinary times; but only as a last resort should controls

be imposed on other financial institutions; and whether they are imposed solely on banks or on a wider range of institutions they are bound to be undermined in the long run by the development of rival institutions. Leaving this somewhat ambiguous principle, which, not surprisingly, was endorsed unanimously by the Committee, it is stated that when you get right down to it the banks must be controlled.[75] However:

> If, in the light of future experience, it should appear desirable to reinforce the authorities' power by raising the minimum liquidity ratios of the banks appreciably above their present levels, the practicability of imposing comparable restraints on other groups of financial institutions should be considered.[76]

The question of controlling other financial institutions was raised with several witnesses, and other individuals expressed their opinions (or those of their organizations) in memoranda to the Committee. The most extensive discussion of this was carried on with M. H. de Kock, Governor of the South African Reserve Bank. Here is how a small part of it went:

> Does it follow from [your] argument . . . that there is a danger that when you operate on the quantity of money the banks as particular financial institutions may be penalized, and that, if you are going to operate a credit squeeze, it should if possible operate widely over the whole field of finance and not narrowly on one set of institutions?——Yes. Years ago, when commercial banks were the main financial intermediaries, the authorities could by contracting bank credit achieve all that they wanted to achieve. In the thirties we considered that that was all that was necessary. Since that time the development of these other financial institutions has been far more active than that of the banks, and they are encroaching more and more on the field of the banks in all sorts of little ways; and today the banks are hampered in their attempts to follow the requests of the central bank.[77]

Roughly similar views were expressed by T. Balogh and by representatives of the Trades Union Congress.[78] There were of course many dissenters, among whom was Winfield Riefler, who was torn between two opposing views: that nonbank intermediaries, when borrowing funds from the public, have no effect on monetary equilibrium; and that such intermediaries, when creating money substitutes, do upset monetary equilibrium.[79] He was not asked to reconcile these views. Others, including M. W. Holtrop, president of The Netherlands Bank, were on the same side. Holtrop stated that, inasmuch as nonbank intermediaries simply redistributed the community's savings, there was no reason to believe that they would create a monetary disturbance, but that his bank, nevertheless, collected data on their activities—why, he did not say.[80]

Debt Management and Monetary Policy

The Committee's views up to this point seem to leave us in a box. The money supply has little to do with the determination of interest rates; changes in these rates have had little direct effect on spending; spending is instead influenced by liquidity, which is increased when financial institutions lend; but only as a last resort should lending by nonbank intermediaries be directly controlled, and only in emergency situations (as we shall see) should bank lending be so controlled. How is spending, then, to be regulated effectively by monetary techniques?

The answer is that the authorities can *indirectly* control the lending of financial intermediaries, and, hence, the liquidity and spending of the public, by changing the level and structure of interest rates. A rise in interest rates, for example, will slow down lending by these intermediaries to the private sector by imposing capital losses on their security holdings. Or, as Sayers put it during the hearings, "you insert the gelatine of uncertainty into their liquidity."[81] Moreover, if the national debt is lengthened at the same time, the liquid-asset base of commercial banks will be limited and thus their lending depressed.[82]

This brings debt management to the head of the class, because it is the principal means of affecting the level and structure of interest rates, and the rate structure should be considered "the centre-piece of monetary action." It is through this mechanism that regulation is exerted on the lending ability of banks and other financial intermediaries and on the public's ability to spend.[83] The authorities, in managing the debt, should not concentrate exclusively on short rates but should give a lead to the market on long rates as well; it is this structure of rates they should keep their eyes on and not "some notion" of the money supply.[84] In principle, during inflationary periods, the debt should be lengthened and interest rates raised: during deflation, the opposite policies should be followed.[85]

Thus the national debt, and not the money supply, becomes the focal point in the economy for the control of interest rates, and through these rates, for the control of institutional lending and thus the economy's liquidity and spending. In this set-up, banks are important because they are key lenders:

> It is the level of bank advances rather than the level of bank deposits that is the object of this special interest; the behaviour of bank deposits is of interest only because it has some bearing, along with other influences, on the behaviour of other lenders.[86]

In looking upon the national debt as the focal point of financial control, the Committee claims that it is following the evidence submitted to it by Kahn.[87] But, when one looks at this evidence, it is apparent that the Committee has gone somewhat further than Kahn did. Kahn stated his main thesis on this point in the following way:

> Within wide limits it is possible to achieve any desired structure of interest rates *by a suitable combination* of monetary policy with management of the National Debt. The Exchequer, by issuing short-dated securities in the place of long-dated, or *vice versa*, can secure the desired shift in relative rates of interest *against the background of a monetary policy which operates on rates in general.*[88]

Now Kahn further added that the authorities, in conducting a monetary policy, should not control the money supply *"as an end in itself"* but only because the money supply, other things given, determines the general level of interest rates.[89] He underlined this by saying:

> It is the lower level of interest rates, not the larger quantity of money, which exercises an expansionist influence . . . it is immaterial what changes in the quantity of money have to occur as part of the process of securing a particular desired behaviour of rates of interest.[90]

Kahn is clearly advocating a monetary policy that controls the money supply for the purpose of setting the general level of rates, and a debt policy that controls the composition of debt for the purpose of setting the rate structure. But, presumably because of Kahn's oft-repeated assertion that the money supply is not important as an end in itself, the Committee seems to have been misled into believing that he was de-emphasizing the link between money and interest rates, and thus removing money from any central role in policy decisions, that he was putting all of his eggs into the debt-management basket, and that he was advocating the structure of rates as the "centre-piece" of monetary action. In any case, the Committee in its *Report* and in its questioning of witnesses seems obsessed with the idea of debt managers "doing something" about the structure of rates, while control of the money supply as a means of influencing the level of rates, or the price level, receives only passing mention, and then usually for the purpose of ridiculing the notion.

Presumably, then, debt management should operate in this way: the managers set the general level of interest rates by forcibly playing on the expectations and confidence of the public; they then go to work on the structure of rates by manipulating the composition of debt. In pursuit of this policy, debt managers may be called upon at times to change the level and structure of interest rates markedly. Also, in view of the record of the 1950's, rates would have to fluctuate very widely to affect spending directly. Are such fluctuations desirable? In answering this, the Committee states that if the wide fluctuations could be confined to the short-end of the rate structure the case for this policy would be fairly strong. But, since movements in short-term rates cannot much influence spending, either directly or indirectly, it is the long-term rates that must move. And there are three reasons why this policy should be rejected. First, while long-term rates can be raised quite high, the reverse policy of lowering them sharply during recessions would require a flood of liquidity into the economy that would play havoc with attempts at stability when the economic climate reversed itself;[91] and this liquidity would at the same time inspire a speculative swing against sterling. Second, widely fluctuating long-term rates would gravely weaken the foundations of financial institutions, by involving them, when rates are rising sharply, in capital losses on large blocks of securities.[92] Third, changes in long-term rates, no matter how marked, probably have little direct impact on spending in the short run.

Inasmuch as short-run movements in interest rates, in the Committee's opinion, can get at spending only through imposing capital losses on financial institutions' security holdings, and inasmuch as this policy is rejected partly because it would "gravely weaken" the foundations of these institutions, where do we go from here? Well, the Committee states, interest rates do have a direct effect on spending in the long run, and they do influence institutional lending in the long run, so they should be used carefully and slowly in a way to set the general long-term tone of the economy.[93]

> Our conclusions on rate of interest policy are therefore that, while there can be no reliance on this weapon as a major short-term stabilizer of demand, the authorities should think of rates of interest—and particularly long rates—as relevant to the domestic economic situation. The authorities should not aim at complete stability of interest rates, but should take a view as to what the long-term economic situation demands and be prepared by all the means in their power to influence markets in the required direction.[94]

To fill the policy gap in the short run, the Committee would like to see more use made of fiscal policy, as a short-run stabilizer (after some of its present defects are corrected), leaving monetary policy to act on the longer-term situation.[95] Thus, the standard policy prescription is turned on its head; it now reads: Use fiscal policy to iron out short-run fluctuations and monetary policy to guide the economy for the longer period.[96]

So much for poor old monetary policy in ordinary times. However, during an emergency, when the danger is that of "headlong inflation," monetary measures should be used vigorously. This does not mean restriction of the money supply—for that is not important—but rather striking "more directly and rapidly at the liquidity of spenders."[97] Now, since most of us are immediately inclined to identify the money supply as a major part of liquidity, these pronouncements seem contradictory, until we remember that, for the Committee, liquidity often refers only to lending (or borrowing). So it comes as no surprise that the monetary measures the Committee has in mind in such an emergency are direct controls of capital issues, bank advances, and consumer credit—and perhaps the control of lending by nonbank intermediaries.[98]

The role envisaged for monetary policy, in ordinary times, as modest as it may be, nevertheless requires that the authorities take positive action from time to time to influence the level and structure of interest rates. The Committee notes that during most of the 1950's the monetary authorities concentrated on short-term rates and were unwilling to admit "there was much scope for the exercise of official influence over long-rates"; it recommends that the authorities give a more positive lead in the long-end of the market.[99]

This seemingly innocent recommendation was actually the upshot of a running debate between representatives of the Bank of England and the Committee that was one of the hottest of the hearings, rivaling even those of recent years in this country between the Federal Reserve and its Nemesis in Congress. The Bank authorities defended, with the greatest of moral fervor, the doctrine that they do not, and most certainly should not, influence in any direct way the level of long-term rates; and, moreover, at times they argued that they should not exert such influence, except on a very temporary basis, in any indirect way, such as by operating at the short-end of the market. They simply "follow the market," permitting the natural forces of supply and demand to determine the level of rates. Spokesmen of the Bank were never ready to concede that operations at the short-end were meant to influence the entire rate structure, though they did think that at times their operations probably did have some impact on long-term rates, undesirable and annoying as that may have been.[100]

At one stage, Bank officials were asked why, in view of strong inflationary pressures, they did not act more energetically in getting long-term rates higher. The answer and subsequent exchange follow:

> I want it to be quite clear that we do not set out to intervene in a trend.

> Even though it was reasonably plain that the reason for the action was to establish a long-term rate of interest that was needed to the

general economic health of the country?——Yes, even doing one's best to make it plain that "it hurts me more than it hurts you."[101]

Bank officials felt that their operations had not in fact pushed up long rates, that these rates had increased because of the public's fear of inflation,[102] and that it was really the impersonal forces of supply and demand that had "a pretty big influence" on long-term rates.[103] Under questioning, however, it was admitted that the Bank could affect both supply and demand, but the officials made it clear that under no conditions would they wish to do this in any direct way, because such a policy would lead the public to cry "stinking fish" at government securities and would damage Her Majesty's Government's credit. But the officials were hard put to defend this position:

> When you say that "it would greatly damage the Government's credit," what effect have you in mind there?——Put briefly, that if we have just issued a new stock at, let us say, 100, and we then proceed actively to sell it down ourselves to 95, we have largely by our own direct actions on that security forced a book loss of five points on the people who took the security at 100.

> It operates in a similar way in your sales of Treasury Bills from day to day; the Bank Rate will very definitely affect the Treasury Bill rate. You impose a loss on all holders of Treasury Bills?——I accept that, but that is the recognized play of the money market.

> Why is the one transaction objectionable and the other not?—— The Treasury Bill and short bond market is a technical market, where these things are clearly understood . . . [The institutional market is different]; if, shortly after you bought [a security] at 100, you found someone else buying it at 92 or 93 your confidence would be very seriously reduced. We cannot afford to impair people's confidence. . . .[104]

The Bank's Status, Sterling, and Statistics

In the foregoing, I have neglected several areas that received much attention in the *Minutes of Evidence* and that were dealt with at some length in the *Report*. There is space only to skip across the high points of three of these areas.

THE STATUS OF THE BANK OF ENGLAND

The Committee rejects the theory that the Bank of England should be completely independent of political influence.[105] It believes that the function of the Bank "is to act as a highly skilled executant in the monetary field of the current economic policy of the central Government," and that "the policies to be pursued by the central bank must be from first to last in harmony with those avowed and defended by Ministers of the Crown responsible to Parliament."[106] The Bank should generate advice, views, and proposals of its own, but the will of the government should be paramount.[107]

The Committee's opinions on the status of a central bank were not shared by Riefler, whose comments on this subject prompted the Committee to ask:

> This means, leaving Congress on one side, that, as between the Administration and the Federal Reserve on an issue of policy, the initiative and the last word rest with the Federal Reserve? Suppose that the Administration want a certain economic climate to be created, they can merely discuss their desires with the Federal Reserve?——The only question that comes up relates to the reading of the business and credit situation. Sometimes there are differences of view. The question then is whose judgment is going to prevail. Our position is that obviously the people who are more specialized in reading the business and credit situation have to make the judgment. It would make no sense to have us try to make a judgment on what the business and credit demand is, and then have somebody else super-imposing another judgment. It ought to be made by whoever is most capable of making it.[108]

Riefler returned to the point later:

> If the System is in this way by statute independent of the executive, and therefore from direct political pressure, and also independent of private interest, is the argument ever heard that, by being so insulated, they are in an ivory tower and out of touch with what is going on in the length and breadth of the United States?—— Yes, Mr. Elliott Bell does say that in *Businessweek* [sic]; anyone wishing to criticize the system is very likely to say that. I do not think it is taken very seriously. The system, through the directors of the Banks and the branches, and through its contacts, is intimately bound into the structure of the economy. In a sense it is the most important recorder of the state of the economy of the country; often the same people who are opposed to some action taken and who raise the cry of the "ivory tower" rush to us to corroborate any judgment they have on economic questions.[109]

The *Report* recommends the formation of a Standing Committee which would be advisory in character; it proposes that changes in the Bank Rate be made in the name of the Chancellor; and that part-time directors of the Bank be retained, a subject that had been discussed at length before the Parker Tribunal.[110]

INTERNATIONAL ASPECTS

The Committee says nothing in this portion of the *Report* that will upset foreign confidence, steps gingerly around many touchy issues, and generally approves of official postwar policy toward sterling.

It has little confidence in the ability of changes in short-term rates to correct balance-of-payments difficulties. "We have had little evidence of actual movements of funds in response to changes in short-term rates . . . ," though it adds that there is some indication that a rise in long-term rates has induced purchases of long-term securities in London. However, "the fact that changes in rates have had only a limited effect on the movements of funds in a period when sterling was weak does not imply that they will be correspondingly ineffective if sterling is strong." Rather than relying on movements of interest rates, it perhaps would be better at times to support the forward rate of exchange, though many weaknesses of this proposal are noted.[111] The Committee favors a fixed parity for sterling, rejecting freely fluctuating exchange rates, which were advocated by James E. Meade, and devaluation as a policy, "though as a way of escape it cannot be excluded."[112]

Despite the recent improvement in reserves, the Committee states that they are still far from adequate; but it is noted that the U.K.'s problem in this respect is really part of a world-wide "shortage" of international reserves relative to levels of trade.[113] This raises the question of whether there should be a substantial increase in the world price of gold, a proposal that is rejected by the Committee as not "immediately necessary [nor] the most helpful approach to the problem of international liquidity." Moreover, an increase in the price of gold would alter the existing distribution of reserves "very much in favour of the countries that are most amply provided."[114]

It is felt that this problem can best be attacked by utilizing existing international machinery, such as the International Monetary Fund, but the Committee believes that in its present form the IMF has many defects. Several suggestions are offered to remedy these defects, including relaxing the requirements on drawing rights, but the Committee seems more enthusiastic in suggesting that the IMF might be turned into an international central bank, with its own unit of account, along the lines originally suggested by Keynes.[115]

The Committee approves the steps taken toward convertibility and nondiscrimination in trade. It is hopeful about the international position of the United Kingdom, and believes that the dollar problem "is likely to be more intermittent and less intractable than is sometimes supposed, and that it has already changed in character, and is likely to continue to do so."[116] It is reported that the Treasury is looking ahead to a larger current account surplus in the early 1960's.[117] This is all to the good, because it is necessary "to maintain a balance of payments sufficiently favorable to leave a margin for loans and other investments. This margin must be correspondingly widened to allow of grants in aid of colonial development." Since, however, it is better for the United Kingdom to use its surplus more to build up reserves than long-term assets, other sterling countries should be encouraged to borrow more in other areas of the world.[118] But the United Kingdom should remain a major source of capital to the Commonwealth even if it has to borrow abroad for this purpose.[119]

FINANCIAL STATISTICS*

Although many trade associations, the Bank of England, the Treasury, and others submitted economic data to the Committee that had not previously been published,[120] the Committee was frequently handicapped by a lack of information on matters into which it was inquiring. The Committee discussed this problem in its *Report* at some length and carefully pointed out the means of correcting it.[121] As anyone who is at all familiar with the paucity of British economic data might guess, the *Report* called for more reporting and publishing of statistical series in almost every field of conceivable interest to the authorities and the informed public.

* * *

Finally, for anyone interested in further pursuit of this matter of statistics, he could do no better than follow the Committee in its quest for the marketable security holdings of the Exchange Equalization Account in 1939, a real thriller with a surprise ending.[122]

Concluding Remarks

An English visitor here, when asked what he thought of the Radcliffe *Report*, replied that it was "woolly." He undoubtedly meant that it was confused and hazy. But there is a colloquial meaning of the word, which is "attended with unusual excitement," as a woolly melodrama. The *Report* is certainly woolly in both senses.

* This section has been abridged by the editor. [R.S.T.]

It is exciting because the Committee's undertaking was hazardous from the very beginning, being nothing less than the development of a general theory of finance that would explain the impact of financial variables on the postwar British economy. And it must be said, considering the string of celebrated witnesses that paraded before it, that the Committee received surprisingly little help in its main task. In view of all this, not to mention time limitations, the *Report* it turned out, for all its deficiencies, is remarkable. The macrocosmic view the *Report* gives of the world of finance will leave many monetary theorists and policymakers uneasy in their self-imposed exile to a small corner of this world. If it does nothing more than open up this larger world to them, it will have served a worthy purpose.

But at the same time, in its analysis of this wide, wide world there seems to be confusion everywhere—in the role of the money supply, in the concept of liquidity, in the analysis of nonbank intermediaries, in the discussion of interest rate determination, in the exalted role assigned to debt managers, and so on. Even so, though this is the *Report* at its worst, it can still be judged an honorable failure. "Honorable" because, as Zarathustra reminded the dying rope-dancer, there is nothing contemptible in making danger one's calling, nor in perishing in that calling. Nothing contemptible; but still, in the way it all ended, something distinctly sad.

NOTES

1. The five volumes of the Committee on the Working of the Monetary System are: (1) *Report* (London 1959), pp. viii, 375; (2) *Minutes of Evidence* (London 1960), pp. ix, 980; (3) *Memoranda 1* (London 1960), pp. vi, 308; (4) *Memoranda 2* (London 1960), pp. vi, 227; (5) *Memoranda 3* (London 1960), pp. vi, 251.

2. Unless otherwise indicated, footnote references have the following meanings: R, 000 refers to the *Report* and its paragraph number; MinE, 000 refers to *Minutes of Evidence* and the number of the question-answer; M-1, 000 refers to the first volume of *Memoranda* and its page number; and similarly for M-2, 000 and M-3, 000.

3. Most of them issued by the Bank of England but some by Scottish and Northern Irish banks. R, 347, 349.

4. R, 388, 478.

5. Partial series, which are either inconsistent with one another, refer to different things, or are for different dates, are scattered around like Easter eggs. The *Report* shows total deposits of London clearing banks (R, 134) and of Scottish banks (R, 149), but only for 1958; net personal deposits in London clearing banks for four postwar years (R, 478);

and a chart of the ratio of the money supply to national income for
1946–58 (R, 478). Elsewhere, data are presented for currency with the
public and net deposits of clearing banks (M-3, 69), note circulation and
clearing bank deposits (M-3, 184), in chart form the ratio of the money
supply (currency with the public and net deposits of clearing banks) to
GNP (M-3, 102), note issues and deposits of all reporting banks and
acceptance houses, with intergroup items not omitted (M-2, 202–3),
and in chart form the ratio of net bank deposits to national income
(MinE, 10433).

6. R, 128–31.

7. R, 131. The Scottish banks appear to treat their deposit accounts
somewhat differently. See R, 153.

8. For example, see MinE, 8033–35 and 8132 for evidence that deposits
in Trustee Savings Banks are more and more being used as current
accounts.

9. R, 125, 504; also 395, 523.

10. R, 143–48, 351; M-1, 9–10.

11. R, 175, 355–58; M-1, 9–10; MinE, 183–89, 1568–96.

12. M-1, 10.

13. MinE, 98. For a similar statement, see MinE, 421, which the
Committee quotes in R, 360.

14. In this and subsequent exchanges quoted here, the first part of
each paragraph is a question from some member of the Committee, and
the second part, after the dash, is the answer by one of the witnesses. I
have not thought it necessary most of the time to identify the interrogators
and respondents.

15. MinE, 2262–70. It should be noted, though, that at times even the
Bank argued that the cash ratio was largely ineffective because it had to
act as a lender of last resort to the discount market (M-1, 38). However,
it was brought out in testimony that this meant only that the Bank, as
lender of last resort, would give the market, *at a price*, all the cash it
wanted; it did not mean that the Bank, as lender of last resort, relinquished
all control over interest rates (MinE, 94–101).

16. R, 120, 376, 430, 583. In fact, in direct opposition to the above
evidence, the *Report* says: "But now that the credit-creating capacity of
the banks is limited by the 30 per cent liquid assets' convention, an increase in cash precisely balanced by a decrease in the Treasury Bill issue
has become irrelevant to the credit-creating power of the banks" (R, 167).

17. R, 376. See also R, 121, 355, 357.

18. R, 120, 167, 175, 505–7. For further discussion of the weaknesses
of the liquidity ratio, see MinE, 183–89, 1568–96, 1654–58, 1909–13, with
supplementary notes to 1909 on pp. 952–54, and 3738–65.

19. R, 411, 417, 422; MinE, 2677 ff., 3265–72, 3523–3645; and M-1,
40. However, if the control over bank advances forces the banks to purchase other earning assets that are more liquid than those they would have
purchased, a given money supply is likely to be associated with a higher
interest rate structure, other things the same.

20. R, 392 and footnote.

21. R, 504; also 385, 397 ff.

22. R, 397. This is also suggested in R, 394.

23. In other words, while there may be a liquidity-preference schedule, drawn against interest rates, the schedule is subject to such wide shifts, as expectations change, that interest rates are in fact little influenced by the amount of liquidity in the system.

24. I admit that it is a tricky business to impute views to the Committee from questions asked and statements made by it during examination of witnesses. But I have done this only when such evidence seems consistent with the final views of the Committee as stated in its *Report*.

25. MinE, 9760–61; also 10220, 10236. My emphasis.

26. See, for example, R, 563, as modified by 565. Note also the Bank's stress on confidence as the prime determinant of interest rates in MinE, 2398–99, qualified slightly in supplementary notes of the Bank, pp. 955–56.

27. R, 395. For Kahn's opinions on this, see M–3, 144.

28. MinE, 10433; M–3, 102, 184–85.

29. MinE, 10431–32, 10434, 10436, 10438.

30. MinE, 10441. See also MinE, 10443–53 for further discussion of these points.

31. See M-3, 66, 179, 183–85, 85, 113, 146–48; and MinE, 10425–512. Outstanding memoranda on this subject were produced by James V. Morgan and J. C. R. Dow.

32. For one flagrant example, see R, 570, where the Committee presents three reasons for the rise in bond rates without once mentioning the money supply or national income.

33. R, 442–43.

34. R, 386.

35. R, 450–51, 489, 495.

36. R, 487. Sayers kept pressing the view on witnesses that an increase in interest rates will raise actual investment in the short run. His theory was that higher rates will lower consumption and so leave more room for investment, given aggregate demand. No witness accepted this, and it does not show up in the *Report*. See, *e.g.*, MinE, 4189–92, 5656–61.

37. Some of this material appears in the *Report*, R, 452–53.

38. M-2, 118-22.

39. R, 453.

40. This is part of the full exchange found in MinE, 5566–5617.

41. M-2, 88–96; R, 453; MinE, 11119 (and footnote).

42. R, 453.

43. R, 453.

44. M-2, 87–88.

45. MinE, 11169–70.

46. MinE, 6266–69.

47. MinE, 6427–29.

48. MinE, 6490–93, 6499.

49. MinE, 6734–47.

50. MinE, 7568–79.

51. MinE, 8149, 8155–67, 8171–75, 8178.

52. MinE, 8188, 8206.

53. MinE, 8263–66, 8276. But see 8279 where this view seems to be modified.

54. MinE, 8544.

55. MinE, 8583–85.

56. MinE, 8918.

57. MinE, 11360–62, 11414.

58. MinE, 11605, 11618–28.

59. MinE, 11726.

60. MinE, 12287.

61. MinE, 12992–96.

62. MinE, 12952–55.

63. MinE, 4976–86.

64. MinE, 3617, 3646.

65. M-3, 178–82, 182–88, 95, 213.

66. M-1, 35–38.

67. R, 125, 389.

68. The monetary system is composed of the Bank of England, the London clearing banks, and the Scottish and Northern Irish banks. The assets of the separate financial institutions for several postwar years are given in the memorandum of the Central Statistical Office (M-1, 130–41), but the most recent data are in the *Report*, Table 20, and referred to in R, 313.

69. R, 390. My italics.

70. R, 316, 389, 390.

71. The possible exception is R, 392.

72. On this last point, the basic difficulty with the Committee's approach stands out most clearly. It is stated that "regulation of the banks is required not because they are 'creators of money' but because they are the biggest lenders at the shortest (most liquid) end of the range of credit markets" (R, 504). That banks lend at the "most liquid end of the range of credit markets" is an argument against controlling them. The more the assets purchased by a financial institution resemble the liabilities it creates, the less need is there to control that institution. An institution, for instance, that purchased money and created money would not have to be controlled. (In another context, the Committee comes to this conclusion with respect to the note issues of Scottish banks which are backed by Bank of England notes.) Nor would one that purchased bonds and issued what the market considered to be identical bonds need to be controlled. Financial intermediaries become potentially more dangerous to the stability of the economy the more illiquid their assets are relative to their liabilities, given the rate and pattern of their growth.

73. R, 394.

74. R, 504.

75. R, 505.

76. R, 509. See also R, 510–11, 527.

77. MinE, 9377. For de Kock's full views on this, see M-1, 289–90.

78. M-3, 37; MinE, 10172–80.

79. This testimony is in MinE, 9822–27. Riefler also dealt with this problem in his memorandum, in which he stated that nonbank inter-

mediaries play a neutral role in the saving-investment process and that control of the money supply has pervasive influences throughout the whole financial structure. See M-1, 301.

80. MinE, 11812–18. For similar, though milder, statements, see the memorandum of The Bank of Australia, M-1, 249, and the British Treasury's statements, MinE, 1607–11.

81. MinE, 9366.

82. R, 374, 393.

83. R, 395, 514, 603.

84. R, 499, 395.

85. R, 562.

86. R, 395.

87. R, 393.

88. M-3, 145. My emphases.

89. M-3, 145. His emphasis.

90. M-3, 144. See also Kahn's testimony, MinE, 10983–87.

91. This statement recognizes the connection between liquidity (lending) and the level of interest rates, and it is therefore in opposition to what I have called the dominant view of the *Report* on this matter.

92. R, 487–91. N. Kaldor, in his memorandum, advanced an additional argument against highly fluctuating rates: namely, that the average rate over time would then be higher, due to risk considerations, which would push the economy more toward consumption and away from investment, and so slow down its growth rate. He also felt that saving, under these conditions, would be allocated less efficiently to investment alternatives. M-3, 148.

93. R, 492–97.

94. R, 498.

95. R, 516–17. See also the Committee's discussion of this with the Treasury, MinE, 13311–22.

96. Along these lines, for what is probably the most extreme statement ever made on the relative merits of fiscal and monetary policies, see the memorandum by I. M. D. Little, R. R. Neild, and C. R. Ross, M-3, 159–67.

97. R, 524.

98. R, 520–29.

99. R, 428.

100. This is noted in R, 428, 552, 583. The Committee states that "we were sometimes assured that the bill rate has practically no connection with long rates."

101. MinE, 1884, 1887. See also MinE, 1792, 1796, 1804, 1845.

102. MinE, 1849–51.

103. MinE, 1870.

104. MinE, 1849, 1855–60. For a fuller discussion of these questions, see MinE, 1762–63, 1792–1805, 1841–98. The Committee's views are in R, 551, 575–76. The Treasury's position was much the same as the Bank's; see MinE, 2387–98, 2953–72, 2799–2995.

Subsequently, the Bank did use open-market operations to influence long-term rates. For a justification of this and a slight modification of its initial position, see MinE, 11919, 12000–01, 12008–14, 13416, 13453. This change is discussed by the Committee in R, 341, 428, 553.

105. R, 768.
106. R, 767, 769.
107. R, 761–62. See also MinE, 256–58.
108. MinE, 9407.
109. MinE, 9454. Compare Riefler's statement with that of the Governor of the Bank of England, who said in part: "I have no doubt that in modern conditions it is proper that Government should have the final word on policy and that the central bank should not be free to pursue a completely independent line." MinE, 12813.
110. R, 771, 773, 778–87; MinE, 262–63, 269. A similar body has been suggested here many times in recent years, but the proposal has been attacked partly because it would jeopardize the independence of the Federal Reserve. Four years ago, before the Joint Economic Committee, Elliott Bell submitted a remedy:

> If . . . it is felt that the Federal Reserve Board is so sensitive that contact with the President would corrupt it, then I suggest there might usefully be formed a National Economic Council without regular representation by the Federal Reserve Board. In this event, the Fed might be invited to send an observer with the express understanding that he could sit near an open door ready to fly to the sanctuary of Constitution Avenue if he felt the danger at any point of political contamination.

See *Hearings before the Subcommittee on Economic Stabilization of the Joint Economic Committee*, on December 10–11, 1956, p. 7.

The Committee received and heard an unusually large amount of evidence concerning the status of the Bank. For the Bank's views, see M-1, 5–9; MinE, 249–86, 752–60, 12813–900. For opinions of part-time directors of the Bank, see M-1, 44–45; MinE, 12066–188. Riefler's statements are found in MinE, 9395–9407, 9422–36, 9452–54. The views of former Chancellors and others are found in M-3, 47–48, 70–71, 207–11, 248–49; MinE, 11250–99, 12301–640.
111. R, 695–702, 703–07. See the Treasury's spirited objection to the support of the forward rate in M–1, 121–22.
112. R, 716, 719–22, 728.
113. R, 670–71; MinE, 2531.
114. R, 672–74.
115. R, 678.
116. R, 684.
117. R, 630, 734.
118. MinE, 2492–2507, and p. 956.
119. R, 741–47. The Bank's views on the international aspects in M-1, 13–17, 34–35; MinE, 833–947, 948–71; the Treasury's in M-1, 105, 112–22; MinE, 2483–2615, 3211–22, 9695–9734. Economists addressed themselves to these issues in M-3, 71–76, 132–36, 243.
120. The Bank presented a memorandum on the current sources of banking statistics (M-1, 66–70); the Central Statistical Office prepared

data on sources of financial and economic statistics relating to the monetary system and on assets of financial institutions (M-1, 129–62); The National Institute of Economic and Social Research presented a comprehensive memorandum on financial and economic statistics (M-3, 3–27); and the many data presented by trade associations are found throughout the evidence.

121. The recommendations are found principally in Chapter 10 of the *Report*; but see also R, 366–67, 580, 582, 629.

122. MinE, 2848–55, 3223.

20 The Report of the Commission on Money and Credit

Karl Brunner *University of Rochester*

The Commission*

* * *

The Commission on Money and Credit[1] was formed in 1958 . . . [Its] mandate implied the following specific obligations:

1. A consensus on economic goals and criteria for an evaluation of the economy's aggregate performance had to be worked out. Ideally, this task required the specification of a social utility function.

2. With the goals accepted, or a social utility function more or less vaguely outlined, a re-evaluation of the existing institutional arrangements became necessary. Different arrangements impose different restrictions on the social goals. The choice of institutions may significantly affect the economy's performance. One might formalize the specific problem faced by the Commission as an optimal choice of restrictions on the social utility function. This task may be broken into four parts: (*a*) evaluation of institutions bearing on policy-making processes; (*b*) assessment of institutions bearing on operation of financial markets and behavior of eco-

Reprinted from *Journal of Political Economy*, Vol. 69 (December 1961), 605–20, by permission of the author and The University of Chicago Press. Copyright 1961 by The University of Chicago Press.
    * The part of this section dealing with the organization and background of the Commission has been omitted. [Editor]

nomic units; (*c*) choice of policy variables, that is, of economic magnitudes which are directly and immediately controlled by actions of responsible authorities; (*d*) choice of economic signals associated with specific operations on selected policy variables.

3. Optimal choice of institutional arrangements relative to a specified social valuation presupposes a rational foundation. The goals on the one side and the appraisal of institutions on the other are linked by our systematic knowledge of the financial environment. A more assured, less speculative, and better validated explicit theoretical comprehension of the financial system's mode of operation in the United States and its connection with the behavior of employment and price was required. The development of theory would appear to form the third major task for a Commission on Money and Credit.

*   *   *

The Report

The report's political impact will be determined by its more than eighty recommendations bearing on the Federal Reserve, the Treasury, commercial banks, thrift institutions, federal credit programs, international arrangements, and the relation between the Congress and the Executive branch of the government. These proposals are accompanied by descriptions and summaries evidently emanating from the contributions made by the staff and numerous subcontractors who submitted research material. Whatever the underlying analysis and substantive contributions may have been, this purely cognitive aspect of the Commission's work is unavoidably muted and appears only in summarized and sketchy form. Still, the report reveals some excellent underlying pieces of research.[2] But it also contains symptoms of thoroughly inadequate analysis and worn-out textbook legends.

The proposals appear, on balance, well conceived. The Commission avoids an easy and fascinating gamesmanship with dubiously founded and obscurely justified institutional innovations. In particular, the Commission shows commendable intellectual self-discipline by avoiding impressionistic recommendations for new controls simply because the morphology of the financial system has changed. The recommendations exhibit a refreshing attempt to question and appraise existing monetary and financial institutions. They effectively point to ill-conceived and redundant arrangements imposed on our financial system. Numerous regulations on the asset portfolios of financial institutions or on the geographic distributions of their operations impair the rational use of our resources and contribute little to an effective monetary policy.[3] The Commission's determined effort to evaluate institutions in terms of their contribution to an efficacious policy mechanism is highly significant. It underscores the importance of appropriate analysis and empirical investigation which provide the necessary foundation for the Commission's judgments.

Numerous recommendations, particularly those on the structure and organization of Federal Reserve authorities and the co-ordinative machinery, are designed to improve the efficacy of the institutional frame within which policy-making proceeds.[4] These proposals, though not unimportant, will not be discussed further here. Their meaning depends on the systematic and validated comprehension of our financial environment.

The core of other proposals is more closely associated with the system's mode of behavior. These recommendations refer to institutional arrangements that influence the choice of policy variables or that affect the *modus operandi* of the financial process. A vast range is covered, including the host of federal credit programs and non-bank financial intermediaries. The subsequent discussion selects some broad problems for more detailed consideration.

The Commission's discussion of national economic goals reveals an ample consensus in the choice of the rate of price change, the rate of economic growth, and the rate of unemployment as major arguments of the social utility function.[5] However, a potentially serious cleavage appears in the mode of evaluating unemployment. The report specifies the volume of unfilled vacancies as setting the tolerance level for unemployment. Expansionary policy would not be applied until the number of those seeking jobs exceeded the number of available jobs. Ruttenberg, on the other hand, insists on 3 per cent unemployment as the tolerance level.[6]

This disagreement in the specification of the social utility function has important ramifications. The two formulations tend to be associated with sharply divergent policy conceptions. A definite percentage for tolerable unemployment focuses attention on inflationary monetary and fiscal policies combined—or compensated—with a complex arrangement of selective controls. The other formulation directs attention to the allocative mechanism and the government's responsibility for the deliberate fostering of an appropriate institutional frame which minimizes the size of the tolerance level.

The Commission seems at least partly aware of this implication of its evaluation of unemployment. On various occasions the report expresses concern for a properly functioning (relative) price mechanism and the suitable discharge of governmental obligations with respect to the construction of an adequate institutional environment.[7] However, the awareness seems spotty and the discussion of the issue uneven. The impact of important legal institutions, for example, the pattern of court decisions on labor issues and the minimum wage laws, is not even mentioned.[8]

The emerging unemployment pattern and the prospect for economic growth are, of course, related to market institutions. The Commission notes the persistent rise in the rate of unemployment. Two factors are adduced in the report to partially explain observed and expected unemployment behavior, namely, (1) the additional load imposed on the absorptive capacity of the allocative mechanism by accelerated rates of introducing new technologies and (2) rates of entry into the labor market. The increase in such load factors raises the level of structural unemployment. This effect is compounded by institutional restrictions, in the form of stiffer union conditions and higher legal minimum wage levels, impairing the mechanism's absorptive capacity. Sustained pockets of unemployment, particularly among Negroes, women, the young, and the old are thus created.[9] A proper identification of the prevalent types of unemployment is of decisive importance for effective policy action. If the analysis briefly summarized above is correct, additional doses of inflationary policy would have a marginal effect on the average rate of unemployment. When the problem is one of structural unemployment a closer attention to our labor-market institutions would assume considerable urgency.

The report conveys an ambivalent impression with respect to economic growth. Some thoughtful passages evidently summarize systematic studies on the relation between growth and inflation, and the Commission specifically disposes of the contention that inflation is a necessary condition for growth.[10] The relation between the performance of the allocation mechanism and economic growth, however, remains shaded in doubt and confusion. Some statements clearly specify lower barriers to resource mobility as a prerequisite to satisfactory growth and may be understood to emphasize the dependence of economic growth on the quality of the allocation process.[11] Other passages, and particularly comments by individual members, refer to growth as an entity determined by processes unrelated to the manner in which markets operate to adjust to new labor entries, to new technologies, and to new demand patterns induced by our rising wealth.[12] Such notions suggest that "dynamic adjustments" are eased and "structural unemployment" removed by sufficient "growth."

The Commission emerges as a strong advocate of monetary and fiscal policies. It suggests that intelligent use of available instruments would substantially moderate economic fluctuations. The

Commission evidently feels that we possess a satisfactory cognitive foundation to formulate a reliable guide for intelligent policy. The report asserts, in particular, that "there is fairly general agreement about the nature of the processes through which monetary policy affects economic activity."[13]

I submit that this is a pleasant delusion and seriously misrepresents our actually established, systematic knowledge. Do we have a widely accepted workable demand function for money which clarifies the effects of wealth, windfalls, income, other transactions, interest rates, and the composition of wealth on the demand for money? Or do we have an adequate and reasonably useful formulation of the supply mechanism which explains the major determinants of the money supply, its response to particular policy changes, and the orders of magnitudes of their effects? Is there useful knowledge of the position of interest rates in this mechanism and the role of feedback from income, together with the meaning for money-supply behavior of a variety of institutional detail? Most important, do we have a satisfactory explanation of the connection between monetary variables and current output and price level? Is the connection dominated by a few interest elasticities, in the tradition of orthodox Keynesianism? Do we mind Patinkin and incorporate a real balance effect? Are there processes associated with the composition of wealth and the relation between wealth and output, vaguely known but not formally developed, which determine the position of monetary variables with respect to the pace of economic activity?

A glance at the literature reveals the existence of two barely connected worlds of intellectual endeavor in the monetary field. In one we find the textbooks on money and banking, where empirical concern is restricted to the description of institutional detail and analysis is replaced most often by a few numerical examples and graphical exercises. In the other we notice a learned pursuit of the esoterica of formal models with no concern for their possible cognitive significance. This description is not fundamentally unfair, since the test is provided, after all, by our list of well-established empirical hypotheses on money demand, money supply, and aggregate demand for output. Yet the description overlooks the developing pattern in recent research activities, to which the Commission itself signally contributed. For some years through systematic investigations researchers have formulated and assessed hypotheses in the field of money demand and money supply. In the field of aggregate demand theory, differently motivated considerations simultaneously suggest a useful reformulation which incorporates stock (wealth) and flow (new production flows) variables with an explicit description of their interrelation.

Money is a component of wealth with two specific properties: it has the smallest transaction costs and, in our contemporary civilization, the smallest ratio of marginal cost to market price. Both costs nearly vanish when compared to the exchange price of money. The first property explains the existence of a positive demand for this asset; the second property explains the government's responsibility for "maintaining the value of money." Money appears thus as an asset competing with other assets, financial and real, for a place in the balance sheet of economic units. These units are usefully visualized as optimizing their balance-sheet positions— subject to some institutional or technological restrictions. This conception evolves into an explanation of the desired balance-sheet position in terms of prevailing market conditions and the inherited position. Such a framework promises to provide new insights into monetary processes and the nature of the connection between policy variables (that is, reserve requirements, Federal Reserve portfolio, and rediscount rate) and the rate of current output or the price level.

Variations in policy variables induce a reallocation of assets (or liabilities) in the balance sheets of economic units which spills over to current output and thus affect the price level. Injections of base money (or "high-powered" money) modify the composition of financial assets and total wealth available to banks and other economic units. Absorption of the new base money requires suitable alterations in asset yields or asset prices. The banks and the public are thus induced to reshuffle their balance sheets to adjust desired and actual balance-sheet position.

The interaction between banks and public, which forms the essential core of money-supply theory, generates the peculiar leverage or multiplier effect of injections of base money on bank assets and deposits and, correspondingly, on specific asset and liability items of the public's balance sheet. The readjustment process induces a change in the relative yield (or price) structure of assets crucial for the transmission of monetary policy-action to the rate of economic activity. The relative price of base money and its close substitutes falls, and the relative price of other assets rises.

The stock of real capital dominates these other assets. The increase in the price of capital relative to the price of financial assets simultaneously raises real capital's market value relative to the capital stock's replacement costs and increases the desired stock relative to the actual stock. The relative increase in the desired stock of capital induces an adjustment in the actual stock through new production. In this manner current output and prices of durable goods are affected by the readjustments in the balance sheets and the related price movements set in motion by the injection of base money. The wealth, income, and relative price effects involved in the whole transmission process also tend to raise demand for non-durable goods.

The above discussion is the barest outline of a promising approach in monetary theory. The Commission contributed to the exploration of these ideas in some of the underlying study papers.[14] The report itself contains partial glimpses at best. Analysis along the lines indicated still needs considerable tightening, suitable formalizations, and empirical evaluation. Still, it seems sufficiently developed to permit a tentative appraisal of a variety of issues presented in the report.

The report discusses in some detail the effect of interest rates on spending decisions, particularly on investment expenditures. It concludes that the irrelevance of interest rates has often been overstated and cautiously admits that interest rates may very likely exert some significant effect on investment expenditures. The survey presented by the Commission appropriately emphasizes the inadequacy of available evidence. It seems worth pondering whether the tenuous character of this evidence partly reflects some unresolved analytical problems.

The usual evidence derives from econometric studies and questionnaires or interviews. The latter evidence is usually caught in a whirlpool of dubious meanings. If we admit the results at face value, they could hardly be interpreted to deny the influence of interest rates on spending decisions.[15]

Econometric studies of investment behavior have usually been of the pure-flow variety with the accumulated capital stock perhaps intruding. Most statistical estimations yield poor results for the interest variables. The regression coefficient is small, even vanishes, relative to its standard error. The portfolio-balance analysis, outlined above, explains this result and clarifies the place of interest rates in the transmission mechanism. The association of some market rates of interest with investment expenditures in the context of a pure-flow analysis, modified at best by the incorporation of the accumulated capital stock (measured at cost), does not provide an adequate test for the significance of interest rates.

A generalized stock-flow analysis would reveal that in the case of new issues of government securities, or improved expectations concerning the rate of return from real capital, the relative price of government securities falls and the relative price of real capital rises. This means that a positive correlation between market rates and investment expenditures is generated by the process. The previous example of base money injection indicated a negative correlation. Isolation of the cost aspect of interest rates with respect to purchases of new durable goods in econometric studies thus requires an appropriate specification of the stock-flow interrelations centered on real capital. An omission of this mechanism makes the interest rate in the standard flow formulation reflect two opposite forces—cost and wealth effect—which tend to cancel each other in the statistical estimation based on this formulation.[16]

The portfolio-balance analysis may resolve an issue between traditional money and banking analysis and monetary theory mirrored to some extent in the report. The "new skepticism" gave new impetus to the controversy over "credit" *versus* "money supply." Monetary processes have often been described as operating essentially on aggregate demand for current output through a magnitude called "credit." This magnitude seems at times to be a stock variable (portfolio of loans, or portfolio of total earning assets of banks) and at times it occurs as a flow variable (rates of change of the above stock variables).[17] "Credit" as a stock variable appears jointly with the components of the money supply in a complete portfolio analysis; "credit" as a flow is simply the by-product of the adjustments in the balance sheets to modifications in "initial" positions.

The report's description of monetary policy lays particular stress on the importance of lenders' reaction as a crucial link in the transmission of policy actions. This emphasis is subsequently qualified by stressing the importance of a sufficiently large borrowers' demand.[18] The discussion is rather confused, but two strands of thought seem to merge in the report's summary. It appears, first, that only "lending flows" (that is, the rate of change in the banks' loan portfolio) matter and, second, that the borrowers' demand for loans is practically insensitive to interest variations. The second point can be reformulated by saying that changes in market conditions will not induce the public to readjust liabilities and assets.

The general balance-sheet analysis immediately disposes of the first point, but a decision on the second requires a detailed empirical investigation. This issue is closely related to another assertion made by the report, namely, that "excess liquidity" endangers the effectiveness of monetary policy. This notion of a "liquidity trap" has been with us for some time and is still expounded occasionally.

A detailed appraisal of monetary developments in the thirties strongly confirms both the absence of a liquidity trap in the banking system's operation and the public's continued willingness to readjust balance-sheet position to new situations.[19] The results also confirm the existence of a marked non-linearity between periods of low excess reserves and high interest rates, and periods of large excess reserves and low interest rates. The operation of this non-linearity generates the asymmetry between the impact of a restrictive policy in a high-interest regime and the impact of expansionary policy in a low-interest regime asserted by the report. However, the evidence assembled emphatically underscores that such asymmetry is accompanied by a sustained efficacy of monetary policy in a deflationary environment. The report's rather tenuous description of these policy mechanisms leads to a strange and very dangerous formulation. Having asserted that "excessive liquidity" impairs monetary policy, the report suggests that in the case of a downswing the authorities should remove such "excess liquidity" and simultaneously accelerate the reduction in interest rates.[20] Portfolio analysis should reveal the stark inconsistency of the two actions and indicate that the removal of "excess liquidity" inserts an amplifying feedback into the mechanism generating fluctuations of economic activity. The very notion of "excess liquidity"—in the absence of price controls—should be clearly understood as a result of inadequate analysis.

The report is permeated by the awareness that institutional reform does not proceed without costs. This awareness prevented recommendations of radical changes where the possible gains to be expected from the modified arrangements are minute. The report should be commended for this balanced appraisal; yet in the case of discount policy some safeguarding qualifications need to be added. These explicit safeguards can be subsumed under the report's general admonition to the Federal Reserve authorities to adjust policies to the maximization of the "social utility function" specified.

The report recommends that discount facilities be continued and that the associated policies and administrative procedures be uniform in the system. Discount facilities have traditionally been conceived as the means of establishing the essential link between a central bank and the commercial banks. This arrangement was supposed to enable the central banker to gauge the varying demand-and-supply pressures on the loan markets. Such a conception may have prompted the Federal Reserve authorities on occasions in the past to prescribe "continued maintenance of contact with the money market" as a guide in policy considerations. The context of these declarations indicates that policy should be adjusted so as "to keep banks closely tied to the central bank," in other words, so that asset and deposit expansion depend on additional reserve funds being made available by the authorities. This conception may be properly conceived in terms of a continuously effective discount policy, particularly if the banks' demand for cash assets is comparatively insensitive to variations in the discount rate. However, such a policy involves a serious confusion of means and ends and endangers the stabilization desired by the Commission.

In the case of a deflationary process, the policy guide inspired by the conception of a "sustained contact with the money market" leads the central bank to sell on the open market or raise reserve requirements in order to force the "market into the bank." Continuation of existing discount facilities, to be compatible with stabilization, requires recognition by our monetary authorities that an effective monetary policy may involve a breakdown in the operation of discount policy.[21]

Open-market policy and changes in reserve requirements are advocated by the report as major policy variables, with the qualification that only sparing use should be made of the second instrument. It is suggested that reserve requirements against demand deposits be imposed on all insured banks, whereas requirements against time and savings deposits should be abolished.

It can be shown that reserve requirements on time deposits do not raise the authorities' degree of control over the money supply. Abolition of differential requirements would undoubtedly simplify our arrangements and probably raise the authorities' degree of control over the money supply. However, I suspect that the Commission exaggerates the expected gain in the precision of monetary control.[22] Still, differential requirements have no pertinent function either, and a uniform requirement is therefore a move in the proper direction.

The report also notes that changes in reserve requirements and open-market operations appear equally effective in shaping the money supply.[23] The comparatively frequent changes in requirement over the postwar period permit an evaluation of this statement. Our investigation determined that injection of a billion dollars of base money or liberation of a billion dollars of reserves by a reduction in the requirements generates on the average the same money-supply reaction. These results suggest the need for a reconsideration of the specific contribution made to monetary control by the Federal Reserve's discretionary power over reserve requirements. The Commission offers no justification for this power. More fundamentally, while it dismisses reserve requirements on time deposits, it presents no case for the continued adherence to a system of fractional requirements against demand deposits.

A possible rationale for the existence of requirements or the institution of discretionary power with respect to the level of requirements may be formulated either in terms of the degree (or precision) of control over the money supply or in terms of the Treasury's net interest cost. Discretionary requirements were granted in the thirties as a means of increasing Federal Reserve power. The Federal Reserve's portfolio was small relative to excess reserves. It was alleged that open-market operations could not prevent serious inflation in these circumstances. However, such discretionary power over requirement ratios is not a necessary condition for preventing inflation.

Maximization of the degree of control and minimization of net interest costs are equally unable to justify the Federal Reserve's discretionary power. Examination of the money-supply mechanism assigns the same degree of control whether the money-supply reaction is generated by variations in reserve requirements or by changes in the monetary base. Minimizing net interest cost could always rationalize a higher, but never a lower, requirement ratio. On what grounds then should the discretionary powers be continued?

The report is equally mute concerning the existence of fractional requirements. An empirical appraisal indicates that elimination of reserve requirements would lower the precision of control, but probably by a comparatively small margin. In the absence of requirements, the possible gain in the degree of control attributable to their introduction would barely balance the social cost of allocating administrative efforts and legislative energies to their establishment. The existence of reserve requirements necessitates a greater injection of base money than would occur in the absence of requirements to obtain a given secular growth rate in the money supply. Gradual elimination of requirements would generate an increase in the money supply of approximately 15 per cent without a change in the base; subsequent changes in the base would have a greater leverage (30 per cent greater). The greater injection of base money under the existing reserve requirement is accompanied by a correspondingly smaller average volume (over a decade) of Treasury debt outside the government sector. This lower volume compresses the net interest cost. Some computations based on the assumption of a 4 per cent growth in the money supply over the past decade yield an annual saving of approximately $50 million a year attributable to the existence of present requirements. Is this the rationale for reserve requirements, and if it is, why not a 100 per cent requirement?[24]

The report is quite explicit as to the basic identity of debt management and monetary policy. In both cases the authorities modify the existing composition of the government sector's outstanding debt; in both cases the transmission mechanism outlined by the balance-sheet equilibrating process operates in the same manner. The Commission is here again consistent with its basic purposes when it recommends the abolition of statutory limitations on debt volume and interest rates.

Awareness of the identity between the Treasury's debt management and the Federal Reserve's open-market operations uncovers the problem of effective policy co-ordination. The report strongly opposes any merger of the two institutions or concentration of all the government's debt-issuing activities in the Federal Reserve Board.

The report makes a variety of recommendations concerning technical points related to the Treasury's debt operations. Among the points mentioned is the appropriate spacing and regularization of the Treasury's debt issues. I suspect that this suggestion is worth serious exploration. A regular spacing of Treasury debt combined with larger and more homogeneous issues would lead to smaller time intervals between outstanding issues. This might be expected to improve significantly the operation of the longer term market and create the environment for smoother arbitrage. A set of rules would have to be formulated to regulate the Treasury's refunding, issuing, and retirement operations according to the specification of a definite debt structure. Among the major advantages to be gained by this institutional reform are the elimination of the Treasury's guessing game with respect to the issuing conditions. The near continuous yield curve determined by the spacing provides a close guide for the new issues. Extended application of auction techniques, as suggested by the report, would be unnecessary to avoid the price-setting problem. Furthermore, market uncertainty would be reduced and the frequency of the Treasury's operations on the market with their attendant restrictions on Federal Reserve policy lowered. Most important, perhaps, long-term market operations would approximate in efficiency short-term operations.

A market structure is likely to emerge which would tend to increase the efficaciousness of the transmission of monetary policy through the financial markets to the stock of real capital and current output. Under such an arrangement no conflicts between debt-management policy and the Federal Reserve's policy could arise. The Treasury would operate within a fixed refunding or issuing procedure and the Federal Reserve Board would change the composition of the government's outstanding debt according to the indications of stabilization policy. This suggestion of a regularized debt structure is not advanced in a spirit of contention, but the report does touch on it, and the arrangement might render most other technical modifications superfluous and contribute significantly to creating an institutional framework that would raise the effectiveness of policy mechanisms.[25]

Most of the institutional recommendations made in the report are quite sensible in terms of the outlined monetary analysis. The liberalizing of branching and investment regulation, a basic feature of the proposals, would improve the allocative efficiency of credit markets and be likely to raise the sensitivity of the transmission process to policy action. Similar properties hold for numerous aspects of the federal credit programs. Insurance and guarantee features seem to make a decisive difference in allocative efficiency at a vanishing social cost.

The report's discussion of fiscal policy is in some respects less detailed and more general than the survey of monetary and credit arrangements. Two considerations dominate the Commission's proposals in the fiscal field. The report notes that discretionary fiscal policy "was hardly ever used as a stabilizer"[26] and stabilizing processes were restricted to the operation of the "built-in automatic stabilizers." The Commission is, therefore, concerned both with strengthening automatic stabilization devices and with achieving proper timed flexibility of discretionary tax and expenditure policy.

The central proposal emerging under the Commission's scrutiny is for changes in the first bracket rate of the personal income tax according to a predetermined formula (the recommendation of "formula flexibility") or according to discretionary judgment. The report justifies this proposal on the basis of its efficacy in affecting the short-run spending decisions of the public.

Unfortunately, recent developments in the theory of the consumption-function associated with the work of Modigliani and Friedman—which contribute to the systematic incorporation of wealth into monetary analysis—give little support for the report's confidence. Short-run changes in the first bracket rate of personal income tax exert a minor effect on a unit's wealth position, and if wealth dominates consumers' expenditure, formula flexibility and discretionary bracket changes, while not useless, could not be expected to make the contribution asserted by the Commission. The case for short-run adjustments in the first bracket rate would improve if windfalls could be shown to exert some effect on consumers' demand. So far analysis and evidence are inconclusive. We have to know considerably more before the report's major fiscal proposal can be properly assessed.[27]

A major aspect of monetary policy is covered implicitly rather than explicitly by the report, namely, the choice of signals for the policy-making bodies to watch. The original mandate given to the Federal Reserve System has a tenuous relation to the goals formulated by the Commission and a reformulation of the mandate in terms of our major economic goals is certainly appropriate. It could be expected to remove some old conceptions which might otherwise confuse public attention. In this manner we might replace the old concern for an "elastic currency" with a clearly defined responsibility with respect to the "general protection of liquidity." A carefully stated mandate aids in resolving the choice of appropriate signals and policy-indicators but cannot determine this choice by itself.

The Federal Reserve authorities have assigned indicative importance to a variety of magnitudes in the past: the index of consumers' prices, interest rates, the volume of free reserves, and "credit." The discussion in a previous section also noted the volume of banks' indebtedness to the Federal Reserve banks among the signals to be considered. The contribution of monetary policy to economic stabilization depends both on the effectiveness of the transmission mechanism and the manner in which the policy function is discharged. The performance of the policy function is crucially determined by the choice of signals.

Are these signals approximately optimal? The report expresses serious doubt with respect to the consumer price index. It observes that this index is substantially lagged relative to the major cycle movement. Close attention to such an index would delay appropriate policy action in a major downswing. Serious reservations also apply to the choice of interest rates, free reserves, and "credit." These indicators do not suitably mirror the policy requirements imposed by growth and stabilization. Linking policy to some of these indicators may well, under quite general circumstances, generate an amplifying feedback endangering our fundamental goal of stabilization.

The choice of a set of rules is an alternative to the choice of signals. Policy action involves *some* choice and we might just as well try to be deliberate and rational about it. This rationality involves the full utilization of our systematic and validated knowledge. The choice of signals or rules, or the choice between the two alternatives, is not an issue which we can safely leave to the limbo of arts, feelings, and flairs. There is a significant theoretical or cognitive component in this issue and no intelligent choice can deny this component. The issue is still unresolved and pressing, and it seems that both monetary authorities and economists should be concerned with obtaining a firmer cognitive base for judging the decision.

Concluding Remarks

This review article has concentrated attention on our domestic institutions and monetary mechanism. One chapter of the report surveys the United States economy's international position.

The nature of contemporary balance-of-payments problems is discussed and solutions considered. The provision of adequate international "liquidity" and the development of an adjustment mechanism are the report's dominant concern in the field of international policy.

The Commission recommends explicitly that restrictive monetary and fiscal policies should not be used to correct a balance-of-payment deficit. Flexible exchange rates are not even mentioned as a possible alternative and exchange or quantitative trade control is evidently undesirable. But the Commission hopefully explores a host of institutional devices. Some unilateral arrangements, mostly dealing with possible information, insurance, and credit programs for United States exporters, are casually indicated. A variety of complex multilateral institutions requiring concerted action and policies is discussed in more detail. These institutions would also supply additional international "liquidity," balancing the increase in demand associated with expanding world trade under a regime of fixed exchange rates. A (more or less) uniform rise in the price of gold as a means of enlarging the trading nations' "liquidity base" is explicitly rejected by the report because of the unequally distributed benefits and the resulting allocation of resources to (an apparently useless?) gold production. The Commission's suggestions in the field of international finance require some critical analysis. It is quite possible that the political collaboration between debtor and creditor countries necessary to work the institutions proposed (for example, an international central bank) may actually emerge. It also may be the case that flexible exchange rates are definitely a suboptimal arrangement. Still, the judgments should rest on explicit analysis and adequate evidence. In particular, gold might appear as a (no doubt costly) substitute for political collaboration (not necessarily costless) and flexible exchange rates (*horribile dictu!*) a conceivably cheap substitute for gold which simultaneously solves the problems of international liquidity and adjustment.

The Commission's central contribution deals with the financial structure of the domestic economy. Most significant in the longer run is the deliberate appraisal of institutions in terms of their effect on the operation of the market mechanism and the economy's aggregate performance. Institutional innovations proposed for their own sake, or simply because "1960 is not 1920," are successfully resisted. Furthermore, the report does not hesitate to recommend the elimination of arrangements with no essential monetary function.

The systematic evaluation of our financial structure depends on a firm cognitive foundation. Intelligent judgment presupposes validated theoretical work, the construction and assessment of meaningful theories incorporating or bearing on important institutional detail. The Commission appears to have been aware of this. A large number of study papers covering many facets of our financial system have been prepared. Ultimate judgment of the Commission's contribution is therefore unavoidably suspended. But if the discussion presented in the report sharpens our awareness of the awkward situation in contemporary monetary theory and simultaneously awakens our appreciation of the potential power of systematic analysis we need not wait for the study papers to express our satisfaction with the Commission's achievements.

NOTES

1. *Money and Credit: Their Influence on Jobs, Prices, and Growth* (a report of the Commission on Money and Credit) (Englewood Cliffs, N.J.: Prentice-Hall, Inc., 1961).

2. A biased selection would be: (1) the section on differential effects of monetary policy (pp. 57–60, esp. the short summary on the lower half of p. 59); (2) the section on non-banking intermediaries (pp. 78–81); (3) the essentially descriptive section on the Treasury securities market (pp. 115–20); (4) the concise description of the working of political institutions in the last chapter.

3. The recommendations on pp. 69, 77–79, 113, 161–68, 204 refer to the Commission's most significant ideas relating to the improvement of the financial structure.

4. Examples of such recommendations are on pp. 87–89, 90, 174, 263, 272–73, 277, 281.

5. See Chapter 2.

6. The disagreement may be formalized as follows: Let p be the numerical value of the rate of change in the price level, $u =$ the rate of unemployment, $v =$ unfilled vacancies as a percentage of the labor force, $g =$ the growth rate; then we may write, for Ruttenberg,

$$U(p, u, g)$$
$$U_p < 0; \; U_u < 0 \equiv u > 3 \text{ per cent}; \; U_g > 0;$$

for the Commission,

$$U(p, u - v, g)$$
$$U_p < 0 \qquad U_{u-v} < 0 \equiv u > v; \qquad U_g > 0.$$

7. See pp. 12, 35–39, 40.

8. Shuman [who is president of the American Farm Bureau Federation] comments on this point on p. 25.

9. An excellent analysis of the problem and the reason for the pattern of "structural unemployment" appears in Harold Demsetz, "Structural Unemployment: A Reconsideration of the Theory and the Evidence," *Journal of Law and Economics* (October 1961). Demsetz analyzes the data

made available by the Council of Economic Advisers and concludes that the data support the contention of structural unemployment and are not consistent with the C.E.A.'s interpretation, which asserts that this type of unemployment is negligible.

10. The report contains a short survey of inflation analysis (pp. 13–21). I wish to make two points with respect to this passage. First, the report grants entirely too much intellectual respectability to the notion of a "cost push." Reference to the Schultze hypothesis, particularly in connection with structural unemployment, is well conceived. Second, I find the discussion of the effects of inflation underlying the assumed negative social marginal utility of inflation quite unconvincing. Until some pertinent evidence has been exhibited, I doubt that the net debtor position of economic units is highly correlated with their total wealth. Without such correlation, inflation would not induce a regressive wealth redistribution. The report also mentions a wasteful allocation of resources. It would be useful to know more precisely what the Commission means by this. One possible interpretation refers to an inflation with a high degree of anticipation. In such a case economic units to a considerable extent will substitute real resources with a positive marginal opportunity cost for money balances with a negligible (social) marginal opportunity cost. Experience indicates that inflation must be quite substantial—and not of the 3–6 per cent variety—before anticipations emerge definitely enough to induce the above substitution process. Finally, the report mentions that inflation "tends to feed on itself." The only systematic study available on this problem, Cagan's analysis of hyperinflation, makes me rather skeptical of this beloved textbook formula.

11. Pages 32–33.

12. See p. 30, both text and notes.

13. See p. 54. The report contains some conflicting pieces of underlying analysis which exemplify the gaps and tenuous aspects of our cognitive comprehension. On pp. 78–81 the position of non-bank financial intermediaries in the financial nexus is appraised. The report considers particularly the notion of "offsetting velocity behavior" allegedly shaped by the evolving financial patterns. Evidently, some detailed empirical investigation led the Commission to reject the idea that non-bank financial intermediaries impair monetary policy by generating an offsetting velocity behavior. In the discussion of the Treasury's debt structure (pp. 102–3) the notion of an offsetting velocity behavior reappears. A high proportion of short debt is alleged to introduce destabilizing processes. Interest elasticity of money demand seems to be higher (numerically) with such a debt structure, and offsetting velocity behavior appears therefore more pronounced. It would be useful to have these ideas adequately explicated in a manner capable of empirical testing.

14. I had the opportunity to read preliminary drafts of two underlying study papers published subsequently by the Commission. One was M. Friedman and D. Meiselman, "The Relative Stability of Monetary Velocity and the Investment Multiplier in the United States, 1897–1958" [*Stabilization Policies* (Englewood Cliffs, N.J. 1963)]; section 6 of this study deals with "The Channels through Which Monetary Policy Works." The other paper was J. Tobin's "Essay on the Principles of Debt

Management" [*Fiscal and Debt Management Policies* (Englewood Cliffs, N.J. 1963)]. Both papers discuss various aspects of the balance-sheet reaction process or of the "portfolio-balance" analysis. See also the paper by P. Cagan which develops an analysis clearly moving in the same direction ("Why Do We Use Money in Open Market Operations?" *Journal of Political Economy*, Vol. 66 [February 1958]). Note also the following papers in the *Papers and Proceedings of the American Economic Association, 1961:* K. Brunner, "Some Major Problems in Monetary Theory"; H. G. Johnson, "The *General Theory* after Twenty-five Years"; J. Tobin, "Money, Capital and Other Stores of Value."

15. The issue turns on a *slope* property, that is, a reaction at the margin. Thus, if five out of one hundred interviewees say they react to interest-rate variations (accepting whatever is said at face value), then the results could hardly be construed to deny the existence of the slope property at issue.

16. The studies published in A. C. Harberger (ed.), *The Demand for Durable Goods* (Chicago: University of Chicago Press, 1960) bear significantly on the discussion in the text. I concur thoroughly with the report's declaration: "Unfortunately, studies of the actual behavior of business investment and interest rates have not reliably isolated the effects of monetary policy from shifts in other determinants of investments" (p. 52).

17. See pp. 48–49 of report. When the effect of a restrictive policy is discussed "credit" appears to play a crucial role in the transmission mechanism. At other places the money supply moves into the center of the policy considerations. See also p. 50.

18. See pp. 52–54.

19. To be published in two forthcoming papers: "The Structure of the Monetary System and the Supply Function of Money" and "Money Stock and Credit Market."

20. See p. 57. "If excessive liquidity positions of banks . . . and the public are not allowed to develop, and if the Federal Reserve and the Treasury take direct action to speed the adjustment process of long-term and short-term interest rates, the impact of monetary policy should be felt sooner." This passage of the report evidences no understanding of the connection between "excess liquidity" and the operation of the interest mechanism.

21. The second paper mentioned in note 19 develops a detailed analysis of the problem discussed in the text. It should be noted that Tobin's proposal to grant interest on excess reserves equal to the discount rate would help to some extent to remove the problem. Still, in the absence of a clear recognition of the problem there remains a good case for the abolition of discount facilities, particularly as "flexible adjustments of reserve positions" do not appear to hinge decisively on the discounting mechanism. Tobin's proposal could still be useful in the absence of discounting facilities.

22. See p. 68.

23. See p. 67. The report's formulation is indirect: "There is little clear evidence to indicate that the effects of open market operations are slower than those following reserve requirement changes."

24. The results concerning reserve requirements and the precision of control are based on an extensive discussion of the problem in the first paper mentioned in note 19. It should be noted that the Commission dismisses secondary reserve requirements and velocity requirements.

25. I was introduced to this idea by A. H. Meltzer, who presented it in an unpublished paper, "Monetary Policy, Debt Management, and the Dealers Market in Treasury Securities." He also referred to T. C. Gaines's *Techniques of Treasury Debt Management* (New York 1962), which appears to develop a similar proposal.

26. See p. 122.

27. It should be noted that the essential point is not affected by the choice of interpretation for Friedman's exponentially weighted average of past incomes, whether we understand it as an index of wealth or, as Klein insists, simply as a distributed lag in the influence of past income on current consumers' demand. The Modigliani-Friedman notion of wealth-dominated consumers' demand has an interesting implication with respect to a possible interpretation of the "burden of the debt," a problem considered by the Commission. A larger debt means a correspondingly large wealth position of the public—assuming that tax liabilities corresponding to the larger debt are not imputed in the wealth evaluations of the public. The greater wealth shifts output absorption from investment to consumption. The discounted yield stream associated with the resources reallocated from investment to consumers' goods may be understood as *some* measure for the burden of the debt.

The report's discussion of automatic stabilizers contains a strange assertion not justifiable in terms of standard (linear) models of income analysis. It is asserted that the strength of the built-in stabilizers depends on the ratio of government expenditures or taxes to national product. What is the base for this assertion—some peculiar non-linearities not considered in standard models?

21 The Lag in the Effect of Monetary Policy: A Survey of Recent Literature

Michael J. Hamburger *Federal Reserve Bank of New York*

During the last ten years the views of economists—both monetarists and nonmonetarists—on the lag in the effect of monetary policy on the economy have changed considerably. This article examines some of the recent evidence which has served as the basis for these changes.

Prior to 1960, quantitative estimates of the lag in the effect of monetary policy were rare. While there had always been disagreement on the effectiveness of monetary policy, a substantial number of economists seemed to accept the proposition that there was sufficient impact in the reasonably short run for monetary policy to be used as a device for economic stabilization. Although this view did not go unquestioned—see, for example, Mayer [26] and Smith [29]—the main challenge to the conventional thinking came from Milton Friedman. He argued that monetary policy acts with so long and variable a lag that attempts to pursue a contracyclical monetary policy might aggravate, rather than ameliorate, economic fluctuations. In summarizing work done in collaboration with Anna Schwartz, he wrote [16]: "We have found that, on the average of 18 cycles, peaks in the rate of change in the stock of money tend to precede peaks in general business

Reprinted from *Monetary Aggregates and Monetary Policy* (New York: Federal Reserve Bank of New York, 1974), 104–13. The views expressed in this paper are the author's alone and do not necessarily reflect those of the Federal Reserve Bank of New York.

by about 16 months and troughs in the rate of change in the stock of money precede troughs in general business by about 12 months. . . . For individual cycles, the recorded lead has varied between 6 and 29 months at peaks and between 4 and 22 months at troughs."

Many economists were simply not prepared to believe Friedman's estimates of either the length or the variability of the lag. As Culbertson [11] put it, "if we assume that government stabilization policies . . . act with so long and variable a lag, how do we set about explaining the surprising moderateness of the economic fluctuations that we have suffered in the past decade?" Culbertson's own conclusion was that "the broad record of experience support[s] the view that [contracyclical] monetary, debt-management, and fiscal adjustments can be counted on to have their predominant direct effects within three to six months, soon enough that if they are undertaken moderately early in a cyclical phase they will not be destabilizing."

Kareken and Solow [5] also appear to have been unwilling to accept Friedman's estimates. They summarized their results as follows: "Monetary policy works neither so slowly as Friedman thinks, nor as quickly and surely as the Federal Reserve itself seems to believe. . . . Though the *full* results of policy changes on the flow of expenditures may be a long time coming, nevertheless the chain of effects is spread out over a fairly wide interval. This means that *some* effect comes reasonably quickly, and that the effects build up over time so that some substantial stabilizing power results after a lapse of time of the order of six or nine months."

However, as Mayer [27] pointed out, this statement is inconsistent with the evidence presented by Kareken and Solow. They reported estimates of the complete lag in effect of monetary policy on the flow of expenditures for only one component of gross national product (GNP), namely, inventory investment, and this lag is much longer than Friedman's lag. For another sector—producers' durable equipment—they provided data for only part of the lag, but even this is longer than Friedman's lag. Thus, Mayer noted that Kareken and Solow "should have criticized Friedman, not for overestimating, but for underestimating the lag."

More recently, it is the *monetarists* who have taken the view that the lag in the effect of monetary policy is relatively short, and the nonmonetarists who seem to be claiming longer lags. This showed up in the reaction to the St. Louis (Andersen and Jordan) equation [4]. According to this equation, the total response of GNP to changes in the money supply is completed within a year.

In his review of the Andersen and Jordan article, Davis [12] wrote "the most surprising thing about the world of the St. Louis equation is not so much the force, but rather the speed with which money begins to act on the economy." If the level of the money supply undergoes a $1 billion once-and-for-all rise in a given quarter, it will (according to the St. Louis equation) raise GNP by $1.6 billion in that quarter and by $6.6 billion during four quarters. In contrast, Davis found that in the Federal Reserve Board-Massachusetts Institute of Technology model—which was estimated by assuming non-borrowed reserves to be the basic monetary policy variable—a once-and-for-all increase in the money supply of $1 billion in a given quarter has almost no effect on GNP in that quarter and, even after four quarters, the level of GNP is only about $400 million higher than it otherwise would be. Thus, he concluded, "what is at stake in the case of the St. Louis equation is not merely a 'shade of difference' but a strikingly contrasting view of the world—at least relative to what is normally taken as the orthodox view roughly replicated and confirmed both in methods and in result by the Board-MIT model."[1]

The Federal Reserve Board-MIT model (henceforth called the FRB-MIT model) is not the only econometric model suggesting that monetary policy operates with a long distributed lag. Indeed, practically every *structural* model of the United States economy which has been addressed to this question has arrived at essentially the same answer.[2]

The most recent advocates of short lags are Arthur Laffer and R. David Ranson [25]. They have argued that: "Monetary policy, as represented by changes in the conventionally defined money supply [demand deposits plus currency], has an immediate and permanent impact on the level of GNP. For every dollar increase in the money supply, GNP will rise by about $4.00 or $5.00 in the current quarter, and not fall back [or rise any further] in the future. Alternatively, every 1 percent change in the money supply is associated with a 1 percent change in GNP."

This article reviews some of the recent professional literature on the lag in the effect of monetary policy, with the objective of examining the factors which account for differences in the results. Among the factors considered are: (1) the type of statistical estimating model, i.e., structural versus reduced-form equations; (2) the specification of the monetary policy variable; and (3) the influence of the seasonal adjustment procedure. For the most part, the analysis is confined to the results obtained by others. New estimation is undertaken only in those instances where it is considered necessary to reconcile different sets of results.

Structural Versus Reduced-Form Models

We turn first to the question of whether it is more appropriate to use structural or reduced-form models to estimate the effects of stabilization policy on the economy. A structural model of the economy attempts to set forth in equation form what are considered to be the underlying or basic economic relationships in the economy. Although many mathematical and statistical complications may arise, such a set of equations can, in principle, be "reduced" (solved). In this way key economic variables, such as GNP, can be expressed directly as functions of policy variables and other forces exogenous to the economy. While the difference between a structural model and a reduced-form model is largely mathematical and does not necessarily involve different assumptions about the workings of the economy, a lively debate has developed over the advantages and disadvantages of these two approaches.

Users of structural models stress the importance of tracing the paths by which changes in monetary policy are assumed to influence the economy. Another advantage often claimed for the structural approach is that it permits one to incorporate *a priori* knowledge about the economy, for example, knowledge about identities, lags, the mathematical forms of relationships, and what variables should or should not be included in various equations (Gramlich [20]).

On the other hand, those who prefer the reduced-form approach contend that, if one is primarily interested in explaining the behavior of a few key variables, such as GNP, prices, and unemployment, it is unnecessary to estimate all the parameters of a large-scale model. In addition, it is argued that, if the economy is very complicated, it may be too difficult to study even with a very complicated model. Hence, it may be useful simply to examine the relationship between inputs such as monetary and fiscal policy and outputs such as GNP.

Considering the heat of the debate, it is surprising that very little evidence has been presented to support either position. The only studies of which I am aware come from two sources: simulations with the FRB-MIT model, reported by de Leeuw and Gramlich [13, 14], and the separate work of de Leeuw and Kalchbrenner [15]. The latter study reported the estimates of a reduced-form equation for GNP, using monetary and fiscal policy variables similar to those in the FRB-MIT model. The form of the equation is:

$$\triangle Y_t = a + \sum_{i=0}^{7} b_1 \triangle NBR_{t-1} + \sum_{i=0}^{7} c_1 \triangle E_{t-1} + \sum_{i=0}^{7} d_1 \triangle RA_{t-1} + u_t \quad (1)$$

where

$\triangle Y$ = Quarterly change in GNP, current dollars.

$\triangle NBR$ = Quarterly change in nonborrowed reserves adjusted for reserve requirement changes.

$\triangle E$ = Quarterly change in high-employment expenditures of the Federal Government, current dollars.

△RA = Quarterly change in high-employment receipts of the
Federal Government in current-period prices.

u = Random error term.

All variables are adjusted for seasonal variation, and the lag structures
are estimated by using the Almon distributed lag technique.[3]

Chart I illustrates the lag distributions of the effect on GNP of
nonborrowed reserves—the principal monetary variable used in the
studies just mentioned. The chart shows the cumulative effects of a
one dollar change in nonborrowed reserves on the level of GNP as
illustrated by four experiments, the reduced-form equation of de
Leeuw and Kalchbrenner and three versions of the FRB-MIT model.
The heavy broken line traces the sum of the regression coefficients
for the current and lagged values of nonborrowed reserves in the de
Leeuw-Kalchbrenner equation (i.e., the sum of the b_i's). The other
lines show the results obtained from simulations of the FRB-MIT
model; FRB-MIT 1969(a) and FRB-MIT 1969(b) represent simu-

CHART I   *Cumulative Effects of a One-Dollar Change in Nonborrowed
Reserves on GNP*

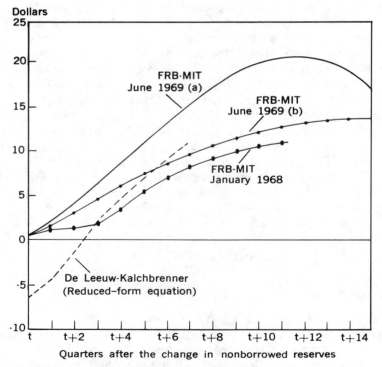

Note: FRB-MIT = Federal Reserve Board-Massachusetts Institute of Technology
econometric model.

lations of the 1969 version of the model, with two different sets of initial conditions.[4] FRB-MIT 1968 gives the simulation results for an earlier version of the model.

Although there are some large short-run differences in the simulation results, these three experiments suggest similar long-run effects of nonborrowed reserves on income. Such a finding is not very surprising; what is significant, in view of the debate between those who prefer structural models and those who prefer reduced forms, is that after the first three or four quarters the de Leeuw-Kalchbrenner results lie well within the range of the simulation results.[5]

Thus, we find that when nonborrowed reserves are chosen as the exogenous monetary policy variable, i.e., the variable used in *estimating* the parameters of the model, it makes very little difference whether the lag in the effect of policy is determined by a structural or a reduced-form model. There is, to be sure, no assurance that similar results would be obtained with other monetary variables or with other structural models (including more recent versions of the FRB-MIT model). In the present case, however, the use of reduced-form equations does not lead to estimates of the effects of monetary policy on the economy that differ from those obtained from a structural model. For the purposes of our analysis, this finding implies that the type of statistical model employed to estimate the lag in the effect of monetary policy may be less important than other factors in explaining the differences in the results that have been reported in the literature.

Specification of the Monetary Policy Variable

Another important difference among the various studies of the lag is the variable used to represent monetary policy. The aim of this section is not to contribute to the controversy about the most appropriate variable, but rather to summarize the arguments and spell out the implications of the choice for the estimate of the lag in the effect of policy.

In recent years, three of the most popular indicators of the thrust of monetary policy have been the money supply, the monetary base, and effective nonborrowed reserves.[6] Monetarists prefer the first two variables on the grounds that they provide the most appropriate measures of the impact of monetary policy on the economy. Critics of the monetarist approach contend that these variables are deficient because they reflect the effects of both policy and nonpolicy influences and hence do not provide reliable (i.e., statistically unbiased) measures of Federal Reserve actions. The variable most often suggested by these economists is effective nonborrowed reserves.[7] In reply, the monetarists have argued that, since the Federal Reserve has the power

CHART II   *Cumulative Percentage Distributions of the Effects of Various Aggregates on GNP*

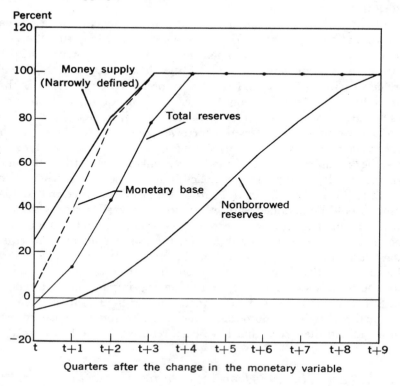

Quarters after the change in the monetary variable

to offset the effects of all nonpolicy influences on the money supply (or the monetary base), it is the movements in the money variable and not the reasons for the movements which are important (Brunner [7] and Brunner and Meltzer [8]). However, this sidesteps the statistical question of whether the money supply or the monetary base qualifies as exogenous variables to be included on the right-hand side of a reduced-form equation. (For a further discussion, see Gramlich [20] and Hamburger [22].)

Chart II presents the cumulative percentage distributions of the effects of various monetary variables on nominal GNP, as implied by the parameter estimates for equations similar to equation 1, that is, reduced-form equations relating quarterly changes in GNP to quarterly changes in monetary and fiscal policy variables. The monetary variables are effective nonborrowed reserves, the monetary base, the narrowly defined money supply (private holdings of currency and demand deposits), and total reserves. The latter is defined as effective nonborrowed reserves plus member bank borrowings from the Federal

Reserve. It is also approximately equal to the monetary base less the currency holdings of nonmember banks and of the nonbank public. Once again, the lag structures for the monetary and fiscal policy variables are estimated using the Almon distributed lag technique. In all cases, with the possible exception of the monetary base, the lags chosen are those which maximize the $\bar{R}^2$ (coefficient of determination adjusted for degrees of freedom) of the equation. Percentage distributions are used to highlight the distribution of the effects over time as opposed to their dollar magnitudes.[8]

The results indicate that the choice of the exogenous monetary policy variable has a significant effect on the estimate of the lag in the effect of policy. If the money supply, the monetary base, or total reserves are taken as the monetary variable, the results suggest that the total response of GNP to a change in policy is completed within four or five quarters. On the other hand, those who consider nonborrowed reserves to be the appropriate variable would conclude that less than 40 percent of the effect occurs in five quarters and that the full effect is distributed over two and a half years.[9]

Thus, the evidence suggests that the relatively short lags that have been found by the monetarists in recent years depend more on their specification of the monetary policy variable than on the use of a reduced-form equation. Whether or not these estimates understate the true length of the lag, they seem roughly consistent with the prevailing view among economists in the early 1960's. They are, for example, essentially identical with Mayer's [26] results which suggested that most of the effect of a change in policy occurs within five quarters. As indicated above, wide acceptance of the proposition that monetary policy operates with a long lag—i.e., a substantial portion of the impact of a policy change does not take place until a year or more later—is of relatively recent vintage and appears to have been heavily influenced by the results of those who do not consider the money supply to be an appropriate measure of monetary policy impulses.

The Seasonal Adjustment Problem

One of the most recent investigations of the effects of monetary and fiscal policy on the economy is that conducted by Laffer and Ranson for the Office of Management and Budget [25]. Perhaps the most striking finding of this study is that every change in the money supply has virtually all its effect on the level of GNP in the quarter in which it occurs. Or, to put this differently, there is little evidence of a lag in the effect of monetary policy. This finding which stands at odds with most other evidence, both theoretical and empirical, is attributed by Laffer and Ranson largely to their use of data that are *not* adjusted for seasonal variation.[10] They contend that the averaging (or smoothing) properties of most seasonal adjustment procedures tend to distort the timing of statistical relationships. Hence, specious lag structures may be introduced into the results.

As shown below, however, the results reported by Laffer and Ranson are much more dependent on their choice of time period (1948–69) than on the use of seasonally unadjusted data. For, if their nominal GNP equation is reestimated for the period 1953–69 (the period employed in the current version of the St. Louis model [3] and in most other recent investigations), it makes very little difference whether one uses seasonally adjusted or unadjusted data. They both indicate that a significant portion of the effect of a change in money does not occur for at least two quarters.

The equation selected by Laffer and Ranson to explain the percentage change in nominal GNP is:[11]

$$\%\triangle Y = 3.21 + 1.10\%\triangle M_1 + .136\%\triangle G - .069\%\triangle G_{-1}$$
$$(4.9)\quad(5.5)\qquad\qquad(6.9)\qquad\qquad(3.3)$$
$$- .039\%\triangle G_{-2} - .024\%\triangle G_{-3} - .046\triangle SH$$
$$(1.9)\qquad\qquad(1.2)\qquad\qquad(3.7)$$
$$+ .068\%\triangle S\&P_{-1} - 9.8D_1 + 2.5D_2 - 3.0D_3 \quad(2)$$
$$(2.2)\qquad\qquad(12.1)\quad(2.6)\quad(4.1)$$

$$\bar{R}^2 = .958 \qquad SE = 1.31 \qquad \text{Interval: 1948-I to 1969-IV}$$

where

$\%\triangle Y$ = Quarterly percentage change in nominal GNP.
$\%\triangle M_1$ = Quarterly percentage change in M_1 (the narrowly defined money supply).
$\%\triangle G$ = Quarterly percentage change in Federal Government purchases of goods and services.
$\triangle SH$ = Quarterly change in a measure of industrial manhours lost due to strikes.
$\%\triangle S\&P$ = Quarterly percentage change in Standard and Poor's Composite Index of Common Stock Prices (the "S&P 500").
D_1 = Seasonal dummy variable for the first quarter.
D_2 = Seasonal dummy variable for the second quarter.
D_3 = Seasonal dummy variable for the third quarter.

All data used in the calculations are unadjusted for seasonal variation. The three dummy variables $(D_1, D_2, \text{and } D_3)$ are introduced to allow for such variation and to permit estimation of the seasonal factors. In principle, joint estimation of the seasonal factors and the economic parameters of a model is preferable to the use of data generated by the standard type of seasonal adjustment procedure. However, in having only three dummy variables, Laffer and Ranson assume that the seasonal pattern in income is constant over the entire sample period. If this assumption is not correct, it becomes a purely empirical question as to whether their procedure is any better or worse than the use of seasonally adjusted data.

Stock market prices are included in the equation on the assumption that the current market value of equities provides an efficient forecast of future income. The variable representing the percentage of man-hours lost due to strikes (SH) is included for institutional reasons.

Aside from these factors, the Laffer-Ranson equation is quite similar to the St. Louis equation. The most important difference is that the former contains only the current-quarter value of money. This implies that a change in the money supply has a once-and-for-all effect on the level of income. Equation 3 shows the results obtained when four lagged values of the percentage change in M_1 are included in the model. Only the coefficients of the money variables are shown below; the rest of the results for this equation as well as those for equation 2 are reproduced in the first portion of Table I.

$$\%\Delta Y = 3.36 + 1.03\%\Delta M_1 - .41\%\Delta M_{1_{-1}} + .49\%\Delta M_{1_{-2}}$$
$$\quad\quad (3.9)\quad (4.4)\quad\quad (1.7)\quad\quad\quad (2.1)$$
$$- .31\%\Delta M_{1_{-3}} + .30\%\Delta M_{1_{-4}}. \;\ldots \quad (3)$$
$$(1.3)\quad\quad\quad (1.3)$$
$$\bar{R}^2 = .961 \quad\quad SE = 1.26 \quad\quad \text{Interval: 1948-I to 1969-IV}$$

Following Laffer and Ranson, the coefficients of this equation are estimated without the use of the Almon distributed lag technique. Although some of the lagged money coefficients approach statistical significance, equation 3—like equation 2—implies that the current and long-run effects of money on income are, for all practical purposes, the same. An increase of 1 percent in M_1 is associated with a roughly 1 percent rise in income in the current quarter and a 1.1 percent rise in the long run.

To test the hypothesis, suggested above, that it is the time interval used by Laffer and Ranson which is largely responsible for this result, equations 2 and 3 were reestimated for the subperiods 1948-I to 1952-IV and 1953-I to 1969-IV. The results (see the two lower sections of Table I) show that: (a) the relationship between money and income in the 1948-52 period is not statistically significant (equations 2a and 3a)[12] and (b) there is a significant lag in the effect of money on income during the more recent period. Indeed, the largest single change in income as a result of a change in money during this period occurs after a lag of two quarters (equation 3b).[13]

Perhaps the most interesting feature of the results is the similarity between the "money coefficients" for the period 1953–69 (equation 3b) and those which have been obtained by other researchers using

TABLE I Regressions Explaining the Percentage Change in Gross National Product

Quarterly seasonally unadjusted data

Equation	Constant	%ΔM₁	%ΔM₁₋₁	%ΔM₁₋₂	%ΔM₁₋₃	%ΔM₁₋₄	%ΔG	%ΔG₋₁	%ΔG₋₂	%ΔG₋₃	ΔSH	%ΔS&P₋₁	D₁	D₂	D₃	R̄² / SE
1948-I to 1969-IV																
2	3.21 (4.9)	1.10 (5.5)					.136 (6.9)	−.069 (3.3)	−.039 (1.9)	−.024 (1.2)	−.046 (3.7)	.068 (2.2)	−9.8 (12.1)	2.5 (2.6)	−3.0 (4.1)	.958 / 1.31
3	3.36 (3.9)	1.03 (4.4)	−.41 (1.7)	.49 (2.1)	−.31 (1.3)	.30 (1.3)	.136 (7.1)	−.073 (3.7)	−.034 (1.7)	−.024 (1.3)	−.045 (3.6)	.095 (2.9)	−9.5 (7.6)	1.3 (0.9)	−2.9 (2.4)	.961 / 1.26
1948-I to 1952-IV																
2a	5.05 (4.8)	.61 (1.6)					.125 (5.7)	−.119 (5.6)	−.022 (1.2)	−.015 (0.6)	−.050 (3.3)	.221 (3.2)	−11.0 (8.8)	−1.5 (0.8)	−2.7 (2.3)	.983 / 0.86
3a	2.38 (1.06)	1.11 (2.0)	−.29 (0.5)	−.18 (0.2)	−.24 (0.3)	.66 (1.4)	.121 (3.7)	−.122 (4.0)	−.024 (0.9)	−.030 (0.9)	−.036 (1.9)	.171 (2.0)	−7.2 (2.3)	3.7 (0.8)	1.0 (0.3)	.983 / 0.86
1953-I to 1969-IV																
2b	4.16 (5.1)	.73 (3.1)					.143 (3.8)	−.008 (0.2)	−.042 (1.1)	−.048 (1.3)	−.022 (1.4)	.061 (1.8)	−11.2 (10.2)	1.8 (1.6)	−4.2 (4.2)	.964 / 1.20
3b	5.18 (5.1)	.64 (2.4)	−.40 (1.3)	.88 (3.1)	−.07 (0.3)	−.05 (0.2)	.160 (4.4)	.002 (0.1)	−.044 (1.2)	−.068 (1.9)	−.026 (1.7)	.079 (2.1)	−11.6 (7.8)	−1.8 (1.0)	−5.2 (3.6)	.968 / 1.13

Note: Values of "t" statistics are indicated in parentheses. For explanation of the symbols other than those shown below, see equation 2 above.
R̄² = Coefficient of determination (adjusted for degrees of freedom).
SE = Standard error of estimate of the regression.

CHART III   *Cumulative Effects of a One Percent Change in Money on GNP*

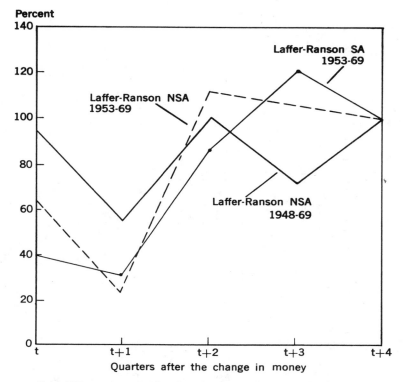

Note: NSA = not seasonally adjusted; SA = seasonally adjusted

seasonally adjusted data for the same period. To demonstrate this, equation 3b was reestimated with seasonally adjusted data for M_1, GNP, and G. The coefficients for the current and lagged money variables for this equation (3b') and for equations 3 and 3b are reported in Table II. Once again the equations are estimated *without* the use of the Almon distributed lag technique. Chart III shows the cumulative percentage distribution of the effects of money on income as implied by these equations. It is clear from the chart that it is the time period chosen by Laffer and Ranson which is largely responsible for their controversial result rather than the use of seasonally unadjusted data. This shows up even more dramatically when the equations are estimated with the Almon procedure. When this is done, there is very little difference between the distributed lag implied by the Laffer-Ranson equations (using seasonally unadjusted data but fitted to the 1953–69 period) and that implied by the St. Louis equation [3], see Chart IV.[14] Thus, once the period through the Korean war is elimi-

TABLE II Selected Regression Results for Equations Explaining the Percentage Change in Gross National Product
Quarterly data

EQUATION	TIME PERIOD	DATA	REGRESSION COEFFICIENTS					$\bar{R}^2$ SE
			$\%\Delta M_1$	$\%\Delta M_{1_{-1}}$	$\%\Delta M_{1_{-2}}$	$\%\Delta M_{1_-}$	$\%\Delta M_{1_{-4}}$	
3............	1948-I to 1969-IV	NSA	1.03 (4.4)	−.41 (1.7)	.49 (2.1)	−.31 (1.3)	.30 (1.3)	.961 1.26
3b............	1953-I to 1969-IV	NSA	.64 (2.4)	−.40 (1.3)	.88 (3.1)	−.07 (0.3)	−.05 (0.2)	.968 1.13
3b'............	1953-I to 1969-IV	SA	.37 (1.8)	−.08 (0.3)	.53 (1.9)	.32 (1.2)	−.21 (1.1)	.541 0.71

Note: Values of "t" statistics are indicated in parentheses. For explanation of the symbols other than those shown below, see equation 2.
$\bar{R}^2$ = Coefficient of determination (adjusted for degrees of freedom).
SE = Standard error of estimate of the regression.
NSA = Not seasonally adjusted.
SA = Seasonally adjusted data are used for M_1, GNP, and G.

CHART IV   Cumulative Percentage Distribution of the Effects of Money on GNP

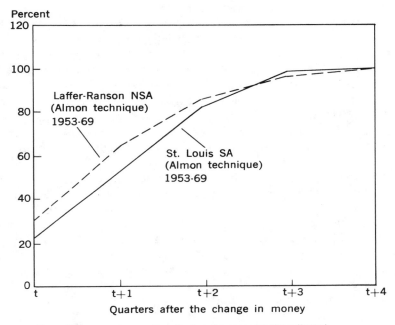

Note: NSA = not seasonally adjusted; SA = seasonally adjusted

nated from the analysis, it makes no difference at all whether the relationship between money and income is estimated with seasonally adjusted data or unadjusted data and dummy variables. Both procedures yield a relatively short, but nevertheless positive, lag in the effect of monetary policy.[15]

The Almon Lag Technique

Finally, it seems worthwhile to say a few words about the use of the Almon technique and its effect on the estimates of the structure (or distribution) of the lag. As noted earlier, this procedure has become quite popular in recent years. It tends to smooth out the pattern of the lag coefficients and makes them easier to rationalize. However, the extent of the differences in the estimates obtained for individual lag coefficients, with and without the use of the technique, provides some reason for concern.

For example, in his experiments with the St. Louis equation, Davis found that either 29 percent or 46 percent of the ultimate effect of money on income could be attributed to the current quarter. The lower number was obtained when the equation was estimated using the Almon technique, while the higher value occurred when the Almon constraint was not imposed on the equation. The explanatory power of the equation was essentially the same in both cases.[16] In the Laffer-Ranson model as well, substantially different estimates of the lag structure are consistent about the same $\bar{R}^2$. In this model the estimates of the current-quarter effect of money on income are 31 percent with the Almon technique and 64 percent with unconstrained lags (compare the Laffer-Ranson NSA curves for the 1953–69 period in Charts III and IV). On the other hand, over the first six months it is the *Almon* technique which yields a faster response of income to money, for both the Davis experiments and the Laffer-Ranson model, than is obtained with unconstrained lags.

The wide divergence in these estimates of the impact of monetary variables over short periods, depending on the nature of the estimating procedure employed, suggests that existing estimates of the underlying lag structure are not very precise. One reason for this may be that the pattern of the lag varies over time.[17] In any event, the uncertainties surrounding the structure (distribution) of the lag are not eliminated by the Almon technique. Thus, use of any existing estimates of the lag structure as a firm basis for short-run policy making would seem rather hazardous at this time.

Concluding Comments

One finding stands out from the results presented above, namely, that there is a lag in the effect of monetary policy. Nevertheless, estimates of the length of the lag differ considerably. Of the three factors considered in this paper that might account for these differences, the most important is the specification of the appropriate monetary policy variable (or variables) in the construction of econometric models. Use of nonborrowed reserves as the exogenous monetary variable suggests that less than 40 percent of the impact of a monetary action occurs within five quarters and that the full effect is distributed over two and a half years. On the other hand, use of the money supply, the monetary base, or total reserves suggests that most of the effect occurs within four or five quarters. The latter estimate of the lag may appear to be relatively short. However, it does not seem to be grossly out of line with the view held by the majority of economists in the early 1960's.

The two other factors considered and found to be less important in explaining the differences in the estimates of the length of the lag are (1) the type of statistical estimating model (structural versus reduced-form equations) and (2) the seasonal adjustment procedure. In both of these instances, though, there is not enough evidence available to draw very firm conclusions; hence further work might prove fruitful.

Finally, more work is also needed to help refine estimates of the distribution of the lag. Existing estimates of the lag structure do not appear to be sufficiently precise to justify large or frequent short-run adjustments in the growth rates of monetary aggregates.

NOTES

1. The properties of the Federal Reserve-MIT model are discussed by de Leeuw and Gramlich [13, 14] and by Ando and Modigliani [6].

2. See Hamburger [21] and Mayer [27]. For a recent discussion of why the lag should be long, see Davis [12], Gramlich [19], and Pierce [28]. The alternative view is presented by White [31], who also gives reasons for believing that the procedures used to estimate the parameters of large-scale econometric models, particularly the FRB-MIT model, may yield "greatly exaggerated" estimates of the length of the lag.

3. Use of the Almon [1] procedure has become quite popular in recent years as it imposes very little *a priori* restriction on the shape of the lag structure, requiring merely that it can be approximated by a polynomial. In the applications discussed in this article, it is generally assumed that a second- or a fourth-degree polynomial is sufficiently flexible to reproduce closely the true lag structure.

4. For the FRB-MIT 1969(a) simulation, the values of all exogenous variables in the model, except nonborrowed reserves, are set equal to their actual values starting in the first quarter of 1964. For the FRB-MIT 1969(b) simulation, the starting values for these variables are their actual values in the second quarter of 1958. The obvious difference between these two sets of initial conditions is the difference in inflationary potential. The quarters during and after 1964 were ones of high resource utilization, and an expansion of reserves at such a time might be expected to stimulate price increases promptly. On the other hand, there was substantial excess capacity in 1958 and a change in reserves under such conditions would be expected to have a minimal short-run effect on prices. The difference in these price effects is significant since it is movements in *current*-dollar GNP which are being explained.

5. De Leeuw and Kalchbrenner do not estimate lags longer than seven quarters. While it is conceivable that the curve representing their results could flatten out (or decline) after period t-7, the shape of the curve up to that point and the results obtained by others, such as those shown in Chart II, make this possibility seem highly unlikely. The initial negative values for the de Leeuw-Kalchbrenner curve arise because of the large negative estimate of b_0 in equation 1; the estimates for all other b's are positive. As de Leeuw and Kalchbrenner pointed out, it is difficult to provide an economic explanation for changes in nonborrowed reserves having a negative effect on GNP in the current quarter. It seems more

reasonable, therefore, that the result reflects "reverse causation," running from GNP to nonborrowed reserve—that is, the Federal Reserve's attempt to pursue a contracyclical monetary policy. This point is discussed at greater length in Hamburger [22].

6. Nonborrowed reserves adjusted for changes in reserve requirements. A similar adjustment is made in computing the monetary base, which is defined as total member bank reserves plus the currency holdings of nonmember banks and the nonbank public. The reserve figure included in the base is also adjusted to neutralize the effects of changes in the ratio of demand deposits to time deposits and changes in the distribution of deposits among banks subject to different reserve requirements.

7. Among others, see de Leeuw and Kalchbrenner [15], Gramley [18], and Hendershott [23].

8. The estimates shown in Chart II are derived from the equations reported by Corrigan [10] and by Andersen and Jordan [4]. Corrigan's results are used for the nonborrowed reserves, total reserves, and money supply curves (the nonborrowed reserves equation is not shown in his article but is available on request). He did not estimate an equation for the monetary base. The fiscal policies variables used in all three equations are the changes in the Government spending and tax components of the "initial stimulus" measure of fiscal policy. The monetary base curve is derived from the Andersen and Jordan results. The fiscal measures used in this study are the Government expenditure and receipt components of the high-employment budget. The criterion used by Andersen and Jordan to select their lag structures is described by Keran [24].

9. A similar conclusion was reached by Andersen [2], who found even longer lags when nonborrowed reserves are used as the monetary policy variable.

10. Other studies which find very short lags in the effort of monetary policy are cited by Laffer and Ranson [25].

11. The numbers in parentheses are t-statistics for the regression coefficients. SE is the standard error of estimate of the regression. A subscript preceded by a minus sign indicates that the variable is lagged that many quarters. In estimating their model, Laffer and Ranson use quarterly changes in the natural logarithms of the variables. This is roughly equivalent to using quarter-to-quarter percentage changes.

12. The contribution of the five money variables to the explanatory power of equation 3a may be evaluated by using the statistical procedure known as the F-test. When this is done, we find that the relationship between money and income is not significant even at the .20 confidence level. It should also be noted that the poor showing of the money variables in the 1948-52 period cannot be attributed simply to the shortness of the period and hence the limited number of degrees of freedom. These conditions do not prevent us from finding statistically significant relationships for most of the other variables included in equations 2a and 3a.

13. In fairness to Laffer and Ranson, it should be noted that even for equation 3b we are unable to reject the hypothesis (at the .05 confidence level) that the current-quarter money coefficient is less than 1.0. However, there appears to be no necessary reason why the current-quarter effect

should be singled out for special consideration. Thus, equation 3b also implies that after six months the cumulative effect of money on income is not significantly different from zero.

The hypothesis that the same regression model fits the entire Laffer-Ranson sample period (1948-69) may be evaluated by means of a procedure developed by Chow [9]. Doing this, we find that the hypothesis may be rejected at the .01 confidence level, that is, the differences in the parameter estimates of equations 2a and 2b and equations 3a and 3b are statistically significant.

14. For comparative purposes, the constraints imposed in estimating the Laffer-Ranson equations with the Almon procedure are the same as those used in the St. Louis equation, i.e., a fourth-degree polynomial with the $t + 1$ and $t - 5$ values of the money coefficients set equal to zero.

15. An almost identical conclusion is reached in a paper by Johnson [23a]. Laffer and Ranson provide an alternative explanation of the difference between their own lag results—shown in equation 3—and the St. Louis results. However, there is no mention in their article that the time period employed to estimate their equations is considerably different from that used in the St. Louis model and most other recent studies.

16. See Davis [12]. The estimates of R^2 are .46 and .47, respectively. The period used to estimate the equation was 1952-I to 1968-II.

17. Some support for this hypothesis is provided by the simulation results for the FRB-MIT model shown in Chart I as well as the results obtained by Warburton [30] and Friedman and Schwartz [17] in their analyses of the timing relations between the upswing and downswing in money and economic activity.

REFERENCES

1. Almon, S. "The Distributed Lag between Capital Appropriations and Expenditures." *Econometrica* (January 1965), pp. 178–96.

2. Andersen, L. C. "An Evaluation of the Impacts of Monetary and Fiscal Policy on Economic Activity." In *1969 Proceedings of the Business and Economic Statistics Section* (Washington, D.C.: American Statistical Association, 1969), pp. 233–40.

3. Andersen, L. C., and Carlson, K. M. "A Monetarist Model for Economic Stabilization." *Review* (Federal Reserve Bank of St. Louis, April 1970), pp. 7–27 (especially p. 11).

4. Andersen, L. C., and Jordan, J. "Monetary and Fiscal Actions: A Test of Their Relative Importance in Economic Stabilization." *Review* (Federal Reserve Bank of St. Louis, November 1968), pp. 11–24.

5. Ando, A., Brown, E. C., Solow, R., and Kareken J. "Lags in Fiscal and Monetary Policy." In Commission on Money and Credit, *Stabilization Policies* (Englewood Cliffs, N. J.: Prentice Hall, Inc., 1963), pp. 1–163 (especially p. 2).

6. Ando, A., and Modigliani, F. "Econometric Analysis of Stabilization Policies." *American Economic Review* (May 1968), pp. 296–314.

7. Brunner, K. "The Role of Money and Monetary Policy." *Review* (Federal Reserve Bank of St. Louis, July 1968), pp. 8–24.

8. Brunner, K., and Meltzer, A. H. "Money, Debt, and Economic Activity." *Journal of Political Economy* (September/October 1972), pp. 951–77.

9. Chow, G. "Tests of Equality between Two Sets of Coefficients in Two Linear Regressions." *Econometrica* (July 1960), pp. 591–605.

10. Corrigan, E. G. "The Measurement and Importance of Fiscal Policy Changes." *Monthly Review* (Federal Reserve Bank of New York, June 1970), pp. 133–45.

11. Culbertson, J. M. "Friedman on the Lag in Effect of Monetary Policy." *Journal of Political Economy* (December 1960), pp. 617–21 (especially p. 621).

12. Davis, R. G. "How Much Does Money Matter? A Look at Some Recent Evidence." *Monthly Review* (Federal Reserve Bank of New York, June 1969), pp. 119–31 (especially pp. 122–24).

13. de Leeuw, F., and Gramlich, E. M. "The Channels of Monetary Policy." *Federal Reserve Bulletin* (June 1969), pp. 472–91.

14. de Leeuw, F., and Gramlich, E. M. "The Federal Reserve-MIT Econometric Model." *Federal Reserve Bulletin* (January 1968), pp. 11–40.

15. de Leeuw, F., and Kalchbrenner, J. "Monetary and Fiscal Actions: A Test of Their Relative Importance in Economic Stabilization—Comment." *Review* (Federal Reserve Bank of St. Louis, April 1969), pp. 6–11.

16. Friedman, M. *A Program for Monetary Stability* (New York: Fordham University Press, 1960), especially p. 87.

17. Friedman, M., and Schwartz, A. J. *A Monetary History of the United States, 1867–1960* (Princeton: Princeton University Press, 1963).

18. Gramley, L. E. "Guidelines for Monetary Policy—The Case Against Simple Rules." A paper presented at the Financial Conference of the National Industrial Conference Board, New York, February 21, 1969. Reprinted in W. L. Smith and R. L. Teigen (eds.), *Readings in Money, National Income, and Stabilization Policy* (Homewood, Ill.: Richard D. Irwin, Inc., 1970), pp. 488–95.

19. Gramlich, E. M. "The Role of Money in Economic Activity: Complicated or Simple?" *Business Economics* (September 1969), pp. 21–26.

20. Gramlich, E. M. "The Usefulness of Monetary and Fiscal Policy as Discretionary Stabilization Tools." *Journal of Money, Credit and Banking* (May 1971, Part 2), pp. 20, 506–32 (especially p. 514).

21. Hamburger, M. J. "The Impact of Monetary Variables: A Survey of Recent Econometric Literature." In *Essays in Domestic and International Finance* (New York: Federal Reserve Bank of New York, 1969), pp. 37–49.

22. Hamburger, M. J. "Indicators of Monetary Policy: The Arguments and the Evidence." *American Economic Review* (May 1970), pp. 32–39.

23. Hendershott, P. H. "A Quality Theory of Money." *Nebraska Journal of Economics and Business* (Autumn 1969), pp. 28–37.

23a. Johnson, D. D. "Properties of Alternative Seasonal Adjustment Techniques, A Comment on the OMB Model." *Journal of Business* (April 1973), pp. 284–303.

24. Keran, M. W. "Monetary and Fiscal Influences on Economic Activity—The Historical Evidence." *Review* (Federal Reserve Bank of St. Louis, November 1968), pp. 5–24 (especially p. 18, footnote 22).

25. Laffer, A. B., and Ranson, R. D. "A Formal Model of the Economy." *Journal of Business* (July 1971), pp. 247–70 (especially pp. 257–59).

26. Mayer, T. "The Inflexibility of Monetary Policy." *Review of Economics and Statistics* (November 1958), pp. 358–74 [reprinted in the previous edition of this book—Ed.].

27. Mayer, T. "The Lag in Effect of Monetary Policy: Some Criticisms." *Western Economic Journal* (September 1967), pp. 324–42 (especially pp. 326 and 328).

28. Pierce, J. L. "Critique of 'A Formal Model of the Economy for the Office of Management and Budget' by Arthur B. Laffer and R. David Ranson." In United States Congress, Joint Economic Committee, *The 1971 Economic Report of the President, Hearings,* Part I (February 1971), pp. 300–12.

29. Smith, W. L. "On the Effectiveness of Monetary Policy." *American Economic Review* (September 1956), pp. 588–606.

30. Warburton, C. "Variability of the Lag in the Effect of Monetary Policy, 1919–1965." *Western Economic Journal* (June 1971), pp. 115–33.

31. White, W. H. "The Timeliness of the Effects of Monetary Policy: The New Evidence from Econometric Models." *Banca Nazionale del Lavoro Quarterly Review* (September 1968), pp. 276–303.

22 *Free Reserves, Total Reserves, and Monetary Control*

William G. Dewald *Ohio State University*

Most textbooks and presumably money and banking courses present a fairy tale about Federal Reserve open-market operations. As the story goes, open-market transactions are made (1) to offset random or regular disturbances in the sources and uses of member-bank *reserves* or (2) to change member-bank reserves and permit monetary expansion or contraction. This is not just an over-simplification. It is wrong. The truth is that the Federal Reserve carries on open-market operations to cushion the money market from a variety of shocks that would, in the absence of offsetting actions, cause member-bank *reserve positions* to change from a policy-determined target level. The *reserve position* is defined as member-bank excess reserves less their borrowings from the Federal Reserve. It is termed free reserves when positive and net borrowed reserves when negative.

I

Behind the walls of the Reserve banks, the reserve position approach to monetary control is the dominating theme. Outside, a chorus of financial reporters and money marketers sing along in close harmony. The accepted approach has its origin in the work

Reprinted from *Journal of Political Economy*, Vol. 71 (April 1963), 141–53, by permission of the author and The University of Chicago Press. Copyright 1963 by The University of Chicago Press.

The article has been slightly abridged where indicated.

of Burgess and Riefler about thirty-five years ago.[1] Since then the principal change is that the reserve positions member banks want are no longer assumed to be always zero but to be a function of such factors as market rates of interest, the discount rate, and the distribution of funds among banks in various size classes.[2]

* * *

II

. . . [As] a framework for comparing the currently used reserve position guide to monetary control with the alternative of a total reserves guide, I hypothesize various supply-and-demand functions upon which the supply of money depends.

SUPPLY OF BORROWED RESERVES:

$$r = r_o$$

In Figure 1a the supply of Federal Reserve discounts and advances to member banks (B) appears as a perfectly elastic function at the prevailing discount rate (r). Though each Reserve bank administers discounting as it interprets the governing regulations, the fact is that borrowers are almost always accommodated with no questions asked.

DEMAND FOR BORROWED RESERVES:

$$B_d = B(r, i); \qquad \frac{\partial B}{\partial r} < 0, \qquad \frac{\partial B}{\partial i} > 0$$

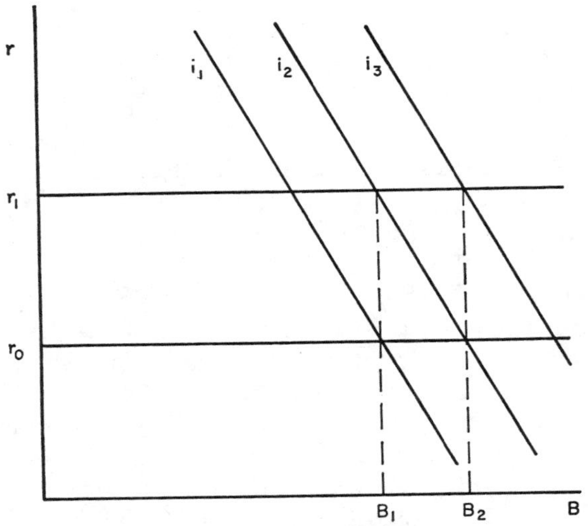

Figure 1a. *Supply and Demand for Borrowed Reserves* (B)

Figure 1a also shows the demand for borrowings as a down-sloping function of the discount rate. The explanation of banks not borrowing indefinitely as long as the discount rate is less than the market rate (i) may be partly the result of official or unofficial ceilings on individual bank borrowing. For a particular market rate, as the discount rate is reduced an increasing number of banks might be willing to approach their limit. Part of the explanation may be that portfolio risks of capital losses increase with increased borrowings. Bankers are presumed to attract deposits or borrow and to buy investments or make loans so as to attain a maximum of expected utility that depends on their subjective evaluation of expected earnings and associated portfolio risk and their preferences with respect to risk and return. It may take a reduction in costs of borrowing, for given market rates, to prompt utility-maximizing bankers to increase their borrowings when not just expected earnings but risks of capital loss are thereby increased.

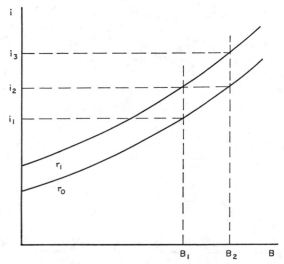

Figure 1b. *Supply and Demand for Borrowed Reserves* (B)

As diagramed in Figure 1b, the demand for borrowings at a given discount rate would increase with increased market interest rates. The demand for borrowed reserves as a function of the market rate would increase at a decreasing rate to the extent that risks of capital loss increase with increased borrowings. Expectations about such factors as receipts and payments, rates of return, and the term pattern of yields also would affect the demand for borrowed reserves. The distribution of funds among banks with different propensities to borrow is another relevant factor.

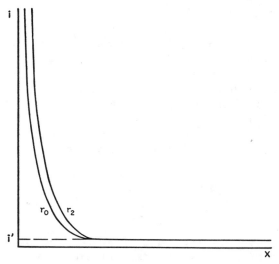

Figure 2. *Demand for Excess Reserves* (X)

DEMAND FOR EXCESS RESERVES:

$$X_d = X(r, i); \qquad \frac{\partial X}{\delta r} > 0, \qquad \frac{\partial X}{\partial i} < 0$$

The demand for excess reserves (X) similarly may be expected to be a function of the discount and market rates, as indicated in Figure 2. There should be an inverse relationship between the interest and the demand for excess reserves for at least three reasons. First, banks hold idle funds for many of the same reasons that non-bank investors hold money for other than transaction purposes. Accordingly increasing interest rates may be expected to lead banks to substitute earning assets for excess reserves up to the point where the added return is not worth the added risk.[3] Second, because there are transaction costs of investing temporarily idle balances, rising interest rates would provide the incentive to reduce any excess reserves that might be held for transaction purposes.[4] Third, the fact that the banks have demand obligations (withdrawal risks) partly accounts for a decrease in excess reserves as interest rates rise.[5] Such risks would account for an increase in demand for excess reserves as deposits rise, a factor ignored in this analysis.

If there is a liquidity trap for banks at some low interest rate (i'), the slope of the demand for excess reserves with respect to the interest rate would decline as the rate fell. A minimum of excess reserves might be approached with increasingly high interest rates. That minimum would depend on such factors as size distribution of banks, length of reserve periods, deposit turnover, speed of communication, and development of money markets. There is evidence that the minimum level of excess reserves is virtually zero for large money-market banks, while it may be a very considerable magnitude for small banks.[6]

To the extent that borrowings and excess reserves are substitute buffers against portfolio and withdrawal risks, the discount rate could also affect the demand for excess reserves. At a given market rate of interest, an increase in the discount rate would be associated with an increased demand for excess reserves.

DEMAND FOR FREE RESERVES:

$$F_d = X_d - B_d$$

For a given discount rate, the demand for free reserves is simply the sum of excess reserves less borrowings at each market rate. Such a summation is shown on the left-hand side of Figure 4a (see below)—a graph where positive units are measured from the origin in every direction except from the origin down (south). Increases in the discount rate could be expected to increase the demand for excess reserves and decrease the demand for borrowed reserves and, hence, increase the demand for free reserves on both counts. Changes in such factors as the distribution of funds, the state of expectations, and the pattern of rates could also shift the demand for free reserves as a function of the market rate of interest.

SUPPLY OF EXCESS RESERVES:

$$X_s = R - qM; \qquad 0 < q \leq 1$$

Though ordinarily not identified as such, the supply of excess reserves is a concept on which a great deal of academic energy in the money and banking field has been spent. Consider a simple example. Suppose that net demand deposits (D) are the only bank liability upon which required reserves are figured and that the required-reserve ratio is q. Required reserves are defined, $Q = qD$. Total reserves (R) are given, $R = R_o$. As a parallel to the consumption function of national income analysis, the banking system is presumed to have a behavior pattern such that $E = (1 - q)D$, where $(1 - q)$ is the "marginal propensity" to acquire earning assets (E). Imposing the equilibrium condition that assets equal liabilities, $E + R = D$, one obtains the familiar solution that $D = (1/q)R_o$. Alternately $Q = qD$ can be considered as a parallel to the saving function and $R = R_o$ as comparable to exogenous spending in a simple national income determination illustration.

Imposing the equilibrium condition that $Q = R$ the identical solution is obtained.

This model can be expressed in terms of the demand and supply of excess reserves. The demand is $X_d = 0$; the supply, $X_s = R_o - qD$ for given total reserves. Imposing the equilibrium condition that $X_s = X_d$ one again obtains $D = (1/q)R_o$. A graphical solution to this problem is shown in Figure 3. $\overline{D}$ is the equilibrium amount of net demand deposits.

The supply of excess reserves in the upper right-hand quadrant of Figure 4a is expressed as a function of the money supply as a whole. The slope of the function is the negative of a kind of average member-bank required-reserve ratio. It equals the ratio of member-bank required reserves to the total money supply and can be thought of as a weighted average of the various member-bank required-reserve ratios. The weights depend on the fraction of money held by the public in currency, the amount of non-member-bank deposits, and the relation between the monetary liabilities of member banks and the liabilities upon which their required reserves are figured.[7] Zero excess reserves, the intercept on the horizontal axis, would be associated with a volume of money supply that can be termed the maximum potential money supply. Maximum excess reserves would be total reserves, which in turn equal the sum of borrowed reserves (B) and unborrowed reserves (U). Under the reserve position guide to monetary control presently employed, one may think of unborrowed reserves as a magnitude that is determined by open-market operations—it is policy controlled.

I shall now show how the demand for free reserves affects the money supply. For given discount rate and unborrowed reserves,

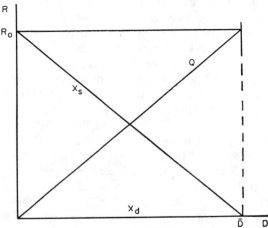

Figure 3. *Excess Reserves Equilibrium*

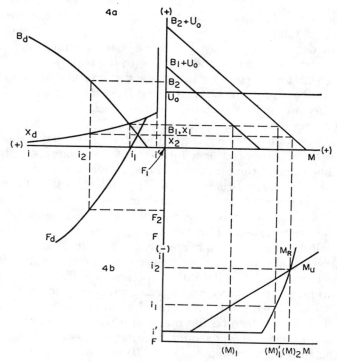

Figures 4a. and 4b. *Supply of Money* (M)

the money supply (M) at each market rate of interest (i) is an
amount such that the demand and supply of borrowed reserves
are equal and the demand and supply of excess reserves are equal.
The money-supply function (M_U), given the particular values of
r_o and U_o, is derived in Figure 4a and recorded as a function of
market rates of interest in Figure 4b. The function depends on the
demand functions for borrowed and excess reserves and the average
required-reserve ratio on money in addition to the policy-controlled discount rate and unborrowed reserves.

To illustrate the process of derivation consider the market rate i_2.
At this rate the demand for borrowed reserves is B_2. Since the
supply of borrowed reserves is independent of the discount rate,
B_2 will also be the equilibrium quantity of borrowings at i_2. Hence
total reserves are $B_2 + U_o$, and the supply of excess reserves for
given average required-reserve ratio (q) is determined. It is the
downsloping line furthest from the origin in the northeast quadrant
of Figure 4a. At i_2 the demand for excess reserves is X_2. Therefore
the money supply must be $(M)_2$ to satisfy the equilibrium condition that the supply and demand of excess reserves be equal.
At the lower market rate i_1 the amount of borrowing is reduced to

B_1 and the supply of excess reserves shifts down to intercept the vertical axis at $B_1 + U_o$. The demand for excess reserves at i_1 rises to X_1, which only coincidentally would be equal to B_1 as indicated in the diagram. Equating supply and demand for excess reserves, one obtains a money supply of $(M)_1$ that is smaller than $(M)_2$. In general, a reduction of the market interest rate, given the discount rate, level of unborrowed reserves, and relevant behavioral relations would be associated with a reduced money supply because there will be (1) a decrease in borrowed reserves that will reduce total reserves and hence the supply of excess reserves and (2) an increase in the demand for excess reserves. In Figure 4b the money supply (M_U) for given r_o and U_o is depicted as a function of market rates of interest. M_R will be discussed below. An increase in unborrowed reserves would shift the supply of excess reserves to the right; this would be reflected in a comparable shift of the money-supply function. For a given interest rate and hence given borrowed and excess reserves, this would lead to a multiple increase in the money supply. In this case $\partial M/\partial U = 1/q$. A decrease in the discount rate would increase the amount of borrowed reserves at each market rate and similarly be associated with an increase in total reserves, an upward shift in the supply of excess reserves, and thus an increase in the amount of money supplied at each market rate of interest.

Presuming in Keynesian fashion that money is demanded for investment (M_2) and transaction purposes (M_1) and imposing the equilibrium condition that money supply and demand be equal, one obtains the familiar relationship between money national income and the market rate of interest. This may be termed the money-equilibrium relation (ME_U) associated with a money-supply function for given discount rate and unborrowed reserves. In Figure 5a a market rate i_2 would be associated with demand for idle balances $(M_2)_2$ and money supply $(M)_2$. If the total money demand and supply are equal, transactions demand must be $(M_1)_2$, that is, $(M)_2 - (M_2)_2$. Only if money income is Y_2 will transactions balances of $(M_1)_2$ be demanded. Hence, for given r_o and U_o, one has the point (Y_2, i_2) on the money equilibrium relation as depicted in Figure 5b. It is associated with particular underlying behavioral relations and policy-controlled magnitudes. At a lower market interest rate i_1 the demand for idle balances increases and the supply of money decreases. On both counts one has lower market rates associated with lower money income on the money-equilibrium curve. The money-equilibrium curve will be more elastic, the more elastic is the investment demand for money and the more elastic is the supply of money. A liquidity trap in either the investment demand or the demand for excess reserves is

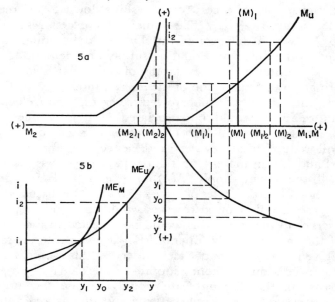

Figures 5a. and 5b. *Money Equilibrium* (M)

sufficient to cause the money-equilibrium relation to be perfectly elastic with respect to the market rate of interest.

III

In Figure 6 a relation between the rate of interest and money income such that income and expenditure are equal is recorded. This is the familiar commodity-equilibrium relation (CE) or investment-equals-saving relation. Ignoring considerations of the price level and aggregate supply, the market rate $(\bar{\imath})$ and money income level $(\bar{Y})$ such that both commodity (CE) and money equilibrium (ME) obtain may be termed their equilibrium levels. Should the commodity-equilibrium curve shift to the right (CE') for some reason, the resulting increase in equilibrium income and interest rate will depend on the money-equilibrium relation. Three basic varieties of such relations are depicted in Figure 6: ME_M, ME_R, and ME_U. ME_U represents a money-equilibrium relation associated with a money-supply function for given discount rate, unborrowed reserves, and relevant behavioral relations. Moving along ME_U a shift from CE to CE' will increase the equilibrium interest rate from $\bar{\imath}$ to $\bar{\imath}_U$ and the level of money income $\bar{Y}$ to $\bar{Y}_U$. This increase in the interest rate will have increased the profitability of making loans and investments and will have prompted utility-maximizing bankers to lend and invest increased amounts;

as a result, when they are "surprised" by withdrawals or additional loan demand they will reduce their excess reserves and/or be "forced" to the Federal Reserve "discount window" to borrow reserves. The increase in the money supply that results dampens the effect of a change in the commodity-equilibrium curve less than would be the case if the money stock were given as is so often assumed in theoretical and econometric studies of national income determination.

In Figures 5b and 6, ME_M is the money-equilibrium relation for a quantity of money fixed at $(M)_1$. It is less elastic than ME_U because rising interest rates are associated with higher income only to the extent that a decline in the demand for idle balances frees money to be held for transaction purposes. ME_R, the money-equilibrium curve associated with the money-supply function for given total reserves, will be discussed in a later section.

At the open-market trading desk of the Federal Reserve Bank of New York, an increase in the commodity-equilibrium curve such as has been hypothesized would be reflected in a money market that feels increasingly tight. Interest rates would rise and free reserves fall in the absence of changes in the behavioral relations governing the supply and demand for money. If the level of free reserves falls below the desired level as he interprets the minutes and off-the-record comments of the last Federal Open Market Committee meeting, the manager of the Open Market Account would purchase sufficient securities to increase free reserves to the

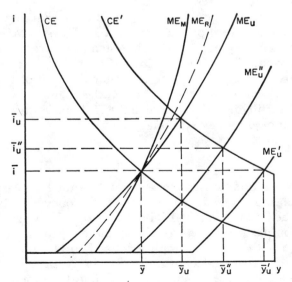

Figure 6. *Income and Interest-Rate Equilibrium*

desired magnitude. The consequence of making the proper amount of purchases is that unborrowed reserves would increase and as a result the money-supply function would move to the right sufficiently to shift the money-equilibrium curve far enough (ME'_U) to reduce the level of the interest rate to its initial level ($\bar{\imath}$) and thereby attain the associated desired level of free reserves. Given the relevant behavioral relations and policy-determined magnitudes, maintaining a free-reserve target in the face of an increased desire to spend prevents rising interest rates from dampening increased spending at all. In the opposite circumstances a cut in planned spending would not be offset at all by a decline in interest rates.

Of course, the target level of free reserves is not permanently fixed. Rather it is increased when the Open Market Committee perceives that an expansionary policy is desirable and vice versa. Of exceedingly great significance is the fact that the Committee often interprets a decline in free reserves and/or an increase in the rate of interest as a contractionary policy, and the reverse developments as expansionary. Whether tight money is contractionary, and easy money expansionary, depends critically on the extent to which economic instability results from instability in investment demand and other determinants of the commodity-equilibrium relation. In response to a destabilizing increase in the commodity-equilibrium curve, there is a substantial danger that the level of unborrowed reserves would not be decreased to offset increased borrowed reserves and, to a lesser extent, decreased excess reserves. In Figure 6 discount and open-market policies that shift the money-equilibrium curve from ME_U to ME''_U are not countering an increase in spending stemming from a shift in the commodity-equilibrium curve from CE to CE' but are contributing to its force in spite of the fact that the rate of interest rises. There is evidence that the Open Market Committee has sometimes not distinguished between tight and contractionary policies or between easy and expansionary policies.

IV

*   *   *

Without question monetary policy aimed at easing money conditions and increasing the supply of money and bank credit through the first half of 1960. The means by which this was to have been accomplished was through an increase in the level of free reserves. Yet the money supply declined substantially—about $4 billion in the year ended in mid-July, 1960. In fact, though free reserves were increased even further during the second half of 1960 the seasonally adjusted average money supply in the second half of November was but a half billion over the minimum value it touched during June and July. Subsequently relatively rapid monetary expansion occurred. But this did not happen until there was a change in required reserve ratios and total reserves; and then it occurred almost simultaneously with a turn in the level of economic activity. This pattern is not a coincidence. It is a natural result of pursuing a reserve position guide to monetary control on the one hand, and on the other of establishing a reserve position target on the basis of what happened in the immediate past.

Though the economic record is most discouraging, it would be possible for the Federal Reserve to vary free reserves and/or interest rates sufficiently to permit money-supply changes to be counter-cyclical even within the framework of the means of monetary control now used. What is required is that reserve positions be increased by sufficient purchases of securities to cause money-supply increases to bolster expenditure when this is less than desired, and vice versa. Despite this fact, a case can be made for an alternative method of monetary control.

v

An alternative to using the presently employed reserve position guide to monetary control is to conduct open-market operations to hit a total-reserves target. Each day the manager of the Open Market Account would consider the same kind of information as he presently does. He would have projections of each of the uncontrolled sources and uses of member-bank reserves and, most important, he would have the reserve-balance data for the portion of the reserve period that had already elapsed. He would authorize sales if the accumulated average of reserves was above the target level for the reserve period and if non-controlled factors were not expected to absorb a sufficient volume of reserves in the remainder of the period to bring about the desired level. By such responses, there is little question that the average level of reserves over a two- or three-week period could be controlled within narrow limits.

To see the implications of manipulating total reserves for monetary control, consider again the demand and supply of excess reserves in Figure 4a. Total reserves are to be considered not a variable but a particular policy-determined amount, say R_o. The interest rate does not affect total reserves now but only the fraction that is borrowed. Let R_o be equal to $B_2 + U_o$ in Figure 4a. In this case $B = B_2$ and $U = U_o$ only coincidentally. At i_2 the quantity of money supplied will be $(M)_2$, a quantity such that the supply and demand for excess reserves are equal as recorded in Figures 4a and 4b. The associated money supply is labeled M_R. The supply and demand for borrowed reserves would also be equal, but this would no longer influence the supply of money. Whatever borrowed reserves are, open-market operations would adjust unborrowed reserves so that $U + B = R_o$. At i_1 the demand for excess reserves would rise and, when equated with the supply of excess reserves, be associated with a decrease in the supply of money to $(M)_1$. This decrease would result only from an increase in the demand for excess reserves, in contrast to the unborrowed reserve case, where a decrease in interest rates not only increased excess reserve demand but also decreased excess reserve supply because of a cut in borrowed reserves.

The supply of money for given discount rate and total reserves is $1/q$ times as responsive to interest-rate changes as is the demand for excess reserves, while the supply of money for given discount rate and unborrowed reserves has that response plus $1/q$ times the increase in borrowed reserves resulting from an increase in interest rates. At a high interest rate, the presumed inelasticity of the demand for excess reserves results in comparable inelasticity in the money supply for given total reserves. At rates above the rate at which the minimum level of excess reserves is reached, the money-supply function would be perfectly inelastic.

Derivation of the money-supply function for given total reserves has not established that total reserves control is preferable to free-reserves control. That argument rests on the proposition that one random variable can be predicted more accurately than a function of that random variable and another one as well. Since the money supply for given total reserves is independent of borrowed reserves, to predict what the money-supply function will be, one only needs predictions of the supply and demand for excess reserves and not predictions of borrowed reserves as is the case under the reserve position alternative. The entire argument is summarized in the following algebraic expressions of the alternative models that have been discussed. $\sigma^2(M_R)$ is necessarily less than $\sigma^2(M_U)$ as long as $2\sigma(BX)$ is smaller than $\sigma^2(B)$ or negative. In the absence of more vigorous discount-rate policy than has been observed in this country $\sigma(BX)$ would in all probability be negative, thus insuring that $\sigma^2(M_R) < \sigma^2(M_U)$.

MONEY SUPPLY WITH DISCOUNT RATE AND

TOTAL RESERVES GIVEN

$$q = q_o$$
$$R = R_o$$
$$r = r_o$$
$$X_s = R - qM$$
$$X_d = X(r, i)$$
$$X_d = X_s$$

$$M_R = 1/q_o[R_o - X(r_o, i)]$$
$$\sigma^2(M_R) = 1/q_o^2 \sigma^2(X)$$

MONEY SUPPLY WITH DISCOUNT RATE AND

UNBORROWED RESERVES GIVEN

$$
\begin{aligned}
q &= q_o \\
U &= U_o \\
r &= r_o \\
R &= U + B \\
B_d &= B(r, i) \\
B_d &= B_s \\
X_s &= R - qM \\
X_d &= X(r, i) \\
X_d &= X_s
\end{aligned}
$$

$$
\begin{aligned}
M_U &= 1/q_o[U_o + B(r_o, i) - X(r_o, i)] \\
\sigma^2(M_U) &= 1/q_o^2[\sigma^2(B) + \sigma^2(X) - 2\sigma(BX)]
\end{aligned}
$$

The variance terms found above may be modified to account for borrowed and excess reserves being estimated more accurately than by their means. If one assumes that $B_d = B(r, i) + v$ and $X_d = X(r, i) + w$ where v and w are dependent random disturbances with zero expected values and finite variances and covariance, then $\sigma^2(M_R) > \sigma^2(M_U)$ only if $\sigma^2(v) < 2\sigma(vw)$.

Meigs has examined evidence leading to the conclusion that a small part of the variation of changes in member-bank net deposits is accountable to variation in the demand for free reserves as a function of market interest rates and the discount rate.[8] Rather, the bulk of the variation in member-bank deposits is due to variation in unborrowed reserves. My own empirical work has established that variation from one semimonthly period to the next in the average required-reserve ratio on member-bank net demand deposits is over 99 per cent accountable to seasonal factors and changes in required-reserve ratios.[9]

VI

In conclusion, there is a substantial case both theoretically and empirically against the presently employed means of monetary control in the United States; I believe that actions of the Federal Reserve Open Market Committee have been conceived and executed with the highest possible motives about the welfare of the American people. But easy and expansionary policies (or tight and contractionary policies) have often been confused because of the free-reserve guide. Certainly the frequently observed slowdown in monetary growth or monetary contraction as the level of economic activity peaks out and begins to fall is not desirable, especially if there is a lag in the impact of money-stock changes on the level of expenditure.

638   *Part VI Monetary Policy*

These recommendations follow from the preceding analysis. First, the Open Market Committee should be persuaded to distinguish between easy and expansionary policies, and tight and restrictive policies. Second, the manager of the Open Market Account should be educated to stop forcing cuts in the money stock when the Open Market Committee calls for monetary expansion and vice versa. Third, the Open Market Committee should direct the manager of the Open Market Account to try to achieve a target level of daily average total reserves (or money supply) during the interim between its meetings.

These recommendations are intended to make monetary policy stabilizing, in contrast to present guides for policy, which often have had destabilizing effects. Stabilizing monetary policy may not achieve the best of all possible worlds, but there is good reason to think that the conduct of monetary policy could bring us closer than it has.

NOTES

. W. R. Burgess, *The Reserve Banks and the Money Market* (New York: Harper & Bros., 1927); and W. W. Riefler, *Money Rates and Money Markets in the United States* (New York: Harper & Bros., 1930).

2. P. D. Sternlight and R. Lindsay, "The Significance and Limitations of Free Reserves," *Monthly Review, Federal Reserve Bank of New York* (November 1958), pp. 162–67.

3. A. D. Roy, "Safety First and the Holding of Assets," *Econometrica*, Vol. 20 (July 1952), 391–405; and J. Tobin, "Liquidity Preference as Behavior towards Risk," *Review of Economic Studies*, Vol. 25 (February 1958), 65–86.

4. W. J. Baumol, "The Transactions Demand for Cash: An Inventory Theoretic Approach," *Quarterly Journal of Economics*, Vol. 66 (November 1952), 545–56; and J. Tobin, "The Interest-Elasticity of Transactions Demand for Cash," *Review of Economics and Statistics*, Vol. 38 (August 1956), 241–47.

5. D. Orr and W. J. Mellon, "Stochastic Reserve Losses and Bank Credit," *American Economic Review*, Vol. 51 (September 1961).

6. W. Dewald, "Money To Spare: Excess Reserves," *Monthly Review, Federal Reserve Bank of Minneapolis* (August 1961), pp. 2–7.

7. W. Dewald, "Monetary Control and the Distribution of Money" (unpublished Ph.D. dissertation, University of Minnesota, 1963).

8. A. J. Meigs, *Free Reserves and the Money Supply* (Chicago: University of Chicago Press, 1962).

9. Dewald, "Monetary Control and the Distribution of Money."

23 Recent Approaches to Dynamic Stability in Macro-Economic Models

Paul E. Smith *University of Missouri*

Ever since Phillips' [11] pathbreaking work of the 1950's on policy and stability in macro-economic models, the theory of control processes has grown rapidly. More recently, economists have utilized some of the new control tools, although the theoretical applications have been largely restricted to models of economic growth.[1] The purpose of this paper is to demonstrate some elementary applications of control theory to three short-run macro-economic models, two of which have been recently discussed by R. G. D. Allen [1, Chapter 9]. In doing so, we will utilize the classical method of the calculus of variations, Pontryagin's maximum principle, and dynamic programming.[2] Section I briefly outlines the nature and methods of control processes; Section II deals with stability in a model, which reduces to a first-order linear differential equation, and an application of Pontryagin's maximum principle, and Section III uses the calculus of variations to impose "stability" on an economic model which can be represented by a second-order linear differential equation. Finally, Section IV provides a simple application of dynamic programming to the stability problem. The illustrations used are both elementary and introductory, and no claim of mathematical originality is made.

Reprinted from *Public Finance,* Vol. 25 (1970/71), 1-21, by permission of the author and publisher.

I. *The Optimalization Problem*

In general, a first-order system can be described by the differential equation

$$\frac{dx}{dt} = \dot{x} = f(x, u, t) \tag{1}$$

where x and u are called the state and control variables, respectively, $\dot{x}$ is the first time derivative of x; and where t denotes time.[3] In the remainder of this paper we shall sometimes follow the economist's jargon and define x as the target variable of the system and u as a policy instrument. Next, the control or policy law may be written as

$$u = g(x, t) \tag{2}$$

i.e., the value of the policy instrument, which is to be selected by policy makers, is dependent upon the magnitude of the target variable and/or the date.

The problem is to select an optimal control law, including the specification of its parameters, in such a way that the performance of the system is, in some manner, "best." In doing so, it is first necessary to set up a cost functional or performance index which is to be minimized or maximized and which represents the desired performance of the model in terms of the target variable(s) and the instrumental variable(s). The generalized version of the cost functional is

$$S = S(x, u, t) \tag{3}$$

For example, the performance index may be stated in terms of maximizing the discounted value of consumption over some future period of time, minimizing the length of time required for the system to reach an equilibrium position, or minimizing the deviations of the target variable around its equilibrium path. Moreover, some cost may be entailed in using the instrument, e.g., the diversion of resources from the private to the public sector, so that it becomes necessary to account for the magnitude of the instrument in the performance index.

Inasmuch as most dynamic control systems are concerned with the stability or instability of economic systems, it may prove fruitful to examine briefly the notion of dynamic stability. A dynamic economic (or any other) system may be said to be stable if its response to a sudden disturbance is bounded in magnitude, i.e., the system is asymptotically stable if it eventually returns to a position of equilibrium. The situation is illustrated in Figure 1 for two state variables, x_1 and x_2 in phase space where their equilibrium values are at the point $(x_1{}^*, x_2{}^*)$. Suppose that x_1 and x_2 are disturbed to point A. Then trajectory a illustrates the case of asymptotic stability. Trajectory b which neither returns to x_1^* and x_2^* nor wanders outside the boundary defined by the circle R is said to be stable, while trajectory c represents an unstable situation. If the system is stable for any displacement in some neighborhood of equilibrium it is said to be stable in the small, i.e., locally stable, and if it is stable for a disturbance of any magnitude from equilibrium the system is said to be stable in the large, i.e., globally stable.

The objectives of a dynamic control system may be to find time paths for the control variable(s) such that an unstable system is made stable or more stable in the sense that the length of time required to reach equilibrium after a given displacement is minimized. The three principal mathematical tools for the control of dynamic systems are the calculus of variations, Pontryagin's maximum principle, and dynamic programming.

The calculus of variations is concerned with finding values of the instrument or instruments such that a functional, usually expressed as an integral with respect to time, is maximized or minimized where the target variable and the policy instrument are related by one or more linear differential equations. The solution entails first obtaining the Euler equation, a necessary condition for an extremum, and then

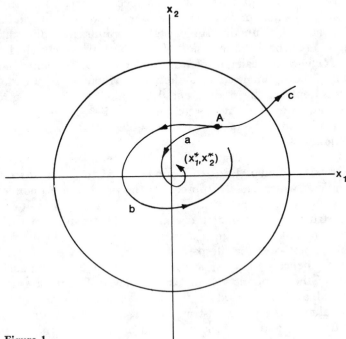

Figure 1.

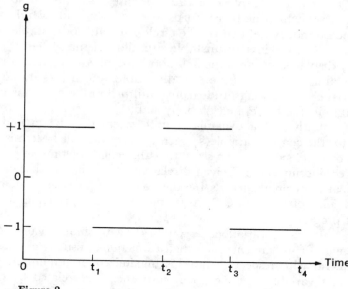

Figure 2.

finding a unique solution to the Euler equation so that the solution provides the desired value of the functional.

Pontryagin's maximum principle is a special extension of the calculus of variations and provides the necessary conditions for finding the extreme value of a function subject to constraints, including differential equations, where the inclusion of the constraints may yield corner solutions. Hence the calculus of variations may not be applicable. The function to be optimalized can often be written as an integral and sometimes replaced by a differential equation so that the problem becomes one of finding a value for the policy instrument which maximizes or minimizes the target variable subject to the system of differential equations.

Bellman's dynamic programming technique is similar to the other methods except that it leads to a model of a sequential *discrete* decision process which closely approaches the process of economic decision making in the real world. Instead of seeking the value of the policy instrument as a function of time as in the calculus of variations the decision maker seeks instructions as to what to do next at any particular point over the lifespan of the control process. The control mechanism hence consists of a multistage decision process such that the state of the economic system, e.g., the level of aggregate demand, is observed at some period of time; a decision is made about the desired value of the policy instrument based on this information and the control law; and the decision has an impact upon the system. As in the other approaches mentioned above, a policy which most effectively attains the desired goal or finds the extreme value of some functional is said to be optimal.

II. *Stability in a First-Order Model*

In this section we utilize Pontryagin's maximum principle in order to illustrate the theory of optimal control. The model is essentially that of Phillips [11], as represented by Allen [1], and may be written where y denotes real aggregate demand; c denotes the demand

$$y(t) = c(t) + g(t) \qquad (4)$$

$$c(t) = \alpha q(t) \qquad (5)$$

$$\dot{q} = \beta[y(t) - q(t)] \qquad (6)$$

for consumer goods; q is output and income; and g denotes autonomous or government expenditures. Equation (6) expresses the hypothesis that output adjusts smoothly and continuously to the difference between aggregate demand and output. If β equals unity, the adjustment is instantaneous; β less than one infers that the adjustment lags; and β greater than one implies that the system overcompensates for any deviation from equilibrium. Solving, we obtain the linear first-order differential equation

$$\dot{q} + \psi\beta = \beta g \qquad (7)$$

where $\psi = 1 - \alpha$, $0 < \psi < 1$, $\beta > 0$.

Taking q to be the target variable and g to be the policy instrument, which is assumed without loss of generality to take a value of zero when the system is in equilibrium at $q = 0$, we postulate that a shock is imposed on the system so that output is displaced from its equilibrium value by the amount $q(0)$. The solution to the homogeneous version of the system is then given by

$$q(t) = q(0)e^{-\psi t} \qquad (8)$$

so that output converges smoothly back toward zero over time. The optimal control problem is then to determine a time path for g in such a way that some cost functional is minimized. We assume that some cost is entailed in using the instrument g and consider two alternative approaches to the problem. The first method entails including g in the performance index, and the second method placed a constraint on the magnitude of g.

A. UNCONSTRAINED INSTRUMENT

Starting from equilibrium, we assume that there is a perturbation so that the initial condition is $q(0) = 1$. The other boundary condition is that output and income eventually fall to zero at some final time T, i.e.,

$$q(T) - 0 \text{ at } t = T \tag{9}$$

Suppose further that the performance index which is to be minimized is quadratic in q and g so that we have

$$S = \int_0^T (q^2 + g^2)dt \tag{10}$$

where no constraint is imposed on the size of g. According to the Pontryagin principle, the performance index must satisfy the differential equations

$$\dot{q} = f_0(q,g) = q^2 + g^2 \tag{11}$$

and

$$\dot{q} = f_1(q, g) = -\psi\beta q + \beta g \tag{12}$$

where q_0 is an adjoined state variable.

We next write the Hamiltonian, which is to be maximized, as

$$H = \lambda_0 f_0 + \lambda_1 f_1 = \lambda_0(q^2 + g^2) + \lambda_1(-\psi\beta q + \beta g) \tag{13}$$

where λ_0 and λ_1 are Lagrange multipliers.[4] Since, as Pontryagin has shown, $\lambda_0 = -1$ is a necessary condition to maximize H, the Hamiltonian can be rewritten

$$H = -(q^2 + g^2) + \lambda_1(-\psi\beta q + \beta g) \tag{14}$$

The first-order condition for H to be maximized is

$$\frac{\partial H}{\partial g} = -2g + \beta\lambda_1 = 0 \tag{15}$$

so that the Hamiltonian is maximized when

$$g = \frac{\beta\lambda_1}{2} \tag{16}$$

Thus, substituting for λ_1,

$$H_{max} = g^2 - q^2 - 2\psi qg \tag{17}$$

In order to put the control law into operation, we first solve for g in terms of output and time and hence must utilize the canonical equations

$$\dot{q} = \frac{\partial H}{\partial \lambda_1} = \psi\beta q + \beta g \tag{18}$$

and

$$\dot{\lambda}_1 = -\frac{\partial H}{\partial q} = 2q + \lambda_1\psi\beta \tag{19}$$

Substituting equation (16) into equation (19), we obtain

$$\dot{q} = -\psi\beta q + \beta g \tag{20}$$

and

$$\dot{g} = \beta q + \psi\beta g \tag{21}$$

which in matrix form is

$$\frac{d}{dt}\begin{pmatrix} q \\ g \end{pmatrix} = \begin{pmatrix} -\psi\beta & \beta \\ \beta & \psi\beta \end{pmatrix}\begin{pmatrix} q \\ g \end{pmatrix} \tag{22}$$

The characteristic roots of equation (22) are given by—

$$\phi_1 = \beta\sqrt{1+\psi^2} \quad \phi_2 = -\beta\sqrt{1+\psi^2} \tag{23}$$

so that the solution to the system is

$$q(t) = c_1 e^{\Phi_1 t} + c_2 e^{\Phi_2 t} \tag{24}$$

and

$$g(t) = c_1(\psi - \sqrt{1+\psi^2})\,e^{\Phi_1 t} + c_2(\psi - \sqrt{1+\psi^2})\,e^{\Phi_2 t} \tag{25}$$

The constants c_1 and c_2 are evaluated by the initial condition $q(0) = 1$, i.e.,

$$c_1 + c_2 = 1 \tag{26}$$

In order for the output to converge to 0, we select $c_1 = 0$ and $c_2 = 1$, obtaining

$$q(t) = e^{\Phi_2 t} = e^{-\beta\sqrt{1+\psi^2}t} \tag{27}$$

and

$$g(t) = (\psi - \sqrt{1+\psi^2})\,e^{\Phi_2 t}$$
$$= (\psi - \sqrt{1+\psi^2})\,e^{-\beta\sqrt{1+\psi^2}t} \tag{28}$$

Since T was not fixed, and in fact is equal to infinity, H should be maximized in the initial period with a value of zero, and substitution indicates that this is indeed the case.

Upon comparing equations (27) and (8), we note that the controlled system converges to equilibrium more rapidly than the uncontrolled system.

B. CONSTRAINED INSTRUMENT

We now consider the same model except that the instrument is dropped from the performance index and a constraint is placed upon the absolute magnitude of the policy variable. Hence the performance index becomes

$$S = \int_0^T q^2 dt \qquad (29)$$

where the instrument must satisfy the relation

$$|g| = 0, 1 \qquad (30)$$

Again utilizing an adjoined state variable, we must satisfy the two differential equations

$$\dot{q} = f_0(q) = q^2 \qquad (31)$$

and

$$\dot{q} = f_1(q, g) = -\psi g + \beta g \qquad (32)$$

The Hamiltonian for the system is

$$H = -q^2 - \lambda \beta q + \lambda_1 \beta g \qquad (33)$$

where λ_1 is once more a Lagrange multiplier. Examination of equation (33) reveals that H will be maximized wherever the sign of the policy instrument g is the same as that of λ_1 since $\psi \beta > 0$ and when the absolute value of its size is equal to the maximum, i.e.,

$$g(t) = F(\lambda_1) \qquad (34)$$

where

$$F(\lambda_1) = \left\{ \begin{array}{l} +1 \text{ if } \lambda_1 > 0 \\ \ \ 0 \text{ if } \lambda_1 = 0 \\ -1 \text{ if } \lambda_1 < 0 \end{array} \right. \qquad (35)$$

Hence g will have the value $+1$ over interval $[0, t_1]$, -1 over interval $[t_1, t_2]$, etc., as illustrated in Figure 2. Or the reverse may be true. This manner of treating the functional equation technique is referred to as "bang-bang" control.

In order to put the control into effect, we need the solution for $\lambda_1(t)$ and hence must derive the Hamiltonian canonical equations

$$\dot{q}_0 = \frac{\partial H}{\partial \lambda_0} = q^2 \qquad (36)$$

$$\dot{q} = \frac{\partial H}{\partial \lambda_1} = -\psi \beta q + \beta g \qquad (37)$$

and

$$\dot{\lambda}_1 = -\frac{\partial H}{\partial q} = 2q + \lambda_1 \psi \beta \qquad (38)$$

with boundary conditions

$$q_0(0) = 0, \ q(0) = 1, \ q(T) = 0, \ \lambda_1(T) = 0$$

so that $q(T) = 0$. Thus we have a two-point boundary problem with the non-linear differential equations

$$\dot{q} = -\psi\beta q + F(\lambda_1) \tag{39}$$

$$\dot{\lambda}_1 = 2q + \psi\beta\lambda_1 \tag{40}$$

and the two boundary conditions that $q(0) = 1$, $\lambda_1(T) = 0$.[5] While there is no general solution to the control law in terms of the level of output, the control rule itself can easily be found.

III. *Stability in a Second-Order Model*

In this section we utilize the calculus of variations to demonstrate the determination of an optimal control law in an economic model which can be expressed as a second-order linear differential equation. To the model of the previous section we add the hypothesis that firms attempt to bring inventories of consumer goods k up to some desired level k^* where k^* is a constant. Combining with equation (6), total output is given by

$$q(t) = [k^* - k(t)] + \frac{\beta}{D + \beta} y(t) \tag{41}$$

where $D = \dfrac{d}{dt}$. Finally, we add an investment-saving identity

$$\dot{k} = \psi q(t) \tag{42}$$

From equations (4), (5), (41), and (42) the reduced-form equation of the homogeneous system, i.e., without a control variable, becomes

$$\ddot{q} + \psi(1 + \beta)\dot{q} + \psi\beta q = 0 \tag{43}$$

with roots given by

$$\Phi_1, \Phi_2 = \frac{-\psi(1 + \beta) \pm [\psi^2(1 + \beta)^2 - 4\psi\beta]^{\frac{1}{2}}}{2}$$

The solution is then

$$q(t) = b_1 e^{\Phi_1 t} + b_2 e^{\Phi_2 t} \tag{44}$$

where b_1 and b_2 are arbitrary constants to be determined from the initial conditions. If $\psi > \dfrac{4\beta}{(1 + \beta)^2}$, the roots are real and negative so that $q(t)$ converges back toward zero after an initial displacement. On the other hand, if $\psi < \dfrac{4\beta}{(1 + \beta)^2}$, the roots are conjugate complex with negative real parts and are equal to $-\alpha + i\omega$ where

$$= \tfrac{1}{2}(1 + \beta)\psi > 0 = \tfrac{1}{2}(1 + \beta)\psi \left[\frac{4\lambda}{\psi(1 + \beta)^2}\right]^{\frac{1}{2}} > 0$$

for $\psi\beta > 0$. Hence q oscillates, one possible solution being

$$q(t) = be^{-\alpha t} \cos(\omega t - \epsilon) \tag{45}$$

where b and e are arbitrary. Inasmuch as $\alpha > 0$, the oscillation is damped with period $\dfrac{2\pi}{\omega}$. Moreover, the oscillation exists except when ψ is large and/or β is much lower or higher than unity. In any case, the length of time required to damp out an arbitrary disturbance might be significantly longer than that desired by policy makers.

Suppose that we first try a control mechanism obtained by setting g equal to some constant proportion θ of the time derivative of q, yielding the differential equation

$$\ddot{q} + \psi(1 + \beta)\dot{q} + \psi\beta q = \psi\theta\dot{q} \tag{46}$$

which, in turn, yields the characteristic equation

$$\Phi^2 + [\psi(1 + \beta) - \theta]\Phi + \psi\beta = 0 \tag{47}$$

By making $-\theta$ a large negative constant, we can make the damping rate as large as we wish. In equation (44), however, we now have $\alpha = \tfrac{1}{2}[(1 + \beta)\psi - \theta]$,

$$\omega = \tfrac{1}{2}[(1 + \beta) - \theta]\left[\frac{4\psi\beta}{\psi(1 + \beta) - \theta^2} - 1\right]^{\frac{1}{2}}$$

so that $q(t)$ is zero at time $t = \dfrac{\pi}{(1 + \beta)\psi - \theta}$ but its rate of change or time derivative at that point in time is

$$\dot{q} = -\alpha be^{-\pi} \tag{48}$$

Hence $|\dot{q}|$ can be very large if θ is large and negative.

Alternatively, we might try a control process of the type

$$\ddot{q} + \psi(1 + \beta)\dot{q} + \psi\beta\dot{q} = G(q, \dot{q}) \tag{49}$$

where $G(q, \dot{q})$ is chosen so that q and $\dot{q}$ converge toward zero at a reasonably rapid rate without violating the condition that neither $|q|$ nor $|\dot{q}|$ be too large. Hence we might try to determine some control function G such that the cost functional

$$\int_0^t (q^2 + \dot{q}^2)dt$$

is small.

Since $G(q, \dot{q})$ is a function of time, we can write

$$\ddot{q} + \psi(1 + \beta)\dot{q} + \psi\beta q = \delta(t) \qquad (50)$$

where $\delta(t) = \beta g(t)$ and then determine $\delta(t)$ by the condition that it minimizes the functional

$$\int_0^t (q^2 + \dot{q}^2)dt$$

Once $\delta(t)$ is determined, it can be described as a function of the state variables $q(t)$ and $\dot{q}(t)$, yielding the desired feedback law for $g(t)$.

Assuming that the functional is a Riemann integral and that q^2 is integrable over the interval from zero to T, it can be shown that the Euler equation for the functional is

$$\ddot{q} - q = 0$$

with boundary conditions $q(0) = 1$ and $\dot{q}(t) = 0$. The general solution of the differential equation is

$$q(t) = b_1 e^t + b_2 e^{-t} \qquad (51)$$

with the boundary conditions

$$b_1 + b_2 = 1, \quad b_1 e^T + b_2 e^{-T} = 0$$

The specific solution is

$$q(t) = b\,\frac{e^{t-1} + e^{-(t-T)}}{e^{-T} + e^T}$$

$$= \frac{be^{-t}}{1 + e^{2T}} + \frac{be^{t-2T}}{1 + e^{-2T}} \qquad (52)$$

It is then a simple matter to substitute back into equation (50) in order to find the optimalizing solution for $g(t)$ in terms of t, T, and the parameters of the model.[6] This was done, the solution being

$$g(t) = \frac{b(1 - \psi)}{\beta(1 + e^{-2T})}\,(e^{-t} + e^{t-2T}) \qquad (53)$$

In passing, we remark that imposing a constraint upon the absolute magnitude of g may again result in a "bang-bang" type of control. Moreover, it should be noted that the inclusion of $\dot{q}$ in the cost functional virtually eliminates the possibility of the system's retaining an oscillation, although this result is not costless since the required absolute value of the instrument is frequently large relative to the magnitude of the target variable.

IV. *Dynamic Programming*

The control processes described in the previous sections are called single-stage processes inasmuch as each required only a single decision on the part of the policy maker. Hence the optimal path of the system is obtained by following a predetermined control rule, the difficulty with this type of approach being that random shocks or changes in the parameters of the system may throw it off the optimal path.

Dynamic programming is a multi-stage decision process, in which we again seek to find an optimum control law as a function of the model's state variables. However, if the system is moved from its optimal path, dynamic programming seeks out a new optimal path rather than attempts to send the system back to the original path. The major difference between the methods discussed previously and the dynamic programming approach is that the former carry out the procedure only once whereas dynamic programming repeats the procedure at many discrete points in time and hence is an optimal control method which utilizes a closed-loop control system by permitting feedback into the control system itself.

As an example, we specify a simple dynamic Keynesian model with discrete time as follows:

$$y(t) = c(t) + i(t) \tag{54}$$

$$c(t) = \alpha y(t) \qquad 0 < \alpha < 1 \tag{55}$$

$$i(t) = \beta r(t-1) \qquad \beta < 0 \tag{56}$$

and

$$r(t) = \mu y(t) + \gamma m(t) \qquad \mu > 0, \gamma < 0 \tag{57}$$

where y again denotes aggregate demand; c is consumption expenditures; i denotes investment outlays; r denotes the interest rate; and m is the stock of money, which is designated as the policy instrument. Equation (57) is of course the familiar *LM* schedule, while the first three equations can be solved to derive the equation for the *IS* schedule, i.e.,

$$y(t) = \frac{\beta}{1-\alpha} r(t-1) \tag{58}$$

Combining the equations for the *IS* and *LM* schedules yields the reduced-form equation for the target variable y

$$y(t+1) = \frac{\beta\mu}{1-\alpha} y(t) + \frac{\beta\gamma}{1-\alpha} m(t) \tag{59}$$

where the dates have been moved up one period. In general, the solution to the homogeneous version of the model, i.e., with $m = 0$, is

$$y(t) = \left(\frac{\beta\mu}{1 - \alpha}\right)^t y(0) \tag{60}$$

and will of course be zero in equilibrium.[7] Since the single root, according to the signs specified for the parameters, is negative, the system oscillates.[8] There are two possibilities. First, if $\left|\dfrac{1 - \alpha}{\beta\mu}\right| < 1$, the state variable converges toward its equilibrium value; second, if $\left|\dfrac{\beta\mu}{1 - \alpha}\right| > 1$, we have a divergent oscillation. Hence a necessary and sufficient condition for stability is that the absolute value of the *LM* schedule's slope be less than that of the *IS* schedule.

Suppose now that we wish to minimize the performance index

$$S = \sum_{t=0}^{T-1} [y(t)^2 + m(t)^2] + y(T)^2 \tag{61}$$

for a process encompassing T periods of time or stages. Since the control system is discontinued in period T, $m(T) = 0$ and $y(T)^2$ is the cost of terminating the control. If $T = \infty$, $y(T) = 0$ and the last term can be dropped from S. Since we wish to minimize S, we have

$$f_T[y(0)] = [S(0) + f_{T-1} \frac{\beta\mu}{1 - \alpha} y(0) + \frac{\beta\gamma}{1 - \alpha} m(0)] \tag{62}$$

where $S(0) = y(0)^2 + m(0)^2$ and which we wish to minimize with respect to $m(0)$ for $T = 1, 2, 3, \ldots$ In general, the optimal control sequence can be found by beginning from the final period and working backwards. Let $\dfrac{\beta\mu}{1 - \alpha} = a$ and let $\dfrac{\beta\gamma}{1 - \alpha} = b$. Then equation (62) can be rewritten for the final time period as

$$\begin{aligned}
f_1[y(T - 1)] &= \min \{[y(T - 1)^2 \\
&\quad + m(T - 1)^2] + f_T[a(T - 1) + bm(T - 1)]\} \\
&= \min \{[y(T - 1)^2 + m(T - 1)^2] + f_T[y(T)]\} \\
&= \min \{[y(T - 1)^2 + m(T - 1)^2] \\
&\qquad\qquad + [ay(T - 1) + bm(T - 1)]^2\} \tag{63}
\end{aligned}$$

In order to find a minimum, we set the derivative of equation (63) with respect to $m(T - 1)$ equal to zero, i.e.,

$$2m(T - 1) + aby(T - 1) + 2b^2m(T - 1) = 0 \tag{64}$$

so that the optimum control law for the final period is

$$m(T - 1) = - \frac{ab}{2(1 + b)} y(T - 1) \qquad (65)$$

substituting

$$m(T - 1) = - \frac{\beta^2 \mu \gamma}{2(1 - \alpha)^2 \left[1 + \left(\frac{\beta \gamma}{1 - \alpha} \right)^2 \right]} y(t) \qquad (66)$$

Inasmuch as the model is linear in time, the optimum control rule is invariant with respect to time so that it can be generalized to

$$m(t) = - \frac{\beta^2 \mu \gamma}{2(1 - \alpha)^2 \left[1 + \left(\frac{\beta \gamma}{1 - \alpha} \right)^2 \right]} y(t) \qquad (67)$$

Contrary to what might be expected, the control mechanism does not have a built-in negative feedback. That is, the optimal money supply will be greater than zero when aggregate demand is positive and less than zero when aggregate demand is negative. This is due to the lag in the effectiveness of monetary policy. Moreover, it should be emphasized that the control law, like those of the previous sections, is not designed to ensure perfect stability. Even though perfect stability might be possible in some models, the cost of implementing the control might make it prohibitive. For example, complete stability of the target variable might be attainable only at the expense of a control rule which would necessitate an explosive oscillation in the policy instrument.

In order to demonstrate the dynamic programming control obtained above and some of the attendant difficulties, a pair of numerical examples may prove illuminating. The first example results in a convergent oscillation, and the second results in a divergent oscillation. For the first case we assume the values of the coefficients to be $\alpha = 0.8$, $\beta = -0.5$, $\mu = 0.32$, and $\gamma = -0.2$. Substituting these magnitudes in the reduced-form equation and the equation for the optimum control rule yields

$$y(t) = -0.8y(t - 1) + 0.5m(t - 1)$$

and

$$m(t) = -0.16y(t)$$

respectively. The results for twelve periods are shown in Table 1 where we assume that $y(0) = 0$ and $m(0) = 0$ and that an exogenous shock in the next period increases aggregate demand to $y(1) = 1$, at which point the control rule is put into operation. The first column provides the time period; the second column traces out the time path of aggregate demand in the lack of any control rule; the third column traces

TABLE 1 Control by Dynamic Programming in a Stable Model[a]

| WITHOUT CONTROL | | WITH CONTROL | | | |
| | | *m In Functional* | | *m Not In Functional* | |
Period	*y*	*y*	*m*	*y*	*m*
0	0.0000	0.0000	0.0000	0.0000	0.0000
1	1.0000	1.0000	0.1600	1.0000	0.8000
2	−0.8000	−0.7200	−0.1152	−0.4000	−0.3200
3	0.6400	0.5184	0.0829	0.1600	0.1280
4	−0.5120	−0.4562	−0.0730	−0.0960	−0.0768
5	0.4096	0.4015	0.0642	0.0576	0.0461
6	−0.3276	−0.3533	−0.0565	−0.0230	−0.0184
7	0.2620	0.3108	0.0497	0.0092	0.0074
8	−0.2096	−0.2634	−0.0421	−0.0037	−0.0030
9	0.1677	0.2317	0.0371	0.0015	0.0012
10	−0.1341	−0.2039	−0.0326	−0.0006	−0.0005
11	0.1073	0.1794	0.0287	0.0003	0.0002
12	−0.0858	−0.1579	−0.0253	−0.0001	−0.0001

[a] All numbers are rounded to four decimal places.

out aggregate demand with the optimum control rule in operation; and the fourth column gives the values of the money supply as determined by the control rule. The fifth and sixth columns repeat the procedure for the case in which the control variable is assumed to have zero cost and is hence left out of the performance index, yielding a control rule of

$$m(t) = 0.80y(t).$$

For the situation in which m is included as a cost in the performance index, the use of the control rule appears to reduce the amount of stability in the system after the first few periods. Moreover, y converges toward its equilibrium value of zero much more slowly when the control is being utilized. On the other hand, if the costs of utilizing the control variable m are ignored in the cost functional, the system converges toward equilibrium quite rapidly.

The results for an unstable system are shown in Table 2. The values assumed for the parameters are $\alpha = 0.8$, $\beta = -0.5$, $\mu = 0.44$, and $\gamma = -0.2$. When m is included in the performance index, the reduced-form and optimal control equations are

$$y(t) = -1.1y(t-1) + 0.50m(t-1)$$
and
$$m(t) = 0.22y(t)$$

respectively.

TABLE 2   Control by Dynamic Programming in an Unstable Model[a]

		WITH CONTROL			
WITHOUT CONTROL		m In Functional		m Not In Functional	
Period	y	y	m	y	m
0	0.0000	0.0000	0.0000	0.0000	0.0000
1	1.0000	1.0000	0.2000	1.0000	1.1000
2	−1.1000	−1.0000	−0.2000	−0.5500	−0.6050
3	1.2100	1.0000	0.2000	0.3025	0.3327
4	−1.3310	−1.0000	−0.2000	−0.1663	−0.1829
5	1.4641	1.0000	0.2000	0.0915	0.1006
6	−1.6105	−1.0000	−0.2000	−0.0503	−0.0553
7	1.7716	1.0000	0.2000	0.0277	0.0305
8	−1.9488	−1.0000	−0.2000	−0.0152	−0.0167
9	2.1437	1.0000	0.2000	0.0084	0.0092
10	−2.3581	−1.0000	−0.2000	−0.0046	−0.0051
11	2.5939	1.0000	0.2000	0.0025	0.0028
12	−2.8533	−1.0000	−0.2000	−0.0014	−0.0015

[a] All numbers are rounded to four decimal places.

If the policy instrument is excluded from the performance index, the control equation becomes

$$m(t) = 1.10y(t).$$

Without any control mechanism, the system diverges quite rapidly from the equilibrium after the initial displacement. The utilization of the more conservative control rule provides a happier result than in the previous example. While aggregate demand does not converge toward equilibrium, neither does it explode away from equilibrium any longer. Moreover, when the control cost variable is dropped from the performance index, the system converges to equilibrium very rapidly.

We may draw two conclusions from the above. In the first place, complete stability in the Phillips' sense of the system's being strictly maintained on an equilibrium path over time may be extremely difficult if not impossible, even when the model is relatively simple, correctly specified, and not subject to uncertainty in that the parameters are known and stochastic terms are absent. In the second place, even if it were obtainable, perfect stability might not be optimum in that the cost of control might well be prohibitive. Optimum control rules are dependent upon the specification of the cost functional which is to be minimized, and the determination of the optimum function from the range of alternative possibilities might well get bogged down in a hopeless welfare muddle.

V. *Summary and Conclusions*

This paper has been concerned with the efficacy of some of the tools used in control processes with respect to short-run dynamic economic stability. We found that the behavior of the relatively simple models used in the previous sections was not necessarily exemplary, even after an optimal control mechanism was imposed upon the system. This result was partly due to the inadequacy of the control tool from the standpoint of maintaining perfect stability and partly due to the necessity of accounting for the costs entailed in supervising the model's behavior.

Three possible extensions of this type of model are apparent. The first relates to the obvious fact that it is probably desirable to control more than one economic variable and that more than one policy instrument is available. Moreover, it may be necessary to impose systems of restraints upon the variables. This type of problem can be handled with the aid of vector-matrix notation although practical limitations may be imposed by the availability of digital computer facilities.

The second possible extension is related to the deterministic nature of the models utilized in this paper. If we admit that measurement of the parameters may not be completely accurate or add disturbance terms to the equations, the type of analysis suggested here may be impractical. Unfortunately, stochastic programming has not yet reached the level of theoretical or computational sophistication required in other than the most elementary models.

Finally, it seems highly probable that any economic model will be subject to substantial specification errors. Consequently, sensitivity analysis of the effects of specification errors upon the efficiency of optimal control rules would be highly desirable.

NOTES

1. For example, see [13].
2. For general treatment of optimal control theory at varying levels of sophistication, see [3, 7, 9, 10]. Possibly the best source on the calculus of variations is [8], and the classic treatment of the maximum principle is in [12]. Dynamic programming is covered in [2, 4, 5, 6].
3. Alternatively, if x and u are sets of state and control variables, the system can be described with the aid of vector-matrix notation.
4. The Hamiltonian for the system

$$\dot{x}_i = f_i(x, \ u, \ t) \qquad i = 1, \ldots, n \qquad x_i(0) \equiv x^0$$

is defined as

$$H[x(t), \lambda(t), u(t)] = \sum_{i=1}^{n} \lambda_i(t) f_i(x, u, t)$$

Maximizing the Hamiltonian is equivalent to minimizing the performance index.

5. If we like, we may include the cost of policy changes, e.g., switching costs, in the functional.

6. For a whole class of related problems and their solutions, see [10: Chapter 1].

7. Any reader who is concerned about the equilibrium level of aggregate demand being zero can reassure himself by adding constant terms of any desired magnitude to the model's specification.

8. The oscillation arises as a consequence of the interaction between the money market and the goods market. For example, starting from equilibrium an increase in the money stock immediately lowers the interest rate, stimulating investment demand and hence total demand after a one period lag. However, the increase in demand for transactions balances drives the interest rate up reducing investment demand in the subsequent period.

REFERENCES

1. Allen, R. G. D., *Macro-Economic Theory* (New York, 1967).
2. Aris, R., *Discrete Dynamic Programming* (New York, 1964).
3. Athan, M., and P. Falb, *Optimal Controls* (New York, 1966).
4. Bellman, R. E., *Dynamic Programming* (Princeton, 1957).
5. Bellman, R. E., *Adaptive Control Processes: A Guided Tour* (Princeton, 1957).
6. Bellman, R. E., and S. Dreyfus, *Applied Dynamic Programming* (Princeton, 1962.)
7. Dorf, R., *Time-Domain Analysis and Design of Control Systems* (Reading, 1965).
8. Gel'fand, I. M., and S. V. Fomin, *Calculus of Variations* (Englewood Cliffs, 1963). Translated from the Russian by R. A. Silverman.
9. Hestenes, M. R., *Calculus of Variations and Optimal Control Theory* (New York, 1966).
10. Lee, E. B., and L. Markus, *Foundations of Optimal Control Theory* (New York, 1967).
11. Phillips, A. W., "Stabilization Policy in a Closed Economy," *Economic Journal*, 64: 290–323 (June 1954).
12. Pontryagin, L. S., V. G. Boltyanskii, R. V. Gamkrelidze, and E. F. Mischenko, *The Mathematical Theory of Optimal Control Processes* (New York, 1962).
13. Shell, K. (ed.), *Essays on the Theory of Optimal Economic Growth* (Cambridge, 1967).

24 Targets, Instruments, and Indicators of Monetary Policy

Benjamin M. Friedman   *Harvard University*

1. Introduction

Keeping one's eye on the ball is often an important precept, familiar in games of skill and games of chance alike. The making of monetary policy, an activity at which success involves both skill and chance, is no exception. For monetary policy, however, a recurring problem has been the difficulty of determining what is the real ball. Indeed, the problem is yet more serious. Monetary policymakers, even with the assistance of monetary economists, have often not known how to set about discovering what is the real ball.

Within the past decade economists have developed two approaches for trying to find the ball which monetary policy makers should watch. First, the literature of targets and indicators of monetary policy (e.g., Brunner [7], Brunner and Meltzer [8], Davis [12], Dewald [20], Hamburger [35], Hendershott [37], Hendershott and Horwich [38], Holbrook and Shapiro [41], Kaufman [46], Saving [57], Starleaf and Stephenson [60], and Zecher [65]) suggested watching not one but two balls simultaneously, suggested how both to characterize and to use these two balls, and attempted to identify the most likely candidates for each. More recently, the application of control methodologies to problems of monetary policy has attracted widespread attention (e.g.,

Reprinted from the *Journal of Monetary Economics*, Volume 1 (1975), 443–73. © North-Holland Publishing Company.

B. Friedman [25], Kareken [43], Kareken et al. [44], Parkin [48], Pindyck and Roberts [49], Poole [50, 51], and Shupp [58]); such applications have typically relied on the familiar structure of targets and instruments (alternatively called state and controller variables, respectively).

Because of the complex nature of the monetary policy process, however, the resulting literature has at times been somewhat confused. The relationship between the recent literature of target and instrument variables and the previous discussions of target and indicator variables, for example, has remained unclear. The distinction between targets as ultimate goals and targets as intermediate operating devices is straightforward enough, but how do instruments and indicators fit into the pattern? Can an instrument be an indicator? Can an intermediate operating target be an instrument?

Even within the recent control applications literature itself, apparent contradictions abound.[1] Is the stock of money a target (e.g., Federal Reserve Bank of Boston [24]) or an instrument (e.g., Federal Reserve Bank of Boston [23])? Should the policy planning framework treat income (or employment) as endogenous (e.g., Poole [50]) or exogenous (e.g., Pindyck and Roberts [49])? Must the central bank manipulate reserve management so as to exert indirect control over interest rates (e.g., Pindyck and Roberts [49]), or can it control interest rates directly (e.g., Kareken [43])? What is the true menu of available instruments?

The objects of this paper are, first, to set forth clearly the basic targets-and-instruments structure of the monetary policy control problem and, secondly, to explore the relationship between this targets-and-instruments structure and the targets-and-indicators discussions. As developed below, the basic targets-and-instruments structure provides a useful framework for defining and understanding the targets-and-indicators concepts.

Section 2 uses a static deterministic model to define the basic elements of the targets-and-instruments structure of the monetary policy control problem. Section 3 shows how the *instrument problem*, which is trivial in the context of the model of section 2, becomes nontrivial when that model is generalized to be stochastic. Section 4 briefly reviews some of the previous literature which has implicitly or explicitly treated the operation of monetary policy as a two-stage control process, showing that some of the confusions and apparent inconsistencies in this literature result from the two-stage representation itself—an approach which may be invalid under actually prevailing conditions. Section 5 uses the targets-and-instruments framework to analyze the *intermediate target problem* in its usual context of lags in the receipt of information about the policy targets themselves. This section first recasts the model of sections 2 and 3 to incorporate the major implications of such a data lag; it then illustrates the use of the money stock as an intermediate target variable, and compares this procedure with optimal operating procedures in the presence of information lags. Section 6 briefly shows that, although the intermediate target problem has typically been associated with data lags, structural lags in the effects of monetary policy may lead to the same considerations as those discussed at length in section 5. Section 7 shows that use of the targets-and-instruments framework renders the *indicator problem* a relatively unimportant aspect of monetary policy making. Section 8 briefly summarizes the paper's principal conclusions.

2. *Elementary Concepts*

Tinbergen's [64] conception of a policy problem in terms of targets and instruments provides a useful starting point for analyzing the structure of the monetary policy control problem. For a linear deterministic system, Tinbergen's expression of the reduced form is

$$\begin{bmatrix} \mathbf{y}_1 \\ \mathbf{y}_2 \end{bmatrix} = \Gamma \begin{bmatrix} \mathbf{x} \\ \mathbf{z} \end{bmatrix}, \tag{1}$$

where

$\mathbf{y}_1$ = a vector of values of endogenous variables which policy makers seek to control (*target* variables),

$\mathbf{y}_2$ = a vector of values of the remaining endogenous variables in the system (*irrelevant* variables),

$\mathbf{x}$ = a vector of values of exogenous variables subject to direct control by policymakers (*instrument* variables),

$\mathbf{z}$ = a vector of values of the remaining predetermined variables in the system, including any lagged values (*data* variables),

Γ = the reduced-form matrix of coefficients which describe the system's behavior.

A simple linear model of an economy with a goods-and-services market and a money market consists of Hicks' [39] "*IS*" relation

$$Y = a_1 r + \mathbf{a}' \mathbf{z}, \tag{2}$$

Hicks' "*LM*", or money demand, relation

$$M = b_1 Y + b_2 r + \mathbf{b}' \mathbf{z}, \tag{3}$$

and a money supply relation

$$M = c_1 R + c_2 r + \mathbf{c}' \mathbf{z}, \tag{4}$$

where

Y = income,
r = the nominal interest rate,
$\mathbf{z}$ = a vector of values of variables exogenous to the monetary policy process (including fiscal policy variables),
M = the money stock,
R = the stock of nonborrowed bank reserves.

The anticipated values of the scalar coefficients are a_1, $b_2 < 0$ and b_1, c_1, $c_2 > 0$; $\mathbf{a}$, $\mathbf{b}$ and $\mathbf{c}$ are vectors of coefficients applicable to all exogenous variables in $\mathbf{z}$, including zeroes for cases in which individual exogenous variables do not appear in individual structural equations.

This three-equation model is determined with any one of the four variables (Y, r, M, R) taken as exogenous.[2] In practice, central bank operations may exert control directly over the interest rate or over the stock of nonborrowed reserves.[3] Taking income as the endogenous variable which monetary policymakers seek to control, the choice of instrument variables leads to two alternative ways of fitting this model into Tinbergen's format.

Variable	"Rate" alternative	"Reserves" alternative
Y	target	target
r	instrument	irrelevant
M	irrelevant	irrelevant
R	irrelevant	instrument
$\mathbf{z}$	data	data

Either of these policy alternatives possesses a distinct reduced-form solution corresponding to eq. (1). For the "rate" alternative, the reduced-form is

$$\begin{bmatrix} Y \\ M \\ R \end{bmatrix} = \begin{bmatrix} \gamma_{11} & \gamma'_1 \\ \gamma_{21} & \gamma'_2 \\ \gamma_{31} & \gamma'_3 \end{bmatrix} \begin{bmatrix} r \\ \mathbf{z} \end{bmatrix}, \tag{5}$$

where

$$\gamma_{11} = a_1, \qquad \gamma_{21} = b_2 + b_1 a_1, \qquad \gamma_{31} = c_1^{-1}(b_1 a_1 + b_2 - c_2), \tag{6a}$$

$$\gamma_1 = \mathbf{a}, \qquad \gamma_2 = \mathbf{b} + b_1 \mathbf{a}, \qquad \gamma_3 = c_1^{-1}(b_1 \mathbf{a} + \mathbf{b} - \mathbf{c}). \tag{6b}$$

For the "reserves" alternative, the reduced form is

$$\begin{bmatrix} Y \\ M \\ r \end{bmatrix} = \begin{bmatrix} g_{11} & g'_1 \\ g_{21} & g'_2 \\ g_{31} & g'_3 \end{bmatrix} \begin{bmatrix} R \\ \mathbf{z} \end{bmatrix}, \tag{7}$$

where

$$g_{11} = (b_1a_1 + b_2 - c_2)^{-1}a_1c_1,$$
$$g_{21} = c_1 + (b_1a_1 + b_2 - c_2)^{-1}c_1c_2,$$
$$g_{31} = (b_1a_1 + b_2 - c_2)^{-1}c_1, \tag{8a}$$
$$\mathbf{g}_1 = \mathbf{a} - (b_1a_1 + b_2 - c_2)^{-1}a_1(b_1\mathbf{a} + \mathbf{b} - \mathbf{c}),$$
$$\mathbf{g}_2 = \mathbf{c} - (b_1a_1 + b_2 - c_2)^{-1}c_2(b_1\mathbf{a} + \mathbf{b} - \mathbf{c}),$$
$$\mathbf{g}_3 = (b_1a_1 + b_2 - c_2)^{-1}(b_1\mathbf{a} + \mathbf{b} - \mathbf{c}). \tag{8b}$$

In the context of the deterministic model, which one of these two operating alternatives the central bank chooses to follow makes no difference. For desired income value Y^* and known data values $\mathbf{z}^0$, the optimal value of the interest rate instrument under the "rate" alternative is

$$r^*|_r = \gamma_{11}^{-1}(Y^* - \gamma_1'\mathbf{z}^0) = a_1^{-1}Y^* - a_1^{-1}\mathbf{a}'\mathbf{z}^0, \tag{9}$$

and from eq. (5) the associated value of the stock of reserves is

$$R^*|_r = \gamma_{31}r^*|_r + \gamma_3'\mathbf{z}^0$$
$$= (a_1c_1)^{-1}(b_1a_1 + b_2 - c_2)Y^*$$
$$\qquad + (a_1c_1)^{-1}\{(c_2 - b_2)\mathbf{a} + a_1(\mathbf{b} + \mathbf{c})\}'\mathbf{z}^0. \tag{10}$$

Similarly, the optimal value of the stock of reserves under the "reserves" alternative is

$$R^*|_R = g_{11}^{-1}(Y^* - \mathbf{g}_1'\mathbf{z}^0)$$
$$= (a_1c_1)^{-1}(b_1a_1 + b_2 - c_2)Y^*$$
$$\qquad + (a_1c_1)^{-1}\{(c_2 - b_2)\mathbf{a} + a_1(\mathbf{b} + \mathbf{c})\}'\mathbf{z}^0, \tag{11}$$

and from eq. (7) the associated value of the interest rate is

$$r^*|_R = g_{31}R^*|_R + \mathbf{g}_3'\mathbf{z}^0 = a_1^{-1}Y^* - a_1^{-1}\mathbf{a}'\mathbf{z}^0. \tag{12}$$

Since $r^*|_r = r^*|_R$ and $R^*|_R = R^*|_r$, the central bank in fact carries out the same actions regardless of whether it operates in the first instance by controlling the interest rate or the stock of reserves.

3. *The Instrument Problem*

Within the context of the monetary policy control problem, the *instrument problem* is the choice of the variable(s) over which the central bank will exert direct control. For the four-variable, three-equation model developed in section 2, the instrument problem is the choice between the "rate" alternative with r exogenous and the "reserves" alternative with R exogenous.

For the deterministic model of eqs. (2)–(4), eqs. (9)–(12) indicate that the central bank's choice of instrument variables makes no real difference for either the policy actions which it takes or the results of these actions for the system's endogenous variables. If the model is stochastic, however, and if an object of monetary policy is to minimize the variance of income about the desired value Y^*, then the instrument problem is nontrivial.

Rewriting structural eqs. (2)–(4) to include additive disturbance terms yields

$$Y = a_1r + \mathbf{a}'\mathbf{z} + u_Y, \tag{2'}$$

$$M = b_1Y + b_2r + \mathbf{b}'\mathbf{z} + u_{MD}, \tag{3'}$$

$$M = c_1R + c_2r + \mathbf{c}'\mathbf{z} + u_{MS}. \tag{4'}$$

For the "rate" alternative, the reduced form of this stochastic system is

$$\begin{bmatrix} Y \\ M \\ R \end{bmatrix} = \begin{bmatrix} \gamma_{11} & \boldsymbol{\gamma}_1' \\ \gamma_{21} & \boldsymbol{\gamma}_2' \\ \gamma_{31} & \boldsymbol{\gamma}_3' \end{bmatrix} \begin{bmatrix} r \\ \mathbf{z} \end{bmatrix} + \begin{bmatrix} \epsilon_Y \\ \epsilon_M \\ \epsilon_R \end{bmatrix}, \tag{5'}$$

where the γ_{ij} and $\boldsymbol{\gamma}_i$ are as defined in eqs. (6) and

$$\epsilon_Y = u_Y, \quad \epsilon_M = u_{MD} + b_1u_Y, \quad \epsilon_R = c_1^{-1}(b_1u_Y + u_{MD} - u_{MS}). \tag{6'}$$

For the "reserves" alternative, the reduced form of the stochastic system is

$$\begin{bmatrix} Y \\ M \\ r \end{bmatrix} = \begin{bmatrix} g_{11} & \mathbf{g}_1' \\ g_{21} & \mathbf{g}_2' \\ g_{31} & \mathbf{g}_3' \end{bmatrix} \begin{bmatrix} R \\ \mathbf{z} \end{bmatrix} + \begin{bmatrix} e_Y \\ e_M \\ e_r \end{bmatrix}, \tag{7'}$$

where the g_{ij} and $\mathbf{g}_i$ are as defined in eqs. (8) and

$$e_Y = u_Y - (b_1a_1 + b_2 - c_2)^{-1}a_1(b_1u_Y + u_{MD} - u_{MS}),$$

$$e_M = u_{MS} - (b_1a_1 + b_2 - c_2)^{-1}c_2(b_1u_Y + u_{MD} - u_{MS}),$$

$$e_r = -(b_1a_1 + b_2 - c_2)^{-1}(b_1u_Y + u_{MD} - u_{MS}). \tag{8'}$$

The solution to the instrument problem emerges from the comparison of ϵ_Y and e_Y. If the structural disturbances (u_Y, u_{MD}, u_{MS}) each have zero mean, then

$$\mathrm{E}(\epsilon_Y) = \mathrm{E}(e_Y) = 0. \tag{13}$$

Hence the optimal instrument variable values under the "rate" and "reserves" alternatives—$r^*|_r$ and $R^*|_R$, respectively—will be certainty equivalents, identical to the values given by eqs. (9) and (11), and

$$\mathrm{E}(Y)|_r = \mathrm{E}(Y)|_R = Y^*. \tag{14}$$

If, in addition, the structural disturbances have respective nonzero variances $(\sigma_Y^2, \sigma_{MD}^2, \sigma_{MS}^2)$ and covariances $(\sigma_{Y,MD}, \sigma_{Y,MS}, \sigma_{MD,MS})$, then

$$E(Y - Y^*)^2|_r = E(\epsilon_Y)^2 = \sigma_Y^2, \tag{15}$$

and

$$E(Y - Y^*)^2|_R = E(e_Y)^2$$
$$= (b_1a_1 + b_2 - c_2)^{-2}\{(b_2 - c_2)^2\sigma_Y^2 + \sigma_{MD}^2 + \sigma_{MS}^2$$
$$-2(b_2 - c_2)\sigma_{Y,MD} + 2(b_2 - c_2)\sigma_{Y,MS} - 2\sigma_{MD,MS}\}. \tag{16}$$

The solution to the instrument problem is to choose the "rate" alternative if $E(\epsilon_Y)^2 < E(e_Y)^2$ and to choose the "reserves" alternative if $E(\epsilon_Y)^2 > E(e_Y)^2$. Hence the choice of instruments depends upon the coefficients of eqs. (2')–(4') and upon the joint distribution of the structural disturbance terms (u_Y, u_{MD}, u_{MS}).[4]

4. Levels of the Monetary Policy Control Problem

For several operational reasons, the current central bank approach to monetary policy planning is essentially a two-level, or two-stage, process.[5] A number of writers have applied control methodologies to monetary policy, and each has typically focused on only one of these two levels. The result has been some confusion in the literature, including a number of specific apparent contradictions, over the precise relationship among the economic variables which appear as targets and instruments in these formulations of the monetary policy control problem. In particular, within the framework of eqs. (2')–(4'), the interest rate, money stock and income variables all constitute distinct sources of confusion and apparent contradiction.

Clearing up this confusion should, in the first instance, facilitate understanding how the Federal Reserve System plans and implements open market policy, as well as understanding how the seemingly divergent elements of the monetary policy control literature relate to one another; to this end, the discussion of this section indicates the nature of the key inconsistencies involved. In addition, the clarification of these issues permits the more fundamental identification of the conditions required for the usual two-level approach to the monetary policy process to be valid and useful.

At the broadest macroeconomic level, Poole [50] has posed the alternative of monetary policy control of nominal income by means of direct control over either the interest rate or the money stock. Poole examined this question by using the *IS–LM* framework consisting of eqs. (2') and (3') above. This two-equation model, which does not include a reserves variable, is determined with any one of the three variables (Y, r, M) taken as exogenous. Again taking income as the endogenous variable which monetary policymakers seek to control, Poole's two alternatives are as follows.

Variable	"Rate" alternative	"Money" alternative
Y	target	target
r	instrument	irrelevant
M	irrelevant	instrument
z	data	data

This formulation of the monetary policy control problem, shown in panel (a) of fig. 1, is especially interesting because it not only indicates a pair of alternatives which policymakers have openly confronted (e.g., Federal Reserve Bank of Boston [23]) but also corresponds to familiar bodies of literature of empirical economics. As Poole has shown in an analysis similar to that of section 3, the choice between the two alternatives depends in general upon the coefficients of eqs. (2′) and (3′) and upon the joint distributions of the structural disturbance terms u_Y and u_{MD}. The consideration of the (dynamic) coefficients of eqs. (2′) and (3′) was the subject of the Andersen-Jordan [2] St. Louis equation and the subsequent literature,[6] as well as of investigations performed with complete macroeconometric models such as the FRB–MIT model (de Leeuw and Gramlich [16]). The comparison of u_Y and u_{MD} was the subject of the Friedman-Meiselman [30] CMC paper and the subsequent literature.[7]

In a more realistic sense than that of this broad macroeconomic approach, however, the money stock is not an exogenous variable in the strict sense required for the control problem. The Federal Reserve System cannot set the money stock directly but rather must affect it indirectly by influencing the actions of commercial banks and the deposit-holding public. The true instruments which it has available for this purpose are open market operations (i.e., purchases or sales of securities in the portfolio of the System Open Market Account), member bank reserve requirements, and the discount rate. If an analysis of eqs. (2′) and (3′) indicates that the "money" alternative is preferable to the "rate" alternative at the broad macroeconomic level, control of the money stock itself therefore constitutes a separate stage of the monetary policy process and hence a second control problem.

At this second, money market level, Pierce and Thomson (Federal Reserve Bank of Boston [24], pp. 115–136) have posed the alternative of control of the money stock by means of direct control over either the interest rate or the stock of nonborrowed reserves. They examined

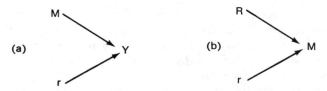

Figure 1. *Levels of the monetary policy control problem.*

this question by using a market-clearing model of the money market consisting of eqs. (3′) and (4′) above. This two-equation model is determined with any two of the four variables (Y, r, M, R) taken as exogenous. In formulating this second stage of the monetary policy control problem, Pierce and Thomson took the money stock as the endogenous variable which policymakers seek to control and assumed that, for purposes of short-term management of the money market, income is exogenous with respect to contemporaneous central bank actions. Their two alternatives, shown in panel (b) of fig. 1, are as follows.

Variable	"Rate" alternative	"Reserves" alternative
Y	data	data
r	instrument	irrelevant
M	target	target
R	irrelevant	instrument
z	data	data

Pierce and Thomson showed that the same analytical methods of section 3 which Poole used also apply to their formulation of this prior stage of the monetary policy control problem, and so the choice between the two alternatives depends upon the coefficients of eqs. (3′) and (4′) and upon disturbance terms u_{MD} and u_{MS}. Like Poole's formulation, this formulation of the problem also indicates a pair of alternatives which policymakers have actually confronted (e.g., Federal Reserve Bank of Boston [24]) and also corresponds to at least some nascent body of empirical work.[8]

As set forth by Poole and by Pierce and Thomson, these two formulations of the monetary policy control problem are distinct, referring to two possible stages of the policy planning process. For at least three reasons, however, there has been much confusion between the two formulations.

One source of confusion is that fact that "the interest rate" enters both formulations in approximately parallel ways. Some writers have distinguished between the two appearances of the interest rate by referring to the three-month Treasury bill or commercial paper rate in the *IS–LM* formulation and to the federal funds rate in the money market formulation, so that the relationship between the two is as in panel (a) of fig. 2. Such a distinction simply clouds the issue, however, since there is no a priori reason for preferring the federal funds rate to either the Treasury bill rate or the commercial paper rate in eqs. (3′) or (4′).[9] Hence fig. 3 is a more accurate representation of the relationship between these two formulations.

An example of this confusion caused by the presence of the interest rate in both formulations of the control problem is the set of experiments in which Pindyck and Roberts [49] used a monthly model of the money market to examine the relative controllability of the Treasury bill rate and the money stock. Their formulation of the monetary policy control problem, shown in panel (b) of fig. 2, supposed a symmetrical treatment of the Treasury bill rate and the money stock as alternative target variables, either of which might in turn be controlled alternatively by the federal funds rate or the stock of nonborrowed reserves. Despite the appeal of the symmetrical decision tree, this formulation is misleading. Since the Federal Reserve System Open Market Account has a portfolio of over $75 billion of U.S. Treasury securities (mostly short maturities) in comparison with only $39 billion of Treasury bills held by nonofficial investors,[10] it is unnecessary for the central bank to use some other variable, such as the federal funds rate or the stock of reserves, to control the Treasury bill rate indirectly. The Federal Reserve's willingness to buy or sell large amounts of bills at an appropriately narrow bid–ask spread is sufficient to determine the Treasury bill rate directly, within the relatively short time horizon employed by Pindyck and Roberts.

A second source of confusion in this two-stage representation of the monetary policy process is the role of the money stock as an instrument variable at the broad macroeconomic level and as a target variable at the money market level. Holbrook and Shapiro [41] and Parkin [48], for example, have posited the model shown in panel (c) of fig. 2, in which the target variable is income and three available instrument variables are the interest rate, the money stock, and the stock of reserves. This conception of the monetary policy control problem is internally inconsistent, however, since money and reserves are not instrument variables in the same sense. Reserves and the interest rate may be parallel variables in that both are subject to direct policy control, and money and the interest rate may be parallel variables with respect to their respective role in the *IS–LM* framework; but reserves and money are not parallel variables in a meaningful control sense.[11]

The contradiction implied by the two roles of the money stock in the two formulations shows clearly that the two stages of the mone-

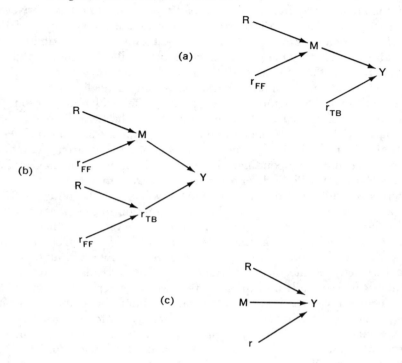

Figure 2. *Incorrect structures of the monetary policy control problem.*

tary policy process are in fact not totally independent in the presence of uncertainty. The solution to the problem of eqs. $(2')$ and $(3')$, based on the assumption that the money stock may be made exogenous, may indicate that the 'money' alternative is the better approach to controlling income. The solution to the problem of eqs. $(3')$ and $(4')$, however, will in general yield a nonzero variance of the endogenous money stock about any desired value M^*. If that variance is sufficiently large, allowing for it may render the "interest rate" alternative the better solution to the problem of eqs. $(2')$ and $(3')$ after all.

A potential third source of confusion in the two-stage formulation of the monetary policy process is the role of income as a target variable at the broad macroeconomic level and as a data variable at the money market level. In other words, income is endogenous with respect to events in the money market at the former level but exogenous with respect to the same events at the latter level. One trend in the literature to date has been to resolve this discrepancy by using different time units for examining the two stages of the problem, using a monthly, or even a weekly model at the money market level and the familiar quarterly model at the broad macroeconomic level.[12] Never-theless, there has been little research to evaluate the adequacy of this schizophrenic approach, which is at best only an approximation to reality. Although some models, such as the FRB–MIT model and the Wharton model (Evans and Klein [21]), may suggest that central bank actions in the money market have only a negligible impact on income in the contemporaneous quarter, the Andersen–Carlson [1] model indicates that a $1 billion addition to the money stock in any quarter yields a $1.22 billion addition to income in the same quarter.[13] If this increase in income occurs throughout the quarter, with per-sonal income correspondingly increasing, the monthly money market model used by Pindyck and Roberts indicates that the feedback in terms of additional demand for money will be of the order of $160 million, or about one-sixth of the initial addition to the money stock.[14] In short, the two-stage representation of the monetary policy process in fig. 3 is incomplete in that it lacks an arrow leading from Y to M.

Like the dual role of the money stock in these two formulations, the endogeneity of income with respect to central bank actions in the money market calls into question the two-stage representation of the monetary policy process. Under what conditions is it appropriate to separate the monetary policy control problem into a broad macro-economic level and a money market level, as is the custom in current central bank practice? As the discussion of this section indicates, at least two conditions are required to justify absolutely such a separa-tion, first, absolute controllability of the money stock within each time period and, secondly, a lag structure which renders income absolutely independent of contemporaneous central bank activity in the money market within each time period. It is unlikely that either condition holds absolutely in reality, and so the errors introduced by using the two-stage approach to monetary policy depend upon the degree to which the assumption of these two conditions may be a close approxi-mation to reality. The closeness of such approximations is itself not a logical question but a proper object of empirical research.

If these two assumptions are not at great variance with the true workings of the economic system, at least the qualitative choices of the "rate" or the "money" alternative at the broad macroeconomic level and the "rate" or the "reserves" alternative at the money market level will still be valid. The true optimal instrument variable values, how-ever, will still differ from the values yielded in the analysis based on the two-stage representation of the monetary policy process. If the two assumptions are further away from reality, then even the qualitative choices of "rate" or "money" and "rate" or "reserves" may be wrong; in this case the two-stage approach would be counterproductive, and policy analysis would do better to rely on a straightforward unified reduced-form framework such as that set forth in section 3.

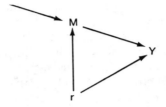

Figure 3. *Two-stage structure of the monetary policy control problem.*

5. *The Intermediate Target Problem*[15]

5.1. THE PROBLEM

A major issue, faced in one form or another during the past decade by central bankers, monetary economists, and financial market participants and observers, has been the role of intermediate operating targets of monetary policy. The targets-and-instruments framework developed in sections 2 and 3 provides a useful vehicle for analyzing the role of such intermediate target variables.

The *intermediate target problem* is the choice of a variable, usually a readily observable financial market price or quantity, which the central bank will treat for purposes of a short-run operating guide, as if it were the true ultimate target of monetary policy. The two-stage representation of the monetary policy control problem in fig. 3 shows clearly how such an intermediate target variable can fit into the planning and implementation of monetary policy; at the same time, it raises useful questions about why an intermediate target variable should play such a role.

Suppose, for example, that empirical and other research on the problem of eqs. (2') and (3') indicated that the "money" alternative is optimal for controlling income, and that similar research on the problem of eqs. (3') and (4') indicated that the "reserves" alternative is optimal for controlling the money stock. If the central bank were then to act, in one stage of the policy process, to manipulate the stock of reserves as if the money stock were the ultimate goal of policy, then the money stock would be playing the role of an intermediate target variable.

Several troublesome questions arise at this point. In light of the uncertain validity of the two-stage representation of the monetary policy process, discussed in section 4, would it be better simply to apply the target-and-instrument methodology based on reduced-form eq. (7') and ignore the irrelevant (in Tinbergen's sense) variable M? Similarly, if research on the problem of eqs. (3') and (4') indicated that the "rate" alternative is optimal for controlling the money stock, would it be better to apply the targets-and-instruments methodology based on reduced-form eq. (5′)? In terms of fig. 3, why is the roundabout policy procedure based on the intermediate target variable M preferable to simply following the conceptual arrow from r to Y? In short, what is the purpose of using the money stock (or any other variable) as an intermediate target variable?

Brunner and Meltzer (Brunner [7], p. 2) defined the intermediate target problem as ". . . the problem of choosing an optimal strategy or strategies to guide monetary policy under the conditions of uncertainty and lags in the receipt of information about the more remote goals of policy"; and subsequent writers have also cited both uncertainty and information lags as either necessary or sufficient conditions for the usefulness of an intermediate target variable.[16] The model used in section 3 is stochastic, but its one-period structure precludes the incorporation of information lags. Rewriting eq. (5′) by inserting a time subscript to emphasize that the single time period in question is one of a series of time periods, yields[17]

$$
\begin{bmatrix} Y_t \\ M_t \\ R_t \end{bmatrix} = \begin{bmatrix} \gamma_{11} & \gamma_1' \\ \gamma_{21} & \gamma_2' \\ \gamma_{31} & \gamma_3' \end{bmatrix} \begin{bmatrix} r_t \\ \mathbf{z}_t \end{bmatrix} + \begin{bmatrix} \epsilon_{Yt} \\ \epsilon_{Mt} \\ \epsilon_{Rt} \end{bmatrix}.
\tag{17}
$$

For simplicity, again let the objective of monetary policy be to minimize the expected variance of the target variable Y_t in each time period about the corresponding desired value of Y_t^*.[18] Given zero expectation for the structural disturbance terms (u_{Yt}, u_{MDt}, u_{MSt}) and therefore zero expectation for the reduced-form disturbance terms (ϵ_{Yt}, ϵ_{Mt}, ϵ_{Rt}), the optimal policy in the presence of additive uncertainty is the certainty equivalent

$$
r_t^* = \gamma_{11}^{-1}(Y_t^* - \gamma_1' \mathbf{z}_t),
\tag{18}
$$

and the resulting expectations of the three endogenous variables are

$$
\begin{aligned}
E(Y_t) &= \gamma_{11} r_t^* + \gamma_1' \mathbf{z}_t = Y_t^*, \\
E(M_t) &= \gamma_{21} r_t^* + \gamma_2' \mathbf{z}_t, \\
E(R_t) &= \gamma_{31} r_t^* + \gamma_3' \mathbf{z}_t.
\end{aligned}
\tag{19}
$$

If the model's structural disturbances are autocorrelated, i.e., if

$$
\begin{aligned}
u_{Yt} &= \rho_Y \cdot u_{Y,t-1} + v_{Yt}, \\
u_{MDt} &= \rho_{MD} \cdot u_{MD,t-1} + v_{MDt}, \\
u_{MSt} &= \rho_{MS} \cdot u_{MS,t-1} + v_{MSt},
\end{aligned}
\tag{20}
$$

where the ρ_i are nonzero, $-1 < \rho_i < 1$, and the v_{it} are serially uncorrelated variables with zero expectation and variances (s_Y^2, S_{MD}^2, s_{MS}^2) and covariances ($s_{Y,MD}$, $s_{Y,MS}$, $s_{MD,MS}$), then the reduced-form disturbances are also autocorrelated in a related way.

In particular, from eqs. (6′) and (20),

$$E(\epsilon_{Yt}) = \rho_Y \cdot u_{Y,t-1},$$
$$E(\epsilon_{Mt}) = \rho_{MD} \cdot u_{MD,t-1} + b_1 \rho_Y \cdot u_{Y,t-1},$$
$$E(\epsilon_{Rt}) = c_1^{-1}(b_1 \rho_Y \cdot u_{Y,t-1} + \rho_{MD} \cdot u_{MD,t-1} - \rho_{MS} \cdot u_{MS,t-1}). \quad (21)$$

Given observations of $(Y_{t-1}, M_{t-1}, R_{t-1})$ at the beginning of time period t, it would be straightforward to calculate the reduced-form disturbances $(\epsilon_{Y,t-1}, \epsilon_{M,t-1}, \epsilon_{R,t-1})$ as the differences between these observations and the corresponding expectations in the analogue of eq. (19) from the previous period. Knowledge of these reduced-form disturbances would, in turn, be sufficient to solve eqs. (6′) for the structural disturbances $(u_{Y,t-1}, u_{MD,t-1}, u_{MS,t-1})$. Then, given these structural disturbance values for the previous time period and the known autocorrelation parameters ρ_i, the "informed" expectation of the structural and reduced-form disturbances in period t would no longer necessarily be equal to zero. In particular, for the reduced-form disturbance ϵ_{Yt} which is crucial to the monetary policy decision for time period t, the "informed" expectation is[19]

$$E_t(\epsilon_{Yt}) = \rho_Y \cdot u_{Y,t-1}, \quad (22)$$

where the notation E_t makes explicit that the expectation in question is an "informed" expectation, conditional on all information known as of the beginning of time period t. The corresponding "informed" optimal policy for time period t would then be

$$r_t^{**} = \gamma_{11}^{-1}(Y_t^* - \gamma_1' z_t - E_t(\epsilon_{Yt})), \quad (23)$$

in contrast to the "uninformed" policy in eq. (18) based on the "uninformed" zero expectation of ϵ_{Yt}. In summary, the informed optimal policy r_t^{**} differs from the uninformed optimal policy r_t^* by an adjustment factor involving the informed expectation $E_t(\epsilon_{Yt})$,

$$r_t^{**} = r_t^* - \gamma_{11}^{-1} E_t(\epsilon_{Yt}). \quad (24)$$

5.2. THE INTERMEDIATE TARGET VARIABLE PROCEDURE

A simplified version of the assumption of an information lag, as is familiar in the literature of intermediate target variables, is to assume that, as of the beginning of time period t, the actual values M_{t-1} and R_{t-1} are known but the actual value Y_{t-1} remains unobserved. This lack of data for Y_{t-1} renders the simple approach of eqs. (22)–(24) infeasible. Under either the "rate" alternative or the "reserves" alternative, lack of knowledge about $\epsilon_{Y,t-1}$ or $e_{Y,t-1}$ renders knowledge of the structural disturbance terms $(u_{Y,t-1}, u_{MD,t-1}, u_{MS,t-1})$ via eqs. (6′) or (8′) impossible.[20] Hence any informed nonzero expectation $E_t(\epsilon_{Yt})$ must follow from the known reduced-form disturbances $(\epsilon_{M,t-1},\ \epsilon_{Rt-1})$. As the following analysis shows, use of the money stock as an intermediate target variable is equivalent to deriving the informed expectation $E_t(\epsilon_{Yt})$ in a particular way from the single known reduced-form disturbance $\epsilon_{M,t-1}$.[21]

The analytic role of an intermediate target variable, therefore, is to provide an effective rule for revising the a priori expectation $E(\epsilon_{Yt}) = 0$ into the (in general) nonzero informed expectation $E_t(\epsilon_{Yt})$. The autocorrelation ρ_Y is of no direct use to this purpose if data describing the recent history of Y are not available. In the presence of such data lags, the central bank may choose to act as if its target is some other variable for which recent data are in fact available.

The uninformed policy for time period t, based on the a priori expectation $E(\epsilon_{Yt}) = 0$, is $r_t{}^*$ in eq. (18), and the resulting expectation of the money stock in that period is

$$M_t^* = \gamma_{21}r_t^* + \gamma_2' \mathbf{z}_t. \tag{25}$$

In other words, M_t^* is the value of M_t which is consistent with the target value of Y_t^*, based on the uninformed expectation $E(\epsilon_{Mt}) = 0$. The essence of the use of the money stock as an intermediate target variable is that, with $\epsilon_{M,t-1}$ known, it is possible to derive an (in general nonzero) informed expectation $E_t(\epsilon_{Mt})$. If the central bank then acted as if its goal were to minimize the expected variance of M_t about M_t^* from eq. (25), its informed optimal policy in the context of the intermediate target approach would be

$$r_t^{**} = \gamma_{21}^{-1}(M_t^* - \gamma_2' \mathbf{z}_t - E_t(\epsilon_{Mt})). \tag{26}$$

Here the informed optimal policy differs from the uninformed optimal policy by an adjustment involving the informed expectation $E_t(\epsilon_{Mt})$,

$$r_t^{**} = r_t^* - \gamma_{21}^{-1} E_t(\epsilon_{Mt}). \tag{27}$$

How can the central bank derive this informed expectation $E_t(\epsilon_{Mt})$? It is clear from eqs. (6′) and (20) that, with full information available about $(Y_{t-1},\ M_{t-1},\ R_{t-1})$,

$$E_t(\epsilon_{Mt}) = \rho_{MD} \cdot u_{MD,t-1} + b_1\rho_Y \cdot u_{Y,t-1}, \tag{28}$$

but the lack of information about Y_{t-1} prevents using this approach, just as it prevents using the direct approach of eqs. (22)–(24). Instead, the central bank must rely upon the limited information which is available—in particular, the reduced-form disturbance $\epsilon_{Mt,-1}$. Again from eqs. (6') and (20), it is possible to write the variance and first-period autocovariance of the ϵ_{Mt} series, respectively, as

$$E(\epsilon_{Mt})^2 = s_{MD}^2 \left(\frac{1}{1 - \rho_{MD}^2}\right) + s_Y^2 \left(\frac{b_1^2}{1 - \rho_Y^2}\right) + s_{Y,MD} \left(\frac{2b_1}{1 - \rho_Y \rho_{MD}}\right),$$

$$E(\epsilon_{Mt} \cdot \epsilon_{M,t-1}) = s_{MD}^2 \left(\frac{\rho_{MD}}{1 - \rho_{MD}^2}\right) + s_Y^2 \left(\frac{b_1^2 \rho_Y}{1 - \rho_Y^2}\right)$$
$$+ s_{Y,MD} \left(\frac{2b_1(\rho_Y + \rho_{MD})}{1 - \rho_Y \rho_{MD}}\right). \quad (29)$$

Hence variance $E(\epsilon_{Mt})^2$ and autocovariance $E(\epsilon_{Mt} \cdot \epsilon_{M,t-1})$ are simply weighted averages of the variances s_{MD}^2 and s_Y^2 and covariance $s_{Y,MD}$, with the weights determined by the autocorrelation coefficients ρ_{MD} and ρ_Y and the coefficient b_1 from the underlying structural economic model. Following a "linear regression" procedure, the ratio of this variance and autocovariance permits deriving the informed expectation $E_t(\epsilon_{Mt})$, given the observed $\epsilon_{M,t-1}$, as

$$E_t(\epsilon_{Mt}) = m \cdot \epsilon_{M,t-1}, \quad (30)$$

and setting the informed optimal policy from eq. (27) as

$$r_t^{**} = r_t^* - \gamma_{21}^{-1} m \cdot \epsilon_{M,t-1}, \quad (31)$$

where

$$m = E(\epsilon_{Mt} \cdot \epsilon_{M,t-1})/E(\epsilon_{Mt})^2. \quad (32)$$

A comparison of eq. (24) and eq. (31) indicates that using the money stock as an intermediate target variable, in the absence of recent data on income, is equivalent to using the assumption

$$E_t(\epsilon_{Yt}) = \gamma_{21}^{-1} \gamma_{11} m \cdot \epsilon_{M,t-1} \quad (33)$$

to supply the informed expectation required for the application of eq. (24). The final two right-hand-side elements in eq. (33) simply state the informed expectation $E_t(\epsilon_{Mt})$; the first two right-hand-side elements in eq. (33) use the reduced-form model of eq. (5') to rotate this expectation from the M dimension to the Y dimension by way of the r dimension.

Using the money stock as an intermediate target variable in this way is therefore equivalent to the covariance assumption

$$E(\epsilon_{Yt} \cdot \epsilon_{M,t-1}) = \gamma_{21}^{-1} \gamma_{11} \left[s_{MD}^2 \left(\frac{\rho_{MD}}{1 - \rho_{MD}^2}\right) + s_Y^2 \left(\frac{b_1^2 \rho_Y}{1 - \rho_Y^2}\right) \right.$$
$$\left. + s_{Y,MD} \left(\frac{2b_1(\rho_Y + \rho_{MD})}{1 - \rho_Y \rho_{MD}}\right) \right]. \quad (34)$$

The true expression for this covariance, however, is easily derivable from eqs. (6′) and (20) as

$$E(\epsilon_{Yt} \cdot \epsilon_{M,t-1}) = s_{Y,MD}\left(\frac{\rho_Y}{1 - \rho_Y \rho_{MD}}\right) + s_Y^2\left(\frac{b_1\rho_Y}{1 - \rho_Y^2}\right). \quad (35)$$

The assumption stated in eq. (34) clearly differs from the true covariance, as stated in eq. (35). Rewriting the assumed covariance and the true covariance in terms of the parameters of the underlying structural system makes it even more convenient to consider the relevant differences between the two. The *covariance assumption implied by use of the money stock as an intermediate target variable is*

$$E(\epsilon_{Yt} \cdot \epsilon_{M,t-1}) = (b_2 + b_1a_1)^{-1}a_1[\rho_{MD} \cdot \sigma_{MD}^2 + b_1^2\rho_Y \cdot \sigma_Y^2$$
$$+ 2b_1(\rho_{MD} + \rho_Y) \cdot \sigma_{Y,MD}], \quad (36)$$

and the *true covariance* is

$$E(\epsilon_{Yt} \cdot \epsilon_{M,t-1}) = b_1\rho_Y \cdot \sigma_Y^2 + \rho_Y \cdot \sigma_{Y,MD}. \quad (37)$$

Comparison of the alternative covariance expressions in eqs. (36) and (37) shows clearly the importance of the assumption of a stable, interest-insensitive money demand function typically associated with proponents of the use of the money stock as an intermediate target variable. In the limit, stability of the money demand function implies $\sigma_{MD}^2 = \sigma_{Y,MD} = 0$. In the limit, interest insensitivity of the money demand function implies $b_2 = 0$. If the money demand function satisfies these two conditions, then both eq. (36) and eq. (37) identically reduce to a value of $b_1\rho_Y\sigma_Y^2$ for the covariance $E(\epsilon_{Yt}, \epsilon_{M,t-1})$. In the absence of these two conditions, the use of the money stock in the role of an intermediate target variable implies the assumption of a covariance $E(\epsilon_{Yt}, \epsilon_{M,t-1})$ which differs from the true covariance.

5.3. OPTIMAL PROCEDURE WITH INFORMATION LAGS

How, then, should the central bank set monetary policy under these conditions of information lags and serially correlated structural errors? Two distinct alternative procedures are apparent for determining the informed expectation $E_t(\epsilon_{Yt})$ required in eq. (23).

First, using the information contained in $\epsilon_{M,t-1}$, the central bank can apply the "linear regression" method of eqs. (30)–(32) but relying on the true covariance $E(\epsilon_{Yt}, \epsilon_{M,t-1})$ from eq. (35).[22] As is clear from eqs. (6′) and (20), however, the relationship between ϵ_{Yt} and $\epsilon_{M,t-1}$ is not in fact linear, and so this "linear regression" method will be misleading when $u_{MD,t-1}$ has dominated $\epsilon_{M,t-1}$.

Secondly, the central bank can ignore the potential information contained in $\epsilon_{M,t-1}$ and use eq. (20) directly to formulate the necessary informed expectation as

$$E_t(\epsilon_{Yt}) = \rho_Y^{T+1} \cdot u_{Y,t-T-1}, \tag{38}$$

where T is the length of the lag in the receipt of information about Y.

One way to evaluate these two alternative procedures is to compare the respective conditional variances of ϵ_{Yt} implied by each. This criterion is useful since, once the central bank uses any given expectation $E_t(\epsilon_{Yt})$ to set its policy instrument by eq. (23), the associated variance enters in a straightforward manner into the resulting variance of income $E_t(Y_t - Y_t^*)^2|_{r_t^{**}}$. If the central bank uses the procedure of eqs. (30)–(32) to derive $E_t(\epsilon_{Yt})$, then, under conditions appropriate to the multivariate normal distribution, the conditional variance of ϵ_{Yt} given $\epsilon_{M,t-1}$ is[23]

$$E_t[\epsilon_{Yt} - E_t(\epsilon_{Yt})]^2\big|_{\epsilon_{M,t-1}} = \sigma_Y^2 - \frac{(b_1\rho_Y \cdot \sigma_Y^2 + \rho_Y \cdot \sigma_{Y,MD})^2}{\sigma_{MD}^2 + b_1^2\sigma_Y^2 + 2b_1\sigma_{Y,MD}}. \tag{39}$$

If the central bank uses the procedure of eq. (38) to derive $E_t(\epsilon_{Yt})$, then the conditional variance of ϵ_{Yt} given $u_{Y,t-T-1}$ is

$$E_t[\epsilon_{Yt} - E_t(\epsilon_{Yt})]^2\big|_{u_{Y,t-T-1}} = \sigma_Y^2(1 - \rho_Y^2)\left(1 + \sum_{\tau=1}^{T-1} \rho_Y^{2\tau}\right). \tag{40}$$

As eqs. (39) and (40) show, both procedures yield conditional variances no larger than σ_Y^2, the variance associated with the uniformed expectation $E(\epsilon_{Yt}) = 0$. (In other words, the value of information, whether contained in $\epsilon_{M,t-1}$ or in $u_{Y,t-T-1}$, is never negative.) The conditional variance in eq. (39) is a fixed function of the parameters of the structural model and its disturbances, while the conditional variance in eq. (40) is positively related to the information lag T. Furthermore, the conditional variance in eq. (40) equals $\sigma_Y^2(1 - \rho_Y^2)$, or s_Y^2, if $T = 0$ (i.e., there is no information lag) and equals σ_Y^2 if $T = \infty$ (i.e., data on Y never become available). Given values of the relevant fixed parameters, therefore, there is some length of information lag, say T^*, such that the conditional variance in eq. (40) is greater/less than the conditional variance in eq. (39) as $T \gtrless T^*$. The length of the information lag on Y therefore determines whether the central bank should apply the procedure of eqs. (30)–(32) and (35), using the information in the previous period's value of the money stock, or the procedure of eq. (38), using the information in the most recent available observation on income itself.[24]

5.4. CONCLUDING REMARKS

In summary, even in the context of the simple model employed above for illustrative purposes, the use of a particular irrelevant (in

Tinbergen's sense) variable in the role of an intermediate target variable does not constitute optimal central bank operating procedure. In the example given here, use of the money stock as an information variable in the general "linear regression" form is superior to use of the money stock as an intermediate target variable, except under very restrictive conditions which render the two procedures identical; and use of the most recent available income data may itself be superior even to the former procedure.

Before leaving this subject, it is useful to consider several specific differences between reality and the restrictive assumptions made in the course of considering the simple four-variable model above. The central bank does indeed face questions such as those posed above, but it does so in a vastly more complex environment.

First, the actual world confronting the central bank contains many more than two irrelevant variables, and the appearance of unanticipated movements in any of them may provide useful information. Except for special cases either of zero covariance or of variables which are linear substitutes (as with ϵ_R and ϵ_M in the model above[25]), the central bank's optimal operating procedure would include the monitoring of all monetary and reserve aggregates and all interest rates, not to mention nonfinancial variables. The approach which Guttentag [34] has described, in which the central bank "looks at everything," is at least partly optimal. To operate optimally, the central bank not only should "look at everything" but should do so in the context of the information-generating procedures illustrated by eqs. (30)–(32) and (35).

Secondly, the simple model used above is explicitly nondynamic except for the autocorrelated error terms. Redefining vector $\mathbf{z}$ to include lagged values of the model's exogenous and jointly determined variables, and substituting higher-order autocorrelation processes in eq. (20), would render the model a more accurate description of actual fact. It is not the purpose of this paper to discuss specific problems involved in policy-making in a dynamic system; as is well known, future impacts of current policy actions render the decision problem significantly more complex. Nevertheless, it is important to be aware that more of past history is relevant to this problem than simply the most recent single set of observations.[26]

Thirdly, the use of income as the single policy target variable in the analysis above is clearly unrealistic. The familiar goals of monetary policy include macroeconomic objectives such as employment, economic growth, price stability and balance-of-payments equilibrium, as well as specifically financial objectives such as market stability. Given a set of preferences to facilitate evaluation of one such goal against another, generalizing the single variable Y in the analysis above to a vector of target variables is a straightforward extension of this analysis. Such a focus of monetary policy on a number of distinct target variables, however, would make the use of any single irrelevant variable as an intermediate target even less likely to be optimal than the analysis above indicates.

6. *Information Problems: Data Lags and Structural Lags*

The intermediate target variable problem, as discussed in section 5, is most familiar in the target-and-indicators literature (e.g., Brunner and Meltzer [8], Holbrook and Shapiro [41] and Saving [57]) in the context of lags in the receipt of data on the ultimate targets of monetary policy. National Income Accounts data, for example, which describe various key income and spending totals, become available only once per quarter; and, until almost two months have elapsed in the subsequent quarter, those data which are available are only preliminary estimates based on severely limited sampling procedures. In contrast, the inherent cohesiveness of financial markets and the active supervision of a number of federal regulatory agencies render financial variables much more readily observable. Data on interest rates are typically available immediately on a daily basis, with little problem of sampling error, and reasonably reliable weekly estimates of reserve and monetary aggregates are available with a lag of only several days.[27] As a result, the central bank may use observations of financial variables to gain information about its policy targets, as section 5 describes.

Nevertheless, the presence of data lags as such is not a necessary condition for the use of an intermediate target variable or the other information-oriented procedures described in section 5. The presence of structural lags, because of which the values of monetary policy instruments in one time period influence the values of monetary policy targets in subsequent periods, can lead to formally equivalent information problems which policy operating procedures must confront. The documentation of such structural lags has constituted a separate literature unto itself (e.g., Ando et al. [3], Cagan and Gandolphi [9], de Leeuw and Gramlich [17], M. Friedman [28], M. Friedman and Schwartz [32], Hamburger [36], Modigliani et al. [47], and Rasche [54], and several writers have followed M. Friedman [27, 28, 29], in stressing the significance of these lags for monetary policy.[28]

In the data lag case, the central bank needs an informed expectation of the reduced-form income disturbance in the current time period, $E_t(\epsilon_{Yt})$, to use in setting the value of its instrument variable in that period. In the structural lag case, the value of the instrument variable in the current period will influence income (or other targets) several periods in the future, say Y_{t+T}, and so the central bank needs an informed expectation $E_t(\epsilon_{Y,t+T})$ to use in determining policy for the current period.[29] Even if the value of Y_{t-1} is known, therefore, given a structural lag the best that the central bank can do without relying on observations of irrelevant variables is to follow the analogue of eq. (38), i.e.,

$$E_t(\epsilon_{Y,t+T}) = \rho_Y^{T+1} \cdot u_{Y,t-1}. \tag{41}$$

The right-hand-side of eq. (40) then gives the conditional variance of $\epsilon_{Y,t+T}$ given $u_{Y,t-1}$.

As in the data lag case, the central bank may be able to do better —i.e., to achieve a smaller conditional variance of $\epsilon_{Y,t+T}$—by taking account of the information in the most recent values of the appropriate irrelevant variables. The parameters of the dynamic structural model, together with the autocorrelation structure of that model's disturbances, will imply an information procedure analogous to that of eqs. (30)–(32). Just as the length of the data lag determines which of the conditional variances in eqs. (39) and (40) is smaller given values of the other parameters involved, the length of the structural lag will similarly determine which of the two analogous procedures is superior.

7. *The Indicator Problem*

The concept of an indicator of monetary policy—defined so as not to be identical with targets or instruments or intermediate targets, all in the senses applied above—is one of the more elusive ideas of recent monetary economics.[30] This confusion remains, despite the voluminous literature devoted to the indicator question during the past decade.

Brunner and Meltzer (Brunner [7], p. 2) defined the *indicator problem* as ". . . the problem of constructing a scale that is invariant up to a monotone transformation and that provides a logical foundation for statements comparing the thrust of monetary policy"; elsewhere (Brunner and Meltzer [8], p. 187) they said that the monetary policy indicator, in their sense of the term, ". . . summarizes in an index the relative degree of monetary ease or restraint." The clearest application of this indicator variable concept is the case in which the central bank seeks to control one target variable (say, Y as above) and has several instrument variables at its disposal for doing so. As in the analysis above, a reduced-form equation relates variable Y to the monetary policy instrument variables, as well as to all other exogenous and lagged endogenous variables in the system. The Brunner–Meltzer monetary policy indicator is then a weighted index of all the monetary policy instrument variables, with each variable's weight equal (or proportional) to its coefficient in the reduced-form equation for variable Y.

Several problems emerge immediately, however, upon any attempt to apply this indicator index concept to a generalized monetary policy framework.

First, such an index ignores any exogenous factors, other than monetary policy, which may influence the target variable. At some levels this direct focus of the indicator index is useful; if the central bank shifts policy in an expansionary way so as to offset the expected effects of a new contractionary fiscal policy, it is useful to be able to say that monetary policy has become expansionary, even if the expected final outcome for target variable Y remains unchanged. At other levels, however, this direct focus becomes misleading. If the central bank uses only one instrument variable, as in the analysis of sections 3–5, the Brunner–Meltzer indicator index is simply a linear transformation of the instrument variable itself. A realistic view of the monetary policy process may argue that the true instrument variable involved in open market operations is the stock of securities in the portfolio of the System Open Market Account, yet it is not very useful to have an indicator index which records monetary policy as being expansionary if the central bank sells securities because of some movement of float, Treasury deposits in Federal Reserve Banks, or the gold stock. Indeed, the basic principle underlying Roosa's [55] delineation of "dynamic" and "defensive" open market operations is that it is useful to be able to talk about monetary policy in a way which abstracts from—i.e., which makes allowance for—certain nonpolicy exogenous influences.

While it is probably clear that a good indicator of the 'thrust' of monetary policy should abstract from offsetting float but should not abstract from offsetting fiscal policy, these two examples represent the extremes of the category of exogenous influences. The actual list of such exogenous influences, equivalent to vector z in the model used in sections 2–5, includes a number of factors, such as financial market events, which lie between these two extremes. Drawing the line between those exogenous factors from which the indicator should abstract and those from which it should not is a necessary step in deriving a Brunner–Meltzer indicator index; and any such index depends fundamentally upon the particular line drawn. The problem is that the actual "thrust" of a monetary policy instrument variable typically proceeds toward the target variable by a transmission process which successively incorporates a number of exogenous and endogenous influences, and the choice of indicator variable is in part a choice of the particular point of that process at which the "thrust" is to be measured.

Secondly, nonlinear economic relationships lead to particular difficulties in defining a Brunner–Meltzer indicator index.[31] If the structure of the system is nonlinear, the system has no reduced form comparable to eqs. (5') or (7') above. In particular, in a nonlinear system the derivatives of Y with respect to the monetary policy instrument variables, which would be the coefficients of these variables in the reduced-form equation for Y if it did exist, are not constant but instead depend on the value of all the variables in the system. Since these derivatives are the weights of the monetary policy instrument variables in the Brunner–Meltzer indicator index, the composition of the index is not invariant but depends on the values of all variables in the system.[32]

Thirdly, as Chase [10] has noted, the Brunner–Meltzer indicator index, constructed as described above, has the intended meaning only in the context of a policy framework with a unique target variable.[33] If in the context of an expanded model the central bank sought, for example, to maximize income Y while minimizing price inflation ΔP, then there would be two relevant reduced-form equations—one for Y and one for ΔP. Any given monetary policy instrument variable would enter both of these reduced-form equations, but with different coefficients in each. What would be the weights of the instrument variables in the indicator index in this case? Brunner and Meltzer suggested solving this problem by, first, computing two individual sub-indicator indices by the usual procedure of weighting each instrument variable by its derivative (coefficient) in the respective reduced-form equations for Y and ΔP and, secondly, computing the overall indicator index by weighting each such subindicator by the respective derivatives of Y and ΔP in the central bank's preference function.

Wholly apart from any difficulties which may be involved in identifying the central bank's preference function, this overall indicator index for the two-variable case fails to meet its intended purpose for several related reasons. Even if the economic relationships in the system are linear, use of a nonlinear preference function would render the weighting of the overall indicator index dependent on the values of variables Y and ΔP. Perhaps more importantly, such an overall indicator index, weighted by the preference function derivatives with respect to variables Y and ΔP, could not support even ordinal inferences about monetary policy associated with concepts such as "easy–tight," "expansionary–contractionary" or "inflationary–deflationary."[34] Given its construction as suggested by Brunner and Meltzer, this overall indicator index could only support inferences associated with concepts such as "good–bad" or "appropriate–inappropriate."

Especially since all of these problems plague an attempted identification of a monetary policy indicator, it is appropriate to confront the basic question of whether having such an indicator is necessary or useful at all. The answer probably depends upon whom the indicator is presumed to serve.

The central bank itself is unlikely to find a monetary policy indicator useful. Sections 2–5 outline a targets-and-instruments conceptual framework for monetary policy decision-making in the presence of additive uncertainty.[35] Use of such a framework by the central bank would require no specific indicator of monetary policy in the sense used here. The central bank must work through the various steps of the decision-making procedure, including the selection of instrument variables and the potential use of irrelevant variables for information purposes. Once having done so, the central bank has no need of a specific monetary policy indicator index.[36]

Market participants typically have their own reasons for wanting to know what actions the central bank is taking and what effects these actions are likely to have. These reasons are usually quite specific, however, and they therefore make the identification of the appropriate indicator a less ambiguous undertaking. In particular, a market participant's reasons for wanting an indicator of the "thrust" of monetary policy typically define the point at which that "thrust" should be measured. A market-maker in six-month Treasury bills, for example, is less directly interested in the likely implications of open market operations for income and price inflation than in the likely implications of these operations for the path of the six-month Treasury bill yield. His optimal monetary policy indicator, therefore, is the set of dynamic expected values of this yield which emerge as irrelevant variables in application of the targets-and-instruments framework outlined above. As is the case for the central bank, no simple shortcut can take the place of working through the steps of the analysis.

Finally, a broad range of observers want to monitor monetary policy for less specific reasons, ranging from political concern to intellectual curiosity. Many persons in this category lack the necessary time or tools for examining the several conceptual steps of the policy-making framework outlined above. Some indicator index of the "thrust" of monetary policy would probably be a useful summary tool for this group. The purpose of this paper is not to derive such a convenient index for popular usage but rather to point out that, should such a device be constructed, it has no significant role to play in the central bank's formulation of monetary policy.

8. Conclusions

Relying on a targets-and-instruments formulation of the monetary policy problem, this paper first clarifies certain confusions and inconsistencies which have plagued several attempts to apply control methodologies to monetary policy. Again using the targets-and-instruments structure, it then analyzes the basic issues involved in previous discussions of monetary policy in terms of a targets-and-indicators conception; much of the targets-and-indicators literature has itself been somewhat confused, if not at times positively opaque. In both efforts the target-and-instruments analytical device makes it possible to identify the key issues involved and to understand the source of previous problems.

In particular, the results of the analysis of this paper support the following five specific conclusions.

(1) As Poole and others have shown, the instrument problem is nontrivial in the presence of uncertainty and merits the serious attention of monetary policy makers.

(2) The two-stage conception of the monetary policy process, which is familiar both in the recent monetary economics literature and in the Federal Reserve System's own descriptions of its operating procedures, contains several internal inconsistencies. Furthermore, given a targets-and-instruments policy planning framework as outlined here, this two-stage conception does not contribute to the efficiency of monetary policy-making. In its planning, therefore, the central bank would do better to abandon this two-stage conception and simply apply the target-and-instruments framework directly to the monetary policy problem as a whole.

(3) Use of a specific noninstrument variable (such as the money stock) as an intermediate target variable does not in general constitute optimal central bank operating procedure. An alternative procedure for using irrelevant (in Tinbergen's sense) variables to gain information is always superior to the intermediate target variable procedure, except under very restrictive conditions which render the two procedures identical. In its operations, therefore, the central bank should "look at everything" in a particular way which yields the maximum useful information and should avoid relying on a particular intermediate target variable.

(4) Contrary to the impression given by some of the previous literature, this problem of information may arise not only in the context of lags in the receipt of data but also in the context of a structural lag by which monetary policy actions affect the ultimate targets of policy. Improvements in facilities for reporting data on policy targets will be useful for monetary policy but will not eliminate the need to use other variables for information purposes.

(5) The concept of an indicator of monetary policy is beset with ambiguities, but this intellectually unfortunate situation presents no problem for monetary policymakers. While some observers outside the central bank might find such an indicator useful if the conceptual ambiguities were resolved, the indicator would not contribute to the efficiency of monetary policy-making.

NOTES

1. The literature of targets and indicators also has its unclear aspects, but it is not the purpose of this paper to rehash them yet again; the references cited above are sufficient.

2. It is possible to preserve the endogeneity of all four of these variables and to render the model determined by adding another constraint. One example of such an additional constraint is a rule requiring that r and R bear some fixed relation to one another (see, e.g., Poole [50, 51] and Parkin [48]; Brainard [6] also discussed the use of a "package" consisting of constrained joint movements of multiple instruments). Another example is a feedback rule relating movements of either r or R directly to income or other endogenous variables of the system.

3. The ability of the central bank to set the nominal interest rate implicitly reflects the focus of the control applications literature on relatively short-run stabilization policy. It also probably indicates an assumption that "the interest rate" is the yield on a short-maturity debt instrument, although opinions differ on the central bank's ability to influence yields on long-maturity assets. In a more general model it would be useful to distinguish between the role of the short-term interest rate in eqs. (3) and (4) and that of the long-term interest rate in eq. 2; the resulting five-variable model would then require an additional constraint, such as a "term-structure" equation relating the values of the two interest rate variables.

4. This treatment is not fully general for several reasons. First, it admits additive uncertainty only, i.e., it assumes that the coefficients of eqs. $(2')$–$(4')$ are nonrandom and known with certainty; hence the certainty equivalence result of Simon [59] and Theil [61] holds. If the model's coefficients were uncertain, the variance expressions in eqs. (15) and (16) would contain an additional term in the difference between the instrument value and its historical or sample-period mean, and the resulting optimal r^*, R^* and $E(Y)$ values would all be different. (See the references cited in footnote 35 below, on the implications of multiplicative uncertainty.) Secondly, in a dynamic model a case of Holbrook's [40] "instrument instability" may render one instrument inferior to another; this one-period model does not analyze dynamic results. Thirdly, the policy authorities may have some preferences about the values of r or R per se, wholly apart from the impact of these variables on the target variable(s).

5. See Axilrod [5] and Davis [14] for an account of the current implementation of central bank open market policy.

6. See, for example, de Leeuw and Kalchbrenner [18], Davis [11] and Hamburger [36].

7. See, for example, Ando and Modigliani [4], de Prano and Mayer [19] and M. Friedman and Meiselman [31].

8. See the list of papers cited by Pierce and Thomson.

9. In fact, the empirical evidence seems to favor either the Treasury bill rate or the commercial paper rate. See de Leeuw [15], de Leeuw and

Gramlich [16], and Thomson, Pierce and Parry [63]; Davis' [13] use of the federal funds rate is something of an exception.

10. Data, which are for June, 1973, are from the Federal Reserve Bulletin.

11. Holbrook and Shapiro [41] acknowledged this inconsistency in a footnote (p. 46) but reported the results of their full analysis anyway.

12. See the monthly model of the money market by Thomson, Pierce and Parry [63] and the weekly model of the money market by Farr, Roberts and Thomson [22].

13. Andersen and Jordan [2] found estimates of the current-quarter impact as large as $1.58 billion.

14. This rough calculation assumes that personal income, which in 1972 was approximately eighty percent of total gross income, rises by $980 million with the $1.22 billion rise income. In the Thomson–Pierce–Parry monthly money market model, a form of which provided the base for Pindyck's and Roberts' experiments, the demand for money is a function of current and lagged values of personal income.

15. Most writers on this subject have simply called this problem the "target problem." The purpose of the extra word "intermediate" or "operating," both of which are typical of more recent usage, is to distinguish this problem from that of identifying the targets of policy in the sense of section 2—i.e., those variables, such as employment and price stability, which enter directly into policymakers' preference functions. The targets-and-indicators literature typically referred to the latter variables s policy "goals."

16. See, for example, Saving [57], p. 448, and Holbrook and Shapiro [41], p. 40.

17. The analysis of this section proceeds in the context of the "rate" alternative for the problem of eqs. (2'), (3') and (4'). The key results are equally applicable to the "reserves" alternatives.

18. See B. Friedman [25] for an analysis of time-linked objectives in which differences between the target variables and their desired values in separate time periods may offset one another.

19. Note that $u_Y = \epsilon_Y$, from eqs. (6'), is particular to the "rate" alternative. Eqs. (8') show that this simplifying property, which is not important for the analysis of this section except for reducing the amount of algebra to be done, does not hold for the "reserve" alternative.

20. Because variable Y does not appear in eq. (4'), knowledge of M_{t-1}, R_{t-1}, r_{t-1}, and z_{t-1} is sufficient to yield the structural disturbance $u_{MS,t-1}$; nevertheless, the structure of eqs. (6') or (8') prevents solving for $(u_{Y,t-1}, u_{MD,t-1})$, despite the knowledge of $u_{MS,t-1}$.

21. The problem is in some ways analogous to the familiar errors-in-variables problem; the central bank cannot observe $\epsilon_{Y,t-1}$ but must infer its value from the observable $\epsilon_{M,t-1}$, which includes $\epsilon_{Y,t-1}$ and another component. At first glance the conclusion of Kareken, Muench and Wallace [44] that the central bank's optimal solution to its information problem is to use all of the information variables available to it, seems to suggest using both $\epsilon_{M,t-1}$ and $\epsilon_{R,t-1}$ for this purpose. A closer look at eqs. (6'), however, shows that the known sum $(c_1 \epsilon_{R,t-1} + u_{MS,t-1})$ simply

equals $\epsilon_{M,t-1}$ and provides no new information; an analogous, though algebraically more complicated, proposition holds for eq. (8′).

22. This procedure is equivalent to using M as an "information variable" in the sense of Kareken, Muench and Wallace [45] since eq. (32) simply states the least-squares estimator of β in the regression equation $\epsilon_{Yt} = \alpha + \beta\epsilon_{M,t-1} +$ disturbance.

23. For reference, see, for example, Rao [53], ch. 8.

24. A mixed procedure, incorporating both pieces of information, would lead to a conditional variance

$$\mathbf{E}_t[\epsilon_{Yt} - \mathbf{E}_t(\epsilon_{Yt})]^2|\,^{\epsilon}_{M,t-1}\,^u_{Y,t-T-1}$$

which would be no greater than the minimum of the alternative conditional variances in eqs. (40) and (41), and would therefore be the true optimum procedure.

25. See footnote 21.

26. A related problem is that the available data themselves often merit only limited confidence; see B. Friedman [25], Axilrod and Beck (Federal Reserve Bank of Boston [24], pp. 81–102) and Poole and Lieberman [52] for an explicit treatment of the implications of inadequacies in data on monetary and reserve aggregates.

27. See the references cited in the previous footnote.

28. See Holt [42], Theil [62] and B. Friedman [26] for a more general treatment of the implications of structural lags for policy decision making.

29. In dynamic policy problems it is typical also to employ an additional parameter, a time-preference discounting factor, to evaluate the importance for current policy decisions of expected effects in future time periods.

30. See Saving [57] for a clear explanation of the rationale for requiring that the indicator and the target be distinct. Sargent [56] denied that the indicator problem as such even exists; his statement is in the spirit of the argument developed in this section.

31. The analysis of sections 3–5 relies exclusively on linear models. Generalizing that analysis to a nonlinear system would preclude the convenience of the reduced form and would therefore render the algebra more complex, but it would not significantly change the key conclusions derived. By contrast, the problem here is of a different order, since a consistently defined Brunner–Meltzer indicator index becomes a logical contradiction in the context of a nonlinear system.

32. Note that a similar logical problem arises, even in a linear model, if the coefficients of the monetary policy instrument variables in the structural model are uncertain. See Goldberger, Nagar and Odeh [33] for the derivation of the variance-covariance matrix of the coefficients of a derived reduced form.

33. Again, the analysis of sections 3–5 proceeds in the context of the unique target variable Y, but extension to multiple target variables is straightforward. By contrast, the problem here is of a different order, involving a logical inconsistency.

34. As the analysis above indicates, there is some ambiguity involved in associating cardinal inferences with the Brunner–Meltzer indicator

index for a one-target case, but ordinal inferences may be unambiguous with only one target. In fairness to Brunner and Meltzer, it is appropriate to note that the context in which they originally suggested the indicator index was the question of accuracy of statements involving ordinal inferences.

35. See, e.g., Brainard [6] and Zellner [66], ch. 11, for a general treatment of the problems introduced by multiplicative uncertainty. B. Friedman (Federal Reserve Bank of Boston [24], pp. 178–184) specifically illustrated the use of the targets-and-instruments framework for monetary policy-making in the presence of multiplicative uncertainty.

36. Saving ([57], p. 450) argued that the central bank would need such an indicator variable if it operated on the basis of an intermediate target variable: "Essentially, the policy-maker requires a separation of the change in his [intermediate] target variable into a policy effect and an exogenous effect. Since observation of the changes in the [intermediate] target variable yields only the total effect, some other variable or combination of variables is required to reflect the policy effect." In the context of the targets-and-instruments framework, however, the central bank's best estimate of the "policy effect" on any endogenous variable—including irrelevant variables used as intermediate target variables—is simply the movement in the instrument variable multiplied by the appropriate reduced-form coefficient.

REFERENCES

1. Andersen, L. C., and K. M. Carlson, "A Monetarist Model for Economic Stabilization," *Federal Reserve Bank of St. Louis Review,* 52: 7–25 (April 1970).

2. Andersen, L. C., and J. L. Jordan, "Monetary and Fiscal Actions: A Test of Their Relative Importance in Economic Stabilization, *Federal Reserve Bank of St. Louis Review,* 50: 11–24 (November 1963).

3. Ando, A., E. C. Brown, J. Kareken, and R. M. Solow, "Lags in Fiscal and Monetary Policy," in *Commission on Money and Credit, Stabilization Policies* (Englewood Cliffs, N.J.: Prentice-Hall, 1968).

4. Ando, A., and F. Modigliani, "Velocity and the Investment Multiplier," *American Economic Review,* 55: 693–728 (September 1965).

5. Axilrod, S. H., "Monetary Aggregates and Money Market Conditions in Open Market Policy," *Federal Reserve Bulletin,* 57: 79–104 (February 1971).

6. Brainard, W. C., "Uncertainty and the Effectiveness of Policy," *American Economic Review,* 57: 411–25 (May 1967).

7. Brunner, K. (ed.), *Targets and Indicators of Monetary Policy* (San Francisco: Chandler Publishing, 1969).

8. Brunner, K., and A.H. Meltzer, "The Meaning of Monetary Indicators," in Horwich (ed.), *Monetary Process and Policy: A Symposium* (Homewood, Ill.: Richard D. Irwin, 1967).

9. Cagan, P., and A. Gandolphi, "The Lag in Monetary Policy as

Implied by the Time Pattern of Monetary Effects on Interest Rates," *American Economic Review,* 59: 277–84 (May 1959).

10. Chase, S. B., Jr., "Comments," in Horwich (ed.), *Monetary Process and Policy: A Symposium* (Homewood, Ill.: Richard D. Irwin, 1967).

11. Davis, R. G., "How Much Does Money Matter? A Look at Some Recent Evidence," *Federal Reserve Bank of New York Monthly Review,* 51: 119–31 (June 1969).

12. Davis, R. G., "Short-run Targets for Open Market Operations," in *Open Market Policies and Operating Procedures: Staff Studies* (Washington: Board of Governors of the Federal Reserve System, 1971).

13. Davis, R. G., "Estimating Changes in Deposits with Reduced-Form Equations," mimeo (New York: Federal Reserve Bank of New York, 1972).

14. Davis, R. G., "Implementing Open Market Policy with Monetary Aggregate Objectives," *Federal Reserve Bank of New York Monthly Review,* 55: 170–82 (July 1973).

15. De Leeuw, F., "A Model of Financial Behavior," in Duesenberry et al. (eds.), *The Brookings Quarterly Econometric Model of the United States* (Chicago: Rand McNally, 1965).

16. De Leeuw, F., and E. Gramlich, "The Federal Reserve—M.I.T. Econometric Model," *Federal Reserve Bulletin,* 54: 11–40 (January 1968).

17. De Leeuw, F., and E. Gramlich, "The Channels of Monetary Policy," *Federal Reserve Bulletin,* 55: 472–91 (June 1969).

18. De Leeuw, F., and J. Kalchbrenner, "Monetary and Fiscal Actions: A Test of Their Relative Importance in Economic Stabilization—Comment," *Federal Reserve Bank of St. Louis Review,* 51: 6–11 (April 1969).

19. De Prano, M., and T. Mayer, "Tests of the Relative Importance of Autonomous Expenditures and Money," *American Economic Review,* 55: 729–52 (September 1965).

20. Dewald, W. G., "Free Reserves, Total Reserves and Monetary Control," *Journal of Political Economy,* 71: 141–53 (April 1963) [reprinted in this volume—Ed.].

21. Evans, M. K., and L. R. Klein, *"The Wharton Econometric Forecasting Model,* 2nd ed. (Philadelphia: University of Pennsylvania, 1968).

22. Farr, H. T., S. M. Roberts, and T. D. Thomson, "A Weekly Money Market Model," mimeo (Washington: Board of Governors of the Federal Reserve System, 1972).

23. Federal Reserve Bank of Boston, *Controlling Monetary Aggregates* (Boston: Federal Reserve Bank of Boston, 1969).

24. Federal Reserve Bank of Boston, *Controlling Monetary Aggregates II: The Implementation* (Boston: Federal Reserve Bank of Boston, 1972).

25. Friedman, B. M., "Tactics and Strategy in Monetary Policy," in *Open Market Policies and Operating Procedures: Staff Studies* (Washington: Board of Governors of the Federal Reserve System, 1971).

26. Friedman, B. M., *Economic Stabilization Policy: Methods in Optimization* (Amsterdam: North-Holland, 1975).

27. Friedman, M., *A Program for Monetary Stability* (New York: Fordham University Press, 1959).

28. Friedman, M., "The Lag in the Effect of Monetary Policy," *Journal of Political Economy*, 69: 447–66 (October 1961).

29. Friedman, M., "The Role of Monetary Policy," *American Economic Review*, 58: 1–17 (March 1968).

30. Friedman, M., and D. Meiselman, "The Relative Stability of Monetary Velocity and the Investment Multiplier in the United States, 1897–1958," in *Commission on Money and Credit, Stabilization Policies* (Englewood Cliffs: Prentice-Hall, 1963).

31. Friedman, M., and D. Meiselman, "Reply to Ando and Modigliani and to De Prano and Mayer," *American Economic Review*, 55: 753–85 (September 1965).

32. Friedman, M., and A. J. Schwartz, *A Monetary History of the United States, 1869–1960* (Princeton: Princeton University Press, 1963).

33. Goldberger, A. S., A. L. Nagar, and H. S. Odeh, "The Covariance Matrices of Reduced-Form Coefficients and of Forecasts for a Structural Econometric Model," *Econometrica*, 29: 556–73 (October 1961).

34. Guttentag, J. M., "The Strategy of Open Market Operations," *Quarterly Journal of Economics*, 80: 1–30 (February 1966).

35. Hamburger, M. J., "Indicators of Monetary Policy: The Arguments and the Evidence," *American Economic Review*, 60: 32–39 (May 1970).

36. Hamburger, M. J., "The Lag in the Effect of Monetary Policy: A Survey of Recent Literature," *Federal Reserve Bank of New York Monthly Review*, 53: 289–98 (December 1971).

37. Hendershott, P. H., *The Neutralized Money Stock* (Homewood, Ill.: Richard D. Irwin, 1968).

38. Hendershott, P. H., and G. Horwich, "Money, Interest, and Policy," in Jacobs and Pratt (eds.), *Savings and Residential Financing, 1969 Conference Proceedings* (Chicago: United Savings and Loan Association, 1969).

39. Hicks, J. R., "Mr. Keynes and the Classics: A Suggested Interpretation," *Econometrica*, 5: 147–59 (April 1937) [reprinted in this volume —Ed.].

40. Holbrook, R. S., "Optimal Economic Policy and the Problem of Instrument Instability," *American Economic Review*, 62: 57–65 (March 1972).

41. Holbrook, R. S., and H. Shapiro, "The Choice of Optimal Intermediate Economic Targets," *American Economic Review*, 60: 40–46 (May 1970).

42. Holt, C. C., "Linear Decision Rules for Economic Stabilization and Growth," *Quarterly Journal of Economics*, 76: 20–45 (February 1962).

43. Kareken, J., "The Optimal Monetary Instruments Variable," *Journal of Money, Credit and Banking*, 2: 385–90 (August 1970).

44. Kareken, J., T. Muench, T. Supel, and N. Wallace, "Determining the Optimum Monetary Instrument Variable," in *Open Market Policies and Operating Procedures: Staff Studies* (Washington: Board of Governors of the Federal Reserve System, 1971).

45. Kareken, J. H., T. Muench, and N. Wallace, "Optimal Open Market Strategy: The Use of Information Variables," *American Economic Review*, 63: 156–72 (March 1973).

46. Kaufman, G. G., "Indicators of Monetary Policy: Theory and Evidence," *National Banking Review,* 4: 1–11 (June 1967).

47. Modigliani, F., R. Rasche, and J. P. Cooper, Central Bank Policy, the Money Supply and the Short-Term Rate of Interest," *Journal of Money, Credit and Banking,* 2: 166–218 (May 1970).

48. Parkin, M., "Optimal Monetary and Fiscal Policy Rules in a Static Stochastic Economy," paper presented to the Fourth Konstanz Seminar on Monetary Theory and Policy, Konstanz, West Germany, June, 1973.

49. Pindyck, R. S., and S. M. Roberts, "Optimal Policies for Monetary Control," *Annals of Economic and Social Measurement* (forthcoming).

50. Poole, W., "Optimal Choice of Monetary Policy Instruments in a Simple Stochastic Macro Model," *Quarterly Journal of Economics,* 84: 197–216 (May 1970).

51. Poole, W., "Rules-of-Thumb for Guiding Monetary Policy," in *Open Market Policies and Operating Procedures: Staff Studies* (Washington: Board of Governors of the Federal Reserve System, 1971).

52. Poole, W., and C. Lieberman, "Improving Monetary Control," *Brookings Papers on Economic Activity,* 4, no. 2, 293–335, 1972.

53. Rao, C. R., *Linear Statistical Inference and Its Applications* (New York: John Wiley, 1965).

54. Rasche, R. H., "Simulations of Stabilization Policies for 1966–1970," *Journal of Money, Credit and Banking,* 5: 1–25 (February 1973).

55. Roosa, R. V., *Federal Reserve Operations in the Money and Government Securities Markets* (New York: Federal Reserve Bank of New York, 1956).

56. Sargent, T. J., "Discussion," *American Economic Review,* 60, 57–58 (May 1970).

57. Saving, T. R., "Monetary-Policy Targets and Indicators," *Journal of Political Economy,* 75: 446–56 (August 1967).

58. Shupp, F. R., "Uncertainty and Stabilization for a Nonlinear Model," *Quarterly Journal of Economics,* 86: 94–110 (February 1972).

59. Simon, H. A., "Dynamic Programming under Uncertainty with a Quadratic Criterion Function," *Econometrica,* 24: 74–81 (January 1956).

60. Starleaf, D. R., and J. A. Stephenson, "A Suggested Solution to the Monetary-Policy Indicator Problem: The Monetary Full Employment Interest Rate," *Journal of Finance,* 24: 623–41 (September 1969).

61. Theil, H. "A Note on Certainty Equivalence in Dynamic Planning," *Econometrica,* 25: 346–49 (April 1957).

62. Theil, H., *Optimal Decision Rules for Government and Industry* (Amsterdam: North-Holland, 1964).

63. Thomson, T. D., J. L. Pierce, and R. T. Parry, "A Monthly Money Market Model," *Journal of Money, Credit and Banking* (November 1975), 411–31.

64. Tinbergen, J., *The Theory of Economic Policy* (Amsterdam: North-Holland, 1956).

65. Zecher, R., "Implications of Four Econometric Models for the Indicators Issue," *American Economic Review,* 60: 47–54 (May 1970).

66. Zellner, A., *An Introduction to Bayesian Inference in Econometrics* (New York: John Wiley, 1971).